The Amesbury Archer and the Boscombe Bowmen

Bell Beaker Burials on Boscombe Down, Amesbury, Wiltshire

by
A.P. Fitzpatrick

The Amesbury Archer and the Boscombe Bowmen

Bell Beaker Burials on Boscombe Down, Amesbury, Wiltshire

by

A.P. Fitzpatrick

with contributions by

Alistair J. Barclay, Jenny Bredenberg, Caroline Cartwright, C.A. Chenery, Bob Clarke,
Rosamund M.J. Cleal, Mike Cowell, Niels Dagless, Mary Davis, J.A. Evans, Richard P. Evershed,
Alex M. Gibson, Phil Harding, T.F.G. Higham, Rob Ixer, C. Kirby, Stephanie Knight,
Jacqueline I. McKinley, Peter Marshall, Anna J. Mukherjee, Stuart Needham, Susan La Niece,
David Norcott, Fiona Roe, R.H. Seager Smith, Alison Sheridan, Pippa Smith,
Lucija Šoberl, Peter Webb, David F. Williams, and Sarah F. Wyles

and illustrations by

S.E. James
with photographs by Karen Nichols and Elaine A. Wakefield

Wessex Archaeology Report 27
2011

First published 2011 by Wessex Archaeology Ltd
Reprinted 2013 (paperback)
Portway House, Old Sarum Park, Salisbury, SP4 6EB
http://www.wessexarch.co.uk/

British Library Cataloguing in Publication Data
A catalogue record for this book is available from the British Library

Produced by Julie Gardiner
Cover design by Karen Nichols

ISBN 978-1-874350-62-0

Printed by Lightning Source

Cover photographs: objects from the grave of the Amesbury Archer (photographs by Karen Nichols)

Contents

PART I

Chapter 1 Introduction

Chapter 2 Grave 25000: the Boscombe Bowmen

Chapter 3. Finds from the Grave of the Boscombe Bowmen

PART II

Chapter 4 Graves 1236 and 1289: the Amesbury Archer and 'Companion'

Chapter 5. Finds from the grave of the Amesbury Archer

List of Figures

List of Plates

List of Tables

Contributors

Alistair J. Barclay

Wessex Archaeology. Portway House, Old Sarum Park, Salisbury, Wiltshire SP4 6EB

Jenny Bredenberg

Formerly Wessex Archaeology

Caroline Cartwright

Department of Conservation and Scientific Research, British Museum, London WC1B 3DG

C.A. Chenery

NERC Isotope Geosciences Laboratory, British Geological Survey, Keyworth Nottingham NG12 5GG

Bob Clarke

Formerly QinetiQ Archaeology, MOD Boscombe Down, Salisbury, Wiltshire SP4 0JF

Rosamund M.J. Cleal

The Alexander Keiller Museum, High Street, Avebury, Wiltshire SN18 1RF

Mike Cowell

Department of Conservation and Scientific Research, British Museum, London WC1B 3DG

Niels Dagless

Formerly Wessex Archaeology

Mary Davis

Archaeology and Numismatics, National Museum Wales, Cathays Park, Cardiff CF10 3NP

J.A. Evans

NERC Isotope Geosciences Laboratory, British Geological Survey, Keyworth Nottingham NG12 5GG

Richard P. Evershed

School of Chemistry, University of Bristol, Bristol BS8 1TS

A.P. Fitzpatrick

Wessex Archaeology

Alex M. Gibson

Division of Archaeological, Geographical and Environmental Sciences, University of Bradford, Bradford, West Yorkshire BD7 1DP

Phil Harding

Wessex Archaeology

T.F.G. Higham

Research Laboratory for Archaeology and the History of Art, University of Oxford, Dyson Perrins Building, South Parks Road, Oxford OX1 3QY

Rob Ixer

Department of Geology, University of Leicester, University Road, Leicester LE1 7RH

S.E. James

Wessex Archaeology

C. Kirby

Formerly QinetiQ Archaeology, MOD Boscombe Down, Salisbury, Wiltshire SP4 0JF

Stephanie Knight
Formerly Wessex Archaeology

Jacqueline I. McKinley
Wessex Archaeology

Peter Marshall
Chronologies, 25 Onslow Road, Sheffield S11 7AF

Anna J. Mukherjee
Formerly, Organic Chemistry Unit, Bristol Biogeochemistry Research Centre, School of Chemistry, University of Bristol, Bristol BS8 1TS

Stuart Needham
Langton Fold, South Harting, West Sussex GU31 5NW

Susan La Niece
Department of Conservation and Scientific Research, British Museum, London WC1B 3DG

David Norcott
Wessex Archaeology

Fiona Roe
Blackthorn Cottage, Vicarage Lane, Hillesley, Wotton-under-Edge, Gloucestershire GL12 7RA

R. H. Seager Smith
Wessex Archaeology

Alison Sheridan
Archaeology Department, National Museum of Scotland, Chambers Street, Edinburgh EH1 1JF

Pippa Smith
English Heritage, Brooklands, 24 Brooklands Avenue, Cambridge CB2 2BU

Lucija Šoberl
School of Chemistry, University of Bristol, Bristol BS8 1TS

Peter C. Webb
Department of Earth Sciences, The Open University, Walton Hall, Milton Keynes MK7 6AA

David F. Williams
Archaeology, University of Southampton, Avenue Campus, Highfield, Southampton SO17 1BF

Sarah F. Wyles
Wessex Archaeology

Acknowledgements

The excavations reported on form part of what is now over 15 years work at Boscombe Down and were commissioned by Bloor Homes, Persimmon Homes, and QinetiQ and Defence Estates and they have funded all the work, including this report. I am grateful to Ron Hatchett, Paul Halfacree and Martyn Clark of Bloors, Paul Bedford, Russell Brewer and Stuart Benfield of Persimmon, Jonathan Wade, Bob Clarke, Colin Kirby, Nicola Jervis and Steve Wilkinson of QinetiQ, and to Christopher Clarke and Martin Miller of Terence O'Rourke for their assistance over this time.

Wiltshire County Council Archaeology Service has provided assistance and constructive comment throughout this period and for this thanks are due to Melanie Pomeroy-Kellinger and Roy Canham and particularly to Helena Cave-Penney. The staff of Salisbury and South Wiltshire Museum Jane Ellis-Schön, Adrian Green, Peter Saunders and Martin Wright have been unfailingly helpful in responding to the many and varied requests relating to these discoveries. All the conservation of the finds was undertaken by Helen Wilmott, Wiltshire County Council Conservation Laboratory.

It has been an immense privilege to be responsible for the excavation, analysis and publication of the finds reported in this volume and to work with everyone who has helped in so many ways. I am grateful to all of the contributors, and especially so to Jane Evans and Carolyn Chenery for their assistance with isotopes, and to my colleagues Rachael Seager Smith, who was responsible for dealing with the finds, and Andy Manning and Dr Alistair Barclay who have respectively assumed responsibility for the fieldwork and reporting of the works at Boscombe Down. As well as being a contributor Alistair Barclay has managed the publication stage of this report and been a patient sounding board, while Andrew Powell assisted with the compilation of the report.

Of my fellow contributors, Jacqueline McKinley would like to colleagues for their thoughts regarding various of the skeletal conditions observed, including Sue Black, Troy Case, Christopher Knüsel, Charlotte Roberts and Christopher Ruff. Fiona Roe would like to thank the many people who assisted with the preparation of her report. They include Ann Woodward and all the Leverhulme 'stone' team. Luc Amkreuz (Leiden), Bernard Pinsker (Darmstadt), Peter Saunders, Martin Wright and Jane Ellis-Schön (Salisbury), Stuart Needham and members of staff at the British Museum, Jill Greenaway (Reading) and Alison Roberts (Ashmolean) helped in museums. In libraries Jenny Colls (Department of Earth Sciences, Oxford) and Elaine Bimpson (Geologists' Association and University College, London) gave invaluable help as did Bridget Franklin and Roger Howell with the fieldwork. Stuart Needham is grateful to successive curators at Salisbury and South Wiltshire Museum – Martin Wright and Jane Ellis-Schön; to Dirk Brandherm for commenting on relationships to Iberian material; to Brendan O'Connor for comments on European basket ornaments, and to Sheridan Bowman for talking through various issues to help shape perspectives.

I am also grateful to colleagues who have helped in many ways including answering queries and providing books and copies of articles in my attempt to do justice to the significance of finds: Dr Barbara Armbruster (University of Toulouse), Dr Josef Bátora (Masaryk University, Brno), Dr Steve Burrow (National Museum of Wales), Dr Jay Butler (University of Groningen), the late Dr Humphrey Case (Wallingford), Neil Carlin (University College Dublin), Matthias Conrad (Landesamt für Archäologie, Dresden), Professor Janusz Czebreszuk (Adam Mickiewicz University, Poznań), Professor Tim Darvill (University of Bournemouth), Dr Andrea Dolfini, University of Newcastle, Professor Alain Gallay (University of Geneva), Dr Alex Gibson (University of Bradford), Professor Richard Harrison (University of Bristol), Dr Frances Healy (University of Cardiff), Dr Volker Heyd (University of Bristol), Dr Frances Lynch (Bangor), Professor Raffaele de Marinis (University of Milan), Bob Mowat (RCHME(S), Edinburgh), Franco Nicolis (Trento), Professor Billy O'Brien (University College Cork), Dr Brendan O'Connor (Edinburgh), Dr Roberto Risch (Autonomous University of Barcelona), Dr Pavel Sankot (National Museum, Prague), the late Ian Shepherd (Aberdeen), Dr Alison Sheridan (National Museums Scotland), Jonathan Smith (Oxford), drs Lisbeth Theunissen (Rijksdienst voor het Cultureel Erfgoed, Amersfoort), Professor Joan Taylor (University of Liverpool), Dr Jan Turek (Institute of Archaeological Heritage, Prague), Dr Ben Roberts (British Museum), Dr Laure Salanova (University of Paris), Dr Peter Suter (Archäologisches Dienst des Kantons Bern), Dr Marc Vander Linden (University of Leicester).

Humphrey Case, Volker Heyd, Stuart Needham, Brendan O'Connor, Alison Sheridan all also kindly provided copies of their work in advance of publication. Professor Mike Parker Pearson (University of Sheffield) and Jim Leary (English Heritage) also generously shared the radiocarbon dates from their own work in advance of publication and Dr Mandy Jay (University of Durham) shared the preliminary results of her isotope analyses undertaken as part of the Beaker People Project.

Much of the research for this volume was done in two libraries, those of the Society of Antiquaries of London and the Römische-Germanisches Kommission, Frankfurt. The opportunity to work in collaboration with the Römische-Germanisches Kommission of the Deutsches Archäologisches Institut was arranged by Dr Knut Rassmann,

providing both accommodation and unrestricted access to incomparable library facilities and I am most grateful for the hospitality and help which was so readily afforded me.

Dr Volker Heyd, Dr Ben Roberts, Dr Laure Salanova, Dr Alison Sheridan and Dr Marc Vander Linden all kindly commented on part or all of the draft of this report.

Finally, I am especially grateful to Niels Daglass, Doug Murphy and David Norcott who unhesitatingly stayed to complete the excavation of the Amesbury Archer in the mistaken belief that we would 'be finished soon.' Dr Nick Cooke visiting out of curiosity on his way home and Rachael Seager Smith, who 'came out to check' also stayed much longer than they anticipated. Sue Davies, Chief Executive Officer of Wessex Archaeology, created space amongst my other responsibilities to allow me to undertake the reporting.

Location of archives

The project archive will be deposited with Salisbury and South Wiltshire Museum, 65 The Close, Salisbury, Wiltshire SP1 2EN under the Wessex Archaeology project numbers 50875 (graves 1236 and 1289, the 'Amesbury Archer' and adjacent grave) and 53535 (grave 25000, the 'Boscombe Bowmen'). The burial of the Amesbury Archer currently forms part of the museum's displays.

Radiocarbon dates

All radiocarbon measurements have been calculated using the calibration curve of Reimer et al. (2004), and the computer program OxCal v4.0.5 (Bronk Ramsey 1995; 1998; 2001; 2009). The calibrated date ranges cited in the text are those for 95% confidence. They are quoted in the form recommended by Mook (1986), with the end points rounded outwards to 10 years if the error term is greater than or equal to 25 radiocarbon years, or to 5 years if it is less. The ranges quoted in italics are posterior density estimates derived from mathematical modelling of archaeological problems (see Chapter 6). Date ranges in plain type have been calculated according to the maximum intercept method (Stuiver and Reimer 1986). All other ranges are derived from the probability method (Stuiver and Reimer 1993).

Abstract

The graves of the 'Amesbury Archer' and the 'Boscombe Bowmen' were found at Boscombe Down, Wiltshire, not far from Stonehenge. The graves date to the 24th century BC and are two of the earliest Bell Beaker graves yet found in Britain. Bayesian modelling of the radiocarbon dates from the graves, other finds at Boscombe Down and nearby sites such as Durrington Walls and Stonehenge has allowed a detailed local chronological sequence to be created. Oxygen and strontium isotope analyses suggest that the Amesbury Archer and some of the Boscombe Bowmen were migrants.

The earliest grave (25000) is that of the Boscombe Bowmen. It was a flat grave that probably had a timber chamber that could be reopened to allow successive burials to be made. Only the last two burials to be made were articulated, the other five or six individuals of Bell Beaker date were represented by some of their disarticulated remains. As the grave had been badly disturbed in modern times and in the Bronze Age it is uncertain why some bones were absent. The bones may have been placed elsewhere during the secondary burial rite or they may have been removed during the reopening of the grave and the rearrangement of the previous burials. Two Early Bronze Age burials associated with a barrow were later cut into the grave.

Remains from at least five adult males of Bell Beaker date, a 15–18 year old teenager who was probably also male, and one, possibly two, children were present. No females were identified. The similarities in the skulls suggest that the men came from a closely related community. Isotope analysis of the only suitable mandibles demonstrated that three of the adults had been resident in one location at about the ages of 5–7 and in a second location between the ages of 11–13. The strontium isotopes indicate that the geologies that underlay these locations comprised very ancient rocks. Their place of burial, Boscombe Down, represented a third location, with a much younger geology. The nearest region that provides comparable biosphere values for the first and second locations is Wales but Brittany, Portugal, the Massif Central and the Black Forest are also possible. Bayesian modelling of the radiocarbon dates suggests that the individuals did not all die at the same time but they may have all been alive at the same time. The first Bowman died between 2500–2340 cal BC.

The grave goods include seven All-Over-Cord Beakers with strong parallels in north-west Europe. One pot was decorated with plaited cord. One Cord-Zoned-Maritime Beaker is also present. Others grave goods include flint scrapers, knives, and barbed and tanged arrowheads, a boar's tusk, and a small antler pendant of a rare but widely distributed European type.

The grave of the Boscombe Bowmen is suggested to have contained the males of a small family group that travelled to Wessex in the 24th century BC. This group practised the collective burial rite that is typical of much of western and Atlantic Europe, and the early date of the grave in the British sequence would suggest that they came from this region rather than Wales. The typology of the grave goods does not allow one possible origin to be preferred over another.

In contrast, the flat grave of the Amesbury Archer (1289), which also had a wooden chamber, contained a single burial, that of a 35–45 year old man. The modelling of the radiocarbon dates suggests that the Amesbury Archer was alive at the same time (2380–2290 cal BC) as the last man buried in the grave of the Boscombe Bowmen. Oxygen isotope analyses indicate that as a teenager the Amesbury Archer lived in a climate colder than that of Wessex. Comparable biosphere values are found from the Alpine region to eastern Scandinavia but the strontium isotopes exclude the older geologies of Scandinavia. A location in the Alpine region is suggested as the Bell Beaker Set was introduced to central and northern Germany and Poland at about the same time as it was introduced to Britain. The objects in the Amesbury Archer's grave also have their closest similarities with finds in western, and not northern, Europe.

Next to the grave of the Amesbury Archer was grave 1236. This contained the burial of a 20–25 year old man who had died one or two generations after the Amesbury Archer (2350–2260 cal BC). The presence of a rare trait in their feet bones demonstrates that the two men were biologically related. Whether this was as grandfather/grandson or father/son etc. cannot be determined. The younger man may also have travelled to continental Europe. He was buried with a pair of gold ornaments and a boar's tusk. A few flint flakes and tools might also have been grave goods.

An exceptional number of grave goods were buried with the Amesbury Archer, making it amongst the 'richest' Bell Beaker burials yet found in Europe. The grave goods include five Bell Beakers, three copper knives, two bracers, a pair of gold ornaments and a shale belt ring. One-hundred and twenty-two pieces of worked flint were found including knives, scrapers, flakes, 17 barbed and tanged and one possible triangular arrowheads. Related finds include an iron pyrite nodule from a fire-making set and an antler pressure flaker for working flint. Other objects placed in the grave were a stone metalworking tool, four boars' tusks, an antler pin, two antler objects of unknown function, and a pendant made from an oyster.

The copper used for the knives (and perhaps the knives themselves) comes from continental European and not Ireland. Two knives could be from northern Spain, the third from western France. Although the style of the gold ornaments is British/Irish, the gold may also be continental European. The black wristguard may also be Continental but the red one may be made from a rock found in south-west Wales. Two Beakers are decorated All-Over with plaited Cord, and one with All-Over-Cord. The other two Beakers are Maritime-Derived.

The presence of the stone metalworking tool (a cushion stone) is suggested to help explain why the Amesbury Archer travelled to Britain and the 'over-provision' of grave goods. His burial is the earliest grave of a metalworker yet found in Britain and over-provision occurs regularly in the graves of Bell Beaker metalworkers and high status graves of Copper and Bronze Age date in Europe.

The graves of the Boscombe Bowmen and the Amesbury Archer are close to some of the most important temples in prehistoric Europe. This may help explain the location of their graves but there is little evidence for contact between Bell Beaker and indigenous Late Neolithic groups. This is partly because of the rarity of early Bell Beaker settlements and burials in Britain but the radiocarbon modelling also suggests little chronological overlap between them.

Evidence for other journeys to Britain and Ireland at this time by groups using the Bell Beaker Set comes from a small number of burials in western and northern Scotland and from the Ross Ireland copper mine in south-west Ireland. Taken together, this evidence suggests a short period of long-distance mobility by groups using the Bell Beaker Set in the 24th and 23rd centuries BC. The burials of the Boscombe Bowmen and the Amesbury Archer seem likely to be those of some of the men involved this international network.

Zusammungfassung

Die Gräber des "Amesbury Archer" und der "Boscombe Bowmen" (jeweils wegen der Beigabe zahlreicher Pfeilzpitzen als Bogenschützen bezeichnet) wurden bei Boscombe, Grafschaft Wiltshire, nicht weit von Stonehenge entfernt gefunden. Die beiden Gräber datieren in des 24. Jh. v. Chr. und gehören zu den frühsten bislang in Großbritannien gefundenen Glockenbechergräbern. Die statistisch modellierten Radiokarbondaten der Gräber, anderer Funde von Boscombe Down und nahegelegener Fundplätze wie Durrington Walls und Stonehenge boten die Möglichkeit, eine detaillierte Lokalchronologie zu erstellen. Analysen von Sauerstoff- und Strontiumisotopen legen nahe, dass der Amesbury Archer und einge der Boscombe Bowmen Migranten waren.

Das früheste Grab (25000) ist jenes der Boscombe Bowmen. Bei diesem handelt es sich um ein Flachgrab, das wahrscheinlich eine hölzerne Kammer besaß, die für Nachbestattungen erneut geöffnet werden konnte. Nur die letzten beiden Bestattungen befanden sich noch im anatomischen Verband, von den anderen fünf oder sechs glockenbecherzeitlichen Individuen fanden sich lediglich Teile des Knochenapparats. Da das Grab sowohl modern als auch in der Bronzezeit stark gestört worden war, muß ugeklärt bleiben, aus welchem Grund die übrigen Knochen fehlten. Möglicherweise wurden die Knochen während des Sekundärbestattungsritus an anderer Stelle platziert, oder sie können bei der Wiedereröffnung des Grabes und der Umordnung der vorangegangenen Bestattungen entnommen worden sein. Zwei frühbronzezeitliche, zu einem Grabhügel gehörende Bestattungen haben später das Grab geschnitten.

Es fanden sich Reste von mindestens fünf glockenbecherzeitlichen adulten, männlichen Individuen, einem 15-18 Jahre alten Teenager (wahrscheinlich ebenfalls männlich) und einem, möglicherweise zwei Kindern. Es wurden keine weiblichen Individuen identifiziert. Ähnlichkeiten der Schädelstrukturen legen nahe, dass die Männer einer eng untereinander verwandten Gemeinschaft entstammten. Isotopenanalysen von Zähnen der einzigen hierfür geeigneten Kieferknochen haben gezeigt, dass drei der männlichen Individuen im Alter von 5–7 Jahren an einem Ort, und im Alter zwischen 11 und 13 Jahren an einem anderen Ort gelebt haben. Aufgrund der Strontiumisotopen zeigt sich, dass diese Standorte im Bereich geologisch sehr sehalter Gesteinsformationen lagen. Ihre Begräbnisstätte, Boscombe Down, liegt als dritter Standort in einem geologisch wesentlich jüngeren Gebiet. Die nächstgelegene Region mit vergleichbaren Biosphären-werten für die ersten beiden Standorte ist Wales, aber die Bretagne, Portugal, das Massif Central und der Schwarzwald kommen ebenfalls in Frage. Die statistisch modellierten Radiokarbondatierungen legen nahe, dass nicht alle Individuen zum exakt gleichen Zeitpunkt gestorben sind, sie haben aber wahrscheinlich alle zur gleichen Zeit gelebt. Der erste Bowman starb zwischen 2500 und 2340 cal BC.

Unter den Grabbeigaben befinden sich sieben totalschnurverzierte Becher (All-Over-Cord Beaker/AOC Beaker) mit deutlichen Parallelen in Nordwest-Europa. Zwei dieser Gefäße sind flechtschnurverziert (plaited cord). Es fand sich auch ein Schnurzonenbecher (Cord-Zoned-Maritime Beaker). Zu den weiteren Grabbeigaben gehören Feuersteinschaber, Messer, gestielte, geflügelte Pfeilspitzen sowie ein kleiner Geweihanhänger eines seltenen aber weit verbreiteten europäischen Typs.

Es wird angenommen, dass im Grab der Boscombe Bowmen die männlichen Mitglieder einer kleinen Familiengruppe bestattet wurden, die im 24. Jh. v. Chr. in die Region Wessex gereist sind. Diese Gruppe praktizierte die Kollektivgrabsitte, die für weite Teile des westlichen Europa und entlang der Atlantikküste typisch ist. Die innerhalb der britischen Sequenz frühe Datierung des Grabes legt nahe, dass die Mitglieder der Gruppe aus dieser Region und nicht aus Wales kamen. Anhand der typologischen Merkmale der Grabbeigaben ist es nicht möglich, zu Gunsten des einen oder anderen möglichen Herkunftsgebiets zu entscheiden.

Das Flachgrab des „Amesbury Archer" (1289), das ebenfalls ein hölzerne Kammer besaß, enthielt eine einzelne Bestattung eines 35–45 Jahre alten Mannes. Nach Ausweis des statistische Modells der Radiokarbondatierungen lebte der Amesbury Archer zur gleichen Zeit (2380–2290 cal BC) wie der letzte im Grab der Boscombe Bowmen bestattete Mann. Die Sauerstoffisotopen-Analyse deutet an, dass der Amesbury Archer als Teenager in einem Klimabereich lebte, der kälter war als Wessex. Vergleichbare Biosphärenwerte finden sich von der Alpenregion bis ins östliche Skandinavien, aufgrund der Strontiumisotopenwerte sind die geologisch älteren Bereich Skandinaviens aber auszuschließen. Eine Herkunft aus der Alpenregion erscheint naheliegend, da das Glockenbecherinventar in Mittel- und Norddeutschland sowie Polen ungefähr zur gleichen Zeit wie in Großbritannien eingeführt wurde. Die Gegenstände im Grab des Amesbury Archer finden ihre besten Vergleiche ebenfalls im westlichen und nicht im nördlichen Europa.

Neben dem Grab des Amesbury Archer lag Grab 1236. Es enthielt die Bestattung eines 20–25 Jahre alten Mannes, der ein oder zwei Generationen nach dem Amesbury Archer gestorben ist (2350–2260 cal BC). Ein seltenes Merkmal, das sich in den Fußknochen beider Männer fand, zeigt, dass sie biologisch verwandt waren; ob es sich hierbei um Großvater und Enkel oder Vater und Sohn handelt, läßt sich jedoch nicht bestimmen. Der jüngere Mann ist möglicherweise auch nach Kontinentaleuropa gereist. Er wurde mit einem Paar goldener Ornamente und einem Eberzahn bestattet. Bei einigen Flintabschlägen und –werkzeugen könnte es sich ebenfalls um Grabbeigaben handeln.

Aufgrund der außergewöhnlichen Anzahl von Grabbeigaben, die mit dem Amesbury Archer beigegeben wurde, handelt es sich um eines der „reichsten" glockenbecherzeitlichen Bestattungen, die bislang in Europa gefunden wurden. Zur Grabausstattung gehören fünf Glockenbecher, drei Kupfermesser, zwei Armschutzplatten, ein Paar goldener Ornamente und ein Gürtelring aus Schiefer. Es wurden insgesamt 122 Stücke bearbeiteten Flints gefunden, u.a. Messer, Schaber, Abschläge, 17geflügelte, gestielte Pfeilspitzen und eine vermutlich dreieckige Pfeilspitze. Zu den damit zusammenhängenden Funden gehört eine Pyritknolle eines Feuerzeug-Sets und ein Druckstab aus Geweih zur Flintbearbeitung. Weitere Grabfunde sind ein steinernes Metallbearbeitungs-werkzeug, vier Eberzähne, eine Geweihnadel, zwei Geweihgeräte unbekannter Funktion und ein aus einer Austernschale gefertigter Anhänger.

Das für die Herstellung der Messer genutzte Kupfer (und vielleicht sogar die Messer selbst) stammt aus Kontinentaleuropa und nicht aus Irland. Zwei Messer könnten aus Nordspanien, ein drittes aus Westfrankreich kommen. Obwohl der Stil der Goldornamente britisch bzw. irisch ist, könnte das Gold selbst ebenfalls kontinentaleuropäischen Ursprungs sein. Die schwarze Armschutzplatte ist vielleicht auch kontinentaler Herkunft, aber die rote könnte aus einer südwest-walisischen Gesteinformation gefertigt worden. Von den fünf Glockenbechern sind drei totalschnurverziert (All-Over-Cord Beakers), von denen wiederum zwei total flechtschnurverziert sind (All-Over plaited Cord). Bei den beiden anderen Gefäßen handelt es sich um Maritime-Derived Beakers.

Die Beigabe des steinernen MetallbearbeitungsWerk-zeugs (ein sogenannter Kissenstein) dient als Erklärungs-ansatz für den Beweggrund der Reise des Amesbury Archer nach Großbritannien sowie die „Überausstattung" mit Grabbeigaben. Sein Grab ist die bislang älteste in Großbritannien gefundene Bestattung eines Metall-arbeiters.Überausstattung begegnet regelhaft in Gräbern glockenbecherzeitlicher Metallurgengräber sowie in kupfer- und bronzezeitlichen Elitengräbern in Europa.

Die Gräber der Boscombe Bowmen und des Amesbury Archer liegen in der Nähe von einigen der wichtigsten Tempel im gesamten prähistorischen Europa. Dies mag zur Erklärung der Lage der Gräber beitragen, aber es lassen sich nur sehr wenige Anhaltspunkte für Kontakte zwischen Glockenbecher-Gruppen und der indigenen spät-neolithischen Bevölkerung aufzeigen. Dies liegt zum Teil an der Seltenheit früh-glockenbecherzeitlicher Siedlungen und Gräber in Großbritannien, aber nach Ausweis des Radiokarbon-Models scheinen diese sich auch chronologisch kaum zu überlappen.

Hinweise für Reisen nach Großbritannien und Irland in diesem Zeitraum durch andere Gruppen, die das Glockenbecherinventar benutzten, finden sich in einigen wenigen Bestattungen im westlichen und nördlichen Schottland sowie der Ross Island Kupfermine in Südwest-Irland. In der Zusammenschau läßt sich durch die bisherigen Ergebnisse auf eine kurze Periode mit weitreichender Mobilität von Gruppen schließen, die das Glocken-becherinventar im 23. und 24. Jh. v. Chr. nutzten. Bei den Bestattungen der Boscombe Bowmen und des Amesbury Archer handelt es sich wahrscheinlich um einige der Männer, die Teil dieses internationalen Netzwerks waren.

Übersetzung: Jörn Schuster

Résumé

Les sépultures du 'Amesbury Archer' et des 'Boscombe Bowmen' ont été découvertes à Boscombe Down, Wiltshire, près de Stonehenge. Ces sépultures datent du 24e siècle BC et constituent deux des plus anciennes tombes campaniformes connues à ce jour en Grande-Bretagne. La modélisation bayésiennne des dates radiocarbone obtenues pour les sépultures, d'autres découvertes réalisées à Boscombe Down et dans des sites proches tels que Durrington Walls et Stonehenge, ont permis la création d'une séquence chronologique détaillée. Les analyses des isotopes d'oxygène et de strontium suggèrent que le 'Amesbury Archer' et certains des 'Boscombe Bowmen' furent des migrants.

La tombe la plus ancienne (25000) est celle des 'Boscombe Bowmen'. Il s'agit d'une sépulture plate qui présentait vraisemblablement une chambre en bois pouvant être réouverte, permettant des inhumations successives. Seules les deux dernières inhumations sont encore articulées, les cinq ou six autres individus n'étant représentés que par une partie de leurs restes désarticulés. Comma la sépulture a été fortement perturbée à date moderne et durant l'Age du Bronze, nous ne savons pas pourquoi certains ossements sont absents. Ces ossements ont pu être placés ailleurs autres l'occasion d'un rituel funéraire secondaire, ou ont pu être enlevés lors de la réouverture de la tombe et la réorganisation des sépultures précédentes. Deux sépultures de l'Age du Bronze Ancien associées à un tertre ont recoupés la tombe principale à date ultérieure.

Etaient représentés les restes de au moins cinq adultes mâles datés de la période campaniforme, d'un adolescent, probablement aussi de sexe masculin, âgé de 15-18 ans, et deux enfants. Aucun individu de sexe féminin n'a été identifié. Les similitudes entre les crânes suggèrent que les hommes proviennent d'un groupe étroitement lié. Les analyses isotopiques des dents provenant des seules mandibules se prêtant à cette méthode ont démontré que trois des adultes ont vécu un endroit donné à l'âge de 5-7 ans et à un second endroit à l'âge de 11-13 ans. Les isotopes de strontium indiquent que les géologies sous-jacentes à ces localisations comprenaient des roches très anciennes. Leur lieu d'enterrement, Boscombe Down, représente une troisième localisation, caractérisée par une géologie bien plus récente. La région la plus proche qui fournisse des valeurs biosphériques comparables aux deux premières est le Pays de Galles, mais la Bretagne, le Portugal, le Massif Central et la Forêt Noire sont d'autres possibilités. La modélisation bayésienne des dates radiocarbone suggère que les individus ne sont pas tous morts en même temps, mais ont pu être contemporains. Le premier individu est mort entre 2500 et 2340 cal BC.

Le matériel funéraire comprend sept gobelets de type All-Over-Cord présentant des parallèles évidents avec l'Europe du Nord-Ouest. Deux de ces vases sont décorés avec une cordelette tressée. Un gobelet maritime mixte était aussi présent. Le reste du matériel funéraire comprend des racloirs, lames et pointes de flèche pédonculées et à barbelures en silex, une défense de sanglier, et un petit pendentif en bois de cerf d'un type européen rare mais largement distribué.

La tombe des Boscombe Bowmen semble avoir contenu les hommes d'un petit groupe familial qui voyagea au Wessex dans le courant du 24e siècle BC. Ce groupe pratiquait le rite de la sépulture collective qui est typique de la plus grand partie de l'Europe occidentale et atlantique, et la datation ancienne de cette tombe au sein de la séquence britannique pourrait suggérer qu'ils provenaient de cette dernière région plutôt que du Pays de Galles. La typologie du matérel funéraire ne permet pas de privilégier une région plus qu'une autre.

Au contraire, la sépulture plate du Amesbury Archer (1289), elle aussi avec une chambre en bois, contenait la sépulture individuelle d'un homme âgé entre 35 et 45 ans. La modélisation des datations radiocarbone suggère que le Amesbury Archer vivait à la même époque (2380–2290 cal BC) que le dernier homme inhumé dans la tombe des Boscombe Bowmen. Les analyses des isotopes d'oxygène indiquent que durant son adolescence le Amesbury archer a vécu dans un climat plus froid que celui du Wessex. Des valeurs biosphériques comparables sont disponibles de la région alpine à la Scandinavie orientale, mais les isotopes de strontium excluent les zones géologiques scandinaves plus anciennes. Une localisation dans la région alpine est donc suggérée, d'autant que le 'set campaniforme' est introduit dans le nord et le centre de l'Allemagne, ainsi qu'en Pologne, plus ou moins en même temps que en Grande-Bretagne. Les comparaisons les plus marquées avec le matériel funéraire découvert dans la tombe du Amesbury Archer sont à rechercher dans l'ouest, et non le nord, de l'Europe.

A côté de la tombe du Amesbury Archer se trouvait la tombe 1236. Celle-ci contenait la sépulture d'un homme âgé de 20 à 25 ans, qui est décédé une à deux générations après le Amesbury Archer (2350–2260 cal BC). La présence d'un caractère discret rare sur les os des pieds prouve que ces deux hommes étaient liés du point de vue biologique, mais la nature exacte de cette relation ne peut être déterminée (grand-père/petit-fils, père/fils, ...). Cet homme, plus récent, a également pu voyager en Europe continentale. Il était enterré avec une paire de parures en or et une défense de sanglier. Quelques éclats et outils en silex peuvent aussi avoir composé le matériel funéraire.

Une quantité exceptionnelle de matériel funéraire était enterrée avec le Amesbury Archer, ce qui en fait une des sépultures campaniformes les plus 'riches' découvertes à ce jour en Europe. Ce matériel funéraire comprend cinq gobelets campaniformes, trois poignards en cuivre, deux brassards d'archer, une paire de parures en or et une boucle de ceinture en schiste. Cent vingt-deux (122) artefacts en silex taillé ont été trouvés et comprennent des couteaux, des grattoirs, des éclats, dix-sept pointes de flèche pédonculées et à barbelure, et une possible pointe de flèche triangulaire. Le reste des découvertes comprend un nodule de fer faisant partie d'une trousse à outils pour faire du feu, et un outil en bois de cerf pour retoucher le silex par pression. D'autres objets placés dans la tombe étaient un outil en pierre pour la métallurgie, quatre défenses de sanglier, une épingle en bois de cerf, deux objets en bois de cerf de fonction indéterminée et un pendentif en coquille d'huître.

Le cuivre utilisé pour la confection des poignards (et peut-être les poignards eux-mêmes) provient de l'Europe continentale et non d'Irlande. Deux poignards peuvent provenir du nord de l'Espagne, le troisième de l'ouest de la France. Bien que le style des parures en or soit britannique/irlandais, l'or provient peut-être également d'Europe continentale. Le brassard d'archer noir peut aussi provenir du continent, mais l'exemplaire rouge peut avoir été réalisé dans une roche trouvée dans le sud-ouest du Pays de Galles. Des cinq gobelets campaniformes, trois sont de style All-Over-Cord, dont deux sont décorés sur l'ensemble de la surface avec une corde tressée. Les deux autres gobelets sont dérivés du type maritime.

La présence d'une pierre liée au travail du métal (sorte de petite enclume) permet probablement d'expliquer pourquoi le Amesbury Archer a voyagé en Grande-Bretagne, ainsi que la 'sur-provision' en matériel funéraire. Cette sépulture est la plus ancienne tombe d'un métallurgiste trouvée à ce jour en Grande-Bretagne, et la 'sur-provision' s'observe régulièrement dans les sépultures de métallurgistes campaniformes et les sépultures de haut rang datées des Ages du Cuivre et du Bronze en Europe.

Les sépultures des Boscombe Bowmen et du Amesbury Archer sont situées à proximité de certains des temples les plus importants de l'Europe préhistorique. Ceci peut aider à expliquer la localisation de ces tombes, mais les traces de contact entre groupes campaniformes et du Néolithique final local sont rares. Ceci s'explique en partie par la rareté des habitats et tombes campaniformes anciens en Grande-Bretagne, mais la modélisation des dates radiocarbone suggère également que la chronologie de ces deux groupes ne se recoupe que peu.

Des données indiquant d'autres trajets vers la Grande-Bretagne et l'Irlande par des groupes porteurs du 'set campaniforme' proviennent d'un petit nombre de tombes de l'ouest et du nord de l'Ecosse, et de la mine de cuivre de Ross-Island dans le sud-ouest de l'Irlande. Prises ensemble, ces données suggèrent une courte période de mobilité à longue distance par des groupes porteurs du 'set campaniforme' durant les 24e et 23e siècles BC. Les sépultures des Boscombe Bowmen et du Amesbury Archer semblent être celles de certains de ces hommes impliqués dans ce réseau international.

Traduction: Marc Vander Linden

Résumen

Las tumbas del 'Arquero de Amesbury' y de los 'Arqueros de Boscombe' fueron halladas en Boscombe Down, Wiltshire, no lejos de Stonehenge. Datadas al siglo XXIV a.C., las tumbas son dos de los enterramientos campaniformes más antiguos encontrados a fecha de hoy en Gran Bretaña. La modelación bayesiana de las dataciones al carbono-14 obtenidas de las tumbas, junto con otros hallazgos en Boscombe Down y en yacimientos cercanos como Durrington Walls y Stonehenge, han permitido la creación de una detallada secuencia cronológica local. Los análisis de isotopos de oxígeno y estroncio parecen indicar que tanto el arquero de Amesbury como algunos de los arqueros de Boscombe eran inmigrantes.

El enterramiento más antiguo (25000) es el de los Arqueros de Boscombe. Se trataba de una fosa plana que probablemente tenía una cámara de madera que podía ser reabierta para permitir enterramientos posteriores. Sólo los dos últimos enterramientos se encontraron articulados, los otros cinco o seis individuos del periodo campaniforme están representados sólo por algunos restos desarticulados. Dado que la tumba ha sido muy perturbada tanto en el periodo moderno como en la Edad del Bronce, no se puede establecer con certeza el motivo de la ausencia de los huesos. Puede que fueran depositados en otro lugar como parte de un ritual funerario secundario o pueden haber sido retirados durante la reapertura de la tumba y la reorganización de los entierros previos. Dos enterramientos de la Primera Edad del Bronce asociados con un túmulo cortaron posteriormente a través de la tumba.

En la tumba se encontraron los restos de al menos cinco hombres adultos del periodo campaniforme, de un adolescente de entre 15 a 18 años probablemente también varón, y de uno o probablemente dos niños. No se identificaron mujeres. Las similitudes en los cráneos sugiere que los hombres provenían de una comunidad estrechamente emparentada. El análisis de isotopos de las únicas mandíbulas adecuadas demostró que tres de los adultos habían residido en un mismo lugar entre aproximadamente los 5–7 años, y en un segundo lugar entre los 11–13 años. Los isotopos de estroncio indican que las geologías subyacentes en estos dos lugares estaban formadas por rocas muy antiguas. El lugar de su entierro, Boscombe Down, representa un tercer emplazamiento, con una geología mucho más joven. La región más cercana con valores biosféricos comparables para la identificación del primer y segundo lugar es Gales, aunque Bretaña, Portugal, el Macizo Central y la Selva Negra son también posibles emplazamientos. La modelación bayesiana realizada con las fechas obtenidas por carbono-14 indica que los individuos presentes no murieron todos en el mismo momento aunque pudieran haber vivido al mismo tiempo. El primer arquero murió entre los años 2500–2340 cal a.C.

El ajuar funerario incluye siete vasos campaniformes con decoración cordada, de fuertes paralelismos en el noroeste de Europa. Dos de estas cerámicas están decoradas con cuerda trenzada. También hay un vaso campaniforme marítimo-cordado. Otros bienes en el ajuar incluyen útiles en sílex como raspadores, cuchillos y puntas de flecha barbadas con pedúnculo, un colmillo de jabalí, y un pequeño colgante de cuerno de un estilo europeo poco común pero de amplia distribución.

La tumba de los Arqueros de Boscombe parece haber sido la de los hombres de un pequeño grupo familiar que viajó hasta Wessex en el siglo XXIV a.C. Este grupo utilizaba el ritual de entierro colectivo típico de la mayor parte de Europa Occidental y Atlántica, y la temprana fecha de la tumba en la secuencia cronológica británica parece sugerir que el grupo provenía de esta región más que de Gales. Sin embargo, la tipología de los bienes en el ajuar no permite preferir un posible origen por encima del otro.

En contraste, la tumba plana del Arquero de Amesbury (1289), que también tenía una cámara de madera, contenía un único enterramiento de un hombre de 35–45 años. La modelación de las fechas al carbono-14 sugiere que el Arquero de Amesbury vivió al mismo tiempo (2380–2290 cal BC) que el último hombre enterrado en la tumba de los Arqueros de Boscombe. Los análisis de isotopos de oxígeno indican que durante su adolescencia el Arquero de Amesbury vivió en un clima más frio que el de Wessex. Valores biosféricos comparables pueden encontrarse desde la región alpina hasta el este de Escandinavia, pero los isotopos de estroncio excluyen las geologías más antiguas de Escandinavia. La introducción del Conjunto Campaniforme en Europa Central y en el norte de Alemania y Polonia más o menos al mismo tiempo que en Gran Bretaña parece indicar una localidad en la región alpina. Los objetos hallados en la tumba del Arquero de Amesbury también tienen sus más cercanos paralelos en Europa occidental, no del norte.

Junto a la tumba del Arquero de Amesbury estaba la tumba 1236, que contenía el cuerpo de un hombre de 20–25 años que había muerto una o dos generaciones después del Arquero de Amesbury (2350–2260 cal BC). La presencia de una rara característica en los huesos de los pies demuestra que los dos hombres estaban biológicamente emparentados, aunque no se puede determinar su se trataba de una relación abuelo/nieto, padre/hijo etc. El hombre más joven bien pudiera haber viajado también a Europa continental. Fue enterrado con un par de ornamentos de oro y un colmillo de jabalí. Unas pocas lascas y útiles de sílex pudieran ser también parte del ajuar funerario.

El Arquero de Amesbury fue enterrado con una cantidad excepcional de bienes funerarios, siendo uno de los entierros campaniformes más ricos de Europa hallados hasta el momento. El ajuar incluye cinco vasos campaniformes, tres cuchillos de cobre, dos muñequeras de arquero, un par de ornamentos de oro, y una hebilla de pizarra. Se hallaron también ciento veintidós (122) piezas de sílex trabajado: cuchillos, raspadores, lascas, 17 puntas de flecha barbadas con pedúnculo, y quizá una punta de flecha triangular. Otros hallazgos relacionados con la tumba incluyen un nódulo de hierro procedente de un juego de útiles para hacer fuego, y un instrumento de cuerno para trabajar el sílex por presión. En la tumba también se hallaron objetos como un instrumento de piedra para trabajar el metal, cuatro colmillos de jabalí, un alfiler de cuerno, dos objetos de cuerno de función desconocida, y un colgante hecho de concha de ostra.

El cobre utilizado para los cuchillos (y quizá los mismos cuchillos) procede de Europa continental y no de Irlanda. Es posible que dos de los cuchillos provengan del norte de España, y el tercero del oeste de Francia. Aunque el estilo de los ornamentos de oro es británico/irlandés, el oro en sí puede ser también de origen continental. La muñequera negra podría ser también de origen continental pero la roja está posiblemente hecha de un tipo de roca encontrado en el suroeste de Gales. Dos de los vasos campaniformes están decorados con decoración cordada con cuerda trenzada, y uno con decoración cordada. Los otros dos vasos campaniformes son de tradición marítima.

Se sugiere que la presencia del útil de piedra para trabajar el metal (un "yunque de piedra") ayuda a explicar el porqué del viaje del Arquero de Amesbury a Gran Bretaña, y la "sobreabundancia" en el ajuar funerario. Su tumba es la tumba de un metalurgo más antigua hallada a día de hoy en Gran Bretaña, y la sobreabundancia de bienes es habitual en las tumbas de los metalurgos del Campaniforme y en aquellas de alto status de la Edad del Cobre y del Bronce en Europa.

Las tumbas de los Arqueros de Boscombe y del Arquero de Amesbury están cerca de algunos de los templos prehistóricos más importantes de Europa. Este hecho puede ayudar a elucidar el emplazamiento de los enterramientos pero hay poca evidencia de contacto entre grupos campaniformes y grupos indígenas del Tardo Neolítico. Esto se debe en parte a que son pocos los asentamientos y enterramientos campaniformes conocidos en Gran Bretaña, pero la modelación estadística de las fechas al carbono-14 también indica que no hubo gran coincidencia cronológica entre los dos grupos.

Un pequeño número de enterramientos en el norte y oeste de Escocia y en la mina de cobre de Ross Ireland al suroeste de Irlanda son evidencia de otros viajes entre Gran Bretaña e Irlanda realizados durante esta época por grupos que utilizaban el Conjunto Campaniforme. Juntos, sugieren un corto periodo de movilidad a larga distancia por parte de grupos que utilizaban el Conjunto Campaniforme en los siglos XXIV y XXIII a.C. Es muy posible que las tumbas de los Arqueros de Boscombe y del Arquero de Amesbury sean las de algunos de los hombres involucrados en esta red internacional.

Traducion: Carmen Vida

PART I

Chapter 1

Introduction

This volume reports the excavation of three early Bell Beaker graves found at Boscombe Down, Wiltshire, in 2002 and 2003 (Fig. 1). All three graves – the 'Amesbury Archer', the 'Companion', and the 'Boscombe Bowmen' – date to the later 3rd millennium BC. Each is, in its own way, unique but all three are linked by a wide-ranging significance relating to the introduction to Britain of the Bell Beaker 'culture' or 'Set'. In addition, the graves lie not far from some of the greatest temples known in prehistoric Europe, the henges at Durrington Walls and Stonehenge (Fig. 2; Pl. 1; pp. 191–2).

The graves were found after more than a decade of investigations in advance of new developments at Boscombe Down and they have been followed by other significant discoveries of both prehistoric and Romano-British date which are reported on in volumes 2 and 3 of this series.

Most of these investigations have taken place before new houses were built. Amesbury lies less than 2 km to the north of Boscombe Down and adjacent to the main road between London and the south-west, the A303 (Fig. 2). In the 1980s Amesbury was identified as both suitable and able to accommodate a significant increase in housing. Most of the developments to provide this new housing stock have been between Amesbury and Boscombe Down, gradually joining the town and the village, while also expanding the area of modern settlement to the west towards the A345 road.

These investigations also chronicle the development of archaeological practice at the turn of the 20th and 21st centuries. The earliest phase of housing development and archaeological investigation was at Butterfield Down. Although archaeological surveys were undertaken in 1990 planning permission had already been granted and, although those surveys demonstrated the presence of a Romano-British village, there was no requirement to undertake archaeological excavations as a condition of the planning permission. Although some excavations were undertaken in advance of house building in 1990–3 (Fig. 3), these were limited in scope with the archaeological remains in some large areas being only planned but not excavated. This archaeological work was undertaken because of the generosity of the developers and the modest subventions from the Archaeology Section of Wiltshire County Council. The report on all these early works was constrained by the very limited funds available (Rawlings and Fitzpatrick 1996).

The implementation of *Planning Policy Guidance 16: Archaeology and Planning* in 1990 marked a sea change in how archaeological matters were dealt with in planning decisions.

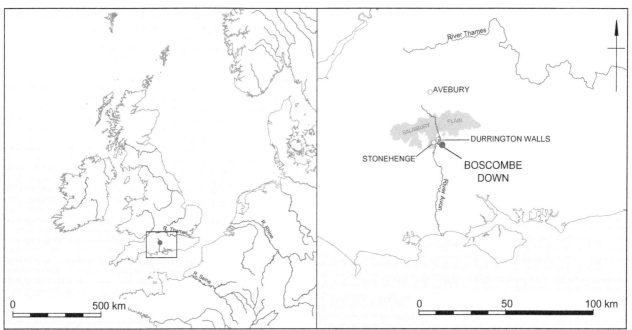

Figure 1 Location of Boscombe Down

Plate 1 View of Boscombe Down from the west with Stonehenge in the foreground (© 2011 TerraMetrics Inc., DigitalGlobe, TomTom, GoogleEarth; reproduced by permission)

Now designated as a 'material consideration' in planning decisions, developers were responsible for establishing the potential impact of proposed developments on archaeological remains and for mitigating the effects of those impacts. The ways in which archaeological remains were considered in the planning process was transformed.

That transformation was often regarded as being encapsulated by the phrase 'preservation by record.' This key phrase in the new Planning Guidance was often interpreted as meaning 'excavation' before destruction. At Boscombe Down this was often the case but the close working relationship that developed between developers, planners, and archaeologists working in both development control and in professional practice also resulted in archaeological sites being preserved. The last surviving area of the Romano-British village was preserved by the land being designated as public open space. An extensive later prehistoric settlement at South Mill Hill was preserved by the land being designated for use as playing fields and public open space, and the design of a new school ensured that the majority of a Romano-British cemetery on the site would remain undisturbed.

In turn the new developments took their name from some of the key discoveries. The first phase of the principal housing development was named *Archer's Gate*. The second phase will be *King's Gate*. The new school became the *Amesbury Archer Primary School* and the Community Centre the *Bowmen Centre*. The *Amesbury Archer* public house was named after a public competition in the local newspaper.

Discovery

The first two of the Bell Beaker graves to be discovered, the Amesbury Archer and the adjacent grave sometimes (and hereafter) called the 'Companion', were found in 2002 in excavations in advance of the new school and a distributor road network which formed the first stage of the principal housing development (Archers Gate) west of Boscombe Down and south-east of Amesbury (Fig. 3). This development lies upon deposits of Upper Chalk (Geological Survey of Great Britain, 1:50,000 Drift Series, Sheet 298). It is situated on the west facing lower slope of the Down

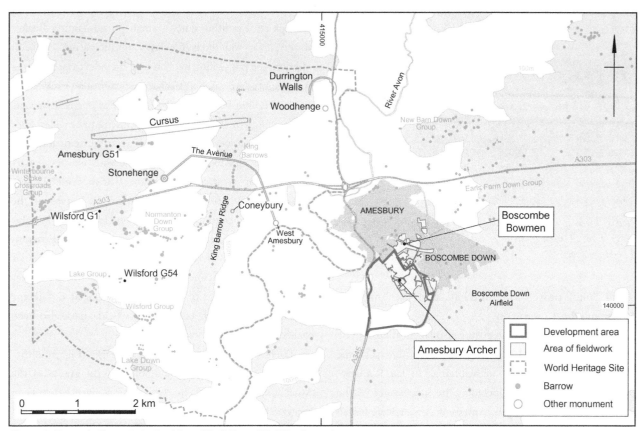

Figure 2 Boscombe Down in its local Late Neolithic and Bell Beaker setting

between approximately 106–116 m aOD. In the years preceding the 2002 excavation the land has been set aside from agricultural use prior to the proposed development. Before this it was used for arable cultivation.

The archaeological potential of the new development had been assessed in both a Desk-Based Assessment and a subsequent Environmental Statement (Terence O'Rourke 2002). Air photographs were transcribed and analysed and geophysical surveys using gradiometry were undertaken. These surveys suggested that relatively few archaeological remains were present but were mindful of the archaeological potential demonstrated by the works at nearby Butterfield Down (Rawlings and Fitzpatrick 1996), the proposed development was preceded by archaeological 'Strip, Map, and Record' fieldwork.

On the 2.45 ha site of the proposed new school, centred on NGR SU 165 405, this work promptly demonstrated that the geophysical surveys had not been able to identify Romano-British inhumation burials. The graves, which had been dug deep into the natural chalk and then promptly backfilled with chalk, did not produce recognisable geophysical anomalies. One effect of this was to demonstrate that what had been thought to be a small undated enclosure

was an enclosed cemetery. The cemetery (Cemetery 1), which was excavated in its entirety, was of late Romano-British date and contained 32 inhumation burials arranged within and around a group of ditched enclosures (Volume 3).

A second group of burials (Cemetery 2) was identified c. 100 m to the west. These graves appeared to continue beyond the excavation area, which was restricted to the footprint of the school building and car park, into the area to be occupied by the school playing fields. The extent of this cemetery was then defined by excavating a closely spaced array of evaluation trenches and the topsoil over it was then removed to expose the cemetery. As it was possible that this second cemetery could be preserved *in situ* under the school playing fields, the burials and other features were surveyed but only a few graves and other features were examined to demonstrate their likely date. The area was covered with a layer of geotextile and then recovered with topsoil (Pl. 2). By altering the design of the drainage system for the playing field it was possible to avoid further damage to most of the graves in the cemetery. However, the two most northerly graves lay beyond the site of the playing field and on the route of a new road that would run past the school. The alignment of the road could not be altered so it was necessary to excavate the

Plate 2 View of Boscombe Down towards King Barrow Ridge. The graves of the Amesbury Archer and the 'Companion' lie just beyond the geotextile cover

graves. These proved to be the burials of the Amesbury Archer and the 'Companion'.

Part of another small enclosure also lay on the route of the new road. This enclosure was *c.* 150 m north-east of the first cemetery and it too contained burials of late Romano-British date. These works, including the latter stages of the excavation of the grave of the Amesbury Archer, were filmed by Topical Television as part of a series of programmes entitled *Past Finders*.

As the 2002 excavations demonstrated that the geophysical surveys had been unable to identify inhumation cemeteries and that the archaeological potential of the area was accordingly higher than anticipated, the area of the proposed housing that would surround the school to the north and east was evaluated in 2003 using mechanically-excavated trial trenches. A number of excavation areas were identified, all to the east of the school, and the areas between them were subject to Strip, Map, and Record where topsoil was removed over the whole area and any archaeological remains were surveyed (or mapped) before being recorded using an appropriate excavation sample. These works were undertaken in 2004. No excavation areas were identified to the north-west of the school and all of this phase of the development was subject to strip, map, and record in 2006–8.

The principal discoveries made in these works, which are reported on fully in Volume 2 (Powell and Barclay in prep.), that are relevant here are: a Late Neolithic pit circle (Pl. 3), a Late Neolithic pit or timber post alignment, several pits containing Late Neolithic Grooved Ware pottery, and several later Bell Beaker graves, one of which was within a ring ditch (Fig. 3). Finds of Late Neolithic and Bronze Age date from the earlier work at Butterfield Down include a Late Neolithic

plaque made from chalk, an undated segmented ring ditch, perhaps of Neolithic date, a small pit containing Beaker pottery, and a ring ditch (Rawlings and Fitzpatrick 1996). In addition, the possibility that some of the unexcavated graves in Cemetery 2 are of Bell Beaker date cannot be excluded.

At the time of writing, work to the west mainly awaits further stages of the housing development, to be called *Kings Gate* (Fig. 3). However, in 2007 during the course of installing a new water pipeline for the houses already built at *Archer's Gate*, part of a large late Romano-British cemetery was excavated some 100 m to the west of the graves of the Amesbury Archer and the 'Companion'. Evaluation has also been undertaken in advance of the southern and eastern length of one of the new roads examined in 2002 and a watching brief maintained over the construction of it. Areas identified as the sites of development associated with the existing housing, such as new sports fields, have also been evaluated.

The cumulative results of these works (Fig. 3) is that *c.* 25 ha to the north, east and south of the graves of the Amesbury Archer and the 'Companion' have either been excavated or stripped of topsoil, mapped, and recorded under archaeological supervision.

In contrast, the grave of the Boscombe Bowmen was found in an archaeological watching brief over a new water pipe some 500 m north of the graves of the Amesbury Archer and the 'Companion' (Pl. 4). That watching brief was part of archaeological works associated with the refurbishment and modernisation of existing housing, mainly built in the 1940s and '50s, associated with the air base at Boscombe Down. This housing, which lies to the west of the base, is commonly known as the 'Lower Camp.' Part of the refurbishment of the Lower Camp entailed renewing the infrastructure and services: relaying roads, replacing water pipes and so on.

In comparison with the extensive evaluations and large excavations in advance of the new housing, the archaeological works in the Lower Camp mainly involved watching narrow water pipe trenches being excavated and old road surfaces being broken out. As the need for a watching brief was intermittent, most of it was undertaken by the QinetiQ staff, Colin Kirby and Bob Clarke (QinetiQ Archaeology), who in addition to their professional skills, are also expert archaeologists. The potential need for archaeological assistance had, though, been recognised and a call-out agreement with Wessex Archaeology put in place. Recognising the pottery as being very similar to that found in the grave of the Amesbury Archer one year previously the works were halted immediately. Colin Kirby contacted Wessex Archaeology and a site meeting was held promptly. An excavation team from Wessex Archaeology was on site by the afternoon where they were assisted throughout by QinetiQ Archaeology.

With so much archaeological work still to be undertaken in advance of proposed new housing to the west of the grave of the Amesbury Archer, there is clearly the potential for further important discoveries.

Organisation of Report

The individual graves – one collective grave and two single graves – have, as far as possible, been reported on and are presented as closed groups. The collective grave of the Boscombe Bowmen is presented first because it is the earliest grave and also allows the differences between the single graves and the perhaps surprisingly complex data from the collective grave to be emphasised.

The range of analyses undertaken in the project attempted to match the significance of the discoveries. As a result some studies whose application in archaeology is not yet mainstream were undertaken. These included isotope but not DNA analysis. There were two reasons for not sampling for DNA. The first is that, at the time of assessment, the likelihood of recovering well-preserved DNA chains from burials of prehistoric date was considered to be low. The second is that, as yet, there is no dataset with which to compare any results. A similar decision not to sample for DNA was reached by the research-funded Beaker People Project (Parker Pearson 2006). As it transpired, osteoarchaeological analysis in this project demonstrated that the two individuals buried in the adjacent single graves 1289 (the Amesbury Archer) and 1236 were genetically related. However, advances in ancient DNA analyses make it probable that successful studies could well be undertaken in the future, particularly on grave 25000 (the Boscombe Bowmen).

Leading British experts were invited to report on the finds from the Boscombe Down graves and to explore their significance. Where the same techniques have been used to report on related materials, for example the burials themselves or isotopes, the methods are only presented once. However, a two-year hiatus in the analysis due to the economic situation meant that it was not possible for the same experts to study

the pottery from the graves of the Amesbury Archer (1289) and the Boscombe Bowmen (25000) or to undertake the associated residue analyses, the work on the Amesbury Archer having already been completed. The radiocarbon dating and the isotope study both contain much comparative material and for this reason they are presented as separate chapters (6 and 7). The final part of this report attempts to draw out something of the significance of the three graves.

Lastly, the individuals buried in graves 1289 and 25000 were named the 'Amesbury Archer' and 'Boscombe Bowmen' for media purposes and this helped in gaining widespread publicity for these internationally important finds. The names have also become firmly established in the archaeological literature with many of the contributors to this report choosing to use them and where they did, this usage has been retained. Questions about nomenclature are not, however, confined to what to call the finds. They also relate to the cultural context, and indeed date, of the burials.

Chronology and terminology: 'Beaker' or 'Bell Beaker'?

In Britain the Late Neolithic period is generally accepted as dating to between c. 2900 and 2200 BC with the Early Bronze Age commencing c. 2200–2100 BC. Bell Beaker or Beaker remains of the type reported here, lie rather uneasily been the two periods. These remains have been variously attributed to the Stone Age (Neolithic) or metal age (Bronze Age), sometimes to a metal using Stone Age (Aeneolithic or Eneolithic), and lately to a separate age (the Copper Age or 'Chalcolithic'). Why this might be is this is discussed below (pp. 192–3).

This British uncertainty about chronological categorisation is echoed in how the remains are described. Throughout continental Europe the terminology used to describe the material reported here is 'Bell Beaker', which reflects the bell-shape of the Beaker pot. In Britain the term 'Beaker' is often – but by no means always – used as shorthand (e.g. Brodie 1997; 1998; Case 2004a). Although the term 'Bell Beaker' is considered here to reflect more clearly the date of the material reported in this volume (c. 2500–2200 BC), its continental European dimensions (where the Early Bronze Age, e.g. Reinecke A1, widely begins c. 2200 BC), and to make the distinction between a pot and what has been considered by many to be an archaeological culture (Harrison 1980, 9–11; Vankilde 2005a, 76; see p. 193 below), the

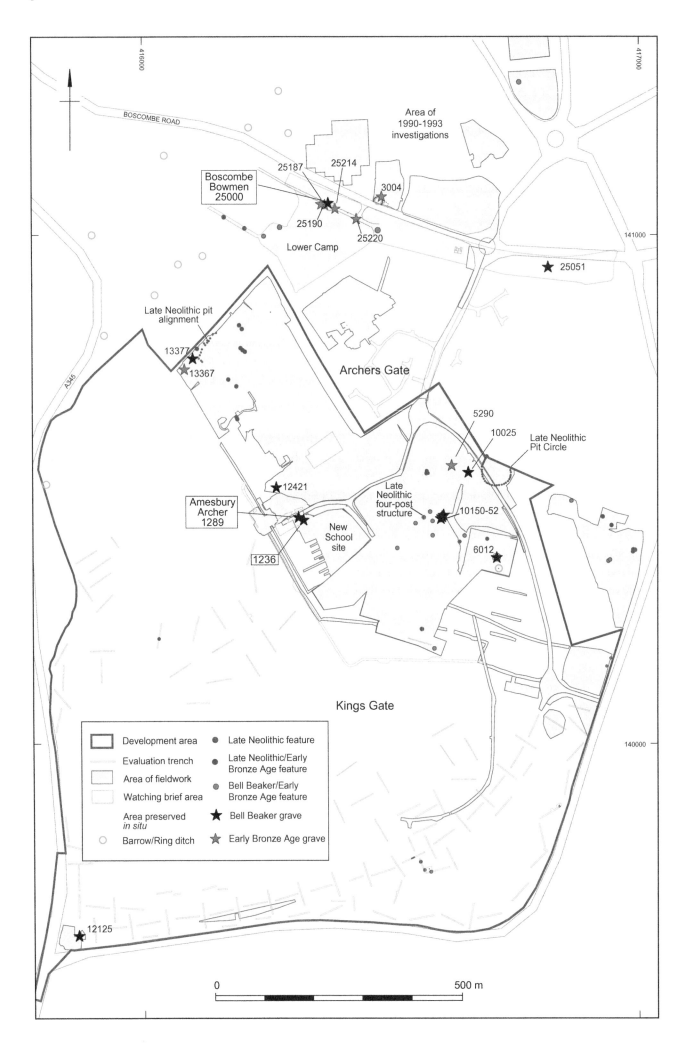

BOSCOMBE ROAD

416000

417000

Area of
1990-1993
investigations

25187   25214

Boscombe
Bowmen
25000

3004

25190

25220

Lower Camp

141000

25051

Late Neolithic pit
alignment

13377

13367

Archers Gate

5290

10025

Late Neolithic
Pit Circle

12421

Late
Neolithic
four-post
structure

10150-52

Amesbury
Archer
1289

New
School
site

6012

1236

Kings Gate

A345

	Development area	●	Late Neolithic feature
	Evaluation trench	●	Late Neolithic/Early Bronze Age feature
	Area of fieldwork	●	Bell Beaker/Early Bronze Age feature
	Watching brief area		
	Area preserved *in situ*	★	Bell Beaker grave
○	Barrow/Ring ditch	★	Early Bronze Age grave

140000

12125

0   500 m

Plate 3 Boscombe Down Late Neolithic pit circle

individual contributors to this report have employed different terms according to their own preference. As these differences reflect something of the current range of thinking in Britain, it has not been considered appropriate to impose an editorial consistency on this diversity. Equally, while the subsequent development of the Bell Beaker Set in Britain is clearly of great interest (Needham 2005), attention has been focused here on finds broadly contemporary with the early burials at Boscombe Down.

Figure 3 (opposite) Distribution of Late Neolithic, Bell Beaker and selected Early Bronze Age burials at Boscombe Down

Chapter 2

Grave 25000: the Boscombe Bowmen

Discovery

By Bob Clarke, A.P. Fitzpatrick, Colin Kirby,
David Norcott, and R.H. Seager Smith

The grave of the Boscombe Bowmen was discovered in the late morning of 22 April 2003 during a watching brief being maintained by Colin Kirby over the excavation of a trench for a water pipe adjacent to Lyndhurst Road. It was found when a small mechanical excavator cut through part of the grave (Pl. 4). The darker fill of the feature was immediately apparent and human bone and Beaker pottery was recovered from the upcast from the trench.

The grave lay on the eastern side of the valley of the River Avon (Figs 2–3) at 104 m aOD as it rises gently from the floodplain towards Boscombe Down (SU 1627 4107). The underlying geology is Chalk. The trench, excavated by the small mechanical excavator, was c. 0.50 m wide and had totally removed the southern part of the grave (Pl. 5); only undisturbed Chalk bedrock was visible in its southern face. The part of the grave that survived was 2.60 m long, at least 0.90 m wide, and a minimum of 0.46 m deep (Fig. 4). It soon became apparent that the northern part of the grave had also been damaged many years earlier when an electricity cable trench had cut across it. As the cable was still operational

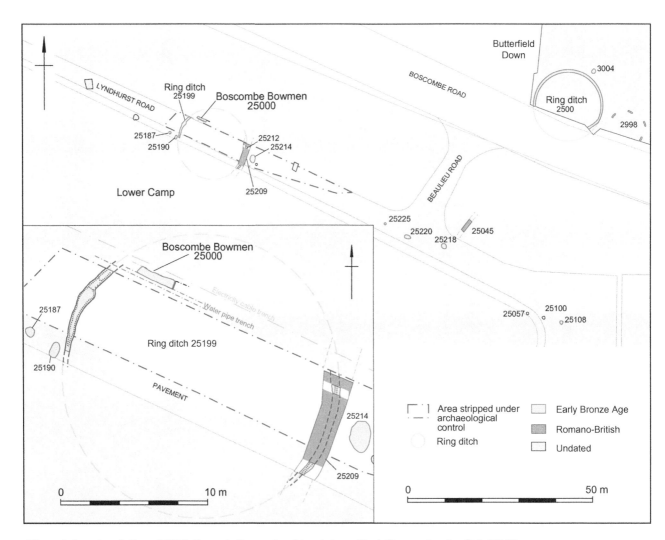

Figure 4 Location of Grave 25000 (Boscombe Bowmen) and its relation to Early Bronze Age ring ditch 25199

Plate 4 View of ?Early Bronze Age ring ditch from the north-west. The grave of the Boscombe Bowmen lies to the left of the photograph

archaeological excavation had to halt at the edge of the cable trench.

The length to width ratio of the wooden chamber in the grave of the Amesbury Archer is 1.32. If, for illustrative purposes, a similar ratio is assumed for the suggested chamber in grave 25000, this would have been 2.60 m long and *c.* 1.95 m wide, so *c.* 0.5 m of the grave and its contents could have been lost on the southern side and *c.* 0.5 m of the northern side before excavation. It is just possible that undisturbed parts of the grave might survive to the north of the electricity cable trench but examination would only be possible when the services are decommissioned in the future. It was, then, a matter of some luck that any of the grave had survived, not least because it had narrowly avoided destruction in the 1950s.

Features Adjacent to Grave 25000

After the excavation of grave 25000 particular care was taken in monitoring further ground works in its vicinity. Most of these involved the resurfacing of Lyndhurst Road and its accompanying pavement and the laying of new kerbs. As

Lyndhurst Road is an access road to a housing estate rather than a highway its foundations and sub-base were not very deep. When it was built in 1951 the road was laid directly onto the natural Chalk.

The make up of the road was carefully removed using a mechanical excavator under archaeological supervision and archaeological remains were found to have survived (Pl. 4). Features in the immediate vicinity of grave 25000 included a ring ditch (25199) and graves 25187 and 25190 of Early Bronze Age date (*c.* 2200–1700 BC; Fig. 4). These are fully reported in Volume 2 (Powell and Barclay in prep.) and are only summarised here.

Ring ditch 25199 had an internal diameter of 18 m (Fig. 4) and was heavily truncated with very little of the ditch fills surviving. The western arc was only 0.07 m deep and while the eastern arc was slightly deeper and could be examined below the footings of the roadside kerb; it was found to have been largely destroyed by a Romano-British ditch (25209). The ditch did not contain any finds or materials suitable for radiocarbon dating.

At the time of its excavation in 2004, ring ditch 25199 was thought to have gone unnoticed when Lyndhurst Road was built although some salvage recording of a nearby barrow

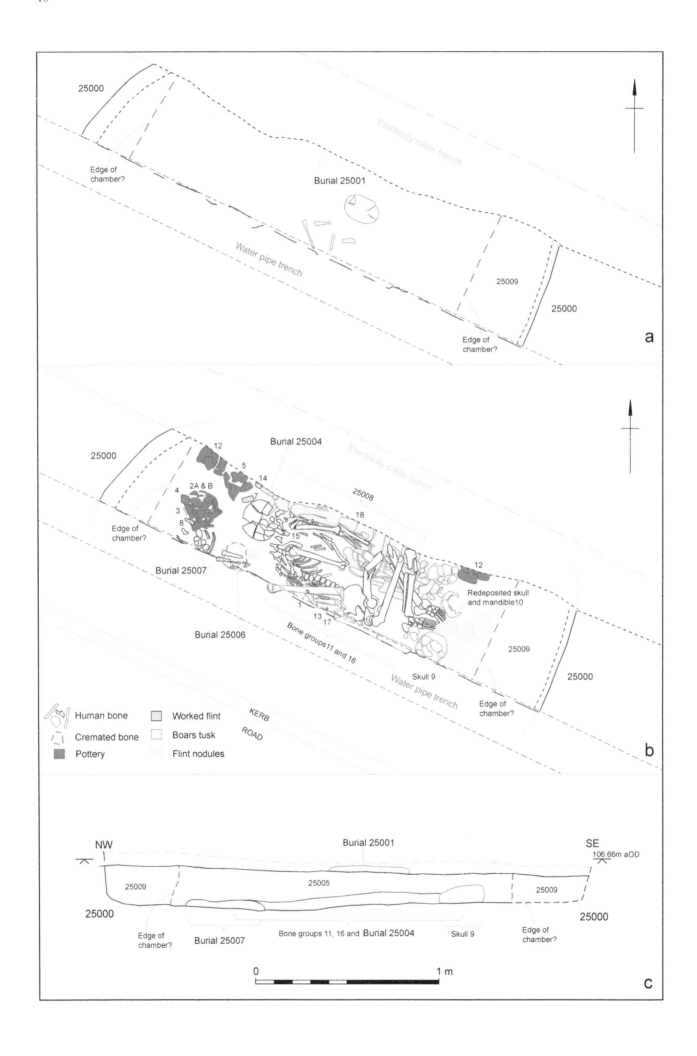

25000

Edge of
chamber?

Burial 25001

Electricity cable trench

Water pipe trench

25009

25000

Edge of
chamber?

a

25000

Burial 25004

Electricity cable trench

12

5

14

2A & B

4

3

8

7

25008

18

Edge of
chamber?

Burial 25007

15

12

Redeposited skull
and mandible 10

Burial 25006

1

13 17

Bone groups 11 and 16

25009

25000

Skull 9

Water pipe trench

Edge of
chamber?

b

Human bone

Worked flint

KERB

Cremated bone

Boars tusk

ROAD

Pottery

Flint nodules

NW

Burial 25001

SE

106.66m aOD

25009

25005

25009

25000

25000

Edge of
chamber?

Burial 25007

Bone groups 11, 16 and Burial 25004

Skull 9

Edge of
chamber?

0

1 m

c

Plate 5 The grave of the Boscombe Bowmen (25000) at the start of excavation

had been undertaken by A. St J. Booth. A brief note on that work was included in the Salisbury and South Wiltshire Museum *Annual Report* for 1952 and more information based on Booth's unpublished notes was included in the catalogue of Bronze Age metalwork in the museum published in 1972. This described the barrow as 58' 6" (17.21 m) in diameter with a central cremation burial in an inverted Collared Urn that was said to have been 'on the surface' (presumably as opposed to being in an excavated grave). A bronze awl was found amongst the cremated bones (Moore and Rowlands 1972, 46, pl. III, G1–2; cf. Longworth 1961, 295, no. 67; 1981, 281, no. 162, pl. 55, c).

Recent records have placed that barrow some 25 m to the south-west of ring ditch 25199. However, a study by Andrew Powell of the earliest records of the location of the barrow

in Salisbury and South Wiltshire Museum strongly suggests that its location has been transposed with that of a 'midden' and that ring ditch 25199 was, in fact, the truncated remains of the barrow recorded by Booth; their diameters are almost identical. The slightly smaller diameter recorded in 1951 as compared to 2003 is presumably because St J. Booth described the diameter of the barrow mound.

Close to the ring ditch and approximately 6 m south-west of the grave of the Boscombe Bowmen (25000) was grave 25187, which contained a cremation burial accompanied by a miniature Collared Urn. Adjacent to and slightly south of grave 25187 was grave 25190. This contained two inhumations and a cremation burial which was accompanied by a small accessory vessel with Collared Urn or Food Vessel affinities. All three individuals in grave 25190 were infants. A number of other burials, probably or certainly of Bronze Age date, were found to the east of ring ditch 25199 including one of a teenager who was buried with an amber necklace (grave 25214).

Another ring ditch or round barrow and, presumably, associated secondary burials, was recorded c. 80 m to the north-east of grave 25000 at Butterfield Down in 1990 (Fig. 4; Rawlings and Fitzpatrick 1996, 10, 38, fig. 6). This (2500) was also *c.* 20 m in diameter and did not appear to have a central burial, unless it too had been placed directly on the ground surface. However, a crouched inhumation burial of probable Early Bronze Age date was found immediately to the north of the ditch. A small undated monument, suggested to be a causewayed barrow or pit ring of Late Neolithic date, was found next to ring ditch 2500 (Rawlings and Fitzpatrick 1996, 37, fig. 6).

Although this evidence is fragmentary, it hints that there may have been a linear barrow cemetery, running approximately east–west, overlooking the Avon valley immediately to the north.

Although antiquarian and most subsequent attention has been directed to the barrow cemeteries around Stonehenge to the north-west of Boscombe Down, there are also extensive cemeteries to the east of Boscombe Down at Earl's Farm Down and New Barn Down (Ashbee 1985; 1992; Clarke and Kirby 2003; Christie 1964; 1967; Darvill 2005, map I; Lawson 2007, 205–10, 376–92, fig. 7.6; Thomas 1956; Fig. 2). It is possible that there was also a cemetery immediately to the south–east within the Boscombe Down airfield (Clarke 2000, 278; Clarke and Kirby 2003).

Figure 5 Plan and profile of grave 25000 (Boscombe Bowmen)

Plate 6 Profile of the grave of the Boscombe Bowmen (25000) looking from the south after initial cleaning (bones visible in section)

Excavation Methods: Grave 25000

The soil from grave 25000 that had been removed by the mechanical excavator was collected (context 25010, sample 100) for sieving for human remains and objects. The remainder of the accessible grave fill (25005) was hand excavated and, in additon to the samples routinely taken for the recovery of human remains, the rest of the fill was retained as a whole earth sample (sample 101).

As soon as the northern side of the trench cut by the mechanical excavator had been cleaned it was apparent that the grave contained multiple deposits (Pl. 6) and, when the complexity of these deposits became clear, recording was undertaken by osteoarchaeologist Jacqueline McKinley.

The deposits within grave 25000 were of two main types; i) articulated skeletons that were probably in the position in which they were laid originally and ii) redeposited disarticulated remains, some of which were deposited in bundles. There was also one cremation burial (Fig. 5). Burials that were considered to be certainly or possibly in their original position were recorded as single contexts. Groups of disarticulated bones and also individual skulls were recorded as objects (ON9, 10, 11, and 16), except in one case where an additional context number (25008) was assigned. For the

purposes of consistency and clarity the numbers that were assigned in the field are retained here. Table 1 summarises all the finds and their assigned object numbers and Table 2 provides a concordance of the burial/bone deposit reference number, isotope samples and radiocarbon measurements.

The Grave

As surviving, grave 25000 was rectangular, 2.60 m long, at least 0.90 m wide and a minimum of 0.46 m deep cut into the natural Chalk (Fig. 5). It was aligned west-north-west to east-south-east and had a flat base. At the eastern and western ends, at least, it had vertical sides. It was filled with a grey–brown silty clay (25005). At the eastern end of the grave several flint nodules up to 0.30 m in size were found in the fill (Fig. 5, b); the four examples seen in Plate 7 are only the ones that lay on the base of the grave. There was also evidence of recent root growth from nearby trees in the grave fill (Pl. 4) and it is suggested below that root action might have moved some of the smaller flint objects in the grave. The upper fill(s) of the grave may have been truncated to some degree but this is unlikely to have removed any bone from the grave.

Table 1: Schedule of objects from grave 25000

Obj. No.	Description	Context
1	Flint end scraper, poss. made from fabricator/strike-a-light, found behind vertebrae of burial 25004	25005
2A–B	2 Beakers, smaller placed within larger, at W end of grave	25004
3	Boar's tusk found with ON 2A–B, ON 4 & ON 8 at W end of grave	25004
4	Barbed & tanged arrowhead found with ON 2A–B at W end of grave	25004
5	Beaker at NW end of grave	25004
6	Beaker at NE end of grave. Sherds were also recorded as ON 23 from spoil of machine trench (25010)	25004
7	Flint end scraper? at NW end of grave next to ON 14 & ON 5	25004
8	Unretouched flint blade found next to ON 2A–B at W end of grave	25004
9	Human skull vault at SE end of grave	25005
10	Human skull vault & mandible, not necessarily from same skull	25005
11	Group of disarticulated human bone in S of grave above burial 25004 & flint flake ON 11	25005
12	Beaker at NW corner of grave	25004
13	Flint knife next to ON 1 behind vertebrae of burial 25004	25005
14	Flint flake by head of burial 25004	25004
15	Flint flake found under left shoulder of burial 25004	25005
16	Group of disartic. human bone in S of grave below burial 25004	25005
17	Flint fabricator/strike-a-light found among group in cervical vertebrae in bones below burial 25004 in S part of grave	ON 16
18	Antler pendant among bone group 25008 in N part of grave	25008
19	Beaker sherds, upcast from water pipe trench	25010
20	Beaker sherd, as above	25010
21	Beaker sherd, as above	25010
22	Barbed & tanged arrowhead, upcast from water pipe trench	25010
23	Beaker sherds, plaited cord, from same vessel as ON 6, upcast from water pipe trench	25010

A thick band of very light brown chalk rubble, which contained sparse pieces of flint up to 0.05 in size and which was 0.40 deep, (25009), extended upwards from the base of the grave to a height of 0.21 m at its eastern and western ends (Fig. 5, c). Although not well defined, it is suggested below that this rubble represents the packing around a wooden chamber in the grave.

Human remains covered the centre of the base of the grave (Bone groups 11, 16, and burial 25004) (Fig. 5, b). Including the bone retrieved from the upcast of the water pipe trench (20510), the remains of at least nine, possibly 10, individuals were represented in this area of the grave. The excavation of the electricity trench some years earlier was not observed archeologically and, while there is no record of bone being found then, it seems likely that some bones and perhaps artefacts also were lost at this time.

One burial, 25001, was at a higher level in the fill of the grave and was of Early Bronze Age date (OxA-13599) (Fig. 5, a). Almost all of the other burials were on the base of the grave, the exception being cremation burial 25006, the bones from which partly overlay and partly intermingled with those from articulated inhumation burial 25007 (Fig. 5, b). Cremation burial 25006 was also dated to the Early Bronze Age (OxA-13972). Two articulated inhumation burials were found on the base of the grave, 25007 and 25004. Burial 25004, which was of an adult male, had been placed amongst disarticulated human bone. Most of this disarticulated bone (25008) was below burial 25004 but some overlay him (25005, ON 11, ON 16; Fig. 6). Two skull vaults and part of a jaw (ON 9–10) lay on the base of the grave at the east of the grave (Fig. 6, a). Remains from a minimum of five, and possibly six, individuals were represented amongst the disarticulated bone. Five individuals were radiocarbon dated to the Bell Beaker period; the two articulated burials 25004 and 25007, one individual represented amongst the group of disarticulated bones recorded as 25008, and two represented amongst the disarticulated remains recovered form the upcast from the water pipe trench (Table 2).

At least eight Beaker pots were present (Fig. 7; Table 1). The Beakers were found mainly at the ends of the grave. A pair of Beakers, one nested (ON 2B) inside the other (ON 2A) was found at the western end of the grave and another two, ON 5 (complete) and ON 12 (incomplete) were found in the north-west. Approximately half of ON 12 was present and, although the electricity cable trench cut through the grave next to the Beaker, it appears that this breakage had occurred in antiquity (pp. 46–7 below). Towards the eastern end of the grave only part of Beaker ON 6 was present. This vessel had certainly been broken in antiquity and parts of it were recovered from the upcast from the water pipe trench

Table 2: Correlation of individuals, isotope samples and radiocarbon dates from grave 25000

Context	Sex	Age	Isotope sample	Radiocarbon date associated	Date
25001	?	6–7	J2	Certain	OXA-13599
25004	M	35–45	A1	Certain	OXA-13624
25006	?	2–4	–	Certain	OXA-13972
25007	?	5–6	J1	Certain	OXA-13598
25010	M	15–18	–	Certain	OXA-13681
25008	M	25–30	A3	*Possibly*	OXA-13543
25010	M	23–30	A2	*Possibly*	OXA-13542

14

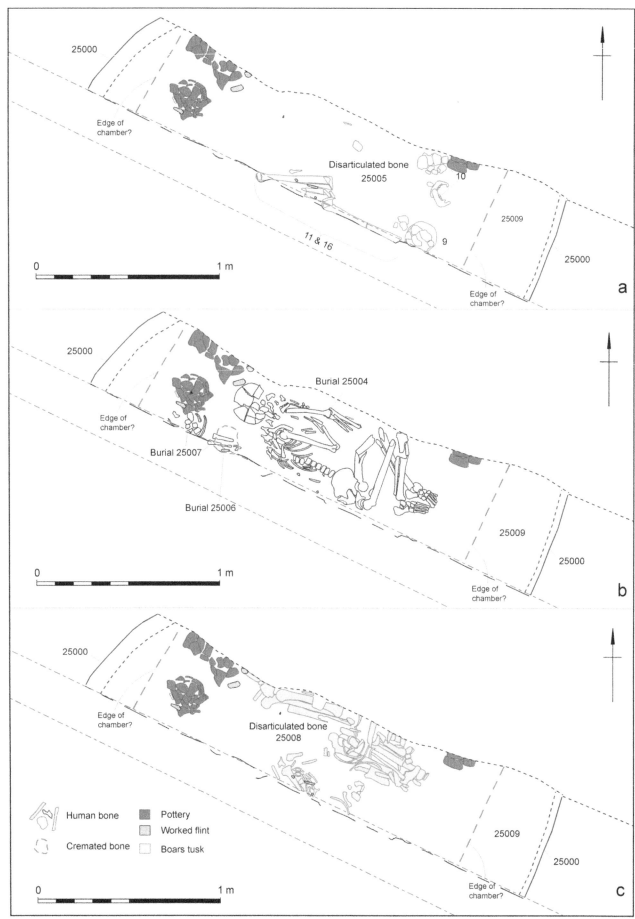

25000

Edge of
chamber?

Disarticulated bone
25005

10

11 & 16

9

25009

25000

Edge of
chamber?

0   1 m

a

25000

Edge of
chamber?

Burial 25007

Burial 25006

Burial 25004

25009

25000

Edge of
chamber?

0   1 m

b

25000

Edge of
chamber?

Disarticulated bone
25008

Human bone   Pottery

Cremated bone   Worked flint

                Boars tusk

0   1 m

25009

25000

Edge of
chamber?

c

Figure 6 Stratigraphic sequence of the Bell Beaker bone groups and burials in grave 25000 (Boscombe Bowmen): a) disarticulated bone group 25005, skulls ON 9 and 10 and groups of bones ON 11 and 16, b) burials 25004 and 25007, c) disarticulated bone group 25008

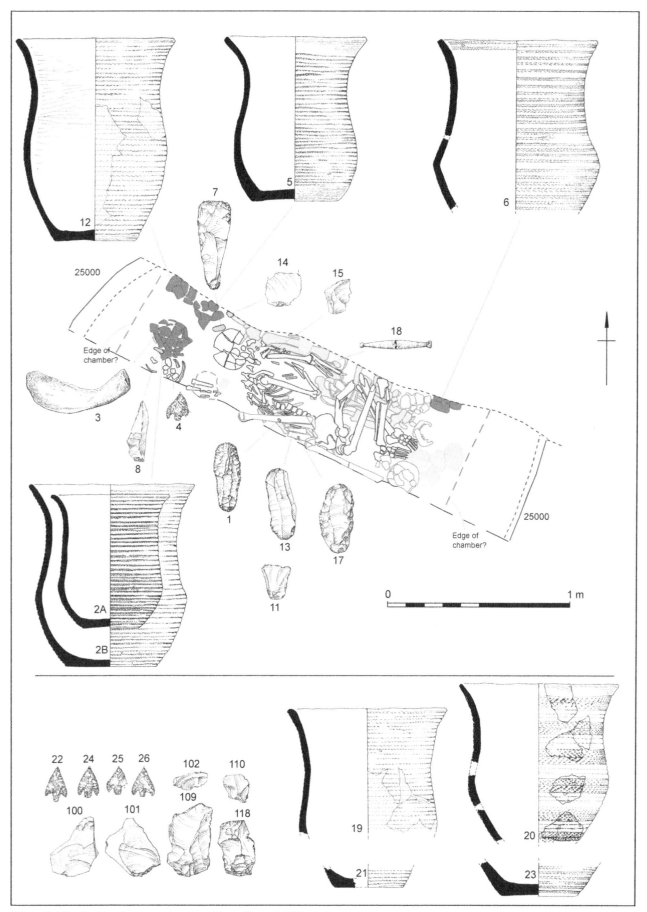

Figure 7 Distribution of grave goods recovered from Grave 25000

Plate 7 The grave of the Boscombe Bowmen (25000)

and recorded as ON 23, indicating that these sherds had lain in the southern side of the grave. Some smaller objects of flint and antler were found amongst the bones (Fig. 7).

Details of the radiocarbon and isotope samples are given in Table 2. As the samples for radiocarbon dating were taken from the femora of individuals, whereas the isotope samples were taken from the lower jaw, it is not possible to be certain that the two sets of samples taken from the four adult males represented in the disarticulated remains are from the same two individuals. The possible – but not certain – sample associations for these men are italicised in the table.

Burials

In situ remains

Four burials were recorded as *in situ* within the grave: 25001, 25004, 25006, and 25007 (Figs 5–6) and are described below in their stratigraphic order, starting with the earliest deposits.

Burial 25004 was an adult male, aged 35–45 years, whose remains lay in the centre of the surviving part of the grave. He was placed on his left side in a flexed position, aligned north-west to south-east, and with his head facing north. His right arm was bent up upwards and it was overlain by his left arm, which was extended downwards. His lower right leg crossed his lower left leg. His torso and chest overlay disarticulated bone group 25008, though his skull and arm bones did not seem to overlie any of this bone. Some disarticulated bones were found on top of this individual (25005, ON 11, ON 16). Two skull vaults and part of a jaw (ON 9–10) lay on the base of the grave at the east end and the feet of burial 25004 lay between these remains. The radiocarbon date from the right femur of burial 25004 (OxA-13624, 3845±27 BP, *2460–2200 cal BC*) is in the Bell Beaker period.

To the south-west of burial 25004, towards the western end of the grave and at the same stratigraphic level on the floor, was inhumation burial 25007. This had been badly disturbed by the machine trench and only the skull and parts of the left upper limb remained *in situ*. The burial was of a 5–6 year old juvenile and it seems probable that they had been buried on their left hand side in a flexed position with their head to the west. Bone attributable to this juvenile was also recovered from the upcast from the water pipe trench (25010) and a radiocarbon date (OxA-13624, 3889±32 BP, *2350–2200 cal BC*) was obtained on the left femur.

Bone deposit 25006 was the remains of the unurned cremation burial of a 2–4 year old infant represented by 7 g of bone in an area 0.15 m long, 0.10 m wide and 0.02 thick. This bone seemed to be partly above burial 25007 and partly amongst it (Fig. 6, b). Burial 25006 had also been disturbed by the excavation of the water pipe trench and 3.6 g of cremated bone was recovered from the upcast from the machine trench. A grave cut for this burial could not be identified in the fill (25005) of grave 25000. The radiocarbon date (OxA-13599, 3613±28 BP, *2140–1970 cal BC*) for burial 25006 places it in the Early Bronze Age.

Burial 25001 was found in the centre of the grave, *c.* 0.2 m above the base of the grave and *c.* 0.1 m above the other burials from which it was separated by soil. It too had been disturbed by the pipe trench (Fig. 5, a). No grave cut (25002) was visible, nor could a separate fill be distinguished from that of the main fill (25005) of the grave. The burial was represented by the upper limbs and skull of a 6–7 year old juvenile, whose head was to the north, facing north-west. The body may have been placed on its right side with the arms flexed. Bone attributable to this juvenile was recovered from the upcast from the water pipe trench (25010) and a radiocarbon date from the left femur is Early Bronze Age (OxA-13599, 3681±30 BP, *2140–1970 cal BC*).

Disarticulated remains

Five groups of bones or individual bones were recorded (ON 9–11, 16, and 25008; Fig. 6). Two crania ON 9 and ON 10 were found towards the eastern end of the burial chamber by the feet of burial 25004. A broken mandible of a 25–30 year old adult male next to cranium ON 10 is not necessarily associated with it. One group of disarticulated bone, largely of long bones (ON 11), overlay the lower spine and upper legs of burial 25004. A second group of disarticulated bone (ON 16) lay below the spine of 25004. The bones recorded as context 25008 partly underlay the spine, patellae, and lower leg bones of articulated burial 25004 but some were on the base of the grave in front of the arm bones and skull of this man. The partial remains of two adult males, a 15–18 year old subadult male and a third possible juvenile (additional to the two juveniles 25001 and 25007) were present in 25008 (all within the burial chamber). A sample from a femur of one of the adults represented amongst 25008 yielded a radiocarbon date of *2470–2310 cal BC* (OxA-13543, 3822±33 BP).

Unstratified remains

Unstratified human bones from the southern part of the grave were also retrieved from the upcast of water pipe trench (25010). These include bones from the articulated burials 25001, 25004, and 25007, and cremation burial 25006; others can be associated with individuals whose remains are present amongst the disarticulated remains that were recorded in the grave, notably the subadult.

Two right femurs from adult males amongst the bone archaeologically excavated (one in ON 11 and one in 25008) and two more from other adult males amongst the material from 25010 show that remains at least four adult males are represented. Samples from one of the adult males (OxA-13542, 3955±33 BP, *2500–2340 cal BC*) and the subadult male (OxA-13681, 3825±30 BP, *2460–2290 cal BC*) represented in 25010 gave radiocarbon dates that fall early in the Bell Beaker period in Britain.

Parts of the body present

Not all the bones from the individuals represented amongst the disarticulated and unstratified remains were recovered and the amount of bone that can be attributed to each of the five, possibly six, people varies greatly. As only part of the grave was excavated, a consideration of the presence or absence of bones must be cautious. Most of the disarticulated remains were large bones, such as leg bones, though some ribs were found, and ribs and small bones from the fingers and toes were found in the upcast from the water pipe trench (25010). The four adults amongst the disarticulated remains were represented by only three major limb bones, their upper and lower left arm bones and their left thigh bones.

It was only occasionally possible to suggest that bones from the same individual occurred in either the same or different group of bones. One example is a right tibia from context 25008, which partly underlay burial 25004, and is considered to form a pair with the smaller of two left tibiae recorded in bone group ON 11 that overlay burial 25004. For the most part there were either no potential matches or no more than one match.

Objects from the Grave

Twenty-three objects were assigned at the time of excavation; eight Beakers, an antler pendant, a boar's tusk, and seven flint tool and flakes including a barbed and tanged arrowhead (Table 1) A further three arrowheads found in the sieving of the fill of the grave and the samples were also assigned numbers in that sequence (ON 24–6). Seven flakes, a fragment of debitage, 46 flint chips and two fragments of burnt flint were also found in this sieving and they were assigned object numbers from 100 onwards (Table 1).

As it is considered highly likely that the grave had been reopened for the placing of successive burials it is possible that residual materials, for example the burnt flint, may have become incorporated into the fill of the grave. The objects of flint were generally in mint condition but a flake and a knapping fragment from the fill of the grave and two flakes from the upcast were dulled and their edges damaged. These pieces are considered to be residual as is a small quantity of animal bone. In general, however, the flint and pottery, whether found in the grave or recovered from the upcast, form a coherent assemblage in both their typology and technology and this suggests that most of them were grave goods.

Although every effort was made to ensure that all finds were recovered, the full extent of the grave could not be determined and part of the grave had already been damaged by an electricity cable. Therefore it is considered unlikely that all the objects present in the grave when it was finally closed have been recovered.

Location of grave goods

Only a partial impression can be formed of where the grave goods had been placed when the grave was closed for the last time (Fig. 7). In addition to post-depositional movement between the disarticulated bones and the decomposing corpses (25004 and 25007), movement may also have been caused by the insertion of burials 25006 and 25001, by root action, and by the recent excavation of the water and electricity trenches.

As already noted, parts of the same Beaker were found in the northern side of the grave (recorded as ON 6) and c. 1 m away on the southern side, recorded as ON 23, among the upcast from the water pipe trench. The distance between these two locations, and also the condition of the breaks in the pot, suggests that it had been broken and moved in antiquity.

Four Beakers, one of which was found inside another, had been placed at the western end of the grave (ON 2A and 2B, 5, and 12). Beakers ON 2A–B were next to the skull of juvenile 25007 and cremation burial 25006, and above the skull of adult male 25004. The complete Beaker (crushed on its side), ON 5, was found 0.08 m to the north-west of the skull of burial 25007. Approximately half of Beaker ON 12 was recovered, crushed, next to ON 5. The rim of Beaker ON 6 lay next to the feet of the adult male 25004. Fragments of the remaining four/five Beakers (ON 19–21, 23) were recovered from the upcast (25010) and so had lain in the outhern part of the grave. They include the base and shoulder of vessel ON 6/23.

The boar's tusk (ON 3) was found near the west end of the grave next to Beakers ON 2A and 2B. Antler pendant ON 18 was found amongst disarticulated bone group 25008 and could have been redeposited along with these bones.

One barbed and tanged flint arrowhead was found within the fragmentary remains of Beakers ON 2A and 2B. The four other arrowheads (ON 22 and 24–6) were recovered from the upcast (25010), indicating that they had lain in the southern part of the grave.

Of the remaining flint objects, blade ON 8 was also found next to Beakers ON 2A and 2B. End scraper ON 1 and knife ON 13 were found behind the spine of burial 25004, while the possible end scraper ON 7 was found at the north-western end of the grave next to the skull of burial 25004 and next to flake ON 14 and Beaker ON 5. Flake ON 15 was found under the left scapula of burial 25004 (25005) and the fabricator/strike-a-light ON 17 was found amongst a group of cervical vertebrae in the bones (ON 16) below burial 25004 in the southern part of the grave. Flake ON 11 is from bone group 11.

Human Remains

by Jacqueline I. McKinley

To achieve a greater understanding of the broader mortuary practices and social composition of the population from which the remains reported in this volume derived, it will be necessary to set them in their wider context. Analysis of these other contemporaneous remains is not yet complete and the full results will be published and discussed in Volume 2 (Powell and Barclay in prep.), though some preliminary comments will be included here. Where data or discussion are relevant to remains from both sets of graves (ie, 25000 and 1236+1285), that information will generally be presented in this section.

Methods

In addition to the procedures for the excavation and recovery of human remains, which includes taking a standard suite of samples, the fill of grave 25000 was retained in its entirety for wet sieving. All osseous and artefactual material was removed from the >5 mm sieved fractions during post-excavation; the smaller fraction residues (2 mm and 1 mm) were retained and scanned by the writer.

Five groups of disarticulated bone were attributed an object number (ON) during excavation (by the writer) including two skulls (ON 9 and ON 10), one group of bone overlying the *in situ* burial 25004 (ON 11) and a second group from below (ON 16) (Figs 5–6). One obviously placed bundle of bone (predominantly long bones) was given an individual context number (25008). The remaining grave fill was recovered as sample number 101 (Table 3).

Recording and analysis of the cremated bone followed McKinley (1994, 5–21; 2004a). The degree of erosion to the unburnt bone was scored following McKinley (2004b, fig. 6). The minimum number of individuals (MNI) was ascertained from the minimum number count of the most commonly occurring skeletal elements in association with clear distinctions in age (*ibid.*). All the bone from this grave was laid out and recorded at the same time to facilitate ease of comparison and potential re-fitting of bone fragments (Pl. 8). Age (cremated and unburnt bone) was assessed from the stage of tooth and skeletal development (Bass 1987; Beek 1983; Scheuer and Black 2000); the patterns and degree of age-related changes to the bone (Buikstra and Ubelaker 1994); and sex was ascertained from the sexually dimorphic traits of the skeleton (*ibid.*). Where possible, a standard set of

Table 3: Summary of human bone from grave 25000

Context	Deposit Type	Quantifi-cation	Age/sex	Pathology	Condition
25001	*in situ* burial	*c.* 12% (s.a.u.)	juvenile *c.* 6–7 yr		4
25004	*in situ* burial	*c.* 85%	adult *c.* 35–45 yr; m	calculus; fracture – left femur; periosteal new bone – right fibula; Schmorl's node – L3-4; pitting – left humerus tubercle; new bone – left humerus tubercle; mv – mandibular M3 5 cusps, overbite	2–3
	R crem. bone	0.2g	infant (=25006)		
25005	R grave fill				
ON 9		*c.* 12% (s.)	adult *c.* 25–45 yr; ??m		3
ON10		*c.* 12% (s.)	adult *c.* 20–30 yr; m	calculus; mv – mandibular M3 5 cusps	2–3
ON 11		*c.* 25% (a.u.l.)	adult <45 yr; m		1–4
ON 16		28 frags. (a.u.l.)	1) subadult *c.* 14–17 yr; ?m 2) adult *c.* 25–35 yr; m		2–4
<101>		*c.* 51 frags	a i) juvenile *c.* 5–6 yr (= 25007) a ii) juvenile *c.* 6–7 yr	calculus	
		c. 60 frags	b i) adult *c.* 18–30 yr; ?m b ii) adult *c.* 18–45 yr; m		
		1.9g	infant (=25006)		
25006	un. burial	7.0g	infant *c.* 2–4 yr		
25007	*in situ* burial	*c.* 25% (s.a.u.)	juvenile *c.* 5–6 yr		3
25008	R placed	144 frags	1) juvenile 2) subadult m 3) adult *c.* 18–30 yr; m 4) adult >30 yr; m	Schmorl's node – T10-11, L2, L4-5, 2L (one adult); op – left distal humerus (one adult)	1–4
25010	R from spoil heap	*c.* 300 frags	1) juvenile *c.* 5–6 yr 2) juvenile 3) subadult 4) min. 2 adults, m	calculus (subadult + 1 juvenile), periodontal disease (subadult); mv – pegged supernumerary (subadult), tooth rotation (subadult), malformed supernumerary (subadult)	1–4
		1.9g	infant (=25006)		

Key: un. – unurned; R – redeposited; cremated bone quantified by weight, unburnt bone by % skeletal recovery or no. frags; s. – skull, a. – axial skeleton, u. – upper limb, l. – lower limb (elements shown only where all are not represented); op – osteophytes, mv - morphological variation; C - cervical, T – thoracic, L – lumbar, S – sacral; bsm - body surface margins (spinal); f = female, m = male

measurements was taken on the unburnt remains (Brothwell and Zakrzewski 2004); stature was estimated in accordance with Trotter and Gleser (1952; 1958) and other indices were calculated according with Bass (1987, 214, 233). Non-metric traits were recorded (Berry and Berry 1967; Finnegan 1978). Full details are held in the archive.

Results

Disturbance and condition

An account of the post-depositional disturbance is given above (pp. 8–9). The unburnt bone is in relatively good condition but much of it is moderately eroded (grade 3) and some of it heavily so (grades 4–5) as a result of root action.

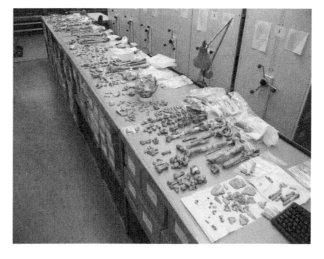

Plate 8 Human remains from Grave 25000 laid out for recording

20

The juvenile bone from the *in situ* burial 25001 was amongst the most heavily eroded, probably due to it being closer to the surface. There are limited signs of abrasion suggestive of repeated manipulation/redeposition and no indication of weathering due to exposure (see *burial formation processes* below). The bone is all fairly heavily fragmented (old breaks), including that from the *in situ* burial 25004, and there are few complete bones in the assemblage. Only *c.* 19% of the skeletal elements from amongst the disarticulated remains are represented by the entire (often fragmentary) bone and most of these are the smaller elements, such as hand and foot bones and some vertebrae (ie, those less susceptible to fragmentation). The long bones are frequently missing their articular surfaces rendering matching or pairing of bones difficult or inconclusive. More of the skeletal elements from the *in situ* remains survive complete (though again, not necessarily intact) with *c.* 65% complete bones, but these are mostly from burial 25004 and, as with the disarticulated material, predominantly the hand and foot bones. Some of the skulls are warped. The cremated bone is in good visual condition and some trabecular bone is present in this very small (11 g) assemblage.

Demographic data

A minimum of nine, possibly 10, individuals is represented; the *in situ* remains of four individuals comprising one infant (25006; cremated), two juveniles (25001 and 25007) and one adult male (25004). A minimum of five, possibly six, other individuals is represented amongst the redeposited bone: possibly an additional juvenile (see below); a subadult (*c.* 15–18 yr), probably male; two adult males of *c.* 23–30 years and *c.* 25–30 years of age; two adults, probably male, who cannot be aged more closely that as greater than 18 years old. The

minimum number was calculated from the number of duplicate skeletal elements (Table 4), the most common of which were the left humerus, radius, and femur. In all except two instances – the left humerus from juvenile 25007 and the left femur from the subadult in 25008 – these skeletal elements were incomplete.

The distribution of bone within the grave is shown in Figures 5–6 and Tables 3 and 5. The placed bundle of bone 25008, which physically underlay the *in situ* remains 25004 (although the arm and face of 25004 may have slumped forwards over the bundle during decomposition), included skeletal elements from a minimum of four of the redeposited individuals; one juvenile, the subadult, and two adults (Table 3). The two skulls and a mandible (25005, ON 9 and 10 – the mandible is probably not associated with the skull recorded under the same object number), possibly deliberately placed at the feet of 25004, appear to belong to the two 23/25–30 year old adult males. The *in situ* remains 25004 both overlay and underlay apparently disorganised groups of redeposited bone (25005, ON 16 and ON 11 respectively) both of which include elements from the subadult and at least one of the adults. Bone from both *in situ* juveniles, the subadult, and at least two of the adults was recovered from the machine spoil (25010), indicating that all lay in the southern portion of the grave.

Recent and possibly ancient disturbance of the *in situ* immature remains, together with the normal actions of bioturbation, had resulted in some bone from all three individuals being recovered from several different contexts including the spoil (25010). The incorporation of burial 25004 may have slightly disturbed the remains of juvenile burial 25007, which radiocarbon analysis indicates pre-dated it, but this cannot be confirmed or refuted with confidence (see Chap. 6: Model 2). Only the skull and parts of the left upper limb of burial 25007 remained *in situ* (Fig. 6). The insertion of the pipe trench would have removed most, if not all, of the *in situ* bone had the individual been laid either supine or on their left side – either of which could have been the case. Some redeposited cremated bone (0.2 g) was recovered from the overall sample associated with burial 25004 but this must reflect the action of bioturbation given the radiocarbon date attributed to the cremation burial indicating that it represents a later addition into the grave.

Table 4: Minimum numbers of major skeletal elements from grave 25000

Skeletal element	Left				Right			
	Juvenile	Subadult	Subadult/adult	Adult	Juvenile	Subadult	Subadult/adult	Adult
Clavicle	1	1	–	3	1	–	1	2
Scapula	2	–	–	4	1	1	–	3
Humerus	2	–	1	5	1	–	1	3
Radius	2	1	–	5	2	–	–	2
Ulna	1	–	1	3	1	1	–	2
Femur	2	1	–	5	2	–	1	3
Tibia	1	–	–	4	1	–	–	2
Fibula	2	–	–	1	1	–	1	3
MNI	2	1	–	5	2	1	–	3

Table 5: Distribution of most commonly occurring skeletal elements from grave 25000

Skeletal element	No. contexts	Juvenile	Subadult	Adult
L. femur	4	25010 (x2)	25008	25004 (*in situ*)
				25005 ON 11
				25008 (x2)
				25010
L. humerus	6	25001 (*in situ*)		25004 (*in situ*)
		25007 (*in situ*)		25005 ON 11
				25008 (x2)
				25010 (x2)
L. radius	6	25001 (*in situ*)		25004 (*in situ*)
		25007 (*in situ*)		25005 ON 11
				25008 (x2)
				25010 (x2)

The small amount of redeposited immature bone recovered from the grave fill (25005) may have derived from either or both of the *in situ* juvenile burials as a result of bioturbation. The three small fragments of immature bone (skull vault, mandibular condyle, and scapula) from the apparently placed bundle 25008 could plausibly reflect the result of similar action, but at least two of the fragments cannot have derived from burial 25007, where they are duplicated, and they are unlikely to derive from the apparently later burial 25001 which was separated from this deposit by a *c.* 0.15–0.20 m depth of soil. On the basis of minimum numbers of skeletal elements, these fragments do not suggest the presence of a third juvenile, however, the contextual data and radiocarbon results suggest that these immature remains could have been disarticulated and redeposited before the insertion of burial 25007; ie, they could represent the sparse remains of a third juvenile.

The majority of the remains comprise incomplete skeletal elements. The adult bone all appears to represent the remains of males, generally of a similar size and robusticity, and, where distinguishable, age. With the exception of the *in situ* burial 25004, and some dental pathology and lesions in the axial skeleton, there are no pathological lesions which may have assisted in matching bones from the same individual. Consequently, in general it was not possible to state with confidence which elements belonged to which of the five adults represented amongst the disarticulated bone.

The *c.* 25–30 year old male is represented by the mandible 25005 ON 10 and the *c.* 23–30 year old by a mandible recovered from the spoil (25010) but neither could be confidently matched with any of the limb bones or the small amount of axial skeletal remains. In a few instances, adjacent skeletal elements from what appear to be the same individual (eg, left tibia and femur in 25005 ON 11 and 25008) were

deposited in the same group of bones. Elements from what are likely to have been the same individual were also distributed between bone groups, for instance, the right tibia from 25008 is likely to be a pair with the smaller of the two left tibiae from 25005 ON 11. In many cases, however, no potential match suggested itself, or more than one possible candidate was suggested, for example, between the left femur from 25008 and the right femur from either 25008 or 25010, and between the large left tibia from ON 11 and the left femur from either 25010 or 25008. Given the incomplete nature of both the skeletal elements and the assemblage there seemed little to be gained from further attempts to ascertain possible matches between skeletal elements by macroscopic examination.

A brief summary of the combined data from the Beaker and Early Bronze Age graves excavated within the immediate vicinity in recent years (to be reported on in Volume 2) gives an overall minimum number of 40 individuals; seven disposed of by cremation and the rest represented by unburnt remains. A large proportion of these individuals were immature (47.5%), most of which were less than 5 years of age at time of death (32.5%). Of the 20 adults identified, 17 (85%) were male. Although not discussed in detail here, these results are undoubtedly of interest. The high proportion of immature individuals, particularly infants, whilst falling within the normal range one might expect to see in a pre-modern 'domestic' population, is well above what is normally present in archaeological assemblages. The other point of note is the extreme paucity of adult females which, particularly in view of the suggested high fertility rate indicating their presence in the population, begs the question of how and where their remains were being disposed of?

Skeletal indices

A summary of the cranial and post-cranial measurements taken from the remains from all three graves – (25000) (Boscombe Bowmen), 1289 (Amesbury Archer) and 1236 ('Companion') – is given in Table 6 for comparative purposes. Stature was estimated for a minimum of three of the adult males, including the two from the *in situ* burials 1238 and 1291, and a minimum of one of the disarticulated adults from grave 25000 (right femur and tibia 25008 and left tibia ON 11, all possibly same individual). There is a close range of 1.74–1.78 m (*c.* 5' 8½"–5' 10"), with an average 1.77 m (1.76 m if all measures on disarticulated bones included). The mean is higher than that of 1.68 m (*c.* 5' 6") recorded by Brothwell for Neolithic males and also slightly greater than his figure of 1.74 m for the Bronze Age but within the same range

Table 6: Cranial and post-cranial measurements (mm) from bone recovered from all three graves (25000, 1291, and 1236). Biometric codes after Brothwell (1972, 79–84)

Measurement	No.	Range	Mean	SD
Cranial				
Cranium: B'	1	115.4		
Cranium: B"	2	123.5–129.7	126.6	3.1
Cranium: MB	3	132.5–155.5	153.7	1.31
Cranium: L	3	186.8–189.0	188.2	0.97
Cranium: H'	1	141.8		
Mandible: GoGo	3	95.5–104	100.0	3.5
Mandible: Cr H	3	67.7–70.2	69.2	1.1
Mandible : H1	3	34.0–37.0	35.6	1.2
Mandible: ML	2	100.6–112.0	106.3	5.7
Mandible: RB'	4	32.4–37.0	34.7	2.0
Mandible: W1	1	126.5		
Mandible: ZZ	3	45.3–51.4	47.5	2.8
facial: G'1	1	56.3		
facial: G2	1	44.9		
Post-cranial				
Sacrum: B	1	110		
Scapula: glenoid L	6 (2R4L)	28.5–40.7	37.4	4.1
Scapula; glenoid W	4 (1R3L)	25.6–31.1	30.4	4.8
Humerus: W distal as	2 (1R1L)	44.0–50.4		
Humerus: epicond. W	4 (1R3L)	59.4–67.6	63.9	3.0
Humerus: VD head	4 (2R 2L)	46.3–52.5	48.8	2.6
Humerus: L	1 (L)	330		
Radius: depth head	1 (L)	10.5		
Radius: diam. head	2 (1R1Us)	22.6–23.0		
Radius: L	1 (L)	247		
Ulna: L	2 (1R1L)	268–287		
Femur: a-p meric	7 (2R5L)	26.5–38.0	31.2	4.2
Femur: m-l meric	7 (2R5L)	29.6–33.7	32.5	1.6
Femur: a-p midshaft	5 (L)	25.4–36.0	25.4	3.4
Femur: m-l midshaft	5 (L)	26.1–28.5	27.4	0.9
Femur: Bi-condylar W	2 (1R1L)	79.2–83.5		
Femur: VD head	6 (L)	46.3–50.0	48.2	1.4
Femur: max L (FeL1)	3 (1R2L)	46.4–48.5	47.6	0.8
Patella: L	1 (R)	42.3		
Patella: W	1 (R)	45.7		
Tibia: a-p cnemic	5 (2R3L)	26.7–40.0	35.6	4.7
Tibia: m-l cnemic	5 (2R3L)	22.8–24.2	23.8	0.5
Tibia: L	3 (1R2L)	38.7–39.6	39.1	0.3
Fibula: L	1 (L)	36.8		

(1973, table 149). Comparison with more recent data from 13 male Beaker period graves from five sites – Barnack, Cambridgeshire (Wells 1977); Amesbury G51 (Brothwell *et al.* 1975/76); Stonehenge, (O'Conner 1984); Chilbolton, Hampshire (Stirland 1990); and Fordington Farm, Dorset (Jenkins 1991) – gives a range of 1.63–1.78 m, with a mean of 1.73 m and a Standard Deviation (SD) of 0.04 m; the figures from Boscombe Down are again towards the top of the range, and have a higher mean.

The crania were insufficiently intact to allow measurements to be taken for the calculation of indices other than the basic cranial index, which was calculated for the three adult males whose remains were *in situ*. There is a range of 81.0–82.4, with a mean of 81.7 and a SD of 0.57; all fall within the brachycranial (round-headed) range. This corresponds with the range most frequently recorded by Brothwell in his study of Bronze Age populations (1973,

Abb. 65), where he demonstrated the general shift from the preponderance of dolichocranial skulls (long-headed) in the Neolithic to brachycranial skulls in the Bronze Age. Cranial index was calculated for three males skulls from the sites mentioned above, giving a broad range of 68.2–80.9, a mean of 75.7 and a SD of 5.5 (Wells 1977; O'Connor 1984; Jenkins 1991); these figures suggest a level of homogeneity within the Boscombe Down group that is not necessarily reflected in the period as a whole.

The platymeric index (demonstrating the degree of anterior-posterior flattening of the proximal femur) was calculated for six left and four right femora, representing the remains of six individuals (left side). The range for the left side is 77.9–96.5 (platymeric–eurymeric), with a mean of 87.1 and a SD of 5.9. The range and SD is slightly reduced if the left femur from 1291 – which had suffered gross plastic deformation/under-development (see pp. 83–6 below) – is excluded; range to 82.8–96.5 (platymeric-eurymeric), mean of 89.0 (eurymeric) and SD 4.5. The range for the right side is 83.4–98.8, with the same mean as for the left side (89.0) and a SD of 6.0. In general the figures for remains from grave 25000 are slightly lower than those from graves 1236 and 1289, which have a left range, mean and SD of 82.8–90.7, 87.1, and 2.9 respectively, and a right range, mean and SD of 83.4–84.8, 84.1 and 0.7. The tighter range and lower SD for the group of four individuals from grave 25000 suggests a closer homogeneity between these individuals than between those from all three graves. Comparative platymeric data was available for only two of the comparative Beaker period sample (seven individuals) giving a range of 65.7–78.2, with a mean of 72.1 and a SD of 4.2 (left side: Wells 1977; Brothwell *et al.* 1975/76).

The platycnemic index (illustrating the degree of meso-lateral flattening of the tibia) was calculated for four left and three right tibia. The range for the left side is 60.2–89.5, with a mean of 71.2 (eurycnemic) and a SD of 11.0. As with the femur, the mean and the SD have probably been skewed by plastic changes to/under-development of the left leg of skeleton 1291 and if this is excluded from the calculation the range is reduced to 60.2–68.4 with a mean of 65.1 (mesocnemic) and a SD of 3.5. The range for the right side is 58.0–67.2, with a mean of 62.8 (platycnemic) and a SD of

3.7. Platycnemia has been linked with plastic changes to the bone as a result of the frequent adoption of a squatting posture and is noted as being more common in prehistoric material in the British Isles (Brothwell 1972, 91). There is, however, no clear link between individual indices and the presence/absence of squatting facets in this assemblage; the latter were seen in tibiae with indices in the mesocnemic range as well as those in the platycnemic. Comparative platycnemic data were again available for only two of the five aforementioned comparative sites (seven individuals) giving a range of 58.6–72.0, with a mean of 66.8 and a SD 4.4 (Wells 1977; Brothwell *et al.* 1975/76).

Non-metric traits/morphological variations

Variations in skeletal morphology may, with other predisposing factors, indicate genetic relationships within a 'population'. The heritability of some traits is open to question (Berry and Berry 1967; Tyrrell 2000) and some have been attributed to developmental abnormalities (Brothwell 1972, 92, 95–8; Molleson 1993, 156). A summary of the presence/absence of the standard variations recorded from three graves is presented in Tables 7–8. Other variations observed during analysis are recorded in Tables 3 and 14. Where variations of the same type/form were observed in remains from graves 1236, 1289, and 25000 they are discussed together here; where specific types of variation were recorded only in remains from graves 1236 and 1289 the data are presented below (pp. 78–86).

Numerous dental anomalies were observed including a five-cusp form to the mandibular 3rd molar (M3), which was noted in four of the five dentitions where these teeth were recovered (Tables 3 and 14). This is a common variation recorded in 34–77% of human populations (Hillson 1986, 268). Shovelling of the maxillary incisors (1291) is also relatively common (24–100%; Hillson 1986, 259). A fragment of the left distal mandibular body from context 25010

Table 7: Scoring of cranial non-metric traits from graves 25000, 1236, and 1289

Vertebra	Total	Schmorl's nodes	Degenerative disc disease	Osteophytes (lone lesions)
C1	6	–	–	–
C2	5	–	–	–
C3	3	–	–	–
C4	3	–	–	–
C5	3	–	–	–
C6	3	–	–	–
C7	3	–	–	–
C gen.	5	–	–	–
T1	2	–	–	–
T2	2	–	–	–
T3	2	–	–	–
T4	2	–	–	–
T5	2	–	–	–
T6	2	–	–	–
T7	2	2	–	–
T8	2	1	–	1
T9	2	2	–	–
T10	3	2	–	1
T11	3	2	–	–
T12	3	1	–	–
T gen.	24	–	–	–
L1	4	1	1	–
L2	4	1	–	–
L3	3	3	–	–
L4	4	3	–	1
L5	4	1	–	1
L gen.	8	2	–	–
S1	5	–	–	–
Total	114	21	1	4

Table 8: Scoring of post-cranial non-metric traits from graves 25000, 1236, and 1289

Trait	Presence		Absence	
Axial skeleton				
Atlas bridging: a) posterior			*2*	*2*
b) lateral			*2*	*2*
Accessory transverse foramen			*2*	*2*
Acetabular crease			2: *1*	1: *2*
Accessory sacral facets			*1*	*2*
Upper limb				
Acromion articular facet	*1*	*1*	2	2
Circumflex sulcus		1	1:*2*	4: *2*
Supra-condyloid process			5: *2*	4: *2*
Septal aperture	*1*		2	3: 1
Lower limb				
Allen's fossa	1		2: *2*	1: *1*
Poirier's facet	2		1: *2*	1: *1*
Plaque		*1*	3: *2*	1
Hypotrochanteric fossa			2: *2*	1: *1*
Exostoses in trochanteric fossa			2: *2*	2: *2*
Third trochanter	1		2: *2*	3: *2*
Squatting facets:				
a) medial	1	2	2: *1*	1: *1*
b) lateral	2	1: *1*	*1*	1
Vastus notch				*1*
Os trigonum			1	2
Medial talar facet			1: *2*	2: *2*
Lateral talar extension			1: *2*	2: *2*
Inferior talar articular surface	1	1	*1*	1: *1*
Anterior calcaneal facet double		1	*1*	1: *2*
Anterior calcaneal facet absent	*2*	*1*	1	2
Peroneal tubercle		*1*	1: *1*	2

Key: data from burials 1238 and 1291 are italicised

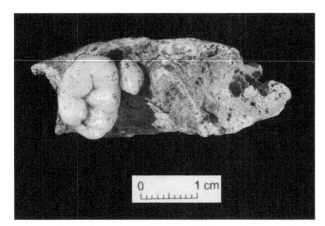

Plate 9 Occlusal view of left dorsal mandible from Grave 25000, context 25010(d), showing rotated, multi-cusped M2, 'pegged' supernumerary and unerupted supernumerary tooth forms

(subadult) shows a variety of more unusual dental anomalies including a large six-cusped 2nd molar (M2), rotated *c.* 90°, and a small, 'pegged' supernumerary tooth erupted against the labio-distal side of the M2 (Pl. 9). The alveolar surface between the M2 and M3 crown crypt shows the presence of a formation within the mandibular body, presenting a smooth bony-texture with convex surface in the occlusal plane. An X-radiograph illustrates the presence of a spherical sub-alveolar formation, *c.* 9.5 mm diameter, sitting in what appears to be a crown crypt. The spherical mass does not have the dense opaqueness of tooth enamel, corresponding more with the appearance of the dentine and roots, but there are no internal structures suggestive of a pulp cavity. The cusp variation in the M2 is relatively rare, occurring in between 0–19% of individuals (Hillson 1986, 268). Supernumerary teeth

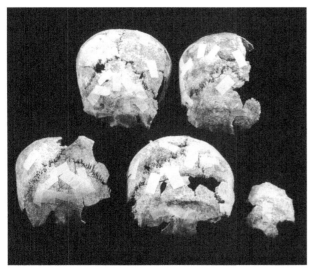

Plate 10 Grave 25000; reconstructed skulls from: 25004 (top left), ON 9 (top right), burial 25007 (bottom left), ON 10 (bottom centre), 25008 (bottom right)

are most frequently found in the maxillary dentition rather than the mandibular, and generally take an aberrant form, the small 'pegged' form seen here being the most common type (Hillson 1986, 270). The sub-alveolar spherical mass seems likely to represent a second supernumerary of aberrant form.

Only one of the crania from grave 25000 – the *in situ* burial of adult male 25004 – was sufficiently complete to allow measurements to be taken (Table 6), but it was possible to reconstruct at least parts of the dorsal portions of five others and thereby formulate an impression of their general shape (Pl. 10). The skulls from all three graves appear to share a relatively short form, broad at the back with flattening of the occipital/distal parietals. This conforms with the tendency towards the brachycranial form illustrated in those for which the cranial index could be calculated. A minimum of three of the skulls from grave 25000 had between two and four relatively small ossicles in the lambdoid suture, predominantly in the left side (Pl. 10). Between one and five lambdoid ossicles were observed in 37% of the Neolithic skulls and 34.8% of the Bronze Age skulls in Brothwell's survey (1973, table 152). Given the frequency of the variant and the possibility of other extrinsic factors being involved in their formation, such ossicles cannot reliably be used as an indication of a genetic link between individuals (Brothwell 1972, 95–6; 1973, 293).

In general, individual non-metric traits cannot be used to indicate possible familial relationships between individuals. The frequency of occurrence of many of the recorded variations is such that the use of individual traits in this way could be, at best, highly misleading. Within this small assemblage, derived from three relatively nearby graves of closely similar date, few metric and non-metric traits could be recorded on a consistent basis rendering interpretation even more problematic. There are a few general indications of broad similarities between the individuals within the assemblage – skull form and fairly close homogeneity in the platymeric index – but indications of closer, possibly broad family relationships are absent or inconclusive. The one exception is the occurrence of the same rare non-metric variation shared by the two males buried in the adjacent graves 1236 and 1289 (p. 80 below).

Pathology

Tables 3 and 14 include summaries of the pathological lesions observed and the bones affected in individuals recovered from all three graves reported in this volume. Where pathological conditions of the same type were observed in remains from all three graves they are discussed together here.

Some specific conditions were recorded only in the remains from grave 1289 and they are reported on pp. 80–6. No lesions were observed in the cremated bone and the following data and rates pertain only to the unburnt bone.

Dental disease

All or parts of two juvenile, one subadult and a minimum of five adult dentitions were available for analysis. A total of 18 deciduous teeth and 10 deciduous tooth positions were recorded and 137 (66 maxillary, 71 mandibular) permanent teeth and 144 (60 maxillary, 84 mandibular) permanent tooth positions. Unlike the permanent dentitions, the deciduous dentition contained more maxillary than mandibular teeth and socket positions.

Dental calculus (calcified plaque/tartar) harbours the bacteria which predispose to periodontal disease and the development of dental caries. The condition was observed in both juvenile, the subadult, and four of the adult dentitions (82% of permanent teeth). Deposits were classified as mild–moderate. There was no consistent increase in severity with age, though deposits in the adult dentitions of greater than 30 years of were both classified as moderate. Roberts and Cox (2003, tables 2.7 and 2.29) give a Crude Prevalence Rate (CPR; ie, number of individuals with the condition) as 11% for the Neolithic and 37% for the Bronze Age in Britain. However, given the tendency of this material to become dislodged from the teeth during excavation and post-excavation processing, these rates should probably be viewed as a minimum.

Periodontal disease (gingivitis) was observed in three dentitions (CPR 37.5%), including that of the subadult from grave 25000 and the adult dentitions 1238 and 1291. Lesions are generally slight to moderate (scored at 2–3 according with Ogden 2005), with indications of an age-related increase in severity, and are generally concentrated in the distal dentitions. The CPR of the condition is given as 14% for the Neolithic and 24.6% for the Bronze Age in Roberts and Cox's survey (2003, tables 2.10 and 2.30).

Dental caries, resulting from destruction of the tooth by acids produced by oral bacteria present in dental plaque, were recorded in two of the adult dentitions (1238 and 1291). Lesions were seen in three mandibular teeth, giving a rate of 2.2% (3/137 teeth) or 4.2% mandibular teeth; CPR 33%. One small ('pin-hole') lesion was seen in the occlusal surface of the right 2nd molar (1238). In 1291 adjacent approximal lesions were seen in the 2nd premolar and 1st molar (M1), exposing the pulp cavities in both. The infection had tracked into the socket of the M1 resulting in the formation of a

dental abscess (rate 0.7%); the infection had subsequently exited buccally through the mandibular body and there is some indication of soft tissue infection. The spread of infection from grossly carious teeth to the supportive structures is a common cause of dental abscesses (Hillson 1996, 316–18). The rates for both caries and abscesses is lower that those for either the Neolithic (caries 3.3%, abscesses 3.8%) or the Bronze Age (caries 4.8%, abscesses 1%) assemblages within Roberts and Cox's samples (2003, tables 2.6, 2.8, and 2.27–8 respectively). This may in part be due to the apparent fairly young age of most of the individuals in the Boscombe Down assemblage, since both these conditions tend to increase in frequency with age.

Dental hypoplasia is a condition represented by developmental defects in the tooth enamel formed in response to growth arrest in the immature individual, the predominant causes of which are believed to include periods of illness or nutritional stress (Hillson 1979). Lesions were seen in the two adult dentitions from graves 1236 and 1289 (33.3% of dentitions); overall rate 4.3%, 3% in the maxillary teeth and 5.6% in the mandibular. In both cases the lesions are slight (single faint hyperplasic lines) and present in only a limited numbers of teeth (1238 canines; 1291 2nd molars). The CPR appears much higher than that of 2% for the Neolithic and 12.3% for the Bronze Age given by Roberts and Cox (2003, tables 2.5 and 2.32). These rates, however, are calculated for the total number of individuals within the populations included in the survey irrespective of whether they were represented by dentitions or not, and consequently are likely to be unrepresentative of the True Prevalence Rates (TPR). For example, the CPR given for the early Neolithic site of Hambledon Hill, Dorset is 2.7% (Roberts and Cox 2003, table 2.5), but only 29 permanent dentitions were recovered, six (20.7%) of which included teeth with dental hypoplasia (McKinley 2008a). The true prevalence rate was available for only one Bronze Age site in Roberts and Cox's survey (2003, table 2.32) with a rate of 8%, higher than the 4.3% from the Boscombe Down assemblage.

The condition of the teeth can give indications as to an individual's diet and, potentially, their general well-being. The low levels of dental hypoplasia suggest relatively well-nourished children who suffered no major stresses during the years of tooth development; this was particularly the case for those buried in grave 25000. The generally slight level of calculus deposits together with the low rates of caries and the other dental conditions to which they may lead (abscesses and *ante mortem* tooth loss: no case of the latter was observed) suggest a high protein, meat-rich diet relatively low in carbohydrates, and generally self-cleaning (Hillson 1986, 286–99).

Trauma

The adult male 25004 had suffered a major, probable multiple, fracture to the proximal third of the left femur, which was well-healed but mis-aligned (Pl. 11). Damage and incomplete recovery of the distal portion of the bone (all of the elements of the left knee joint are missing; see below) renders it impossible to ascertain the full impact of the injury. The X-radiograph suggests the bone may have fractured in two places; there is a clear oblique or spiral fracture at the proximal and distal ends of the central segment of shaft, with dorsal angulation of at least the proximal fragment. There appears to be c. 62 mm overlap of the broken fragments at the proximal end. The medullary cavity has partially in-filled with cancellous bone. There are several small sinuses around the dorsal bony extension but no sign of infection. The macroscopic appearance is one of anterior and lateral 'bowing' of the bone with a gross but smooth bony callus, 43 mm (medio-lateral) x 32 mm (anterior-posterior). The *linea aspera* has atrophied and the only marked muscle attachment is at the upper margin of the *vastus intermedius* (extends leg at knee joint). Most of the left innominate and tibia were recovered and appear normal; the latter does have a markedly stronger *soleus* muscle (planter extension of foot) attachment than the right tibia.

Fractures to the femur shaft are usually the result of severe violence such as may be caused in the present day by a road or aeroplane accident (Adams 1987, 222). The type of activities leading to the equivalent violent impact force in the Beaker period could include a fall from some height or, possibly, from a horse (if they were being ridden at these times) moving at speed. The broken fragments were subject to mal-union with shortening and lateral bowing; this would have had a major effect on the mobility of the individual and the angulation may have lead to osteoarthritis in the knee (*ibid.*, 231). Other likely complications of such a major injury include damage or severing of blood vessels and/or nerves; though the normal appearance of the surviving tibia and fibula suggest that if such injuries had occurred they were either minor or temporary since the leg clearly continued to function. There was clearly no (successful) splinting of the bone but the individual would have required long-term convalescence (union of the adult femur normally taking about four months: *ibid.*, 230) and continued support of the community, with what would have been a long term subsequent disability.

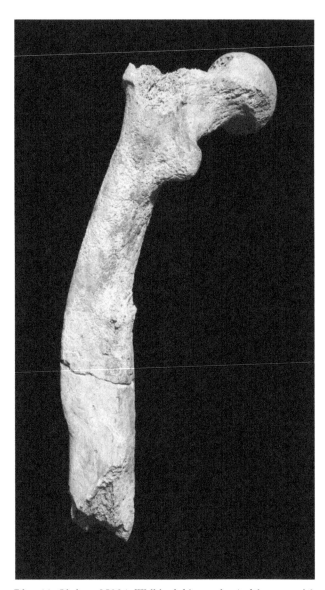

Plate 11 Skeleton 25004: Well-healed but mal-united fracture to left femur with lateral bowing

Joint disease

The various forms of joint disease represent the most commonly recorded conditions in archaeological skeletal material. Similar lesions – osteophytes and other forms of new bone development, and micro- and macro-pitting – may develop as a consequence of one of several different disease processes, some also occurring as lone lesions largely reflective of age-related wear-and-tear (Rogers and Waldron 1995). Tables 9–10 summarise the lesions and conditions affecting the various spinal and extra-spinal skeletal elements for the contents of all three graves.

Schmorl's nodes (a pressure defect resulting from a rupture in the intervertebral disc; Rogers and Waldron 1995, 27), were observed in between two and eight vertebrae in four adult spines, with an overall rate of 18.4% (TPR). No lesions

Table 9: Summary of vertebrae and lesions observed in all remains from graves 25000, 1289, and 1236

Vertebra	Total	Schmorl's nodes	Degenerative disc disease	Osteophytes (lone lesions)
C1	6	–	–	–
C2	5	–	–	–
C3	3	–	–	–
C4	3	–	–	–
C5	3	–	–	–
C6	3	–	–	–
C7	3	–	–	–
C gen.	5	–	–	–
T1	2	–	–	–
T2	2	–	–	–
T3	2	–	–	–
T4	2	–	–	–
T5	2	–	–	–
T6	2	–	–	–
T7	2	2	–	–
T8	2	1	–	1
T9	2	2	–	–
T10	3	2	–	1
T11	3	2	–	–
T12	3	1	–	–
T gen.	24	–	–	–
L1	4	1	1	–
L2	4	1	–	–
L3	3	3	–	–
L4	4	3	–	1
L5	4	1	–	1
L gen.	8	2	–	–
S1	5	–	–	–
Total	114	21	1	4

Table 10: Summary of extra-spinal joints and lesions observed in all remains from graves 25000, 1289, and 1236

Joint	Right Total	Osteo-arthritis	Lone osteophytes	Left Total	Lone osteophytes
Temporo-mandibular	5	–	–	8	–
Costo-vertebral (ribs)	26	2	–	23	2
Sacro-iliac	4	–	1	4	1
Acromio-clavicular	1	–	–	1	–
Sterno-clavicular	2	–	–	1	–
Shoulder - Glenoid	6	–	–	5	–
Shoulder – humerus	4	–	–	6	–
Elbow – humerus	4	–	–	5	1
Elbow – radius	1	–	–	1	–
Elbow – ulna	4	–	–	5	–
Wrist – radius	2	–	–	2	–
Wrist – ulna	2	–	–	3	–
Hand – carpals	8	–	–	11	–
Hand - carpo-meta	6	–	–	7	–
Hand - meta-phalangeal	4	–	–	7	–
Hand - proximal IP		–	–	9	–
Hand – distal IP	2	–	–	5	–
Hip – pelvis	4	–	–	5	1
Hip – femur	4	–	–	8	–
Knee – femur/patella	3	–	–	3	–
Knee – lateral	7	–	–	4	1
Knee – medial	5	–	–	4	–
Ankle	5	–	–	6	–
Foot – tarsals	20	–	–	23	–
Foot – tarso-meta	19	–	–	13	–
Foot – meta-phalangeal	9	–	–	11	–
Foot – proximal IP	7	–	–	9	–
Foot – distal IP	5	–	–	1	–

were observed above the 8th thoracic, and the 7th and 9th thoracic and the 3rd lumbar were most commonly affected. The lesions are most frequently seen in the lower thoracic and lumbar vertebrae, and stress-related trauma is implicated as a major cause of the condition (Roberts and Manchester 1997, 107). Unlike many of the other forms of joint disease this condition commonly develops in young adults. The CPR given by Roberts and Cox is 7.6% for the Neolithic and 16.3% for the Bronze Age (2003, table 2.17 and 2.23); however, the potential abnormally low rate suggested for the former is demonstrated by the true prevalence rate (TPR) for the early Neolithic site of Hambledon Hill, Dorset, which is 14.4% (McKinley 2008a; most of the individuals at Hambledon Hill were represented by skull or long bone shaft fragments only), ie, much closer to the TPR from Boscombe Down and the CPR for the Bronze Age sample.

Degenerative disc disease results from the breakdown of the intervertebral disc and reflects age-related wear-and-tear (Rogers and Waldron 1995, 27). Lesions were observed in only one vertebra (0.9%). The low rate probably reflects the relatively young age of most of the individuals within the assemblage.

Lesions indicative of minor osteoarthritis (Rogers and Waldron 1995, 43–4) were seen in two joints (all extra-spinal) from one individual (1289), giving an overall rate of 0.6%. The CPR for the Neolithic (2.8%) and Bronze Age (12.2%) in Roberts and Cox (2003, tables 2.12 and 2.20) again suggest a probable abnormally low rate for the Neolithic (see above); for example, the TPR of lesions in the costo-vertebral joints from Hambledon Hill is 21.5% (McKinley 2008a) compared with the *c.* 4% from the early Beaker burials at Boscombe Down (Table 10).

Lone osteophytes (new bone growth on joint surface margins) often appear to be a 'normal accompaniment of age' (Rogers and Waldron 1995, 25–6). Slight lesions were seen on the vertebral body surface margins or synovial joint surface margins of three individuals, each with lesions in between one and 10 joints (3.5% spinal joints, 1.9% extra-spinal joints). In the case of skeleton 1291, the lesions in the left knee and acetabulum were probably related to the mobility difficulties experienced in that leg (pp. 82–6). Lone macro- and micro-pitting lesions were seen in single extra-spinal joint surfaces in two individuals (0.5% extra-spinal joints).

Infection

Periosteal new bone was observed in the remains of the adult male 25004. There is fine-grained (active) woven new bone, indicative of a non-specific infection, on the dorsal side of the right proximal fibula. The aetiology of such non-specific lesions is difficult to ascertain but the infection most likely spread from a focus elsewhere in the body.

Cremation rite

The cremated bone is all white in colour, indicating a high level of oxidation (Holden *et al.* 1995a and b). The small overall quantity of bone recovered, 11 g, may not necessarily reflect the total weight of bone included in the burial as there has clearly been some bioturbation and modern disturbance with potential loss of bone (see above); however, the recovery of such low weights is a fairly common feature with the burials of such young individuals. Elements from all skeletal areas are represented within the deposit and there is no indication of preferential selection of particular elements. A small fragment of cremated bird bone, that could not be identified to species, probably the remains of a pyre good, was recovered with burial 25006. The inclusion of animal remains on the pyre was a relatively common part of Bronze Age rites and bird remains have been recovered from a number of burials of this date (McKinley 1997, 132).

Burial formation processes in grave 25000

The distribution of the remains within grave 25000 was outlined above (pp. 20–1). Radiocarbon dating has demonstrated that juvenile 25001, recovered *c.* 0.2 m above the base of the grave and separated from the underlying bone by a layer of soil, represents one of the latest burials made within the grave, potentially up to 200 years after the burial of adult 25004. The remains of the cremated infant 25006, which appeared to lie directly over, and to have intermingled with, the upper limb bones of juvenile 25007 laid on the base of the grave, were also a later insertion of Early Bronze Age date. No separate grave cuts for either of these later burials were evident within the general grave fill.

The lack of soil between the cremated bone 25006 and the juvenile 25007 suggests one of two possibilities for the burial. Either a cut was made – such a cut made through and immediately backfilled with the general grave fill could be indistinguishable in excavation – and those making the burial managed to avoid disturbing the juvenile bones despite exposing them; or at this stage it was still possible to remove whatever form of lid was covering the chamber and place the cremation burial directly over the *in situ* remains. Soil separated 25001 from the underlying deposits and again two possibilities are suggested; either a subsequently indistinguishable grave cut was made, as outlined above, or this burial was made as grave 25000 itself was finally being filled with soil, the burial representing a deposit associated with final 'closure' of the grave. The latter may be the more plausible given the evidence for the slumping of 25004 which suggests that there had been no soil in the grave when it was deposited.

The *in situ* adult burial 25004 may represent the final deposition of articulated remains made at the base of the grave (see radiocarbon Model 2, p. 172), and the burial may have been made either shortly after or several decades later than that of the juvenile 25007 which it appears to respect (though the modern disturbance obscures the exact relationship). The burial was made with the body loosely flexed on the left side, and there had been subsequent slight forward slumping suggesting an absence of soil immediately around the body in the original burial environment. The pattern of skeletal recovery – or rather loss – in this case is interesting; the skeleton is fairly well represented (*c.* 85%) with some general loss/degradation of bone from most skeletal areas but there is a discrete area of bone loss around the knees where the left wrist/hand would also have been located. Here a *c.* 0.1 m diameter area is devoid of bone including both distal femora and patellae, the left hand, and forearm. This 'void' could be indicative of post-depositional manipulation subsequent to skeletalisation. According to the radiocarbon models this burial (25004) appears to be contemporary with grave 1236, whilst the individual in grave 1289 is of a similar, possibly slightly earlier, date to the juvenile 25007.

The redeposited bone appears to represent both placed deposits of skulls and bundles of long bones, and more random bone deposits placed around and above the *in situ* remains 25004. Although the arms and legs of the latter overlay some bone deposits they may have partly slumped into this position; alternatively, the lower limbs could have been propped against some of the underlying bone. It is also possible that some of the bone lying above the *in situ* burial

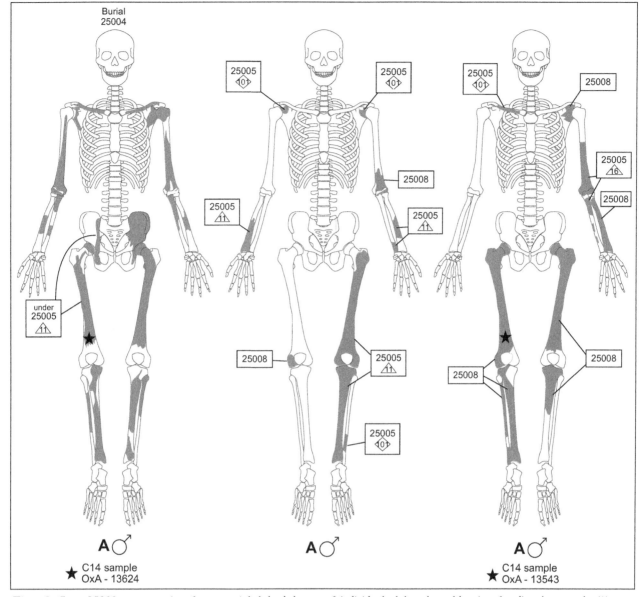

Figure 8 Grave 25000: representation of post-cranial skeletal elements of individual adult males and location of radiocarbon samples (1)

remains were originally placed on a lid covering the possible chamber and that they subsequently fell into position rather than being deposited directly over the body at the time of burial.

The redeposited bone comprises the disarticulated remains of a minimum of five individuals, possibly six, some of which are represented within the surviving assemblage by fewer skeletal elements than others. Any discussion of the potential significance which may be attributed to this and the skeletal elements recovered must be tempered by the fact that we do not have the entire contents of the grave. Figures 8–10 and Tables 3–4 and 9–10 illustrate how poorly represented some of the disarticulated individuals were within the assemblage. All four adults were represented by only three skeletal elements (the left humerus, radius, and femur); a

maximum of three were represented by six other major skeletal elements, and a maximum of two by four others (Table 4; including skull). Most of the redeposited bone comprised these larger skeletal elements and very few disarticulated vertebrae (parts of *c.* 30) or hand/foot bones (parts of *c.* 36) were recovered. This indicates that either the disarticulated bone was introduced to the grave from the remains of burials made elsewhere and from which only 'selected items' were extracted, or, if the disarticulated remains represent those of the earliest occupants of the grave, that some of their remains were removed (either by deliberate action or by inconsequential dumping such as leads to the build-up of 'cemetery soils' in many medieval/post-medieval cemeteries) for disposal elsewhere. One other striking feature illustrated in Table 4 is the dominance of the

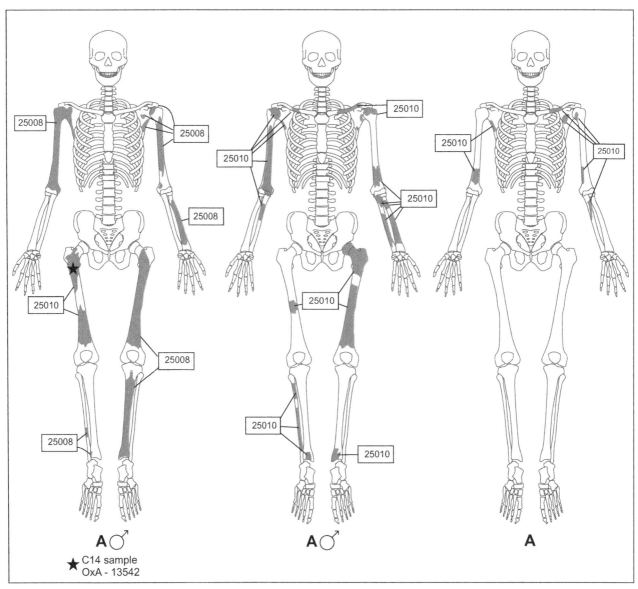

Figure 9 Grave 25000: representation of post-cranial skeletal elements of individual adult males and location of radiocarbon samples (2)

left side over the right in the recovery of most of the major elements; a minimum of six of the eight elements (75%) compared with only one (12.5%) where the right side dominated. Variable levels of erosion recorded in different skeletal elements from the same bone group, together with occasional staining to individual bones, is indicative of their deposition within a slightly different burial environment at some stage. These implied changes in burial environment could, however, have all occurred within grave 25000 at different times and localised micro-environmental variations may even have affected the same *in situ* deposit.

The earliest radiocarbon dates from the grave are from the redeposited remains, the results from which covered a span of 20–120 years. The most recent of the three dated individuals could, just, have been contemporaneous with the *in situ* juvenile 25007 (radiocarbon Model 1). Were this grave

to have been used as the original place of deposition for all the individuals recovered from it, the earliest burial could have occurred 225 years prior to the last *in situ* deposit made at the base of the grave, and 375 years before the last known burial (25001) was made. If it is assumed that this latter Early Bronze Age burial was deliberately made in grave 25000, the dates from the *in situ* deposits give a potential 300 years of use, during which time its location must have been known if not clearly marked. It is possible that some, if not all of the disarticulated remains, which pre-dated the burial made in grave 1289, were brought in from elsewhere, curated 'ancestral remains' carried and finally deposited to give a sense of place and context within a new settlement area; but it is equally possible that the grave itself, perhaps with an intermittently renewed wood lining, remained functional over the period indicated.

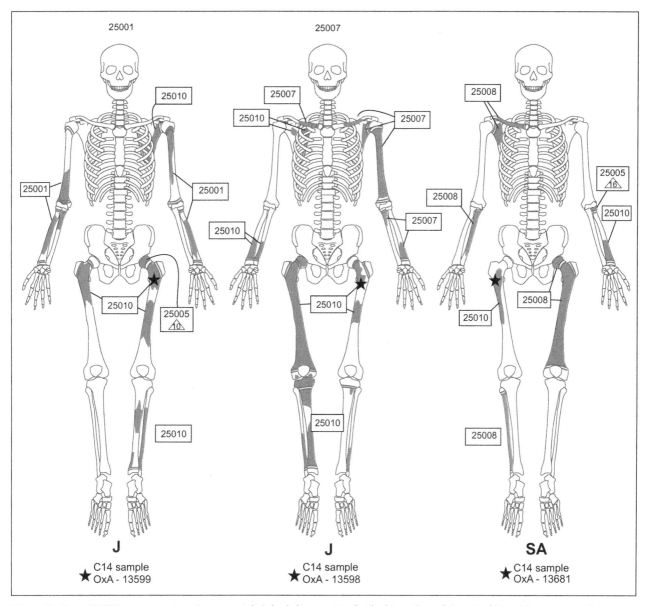

Figure 10 Grave 25000: representation of post-cranial skeletal elements of individual juveniles and the sub-adult and location of radiocarbon samples

The disarticulated bone assemblage, with its emphasis on fragments of skull and long bone shaft, bears striking similarities to those recovered from the Neolithic causewayed camp at Hambledon Hill, Dorset and other Early Neolithic (Smith 1959, 161; 1965, 137; McKinley 2008a) and Late Neolithic sites (Wainwright 1979; Wainwright and Longworth 1971). To a large extent, this assemblage composition is a feature of assemblages across later prehistory, the same elements being seen amongst disarticulated remains from Early Iron Age sites (eg, Wilson 1981; Whimster 1981; Wait 1985; McKinley 2008b), where there is a predominance of elements from the right side.

A tradition of communal burial in the Early Bronze Age – in a variety of forms including disposal by cremation and inhumation of an unburnt corpse – is well recognised and considered by some indicative of a continuation of the Early Neolithic tradition of group or communal burial, or reburial (Lynch 1970, 117–8; Savory 1972; Petersen 1972; Mount 1995);

> '... multiple burial in the same grave, often involving a burial routine entailing the deliberate re-opening of filled graves and the disarrangement of older internments in a manner strongly recalling the analogous customs recorded from many Neolithic chambered tombs' (Petersen 1972, 27).

Petersen cites up to 70 examples, mostly from the Yorkshire Wolds but also from Wessex, of graves incorporating both articulated and disarticulated human remains with a maximum of 13 individuals per grave and an average of 3.7, only three contained more than eight individuals (*ibid.*, 28). As at Boscombe Down, additional burials were sometimes made within the fill of the grave (*ibid.*, 32). There are similar proportions of immature to adult individuals (either of which may be articulated or disarticulated) as noted at Boscombe Down, but unlike here both males and females are clearly represented. (*c.* 50% of the adults were unsexed so any comment on relatively proportions could be misleading). The *in situ* remains of cremated and unburnt bone, in direct physical contact and apparently made contemporaneously, has been observed at various sites (*ibid.*, 34). Petersen refers to these as 'paired' deposits, suggesting a deliberate intention in their placing. The radiocarbon dates from grave 25000 where two burials, 25006 and 25007, appeared to be in direct contact but which proved to be up to 225 years apart in date, demonstrates that physical context can sometimes be stratigraphically misleading in graves which have been 'revisited' and emphasises the value of radiocarbon analysis. It does not necessarily follow, however, that the association of the two deposits in grave 25000 was not intentional. None of the 'pairs' cited above include the combination of an infant and a juvenile as seen at Boscombe Down, and there is no indication that individuals of a certain age or sex were assigned a different mortuary rite from others within the group.

Petersen regards these graves as 'family vaults' (*ibid.*, 39), as indeed they may have been, though the 'family' may have been an extended one. In the case of grave 25000 at Boscombe Down, the demographic make-up of the assemblage is not entirely suggestive of a 'normal' family group as there is no clear evidence of the presence of any adult females. We may, of course, have a not entirely representative sample of the occupants of the grave since it was not excavated in its entirety and some bone had undoubtedly been lost due to disturbance. The paucity of adult females amongst the other burials of similar date from the area (see p. 21 above) does, however, suggest a gender difference in mortuary practice. Although there are indications of at least some morphological homogeneity within the assemblage, there is currently no proof of familial relationship between the individuals.

Isotope Studies

by J.A. Evans and C.A. Chenery

Oxygen and strontium isotope analyses were undertaken on five individuals from grave 25000 and the methods and results are set out in Chapter 7 and in Evans *et al.* 2006.

Two teeth were selected (a 2nd premolar and a 3rd molar) from the three adults whose jaws were present in order to assess the environment of the individuals at two time points in their development. These were from adult male 25004 (isotope sample A1), the disarticulated mandible ON 10 (isotope sample A3) from 25008, and from amongst the unstratified bones (25010, isotope sample A2). Unerupted premolars were sampled from the two articulated juvenile burials (25001: isotope sample J2 ((of Early Bronze Age date)) and 25007: isotope sample J1) but no samples were available from the 15–18 year old subadult male, whose remains were present amongst the disarticulated bones from 25008 and 25010 (Tables 2–3). Jaws A2 and A3 do not come from articulated burials and so cannot be associated with particular individuals.

The three adults were shown to have a significant difference in $^{87}Sr/^{86}Sr$ isotope composition between their premolar and 3rd molar teeth reflecting a change in environment between the formation of these two teeth. The children, for whom there is only one datum point, cannot be classified by this method.

The adult males had moved during their childhood, from an area of radiogenic rocks to a second site before journeying to Wessex where they were buried together. These people record a pattern of movement, which suggests that they each made the same journey, or rather spent the same parts of their lives in the same places. Wales is the nearest area that can supply the appropriate $^{87}Sr/^{86}Sr$ values for the early childhood values, which means they travelled at least 150–200 km during their lives, more if they travelled from continental Europe where a number of regions provide appropriate values, and these are discussed further below (pp. 188–90). The two juveniles, whose Sr data are so similar, did not make the same journey, but they too were not immediately local to Boscombe Down.

Stable isotope analyses to assess diet (carbon and nitrogen) undertaken on burial 25004 (the articulated burial of an adult male) by Dr Mandy Jay as part of the ongoing Beaker People Project (Jay and Richards 2007) suggest that he ate a mixed a diet (M. Jay, pers. comm.). A similar conclusion was suggested by the strontium concentrations (Evans *et al.* 2006, 318–19).

Chapter 3

Finds from the Grave of the Boscombe Bowmen

Flint

by Phil Harding

A small assemblage, comprising 10 retouched tools, 17 flakes and blades, and 47 chips (Fig. 11), was recovered from the excavated grave 25000, the fill of the grave 25005 and the machine-disturbed material 25010 (Fig. 12). Of these artefacts, the retouched tools and some of the flakes and blades were clearly included as grave goods. Of the remainder, most are likely to be residual. The assemblage is unlikely to be complete due to the modern disturbance to the grave (Chapter 2 above). The flints are described in relation to the nearest skeleton and/or bone group, though any attempt to assign objects to particular indiviual burials is problematic due to the nature of the grave.

Objects found in Grave 25000

A well-made implement (ON 1) retouched at one end into an end scraper but heavily worn at the other in the fashion of a fabricator/strike-a-light was found behind the vertebrae of the adult male 25004 (Fig. 12). It was accompanied by a knife (ON 13), made on a blade. Retouch is minimal to retain the general effectiveness of the edges, one of which is dulled, probably by use. One edge is also heavily iron stained. A

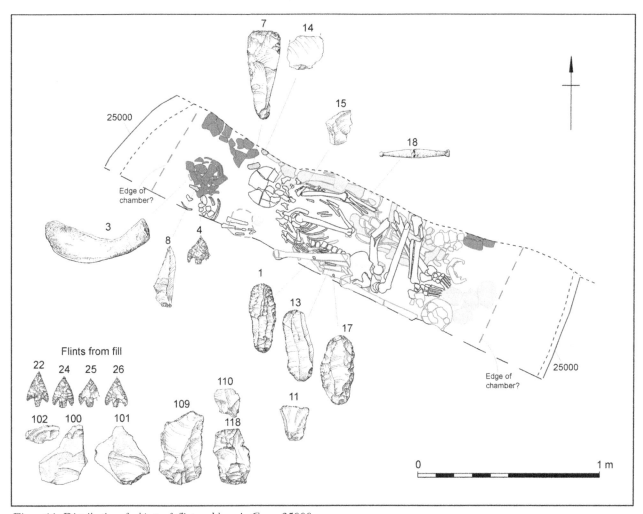

Figure 11 Distribution of objects of flint and bone in Grave 25000

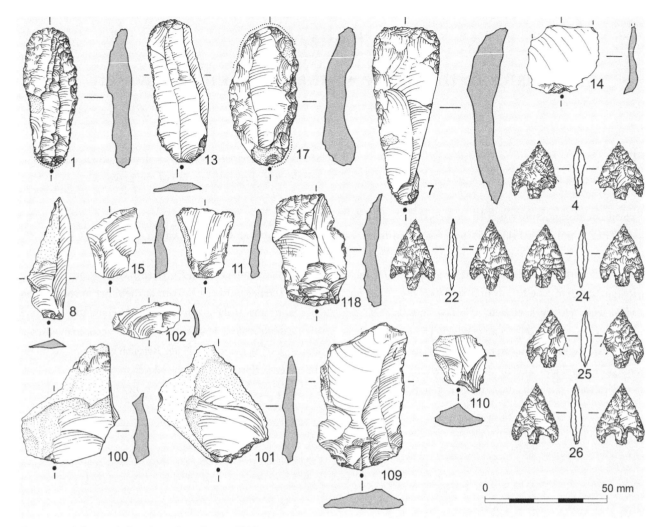

Figure 12 Selection of flint objects from Grave 25000

fabricator/strike-a-light (ON 17) with a characteristic 'D' shaped cross-section, heavily worn ends, and a small area of iron staining along one edge, was also found with these objects.

The heavily worn ends of the two implements, ON 1 and 17 (Fig. 12), is a feature frequently associated with strike-a-lights. These implements are often found in Beaker graves with an accompanying nodule of pyrite (or bog iron) and are believed to represent fire-making sets. Iron pyrite occurs naturally in Chalk and nodules were found in the fill of the grave, as were minute fragments that were found in the samples from bone group 25008 and from the grave fill (25005, sample 101). An implement (ON 7) that had possibly been used as an end scraper, with retouch that extended along the edge, was found by the skull of burial 25004, near Beaker ON 5, with a flake (ON 14; Fig. 12). These objects are also both heavily encrusted with iron staining. It is possible that these objects, behind the back and by the head of 25004, represent the only surviving parts of groups of finds that

were removed by the excavation of the water and electricity trenches.

An isolated flake (ON 15) was plotted under the left shoulder of the burial 25004 and a broken flake, possibly residual, was found among an assemblage of long bones (25008) immediately north of this burial (Fig. 12). A flake and unintentional chip were found subsequently in the sieved residue from a sample around the head (sample 105A, 25004).

At the west end of the grave a barbed and tanged arrowhead (ON 4) was found with the crushed remains of Beakers ON 2A–B and with a small, unretouched blade (ON 8), with partial natural backing, that may have been included as a knife (Fig. 12).

Worked flint recovered from grave fill 25005

The sieving of the fill of the grave (25005) produced an end scraper that was partially iron stained. It was retouched by pressure flaking at the distal end, but shows damaged edges, as if used as a knife (ON 118; Figs 11–12). There are also seven flakes (ON 11, 100–2), including a platform preparation/rejuvenation flake (ON 100) and a fragment of debitage (Figs 11–12). The grave fill also contained two fragments of burnt flint (33 g) and 26 undiagnostic chips, including some that may not be man-made, that were all recovered from sieved residue.

Worked flint recovered from the machine disturbed frave Fill 25010

Four barbed and tanged arrowheads (ON 22, 24–6), a blade (ON 8), four undiagnostic flakes (ON 109–10), and 20 undiagnostic chips, some, but not all, products of debitage, were recovered from 25010 (Fig. 11–12).

These barbed and tanged arrowheads, including that found with Beakers ON 2A–B, are all of Green's (1980) Sutton b and c types. They are of a similar size and form and may have been produced as a set.

They are slightly smaller than the arrowheads placed with the Amesbury Archer (pp. 90–1 below) but well within the average dimensions calculated by Green for Sutton arrowheads (1980, table ii.24). The arrowhead (ON 4), which was found in the grave, lacks its tip and a barb. The loss of the tip may have been due to impact but the barb had broken in manufacture. One other arrowhead (ON 25) lacks a barb that had also snapped in manufacture.

The flakes are generally undiagnostic. Two unlocated pieces from the grave fill, including a rejuvenation or platform preparation flake (ON 100), are of similar character and cortex that suggests they might have been removed from the same nodule; neither possesses any usable edges.

All the objects are patinated with the exception of one barbed and tanged arrowhead (ON 25), which shows that it was made of good quality black flint speckled with grey inclusions; flint of this type can be found locally. The artefacts are generally in mint condition; however, the dorsal ridges of a flake (ON 11) and knapping fragment from the grave fill (25005), and two flakes (ON 109–10) from 25010 are dulled and the edges damaged, suggesting that they were residual. The larger of the two flakes (ON 109) has been removed from a well-dressed core with prepared striking platform and is probably of Late Neolithic date, with which the use of this early Beaker grave overlaps. Both flakes are also slightly 'soapy' to the touch. This surface texture is present on other artefacts from the grave, which otherwise show no indications that they might be residual.

Most of the chips, only 21 of which are patinated, are undiagnostic and undoubtedly include a number that resulted from natural impact or crushing of flints in the soil. There is

nothing to indicate that flaking took place at or near to the grave side.

Discussion

Although the grave was a collective one, there were relatively few flint objects; some may have been removed when new burials were made, but it is just as likely that they were not included in the first place. Other flints could have been lost when the grave was disturbed in more recent times. Clarke (1970), followed by Brodie (1998; 2001), showed that Beaker graves were frequently poorly furnished with grave goods, including flints, and that some contained no grave goods.

The artefacts whose locations are known were found either behind the back of burial 25004, among redeposited bones, or with the Beakers at the west end of the grave (Fig. 11). It is uncertain whether the three retouched tools (ON 1, 13, and 17) are part of a group as they could relate either to the redeposited bones (25008) from disturbed earlier inhumation burials or to the articulated burial 25004. Knife ON 13 was recorded with the upper level of disarticulated bones (ON 11), whereas the fabricator/strike-a-light (ON 17) was found on the base of the grave and was revealed only when the bones of burial 25004 had been lifted.

This vertical variation in the recorded positions of these objects may hint at some degree of post-depositional movement, either when the burial chamber was reopened, when it was infilled, and/or during episodes of bioturbation such as more recent root activity. These activities may account for some displacement of the vertical relationships of some objects, especially where they were not protected by bones. Minor displacement within the surviving grave fill may also have resulted from the adjacent modern disturbances. However the position of groups of objects, including flint tools, behind the body was a favoured location for grave goods in Beaker funerary rites. The small cluster of ON 1, 13, and 17 also suggests that they may have been associated with burial 25004, although there is no way of being sure.

The flint artefacts at the west end of the grave, with the Beakers, might be thought more likely to be in a primary position. They were found at the greatest depths hinting that, although they might have migrated downwards, they had probably been placed on the floor of the grave. It is possible that end scraper ON 7 and flake ON 14, which lay between Beaker ON 5 and the head of burial 25004, were associated with this burial. Blade ON 8, which is sufficiently well made to consider it a deliberate grave item, and arrowhead ON 4 may also be associated with this burial but may equally represent grave goods placed with the burial of the juvenile 25007. Flake ON 15 was found under the left shoulder of the articulatcd adult burial 25004 and may originally also have been on the floor of the grave. However, some or all of these objects could already have been in the grave when burials 25004 and 25007 were placed and may have been moved as the bodies were interred.

The original location of the four arrowheads found in 25010 can only be said to have come from the southern part of the grave. It is possible that they were originally behind the *in situ* burial of the adult male, 25004, a position that would be consistent with other Beaker burials. If this is so it may imply that they were originally deposited together in a bundle or quiver, as at for example Mucking, Essex, where five arrowheads were found in a group behind the body pointing towards the feet (Jones and Jones 1975, 138–9, fig. 45a–b, 47), or at Barrow Hills, Radley, Oxfordshire where, in grave 206, five arrowheads were found at the feet (Barclay and Halpin 1999, 136, 140, fig. 4.76).

The recovery of objects from the surviving grave fill (25005) was comprehensive and meticulous, with only one tool, an end scraper (ON 118), being recovered from a position that could not be plotted (Fig. 11). However, a localised patch of iron staining, possibly related to decayed pyrite (see Heyd 2007a, 352, for a similar argument) suggests that it may have been related either to adjacent retouched grave goods ON 1 and 13 behind the vertebrae, or to objects ON 7 and 14, which were also iron-stained, at the head. These two pairs of objects were the only pieces from the grave that were stained; nothing similar was noted on any of the human bone or on any of the pottery. This, therefore, suggests proximity of the flint items to iron pyrite. Only four flakes and a blade were found from 25010, of which two pieces were probably residual and unlikely to represent deliberately placed grave goods.

Even though the grave is a collective one, the flint component from the grave also conforms to the range that might be anticipated from a single well-furnished Beaker burial. The largest component comprises the five barbed and tanged arrowheads, of which only one was found *in situ* at the head of the grave. This situation is reminiscent of the Amesbury Archer burial where arrowheads were found near the feet with one amongst a cache of flints near the head (see below). Barbed and tanged arrowheads are most frequently found singly or in pairs (Green 1980). Other than Beakers, they consistently form the most common grave goods in Beaker graves in Britain and stress the relationships between Beaker users and archery equipment. It may be argued that the arrowheads represent single items from separate

individuals in the grave; however, they are of a similar size and form that suggests they may have been produced as a set. The arrowheads were accompanied with flakes, knives, scrapers, and fabricators/strike-a-lights, a range of objects that is also often present in graves, as in flat grave 9 at the Drayton North Cursus, Oxfordshire (Barclay *et al.* 2003, 84–6, fig. 4.33–4, pl. 4.7) where an All-Over-Cord Beaker was associated with a barbed and tanged arrowhead, a fabricator, and a small group of unretouched elongated flint flakes.

The four retouched tools from Boscombe are notable in that they demonstrate a distinct preference for the selection of elongated blanks, including two blades, as supports for the retouch. ON 13 (Fig. 12) is made on an especially competent blade. This technology has been regarded as being in decline (Smith 1965; Pitts 1978) by the 3rd millennium BC, a conclusion that has been confirmed in many subsequent analyses (Wainwright and Longworth 1971; Harding 1992). In contrast, Clarke demonstrated that blades continued to form part of the burial tool kit in Beaker burials (1970, app. 3.1). Bradley (1970) also recorded blades at Belle Tout, Sussex, a feature that he attributed to 'conservatism' in technology. Blades also featured in a Beaker pit at Dean Bottom on the Marlborough Downs (Harding 1992), although manufacture omitted features normally associated with deliberate blade production, such as carefully prepared cores, platform abrasion, or systematic rejuvenation. It is possible that the use of blades does indeed reflect 'conservatism' within the Beaker community, but it is equally possible that some of those well made items selected for use as grave goods represent symbolic heirlooms.

Using Humble's (1990) approach from Raunds (Irthlingborough), Northamptonshire, where he assigned grave goods into five categories that reflected their function in the burial ceremony, it is apparent that the grave goods from the multiple burial at Boscombe are primarily personal possessions of the deceased or redeposited items. The two unretouched flakes and the blade, which were plotted, and the flakes from the fill, which were not, may have represented items made especially for deposition, items used in mortuary rites or additional redeposited pieces. Either way the flakes do not comprise large-scale caches.

Pottery
by Alistair J. Barclay

The fragmentary remains of eight Beakers (ON 2A–B, 5, 6/23, 12, 19–21) (Fig. 13), in various states of completeness, were recovered. Seven of the pots belong within the All-

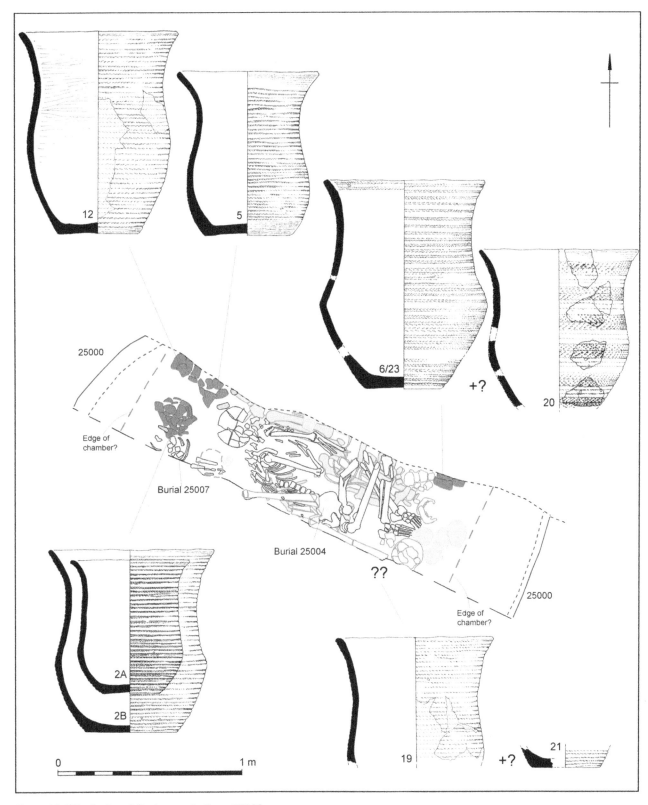

Figure 13 Distribution of Beaker pots in Grave 25000

Over-Cord (AOC) style of early Beaker and one (ON 20) is a Cord-Zoned-Maritime (CZM) vessel (Fig. 14). Some of the vessels could have been placed in pairs, with one pair, vessels ON 2A–B, nested together, one inside the other (Fig. 13). It is possible to suggest that some of the pots were associated with particular individuals on the basis of their proximity to the *in situ* burials and the redeposited remains. However, this reading of the evidence is not without ambiguity as it is possible that some or all of the pots have been moved out of position. All of the pots were recovered broken and were either crushed *in situ* or had suffered one or more episodes of post-depositional disturbance. Four pots have been

38

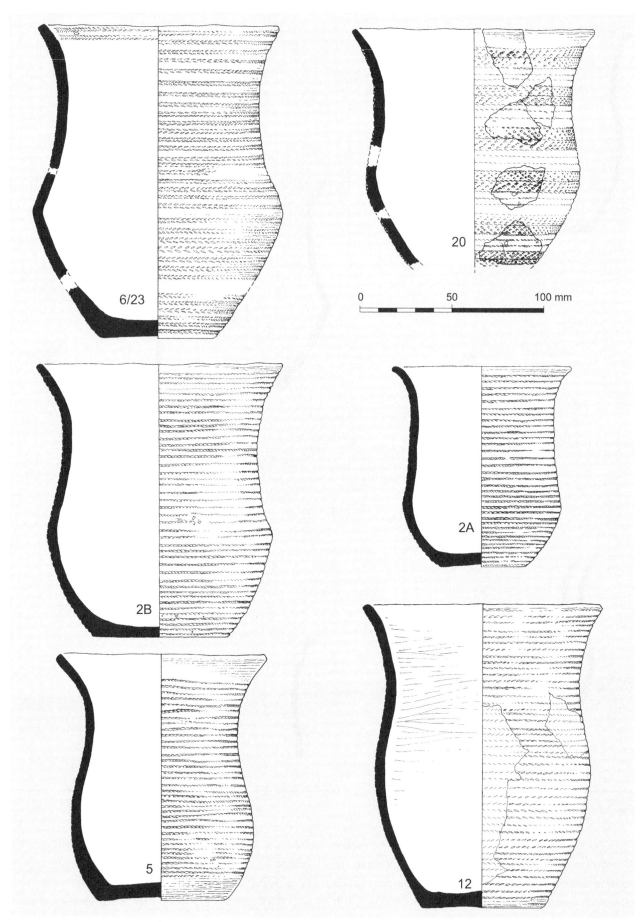

Figure 14 Beaker pottery ON 6/23, 20, 2B, 2A, 5 and 12 from Grave 25000

completely reconstructed (ON 2A–B, 5 and 12). Six of the pots were sampled for lipid analysis (pp. 54–8 below).

Methods

The pottery has been quantified by sherd count and weight. Where possible, fresh breaks were excluded from the overall sherd count, although due to post-depositional disturbance this was not always practicable. Fabrics were defined on the basis of the identification of inclusions present. A record was made of form, decoration, surface treatment, firing colour, evidence for manufacture, use wear, and completion.

Great care was taken to ensure that the vessel reconstructions are correct and true to the original profile. However, in the case of the less complete vessels, ON 12 in particular, some alteration of the profile remains possible. Drawings and photographs were taken of the pots both before and after reconstruction for display purposes and sherds (rim, shoulder, and base) from all the vessels were reserved for future analysis.

Fabrics

The Beakers are manufactured from two (F1–2) very different and distinct fabrics. One is iron-rich and contains relatively few inclusions and probably has little or no added temper and the other, F2, is heavily grog-tempered and potentially a calcareous rich clay. Fabric 1 tends to be fired to a reddish-brown, while Fabric 2 is more yellowish-red to yellowish-brown. All sherds have a typical non-oxidised black core, a slightly wider oxidised outer margin, and a narrower inner one (see Clarke 1970, 256). Fabric 1 is generally well made and fired, while Fabric 2 is relatively poor in comparison. In general the majority of the vessels are made from a good fabric that is well finished and fired.

Fabric 1: Vessels ON 2A–B, 5, 20, 21 and 6/23

Hard fabric with a hackly fracture and no added temper. The clay matrix contains rare quartz sand (<0.5 mm), very rare flint, and sparse organic matter (charred plant). In vessels ON 2A–B there are also rare fragments of chalk, shell, and ironstone. Vessel ON 5 also has rare clasts of clay/?grog. Of the two fabrics, 1 is generally well prepared and the firing and finish of the vessels is generally of a high quality (but see description of ON 6/23 below).

Fabric 2: vessels ON 12 and 19

Soft soapy fabric with common sub-angular grog fragments (mostly 1–3 mm). Flat surfaces, variation in colour, and the possible presence within the grog of inclusions indicate that this could be crushed pottery. Very rare flint chips occur in the matrix, which is otherwise clean of other visible inclusions (ie, chalk and quartz sand).

Forms

There is no published detailed study of Beaker vessel shape relating to Britain beyond the basic systems offered by Clarke (1970), van der Waals and Glasbergen (1955), Lanting and van der Waals (1972), and Needham (2005) (see Salanova 1998a; 2001 for examples of the vessel range for Brittany and France in general, the latter with up to 27 forms).

It was inherent in Clarke's work that sub-types exist beyond the basic categories he defined, a point that Case has made, in particular when describing All-Over-Cord vessels (2004b, 20–1, fig 3; p. 49 below; see Riley 1957, fig. 7, 2–3 for examples of squat and slender All-Over-Cord forms). There is a probable continuum between squat bell-shaped vessels, where the mouth diameter is closer to that of the waist, and taller slender vessels where the height is significantly more than that of the mouth (Needham 2005, 172; Boast 1998). Within this range of basic shapes the potter had a choice between forming a round belly or an angular waist, and where to position this relative to the rest of the vessel.

Two basic shapes are recognised here (Figs 14–15): tall slender pots (Form 1) and squatter vessels (Form 2), which can be further sub-divided into slender pots with a symmetrical smooth S-profile (with a relatively high belly) (1a) or a carination (1b) and squatter pots with S-profiles and low bellies (2a) or a carination (2b). Variety 2b includes a so-called 'Breton-like' variant with very low carination and out-curved rim (Clarke 1970, 79). Further sub-division is possible as some vessels have smooth profiles and others have one or more points of inflection. Such subtle details are important for both characterising vessel form and for understanding the choices available to the potter.

Beakers

There is an argument that at least some of the Beakers were deposited in the grave in pairs (Figs 13–15), a practice that occurs nearby in the grave of the Amesbury Archer and in a pit with a skull at Boscombe Down (Pit 10151; Fig. 3; Powell and Barclay in prep.), and elsewhere. In this report 'pair' refers to physical association; it is not meant to suggest that the pots were made by the same potter and/or that they are identical or closely similar. The vessels are described in this order according to this interpretation of the mortuary sequence, the radiocarbon dated sequence and through typological analysis of the vessels. However, it must be noted that other interpretations, such as some of the pots having been placed in multiples of four (eg, ON 2A–B, 5, and 12), individually (ON 20 and 23), and sequentially (eg, ON 23, 20, and 2A/B) are equally possible.

Beakers ON 6/23 and 20

ON 6/23 (25004): All-Over-Cord, plaited variant (Fig. 14; Pl. 12)
(21 sherds, 178 g). Rim diam. 130 mm, carination diam. 120 mm,
base diam. 60 mm. Height reconstructed as 167 mm, although a shorter
measurement of c. 135 mm is equally possible
Residue samples 9 (base), 10 (body), and 11 (rim)

The rim (ON 6) was found near disarticulated skull ON 10 in the north-east of the grave. The shoulder and base sherds (ON 23) were found in the upcast from the mechanical excavator and so came from the southern side of the grave. The sherds are almost certainly from the same vessel despite the fact that no refits could be found between the different portions of the surviving vessel (Fig. 14). A neck sherd that refits to the drawn rim portion appears to show the edge of what could be a carination. This evidence is slight but would indicate a much squatter profile from that depicted with the vessel height approximately equal to the rim diameter. The problem is that too little of the vessel survives to be sure of the exact profile. Breaks are both fresh and recent (modern disturbance), fresh but slightly worn (post-depositional breakage in antiquity), and contemporaneous with the firing of the vessel. New and old breaks are evident on all portions of the vessel. An old break or crack contemporaneous with the firing of the vessel occurs on the base (Pl. 12, a). This crack runs across the base and up the wall of the vessel and could have formed as a result of shrinkage, during drying and pre-firing (Rye 1988, 66, fig. 46). Fire clouds (indicators of fuel touching the pot during firing or the uneven distribution of air) (*ibid.*, 121, fig. 109) and a hazard of open firing (Rice 1987, 155–6) are present on the surviving rim (Pl. 12, b), shoulder, and base portions. These imperfections would have occurred at different stages of manufacture and indicate that the potter chose to complete the vessel. As the pot was recovered in a broken state and not all the grave could be

Plate 12 The Boscombe Bowmen (grave 25000), Beaker ON 6/23: a) detail of the possible shrinkage crack through the base; b) the fire cloud on the rim and detail of the impressed plaited cord, and c) detail of the impressed cord on the interior of the rim

excavated it is unclear how complete it was when it entered the grave. However, regardless of its state of completeness the crack, which may have gone right through the base, would have limited its usefulness and possibly its life. As with the two similar vessels from the grave of the Amesbury Archer (ON 6609–10; Fig. 46, below), it could have been made specifically as a grave item and, therefore, its usefulness as an everyday vessel for holding liquids may have been of little or no importance. With this in mind, it is of interest that this was only one out of two vessels that produced positive traces of lipid residue. Traces of what could be a plant oil of unknown origin as well as animal fat were found in the sample

(9) from the base, while the body sherd (10) produced only traces of animal fat (see Šoberl and Evershed below). These traces indicate that the vessel was whole enough to use, although whether this was prior to deposition or during the funerary ritual remains uncertain.

The exterior of the vessel is decorated all-over with impressed plaited cord (*Flechtschnur*: Gersbach 1957), while on the inside of the rim there are two circumferential rows of plaited cord impressions (Pl. 12, c). Experimental replication of these impressions undertaken by the author indicates that plaited rather than crocheted (*Häkelmaschen*) cord was most likely to have been used. This is the only vessel from the grave of the Boscombe Bowmen to carry internal rim decoration. The plait impressions run mostly in a clockwise direction. Plaited cord is a variant of All-Over-Cord impressions and occurs along with other variants such as paired (double) cord (Clarke 1970, 53–4) in Britain and across western Europe (Gersbach 1957; Jorge 2002).

The form of ON 6/23 as drawn is that of a relatively slender pot with a long neck and low set carination (Form 1b). However, a squatter profile where the rim and height are of similar proportions is also possible (Form 2b). The two plaited cord-impressed pots from the grave of the Amesbury Archer could have been of similar size, although their precise form is also uncertain. As depicted in Figure 14, comparisons can be made between the form of ON 6/23 with two All-Over-Cord Beakers that are illustrated by Clarke; Forglen, Aberdeenshire (Clarke 1970, 16, AOC 1582) and Aldro, North Yorkshire (*ibid.*, 28, AOC 1215). The form is also similar to that of a Comb-Zoned-Maritime Beaker from Barrow Hills, Radley grave 4660 (Barclay and Halpin, 1999, 63, 204–6, fig 4.23, P27), while the form and decoration are similar to plaited All-Over-Cord vessels from Hasbergen Lkr. Osnabruck, Lower Saxony (Lanting 2007, 13–14, fig. 1, 4–5) and from Dolmen d'Ustau de Loup, St-Gervazy, Puy-de-Dôme (Bill 1984, 164, Abb. 1, phase 1).

ON 20 (25010): low-carinated, Cord-Zoned Maritime (Fig. 14: Pl. 13) *(5 sherds, 18 g). Rim diam. 130 mm, shoulder diam. 116 mm, base diam. <65 mm. Height estimated as* c. *135 mm* *(Not sampled for lipid residues)*

Seven rim, neck, shoulder, and lower body sherds from a probable low-carinated vessel belonging to Clarke's (1970) European group and Cord-Zoned-Maritime type. Decorated with alternating horizontal zonal bands of four parallel impressed twisted cord lines and paired bands of obliquely

Plate 13 The Boscombe Bowmen (grave 25000), Beaker ON 20: detail of the impressed cord and comb decoration

impressed and diagonal short comb marks, separated and bounded by single impressed lines of twisted cord (Pl. 13). The paired bands of diagonal impressed comb marks appear to form a typical chevron pattern, although on ON 20 this is not always clear or well-executed (Clarke 1970, 424 motif group 1, no. 3; eg, Harrison 1980, fig. 9). The individual comb teeth impressions are either square (*c.* 1.0 x 1.0 mm) or slightly rectangular (*c.* 1.0 x 1.5 mm) with the exception of the lowest surviving band of decoration that is made with a much finer comb (*c.* 0.50–0.75 mm). Some of the teeth of the latter comb are pointed. The suggestion by Laure Salanova (pers. comm.) that the marks could have been made with the edge of a mollusc sherd was considered, tested by undertaking a small programme of experimental work using the edges of various *cardium* and *pecten* shells, and found not to be the case (work carried out with S. Wyles). Instead the marks seem to have been made with a form of denticulate stamp.

The incomplete and fragmentary nature of the vessel means that the dimensions and profile are a best approximation. The suggested form (2b) is that of a squat bell-shape (Clarke 1970, 423: form I) in which the height and mouth diameter are broadly equal, somewhat similar to the two comb-impressed vessels from the grave of the Amesbury Archer (ON 6590 and 6597; Fig. 46, below). Given the small number of surviving sherds, other reconstructions are possible; the vessel could have been taller than depicted. It is estimated that the base is likely to have been approximately half the width of the rim diameter.

The vessel was generally well finished, manufactured from Fabric 1 with burnished surfaces fired to a reddish-brown colour (2.5YR4/6).

Clarke (1970) lists a number of similar Cord-Zoned-Maritime and the variant Comb-Zoned-Maritime vessels from Britain including ones from the Avebury Avenue, Wiltshire (1970, 288, fig. 62, E 1070), Stanton Harcourt, Oxfordshire (288, fig. 64, E 770), Thickthorn Down, Dorset (288, fig. 65, E 184), Barrow Hills, Radley 4A (288, fig. 63, E 33), Christchurch, Hampshire (290, fig 78, E 313), and Brean Down, Somerset (293, fig. 112, E 778).

Within the immediate area of Boscombe Down there are vessels from the Wilsford barrow cemetery (*ibid.*, fig. 67, E1155; 60, E1173). From Scotland there is an important Cord-Zoned-Maritime vessel from Upper Largie, Kilmartin, Arygll and Bute, which was found with a low-bellied All-Over-Cord Beaker and a second, less typical, comb impressed zoned pot (Sheridan 2008a, 24–52, fig. 21.3–5). What is quite striking is the similarity of that grave to that of Wilsford G54, if the so-called 'ring of solution pipes' at Wilsford is seen as a ditch with post-holes, and the fact that the grave also produced the fragmentary remains of a Cord-Zoned-Maritime Beaker, an All-Over-Cord Beaker and a carinated comb-zoned vessel of possible squat bell-shaped form (pers. obs.: an alternative shorter reconstruction than the one illustrated is possible; see Smith 1991, 27–9, fig. 12, P8). It is possible, but not certain, that these sherds came from a disturbed primary burial, while the other remains belonged with a later phase of burial (*ibid.*, 23–7). The Cord-Zoned-Maritime Beaker from G54 was illustrated by Smith as relatively tall with an S-profile, while Clarke (1970, 287, fig. 60, E 1173) interpreted the same vessel as slightly shorter with a smoother S-profile and Annable and Simpson show the same vessel as having a much squatter profile (1964, 97, fig. 144). A much shorter low-bellied and wider mouthed profile is possible (pers. obs.).

The Cord-Zoned-Maritime group (including the comb variants) of vessels from the Wessex region can be seen to include relatively tall pots with S-profiles and squatter ones with low bellies or carinations. Motifs vary from single (eg, Wilsford G54) or paired bands of oblique lines (eg, Avebury Avenue, Brean Down, and Christchurch) with alternated blank zones to more complex zonal patterns (Barrow Hills, Radley, barrow 4A: Clarke 1970, 288, fig. 63, E 33; cf. Fig. 74 here, and grave 4660; Barclay and Halpin 1999, 65, fig. 4.23, P27), and Stanton Harcourt (Clarke 1970, fig. 64, E 770).

The comb-bounded chevron motif is also found on the 'Breton'-like vessel from Thickthorn Down, Dorset (*ibid.*, fig. 65, E184). On the same vessel this motif is paired, in

alternating bands, with the bounded cross-hatched motif, while the rim interior carries lines of twisted cord impressions. The Thickthorn Down vessel is important as it has stylistic links with a small group of vessels with the Cord-Zoned-Maritime group, including a vessel of similar form from Wick Barrow, Stogursey, Somerset (St George Gray 1908, 25; Clarke 1970, fig. 54, E 818), a second vessel from Thickthorn Down (*ibid.*, fig. 66, E 183), one from Blackbush, Dorset (*ibid.*, fig. 69, E 169), a vessel from Mere G6a, Wiltshire (*ibid.*, 296, fig. 130, W/MR 1125), one from Wilsford G52 (Smith 1991, 22, fig. 8: P4), and one from Chilbolton, Hampshire (Russel 1990, 161, fig. 5, 1).

The Cord-Zoned-Maritime vessel ON 20 may have been similar to that from Wilsford G54 in shape but it is closer in decorative style to the Comb-Zoned-Maritime vessels from Barrow Hills, Radley (barrow 4A and grave 4660) in particular, and the Cord-Zoned-Maritime ones from Christchurch, Avebury Avenue, and Upper Largie. The date of Beaker ON 20 is important, despite the uncertainty over its precise position within the burial sequence in the grave of the Boscombe Bowmen as there are relatively few radiocarbon dates associated with vessels of this type. Apart from this grave, only graves barrow 4A and 4660 at Barrow Hills, Radley and Upper Largie have radiocarbon dates, all of which reinforce the generally accepted idea that they belong early within the sequence of Beaker use (Lanting and van der Waals 1972, Step 1; Needham 2005, 179). Similarly, the date for Barrow Hills, grave 4660, where an unusual Comb-Zoned-Maritime Beaker was found with a copper knife, is slightly later than expected and again its true date would be expected to be earlier and fall nearer to that of Barrow Hills, barrow 4A (p. 178 below). Cleal (1999, 206) noted that pot 27 at Barrow Hills is similar in form to vessels from Thickthorn Down and Blackbush while a variation of pot 27's key motif can be found on a similar shaped vessel from the West Kennet long barrow in Wiltshire (Clarke 1970, 289, fig. 76, E 1067; Piggott 1962, 45, fig 14, B8). The Cord-Zoned-Maritime Beaker ON 20 is therefore of similar date to the one from Upper Largie (approximating to Step 1) but potentially slightly earlier than that from Barrow Hills, barrow 4A and other Maritime-Derived forms of vessels, for example Chilbolton (Step 2).

Nested pair: ON 2A–B (25004)
All-Over-Cord, low carinated (Fig. 14; Pl. 14, a–b) *(126 sherds, 661 g: both vessels)*
ON 2A: rim diam. 92–6 mm, carination diam. 82–4 mm, base diam. 47–8 mm. Overall height 104–6 mm, carination height 33–5 mm
Residue samples: 1 (base), 2 (body) and 3 (rim)

Plate 14 The Boscombe Bowmen (grave 25000), Beaker ON 2A-2B: a) difference in profiles; b) ON 2A inside 2B and, c) detail of the S-impressed (Z-twisted) cord

ON 2B: rim diam. 133–5 mm, carination diam 120–1 mm, base diam 76–9 mm. Overall height 141 mm, carination height 46–50 mm Residue samples: 4 (base), 5 (body) and 6 (rim)

These two pots were found one inside the other as a nested pair at the west end of the grave. All the fragments from the two vessels came from a single group of sherds (Fig. 13) indicating little post-depositional disturbance after breakage. Both pots had been crushed flat, presumably by the collapse of the burial chamber. It is almost certain that they were originally placed upright. A barbed and tanged arrowhead (ON 4), a boar's tusk (ON 3) and a flint blade (ON 8) were found to the immediate south-west. This cluster of finds was close to burial 25007 and may have been associated with it.

The smaller pot (ON 2A) fits quite tightly within the larger one (ON 2B) (Pl. 14, b). The two vessels are of a similar but not identical All-Over-Cord design (Pl. 14, a). The smaller vessel, ON 2A, has a long sinuous profile with a relatively low carination (25% of total height) and out-curved rim (Form 2b- 'Breton'-like in Clarke's terms 1970, 79). Both

pots are of good quality. Given the small size of ON 2A, it is possible that this vessel was made specifically for a child and its position in the grave next to the head of the juvenile burial (25007) may be no coincidence. The high quality of the vessel could also indicate the importance of the individual with whom it was buried.

The larger vessel, ON 2B, has a more tripartite profile with a flaring rim and a slightly higher set carination (at 40% of the total height) than ON 2A (Form 2b). Both vessels are decorated all-over with a single strand of impressed Z-twisted cord (reversed as S-impressions) (Pl. 14, c), which had been wound in an anti-clockwise direction around the pot. The presence of Z-twisted cord impressions tends to suggest that the cord – if not the vessels – had been made by a right-handed potter as it is easier for a right-hander to twist cord clockwise (see Riley 1957, 52 and experimental work undertaken by the author).

The base of ON 2A is slightly concave, while that of ON 2B is completely flat. The latter carries a number of incidental impressions that include three short lengths of cord impression made with at least two types of thread, the larger of which matches the cord used to decorate the vessel. Both vessels have been fired to a near consistent reddish-brown colour with their interior surfaces having been smoothed but not burnished. Their condition is good, with no obvious signs of damage and with only slight evidence for wear. Both were complete or near-complete when deposited.

Vessels ON 2A–B are of a relatively hard fabric (F1) with a hackly fracture that contains no added temper. It is very similar to the fabrics used to make vessels ON 6/23 and 20. As with all the vessels made from fabric 1, ON 2A–B are fired to an oxidised, reddish-brown colour (2.5YR5/6) and have an incompletely oxidised (black) core.

The smaller vessel ON 2A is similar to a pot from Cassington, Oxfordshire (Clarke 1970, 282, fig. 14, AOC 730) and one from Drummelzier, Scottish Borders (*ibid.*, 284, fig. 29, AOC 1735), both of which have quite low-set carinations with tall necks and out-curved rims. The form is also associated with other styles of Beaker. It is close in shape to one of Clarke's so-called 'European' Beakers from Thickthorn Down (*ibid.*, 288, fig. 65 E 184; Drew and Piggott 1936, 83, fig. 2). That vessel has internal rim decoration of impressed cord and body motifs that are Maritime-Derived. Interestingly, Clarke considered the Thickthorn Down vessel to be 'most Breton-like' and a similar case can be made for ON 2B (see also vessels from Machrie North, Arran, North Ayrshire: Sheridan 2007, 99, 115, fig 11.8, 4; and Dalkey Island, Co. Dublin, Ireland: Case 1995a, fig. 11, 6). A further example comes from site IV at Mount Pleasant, Dorset (Longworth 1979, fig. 47, P134). This vessel has zonal bands

of twisted cord impressions, a type of decoration that is generally rare in Britain (Clarke 1970, 281–4) but has affinities with Cord-Zoned-Maritime vessels found in France (eg, Augy, Yonne: L'Helgouach 1984, fig. 5, 4). A further possible example from Wessex occurs at Dean Bottom, Wiltshire, a site that also produced a Comb-Zoned-Maritime vessel (Cleal 1992a, 65, fig. 45, 1; 46, 6).

Pot ON 2B has a more typical Beaker shape and is similar to vessels from Bathgate, West Lothian (Clarke 1970, fig. 1, AOC 1789) and Torphins, Aberdeenshire (Clarke 1970, fig. 7, AOC 1499). No significant lipids were found (see Šoberl and Evershed below).

Possible pair: ON 19 and 21

ON 21 (25010): All-Over-Cord (1 sherd, 11 g) (Fig. 15). Base diam. 50 mm
Residue samples: not sampled for lipids
ON 19 (25010): All-Over-Cord, ?low-carinated (Fig. 15). Rim diam. 140 mm, shoulder diam. 115 mm
Residue samples: 15 (body) and 16 (rim)

Fragmentary vessels ON 21 and 19 were recovered from upcast from the water pipe trench and are grouped as a possible pair purely on the basis that they are similar in size and style to the certain pair ON 2A–B (Fig. 13).

Beaker ON 21 is represented by a single base fragment from a small vessel of near-identical size to vessel ON 2A. Decoration is very similar to ON 2A–B (fine twisted impressed cord, set 3.25 mm apart, comparable with that of 2.75 mm for ON 2A–B) and also runs in an anti-clockwise direction. The base is flat and carries a single short length of impressed twisted cord. As only a single sherd was recovered little comment can be made on the pot's condition or degree of completeness when deposited, other than to note that the broken edges are quite fresh but not new, which could indicate that more of the vessel was once present in the grave. Firing and fabric (F1) are very similar to ON 2A–B. The possible association of the similar 'child'-sized ON 2A with a juvenile (25007) discussed above is of note as the disarticulated remains of another possible juvenile were also found (see McKinley, p. 21 above).

Vessel ON 19 was recovered in an incomplete and very fragmentary state, almost certainly as a result of the recent disturbance. The vessel could only be partially reconstructed with any accuracy. In addition to what is shown in Figure 15, there are three small base fragments that show that the decoration continued right down to the base and one small carinated sherd that demonstrates that the vessel was

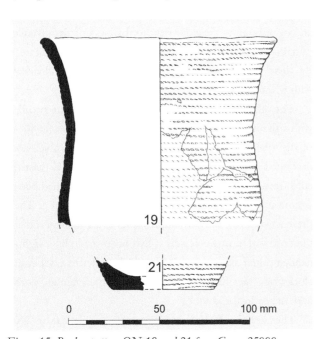

Figure 15 Beaker pottery ON 19 and 21 from Grave 25000.

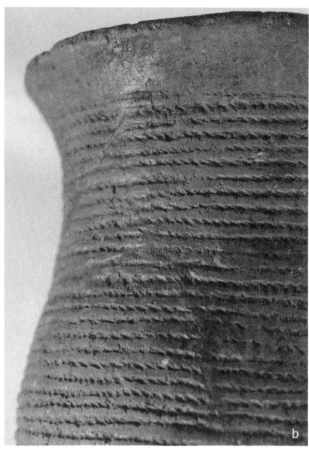

Plate 15 The Boscombe Bowmen (grave 25000), Beaker ON 5: a) note the S-profile and blank margins at the rim and base and, b) detail of the deeper S-impressed cord

probably similar in profile to ON 2A–B (Form 2b). Despite the similarity in size, shape and decoration to ON 2B there are subtle differences. The upper vessel profile has a number of points of inflection and lacks the smoother profiles of both ON 2A–B. It also lacks their consistent reddish-brown colour, suggesting that the clay is perhaps less iron-rich and contains more calcium carbonate. The exterior surface is very patchy varying from reddish-brown to a yellowish-brown, while the interior is a consistent yellowish-brown and unlike most of the other vessels it is in fabric F2, which is heavily grog-tempered (see ON 19 below).

The vessel is fired on the outside to a patchy reddish-brown (5YR5/6) and yellowish-brown (7.5YR6/6). It has a typical non-oxidised black core and its interior surface has been smoothed and fired yellowish-brown (10YR6/4).

As noted above, the form is close to that of vessel ON 2A (see above for discussion of similar types of vessel) but slightly different in that the rim profile has two points of inflection. This type of profile is also evident in the Cord-Zoned-Maritime vessel ON 6/23. As with a shoulder carination, such features could be significant or simply represent a method and choice of pot manufacture. No significant lipids were found (see Šoberl and Evershed below).

Beakers ON 5 and 12

ON 5 (25004): S-profile, low-bellied, All-Over-Cord, 48 sherds, 463 g (Fig. 14; Pl. 15). Rim and belly diams 105–110 mm are approximately equal but in places the rim is wider than the belly and vice versa; base diam. 68 mm. Overall height 127 mm, belly height 40–50 mm.

Residue samples: 7 (base) and 8 (rim)

ON 12 (25004): weak S-profile, All-Over-Cord(alternating twist)/false plaited cord (77 sherds, 252 g) (Fig. 14; Pl. 16). Overall height 148–50 mm, rim diam. 150 mm, belly diam. 120 mm, and base diam. 65 mm

Residue samples: 12 (base), 13 (body), and 14 (rim)

Vessels ON 5 and 12, the only two S-profiled pots, were found close together at the western end of the grave, close to the pair of nested Beakers ON 2A-B (Fig. 13). They could have been placed with burial 25004, although other interpretations are possible. Both vessels had been crushed in the ground, possibly lying on their sides and in the case of vessel ON 5 with the rim facing the top of burial 25004's cranium.

Unlike vessels ON 2A–B, ON 5 has a smooth sinuous (S-profiled), slightly asymmetrical form and a relatively low belly

Plate 16 The Boscombe Bowmen (grave 25000), Beaker ON 12: a) note the S-profile (which reconstruction may have slightly flattened); b, detail of the S- and Z- impressions or false-plated-cord and, c, the vesicular nature of the base- compare with a and b

(Form 2a; Pl. 15, a). It is slightly thicker-walled and of relatively heavier design to ON 2A–B. The cord impressions are generally thicker, more deeply impressed (Pl. 15, b) and more closely spaced than those found on the other vessels in the grave. There are undecorated zones above the base and below the rim (Pl. 15, a), which are considered by Lanting and van der Waals (1972) to be a slightly later trait, of near equal width (c. 15 mm). The cord (Z-twisted reversed as S impressions) appears to have been wound in a clockwise direction. The base is slightly hollowed. The vessel has been fired to a consistent reddish-brown colour. The surfaces have been smoothed all over and lightly burnished in places, on the rim and interior. Traces of what could be a plant oil were found in the lipid residue analysis of the rim.

The fabric (F1) is very similar to that of ON 2A–B but with the addition of rare sub-round clay clasts/?grog. It is fired on the outside to an oxidised, yellowish-red to yellowish-brown (5YR5/6), with an incompletely oxidised (black) core and on the inside to a yellowish/reddish-brown.

The form of this vessel is 'bottle'– shaped with a low rounded belly and relatively long out-curving neck and rim. It is quite similar but smaller in size to vessel ON 6596 from

the grave of the Amesbury Archer. Other than its size the one notable difference with ON 6596 is the blank margins at the rim and base. A very similar vessel was found at Bulford Camp, only 3 km to the north-east of Boscombe Down (Clarke 1970, fig. 11, AOC 1085), although this vessel has only one blank margin at the rim and the cord impressions are circumferential (de Shortt 1946, 382, fig. 3). The low bellied form is also found associated with some of the Cord-Zoned-Maritime Beakers, eg, Christchurch (Clarke 1970, fig. 78, E 313) and 'European' Beakers such as Stanton Harcourt (*ibid.*, fig. 109, E 768, 110, undecorated 769). A somewhat similar but larger vessel was found in grave 206 at Barrow Hills, Radley (Barclay and Halpin 1999, 138–9, 204, fig 4.75, P74). Traces of a fatty residue was found in the sampled rim of ON 5 (see Šoberl and Evershed below).

Vessel ON 12 is an incomplete (50%) vessel with only one side and the base present. The vessel might have been damaged when the trench for the electricity cable was dug, although the relatively poor fabric, which is both pitted and vesicular, suggests that the incompleteness of the vessel could be partly due to post-depositional preservation. The vessel was found crushed in the grave and it is therefore likely that it had become broken in half as a result of reopening of the grave. However, one cannot rule out the possibility that it was deposited in a fragmentary state.

The complete profile indicates that the pot was of a sinuous shape, less pronounced than ON 5 and with a relatively low to mid–high belly (40%). The process of reconstruction has smoothed out the original profile (Pl. 16, a). The original rim and upper vessel profile are similar to vessel ON 19 and, in the grave of the Amesbury Archer, ON 6596, that is with a slight inflection in the profile where the neck joins the upper belly (around ⅔ of the overall vessel height). Decoration consists of alternating rows of Z- and S-twisted cord impressions (Pl. 16, b). These impressions are spaced equidistantly (2.5 mm) and are wound in an anti-clockwise direction around the vessel. The decoration is therefore different in appearance from the plaited cord found on ON 6/23 (Pl. 12, b–c), although it is possible that plaited cord provided the inspiration. In terms of style of decoration it therefore falls between the All-Over-Cord and the plaited/paired All-Over-Cord impressed vessels in the grave. The gentle S-profile (Form 1a) also sets it apart from ON 2A–B but links it as a possible pair with the S-profiled ON 5 (Fig. 14). It can be noted that the direction of the cord impressions is occasionally and randomly reversed in the plaited cord vessels in this grave (ON 6/23) and in the grave of the Amesbury Archer (ON 6609–10) (Fig. 46, below).

Vessel ON 12 is manufactured from Fabric 2 and is harder fired than ON 19. Its matrix is also more vesicular (Pl. 16, a–b). The underside of the base of ON 12 is strikingly more vesicular (Pl. 16, c) than the rest of the vessel. Voids vary from rounded amorphous, lenticular, and stem-like and could represent a variety of plant matter and inorganic substances that were burnt out during the firing process. The higher frequency of voids on the base suggests that the pot was made and accidentally pressed into an unclean surface. However, the even spread of voids throughout the vessel indicates that a certain quantity of material (?plant matter) was either present in the clay or deliberately added as temper/opener. It is fired on the outside to an oxidised yellowish-brown (10YR5/6). It has an incompletely oxidised (black) core and a pale brown (10YR6/3) interior surface.

The decoration is without close parallel in Britain and is perhaps best seen as either false-plaited cord or a variation of all-over single twist cord. Two published sherds from the immediate Stonehenge area can be cited, while others may exist as secondary finds from barrow investigations in particular. One of these sherds is a rim from the excavation of Barrow 38 in the Lake Group and was recovered from the central disturbed area over the primary grave (Grimes 1964, 107, fig. 7, 2). The illustrated sherd is a fragment of rim from a fine Beaker. As drawn, the cord impressions are relatively wide and almost equally spaced and therefore appear to be false-plaited. The second sherd was recorded from Stonehenge itself (Cleal *et al.* 1995, 363, fig. 195, P31) and was recovered from the base of the so-called 'Stonehenge layer' in a cutting around stone 27 of the Sarsen Circle. This sherd also appears to be false-plaited. These examples highlight the apparently localised distribution of this type of decorated vessel which appears to be only poorly represented in Britain (Clarke 1970, 53–4; Gibson 1982; both of whom only illustrate a relatively small number of examples). It is possible that a review of All–Over-Cord material from Britain would identify further examples of the plaited/double or false-plaited version. A number of All-Over-Cord vessels from site IV at Mount Pleasant (Longworth 1979, 103–4, fig. 47, P132, 136, 139) could also be seen as another example of false plaited cord in which the cord impressions are paired and run in the same rather than opposed directions.

Examples of this type of cord-impressed pattern occur outside Britain. Salanova illustrates two examples from the central Atlantic coast of France at Ancenis, Loire-Atlantique (2000, 284, 74 PLC 12, and La Pierre-Folle, Thiré, Vendeé (*ibid.*, 294, PLC 80). At Ancenis the false-plaited cord vessel occurred alongside others of Cord-Zoned-Maritime type in which the cord impressions are mostly plaited (*ibid.*, 284, PLC 07-11). At La Pierre-Folle 21 vessels were recovered from a megalithic grave. Most of the vessels were of Comb-Zoned-Maritime type, although at least one is of plaited Cord-Zoned-Maritime type (*ibid.*, 294, PLC 81). These sites are of particular interest as their Beakers share a similar range of decorative traits (Cord-Zoned-Maritime, plaited cord, and alternating Z and S-twisted cord) with ON 12 from the grave of the Boscombe Bowmen.

The S-profiled form is less pronounced than that of vessels ON 5 here, or ON 6596 in the grave of the Amesbury Archer. Its relatively tall and slender form is in sharp contrast to the squat forms of ON 2A–B and 20. This type of S-profiled form is a rare occurrence amongst All-Over-Cord vessels from Britain (Clarke 1970, 281–5). It would be less out of place in his 'European group' and would certainly match forms illustrated as belonging to his Wessex/Middle Rhine group (*ibid.*, 296–7).

Context and comparanda

The assemblage from the grave of the Boscombe Bowmen represents one of only a few early groups (c. 2425–2300 BC) of Beaker pottery from Britain and Ireland. It is not certain that all eight vessels were deposited as part of a single event; they could have been placed in pairs and/or as singletons associated with the various individuals buried in the grave (Fig. 13). It is very likely, given the level of post-depositional and modern disturbance, that the original grave assemblage is incomplete. There is a good argument on chronological grounds that at least the plaited All-Over-Cord vessel ON 20 was placed with one of the four adult males, parts of whose disarticulated remains were found, and it is possible that the Cord-Zoned-Maritime vessel ON 6/23 was as early, possibly being deposited at the same time as ON 20, perhaps as a pair or as part of the same burial event (Fig. 14). The nested pots ON 2A–B, one of which was a small ('child-sized') Beaker, might be associated with child burial 25007 and the S-profile pair (ON 5 and 12) either with that burial, making four pots in total, or with adult burial 25004. The position of these pots relative to the burials would be unusual in Britain and, therefore, it is equally possible that they are not directly associated with the nearest individual. The possibility that some if not all of the pots have been moved from their original position must be considered. In the case of ON 2A–B and 5 any movement occurred while the pots were still whole, as they were found in a complete but fragmentary state. In contrast ON 12 was recovered with one half of the vessel missing. Assuming the pot was more complete when placed in the grave then breakage had to have happened before the vessel had been crushed.

Unfortunately the original associations of the Cord-Zoned-Maritime Beaker (ON 20) is not known or those of the fragmentary remains of the possible pair of vessels ON 19 and 21 which are similar to ON 2A–B. Given that the Cord-Zoned-Maritime vessel is represented by rim, shoulder, and base fragments it is possible that more was once present in the grave. What is noticeable is that less of this vessel is present than of the other fragmentary vessels and that the fragments that survive from this vessel have undergone further breakage. The conclusion, then, is that the sherds are more likely to have undergone greater post-depositional disturbance than any other vessel, having been subjected to at least two and possibly more episodes of breakage. One possibility is that the pot was buried with one of the individuals whose disarticulated remains are present. Alternatively, the sherds could have been placed in the grave in an old and already fragmentary state, perhaps having been curated along with some of the disarticulated human bones. The Cord-Zoned-Maritime vessel from the grave adjacent to stone 29a in the Avebury Avenue was also recovered in a

Plate 17 Comparison between Beakers in the graves of the Boscombe Bowmen (25000) and the Amesbury Archer (1289)

fragmentary state (Smith 1965, 230, 350) as was the vessel from Wick Barrow, Stogursey (St George Gray 1908, 25; Clarke 1970, 287, fig. 54, E818) and there are numerous references to damaged or incomplete vessels from graves in Britain (eg, Clarke 1970; Case 1982).

The eight Beakers from the grave of the Boscombe Bowmen share a number of similarities with the five vessels from the grave of the Amesbury Archer (pp. 140–54 below) (Pl. 17). Both graves contained a combination of paired and/or single vessels. The pair of plaited All-Over-Cord vessels (ON 6609–10) from the grave of the Amesbury Archer are of similar design to the ON 6/23, although it is not known whether ON 6609–10 had carinated profiles like ON 6/23. All belong to the Form 1 defined here. However, only ON 6/23 exhibits internal rim decoration, which could indicate a slightly earlier date.

The low-bellied S-profiled All-Over-Cord vessel (ON 5) is somewhat similar to ON 6596 from the grave of the Amesbury Archer (Fig. 46, below) (both Form 2a). The squat carinated form found in the two comb-zoned 'European' style Beakers in the grave of the Amesbury Archer (ON 6590, 6597) is also similar to the form of the Cord-Zoned-Maritime vessel ON 20 (all Form 2b). These three vessels are the only ones from the two graves to carry comb impressions.

Taking the assemblages from the two graves together, three and a possible further two vessels have S-profiles and, of the rest, seven have carinations. With the exception of one vessel, all have low bellies or carinations which occur with either tall or squat forms. There is a noticeable correlation between form and style of decoration but not with the choice between a carination or a round belly. The variation in forms described here is also evident in Clarke (1970), in particular with his 'European' group. Whilst his depiction of All-Over-Cord vessels tends to give the appearance of a near absence of slender forms, to some extent this could simply reflect what was available for illustration as a number of taller vessels are known (eg, Stanton Harcourt and Clifton Hampden, Oxfordshire (Case 1963, 25–6; Clarke 1970, AOC 774 and 732). Cord-Zoned-Maritime and the comb-zone variant were also made in a similar range of forms. Of the five classic Cord-Zoned-Maritime vessels illustrated by Clarke, two, possibly three, have slender S-profiles (Brean Down, Christchurch, and Wilsford, although it can be argued that the Wilsford vessel may have had a more squat shape, see above) and two have squatter profiles (Brampton, Cambridgeshire, and Avebury Avenue: Clarke 1970, 288, 61b, E 363.1; 62, E 1070); the same point can be made with the comb-impressed variants. It is possible to trace these basic forms into Clarke's Wessex/Middle Rhine Group when the overall range of pots also included taller and more slender examples. Not only is this apparent in graves but also in deposits from pits and monuments.

The arguably early group of pottery from Mount Pleasant appears to include a range of shapes as discussed above, including one which is 'Breton-like' with zonal cord decoration (Longworth 1979, 101, fig. 47, P134; p. 39 above). That assemblage is also characterised by plain wares and finger-nail impressed decoration, and there is one example of a perforated and cordoned rim (Longworth 1979, 114, fig. 51, P214) of a type familiar in continental Europe (eg, Besse 2001, figs 1–2). The same is true of the arguably slightly later pit group from Dean Bottom, which again includes slender

and squatter forms, some plain vessels and one very low-carinated example that could be a derived 'Breton-like' type (Cleal 1992a).

The radiocarbon analysis (p. 180 below) indicates that the latest dated disarticulated burial from the Bowmen grave is earlier (pre-2350 BC) than the Amesbury Archer, while the Amesbury Archer is probably of a similar age (2350–2300 BC) to the child (25007) and older than the adult (25004) in the grave of the Boscombe Bowmen (2325–2275 BC). The plaited All-Over-Cord vessel ON 6/23 is, on the basis of its broken state and the fact that its position relative to the burials is partly known, likely to have been the earliest one to have been deposited. It is tempting to pair the Cord-Zoned-Maritime Beaker ON 20 with this one, based on the associations suggested above, although this is far from certain. The occurrence in continental Europe of plaited Cord-Zoned-Maritime vessels indicates that that All-Over-Cord and Cord-Zoned-Maritime vessels could be broadly contemporaneous (eg, Salanova 2000, 284). This would also be in agreement with Lanting and van der Waals' (1972) scheme for Wessex as they would expect both types to occur in Step 1. If the nested pair, ON 2A–B, are seen as having been placed with burial 25007, then they could be later than ON 6/23 and, on the basis of the radiocarbon dates, of a similar date to the vessels in the grave of the Amesbury Archer. On a similar basis (radiocarbon results and possible association with adult burial 25004) the S-profiled pair (ON 5, 12) could be slightly later than ON 2A–B. This possible chronological sequence is shown in Figure 16. This sequence would also approximate to Lanting and van der Waals' Steps 1–3 (1972). The more slender and higher bellied form of vessel ON 12 is shared with some of Clarke's Wessex/Middle Rhine group (1970, app. 1.2, form II).

In terms of typo-chronology the Wessex/Middle Rhine vessels from grave 1502 at Wilsford G1 (Leivers and Moore 2008, 25–30) and Shrewton 5K (Needham 2005, 191, table 4, fig. 8, 1), both in Wiltshire, are unlikely to be earlier than those in the graves of the Boscombe Bowmen and the Amesbury Archer and are probably slightly later.

Overall it can be seen that a variety of S-profile and Carinated bell-shaped vessel forms were current at an early stage in Wessex (before 2300 BC), which included All-Over-Cord, Maritime, plaited cord and comb impressed decoration. This would confirm the suggestion made by various authors that these vessels should be amongst the earliest forms in Britain (eg, Clarke 1970; Case 1977a; Harrison 1980; Lanting and van der Waals 1972). At Boscombe Down these forms pre-date a group of rusticated vessels and mid-

50

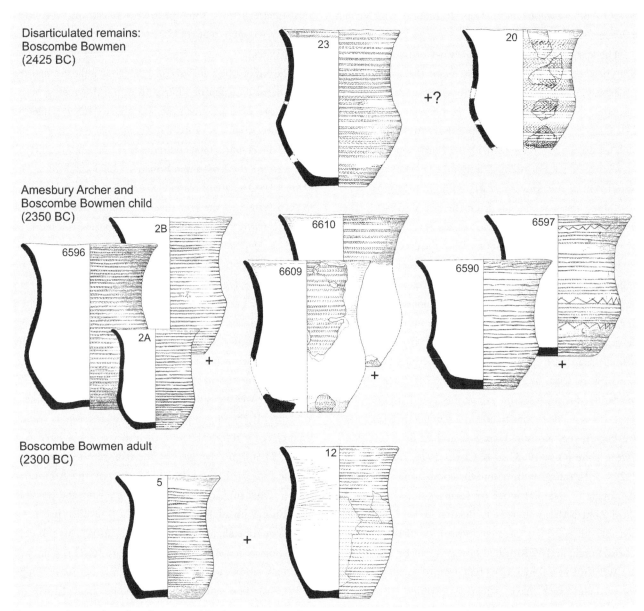

Disarticulated remains:
Boscombe Bowmen
(2425 BC)

Amesbury Archer and
Boscombe Bowmen child
(2350 BC)

Boscombe Bowmen adult
(2300 BC)

Figure 16 Suggested typological sequence of Beaker pottery from Graves 25000 (Boscombe Bowmen) and 1289 (Amesbury Archer) based on the possible burial associations and Radiocarbon Model 1

carinated/Wessex Middle Rhine forms that appear to have been deposited after 2300 BC (pp. 178–80 below).

Within a quite short and tight sequence, there is the possibility that the use of All-Over-Cord in all its variants was early but continued over a few generations, while the use of comb impressions was slightly later. Internal rim decoration, as seen on ON 6/23, is certainly early, while the appearance of S-profiled pots and the occurrence of undecorated margins and zones are also early developments. What the graves of the Boscombe Bowmen and Amesbury Archer show (see Cleal pp. 148–53 below) is that within a relatively short period of time a variety of styles and forms were in use. All of the forms in the grave of the Boscombe Bowmen

grave can be seen to be of direct continental European origin and inspiration. A similar combination of vessels occurs in the early grave at Upper Largie (Sheridan 2008a) and arguably also at Wilsford G54 (Smith 1991). The Boscombe Down graves, Upper Largie, and Wilsford G54 support the suggestion that these should be amongst the earlier forms and most importantly all three graves contain both All-Over-Cord and Cord-Zoned-Maritime vessels.

The temporal relationship between Cord-Zoned-Maritime vessels (Lanting and van der Waals form 2Ia) and those that can be considered to be copies or derived forms using comb rather than cord (Comb-Zoned-Maritime; Lanting and van der Waals form 2Ib) is difficult to evaluate in the absence of further high quality radiocarbon dates, not just from Britain but from north-west Europe as a whole. However, the suggestion made by Lanting and van der Waals (1972) that they should be slightly later is an attractive one, especially when their distribution in Britain is considered. The mostly coastal distribution of the Cord-Zoned-Maritime vessels in south-west England contrasts with a more widespread distribution of the derived forms that share the same basic motifs that are generally executed in impressed comb. Examples of these derived forms include Barrow Hills, Radley, barrow 4A and grave 4660 (Barclay and Halpin 1999, 156, 206, fig. 5.2, P76; 63, 204–6, fig 4.23, P27), Stanton Harcourt, Vicarage Field grave 2 (Case 1982, 105, fig. 60, 11) and Wellington Quarry, Marden, Herefordshire (Harrison *et al.* 1999, 6–7, fig. 5).

It is widely accepted that All-Over-Cord vessels probably had their origins in the area of the Lower Rhine (Case 2004b, 21; Needham 2005, 176–9, fig. 3). The Boscombe Bowmen assemblage of All-Over-Cord vessels is very heterogeneous in character as not only does it include a range of forms but also two variants of the style (plaited and false-cord). The All-Over-Cord vessels from this grave, along with the three from the Amesbury Archer's grave, reinforce the suggestion that this was one of the Beakers of choice in early Wessex graves. The presence of the Cord-Zoned-Maritime vessel in the grave of the Boscombe Bowmen indicates that it could have been in co-existence with those of the All-Over-Cord group in at least the coastal and adjoining inland areas of Wessex. A similar situation has been recorded in France (Needham 2005, 176). It is probable, therefore, that connections existed with the emerging Beaker network in France, the Lower Rhine and Wessex. Whether Needham's 'Fusion Corridor' (2005, 177, 182, fig. 3) is the best way of describing this situation is a moot point as comparisons can be made between some of the vessels within the Boscombe Bowmen assemblage and ones from Brittany and the Atlantic coast of France. In general no single place of origin can be selected for the Boscombe Bowmen Beaker assemblage (see below) with areas of likely contact probably extending beyond Northern France and the Lower Rhine.

Vessel selection and funerary use

The vessels found in the grave of the Boscombe Bowmen are likely to have been placed as pairs or singletons although, as a result of the apparently successive interments and subsequent post-depositional disturbance, the original location of many of the vessels is uncertain. The known pairing of ON 2A–B and the possible pairing of pots ON 5

and 12 and ON 20 and 6/23 has been set out above as has their possible associations with burials. The positioning of pots above and to one side of the head would be unusual in Beaker burials in Britain– virtually all of which are later – and is difficult to parallel (Clarke 1970, 257, app. 3). However, this position is perhaps not dissimilar to that of the pair of plaited All-Over-Cord Beakers ON 6609–10 in front of and slightly above the face of the Amesbury Archer (Fig. 45, below). Mention could also be made of the early Beaker grave at Sorisdale, Isle of Coll, where the Beaker might have been placed in a similar position (Ritchie and Crawford 1978). In the case of the grave of the Boscombe Bowmen an allowance has also to be made for the placing of some of the disarticulated remains of at least four individuals and any associated grave goods such as vessels ON 6/23 and 20. This would have restricted the space available on the floor of the grave. It is also possible that all the Beakers have simply been moved out of position and therefore predate either one or both of the two articulated burials, 25004 and 25007. This would imply that both of these articulated burials did not have Beakers placed with them as grave goods, as was the case of the burial of the 'Companion'. However, the slight typological differences that can be seen between the individual Beakers in the grave of the Boscombe Bowmen suggests that the proposed sequence is a possibility.

The placing of multiple pots, mostly pairs but sometimes in threes, is a relatively common practice within early Beaker graves and one that appears to continue for at least the first 200 years of Beaker usage in Britain (pp. 152–3 below; Sheridan 2008a). The grave of the Amesbury Archer contained five pots, while Wilsford G54 and possibly Winterbourne Gunner, near Boscombe Down (Musty 1963; p. 152 below) contained two. At the latter sherds from two possibly low-carinated Beakers were recovered as redeposited finds. It is possible that the two pots derived from a disturbed grave (Musty 1963). The smaller of the two vessels would have been of comparable size to ON 2A in the grave of the Boscombe Bowmen. Like ON 2A it was well made and finished possibly burnished and fired to a deep-reddish-brown. Unlike ON 2A it was decorated all-over with lines of impressed comb and was manufactured from a fabric that contained fine grog (pers. obs.). The second, larger vessel is more fragmentary but is of a similar appearance and fabric and is also decorated all-over but in this case with impressed cord. It could have been low-carinated and only slightly smaller than ON 2B. A noticeable inflection on a neck sherd indicates a profile possibly similar to ON 2B. If these two vessels were indeed a pair then they provide a good parallel for ON2A–B and one that would link the use of All-Over-Comb and All-Over-Cord.

Sometimes the paired pots form a possible set and occasionally such vessels are placed or nested together (eg, ON 2A–B). This could indicate that they were a set and intended for use perhaps as a container for serving and cup for drinking. Paired pots in graves are reasonably common both in Britain and continental Europe. However, perhaps the best parallel for ON 2A–B comes from a probable flat grave from Stanton Harcourt, Oxfordshire (grave 1: Case 1982, 105, fig. 60, 7–8; Clarke 1970, fig. 109–10, E 768–9). A second grave close by also contained parts of two vessels, a Comb-Zoned-Maritime Beaker and sherds from an All-Over-Cord one (Case 1982, fig. 60, 11–12).

It is probable that these vessels were selected for inclusion in the grave from a larger assemblage in regular use. Examples of these assemblages include Mount Pleasant (Longworth 1979) and Dean Bottom (Cleal 1992a), and another early assemblage comes from Yarnton, Oxfordshire (Barclay and Edwards forthcoming). Variations in form, manufacturing technique (fabric paste and firing), design, and decoration indicate that the vessels in the grave of the Boscombe Bowmen were made by several potters. Slight wear on ON 2A–B indicates probable use prior to burial. It is also possible that some vessels entered the grave in a broken and/or incomplete state. Of particular note here are the fire clouds and potential pre-firing crack in vessel ON 6/23, which could indicate a vessel that was never intended for daily use and one that could have been made for the grave. This vessel contained traces of animal fat and plant oil but these could have part of the grave offerings, as in ON 6590 and 6609–10 in the grave of the Amesbury Archer. Plant oil of unknown origin was also found in ON 5, one of the vessels with slight signs of wear.

Chronological implications

On Boscombe Down, Grooved Ware appears not to have been deposited in great quantity beyond the end of the 25th or early 24th centuries BC and may mostly have gone out of use before the wider uptake of Beaker pottery (see Chapter 6 below). The uptake of Beaker pottery may have been quite rapid, occurring within only one and possibly no more than two generations (ie, 25–50 years). How typical this is of the immediate area and Wessex generally is a moot point. The radiocarbon dating from the grave of the Boscombe Bowmen suggests that the assemblage represents sequential deposition over 25–50 or more years. Together with the group from the grave of the Amesbury Archer they represent the earliest currently dated Beaker pottery in Britain.

The presence of old disarticulated human bone with the articulated Bowmen burials could indicate that the primary use of Beaker pottery could also be older than the date suggested above. The 'death' or grave assemblage of pots (Orton *et al.* 1993, 17, 166; Needham 2005) from these two graves at Boscombe Down may not be a true reflection of what was current in daily use: compare the probably contemporaneous element of the Beaker assemblage from Mount Pleasant (Longworth 1979, fig. 47, P131–45). However, what the two Boscombe Down graves provide are snapshots of what was current over a relatively short period. The evidence from the grave of the Boscombe Bowmen indicates that the 'total assemblage' comprised new vessels (including at least one (ON 6/23) that could have been purpose-made as a grave good), vessels with signs of wear (ON 5, 2A–B), and possibly also old and/or curated vessels/broken vessels (?ON12 and 20).

There is little comparable contemporary pottery from the extensive excavations at Boscombe Down to date other than two All-Over-Cord sherds from pit 8316 *c.* 1 km to the south-east of the grave of the Boscombe Bowmen. Finds from Bulford, Stonehenge, Wilsford G54, and Winterbourne Gunner have been mentioned above, to which may be added other All-Over-Cord Beaker sherds found at Durrington Walls (Longworth 1971, 150 and P568–9) and from barrow sites near to Stonehenge, for example Lake (Grimes 1964, 107, fig. 7, 2), and Wilsford Down (Raymond 1990, 170, fig. 119, P110, P114). Slightly further afield there are sherds with zonal paired cord impressions from the settlement at Downton, Wiltshire (Rahtz 1962, 129, fig. 13, 15–16).

Seen in this light, the early radiocarbon date for the short-necked Beaker from the Shrewton 5K burial (2480–2280 BC (92.5%), BM-3017, 3900±40 BP; Needham 2005, table 4) appears too early and it seems likely that its true age could fall slightly later; probably after 2350 cal BC (*ibid.*, 191; Sheridan 2007). However, this vessel is not too dissimilar to a Wessex/Middle Rhine Beaker from grave 1502 next to the Wilsford G1 barrow, which has an equally early radiocarbon date of 2465–2285 BC (95.4%, NZA-29534, 3878±20 BP: Leivers and Moore 2008, 28, fig. 15). These are single radiocarbon dated burials and further dates would be required to clarify their actual date. As with Barrow Hills, Radley, grave 919 in particular, discussed below, acceptance of these dates would indicate that other types of vessel (short-necked and some Wessex/Middle Rhine Beakers) were equally early.

If the dates from Boscombe Down are viewed as a group against all the currently available early Beaker radiocarbon results for Wessex (Fig. 63, below; Barclay and Marshall in prep.) some of the results (eg, Fig. 63: Radley, grave 919,

OxA-1874–5) could be seen as possible outliers with the true ages slightly later. How late is a matter of debate (Sheridan 2007, 93) although it is tempting to see the graves of the Boscombe Bowmen and the Amesbury Archer, along with one such as those at Wilsford G54 and Upper Largie, as belonging to a primary phase which was followed within one or two generations by the rapid emergence of derived forms (such as Short-necked Beakers, mid-carinated/bellied types and Maritime derived types), new styles of decoration, and the elaboration of primary motifs. In other words, one could suggest that the beginnings of Needham's 'fission horizon', the onset of which he placed at *c.* 2250 BC, may have been reached slightly earlier than originally proposed (Needham 2007, 205) as Sheridan argues for Scotland (2007, 99), at least in certain regions such as Wessex (for example at Avebury, Barrow Hills, Mount Pleasant, Stanton Harcourt, and Stonehenge).

Similarly the uptake of Beaker pottery is also likely to be slightly later than Needham suggested (perhaps nearer to 2400 BC), especially if the primary position of Barrow Hills, Radley, grave 919 is rejected on the grounds that the type of pots should be later that the radiocarbon measurements. Grave 919 contained an atypical mid-carinated incised-zoned small ('child'-sized) Beaker, a low-carinated comb-zoned Beaker also of unusual form in that is has a long cylindrical neck, and three copper rings. It now seems unlikely to be as early as the radiocarbon results suggest (OxA-1874–5, see Table 30; cf. Needham 2005, 206, fig. 13, table 1; 3). Period 1, as illustrated in Needham's figure 13, should arguably be shorter and the sequence of vessel shapes probably reversed. This issue can only be resolved with further radiocarbon dates but the two earliest vessel shapes are evidently out of sequence and would be better placed on or after his 'Fission horizon'. By the time that the grave of the Boscombe Bowmen grave was closed, the use of Beaker pottery was dominant, if not exclusive.

The emerging sequence from Boscombe Down (with complementary results for the later part of the Beaker sequence being discussed in Volume 2; Powell and Barclay in prep.) can also be compared with other sequences, most notably that at Barrow Hills, Radley (Barclay and Halpin 1999). If the Boscombe Down sequence is correct then it provides further support for questioning the radiocarbon dates from Radley, and these are noted below (p. 178). On this basis, the earliest burials there are more likely to include barrow 4A and 4660, both of which contained Comb-Zoned-Maritime Beakers, and probably flat grave 206 which contained an S-profiled All-Over-Cord Beaker; with Grave 919 of a similar if not slightly later date.

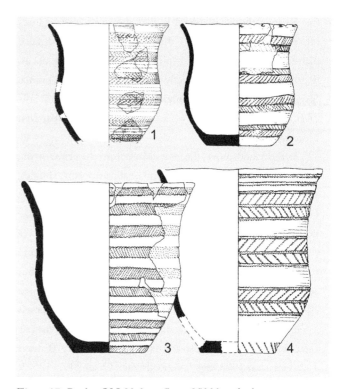

Figure 17 Beaker ON 20 from Grave 25000 and other comparative Cord-Zoned-Maritime Beakers from Britain

Connections and affinities

The link between Cord-Zoned-Maritime Beakers and continental Europe has long been recognised and direct comparisons have been made with the Netherlands and Germany in particular (Clarke 1970, 82; van der Waals 1984, 13–14; Lanting 2007, 41–2), although connections with other regions such as the Channel Islands and France are also possible (Salanova 1998a; 2000). While close continental European parallels to the vessels from Christchurch, Brean Down, and Upper Largie have been suggested (Clarke 1970, 79; Sheridan 2008a) (Fig. 17), this is more difficult for ON 20 with its more complex decorative scheme. It is possible to see this vessel combining a paired line motif, seen for example at Vila Nova de São Pedro, Azambuja, Lisboa, Portugal: Cardoso 2001, 140, fig. 3), with the more typical comb impressed cord-zoned motif (*cf.* Lanting 2007, 35, 48). Alternatively it could be a variant where double rather than single cord (sometimes comb) lines are used (eg, Halliade, Bartrès, Hautes-Pyrénées and Dolmen de la Madeleine, Monze, Aude: Guilaine *et al.* 2001, 232–3, fig. 1, 3–4, and Monze, Les Champs-Galottes, Champs-sur-Yonne, Yonne: Needham 2005, fig. 4a, 10). An interesting variant of the motif found on ON 20 occurs in plaited cord (at Blömkeberg, Quelle, Kr. Bielefeld, Nordrhein-Westfalen; Gersbach 1957, 7, Abb. 5, Taf. 3, 6–8 and Siejbekarpsal-De Veken, Noorderkoggenland, Nord Holland; Lanting 2007, 16, fig. 5); it is therefore possible that the double cord lines represent an alternative to the use of plaited cord/false plaited cord. However, the inspiration for ON 6/23 is just as, if not more, likely to lie directly across the Channel in France (as represented, for example, by the find from Ancenis discussed above) than anywhere else (Salanova 1998a, 284; Needham 2005, 179).

As described above, the assemblage from the grave of the Boscombe Bowmen has close continental European affinities, with parallels for individual vessels occurring in France, Germany and the Netherlands as well as in Britain (Case 2004b). What is evident is that, as is also argued for the grave of the Amesbury Archer (pp. 148–52 below), the inspiration for the vessels was not from one geographical area but several. To take the Cord-Zoned-Maritime (ON 20), plaited All-Over-Cord (ON 6/23) and 'Breton-like' (ON 2) vessels as examples, these are widely distributed not only in parts of continental Europe but also across Britain (Clarke 1970, maps 1–2; Harrison 1980, figs 5–6; Rodríguez Casal 2001, 125–6, fig. 1; Jorge 2002, 34, est. v–vi). Finds in Britain and Ireland are generally scarce but often, and not surprisingly, coastal such as the Cord-Zoned-Maritime Beakers from Bridgwater Bay and Brean Down in Somerset and Christchurch, at the mouth of the River Avon. The similarities between the Cord-Zoned-Maritime Beaker from the grave of the Boscombe Bowmen in Wessex and that from Upper Largie in south-west Scotland can only occur if people and ideas, values, and culture are moving between distant places, as discussed below (Chapter 13).

Cord-Zoned-Maritime vessels were used not just for burial but also in ceremonies at monuments, as examples have been found at Windmill Hill (Smith 1965, 80, fig. 35, P292) and Mount Pleasant, and for deposition in pits, as at Brean Down where the Cord-Zoned-Maritime vessel was found with a rusticated Beaker. The evidence for All-Over-Cord vessels (including plaited/paired variants) being used in a variety of contexts – at henges at Mount Pleasant and Stonehenge (a single cord decorated sherd: Cleal et al. 1995, 354–6, 365, P31, fig. 195, P31), at tombs at West Kennet, and at settlements at Downton (Rahtz 1962) – is well accepted, as is also the occurrence of what are considered to be more 'domestic' forms. The Mount Pleasant assemblage includes an early component and contrasts with that from Stonehenge, which is arguably of slightly later, post-2300 BC, date (Case 1997a) despite, as has been noted, the occurrence of a few potentially earlier sherds (Cleal et al. 1995, 354–6, fig. 195, P31). The assemblage of Beaker pottery from the settlement at Downton, Wiltshire, which includes two sherds with zonal

paired cord impressions, also provides a possible link with Mount Pleasant and Stonehenge. However, it is uncertain whether the two sherds are contemporaneous with the rest of the assemblage from Downton, which also includes zonal comb, finger-nail impressed, and heavier cordoned sherds (ApSimon 1962, 129, fig. 13, 15–16).

At present there is no conclusive evidence from Wessex at least that Beaker pottery was in 'daily use' prior to the practice of placing it in graves. The occurrence of plaited All-Over-Cord Beakers in the two early Beaker graves at Boscombe Down but, to date, in no other graves elsewhere in Britain, is in sharp contrast to the restricted distribution of Cord-Zoned-Maritime Beakers that are mostly found along the south-western coasts of England with a few notable exceptions. This is in contrast to the more widespread distribution of All-Over-Cord Beakers from various contexts (eg, Case 2001). The occurrence of all three types in the grave of the Boscombe Bowmen perhaps encapsulates how interconnected networks of contact between distant places were during the late 25th and early 24th centuries BC.

Finally, it can be noted that the rather homogeneous assemblage of mostly All-Over-Cord impressed Beakers from the collective grave of the Boscombe Bowmen is in contrast to the more heterogeneous assemblage (All-Over-Cord and zoned comb) from the grave of the Amesbury Archer with its single occupant, despite some similarities in vessel form between the two graves. If it is accepted that the Beakers in the grave of the Boscombe Bowmen were placed with successive burials, then we are seeing the occurrence of a less typical practice of placing similar, rather than different vessels in the same grave that is difficult to parallel in other areas of Britain. If the sequence of burials and pots outlined here is correct – and other interpretations can be proposed – then the early development of All-Over-Cord Beakers in Wessex would appear likely.

Organic Residue Analysis
by Lucija Šoberl and Richard P. Evershed

Lipid residues of cooking and the processing of other organic commodities have been found to survive in archaeological pottery vessels for several thousand years as components of surface and absorbed residues. The components of the lipid extracts of such residues can be identified and quantified through solvent extraction and using a combination of analytical techniques capable of achieving molecular level resolution, ie, high temperature-gas chromatography (HTGC), GC/mass spectrometry (GC/MS; Evershed *et al.* 1990), and GC-combustion-isotope ratio MS (GC-C-IRMS; Evershed *et al.* 1994). Characterisation of lipid extracts to commodity type is only possible through detailed knowledge of diagnostic compounds and their associated degradation products formed during vessel use or burial. For example, triacylglycerols (TAGs) are found in abundance in modern animal fats and plant oils but they are rapidly degraded to diacylglycerols (DAGs), monoacylglycerols (MAGs), and free fatty acids during vessel use and burial, such that in archaeological pottery the free fatty acids tend to predominate; this has been observed in numerous pottery vessels (Evershed *et al.* 2002) and verified through laboratory degradation experiments (eg, Charters *et al.* 1997; Dudd and Evershed 1998; Evershed 2008).

Furthermore, modern cooking experiments have helped to understand the accumulation of lipids resulting from different cooking practices and/or vessel use. Analysing lipid extracts from potsherd samples taken along the profile of the vessel enabled us to differentiate between boiling, roasting, or waterproofing on the basis of varying lipid concentrations (Charters *et al.* 1997). The lipid concentration of 10 mg g⁻¹ for potsherd's maximum capacity of lipid absorption has been estimated by boiling modern foodstuffs repeatedly in replica vessels. If we take into consideration that an average concentration of preserved lipids in archaeological pottery is around 100 µg g⁻¹ it is quite clear, that only 1% or less of the original concentration survives the post-depositional degradation (Evershed 2008). The initial lipid absorption also depends on the lipid contents of processed food (animal vs plant products) and modes of food preparation or storage. Variations in long term lipid preservation can also occur due to differences in fabric types.

An increasing range of commodities is being detected in pottery vessels, including animal products (eg, Evershed *et al.* 1992; Copley *et al.* 2003), leafy vegetables (Evershed *et al.* 1991; 1994), specific plant oils (Copley *et al.* 2005a) and beeswax (Evershed *et al.* 1997). Animal fats are by far the most common class of residue identified from archaeological pottery with compound-specific stable carbon isotope analysis allowing detailed characterisation of their source. GC-C-IRMS allows the carbon stable isotope (δ^{13}C) values of individual compounds (within a mixture) to be determined. We have found that the δ^{13}C values for the principal fatty acids ($C_{16:0}$ and $C_{18:0}$) are effective in distinguishing between different animal fats, eg, ruminant and non-ruminant adipose fats and dairy fats (Evershed *et al.* 1997; Dudd and Evershed 1998), as well as in the

identification of the mixing of commodities (Evershed *et al.* 1999; Copley *et al.* 2001). It has been demonstrated that dairy products were important commodities in prehistoric Britain, as illustrated through the persistence of dairy fats in pots (Copley *et al.* 2003; 2005b; 2005c; Dudd and Evershed 1998). An important but unresolved issue, relating to the abundance of retrieved dairy lipids from archaeological pottery, comes from ethnographical accounts of using milk as a pottery surface sealant and part of the post-firing treatments (Messing 1957; Rice 1987).

Materials and methods

Lipid analyses were performed using established protocols which are described in detail in earlier publications (Evershed *et al.* 1990; Charters *et al.* 1993). The identification of individual compounds was based upon eluting order, comparison of retention times to standards and comparing the mass spectra with known fragmentation patters and NIST spectra library. The analyses proceeded as follows:

Solvent extraction of lipid residues

Lipid analysis of the potsherd involved taking a 2 g sample and cleaning the surface using a modelling drill to remove any exogenous lipids (eg, soil or finger lipids due to handling). The sample was then ground to a fine powder, accurately weighed, and a known amount (20 µg) of internal standard (n-tetratriacontane) added which enables later quantification of lipid concentration. The surface residues were not cleaned because of their fragile nature, but were

Table 11: Sherds analysed for organic residues from grave 25000

Vessel ON	Sample no.	Weight (g)	Description
2A	1	1.629	Base
2A	2	2.010	Body
2A	3	1.456	Rim
2B	4	1.877	Base
2B	5	1.727	Body
2B	6	1.840	Rim
5	7	2.393	Base
5	8	1.800	Rim, visual residue on edge
23/6	9	2.296	Base
6/23	10	2.190	Body
6/23	11	1.978	Rim
12	12	1.869	Base
12	13	1.635	Body
12	14	2.024	Rim
19	15	1.506	Body
19	16	2.326	Rim

Table 12: Summary of the results of organic residue analysis of Beakers from grave 25000

Vessel ON	Sample no.	Lipid concentration ($\mu g\,g^{-1}$)	Lipids detected	$\delta^{13}C_{16.0}\pm0.3$ (‰)	$\delta^{13}C_{18.0}\pm0.3$ (‰)	Predominant commodity type
2A	1	0.00	Nd	n/a	n/a	n/a
2A	2	0.80	Nd	n/a	n/a	n/a
2A	3	0.00	Nd	n/a	n/a	n/a
2B	4	0.00	Nd	n/a	n/a	n/a
2B	5	0.60	Nd	n/a	n/a	n/a
2B	6	0.00	Nd	n/a	n/a	n/a
5	7	0.46	Nd	n/a	n/a	n/a
5	8	5.00	FA (16<18), DAG 32, TAG	in process	in process	?plant oil
23	9	11.10	FA (16<18), MAG, TAG	in process	in process	?mixture of plant oil and animal fat
6	10	5.79	FA (16<18)	in process	in process	animal fat
6	11	1.46	Nd	n/a	n/a	n/a
12	12	1.30	Nd	n/a	n/a	n/a
12	13	3.36	Nd	n/a	n/a	n/a
12	14	0.00	Nd	n/a	n/a	n/a
19	15	0.94	Nd	n/a	n/a	n/a
19	16	0.95	Nd	n/a	n/a	n/a

sub-sampled and ground to a fine powder and weighed; again an internal standard was added. The lipids were extracted with a mixture of chloroform and methanol (2:1 v/v). Following separation from the ground sample the solvent was evaporated under a gentle stream of nitrogen to obtain the Total Lipid Extract (TLE). Portions (generally one-third aliquots) of the extracts were then trimethylsilylated and submitted directly to analysis by HTGC. Where necessary combined GC/MS analyses were also performed on trimethylsilylated aliquots of the lipid extracts to enable the elucidation of structures of components not identifiable on the basis of HTGC retention time alone.

Preparation of trimethylsilyl derivatives

Portions of the total lipid extracts were derivatised using *N,O*-bis(trimethylsilyl) trifluoroacetamide (40 μl; 70°C; 60 minutes; T-6381; Sigma-Aldrich Company Ltd, Gillingham, UK) and analysed by HTGC and GC/MS).

Saponification of total lipid extracts

Methanolic sodium hydroxide (5% v/v) was added to the TLE and heated at 70°C for 1 hour. Following neutralisation, lipids were extracted into chloroform and the solvent reduced under gentle stream of nitrogen.

Preparation of methyl ester derivatives (FAMEs)

FAMEs were prepared by reaction with BF_3-methanol (14% w/v; 100 μl; B-1252; Sigma-Aldrich Ltd, Gillingham, UK) at 70°C for 1 hour. The methyl ester derivatives were extracted with chloroform

and the solvent removed under nitrogen. FAMEs were redissolved into hexane for analysis by GC and GC-combustion-isotope ratio MS (GC-C-IRMS).

Pottery samples

Sixteen sherds, from pots ON 2A, 2B, 5,6, 12, and 19 from grave 25000 were analysed and where possible, samples were taken from different parts along the vessel profile in order to asses the lipid accumulation as well as general lipid preservation (Table 11).

Results and discussion

HTGC and GC/MS analyses serve to quantify and identify compounds present in lipid extracts, such that it is possible to determine the origins of preserved lipids and other compounds indicative of heating the vessels to high temperatures (Evershed *et al.* 1995; Raven *et al.* 1997). GC-C-IRMS analyses can distinguish between ruminant and non-ruminant adipose fats and dairy fats by investigating the $\delta^{13}C$ values of most abundant free fatty acids, namely $C_{16:0}$ and $C_{18:0}$. Table 12 lists the samples, the concentrations of lipids detected, and the preliminary assignments of the broad commodity groups based on the molecular data retrieved. Isotopic analyses of lipid extracts will be carried out at a later date in case of a sufficient lipid concentration.

The Beakers from grave 25000 display a poor lipid preservation with only three sherds yielding significant lipid concentrations (ie, >5 μg g⁻¹), which represents 19% of the sherds analysed. The lipid concentration limit of 5 μg g⁻¹

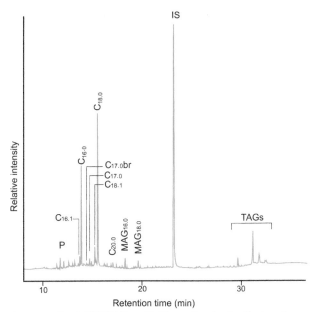

Figure 18 Partial HTGC profile illustrating the distribution of components characteristic of degraded animal fat in the lipid extracts from Beaker ON 6/23 in Grave 25000 (Boscombe Bowmen)

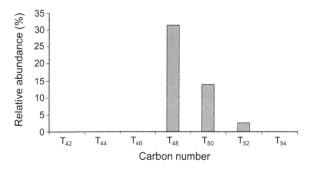

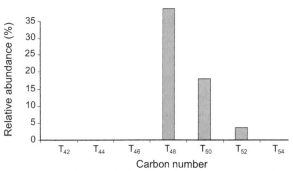

Figure 19 Distributions of triacylglycerols in the lipid extracts from the Beaker ON 5 (upper) and ON 6/23 (lower) in Grave 25000 (Boscombe Bowmen)

represents the minimum concentration which can be reliably interpreted as remnants of ancient food processing, rather than as contamination from the surrounding soil or post-excavation handling. The preservation of lipids in pottery is heavily influenced by the degradative alterations that may occur during vessel use or due to post-burial conditions in the soil (Evershed *et al.* 1999; Evershed 2008).

Figure 18 shows a typical partial gas chromatogram for the total lipid extract (TLE) of the absorbed residue from the base of Beaker ON 23 (sample 9, from the same pot as ON 6; Fig. 14), indicating the compounds detected, namely: predominant free fatty acids, with saturated $C_{16:0}$ and $C_{18:0}$ components. Mono- and diacylglycerols (MAGs and DAGs) were present in trace amounts only, which confirms the high degree of degradation, mainly due to the hydrolytic breakdown of acylglycerols into free fatty acids. The chromatogram also shows traces of odd carbon number saturated fatty acids ($C_{15:0}$, $C_{17:0}$) with their *iso-* and *anteiso-* branched varieties ($C_{17:0br}$), which generally indicate ruminant lipid source (Mottram *et al.* 1999; Evershed *et al.* 2002).

Triacylglycerols (TAGs), which are also present in the TLE of Beakers ON 5 and ON 23, are the most abundant constituents of fresh fats and oils and they degrade quickly through microbial degradation and weathering. Comparison of the TAG distributions with those of modern reference fats has shown that specific distributions can be linked to different lipid sources, and can thereby allow preliminary differentiation of their origins from the two major classes of

domestic animals (ruminant and non-ruminant/ porcine) and between ruminant dairy and adipose fats. Ruminant animals show a characteristic distribution of TAGs with carbon numbers ranging from C_{44} to C_{54} with a maximum concentration at C_{52}; whereas non-ruminant animals display a slightly shorter distribution with carbon numbers between C_{46} and C_{54} with a low concentration at C_{46} and C_{54} and a maximum again at C_{52}. Dairy fats show the widest TAG distribution with carbon numbers range C_{42} until C_{54}, usually with two maxima at C_{50} and C_{52} (Evershed *et al.* 1997; Dudd and Evershed 1998; Mottram *et al.* 1999).

However, laboratory experiments have shown that TAG distributions can be skewed by degradation. The wide TAGs distribution characteristic of fresh ruminant dairy fat is considerably narrowed due to preferential degradation of compounds with lower carbon numbers, and it thus comes to resemble the narrower distribution seen in the ruminant adipose fat TAGs distribution (Dudd *et al.* 1999). Therefore conclusions drawn from TAG distributions have to be made with caution and complemented with measurements of $\delta^{13}C$ values. The TAG distributions for the extracts of the samples are shown in Figure 19.

The TAG distributions detected in the two Beakers are very unusual in British finds and reflect neither typical ruminant nor non-ruminant animal fat TAG distributions.

TAGs and free fatty acids detected in the samples from the rim of ON 5 (sample 8) and the base of ON 23 (sample 9) (Fig. 14) more closely resemble a plant oil residue than animal fat. The biomarker approach usually exploits the presence of specific compounds such as genus-specific alkanes, alcohols, ketones, and sterols (Charters *et al.* 1997). Unfortunately, due to the absence of these compounds in samples 8 and 9 it is difficult to identify the specific plant origin. A similar distribution has been observed previously in pithoi from Isthmia, Greece, which were presumed to contain some kind of unidentified plant oil (Evershed *et al.* 2003). Plant lipids are mainly comprised of saturated and unsaturated straight even-numbered carbon chain fatty acids (Hitchcock and Nichols 1971) with high abundances of polyunsaturated fatty acids. The reactivity of double bonds in unsaturated fatty acids means that they are readily oxidised into diacids and dihydroxy-fatty acids. Due to the higher polarity of these compounds, they are strongly bound to the ceramic matrix and can only be retrieved by base extraction. Unfortunately the plant derived oxidised fatty acid derivatives closely resemble those extracted from mummified skin samples (Makristathis *et al.* 2002; Clark 2006). Since we only have free fatty acids preserved in the Beakers from grave 25000, the interpretation of the TLEs has to be approached with great caution.

The preserved lipid concentration in Beakers ON 5 and ON 23 was too low to proceed with further compound specific stable isotope analysis. However, the hydrolysed and saponified TLEs revealed that the TAG distributions were dominated by $C_{16:0}$ and $C_{16:1}$ fatty acyl moieties. Especially the latter (palmitoleic acid) is a naturally occurring component of complex mixtures of fatty acids in human, animal and vegetable fats and waxes. Unfortunately it is also a very useful and common component for cosmetic and pharmaceutical compositions (Pelle and Mammone 2005).

Conclusions

Lipid residue analyses of the Beakers from the grave of the Boscombe Bowmen revealed a relatively poor preservation of lipids absorbed within the vessel walls, with only three of the 16 samples revealing an appreciable lipid concentration (ie, >5 µg g¹). Gas chromatograms of extracts with appreciable lipid concentrations showed the presence of free fatty acids (palmitic and stearic acid, respectively), confirming the presence of degraded fat. One sample (9) from the base of Beaker ON 23 (Fig. 14) also displayed the presence of odd-carbon number fatty acids with their branched varieties that indicate the presence of ruminant animal fat. Due to the insufficient lipid concentrations, their origin could not be determined more precisely and could be from either ruminant adipose or dairy fat. Extensive hydrolytic degradation of acylglycerols, usually abundant in fresh fats, was evident from the trace amount present. The TAG distributions from the samples from the rim of Beaker ON 5 (sample 8) and the base of Beaker ON 6/23 (sample 9) (Fig. 14) are very ambiguous and may indicate the presence of unknown plant oil or degraded human lipids. However, due to the absence of any oxidation products of fatty acids, typical for the aforementioned lipid sources, the interpretation of the results has to be taken with caution, especially since the high abundance of palmitoleic acid moieties could indicate the presence of modern contamination, which can easily occur during the excavation and post-excavation handling.

The absence of preserved lipids and their extensive degradation could be the result of conditions within the soil or may simply reflect the way these Beakers were used. They have been traditionally associated with the consumption of alcoholic beverages (eg, Sherratt 1987a; Rojo-Guerra *et al.* 2006), which could be the reason for the lower lipid absorption, since higher lipid concentrations commonly reflect cooking, at high temperatures (Charters *et al.* 1993; Evershed 2008). The preserved ruminant fat residues in Beaker ON 23 would fit well with the results of a currently undergoing large scale research of British Early Bronze Age pottery, where a high proportion of vessels (including Beakers) have revealed the presence of ruminant dairy fats. (Šoberl, unpubl. data).

Antler Pendant

ON 18. A long, thin, antler pendant, whose ends taper before ending in expanded, collar-like, terminals (Pl. 18; Fig. 20). A hole 2.2 mm in diameter has been drilled, slightly off-centre, through the middle of the shaft leaving a very delicate and slightly expanded suspension loop. Length 58 mm, max. diam. 7 mm. The identification as antler was confirmed by Pippa Smith and Stephanie Knight; it is not of ivory, as has

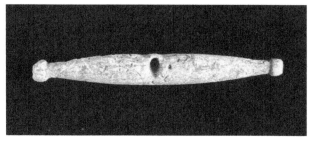

Plate 18 Pendant ON 18 from the grave of the Boscombe Bowmen (25000)

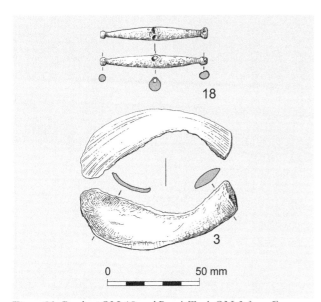

Figure 20 Pendant ON 18 and Boar's Tusk ON 3 from Grave 25000 (Boscombe Bowmen)

been suggested for a related find from Barnack, Cambridge-shire (below). The pendant was found in the group of disarticulated bone 25008, underlying the lower arms of articulated burial 25004 (Fig. 11).

Discussion

The type of object was first discussed by Hájek in the context of his study of bow-shaped pendants made from either antler, bone, or boar's tusk and then later of metal, which have a perforation at or near to the apex of the bow to allow for suspension. These pendants are typically found in Bell Beaker burials in central Europe and are much more frequent than straight pendants like ON 18 (Hájek 1939, 27–8, obr. 4).

Most of the straight continental European pendants are 30–40 mm long and usually have enlarged terminals. A small number are, like ON 18, larger, being up to 70 mm long. There are three types of attachment device on the pendants; (a) a centrally located perforation, often v-bored; (b) a centrally located loop, probably for suspension, as seen on ON 18; or (c) a central groove or waisting, presumably to allow a cord to be seated.

Pendants with a central perforation (variety a) are found most widely, with examples in France, Germany, Italy, and also Greece where they have been found at Lerna (Hájek 1939; Maran 1998, 371–2, Taf. 55; 74; Nicolis 2001a, 217–18, n. 12, fig. 9; 2002, 113–15, fig. 2–3; Fig. 21). The varieties with a suspension loop (b) or a central waisting (c) are known only from Britain and Spain respectively, with the latter

represented by a find from the multicultural Copper Age settlement at Almizaraque, Almería (Hájek 1939, 28, obr. 4, 1; not shown in Fig. 21).

There is some regional variety amongst pendants with a central perforation. Italian examples seem to be shorter with pronounced terminals (Maran 1998, Taf. 55, 9–21) but, in view of the small number of known finds (c. 50 across all of Europe), it is not possible to place much emphasis on difference in shape.

The dating of the pendants is not well established. The contexts of many French finds are poor and in Greece and Italy many examples are found in Bronze Age contexts (Maran 1998, 371–2; Nicolis 2001a, 213–14). The Ilvesheim and Flomborn burials that contained pendants also included Beakers of Monsheim type (Köster 1966, Taf. 20, 10–11; Gebers 1978, Taf. 30, 6, 10) and Lanting has noted that a burial from Bad Nauheim that contained a Beaker of this type was dated to 2470–2290 cal BC, Hd-22049, 3891±19 BP; Lanting 2007, 31–2; Wiermann 2004, no. 74, Taf. 4, 7).

Related finds from Britain come from the Bell Beaker grave at Barnack, Cambridgeshire, dated to 2330–2130 cal BC (Needham 2005, 187 and table 2: 2300–2040 cal BC, BM-2956; 3770±35 BP; Donaldson 1977, 208, fig. 9, 3). Other examples, including one from Driffield (Kelleythorpe 2), East Yorkshire (Abercromby 1912, pl. lix, O.16.3; Kinnes and Longworth 1985, 145, fig. UN. 101, burial 1, 3) are Bronze Age or possibly even later in date (Kinnes 1977, 214–15). The small suspension loop on ON 18 is seen on the later Bell Beaker example from Barnack. Later examples, such as the Driffield find, do not have the expanded terminals seen on ON 18.

In discussing the antler pendant from Barnack, Kinnes commented 'It is unique in a British Beaker context... The most plausible ancestry might be sought in the series of perforated pendants from the upper Danube region' (*ibid.*).

On the basis of their appearance, size, and Bell Beaker associations, the straight pendants from Britain and the Continent seem likely to be related to these bow-shaped pendants in some way. While many bow-shaped pendants are slightly later in date, the distribution of pendants is, in general terms, mutually exclusive of bow-shaped pendants in that only one possible example, from Altenmarkt grave 11 (Schmotz 1994, Abb. 15, 6), is currently known from southern Germany, Austria, the Czech Republic, or Slovakia (Hájek 1939, obr. 5; Piggott 1971, fig. 2; Heyd 2000, 286, Liste 12, Taf. 77–9; Růžičková, 2008) (Fig. 21). However, some of the most simple pendants can be compared with bow-shaped pendants and in one instance, in grave 11, Altenmarkt, Lkr.

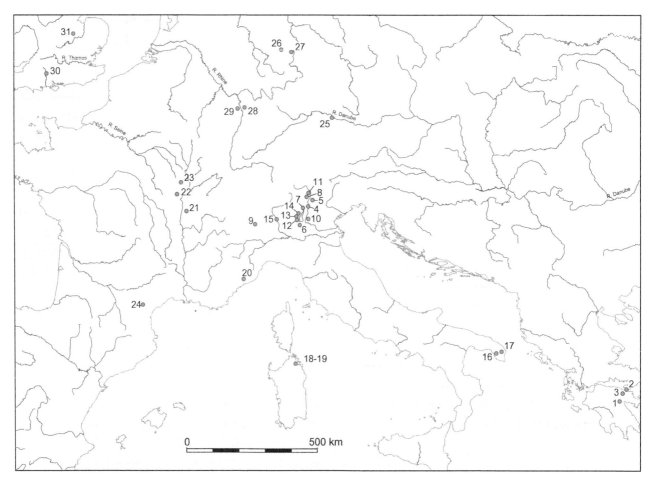

Figure 21 Distribution of pendants in central and western Europe (Iberia not plotted). 1 Lerna IV; 2 Korakou; 3 Zygouries; 4 Colombo di More; 5 La Rupe di Mezzolombardo; 6 Lavagnone; 7 Ledro; 8 Nogarole di Mezzolombardo; 9; Romagnano. 10 Madonna Bianca; 11 Vela Valbusa; 12 Lucone; 13 Polado; 14 Porto Galeazzi; 15 Tomba dei Polacchi; 16; Grotta dei Cappuccini, Galatone; 17 Grotta della Trinita, Ruffiano; 18-19 Padru Jossu; 20 Grotte Barriéra, La Tourbie; 21 La Baume-sous-Rouche, Loisia; 22 Chagny, Vertempierre; 23 Collonges-Lès-Bévy; 24 Grotte de la Treille, Mailhac; 25 Altenmarkt grave 11; 26 Erfurt-Gispersleben; 27 Weimar; 28 Ilvesheim; 29 Flomborn; 30 Boscombe Down (grave 25000); 31 Barnack.

Deggendorf, Bavaria, a simple bow-shaped pendant was associated with four decorated ones (Schmotz 1994, Abb. 15, 6). This suggests that pendants like the one found in grave 25004 and the bow-shaped pendants were variants on a theme, possibly representing different types of bow. Boars' tusks that were perforated, presumably for suspension, are also found in these regions.

Although Hájek suggested that the bow-shaped pendants were belt fittings they are now widely considered to be decorative pendants, made in the shape of a miniature recurve bow. In considering burials from central Europe, Heyd noted that where information was available, bow-shaped pedants were found in two principal positions relative to the body. The first area was at the neck, chest, and front of the torso and the second was behind the back, where a significant number had been found (2000, 286).

Two recent finds of bow-shaped pendants from graves in Bavaria further suggest that these objects may have been quiver ornaments. Five pendants were found in Oberstimm grave 2. Two were over the head and right shoulder of the dead man and the remaining three were between and under the right shoulder and forearm with two arrowheads, points downward, by the feet (Rieder 1987, Abb. 19; 21). At Irlbach, six bow-shaped pendants were found on and over the right shoulder and chest area, and there was also an arrowhead by the feet although the distribution within the grave is not as compact as at Oberstimm (Koch 2006, 26, Taf. 23; 24, 1–6; 25). These suggests that the pendants ornamented a costume or object by the right shoulder, perhaps a quiver.

There is less information regarding the location of pendants in graves. In Britain, the Barnack example was found at the left elbow, next to the copper knife, and on the left forearm there was a wristguard decorated with gold rivets (Donaldson 1977, 208–9, pl. xxix, fig. 8). Of the continental European finds the French examples are, like pendant ON 18 found with the Boscombe Bowmen, from collective graves, while those from Germany come from single graves.

Of these, Weimar and Erfurt-Gispersleben (Gall and Feustel 1962, 225, Abb. 5, 1; Lippmann and Müller 1981, Taf. 37e; Behrens 1973, 156, Abb. 63, g) are certainly or probably male graves. The Erfurt-Gispersleben and Weimar graves both contained bracers or wristguards, with the former containing three arrowheads. The pendants at Flomborn and Ilvesheim were both found near the waist, leading Gebers to suggest that the objects were a costume fitting (Gebers 1978, 64). Another possibility is that the pendants, like the bow-pendants, decorated the carrying strap of a quiver and symbolised archery.

Other possible archery-related uses that have been suggested include release aids (Webb 1994) or as a bowstring winder where the string was attached to the middle of the pendant, knotted, and twisted before being threaded onto the bow (K. Adams, pers. comm.), although this would put excessive strain on the loop bridge.

Although the function of these pendants remains uncertain, it is possible that they were associated with or symbolised archery. They are found widely across western Europe but on the evidence currently available the example from the grave of the Boscombe Bowmen is the earliest find.

Boar's Tusk

ON 3. Boar's tusk: 86 mm long, worked into a scoop or spoon-like implement (Fig. 20). It was found at the west end of the grave adjacent to the nested pair of Beakers ON 2A–B (Fig. 11).

Pippa Smith and Stephanie Knight identified the tusk as having come from the right side of an adult male's mandible. Not enough cement survives to allow the tusk to be aged; modern male boars develop tusks by the age of 2 years, though permanent teeth erupt at 12 months in late maturing breeds. Despite the shaping of the tusk, no obvious traces of use wear were evident.

Boars' tusks are not common finds in Beaker graves in Britain so it is noteworthy that they are present in all three of the early graves at Boscombe Down; the Boscombe Bowmen, the Amesbury Archer, and the 'Companion'. Elsewhere in Britain they have been found with burials at Sutton Veny 11a (two) and Wilsford G1, both in Wiltshire, (the tusk being perforated in the latter case), at Pershore, Worcestershire (with an N3 Beaker; Smith 1957, 20, fig. 7, 1; Clarke 1970, app. 3.1, 504, no. 1209), and at Raunds barrow 1 (Irthlingborough), Northamptonshire (Healy and Harding 2004; Harding and Healy 2007; Brodie 2001). The example from Raunds is hundreds of years earlier than the burial and it is suggested that it was either an heirloom or may have been recovered from what was already an archaeological context (Healy and Harding 2004, 186). The radiocarbon dates from the tusks in the grave of the Amesbury Archer show that they were contemporary with the burial.

In central Europe tusks, sometimes perforated for suspension, were regularly placed in graves (eg, Heyd 2000, 298–9; Turek 2004, 150), and they may represent hunting trophies, as it takes skill and courage to fell a boar. However, they also occur regularly in the graves of metalworkers there and in several cases tusks, some of which have also been modified, have been found in direct association with stone tools suggesting that they were also used as tools, perhaps for planishing or burnishing object. Two of the tusks associated in the grave of the Amesbury Archer were adjacent to a metalworker's stone tool suggesting a similar function and it is possible that ON 3 in the grave of the Boscombe Bowmen was also used in metalworking (p. 222 below).

Animal Bone
by Jenny Bredenberg

A small quantity of animal bone was found. This includes poorly preserved cattle bone fragments (25001 and 25010), a sheep/goat tooth (25005), and a fragment of bird bone (25005), not necessarily from the same individual represented in Early Bronze Age cremation burial 25006. It is possible that some or all of this bone is redeposited. A cat tooth (25010, the upcast of the water pipe trench) and rodent bone (25005) are likely to be intrusive.

PART II

Chapter 4

Graves 1236 and 1289: the Amesbury Archer and 'Companion'

Discovery

The graves of the Amesbury Archer (1289) and 'Companion' (1236) lay to the north-west of Romano-British cemetery 2 (p 3 above) (Fig. 22). The two graves were 3 m apart. As they were different in plan and in their fills from the Romano-British graves there was initially some uncertainty whether feature 1289 was indeed a grave. The colour of the fill was closer to those of the numerous tree throw-holes on the site. Accordingly, the initial excavation was by half-section but this was stopped when the adjacent, but much shallower, feature 1236 was shown to be a grave.

The excavation followed standard methods with a suite of soil samples being taken from each grave to ensure the collection of smaller bones, ossified tissue, foetal bones, gall stones, etc. Samples were taken from the head, thorax, pelvis, hands, and feet, and from beneath the skeleton after it had been lifted.

The excavation of the graves had started on a Friday and it was anticipated that this would be completed in the course of the day, and this was the case with grave 1236. However, the discovery in the early afternoon of a gold ornament in grave 1289 put a different complexion on the excavation.

On the basis that these ornaments might be anticipated to occur in pairs and that they were also likely to be found in a burial of high social status it was decided to retain all the soil from grave 1289 as a whole-earth sample in addition to the samples taken routinely (Pls 19; 52). All spoil that had already been removed from the grave and deposited nearby was retrieved. All the soil from the grave was subsequently wet-sieved for artefact retrieval.

Throughout the course of the day, which was the Friday before a Bank Holiday weekend, it was anticipated that the excavation of grave 1289 would be completed that afternoon but as more and more finds were revealed, it became apparent that the work would not be completed until the early evening. The experience of two months' excavation on the site had shown that it could not be made secure and as news of the discovery of a gold object had already found its way to

Plate 19 Excavation of the graves of the Amesbury Archer (1289) (in the foreground) and the 'Companion' (1236)

passers by, it was decided – by the Project Manager – that the work should be completed that day. While most of the excavation and the recording was completed in daylight, the painstaking process of assigning object numbers to the unparalleled – and unforeseeable – number of objects, completing the paper records for them, recording their locations with a Total Station, lifting the objects, packing and bagging them meant that the final stages of the excavation were completed late at night using light from torches and vehicle headlights. The excavation of chalk packing around the sides of the grave was completed on the Tuesday morning.

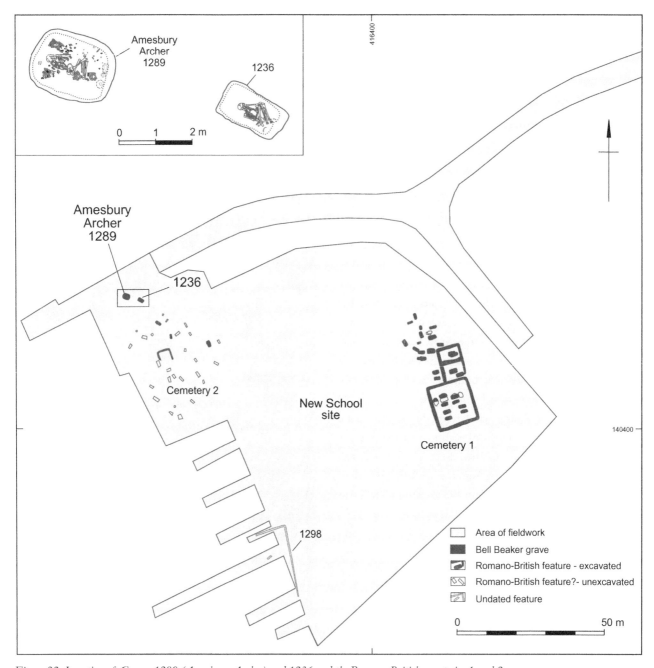

Figure 22 Location of Graves 1289 (Amesbury Archer) and 1236 and the Romano-British cemeteries 1 and 2

Grave 1236: the 'Companion'

The Grave

This grave was sub-rectangular in plan with sloping sides, almost vertical in places, and a flat base (Pls 20–1; Fig. 23). Orientated west-north-west to east-south-east, it was 1.86 m long, 1.05 m wide and 0.37 m deep. The fill (1237) was a dark brown silty clay that was rather more loamy in the upper part.

The Burial

Burial 1238 was the flexed inhumation of an adult male aged 20–25 years, placed on his left side with the head facing north-east (Pl. 21). The arms lay across the torso. During the excavation the burial was considered to be undisturbed (90% present) and the bone in good condition, although several of the lower ribs were absent.

Evidence for post-depositional movement is provided by the presence of hand bones and teeth in the sample from the

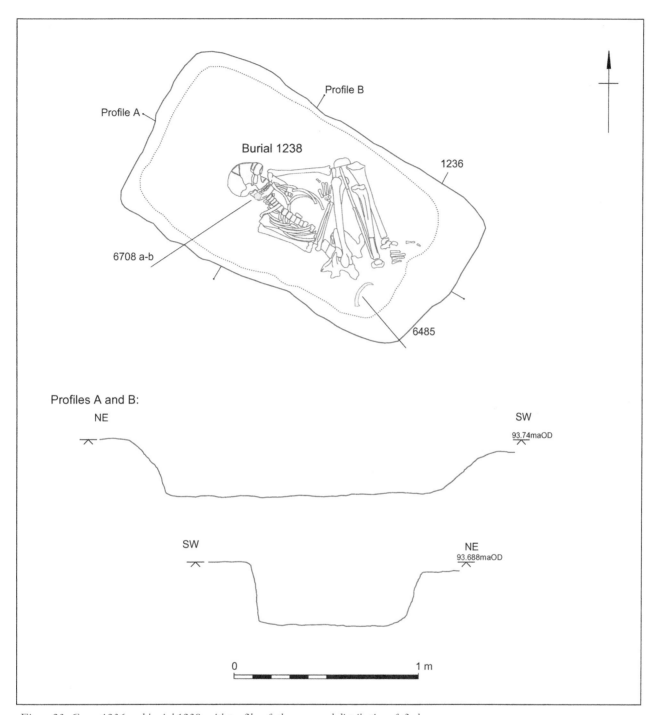

Figure 23 Grave 1236 and burial 1238, with profiles of the grave and distribution of finds

thorax; of hand and foot bones in the sample from the pelvis; and hand bones from the single foot sample.

A single tooth – a deciduous incisor, probably from another individual – was found in the sample taken from around the skull. Deciduous or milk teeth are usually lost by the age of 6 although they can be retained. In the case of burial 1238, all the adult teeth were present so the tooth is likely to have come from a child aged approximately 3–5 years old. This tooth may be residual or intrusive, but it is also possible it was deliberately included in the grave.

Objects from the Grave

A boar's tusk (ON 6485) was found behind the feet, and a number of flint flakes and tools were recovered from the grave fill, but during the excavation these were not considered to be grave goods (Fig. 23). Four small and undiagnostic fragments of fired clay weighing 9 g were found in the upper part of the grave fill.

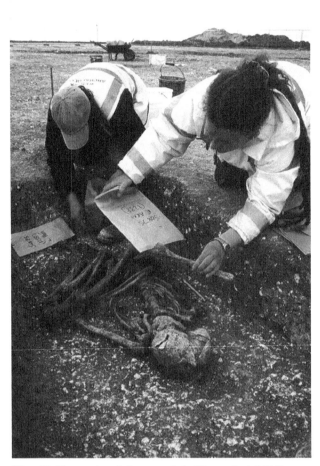

Plate 20 Excavation of the grave of the 'Companion' (1236)

Plate 21 The burial of the 'Companion' (1238)

Flint

One flake with edge-use (Fig. 24, 2), one retouched flint flake (Fig. 24, 4), and three other flakes (Fig. 24, 1, 3, 5) were recovered from the grave fill. In addition, a flint chip, five small broken flakes, and a piece of burnt flint were found in the sieved residue from the samples.

All the flints are in mint condition with the exception of one broken flake which is considered to be probably residual. It is possible that the flints were included in backfill of the grave accidentally and derive from knapping in the immediate vicinity shortly before the burial was made. However, as the range of material is similar to the much larger assemblage in grave 1289, the possibility that they were grave goods cannot be excluded.

Gold ornaments

During the cleaning of the skeleton a pair of gold ornaments, one placed inside the other (ON 6708a–b), was found inside the lower right jaw (Pl. 22). It is possible that they were originally at the dead man's neck, perhaps suspended on a cord, or were placed in his mouth. The conservation advice was not to separate the objects and they were left as found until they were separated at a late stage in the analysis. The ornaments are fully described and discussed on pp. 130–8 below with the similar objects found in grave 1289 (Fig. 25).

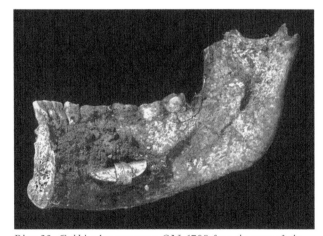

Plate 22 Gold basket ornaments ON 6708 from the grave of the 'Companion' as found

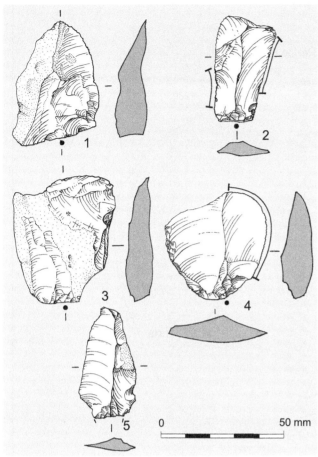

Figure 24 Flint objects from Grave 1236

Boar's tusk

A complete boar's tusk (ON 6845), 103 mm long, from the right side of an adult male animal, was found behind the dead man's feet (Fig. 26). The tip has not been worked into the spoon-like scoop shape seen in the example from the grave of the Boscombe Bowmen (ON 3) and one of those from the grave of the Amesbury Archer (ON 6627). As set out on ppp. 61 and 222. it is possible Boar's tusks were associated

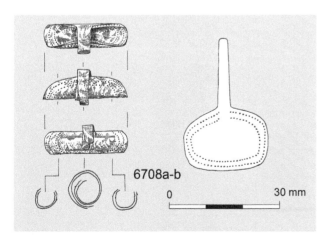

Figure 25 Grave 1236; pair of gold ornaments (ON 6708).
During analysis the two ornaments were left as found and not unrolled

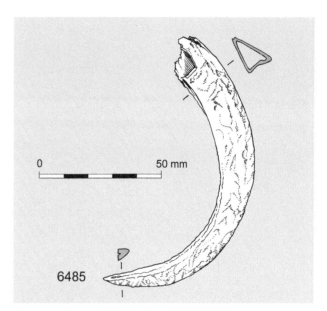

Figure 26 Grave 1236; Boar's tusk (ON 6845)

with metalworking although how they might have been used is not yet clear.

Grave 1289: the Amesbury Archer

by Niels Dagless, A.P. Fitzpatrick, and David Norcott

The Grave

Grave 1289 was sub-rectangular in plan and was oriented close to north-west to south-east (Fig. 27). There was no evidence of an encircling ditch or related feature. As excavated, the grave was 2.35 m long, 1.77 m wide, and 0.58 m deep below the surface of the natural chalk.

The sides of the grave were very steep, almost vertical. The junction between the sides and the floor was slightly concave. The floor was mostly flat but it was uneven at the centre.

All around the sides of the grave, from the top to the base, was a very light brown deposit of chalk (1325) between 0.10 m and 0.15 m thick. It mostly comprised small lumps of chalk less than 40 mm in size with occasional flecks and lumps of charcoal up to 5 mm in size. The chalk rubble had become consolidated within a calcareous silt matrix that is typical of broken and/or rammed chalk that has been subject to water percolation over time. The inner faces of this chalk matrix (1358) were vertical and they defined a more rectangular shape than the cut of the grave (1289).

At the western end of the grave floor there was a small stake-hole (1317) which was 0.09 m in diameter and 0.10 m deep. At the other there were three similar shallow

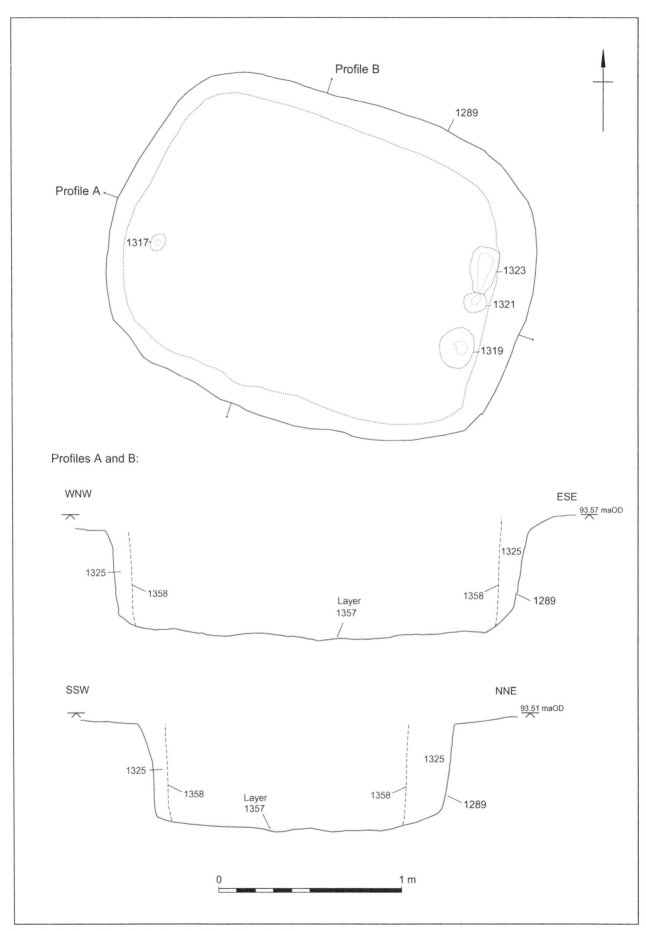

Figure 27 Plan and profiles of Grave 1289 (Amesbury Archer)

depressions in a row (1319, 1321, and 1323). Feature 1319 was sub-circular with shallow concave sides and a concave base. It was 0.20 m in diameter and 0.08 m deep. Depression 1321 was circular with moderately shallow sides and a concave base, measuring 0.12 m in diameter and 0.08 m deep. Depression 1323 was more rectangular with shallow sides and a concave base. It was 0.20 m long, 0.13 m wide and 0.08 m deep.

The fills of all four small features (1318, 1320, 1322, and 1324, respectively) were indistinguishable from a thin layer of mid-brown grey silty loam with occasional pea grit (1357) that covered of the floor of the grave. Although layer 1357 was patchy, it was generally 0.02–0.03 m thick. It was not possible to distinguish with certainty whether the corpse had rested on this layer.

The grave was filled with a mid-brown silty loam (1290) that was quite friable and loose in places and which contained occasional large flint nodules <0.10 m in size that were concentrated in the upper central portion of the fill. Patches of a darker, more loam-like soil were noted in the top of the fill at both ends of the grave. One small fossil (ON 6576) was recovered from the fill during excavation, but as 15 small fossil sponges, a shark's tooth, and four other fossils were recovered from the sieving of the grave fill, it is not considered likely that the fossil was deliberately placed in the grave. A few small fragments of burnt flint were also recovered from the fill of the grave during sieving.

A shallow sub-circular scoop (1326), 0.50 m in diameter and 0.20 m deep with concave sides, was cut into the top of the grave fill at the centre. It was filled with a mid–dark grey brown silty loam (1327) that contained a few snail shells, a fragment of comb-decorated Beaker pottery (8 g), and a fragment of abraded bone or antler. In the initial half-sectioning of the grave, this scoop was initially thought to be a posthole cut into the top of the fill of the grave.

Interpretation
It seems likely that the compacted chalk (1325) around the edge of the grave represents packing material between the grave and a wooden chamber; such deposits have been noted in other Bell Beaker graves in the region and beyond (pp. 199–201). The displacement of some smaller bones of the skeleton (p. 73), which are typically the first to become separated from the major limbs during decay, is consistent with the chamber having survived for some time. How long that might be is difficult to assess but it unlikely to have been longer than 5 years. Some of the displacement recorded might be due to animal activity.

The interpretation of the stakehole and intercutting scoops in the base of the grave is not certain. They could have been created while the grave was being dug, or be associated with the construction of the chamber – if it was built *in situ*. Other possibilities include some form of markers that were placed in the grave before the chamber was constructed. It seems unlikely that a chamber would have needed posts to secure it in place.

Also uncertain is the origin of the fine silt (1357) on the base of the grave. It might represent fine sediment filtering down into the chamber, the decayed remains of the chamber, or possibly some form of bedding in the chamber, such as a mat, perhaps of rushes. The patches of a darker loam-like fill near the top of grave fill 1290 might also represent fine sediments that accumulated naturally.

Because of the insertion of the wooden chamber, not all the chalk dug out of the grave could have been returned when it was closed. It is possible that the grave was marked by this material, perhaps as a small cairn or barrow, and the larger flint nodules found in the centre of upper fill could derive from such a cairn. However, the nodules could also have accumulated naturally in the depression created when the chamber collapsed. The shallow scoop (1326) in the centre of the grave fill might relate to the collapse of the chamber, its possible reopening, or be from animal disturbance of the soft fill.

Several highly degraded cereal grains, a fragment of hazelnut shell, and a single seed of vetch/tare were recovered from the fill of the grave. However, as several modern seeds of the relatively large seeded ivy-leaved speedwell were also recovered, it is considered that all these remains are probably intrusive rather than being contemporary with the burial.

The Burial

Burial 1291 was the flexed inhumation of an adult male aged 35–45 years. He had been placed on his left side with his head facing towards the north (Pl. 23; Fig. 28). The right arm was flexed with the right hand by left shoulder. The left arm was extended, though flexed slightly, with the hand close the right elbow. The legs were bent with the right one overlying the left.

The torso appeared to have slumped forward to the north-north-east and this may well have occurred during decomposition of the corpse. All five Beaker pots lay on their side with the mouths to the north and they may have been knocked over when the chamber collapsed and before the

72

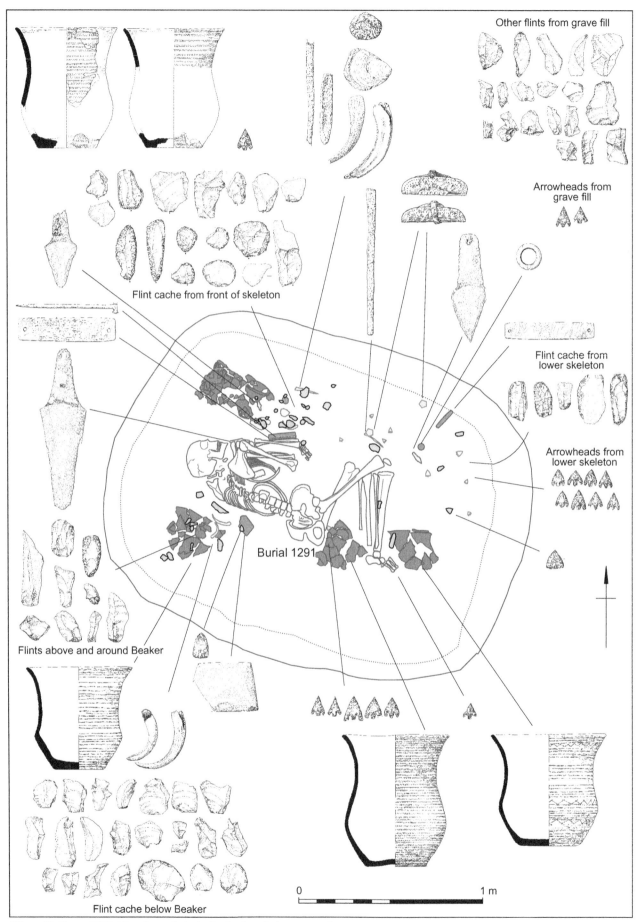

Other flints from grave fill

Arrowheads from grave fill

Flint cache from front of skeleton

Flint cache from lower skeleton

Arrowheads from lower skeleton

Burial 1291

Flints above and around Beaker

Flint cache below Beaker

0   1 m

Figure 28 Grave 1289 (Amesbury Archer); distribution of the grave goods

Plate 23 The burial of the Amesbury Archer (1291)

grave filled with sediment. Such a collapse might also have moved the corpse.

During excavation it was considered that the bone was in good condition with almost all of the skeleton was present, although some displacement of bones was noted, as was the fact that the left knee cap (patella) was not in position. It was not until the osteological analysis, however, that it was recognised that left first rib (the one nearest to the shoulder) was also absent.

The movement of some bones within the grave was subsequently demonstrated by the discovery of fragments of pelvis, rib and vertebrae in the soil sample taken from around the skull; of hand bones from the sample taken around the pelvis; and of hand bones from the sample by the feet.

Despite the whole-earth sampling (with the fill collected as samples 7338 and 7348 and the remaining soil from around the body as samples 7342 and 7345), which was additional to the samples taken for osteological purposes, some smaller bones, such as a number of hand and feet bones, are absent, as are some fragile or highly cancellous bones which are typically less dense and softer than compact bone. The absence of the left patella, at least in any recognisable form, was confirmed by the osteological analysis.

Further evidence for movement within the grave might be reflected in the distribution of the flint arrowheads (Fig. 28), which were found at slightly different levels within the fill, but consistently *c.* 0.10 m above the finds on the base of the grave. It may be suggested that the equivalent of a quiver full of shafted arrows had been placed or scattered over the lower body of the dead man. A single arrowhead was found towards the head. The presence of flint arrowheads above the base of the grave has been noted in other broadly contemporary graves in Britain (eg, Barrow Hills, Radley, barrow 4A; Williams 1948, 5) but it is possible that this distribution in the Amesbury Archer's grave represents the dispersion of a group of arrows that were placed in the grave as a group.

Objects from the Grave

Five Beakers were arranged around the body (Table 13). Two (ON 6609–10) were in front of the face and one (ON 6590) behind the head and shoulders. The other two were either side of the feet, ON 6596 placed between the feet and the pelvis and ON 6597 in front of the feet (Fig. 28; Table 13).

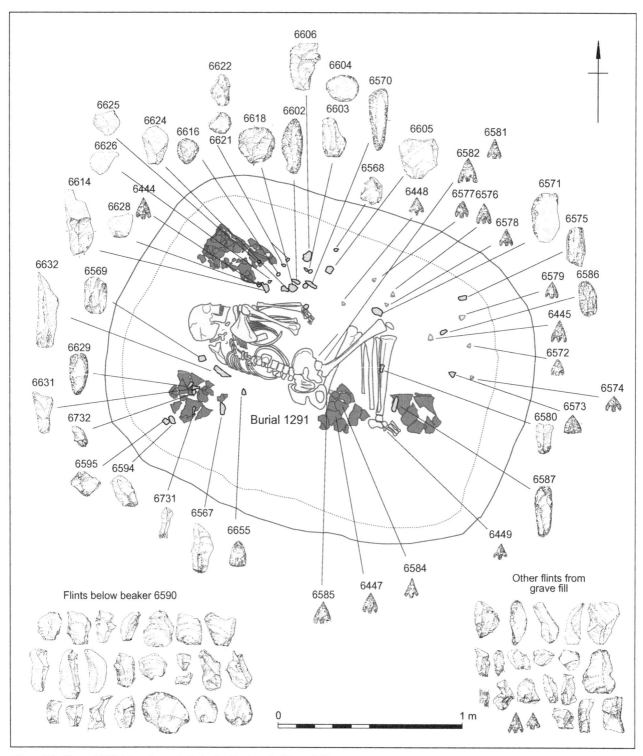

Figure 29 Grave 1289 (Amesbury Archer); distribution of objects of flint

On the outside of the lower left forearm was a black stone bracer or wristguard (ON 6600). An antler pin rested on it (ON 6601; Fig. 28). Below the right shoulder was a copper dagger or knife (ON 6613). Next to the Beakers in front of the head there was a cache of worked flints, two boars' tusks, a second copper knife (ON 6620), a nodule of iron pyrites (ON 6608) that was probably used with a flint fabricator/strike-a-light as a fire making set, an antler spatula

(ON 6612), an antler strip (ON 6607), and a perforated oyster shell (ON 6623).

There was a second cache of worked flints and boars' tusks behind the head and shoulder, some of the flints being recovered from below Beaker 6590, others from above it. A stone metalworking tool (a cushion stone; ON 6593) had also been placed behind the man's back.

Table 13: Schedule of finds from grave 1289 (Amesbury Archer)

Material	Obj. No.	Description	Location in grave
Gold	6446	Basket-shaped ornament	In front of knees
	6589	Basket-shaped ornament	In front of knees
Copper	6598	Knife	In front of knees
	6613	Knife	Left shoulder/arm
	6620	Knife	In front of chest
Pottery	–	1 Beaker sherd with combed decoration	Grave fill
	6590	Beaker	Behind head
	6596	Beaker	Between feet and pelvis
	6597	Beaker	In front of feet
	6609	Beaker	In front of face
	6610	Beaker	In front of face
Shale	6583	Belt ring	In front of knees
Stone	6588	Bracer: red stone; found with flatter side uppermost	In front of knees
	6600	Bracer: black stone; found with flatter side uppermost	On outside of left arm
	6593	Cushion stone	Behind back
	6608	Iron pyrite nodule	In front of chest
	–	1 small complete & 17 frags outer shell of iron pyrite nodules	1 from grave fill; rest from samples 7342 & 7348
Shell	6623	Perforated oyster shell	In front of chest
Antler & tusk	6591	Boar's tusk	Behind back
	6592	Boar's tusk	Behind back
	6599	Antler object	In front of knees
	6601	Antler pin	By left arm
	6607	Antler object	In front of chest
	6611	Boar's tusk	In front of chest
	6612	Antler pressure 'spatula' or flaker	In front of chest
	6627	Boar's tusk	In front of chest
Flint: arrowheads	6444	Sutton b	In front of chest with cache nr Beaker 6609
	6445	Sutton b	Arc around knees
	6447	Sutton b	Among pelvis
	6448	Sutton b	In front of waist
	6449	Sutton b	Behind feet
	6572	Sutton b	Arc around knees
	6573	Triangular	Arc around knees
	6574	Sutton b	Arc around knees
	6576	Conygar Hill	Arc around knees
	6577	Sutton b	Arc around knees
	6578	Sutton c	Arc around knees
	6579	Sutton b	Arc around knees
	6581	Sutton b	By pelvis
	6582	Green Low	By pelvis
	6584	Sutton b	Among pelvis
	6585	Conygar Hill	By pelvis
	6711	Sutton b	From sample 7342
	6712	Sutton c	From sample 7342
cache near Beaker 6590	6567	Blade	Behind shoulders
	6569*	Flake tool	
	6594	Flake	
	6595	Flake	
	6629	Knife	
	6630	Flake	
	6631	Naturally backed flake	
	6632*	Naturally backed blade	
	6633*	End scraper	
	6634	Flake	

Table 13 (continued)

Material	Obj. No.	Description	Location in grave
	6635	Flake	
	6636	Flake	
	6637	Flake	
	6638	Naturally backed blade.	
	6639	Naturally backed blade	
	6640	Naturally backed flake	
	6641	Flake	
	6642*	Side scraper	
	6643	Flake	
	6644	Broken flake	
	6645	Broken flake	
	6646	Retouched flake/scraper	
	6647	Flake	
	6648	Flake	
	6649	Naturally backed flake	
	6650	Broken flake	
	6651	Flake	
	6652	Naturally backed flake	
	6653	Flake	
	6654	Flake	
	6655	Unfinished arrowhead	
	6731	Broken flake/blade	
	6732	Flake	
	–	Chip (lost)	
cache near Beaker 6609	6568	Flake	In front of chest
	6570	Scale flaked knife/dagger	
	6602	Plano-convex knife/dagger	
	6603	Utilised flake	
	6604*	Discoidal scraper	
	6605*	Utilised flake	
	6606*	Utilised flake	
	6614*	Blade	
	6616*	Discoidal scraper	
	6617	End scraper	
	6618*	Discoidal scraper	
	6621	End scraper.	
	6622*	Flake	
	6624	Flake	
	6625	Flake	
	6626	Flake	
	6628	Flake	
Flints tools at lower skeleton	6571	Knife	Arc around knees
	6575*	Knife	Arc around knees
	6580	Flake	At lower legs
	6586*	Fabricator/strike-a-light	Arc around knees
	6587	Fabricator/strike-a-light	At feet
Other flint from grave fill	7342.1	Flake	Grave fill
	7342.2	Retouched flake	
	7342.3	Knife edge flaked in rep	
	7342.4	Edge flaked knife made on naturally backed blade	
	7342.5	Flake with inverse retouch/use unretouched in rep	
	7342.6	Naturally backed blade	
	7342.7	Flake	
	7342.8	Microdenticulate on naturally backed blade	
	7342.9	Flake with edge damage/use	
	7342.10	Flake	

Table 13 (continued)

Material	Obj. No.	Description	Location in grave
From spoil	7348.1	Flake	From spoil heap
heap	7348.2	Flake	
	7348.3	Naturally backed flake, burnt	
	7348.4	Flake	
	7348.5	Denticulate	
	7348.6	Flake	
	7348.7	Broken flake	
Sieved	7338.1	Flake	Residue from near skull
	7345.1	Fabricator	Residue from near body
	–	Thirteen flake fragments and fifteen chips	Residue
Bone	6619	Probably a hand bone from the skeleton itself	
Bone/antler	–	Degraded bone or antler fragment	
Fossil	–	Small, elongated oval fossil	

* Flint object assessed for microwear analysis

In front of the man's knees was another stone bracer, this time red (ON 6588), a third copper knife (ON 6598), a shale belt ring (ON 6583), two gold basket-shaped ornaments (ON 6446, 6589), and another antler strip (ON 6599) similar to ON 6607. The antler strips were oriented in the same direction but their function is not known.

Arranged predominantly around the foot of the grave were 14 barbed and tanged arrowheads and one probable triangular arrowhead (Fig. 29). These were dispersed at different levels throughout the fill of the grave, suggesting that they may have been shafted and then thrown into the grave upon burial. It was not possible to record accurately the orientation of all the arrows as the first discovery of the objects sometimes slightly displaced them. A further barbed and tanged arrowhead was found towards the western (head) end of the grave, and a further two were recovered from the grave fill.

Human Remains (graves 1236 and 1289)

by Jacqueline I. McKinley

To avoid unnecessary repetition, data and discussion relevant to the remains from these two graves and those from grave 25000 (the Boscombe Bowmen), including the methods of analysis, have been presented earlier (pp. 18–28) Table 14 provides a summary of the results from the analysis of human bone from graves 1236 ('Companion') and 1289 (Amesbury Archer).

Results

Disturbance and condition

Both graves had survived to a relatively substantial depth: grave 1236 to 0.37 m and 1289 to 0.58 m. Although the upper fills had undoubtedly been truncated to some degree this will not have had a direct impact on the skeletal material in term of removing any bone from the graves. There was visual evidence to indicate that the contents of both graves had been subject to disturbance resulting in displacement of some bone (generally ribs and some vertebrae) (Fig. 28). Other evidence for post-depositional movement of bone is suggested by the skeletal elements recovered from the samples. In grave 1289, for example, fragments of pelvis, rib, and vertebrae were recovered from the skull sample, hand bones from the pelvic sample, and hand bones with those of the foot. In grave 1236, hand bone and teeth were recovered with the thorax sample, hand and foot bones with the pelvic sample and hand bone from the foot sample. Although much of this movement was probably the result of animal activity other factors are also considered likely to have been involved.

The bone from grave 1236 is in noticeably poorer condition than that from 1289, as reflected in both the higher grade of erosion (due to root etching) and the lower percentage skeletal recovery (Table 14). The bone from these two graves is less fragmentary than that from 25000 (the Boscombe Bowmen), particularly that from the deeper grave 1289, though here the skull was cracked and warped (Pl. 24).

Table 14: Skeletons 1291 and 1238: summary of results from analysis of human bone

Grave	Context	Deposit type	Quanti-fication	Age/sex	Pathology	Condition
1289	1291 Amesbury Archer	c. 99%	c. 99%	adult c. 35–45 yr; m	caries; abscess; hypoplasia; periodontal disease; calculus; osteoarthritis - 11-12 costo-vertebral; infection – mandibular body, left knee; plastic changes – left femur & tibia; calcified tissue – ovoid from thorax region; Schmorl's node – T7, T9, L3-4; op – right sacro-iliac, left acetabulum, left knee, T8 & 10 bsm, L4 bsm, L5 ap, T11-12 rib facets; pitting – 3rd Mt, L1 bsm, T11-12 rib facets; exostoses – right patella, calcanea; mv - *os acromiale*, mandibular left M3 5 cusps, shovelled maxillary I2, T11 spinal process absent, non-fusion posterior synchondrosis T10-11, calcanonavicular tarsal non-osseous coalition (bi-lateral), ?lateral cunieform-3rd metatarsal non-osseous coalition (bi-lateral), *spina bifida occulta*	2–3
1236	1238 Comp-anion	*in situ* burial ?redep.	c. 90% 1 frag. (s.)	adult c. 20–25 yr; m + infant c. 3–5 yr	caries; hypoplasia; calculus; periodontal disease; op – C1; Schmorl's node – T7-12, L1, L3; pitting – 4th left metatarsal; mv – mandibular M3 5 cusps, calcaneonavicular tarsal coalition (left)	3–5

KEY: s. – skull, a. – axial skeleton, u. – upper limb, l. – lower limb (elements shown only where all are not represented); op – osteophytes mv - morphological variation; C- cervical, T – thoracic, L – lumbar, S – sacral; bsm – body surface margins (spinal). Bone condition from grade 1(good)–5(heavily eroded); m = male

Demographic data

A minimum of three individuals is represented. Graves 1236 and 1289 each contained the *in situ* remains of an adult male (Table 14). A single deciduous mandibular incisor recovered from the skull area of the *in situ* remains within grave 1236 appears to represent the redeposited remains of an infant. Although deciduous teeth may be retained into adulthood, the full dentition from skeleton 1238 (the 'Companion') survives and there was no place in the dental arch for an additional tooth. This singular occurrence suggests that earlier burials may have been present in the area and subject to disturbance. It cannot be discounted, however, that the tooth was a deliberate inclusion, a retained 'token' from an infant known to the deceased.

Skeletal indices

These data have been presented and discussed together with that from grave 25000 above (pp. 21–2) to facilitate easier comparison between the graves and contemporaneous burials.

Non-metric traits/morphological variations

A summary of the presence/absence of the standard variations recorded is presented in Tables 7–8 (Chap. 2), and some others are noted in Table 14. Where variations of the same type/form were observed in remains from these two

graves and grave 25000 they are discussed together above (pp. 23–8), to which the reader is referred in the first instance. This section covers only those variations noted exclusively in remains from graves 1236 and 1289.

Bi-lateral *os acromiale* (non-fusion of the tip of the acromion process of the scapula) was recorded in skeleton 1291. Only three other acromion processes were recovered

Plate 24 The Amesbury Archer (1291): view of skull from dorsal right showing post-depositional crack across dorsal parietal bones and associated slightly warping

amongst the remains discussed in this volume (one left and two right from grave 25000) and none shows the presence of this trait. The variant occurs in *c.* 3–6% of individuals though there are, in some cases, indications that activity-related stress may be a factor in its occurrence (Stirland 1987; Knüsel 2000, 115–16). One activity with which an increased frequency of *os acromialie* has been linked is archery (Stirland 1987). Since archery equipment was buried with the individual in grave 1289, the presence of this variant was deemed of particular interest. The studies which have been undertaken on the plastic changes occurring to bone as a result of archery have concentrated on medieval and early post-medieval assemblages, where any affected individuals would have been employing the powerful medieval longbow (Stirland 1987; 2000, 118–30; 2005, 532–7; Knüsel 2000, 108–9, 115–16). In the use of such bows both arms and shoulders are placed under great stress; the bow arm in supporting the weight of the bow and arrow, the dominant shoulder of the draw arm in bending the bow away from the body (Knüsel 2000, 108–9). Consequently, the upper body and both arms develop strong musculature, and, the shoulder joints in particular, are prone to injury especially in the novice (*ibid.*).

Modern composite bows have a draw-weight of *c.* 45 lb (20.4 kg; Stirland 2000, 123), which is considerably less than the predicted 100–172 lb (*c.* 45.4–78.0 kg) of the medieval longbow (*ibid.*, 124). Reconstructions and experimental work on prehistoric self-bows suggest a draw-weight closer to that of the modern composite bow than the more physically demanding medieval longbow; *c.* 45–90 lb (*c.* 20.4–40.8 kg) has been suggested (Clark 1963; Prior 2000) though somewhere between 35 lb and 60 lb (*c.* 15.9–27.2 kg) is perhaps more likely (A. Sheridan, pers. comm.). This being the case, one may not expect to see the same degree of plastic changes in the remains of a prehistoric archer as in later proponents, though undoubtedly regular usage of a lighter weight bow would affect muscular development and, thereby, the supporting bone structure. The measurements taken on the humeri from 1291 show the right side to be slightly larger than the left in most respects suggesting the individual favoured his right hand (Table 15). The upper limb in general, however, does not appear to have been markedly robust. The

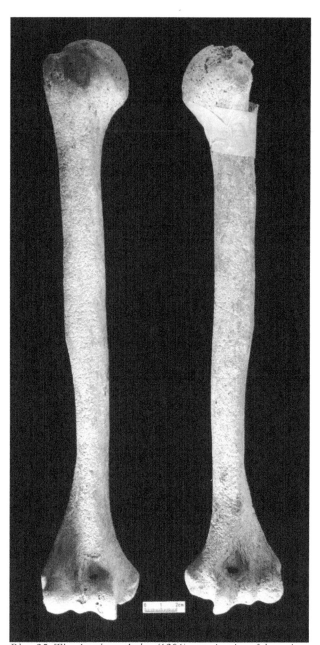

Plate 25 The Amesbury Archer (1291): anterior view of humeri

clavicles and scapulae are relatively small and gracile. Although the deltoid tuberosities (insertion for the *deltoideus* – actions include flexion/extension, rotation and abduction of the arm) of the humeri are fairly robust they are not massively so and there are no enthesophytes, strongly marked muscle attachments or changes in the tubercles (Pl. 25, a–b). The *pronator quadratus* attachments (pronates forearm and hand) of the ulnae are very pronounced, and the hand bones are generally small–medium in size. There is no indication that this individual was of greater upper body strength or was engaged in any more strenuous upper body activity than the other adults within the overall assemblage discussed in this volume. Whilst he, and the others, may well have undertaken

Table 15: Measurements (mm) on humeri from skeleton 1291

	Length	Epicondylar width	Width distal articular surface	Max. mid-shaft diam.	Min. mid-shaft diam.
Left	330	59.4	44.0	24.2	20.0
Right	337	60.5	45.6	25.7	19.2

80

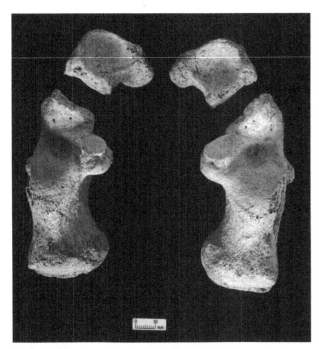

Plate 26 The Amesbury Archer (1291) and the 'Companion' (1238): calcaneonavicular non-osseous coalition 1) bi-lateral skeleton 1291 b) left tarsals skeleton 1238 (right missing)

archery as one of their general activities, their osteological condition does not clearly demonstrate this or suggest it was their primary activity. In the case of skeleton 1291, the strong pronator attachments may suggest the individual was more engaged in the fabrication of some artefact(s) or other activity that required strong wrist control accompanied by forceful movement. There is also the question of the mobility difficulties this individual had to overcome which may have enforced a relatively sedentary lifestyle for much of his life (see below).

Skeleton 1291 has bi-lateral non-osseous calcaneo-navicular coalition, a condition also observed in the left tarsals (right missing) of skeleton 1238 (Pl. 26). Non-osseous coalition may take two forms, cartilaginous (synchondrosis) and fibrous (syndesmosis; Burnett and Case 2005). Given the relatively smooth appearance of the coalition surfaces here, they are likely to represent the fibrous form (D. Case, pers. comm.). Although the condition may lead to pain and swelling reflective of peroneal spastic/rigid flat foot (Leonard 1974; Regan *et al.* 1999), most cases appear to be asymptomatic, and neither individual here shows the osteophyte formation on the head of the talus often associated with the pathological condition (D. Case, pers. comm.). The variation is relatively rare, with recorded frequencies of 1.2–2.9% in modern and medieval European populations (Case and Burnett 2005; Vu and Mehlman 2010), and shows high heredability within immediate families and

over several generations within a family (Case 2003, table 4.2). Studies undertaken in Scotland in the mid-20th century demonstrated a relatively high proportion (25%) of affected first degree relatives (parents, children, and siblings) and no significant difference between the sexes (Leonard 1974).

Skeleton 1291 may also have non-osseous coalition between the 3rd metatarsal and the lateral cuneiform (bi-lateral); although the characteristic pitting was observed in the planter surface of the 3rd metatarsal (Regan *et al.* 1999, fig. 1), no corresponding changes were recorded in the cuneiform. Individuals with one coalition between foot bones are often observed to have others.

As noted above (p. 24), individual non-metric traits generally cannot be used to indicate possible familial relationships between individuals since the frequency of occurrence of many of the variations is too high to render this a reliable practice. The one exception within the burials considered in this report is the occurrence of the same rare non-metric variation shared by the two males in the adjacent graves 1238 and 1291. Here, the similarities in skeletal form, coupled with the proximity in burial place and the presence of gold ornaments in both graves, conspire to indicate a close familial link between the individuals. How close a tie this may have been is not known. Radiocarbon dating indicates the two individuals could have been contemporaries, though of different generations, or there could have been a gap of up to six generations between them (see Chapter 6).

Pathology

Table 14 contains a summary of the pathological lesions observed and the bones affected. To avoid repetition and facilitate easier comparison between both the burial remains recorded in this volume and those from contemporaneous assemblages, where the same type of pathological conditions were observed in remains from graves 1236, 1289 and 25000 (Boscombe Bowmen), they are discussed together on pp. 24–8. This section covers only those conditions exclusive to the remains from grave 1289.

Infection

Infection of the periosteal membrane of the buccal mandible from skeleton 1291, secondary to the formation of a dental abscess (Pl. 27), has already been mentioned (Chap. 2). There is also visual and radiographic evidence for a chronic infection in the left knee joint, possibly associated with gross plastic changes to the left limb bones. The left distal femur has a smooth margined 'patella groove' (see below) at the distal end of which lies a deep depression (10 x 7 mm, *c.* 9 mm deep) in

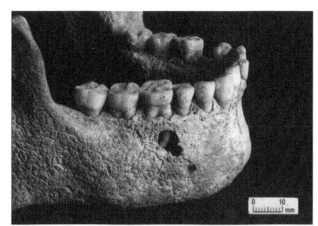

Plate 27 The Amesbury Archer (1291): dental abscess and associated periosteal new bone in mandibular body

what would have formed the medial face of the patellar surface (Pl. 28). The margins of the depression are more open and uneven than those of the groove, and it appears to be associated with internal lesions disclosed radiographically. The X-radiograph shows two, possibly three, spherical areas (*c.* 4–5 mm diameter and *c.* 16 x 14 mm – possibly two coalesced lesions) of decreased bone density in the central area of the articular surface, indicative of foci of infection (osteomylitis). The margins of the lesions are not strongly defined suggesting that the condition was active at the time of death. There is a further small, shallow depression (*c.* 7 x 5 mm, *c.*

1.5 mm deep) in the central medial margin of the left tibia medial condylar surface. X-radiograph of the joint surface shows two spherical areas – *c.* 8 mm diameter, almost coalesced – of decreased bone density (indicative of foci of infection) in the medio-central area close to the intercondylar eminences, with some marginal density suggestive of sclerosis (healing). In neither case is there evidence of periosteal new bone either within or external to the joint capsule, including around the possible sinus associated with the lesions in the distal femur (there are slight osteophytes on the anterior margins of tibia lateral condyle). These lesions could be indicative of a non-specific infection seated in the knee joint spread via the bloodsteam from a focus elsewhere in the body. Their location in the left knee joint of this individual, who had numerous skeletal anomalies and plastic changes to the left lower limb, present the possibility of a traumatic origin to the lesions which will be discussed further below.

A small fragment of calcified tissue (7.6 x 5.0 mm, *c.* 1.4 mm thick), of ovoid form and with an uneven surface, recovered from a sample taken from the thorax area of skeleton 1291, may be a fragment of hydatid cyst indicative of tape worm (genus *Echinococcus*) infestation (Manchester 1983, 49–50). The worm develops multi-cystic structures which may inhabit various of the body's organs, predominantly the liver and, less frequently, the lungs (*ibid.*).

Skeletal abnormalities

Skeleton 1291 has numerous skeletal anomalies, at least some of which, individually, would normally be classified as

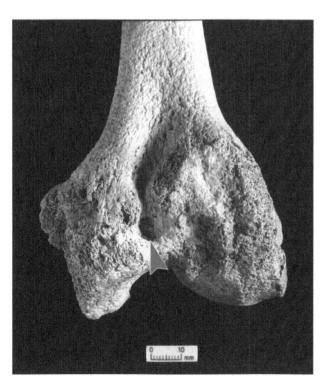

Plate 28 The Amesbury Archer (1291): detail of left femur distal articular surface (patella groove and depression indicated by arrow)

Plate 29 The Amesbury Archer (1291): detail of left tibia proximal articular surface

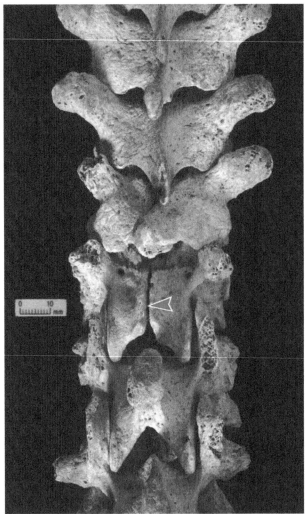

Plate 30 The Amesbury Archer (1291): posterior view of thoracic vertebrae. The arrow indicates the absence of spinal process and non-fusion of the posterior synchondrosis in T11

Plate 31 The Amesbury Archer (1291): dorsal view of spine from mid-thoracic to sacrum showing the slight curve to left in lower lumbar region

morphological variations/non-metric traits or as congenital conditions and not strictly pathological in nature. Given that the anomalies are so numerous, and either demonstrate or are potentially linked with changes in the lower limbs, they are presented together here.

Several anomalies were observed in the spine which may either have affected the enhanced skeletal development seen in the right lower limb, or have developed in response to the indicated increased function on the right side. The spinal process of the 11th thoracic (T11) vertebra is absent and there is non-fusion of the posterior synchondrosis both here and in the 10th thoracic (Pls 30–1). Several of the muscles of the trunk have their origin and/or point of insertion in the spinal process of the T11; the *spinalis thoracis* and the *interspinales* (spinal extensor muscles), and the *serratus posterior inferior* (pulls the ribs down against the force of diaphragm). There was clearly a reduction in the area of bone available

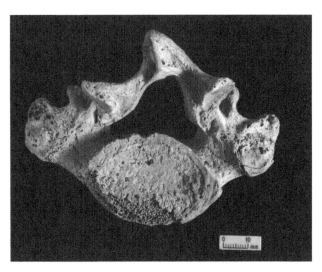

Plate 32 The Amesbury Archer (1291): inferior surface of L5 showing malformation of foramen and spinal process (ie, non-osseous coalition surfaces; see Pl. 33)

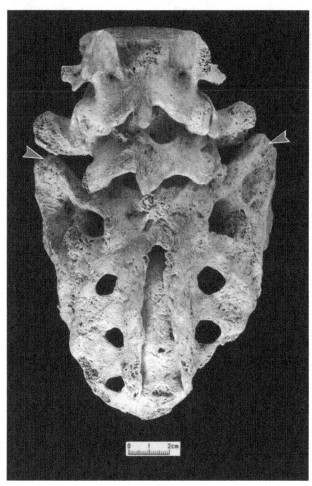

Plate 33 The Amesbury Archer (1291): posterior view of sacrum and L4–5 showing spina bifida occulta in the sacrum and non-osseous coalition between L5–S1 (indicated by the arrow)

Table 16: Dimensions (mm) of left and right femora and tibiae from skeleton 1291

Femur

	Length	m–l diam. proximal	a–p diam. proximal	m–l diam. midshaft	a–p diam. midshaft	Angle torsion neck
Left	464	38.0	29.6	25.4	26.1	72.7 (21°)
Right	477	34.0	30.4	29.2	35.5	61.2 (5°)

Tibia

	Length	m–l diam. nutrient foramen	a–p diam. nutrient foramen	m–l diam. midshaft	a–p diam. midshaft
Left	387	23.9	26.7	21.7	23.7
Right	390	24.2	38.3	22.3	35.2

key: m-l = medio-lateral; a-p = anterior-posterior

a very slight curve to the left (Pl. 31). Spinal *bifida occulta*, involving incomplete fusion of the posterior neural arch below the S1 level, was observed in the sacrum (Pl. 33); this condition is generally symptomless (Aufderheide and Rodríguez-Martín 1998, 61).

There are major plastic changes evident in both femora and tibiae, mostly indicative of decreased activity in the left side and enhanced activity in the right. Whilst showing only a *c.* 2.7% reduction in length, the left femur shaft is considerably more gracile than the right (*c.* 13–26.5% at mid-shaft level; Table 16; Pl. 34). The *linea aspera* is so under-developed as to be almost absent, indicating limited development of the muscles associated with adduction of the hip, and extension and flexion of the knee. Conversely, the gluteal tuberosity is pronounced in the superior and inferior aspects giving the appearance of the proximal part of the shaft being 'pulled' laterally (Fig. 34c). The major muscle attachments here are for the *gluteus maximus* (extends and laterally rotates hip joint, extends trunk) and the *vastus lateralis* (extends leg at knee; one of several which normally work together). The angle of torsion in the left neck is acute, resulting in it lying *c.* 15 mm anterior to the right. The left tibia is similarly thin and gracile compared with the right (Table 16), with no pronounced muscle attachments; 0.8% reduction in length, 1.2–2.7% reduction in medio-lateral diameter, but 30.3–32.8% reduction in anterior-posterior diameter. The proximal condylar surfaces, which are normally angled close to the horizontal, are both angled dorsally by *c.* 25–30° (lateral) and *c.* 30–35° (medial) (Pl. 35).

The other notable changes to the left distal femur included a broad (5.5–14.0 mm), smooth-surfaced groove extending from the anterior superior margin of the capsule attachment to the medial edge of the medial condyle. The

for muscle insertion in this part of the spine. However, since the majority of these muscles have multiple attachments, the individual may have had no noticeable symptoms associated with this condition (S. Black, pers. comm.). The 4th and, particularly, the 5th lumbar vertebrae (L4 and L5) have mis-shapen foramina (Pl. 32). The spinal portion of the L5 is skewed with the process angled to the left and slight bowing-out of the lamina on the right side creating an irregular shaped foramen, narrow on the left side and enlarged/off-set to the right. The foramen is also very slightly skewed in the L4. The neural foramina on the right side of the sacrum are also enlarged. These changes all indicate an enhanced nerve supply to the right lower limb (S. Black, pers. comm.: Pl. 33). There is non-osseous coalition between the L5 and the 1st sacral (S1) via the inferior-lateral surfaces of the L5 transverse processes and the superior surfaces of the S1 lateral mass which are extended superiorly (Pl. 33). These lateral extensions are very slightly higher on the right side than the left resulting in the lower part of the lumbar spine having

84

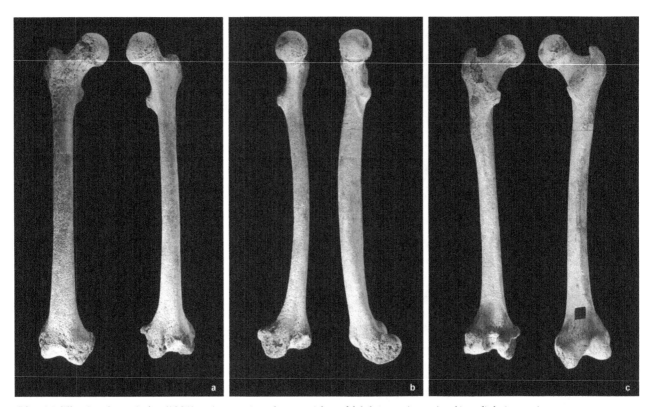

Plate 34 The Amesbury Archer (1291): a-c) comparisons between right and left femora: a) anterior; b) medial; c) posterior

medial face of the patellar surface is absent, as is the central concavity which was replaced by a *c.* 15 x 9 mm surface depression (Pl. 28). The lateral 'face' is abnormal, presenting an uneven surface, with a smooth central bony ridge extending anterior-posterior. The bone is damaged and poorly preserved in this area but there is some suggestion of the retention of a partial articular surface in the superior-lateral area, but if so the patella served must have been small or incomplete. The medial and lateral femoral condyles (former damaged) also appear to have central bony ridges with slight angulation in the surfaces to either side. Many of these changes are consistent with those seen in a knee joint where the patella was absent in life, the deep groove being formed by the *quadriceps femoris* tendon which would normally be distanced from the joint surface by the patella which lies within the tendon (Jerome *et al.* 2009; Patrick and Waldron 2003; Scheuer and Black 2000, 395–9; Sakamoto *et al.* 1999). The left patella was not present within the grave – the normal right patella was found *in situ* – and the condition of the distal femoral surfaces suggest it probably did not exist, or if it did then only in a much reduced form.

The atrophied appearance of the left femur and tibia and consequent increased robusticity in the right limb show that the individual remained mobile, with increased reliance on the right leg and a limited range of movement in the left. The only noticeable muscle attachment in the left femur is for the *gluteus maximus* which would facilitate lateral rotation and extension of the leg at the hip, effectively resulting in the leg being thrown out and forward – a gait commonly adopted by those who are unable to easily or comfortably bend the knee in order to walk. That some movement was retained in the knee joint is indicated by the presence of the patellar groove and the relatively normal tibial tuberosity which provides the insertion for the *quadriceps femoris*. A long-term adjustment in the normal resting stance is suggested by the plastic changes in the angle of the femoral head and the proximal tibia. The change in the angle of the head would have developed from the adoption of a turned-out leg, which may have helped stabilise the individual when in a standing position. The increased dorsal angulation of the tibia proximal articular surface suggests that the force of the body weight was predominantly passing through the dorsal part of the joint rather than being more evenly distributed.

All these plastic changes appear to be of long standing, but their cause is uncertain. There are several congenital conditions, all extremely rare, which are characterised by absence or severe reduction in the size of the patellae (Dellestable *et al.* 1996; Patrick and Waldron 2003). Although there are similarities between some of the features observed here and the characteristics of these various syndromes, the

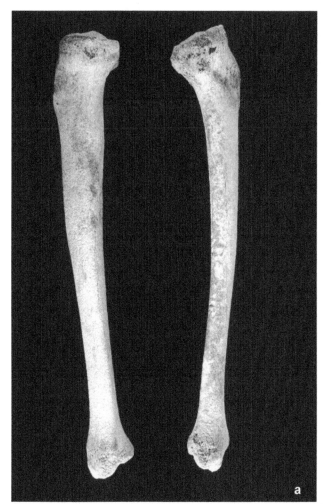 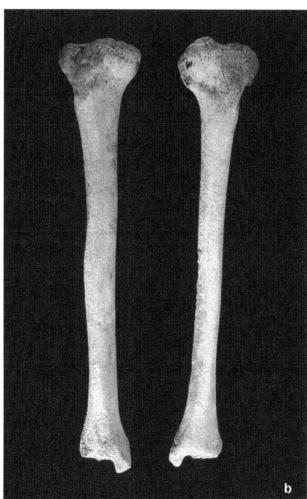

Plate 35 The Amesbury Archer (1291): a-b) comparisons between right and left tibiae: a) medial; b) anterior

case of 1291 does not conclusively fit with any one diagnosis. A noticeable departure from all the known syndromes is the unilateral nature of the condition in this case.

Congenital absence of the patella as an isolated entity is very rare and is bi-lateral in 70% of cases (Nugent *et al.* 1995). The condition is frequently asymptomatic, the affected individual retaining full flexion and activity where the *quadriceps* are intact and of normal strength (Bernhang and Levine 1973; Nugent *et al.* 1995). The condition has, however, been found to be accompanied by an absence of the distal third of the *quadriceps* muscle (as is suggested but the lack of muscle attachments in the distal femur of skeleton 1291) or severe lateral dislocation of the extensor mechanism, resulting in a fixed flexion deformity (eg, 30–80° in the case presented by Jerome *et al.* 2009) and impaired mobility (eg, inability to run, jump, or extend the back whilst standing; Sakamoto *et al.* 1999). These reported mobility problems result not so much from the absence of the patella itself but from the associated dysfunctional soft tissue conditions and resultant instability in

the joint. In modern cases corrective surgery to realign the tendons generally redresses the problem and full mobility is regained; this would not, of course, have been an option in the case of a Beaker individual, who would have had to adjust his movement to accommodate the reduced muscle mobility in his left leg. Only one archaeological case of this condition has been recorded in the British Isles, that of a young Anglo-Saxon female who, in common with most of the recorded clinical cases, was affected bi-laterally but appeared to have had no associated mobility problems (Patrick and Waldron 2003).

Most clinically recorded cases of agenesis of the patellae are related to nail-patella syndrome (Aufderheide and Rodríguez-Martín 1998, 71). This rare hereditary condition, the current prevalence rate of which is variously placed at 1:50,000 (Choczaj-Kukula and Janniger 2009) and 4.5 per million (Patrick and Waldron 2003), features fingernail dysplasia, absent or hypoplastic patellae in 90% cases, posterior conical iliac horns in of 80% cases (considered pathognomonic for the syndrome), deformation or luxation of the radial heads, and various other soft tissue anomalies (Nugent *et al.* 1995). The clinical symptoms are generally knee pain or an inability to extend the knee completely, and there is no reported preferential age of onset (Choczaj-Kukula and Janniger 2009). Although skeleton 1291 does have a number of skeletal anomalies, the changes in the elbow and ilium characteristic of this condition were not observed.

Small patella syndrome is characterised by a small or absent patellae, generally bi-laterally (Dellestable *et al.* 1996). There is a recorded familial link to the condition which is associated with numerous other skeletal anomalies including defective ossification in the ischiopubic junction, hypoplasia of the lesser trochanter, hypertrophy of the talar neck, and planter calcaneal exostoses. The small, laterally placed patella illustrated in Dellestable *et al.* (1996, figure 2, a), appears about normal size and is located superior-lateral within the joint; this is a similar position to that suggested by the possible remnant patella facet in skeleton 1291 but, yet again, the latter shares none of the other skeletal anomalies characteristic of this condition.

One other possible cause for some, if not all the changes seen in this case, could be indicated by the depression at the base of the patella groove apparently associated with the osteomyelitic lesions in the joint described above. These lesions could represent the seat of a well-healed penetrating injury which could have shattered the knee-cap and resulted in direct infection of the joint. Violent fractures to the patella may result from a fall or direct blow, causing either a crack or comminuted fracture, often with associated displacement due to contraction of muscles pulling the segments apart (Adams 1987, 236–7). The separated fragments cannot be reunited without surgical intervention and, where comminuted, there is no chance of restoration of the articular surface. Consequently, in present day cases the fragments are generally surgically removed (*ibid.*). Such an injury would result in severe pain, a long period of convalescence, and permanent disability. The subsequent chronic infection would have caused persistent pain, swelling of the joint, and the ever-present danger of the infection spreading to one of the vital organs; whether anyone could have survived such a condition for a sufficiently long time to allow such plastic changes to develop is debatable.

Whatever the cause, and more than one factor could have been involved, this individual clearly had a very long-standing disability in his left leg which probably included some degree of fixed flexion in the knee joint and affected his mobility. The strength of the right leg demonstrates that he continued to be physically active despite this problem, placing extra

reliance on the right side. The infection, which could have been secondary to this long-standing disability, would been painful, debilitating, and have further aggravated an already difficult situation.

Miscellaneous conditions

Enthesophytes are bony growths which may develop at tendon and ligament insertions on the bone. Causative factors include advancing age, traumatic stress, or various diseases (Rogers and Waldron 1995, 24–5). It is not always possible to be conclusive with respect to the aetiology of particular lesions, but they are commonly seen – as here – in the anterior surface of the patella and posterior surface of calcanea where they reflect activity related stress.

Burial formation process: grave 1289 (Amesbury Archer)

The majority of the bone from the burial made within grave 1289 was found *in situ*, and whole-earth collection of the grave fill for wet-sieving ensured full recovery of all the bone that remained in the grave. The bone is generally in good condition (grade 2, except left hand at grade 3) with fairly minimal fragmentation (Table 14). The few bones which are missing are generally those most frequently 'lost' from burials including the xiphoid process (base of sternum), coccyx, 35% of the hand bones (mostly phalanges), and 29% of the foot bones (phalanges). The unfused tips of the acromion processes, some fragments of the sphenoid bone (skull base), and a few small fragments of the sternal ends of the ribs are also absent; all represent either fragile and/or highly cancellous bone. The absence of the one other missing bone – the entire left 1st rib – does, however, seem anomalous. All the other ribs were recovered, most in their entirety, and survived in good condition. Why this one rib should not have survived when all the others did is not easily explained by either poor preservation or animal disturbance/bioturbation. The implication is that there was deliberate post-depositional manipulation of the remains involving, possibly amongst other activities, removal of some bones.

The individual had been buried laid loosely flexed on his left side, but the upper body had slumped forwards during decomposition (Pl. 23; Fig. 28). The right arm (upper-most) lay against the side of the body, being tightly flexed at the elbow to bring the hand back up to shoulder level. The left arm was extended across the body at shoulder height and flexed at the elbow, bringing the forearm almost parallel with the right arm and the hand resting at the level of the right elbow. The lower thoracic and upper lumbar region of the spine was disrupted in antiquity, with marked rotation of at least two vertebrae (T12 and L1); one right rib was also displaced. The opportunity for such post-depositional movement (slumping and displacement of individual bones) suggests that the burial was initially covered in some manner which kept the grave fill away from the body. The rate of decomposition of the soft tissues can vary dependent of a number of factors including the time of year and length of time between death and burial (heat, bacterial activity, parasite access), mode of dress and other inclusions in the grave (Evans 1963; Henderson 1987). Decomposition times can range from as little as a few months to c. 5 years. Access to the underlying left rib without undue disturbance of the rest of the articulated skeleton would have required care but would not have been impossible. Disruption to the spine could have occurred as a result of such manipulation or could be indicative of animal activity.

Isotope Analyses
by C.A. Chenery and J.A Evans

Oxygen and strontium isotope analyses (Chapter 7 below) were undertaken on the Amesbury Archer and the oxygen isotope composition is diagnostic of an origin outside Britain. The drinking water value of −10 is found in south-east or west Germany and up into Scandinavia. His strontium isotope composition is typical of many of the Copper–Bronze Age populations from such Alpine areas.

The 'Companion' has a combined oxygen and strontium signature that is consistent with an early childhood in southern England in a Chalk founded area but later childhood values suggest a domicile closer in conditions to that of the Amesbury Archer.

Stable isotope analyses to assess diet currently being undertaken as part of the Beaker People Project (Jay and Richard 2007) indicates that both individuals ate a mixed a diet (M. Jay, pers. comm).

Chapter 5

Finds from the Grave of the Amesbury Archer

Flint
by Phil Harding

The excavation of the grave of the Amesbury Archer (1289) produced 122 pieces of worked flint, the largest category of material from the grave, constituting 82% of all the artefactual finds. The grave goods included 35 retouched tools and 37 unretouched flakes that were recorded, in three dimensions, in three broad areas immediately around the skeleton (1291) (Figs 28–9). The remaining 50 items, including pieces recovered from bone and whole-earth samples, were found in the fill of the grave (1290).

A sample of 13 objects, comprising flakes, blades, scrapers, a knife, and a fabricator/strike-a-light (Table 13),

was examined for microwear by Dr Linda Hurcombe, University of Exeter. It was found that the surfaces had been affected by post-depositional processes in the soil preventing microwear traces being seen, even where the objects had edge damage that was consistent with use.

Finds Recorded with the Skeleton (1291)

A spread of 14 barbed and tanged arrowheads and a triangular arrowhead was found near the lower parts of the body (Fig. 29). In addition, four retouched tools, including two heavily worn fabricators/strike-a-lights (ON 6586–7) with rounded ends, two flake knives (ON 6575, 6571), and a

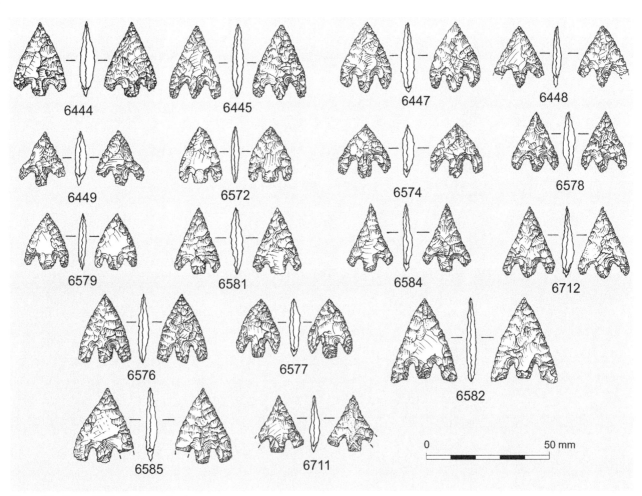

Figure 30 Grave 1289; flint arrowheads

flake were found in the same area, lying in an arc surrounding the knees and feet.

Two discrete caches of flints lay towards the head end of the grave; one behind the head and shoulders, associated with Beaker ON 6590, the other in front of the chest, associated with Beaker ON 6609. The caches comprised 34 and 18 pieces respectively and were of contrasting composition. The cache behind the body contained three scrapers, an unfinished arrowhead, a knife, and a retouched flake, but was principally composed of unretouched flint flakes in mint condition. The cache in front of the body comprised five scrapers, a plano-convex-knife/dagger, an edge flaked knife/dagger, and flakes, some of which appeared to have been utilised; a further barbed and tanged arrowhead was found among this cache. Both caches were of sufficient quantity and limited extent to indicate that they had not undergone significant post-depositional movement following the completion of the burial. This was particularly true of the cluster of unretouched flakes behind the back, which had been covered and protected by Beaker ON 6590, which may have been pushed over by the collapse of the wooden chamber.

In addition, a fabricator (ON 7345; Fig. 35) was extracted from residue sieved from a sample recorded as having come from around the area of the body. Sieving also produced a flake (ON 7338.1) from near the skull and an unallocated broken flake and a chip from other sieved residue in the grave.

Finds from the fill of the grave (1290)

Samples taken from around the skeleton during the excavation also produced two barbed and tanged arrowheads, a microdenticulate, two edge-flaked knives, a retouched flake, and six flakes (Fig. 30, ON 6711–2). Although these objects could not be located precisely, most were in mint condition and probably formed part of the main burial. Thirteen broken flakes and 15 chips were also recovered from the samples (Fig. 35, sample 7542), as well as six flakes and a denticulate from the bulk sieving of the whole-earth sample (Fig. 35, sample 7348) of the grave fill (1290).

Raw Material

The entire assemblage is patinated, which did not permit detailed examination of the raw material through any unbroken surfaces; however, it is most probable that the flint

is from the local Chalk. It is generally of good quality with few obvious thermal flaws. Blotches in the surface of the patination can be attributed to grey inclusions that are frequently present in flint. It is very difficult to calculate how many nodules were involved or over what timescale tools for the burial had been produced. The raw material, size, technology, unused condition, and composition of the cache sealed by Beaker ON 6590 make it likely that these flakes were derived from a single nodule or limited number of nodules that were flaked soon before they were placed in the grave. However, variations in the composition of the retouched tool component and the presence of retouched tools with heavily worn edges, especially fabricators ON 6586–7 (Fig. 34), suggest that other pieces were relatively old when they were included in the burial.

The cortex is frequently the most variable and distinctive material in this assemblage. Although it is possible for variations to occur in the composition of the flint and the thickness and character of the cortex in the same nodule, the frequency of these variations suggests that it is more likely that a number of nodules are present. The cortex ranges from fresh thick chalky material (ON 6587), which may have been taken as fresh flint from the Chalk to thin, weathered cortex (ON 6604, 6655) that is more likely to have originated from surface nodules. There is also a barbed and tanged arrowhead (ON 6711) that is stained orange beneath the cortex, and a fabricator (ON 7345.1) with heavily weathered cortex that may have originated from a gravel source, most locally the River Avon. There were also seven other pieces, including a barbed and tanged arrowhead (ON 6572), a knife (ON 6575), and a plano-convex knife/dagger (ON 6602) that are partially stained by iron, although it is likely that some of this may be post-depositional and related to iron pyrite nodules in the Chalk.

Technology

There were no cores from either the Amesbury Archer's grave or that of the 'Companion'. However, it was possible to reconstruct some aspects of the technology used to manufacture the unused flakes included with the burial. The results are, to some extent, repeated in the blanks for the retouched tools. Blank production was undoubtedly undertaken using direct percussion. Hard hammers, probably of flint, appear to have been preferred, although soft hammer characteristics are also present. There is nothing to indicate that there was large scale use of soft hammers; it is more likely that the characteristics were created by the use of cortical surfaces on flint hammers, which can mimic the effects of soft hammers (Ohnuma and Bergman 1982). Flakes were normally removed without preliminary platform abrasion. Only six examples with abraded striking platforms were recorded among 53 unretouched flakes. The procedure was used inconsistently and was primarily to tidy the edge of the core. It did nothing to strengthen the edge of the core before percussion was undertaken. The technique was to some extent unnecessary for this function due to the fact that the point of percussion was usually placed well onto the striking platform, rendering the use of abrasion obsolete.

Cores were probably prepared initially with a single striking platform and a relatively flat flaking face to produce broad expanding flakes. This technology is entirely consistent with Late Neolithic and Beaker flint working. The analysis indicated that although flakes from all phases of flake production were present, fully cortical preparation flakes were generally scarce. Similarly naturally backed flakes with cortex along one edge were relatively frequent.

Arrowheads

Fifteen barbed and tanged arrowheads and a probable triangular arrowhead were recorded in three dimensions and two others were found in samples taken from around the skeleton (1290) (Pl. 36; Figs 28–30; Table 13).

Distribution

Fourteen of the barbed and tanged and the triangular arrowheads were found towards the eastern end of the grave in a scatter extending from the pelvis to the feet. The

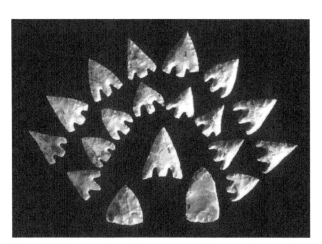

Plate 36 Flint arrowheads from the grave of the Amesbury Archer (1289)

horizontal distribution of these arrowheads hints at two distinct groups. A cluster of nine lay in front of the knees and was separated by a strip, 0.30 m wide, from the remaining six that lay over the pelvis, the lower legs, and Beaker ON 6596. These six arrowheads were found at a slightly higher level than the remainder of the grave goods and clearly overlay the skeleton, which suggested that they had been added to the grave as a final act of burial. They showed no specific alignment or orientation, suggesting that they had not been held in a quiver or bundle, but had been scattered across the foot of the grave. Most arrowheads were inevitably disturbed by the trowel during excavation so that no record could be made of the orientation of individual items. It is likely, in any case, that they had undergone some post-depositional movement as the grave collapsed and it is, therefore, impossible to demonstrate conclusively whether the arrowheads were hafted, the hafts ritually snapped, or the heads inserted without hafts at the time of the burial. The fact that arrowheads were located over the pelvis suggests that shafts were present. This would prevent an arrow, balanced against the body, from falling to the floor of the grave when it was backfilled. The scarcity of arrowheads in the areas between the elbow and knees and behind the lower legs is also noticeable. Their absence in this area may imply that any arrows were laid across the lower legs with their tips aligned in opposing directions. It may also have resulted from some form of structure, clothing, or shroud that was present preventing arrowheads from collapsing into this area. The band with no finds extends as a virtual corridor along the length of the body and may have been filled by a bow. Only one arrowhead (ON 6444) was found towards the western end of the grave, associated with the cache of flints associated with Beaker ON 6609.

Typology

The most prevalent arrowhead type in the grave is Green's (1980) Sutton b type, of which there are 12, with one Sutton c (ON 6577). Green included Sutton arrowheads as those that fell within 'a broad spectrum of miscellaneous arrowheads' and were listed as the most common form of barbed and tanged arrowhead throughout most areas of England and Wales, including Wessex. The remaining four arrowheads comprise 'fancy' arrowheads of Green's Green Low type (ON 6582), two Conygar examples (ON 6585 and 6711), and one classified as a Sutton b/Conygar type (ON 6576). The uncertainty of the final example highlights the difficulty of applying a typology to material that is particularly susceptible to breakage during manufacture. Two of these 'fancy'

Table 17: Metrical analysis (mm) of arrowheads in grave 1289 in relation to Green's nationwide analysis of 448 Sutton type arrowheads

	Max.	*Green*	*Min.*	*Green*	*Mean*	*Green*	*SD*	*Green*
Length	34	58.0	21	14	26.16	29.04	3.96	8.37
Breadth	26	34.0	17	11	20.58	19.71	2.41	3.93
Thickness	5	7.5	2	1	3.89	4.55	0.88	1.34

SD = standard deviation. Source: Green 1980, table II.24

arrowheads (ON 6582, 6585) were found close together above the hips.

The quantity of arrowheads associated with the burial ranks it as one of the largest assemblages yet recovered from a Beaker burial, providing metrical, technological, and typological data for comparative study. The results of the metrical analysis of the arrowheads from the grave of the Amesbury Archer are presented in Table 17 and are shown with the results obtained by Green (1980, table ii.24) from a nationwide analysis of 448 Sutton type arrowheads.

These results show that the 'typical' arrowhead from the burial measures 22–30 mm in length, 18–22 mm in width, and 3–5 mm in thickness, falling well within the metrical parameters obtained by Green. He showed that arrowheads of Green Low and Conygar types, with more finely shaped barbs and tangs, were consistently larger and thinner than other types. These characteristics, which are present in the arrowheads buried with the Amesbury Archer, make it easier to insert the notches forming the barbs and tangs of the arrowhead and consequently preserve their shape. It is perhaps not surprising that the largest, best-formed arrowhead (ON 6582) was produced on a thin blank and that one of the thickest (ON 6444) has relatively short barbs.

The arrowheads from the burial were all made on flakes, using pressure to shape and thin the blank. They were competently made, consistent in their style of manufacture, and, irrespective of variations in size, may have represented the output of a single knapper. Variations in cortical remnants indicate that they are unlikely to have been made at the same time. The majority have covering retouch across both sides which has removed most of the traces of the blank form. However, they are frequently characterised by an eccentric profile, which has preserved the respective dorsal and ventral surfaces of the blank. Knowles (1944) suggested that the preferred arrowhead blank should be a relatively broad, flat flake with ridges sufficiently near the edges (Gingell and Harding's (1981) type 2) to provide a strong edge against which pressure could be applied. Seven flakes of this description and large enough to manufacture arrowheads were present in the cache of flakes associated with Beaker ON 6590. However, the arrowheads found with the burial suggest that flakes with a single centrally placed dorsal ridge were preferred by the knapper for arrowhead manufacture. None of the arrowheads shows a broken tip indicative of impact against a hard surface, although three have broken barbs consistent with manufacturing snaps.

The triangular arrowhead (ON 6573; Fig. 34) was found with the other barbed and tanged arrowheads. Its location may indicate that it represents a finished object rather than an unfinished barbed and tanged example. It was of similar dimensions to the other remainder of the group, with convex edges, but merely lacked the notches to create the barbs and tang.

Groups

Cache associated with Beaker ON 6590

The cache of 34 flint objects found with Beaker ON 6590 behind the back of the burial includes three scrapers (ON 6633, 6642, 6646), a knife (ON 6629), a miscellaneous flake tool (ON 6569), an unfinished arrowhead (ON 6655), 27 flakes, and an unnumbered chip (Figs 28–9; 31–2; Table 13). The cache formed a tight oval spread approximately 0.45 m long and 0.30 m across centred around the Beaker. Towards the north-east edge of the cache a cluster of flakes in mint condition had been sealed beneath the Beaker as it collapsed. These objects, numbered ON 6633–54, were found as a pile of flakes, one physically above the other. They were allocated to the survey points given to flake ON 6632 and the unfinished arrowhead ON 6655. Their consistent condition and morphology indicates that they unquestionably formed a single group that was probably placed in the grave in a bag or similar form of organic container.

Retouched tools

The three scrapers included a side scraper (ON 6642), a side and end scraper (ON 6633), and a broken bifacial, discoidal implement (ON 6646), classified as an 'other' scraper, which may have been snapped in manufacture. The edge of scraper ON 6633 appeared to have been slightly worn by use but was otherwise in mint condition. All three tools were made on relatively broad blanks using direct, semi-abrupt retouch to construct a functional convex scraping edge. The knife (ON

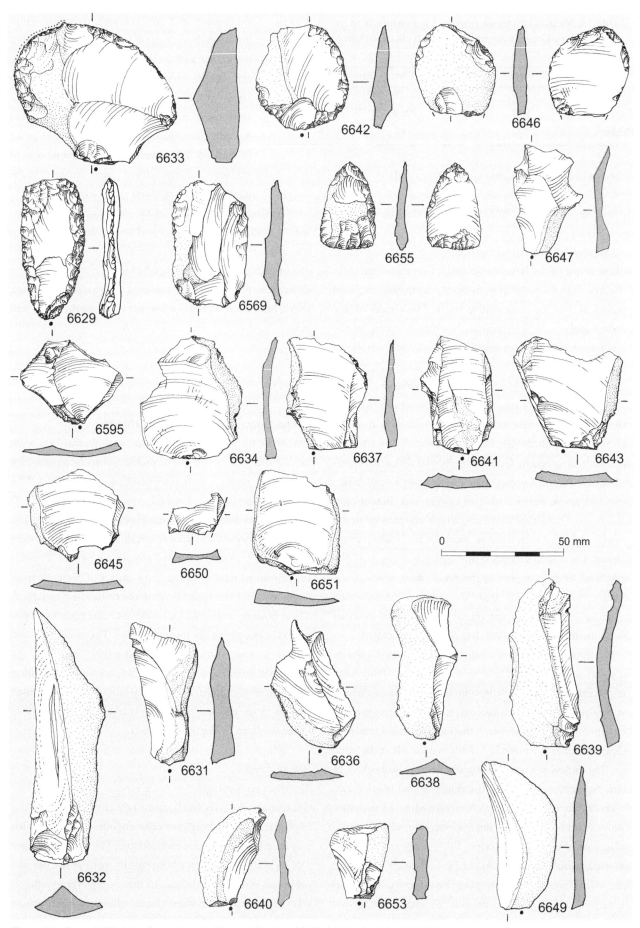

Figure 31 Grave 1289 (Amesbury Archer); objects of flint found behind the back of burial 1291

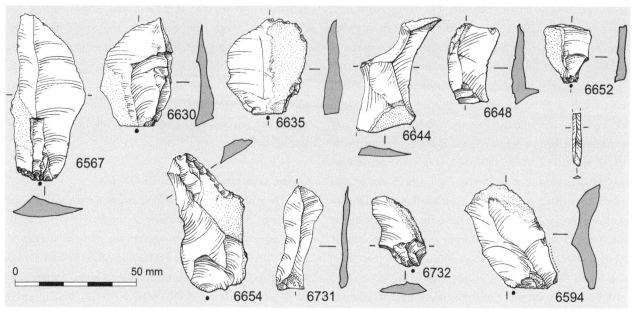

Figure 32 Grave 1289 (Amesbury Archer); objects of flint found behind the back of burial 1291

6629) was made on an elongated flake with a hinged distal end. The abrupt retouch along the left edge appeared to serve as backing for the semi-abrupt retouch on the right edge. The miscellaneous flake tool (ON 6569) is a naturally backed 'knife' and is unretouched except for short lengths of marginal retouch at both ends. The unfinished arrowhead (ON 6655) was made on a cortical flake. The flaking angle along the right edge is relatively steep which may have made it difficult to thin the blank successfully. This is the only piece in the group that is likely to have been modified by pressure flaking.

Unretouched flakes

The cluster of unretouched flakes included three blades (length=twice breadth) and had developed a dark blue patina. The flakes are of similar raw material with a weathered cortex and are in mint condition. There was a general absence of broken material: only five flakes were classified as broken, the breakage mainly in the form of crushed butts; two have small Siret fractures (indicating accidental breakage). The flakes were produced with plain butts using hard-hammer percussion.

The initial examination of the material indicated that, apart from a number of small pieces including ON 6650 and 6732, there is not only a consistent level of size but also two types of flakes are present that are not normally a significant part of an assemblage (Table 18). Particularly noticeable are eight flakes (Fig. 31, 6595–6651) characterised by double ridges on the dorsal surface that give the flake a crescentic cross-section (Gingell and Harding's (1981) type 2) and eight

flakes (Fig. 31, 6631–49) that were partially or totally naturally backed pieces (Harding's (1991, 79) side-trimming flakes). The 'type 2' flakes are all similar in size and form. One is broken by a Siret fracture and another was apparently too small to be of use in tool manufacture. They can be produced by an intentional blow immediately behind the previous point of percussion, as with 'double back' blades manufactured by gun flint knappers at Brandon (Forrest 1983, 10), but can also result accidentally from two points of percussion landing

Table 18: Variations in flake dimensions (mm) by category of unretouched flakes associated with Beaker ON 6590

	Max.	Min.	Mean	SD
Double ridged (Type 2) (Gingell and Harding 1981)				
Length	48	17	39.00	10.58
Breadth	43	25	35.30	6.70
Thickness	6	3	5.00	1.00
L:B ratio	1.62	0.68	1.11	0.30
Naturally backed				
Length	99	29	56.00	20.92
Breadth	32	24	28.00	2.32
Thickness	13	6	9.13	2.42
L:B ratio	3.54	1.21	1.99	0.73
Unclassed				
Length	63	23	39.17	11.33
Breadth	41	17	28.50	7.39
Thickness	11	3	6.25	2.30
L:B ratio	2.29	0.89	1.42	0.43

simultaneously on a striking platform. Given the narrowness of the butts it is difficult to be certain whether these flakes were of deliberate or accidental manufacture. There is nothing to indicate that they were ever manufactured intentionally and flakes of this type do not normally occur in large numbers from any period. Beaker pit 23 at Dean Bottom on the Marlborough Downs, Wiltshire, contained 686 measurable flakes, of which 'type 2' flakes contributed only 10% of the total (Harding 1992, M:1, D3). This type of flake was consistently the most infrequent form of flake from assemblages of all periods across the Marlborough Downs, averaging only 6%. It suggests that the flakes found at Boscombe Down were selected from a large assemblage of debitage. Knowles (1944) regarded this type of thin flake, with broad flat surfaces and sturdy edges against which to apply pressure, as the most suitable blanks for conversion into arrowheads. However, the arrowheads found with the Amesbury Archer are, in general, marginally thicker than these flakes and are characterised by a domed profile, which suggests that they were not used for this purpose.

The eight naturally-backed flakes, characterised by a strong dorsal ridge, appear to have been selected for the relatively straight, opposite edge. They function admirably as unretouched knives. A cache containing four flakes of this type, including a retouched knife, had been placed near one of the hands and face of a male inhumation burial that was excavated with six Green Low arrowheads at Easton Lane, Winchester, Hampshire (Harding 1989).

The remainder of the cache cannot be allocated to a specific group with as much confidence. However flakes ON 6594, 6644, and 6567 all have relatively straight edges, which makes them similar in shape and size to the naturally backed pieces.

All flakes from the cache were analysed to confirm that they were of a consistent size and shape that might indicate intentional selection for immediate use or as potential tool blanks. The results of this analysis, shown in Table 19 as variations in flake dimensions and as dimension ranges for archetypal flakes, confirm that, despite variations in the

Table 19: Dimension ranges (mm) for the archetypal flakes by type associated with Beaker 6590

	Type 2	Naturally backed	Unclassed
Length	36–48	37–66	30–42
Breadth	29–42	27–30	20–32
Thickness	5–6	7–12	4–9
L:B ratio	0.92–1.33	1.21–2.36	0.98–1.90

extreme limits of size, there is overall consistency in the cache. This is not only evident in the type 2 flakes and naturally backed pieces but is also respected in the unclassed material. The results also show that although individual flakes, such as ON 6635, might serve as a suitable blank for scraper ON 6642, the remainder bear no resemblance in size or shape to any of the other retouched tools from the burial, except the arrowheads.

Cache associated with Beaker ON 6609

The 18 items forming the cache in front of the burial covered an area of similar size to that of the cache behind the burial and had probably been arranged in the grave as a series of single items (Figs 28–9). The cache comprised a plano-convex knife/dagger (ON 6602), a scale-flaked knife/dagger (ON 6570), five scrapers (ON 6604, 6616–18, 6621), and a retouched flake (ON 6606) (Fig. 33; Table 13). There were also two flakes (ON 6603, 6605) with damaged or used edges and seven unretouched flakes. Although there was nothing to indicate that any objects had been placed in bags there was a distinct division between the retouched tools, which generally lay towards the east end of the group, and the flakes, which were more prevalent to the west, close to the Beaker and arrowhead ON 6444.

Tools

The two knives/daggers are undoubtedly the finest flint objects from the burial. Knife/dagger ON 6602 was found near the left hand of the burial although there was nothing to indicate that it had been held in the hand. Both objects are made on strongly ridged blades, 73 mm and 83 mm long respectively, which were retouched by well-executed direct pressure flaking. A slight notch at the proximal end of ON 6602 may have assisted in attaching a haft but its formation is likely to have resulted as much from a negative flake scar in the flaking face of the core rather than being a feature of deliberate manufacture. It is in any case very likely that, as the discovery of 'Ötzi the Ice Man' (Spindler 1994; Egg and Spindler 1992, 58–61, Abb. 21–2, Farbtaf. xiii) demonstrated, blades of this type were frequently hafted in bound wooden handles.

The five scrapers include two with broken blades, one of which (ON 6621) was broken during or after manufacture. They were all made on broad flakes using direct retouch to produce a convex scraping edge. Three of the scrapers are discoidal or semi-discoidal with some use of bifacial flaking to thin the butt.

A retouched flake (ON 6606) and two other flakes with used or damaged edges (ON 6603, 6605) were also found in

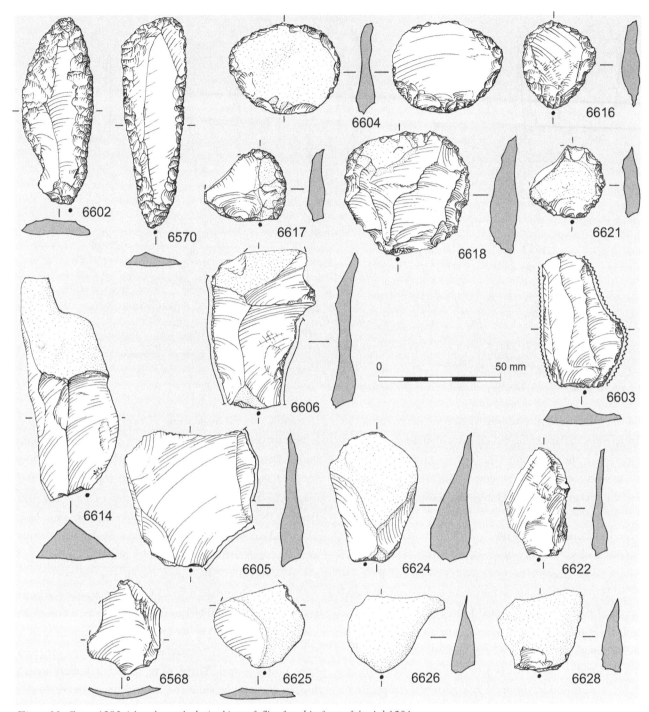

Figure 33 Grave 1289 (Amesbury Archer); objects of flint found in front of burial 1291

close proximity with the retouched tools. Apart from lengths of relatively straight edges they show no other recurring characteristics that might have accounted for their selection. Similarly the unretouched flakes, which include three small primary flakes, appear to represent random or symbolic selection, rather than practical or functional choice.

A fragment of pyrite found towards the east end of the cache (ON 6608) (Fig. 39) had stained parts of knife/dagger (ON 6602), retouched flake (ON 6603), and scraper (ON 6621) with traces of iron. The pyrites is damaged through use as part of a fire-making set but although three strike-a-lights were found in the grave (ON 6586–7, 7345.1), none was close to this fragment of pyrite (p. 118 below).

Material from around the lower body

Two fabricators/strike-a-lights (ON 6586–7) with heavily worn ends were found near the lower legs (Figs 28–9). Implement ON 6586 (Fig. 34) also shows traces of iron

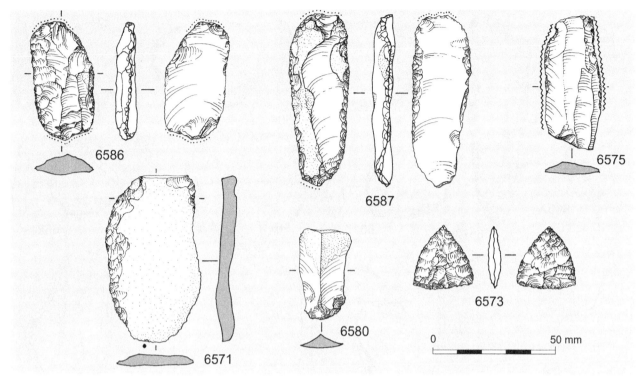

Figure 34 Grave 1289 (Amesbury Archer); objects of flint found around the lower body of burial 1291

staining near the tip, probably deriving from the proximity of iron pyrites. A flake knife (ON 6575), with utilised edges was found with the fabricator ON 6586. A knife (ON 6571), made on a cortical flake, an unretouched flake (ON 6580), and the triangular arrowhead were also found in this area.

Material from the grave fill

A fabricator (ON 7345.1) was extracted from residue sieved from a sample recorded as from around the area of the body (Figs 28–9; 35). It was made on a flake with heavily abraded cortex that may have originated from a gravel source. The ends are heavily worn and the surface texture, which is slightly soapy, suggests that it might have been residual or old when it was placed in the grave. As two other fabricators/strike-a-lights were found in the grave it is perfectly acceptable to consider that this implement formed part of the original grave deposit.

Sieving also produced a flake (7338.1) from near the skull and an unallocated broken flake and a chip from other sieved residue in the grave (Fig. 35).

Two barbed and tanged arrowheads (ON 6711–12; Fig. 30), a microdenticulate (ON 7342.8), two edge flaked knives (ON 7342.3–4), a retouched flake (ON 7342.2), and six flakes were recovered from samples taken from around the skeleton during the excavation (Fig 35). Although these objects could not be located precisely or assigned to specific caches within the grave, most are in mint condition, patinated, and frequently covered by deposits of calcium concretion and it is safe to assume that they also formed part of the main burial. Two unretouched pieces (ON 7342.5, 7342.9) show traces of slight edge damage, which may result from use and may suggest that they were originally part of the cache near Beaker ON 6609 where edge damage was more prevalent. Thirteen broken flakes, mainly small fragments, and 15 chips were also recovered from the samples as well as six flakes and a denticulate (ON 7348.5) from the fill (Fig. 35).

The retouched flake (ON 7342.2) from around the body and two flakes (ON 7348.4 and 7348.6) from the whole-earth sample are more heavily weathered and characterised by a glossy, 'soapy' surface texture, which suggests that they may have been residual. There were no other indications to suggest that large quantities of residual material were present in the immediate area of the burial although prehistoric activity locally is well known from the Neolithic onwards.

Microdebitage

The sieving programme produced a small number of pieces of microdebitage. The rarity of this material and the absence of significant quantities of broken flakes and flaking waste suggest that flint working did not take place at the grave side. Most of the chips are undiagnostic. However, the presence of a bulbar scar from the grave fill is a diagnostic type fossil of flaking (Newcomer and Karlin 1987). Its presence may indicate that flint knapping was taking place beyond the spoil

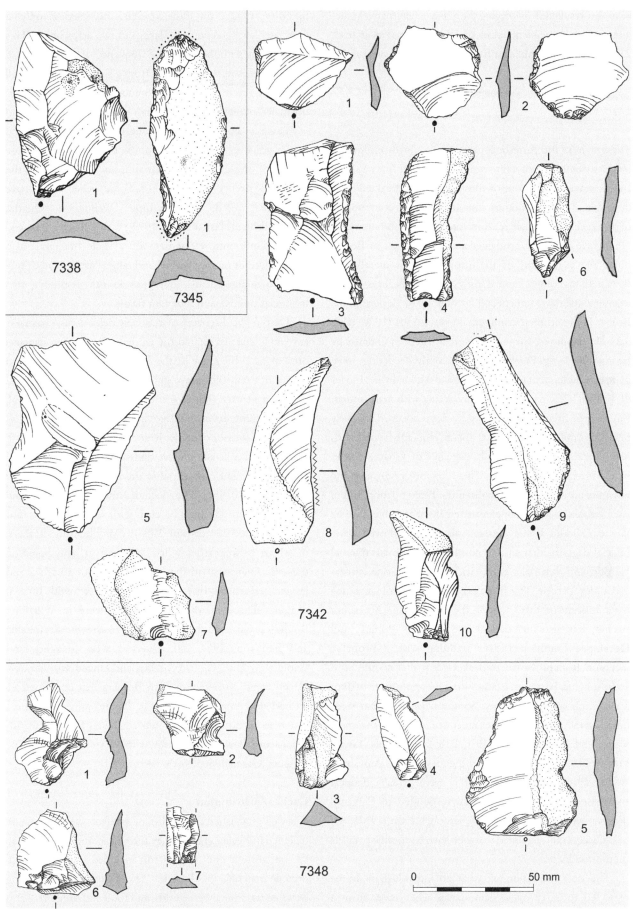

Figure 35 Grave 1289 (Amesbury Archer); objects of flint found in the fill of the grave from samples 7338 (whole earth) and 7345 (around the skeleton), sample 7342 (around the skeleton) and sample 7348 (whole earth).

heap that resulted from digging the grave or, alternatively, that it represents an incipient bulbar scar that detached itself from a freshly knapped flake that forms part of the grave goods.

Discussion

The grave of the Amesbury Archer contained one of the largest assemblages of flint artefacts yet found from a single Beaker grave; it is also one of the earliest single Beaker graves in Britain. The collection of flint artefacts, the components of the caches, and their relationships to one another and to other grave goods, have provided a unique example of Beaker burial rite at the time of the introduction of metals into Britain. In his comprehensive study of British Beakers, Clarke examined the development and distribution of Beakers in the British Isles and their continental associations (1970, table 3.2). He also listed, in a catalogue that has been updated by Brodie (2001, fig. 2), the most frequently occurring grave goods, including flint implements, found with individual styles of Beaker. This material invariably occurs with male burials. Burials containing All-Over-Cord Beakers contained relatively few flint implements but were most frequently found with barbed and tanged arrowheads, primarily of Green's Sutton type, with flakes and scrapers. These flint objects recur as the most prevalent objects throughout the Beaker period, but in later burials they are supplemented by other objects. The Wessex/Middle Rhine Beakers also included well-made bifacial daggers, that carried connections with continental Europe, and flint flake knives with non-flint stone bracers and antler spatulae. This more expansive flint tool kit, which is reminiscent of that found in the grave of the Amesbury Archer, was also included in both Clarke's Primary and Developed Southern Beaker tradition with a probable inclusion, from his Northern Beakers, of pyrites nodules with strike-a-lights. However, Clarke noted the appearance of flint arrowheads with Developed Southern Beakers that were more ogival in outline with exaggerated, obliquely trimmed, square-ended barbs (Clarke 1970, 218; Green's 1980 Green Low type), a type also present in the grave of the Amesbury Archer. Clarke pointed out that they were virtually identical to Wessex 1 arrowheads and corresponded to Piggott's 'Breton' type (Piggott 1938, 70), although Case (1977a, 83) has subsequently suggested that they have no specific parallels on the continent.

The only indication of what an individual might be expected to carry on a 'daily' basis, when away from a settlement, comes from 'Ötzi' (Spindler 1994; Egg and Spindler 1992). As flint objects, he carried only a knife/dagger, scraper, drill, flake, and two arrowheads. This is in keeping with the range and frequency of flints found in Beaker burials in Britain. Apart from a small number of well furnished, 'rich' graves, the number of pieces of flint normally found in a grave does not exceed three or four, and is frequently smaller than that. The small assemblage found in the grave of the 'Companion' is therefore much more typical of Beaker graves in Britain, and the grave of the Amesbury Archer is the exception. Some 'richer' burials have been discovered, for example Wellington Quarry, Herefordshire (Harrison et al. 1999), with a Beaker, a tanged copper knife, and a fragment of a shale bracer. It also contained four unused barbed and tanged arrowheads, three unfinished arrowheads, five flint knives (including two triangular points), and four flint flakes.

Despite the discovery of relatively rich burials, it remains extremely unusual to find the entire range of flint artefacts present, as in the grave of the Amesbury Archer, associated with other non-flint grave goods, and to encounter several examples of each flint tool in the same burial. The rarity of such large flint tool assemblages in association with All-Over-Cord and Wessex/Middle Rhine Beakers is particularly marked. Clarke listed only five findspots with All-Over-Cord Beakers and flint objects, all in the north of England and Scotland (1970, 438). They included three with barbed and tanged arrowheads and one each with scrapers and a flint flake. He listed 22 sites with Wessex/Middle Rhine Beakers, of which 10 were from Wiltshire. However, only seven of these 22 findspots had flint tools, three with a barbed and tanged arrowhead, two with knives, and two with bifacial daggers. Three of these seven sites were in Wiltshire: Roundway barrow 8 (barbed and tanged arrowhead: Annable and Simpson, 1964, 38), Overton West (dagger), and Winterslow Hut (11) (two barbed and tanged arrowheads). Green listed 30 findspots with Beakers that contained 91 barbed and tanged arrowheads. There were only three instances of Sutton type arrowheads being found with All-Over-Cord Beakers and three with Wessex/Middle Rhine Beakers (Green 1980, 244).

Caches/distribution

It is well established that caches of artefacts were frequently included in Beaker graves. They formed an important part of the burial ritual and undoubtedly included a wide range of organic materials that have left few, if any traces, including bows, hafts, animal hide goods, and food and drink. It is also frequently difficult to determine from the positions of individual flakes whether they formed part of a deliberate cache. Excavations, including that of the Boscombe Bowmen (grave 25000), have indicated that graves were sometimes used more than once. The distribution of individual objects and the identification of discrete caches therefore forms an important consideration in the interpretation of grave goods. Improved standards of excavation now provide more accurate records of the presence and distribution of both used and unused flakes, caches, and other flint artefacts in Beaker burials. There is also greater understanding of post-depositional processes that can influence the distribution of individual objects.

There is nothing to indicate that any major reorganisation of artefacts had taken place in the grave of the Amesbury Archer. The objects behind the back comprised a particularly large group (Figs 28–9). However, this is a common location for grave goods later in the Beaker period, such as at Overton Hill, where a long necked Beaker was found with an antler spatula, a slate object, a bronze awl, flint knife, and flint flake (Smith and Simpson 1966). At Amesbury 51, a similar assemblage comprising a Beaker, a bronze awl, flint scraper, and a roe deer antler was also found behind the man's head (Ashbee 1978). The tightly cached group of unretouched flakes associated with Beaker ON 6590 had been included together and showed no indication of having been disturbed by the collapse of the Beaker.

Grave goods in caches or as spreads of objects, particularly arrowheads, were also placed near or at the feet, as at Irthlingborough, Northamptonshire, where an assemblage including a long necked Beaker, bifacial flint dagger, five buttons, a bracer, whetstone, triangular arrowhead, boar's tusk, and nine flint flakes that were placed together, probably in a bag (Halpin 1987, 331; Healy and Harding 2004). More recently, Barclay and Halpin described a male burial accompanied by a Beaker of Clarke's (1970) Final Southern (S4) type from grave 203 at Barrow Hills, Radley, Oxfordshire: a cluster of arrowheads, thought to be in a quiver, were found behind the feet, with a side scraper, bone awl, and antler spatula behind the waist. A small group of flakes was located beneath the legs and two other small groups, including flakes, retouched flakes, a broken scraper, and a piercer, had been placed close to the knees (Barclay and Halpin 1999, 136, 140, fig. 4.76). However, spreads of arrowheads have also been recorded, including the burial at Wellington Quarry (Harrison *et al.* 1999) where four arrowheads were found spread across the lower part of the grave. The arrowheads in the grave of the Amesbury Archer

were found towards the lower part of the body and some overlay the bones.

Caches placed in front of the body are also known. Harding (1989, 100) listed 47 flakes and broken flakes from a Beaker burial at Easton Lane, Winchester, although only four naturally backed 'knives' and a retouched knife formed a distinct cache near one of the hands in front of the body. Two flakes from the cache, which was apparently made especially for the burial, could be refitted. The structure of the group of objects placed in front of the Amesbury Archer also does not appear to have undergone any significant reorganisation. The best made implements were found near one of his hands, although it is by no means certain that they were buried in this way, and there was an apparent grouping of the retouched and unretouched pieces.

Additional flakes in mint condition were found in the grave fill at Easton Lane, which might have been displaced by post-depositional movement although it was thought more likely that they had been thrown in with the original backfill. A similar explanation may be offered for flakes in mint condition that were recovered from the grave fill of the Amesbury Archer. It is equally possible, indeed very likely, that in some instances small caches of artefacts that were not contained in bags were disturbed during the grave's backfilling or subsequently.

Barbed and tanged arrowheads

The assemblage of barbed and tanged arrowheads from the Amesbury Archer's grave also ranks as one of the largest yet recorded from Britain (Pl. 36; Fig. 30). They are an accepted accompaniment to male Beaker burials, but are normally found singly or in pairs. Green (1980, table viii.1) listed 88 burials with arrowheads, of which 48 were associated with a single barbed and tanged arrowhead and 13 with two arrowheads. At the higher end of the list he noted only two instances of 11 arrowheads, including Mucking, Essex, where five were thought to be in a quiver (Jones and Jones 1975), and two instances of 13 arrowheads, including Breach Farm, Llanblethian, South Glamorgan, where 11 arrowheads were of Conygar type and two were of Green Low type. A collection of 18 barbed and tanged arrowheads was found at Thames Valley Park, Reading, Berkshire (Harding 1997), with a flint knife and sherds of a comb-decorated Beaker, possibly of Clarke's European or Wessex/Middle Rhine styles.

The barbed and tanged arrowheads from the Amesbury Archer grave were dominated by Green's Sutton type, specifically Sutton b, which are the most common type in

Wessex (1980, 119). A Sutton b arrowhead was found with a tanged copper dagger in the Roundway 8 barrow.

The presence of Green Low and Conygar arrowheads is more significant. Green (1980, 120) concluded that, considering the frequency with which these arrowheads were related to the Early Bronze Age cultures of Wessex, it was surprising that they were of below average density in that area. He showed that Green Low arrowheads were known from Beaker contexts, but that they occurred principally from late graves (of Lanting and van der Waals' (1972) Steps 4–7 or Clarke's (1970) S1–S3 Southern Beakers). The evidence for Conygar Hill arrowheads with Beakers was considered to be more uncertain. Examples from Stanton Harcourt, Oxfordshire and Mucking were classified as crude and contrasted with the finely-made examples that were representative of the type associated with Food Vessels (Green 1980, 130). Green also noted that, although Conygar Hill arrowheads were only rarely associated with British Beakers, especially early ones, they were recorded from relatively early Beaker contexts in Ireland at Newgrange, Co. Meath and Slieve Gullion, Co. Armagh. He also noted a potential 'Irish connection' at Winterslow Hut, where two Ballyclare arrowheads were associated with a Step 3 (Wessex/Middle Rhine) Beaker and a tanged copper dagger, suggested to be of Irish origin (op. cit., 129). This suggests that it may be hard to identify any sequence or development of arrowhead types through the Beaker period or the development of a range of tools. The range of artefacts from the burial of the Amesbury Archer suggests that not only were Green Low and Conygar arrowheads in use simultaneously, but that the complete range of associated artefacts were also in existence from the introduction of the earliest Beakers to Britain.

While the barbed and tanged arrowhead, perhaps introduced into Britain at the same time as Beakers, is the ubiquitous form of projectile point of the Beaker period in 'western' Atlantic Europe (Case 2004b, 28), triangular arrowheads have received considerably less attention in Britain. In his study of arrowheads Green (1980) examined 465 examples from across England and Wales. Although most were poorly stratified a few, as at Eyebury, Cambridgeshire, Aldwincle, Northamptonshire and Breach Farm, South Glamorgan were included as grave goods. Others were frequently found in areas of production, especially East Anglia, but also with relatively large numbers in Wessex, and were regarded as blanks for barbed and tanged arrowheads (Green 1980, 118). Green stressed that the evidence for their function was not completely clear but was confident that they

were of second millennium date. Triangular arrowheads of similar form to that from the Amesbury Archer's grave are also present in continental Europe, including the Netherlands (eg, Butler and van der Waals 1966, fig. 4a) where they are seen as a distinct form and occur with Beakers and with hollow-based and barbed and tanged arrowheads. If the triangular arrowhead is not viewed as an unfinished blank for a barbed and tanged arrowhead, it may indicate an additional link with continental Europe.

Arrowheads are found in Beaker graves both as scatters of loose implements and in distinct concentrations that imply that bundles or quivers of arrows were placed in the grave. The discovery of 'Ötzi' has provided some evidence of the numbers, construction, dimensions, and raw materials of arrows that might be carried on a day-to-day basis. Twelve arrows, between 0.84 m and 0.89 m long, made from dogwood (*Cornus* sp.) and wayfaring tree (*Viburnum lantana*), were found in a hide quiver. Only two arrows were armed with flint heads, the remainder being untipped (Spindler 1994, 127; Egg and Spindler 1992, 118). This is in keeping with the evidence from Beaker graves, where the presence of only one or two arrowheads is normal; however, larger numbers are known, including groups of 'fancy' arrowheads that were clearly made as sets. The consistent standards of workmanship suggests that these were probably produced by individual craftsmen, as at Easton Lane, Winchester (Harding 1989), where six Green Low arrowheads were found, and at Conygar Hill, Dorset (RCHM 1970), where six of eponymous type accompanied a male burial. Elsewhere, as with the grave of the Amesbury Archer, it is less clear whether the presence of larger numbers of Sutton type arrowheads, displaying the influence of less standardised workmanship or the effects of reworking broken arrowheads, indicates that we are dealing with collections that were built up over time. It was apparent that the arrows or arrowheads in the grave of the Amesbury Archer had been placed there after the body. The general arrangement of individual pieces suggests that they had probably been hafted at the time of deposition. A similar scenario was evident at Wellington Quarry where, although the body had completely decomposed, the arrowheads, which included one of Conygar Hill type, were found scattered across the grave at a higher level (Harrison *et al.* 1999). In barrow 4A at Barrow Hills, Radley, three barbed and tanged arrowheads were found above the skeleton (Williams 1948); Barclay has suggested subsequently that these may not have belonged to the deceased but were added to the grave by participants in the funeral (Barclay and Halpin 1999, 154).

Discrete concentrations that might indicate the presence of quivers were detected at Dairsie, Fife, and at Mucking, where 11 arrowheads of similar form were found, of which five were found in a group behind the body with points aligned towards the feet (Jones and Jones 1975). A similar arrangement was encountered at Barrow Hills, Radley, where, in the central grave 203 of ring ditch 201, five Green Low arrowheads were found at the feet (Barclay and Halpin 1999, 140, fig. 4.76). It cannot be overlooked that the grave of the Amesbury Archer included a small cluster of arrowheads immediately behind the pelvis, including one of Green Low type and one of Conygar type.

Irrespective of their use as status items, there is sufficient evidence that barbed and tanged arrowheads were extremely efficient projectiles although none of those from the Amesbury Archer's grave showed signs of impact. At Stonehenge, however, a barbed and tanged arrowhead was found embedded in the skeleton of a man (Evans 1984). Possibly similar evidence was found at Barrow Hills, grave 203 (Barclay and Halpin 1999, 140), where an arrowhead of probable Sutton type, with an impact fracture, was found among the bones of an individual that had been buried with a quiver of arrows tipped with Green Low arrowheads. Evidence for the use of barbed and tanged arrowheads in a hunting, social, or sporting context was supplied by the remains of a butchered aurochs that was found in 1987 in a pit at Holloway Lane, Harmondsworth, Middlesex (Cotton *et al.* 2006) with six barbed and tanged arrowheads embedded in it.

Green (1980, 129; table vi.4 and 7) demonstrated that barbed and tanged arrowheads are the only form of projectile point found in Beaker burials and that they also occur on settlement sites where they can provide valuable chronological indicators along with other forms of flint implement. Stratified evidence from settlement sites is limited, although at Downton, Wiltshire (Rahtz 1962) Green (1980, 120) was satisfied that the evidence was sufficiently reliable to demonstrate that users of All-Over-Cord Beakers also continued to use Neolithic leaf-shaped arrowheads. He extended this association to sherds of finger-nail impressed Beaker (which are frequently found with All-Over-Cord Beakers) that were found unstratified with a leaf-shaped arrowhead at the flint mine site at Easton Down, Wiltshire. In any case, Green considered that there may be a link between the manufacture of triangular arrowheads as blanks for the manufacture of 'fancy' arrowheads and flint mining sites particularly in East Anglia, where 'fancy' arrowheads are more common (*op. cit.*, 118). Some of these appear to have

been included as grave goods at Eyebury (Cambridgeshire), Aldwincle (Northamptonshire), and possibly Breach Farm (South Glamorgan). The suggestion that flint mine sites provided a ritual/symbolic function during the Neolithic, in addition to an economic one, has been discussed by Barber *et al.* (1999, 61). Antler picks found by Stone, between 1930 and 1934, in a gallery of a mine, provided a radiocarbon date of 3630–2700 BC (BM-190, 4480±150 BP, Barber *et al.* 1999), suggesting that mining at Easton Down was being undertaken during the later part of the Neolithic. This date is clearly insufficient to confirm the range of mining at the site, although the discovery of Beaker pottery indicates some continuity of activity into the Beaker period. Analysis has shown that many of the non-flint items from the grave of the Amesbury Archer were not local and may have carried some ritual or symbolic meaning. Assuming that large scale extraction had ceased at Easton Down at the time of the burial it is possible that flint from the site, or from the apparently abortive Late Neolithic mines from Durrington Walls (Booth and Stone 1952), continued to hold value and to be of special significance. In any case, it seems unlikely that the Amesbury Archer was unaware of the Easton Down site, which lies only 9 km south-east of Boscombe Down on the eastern side of the valley of the River Bourne. At present there is no known method by which the flint can be chemically tested to establish whether any flint originated from this source or was of special significance.

Knives and flakes
The objects buried with the Amesbury Archer included not only a large number of barbed and tanged arrowheads but also knives/daggers of varying forms, scrapers, fabricators/strike-a-lights, flakes with edge retouch, and two caches of unretouched flakes including 'naturally backed knives'. If these naturally backed knives are also classified as diagnostic tools, it is clear that knives formed a significant component to the overall total. Clarke tabulated individual types of Beaker pottery with associated artefacts and demonstrated that the 'basic' flint tool kit common to all types of Beaker comprised flakes, arrowheads, and scrapers (1970, 448, table 3.2). Flint flake knives were generally scarce with his Early and Middle Rhenish Beakers but became prevalent with his Northern and Southern Beakers, especially N2 and S2. Clarke also tabulated results showing grave goods associated by sex and demonstrated that knives were more frequently associated with male graves (19 of 23) as were male graves with flakes (14 of 19) and scrapers (10 of 11) (*op. cit.*, 448, tab. 3.3). The role of the knife as a predominantly male item

is also reflected in the discovery of 'Ötzi', who carried not only arrowheads and arrows but also a hafted flint knife/dagger and a strike-a-light.

There is often nothing to indicate whether flint flakes may have been under-represented or ignored by antiquarian excavators or by more recent scholars. Clarke (1970, 438) himself listed only a gold basket-shaped ornament and a barbed and tanged arrowhead from a barrow at Alston, Kirkhaugh, Northumberland, whereas the excavator (Maryon 1936) illustrated a saw/knife, two cores, and six flint flakes from the grave. However, Clarke's catalogue of items from individual graves with associated Beakers showed that normally no more than one or two flakes occur in a single grave, although 25 flakes were found with a male burial accompanied by a Beaker of his Northern type at Hanging Grimston, North Yorkshire (Clarke 1970, app. 3). Flakes may be accompanied by other tools, when there is often very little to show whether they were part of a cache, or occur in isolation, in which case it is difficult to know whether the position in the grave is significant.

Strike-a-lights

The creation and control of fire was important not only as a means of cooking and heating but also as a symbol of power, especially as it related to the newly discovered metal technologies. The ability to create this essential element is entirely consistent with male Beaker burials, as demonstrated by the fact that Clarke (1970, 448) could list no fire making equipment with female burials.

Fabricators/strike-a-lights are frequently found with nodules of pyrite or marcasite at the waist or below the thorax to form fire making kits. In his review of the British evidence Clarke could list nine certain and two possible examples of this association and they were found together more frequently than either strike-a-lights or iron nodules were found on their own, where there was a combined total of six or possibly seven single finds. The number of burials where the sex could be identified was much smaller but in the case of both strike-a-lights and what was described as 'pyrites', they were found exclusively with males (Clarke 1970, 448, app. 3.3). In several cases the items were found at the chest or waist.

Most of these burials are later in date than the Amesbury Archer but at the broadly contemporary but re-arranged primary burial at Chilbolton, a strike-a-light and what was described as a fragment of marcasite nodule were found together below the hips and formed a fire making kit that was probably kept together (Fig. 71, below). Marcasite is also an iron sulphide with similar properties to pyrite, with which it

is often confused (Russel 1990, 156, fig. 3, 7). In the primary burial at Overton G6b, Wiltshire, which is relatively close to the grave of the Amesbury Archer, although later in date, a ball of marcasite and a strike-a-light were also found by the chest though they were not associated (Smith and Simpson 1966, 127, 131, fig. 3, 6). Closer still, but again later, of Bronze Age date, the fragment of iron pyrite from the primary burial in Amesbury G58, Wiltshire, is approximately the same size as that buried with the Amesbury Archer (Ashbee 1985, 70, fig. 33–4c). Slightly further afield, a fragment of broken pyrite was found at the base of the ribs in grave 203 at Barrow Hills, Radley, a grave which also contained an antler spatula and a bone point (Barclay and Halpin 1999, 136, 140, fig. 4.47; 4.79, s4).

The location of these objects is consistent with the evidence preserved in the body of 'Ötzi', where fire making equipment was stored in a pouch strapped to the stomach. It is unusual to find three strike-a-lights in one grave and to find that the pyrite nodule, which was included with the cache in front of the body, was not directly associated with the body and the strike-a-lights, even though strike-a-light ON 6586 is iron stained.

Who is he?

Two general approaches have been adopted in the study of Beaker graves. In one Case (1977a, 81) attempted to examine the social status of the individual, while in the other (Humble 1990) focused on the function and status of the grave goods. Case used the contents of comparatively well-furnished or 'rich' Beaker graves to classify them into three types: 'artisans burials' associated with flint axeheads, antler picks or tines; arrowhead burials, which occur infrequently but were considered to indicate feuding in Beaker society; and the rare, exceptionally well-furnished burials, which were considered to be of high status and frequently associated with stone bracers.

There is no doubt that the grave of the Amesbury Archer belongs primarily with the group of well-furnished, high status burials. However, the inclusion of an antler spatula, if interpreted as a pressure flaking tool, also indicates that he was probably a flint knapper and therefore also an 'artisan', capable of arrowhead production. It is impossible to know whether the retouched tools were made by the Amesbury Archer, although the method of blank selection and approach to production for most of the arrowheads suggests that they could have been produced by one capable knapper. It is almost inconceivable that an adult male living at the time did not have some practical flint working skills. The technology used to produce the flakes and scrapers has roots in Late

Neolithic Britain with the manufacture of squat flakes (Pitts 1978). However, the cluster of unretouched material placed behind the body of the Amesbury Archer was probably made for the grave and is likely to have been made *post mortem*.

The two knife/daggers also show much higher levels of manufacture and were undoubtedly valued artefacts as status items, personal possessions, heirlooms or as functional tools. They were placed close together near the body. The knives/daggers from the Amesbury Archer's grave do not exhibit the same levels of flaking skill as bifacial daggers, which also occur in Britain and replicate in flint the form of early copper daggers. However, it is possible that the knives/daggers in the grave were produced by craftsmen who were sufficiently skilled to remove blades, which are generally scarcer in the Early Bronze Age, of sufficient quality to produce these objects.

Humble (1990) adopted a different approach at Raunds (Irthlingborough) barrow 1, Northamptonshire, preferring to place grave goods into groups that reflected their function in the burial ceremony. He assigned flint artefacts to one of five categories: personal possessions of the deceased; items made especially for deposition; items used in mortuary rites; instruments of death; and redeposited or intrusive items. The most personal items in the Amesbury Archer's grave are likely to have included the two high status knife/daggers found in front of the body. It is also reasonable to assume that the flake knives and strike-a-lights around the feet were personal possessions. As we have seen, knives and strike-a-lights were found with the body of 'Ötzi' (Spindler 1994; Egg and Spindler 1992, 125) and may be considered to represent everyday necessities of life. Similarly scrapers and arrowheads, especially when found in a quiver, may have represented personal items.

There is less certainty about the arrowheads that were scattered in graves, as in that of the Amesbury Archer. Barclay has suggested that these might be added by participants in the funerary ceremonies and considers them as individual gifts or offerings to the dead that reflected the importance of archery in the community (Barclay and Halpin 1999). This approach may help to explain variations in the quality of arrowhead manufacture, especially the presence of the better made Green Low and Conygar Hill type arrowheads.

Significant differences were apparent in the composition of the caches of flints found in the grave around Beakers ON 6590 and 6609, although both primarily contained scrapers and flakes. Some of the scrapers associated with the knife/daggers in front of the body may be seen as personal items and were found with flakes that exhibited traces of edge

damage, possibly from use in the mortuary ceremony. Case (2004b, 29) offered an alternative explanation for the frequent inclusion, as at Wellington Quarry (Harrison *et al.* 1999), of worn or broken implements, flints in particular, as grave goods. He emphasised the close relationships of the Beaker tradition with burial practice and postulated that objects were included for impractical, symbolic roles that might be associated with hunting. In the grave of the Amesbury Archer, flint flakes with edge damage, broken scrapers and strike-a-lights with ends polished by use were included with a heavily worn antler spatula. One of the scrapers behind the back (ON 6633), associated with a cluster of flakes in mint condition, also appeared to have been used, possibly in the mortuary rituals. That cluster of unretouched flakes comprised primarily naturally backed flakes/knives or flakes with double ridges. The naturally-backed pieces may have been employed to process soft material, although the total lack of edge damage suggests that they were probably not used but were made, selected and deposited as blanks. The idea that these flakes represent unused tool blanks can be extended to the flakes with two ridges. There is a view that these flakes provide the most suitable blanks for arrowhead manufacture, although the arrowheads in the grave were mostly thicker than the double ridged flakes and retained a distinctly plano-convex section. The unfinished arrowhead from the cache behind the back was unquestionably made on a relatively thick cortical flake. A possible explanation might be that the double ridged flakes were selected for the manufacture of a set of 'fancy' arrowheads of Conygar Hill or Green Low type, which were thinner and characterised by a more lenticular cross section.

Bracers
by Fiona Roe

Two bracers (or wristguards) were found (Fig. 36). One, red in colour (ON 6588), was found by the knees with the slightly flatter side uppermost (Pl. 37; Fig. 37). The other, black or dark grey, example (ON 6600) was next to the outside of the left forearm, again with the flatter face uppermost (Pl. 38; Fig. 37).

The two bracers or wristguards are striking in appearance, and, as explained below, do not appear to relate closely to other examples found in Britain and Ireland. They are in good condition, well made, flat in appearance, rectangular in shape but elongated in proportion, and with one hole at either end. The holes are slightly hour-glass shaped, and wider on the

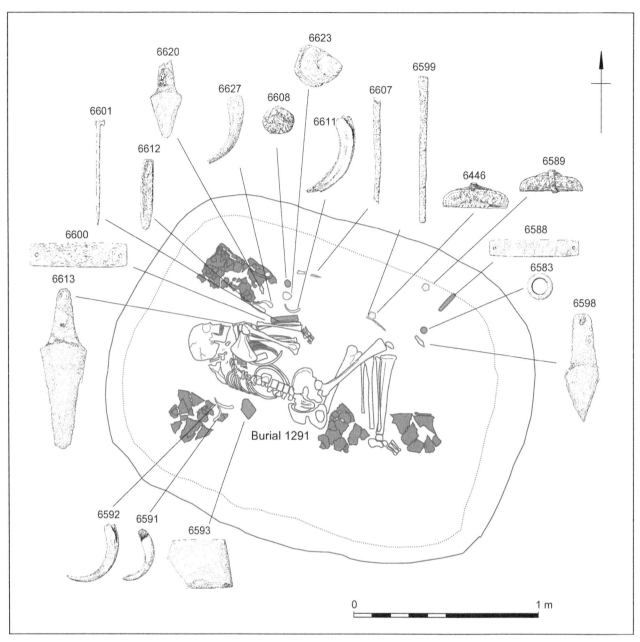

Figure 36 Grave 1289 (Amesbury Archer); distribution of objects of iron pyrites, stone, copper, gold, antler and tusk

under sides, while the surfaces are smooth, especially on the upper sides. The longer sides appear to be straight, but are in fact slightly convex, tapering at either end, so that the maximum breadth is central, while each end narrows slightly. The edges are flattened along the longer sides, but tapered at the ends. Each bracer can be assigned to Atkinson's B[1] group of bracers according to the typology outlined by Clarke (1970, 570, n. 39).

Such finely made artefacts are not suitable for thin-sectioning. They have, however, been included in a study of British bracers, as part of a multi-disciplinary project on *Ritual in Early Bronze Age Grave Goods* (Woodward and Hunter 2011).

This has enabled the bracers buried with the Amesbury Archer to be analysed by portable X-ray fluorescence spectrometry, a method which is non-destructive and provides a chemical fingerprint of the rock (see Ixer and Webb below for details). During a pilot project 26 bracers, including those buried with the Amesbury Archer, were examined by the same method (Woodward *et al.* 2006). In addition, detailed petrographic descriptions have been provided by Rob Ixer, while results of portable X-ray fluorescence spectrometry by Phil Potts and John Watson of the Open University are reported on by Peter Webb (*cf.* Ixer and Webb 2011).

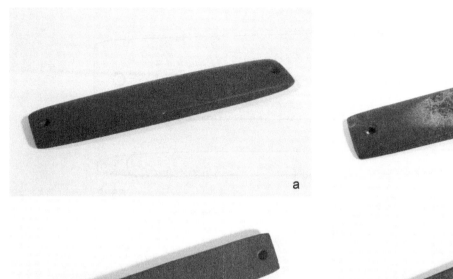

0   10 mm

b

Plate 37 Bracer ON 6588 from the grave of the Amesbury Archer (1289); a) 'front'; b) 'back'

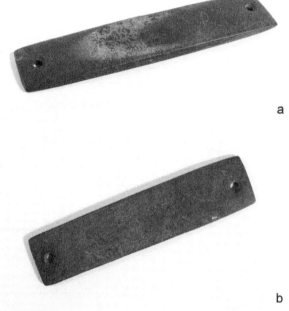

a

b

Plate 38 Bracer ON 6600 from the grave of the Amesbury Archer; a) 'front'; b) 'back'

Description

ON 6588

The red bracer is the smaller of the two, measuring 126 mm in length, 23 mm maximum breadth, and 7 mm maximum thickness, with a weight of 43.95 g. There are traces of striations from the original working of the artefact, especially on the underside (or rear face) while, on the upper surface (or front face), they have mostly been smoothed over. The upper surface is slightly convex, while the lower one is flat. The edges of the long sides have been worked into flat surfaces and the sides of the holes have rings left from the boring process, which was done from both sides. This bracer is made from a fine-grained, banded wine-red stone with the appearance of a well-cemented or metamorphosed sedimentary rock that can be compared with a Welsh Cambrian mudstone, as discussed below.

ON 6600

The black bracer is 134 mm in length, 32 mm in maximum breadth, 5 mm maximum thickness, and weighs 51.79 g. The top surface (or front face) has been smoothed, while the underside (or rear face) has been less carefully finished and longitudinal striations can be seen here, the likely result of the process to work the stone into shape. As with the red bracer, the edges of the long sides have been worked into flat

surfaces. The holes, which have an hourglass shape, have traces of internal rings, left from the boring operation. This bracer appears to be made from a black silty mudstone or slate-like material; see below regarding the issues surrounding its sourcing. There is a lighter coloured patch on the upper surface where the rock has weathered or otherwise altered, perhaps in the grave.

Comparisons with British and Irish Bracers

Altogether some 109 bracers, including eight from Ireland, have now been recorded in museums in England, Scotland and Wales by the aforementioned project (Woodward and Hunter 2011) and the data collected include details of colour, shape, size, and proportions and the varieties of stone that were selected to make them. It had already been suspected that the majority of bracers found in England, and indeed also in Scotland and Wales, are greenish-grey or sometimes a more bluish-grey in colour and this fact has been confirmed by the findings of the project. Thus the differing colours of the bracers placed with the Amesbury Archer stand out in contrast to the general pattern.

Only two other reddish bracers were recorded and since the materials used to make them are different, neither compares with the red mudstone of ON 6588. Both of these

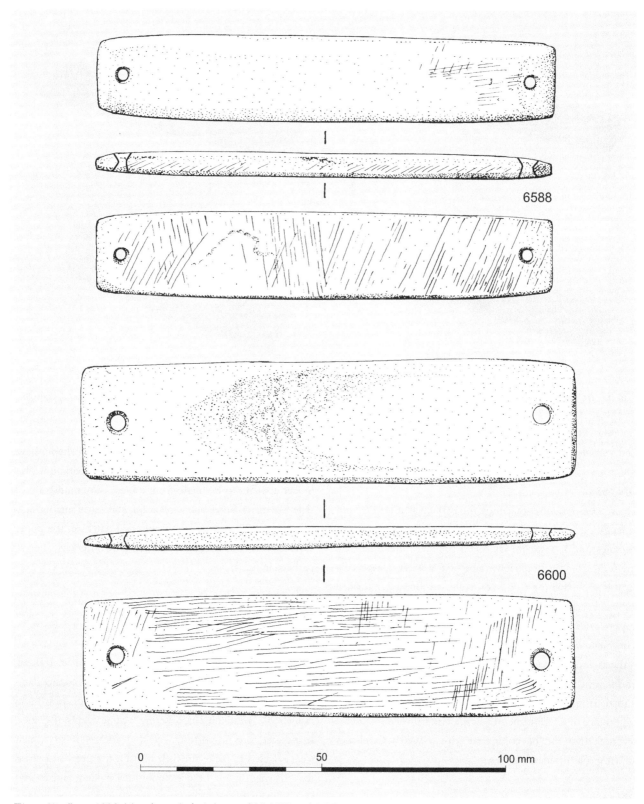

6588

6600

0   50   100 mm

Figure 37 Grave 1289 (Amesbury Archer); bracers ON 6588 and 6600

other bracers appear to be made from Old Red Sandstone which, in each case, is local to the findspot. One of these, from Dornoch Nursery, Highland (location on Fig. 72, below), was found in a cist with a Low Carinated All-Over-Cord Beaker (Ashmore 1989) and is, in fact, not unlike the red bracer buried with the Amesbury Archer in form, although smaller. The burial is relatively early, and one of the earliest in Scotland (2470–2150 cal BC, GrA-26515, 3850±40

BP; Sheridan 2007, 109; table 31; see Fig. 71 for the location of the site). Also made from reddish Old Red Sandstone is a bracer with a rounded outline (of Atkinson form A[1]) and of probable later date from central Wales, found in a cairn at Carneddau, Powys (Gibson 1993).

Nor do the three other black bracers recorded from Britain compare any better with the black example buried with the Amesbury Archer, since all are A[1] varieties with a rounded outline. The Stonehenge bracer (Evans 1984, 17) is altogether different in form, while its X-ray fluorescence spectrometry analysis has shown that it also differs in composition, having a high iron content (Woodward *et al.* 2006), as opposed to the low iron content of ON 6600 detailed below. There is also a difference in grain size between the two materials. The date range for the Stonehenge burial, *2350–2190 cal BC* at 91% probability (p. 180 above) (Cleal *et al.* 1995, 532–3; Parker Pearson *et al.* 2009, 24; Fig. 61, below) suggests that this burial was somewhat later in date than the Amesbury Archer's. The small black bracer from Ben Bridge, Chew Valley Lake, Somerset (Rahtz and Greenfield 1977, 187) is also made from stone with a relatively high iron content (*ibid.*, 343; Ixer and Webb 2011). A third black bracer, from Cliffe, Kent (Kinnes *et al.* 1998) is similar in shape but is made from black shale, possibly from Kimmeridge in Dorset. When it comes to plotting the chemical compositions of the bracers according to the principal components, it may be noted that ON 6600 plots very much on the edge of the diagram, again suggesting that it differs from other British finds (Woodward *et al.* 2006, fig. 6; Ixer and Webb 2011).

In Ireland there was a tradition of bracers made from red stone, with others that are black, grey or brown. The majority of the Irish bracers are two-holed (Harbison 1976, app. A), but an investigation into the materials used to make them has shown that they too do not compare with the bracers buried with the Amesbury Archer (Roe and Woodward 2009). The numerous red Irish bracers were for the most part made from jasper and X-ray fluorescence spectrometry analyses have confirmed that the one buried with the Amesbury Archer was not made from this rock type (Ixer and Webb 2011). The Irish bracers closest to black in colour were made from a stone axe material, porcellanite from Tievebulliagh or Rathlin Island, both Co. Antrim, which again does not compare with ON 6600 (Harbison 1976, 6; Ixer and Webb below). Another point of interest is that the Irish bracers appear to belong to an altogether different burial tradition, one of insertion into megalithic tombs (Roe and Woodward 2009), as can also be demonstrated for Beaker pottery in Ireland (Case 2004a, 197; N. Carlin, pers. comm. and 2011) and for some V-perforated

buttons (Harbison 1976, 14). By contrast, nearly all the British Beaker burials with bracers, including that of the Amesbury Archer, are individual burials (Roe 2011).

Both the bracers buried with the Amesbury Archer are unusually long and slender by comparison with most of the examples of Atkinson's B[1] form found in Britain. ON 6588 in particular is notable for this feature, being in length some 5.5 times its breadth. However, it can be compared with the aforementioned reddish bracer from Dornoch, which has a length/breadth ratio of 6.2, while that for a greenish amphibole-bearing bracer from Llantrithyd, South Glamorgan (Savory 1977, 57) is 5.3. The black bracer, ON 6600, is a little less extreme in its proportions, with a length that is 4.2 times its breadth, an index that that approximates to other B[1] examples from Sturry, Kent (4.3; Jessup 1933, 177) and Hockwold, Norfolk (4.1; Clough and Green 1972, 138, fig. 14). Another feature, which is altogether less common on British bracers, is the treatment of the edges on the long sides. On both the bracers buried with the Amesbury Archer these are flat, whereas rounded edges have more usually been noted on English bracers of the B variety. So far, then, it can be seen that ON 6588 and 6600 differ from most British examples in their colour, in manufacturing details and in the choice of stone used to make them.

Comparison with Continental Bracers

Flat bracers with two holes are a common type on the Continent, as was originally demonstrated by Sangmeister in his paper on narrow bracers. He showed that numbers of such bracers, potentially comparable with those buried with the Amesbury Archer, occur in western Europe and especially in parts of Portugal, Spain, the south of France and Brittany (Sangmeister 1964a, 95, Abb. 2). However these finds all come from areas where Bell Beaker burials tend to occur in megalithic tombs, a tradition which seems ultimately to have reached Ireland via the Atlantic but which apparently had little to do with the establishment of Beaker customs in Britain. Sangmeister then went on to examine bracers from central Europe in more detail and showed that ones comparable to ON 6588 and 6600, his type G, are known here too, with notable concentrations in the Rhineland due to the number of burials discovered there (Sangmeister 1974). These bracers occur in the middle Rhine region around Koblenz, to the south of Mainz and also along the Moselle around Trier, while further examples are concentrated in the Lower Rhineland (Sangmeister 1974, 128, Abb. 9). More recently, a

108

number of bracers have been found during excavations in Bell Beaker cemeteries in southern Germany (Heyd 2007a, 348, fig. 12, b). All such finds from Germany belong within the western part of the Bell Beaker East Group (*ibid.*, 330, fig. 2).

It is especially pertinent to this enquiry that Sangmeister demonstrated that the central European bracers are, in most cases, made from varying shades of either black or red stone (1974, 114). This applies in particular to his group G bracers with two holes, which are often recorded as being made from grey or black stone, while only two of the finds recorded by him appear to be red (1974, 149, Tab. 4g). The red bracers found in continental Europe have, as it happens, proved to be more problematical, since most of the known examples appear to be of the later, markedly curved, 4-holed variety, Sangmeister's group A (1974, 144, Tab. 4a), a variety that is altogether less likely to relate to ON 6588. As for the questions of size and proportions, both ON 6588 and 6600 are longer than those recorded by Sangmeister (1974, 152, diag. 5). Bracer ON 6588 is also considerably more slender in proportion than the continental examples in group G, though ON 6600, with a breadth/length index of 4.2, has proportions comparable to a number of the black group G bracers (Sangmeister 1974, 149, Tab. 4g).

The detail of shaping the edges of the long sides of bracers into flattened surfaces is also to be found on Continental bracers, as for example ones from Andernach in the middle Rhineland (Anon. 1953, 114, Taf. 12, 1), Augsburg, Bavaria (Kociumaka and Dietrich 1991, 68, Abb. 42), and Lunteren in the Netherlands (Butler and van der Waals 1966, fig. 46, 16). The latter, together with a further seven two-holed bracers, was examined at the Rijksmuseum, Leiden, Netherlands, where it was confirmed that all had flattened long sides. One of these was made from shiny black lydite and the other seven from very fine-grained silty mudstone that was probably originally dark grey or black but had since weathered to shades of grey-brown. A common source area for the stone may be presumed. Geologically a good potential parallel for the black Amesbury Archer bracer could be the example of dark, fine-grained stone from Tumulus I at Speulde, Gelderland (Bursch 1933, 45, Taf. vi, 16). In short, ON 6600 seems to have the best potential for continental parallels in areas of single burial, since examples of a similar colour, shape and proportions and possibly even stone are known to be distributed in parts of both the Netherlands and Germany.

The suggestion that there were links between Beaker pottery styles in Wessex and the Rhineland is not a new one, running back to Abercromby (1912, 9, 15, 66–7; Clarke 1970, 84). In addition to the Wessex/Middle Rhine Beakers of Clarke's designation, Needham has commented on stylistic links between Low-Carinated Beakers from the middle Rhine area and British All-Over-Cord Beakers (Needham 2005, 179). Clarke chose to illustrate a Barbed Wire Beaker found with a two-holed, black bracer at Mülheim-Löschacker, Rhineland-Pfalz (1970, 324, fig. 358), while a similar bracer from Mülheim-Kärlich was found with a Low-Carinated Beaker illustrated by Needham (2005, 181, fig. 4b, 27). A further indication of continental European connections could be the plaited cord ornament found on Beakers in the graves of the Boscombe Bowmen and the Amesbury Archer, since this is a decorative style also found in continental Europe, including examples from the Rhineland and beyond (Gersbach 1957).

Geological Considerations

The identification of the two varieties of stone used to make the bracers buried with the Amesbury Archer is crucial to the question of their possible continental connections. The possibility of both insular and continental sources of stone was considered and for this an important factor was the availability of X-ray fluorescence spectrometry analysis through the *Early Bronze Age Grave Goods Project*. It has been possible to show through this analysis that the majority of the English bracers fall into two main groupings of green-grey or blue-grey stone (Woodward *et al.* 2006; Woodward and Hunter 2011). Curved bracers, mainly of Atkinson's form C^1, tend to be made of Langdale tuff from the Lake District, while flat bracers, mainly Atkinson's B^1, B^2, and B^3 forms, are frequently made from a fine-grained amphibole-bearing metasediment which resembles impure nephrite, although it is unlike the Alpine variety of nephrite known to have been used to make some stone axes (P. Pétrequin and M. Errera, pers. comm.). These two groups of stone clearly do not relate to the finds from the grave of the Amesbury Archer, but what is of relevance here is the fact that the choice of lithic materials in Britain was not random, since it was found that nearly two thirds of the bracers examined had been made from these two specific rock types (Woodward *et al.* in press). It seemed likely that some of the continental European bracers would also prove to have been made from specially selected materials.

The task of identifying potential Continental sources of the stone used for the Amesbury Archer's bracer(s) was not expected to be easy, but the chosen starting point for the author's geological fieldwork in continental Europe was in the middle Rhineland, since it was known that both black and red rocks occur in the Rhenish Schiefergebirge (Tilmann 1938), while, as indicated above, there was also the possibility of archaeological links with the same area. Samples were collected from lower Devonian rocks along the Rhine gorge as it passes through the Hunsrück, within the area of the Frankfurt am Main-West geological sheet (CC 6310), but initial results from X-ray fluorescence spectrometry analysis were not encouraging (Table 20).

One dilemma was the realisation that only two of Sangmeister's examples of flat bracers with two holes are made from red stone (1974, 135, no. 197, 136, no. 216), and the material(s) used for these are uncertain. The case for a continental European link here appeared to be in question and this prompted further fieldwork. Although reddish mudstones in general are fairly widespread, very fine-grained, indurated rocks in shades resembling red wine are not of common occurrence in the United Kingdom. There are limited outcrops of reddish Devonian rocks in south-west England but the ones investigated proved to be altogether too micaceous for comparison with ON 6588 (Hobson 1978, 31). The best potential for a match in hand specimen appeared to be a red Cambrian metasediment known as the Caerfai shale, collected from Caerfai Bay, near St David's, Pembrokeshire (Williams and Stead 1982, 38, fig. 5; see Fig. 72 for the location of Caerfai Bay) and subsequent detailed X-ray fluorescence spectrometry analysis showed a good match (Table 20). This small bay on the south coast of Pembrokeshire is striking in appearance, since all the bands of contrasting strata have been upended into a near vertical position. The red bands show up clearly and could easily have been noticed by fishermen and others making journeys that way by sea. This red outcrop is not large but is of further interest because of the known links between Pembrokeshire and Stonehenge. Curiously, the proposed utilisation of this unusual stone for a bracer appears to have been a one-off event.

Black fine-grained rocks are of more common occurrence than red ones but are not necessarily any easier to study and they too have potential British and Continental sources. Rocks from Old Red Sandstone strata would in all probability be too micaceous, as was the case with the Hunsrück slate from the Rhenish

Schiefergebirge, which also proved to have a higher iron content that ON 6600 (Table 20). The possibility was considered that this bracer could be made from a black Welsh slate. However, samples of Ordovician shale from the Breidden, Powys, did not compare particularly well under the binocular microscope, while the single sample submitted for X-ray fluorescence spectrometry analysis again proved to be higher in iron content than the stone used to make ON 6600. A possibility for a match that seems worth considering is a black axehead material, a quartz pelite quarried at Plancher-les-Mines (Haute Saône) in the southern part of the Vosges, a location that is not far either from the river Rhine or from the headwaters of the Meuse (Pétrequin and Jeunesse 1995). This source area has apparent potential, both because it supplied a stone axehead material and also because it is in a mountain location, two factors also relevant for the use of Langdale stone for bracers. Additionally the quartz pelite was worked in the form of long narrow blades, which would be appropriate for bracer manufacture and it weathers to lighter shades of grey and brown, a detail that was observed on bracers seen in Leiden. However, the suggestion that this variety of stone may have been used to make bracers need not exclude other rocks and other potential source areas and clearly there is much further work that could be done. Nevertheless, on balance, there seems no good reason why the black bracer buried with the Amesbury Archer should not have been brought from continental Europe by him. In this case, X-ray fluorescence spectrometry analysis of black, two-holed bracers in continental European museums could lead to the definition of one or more specific materials used to make them, which could in their turn be tested for resemblance to ON 6600. At present, though, the best

Table 20: Composition of the bracers from grave 1289 (Amesbury Archer)

		The Breidden, Powys D1992.18	Red German Devonian DGERDEV	Black German Devonian DRHINDE	ON 6588 (red)	ON 6600 (black)	Red Caerfai Cambrian mudstone 2004.16-2
K	% m/m	1.83	2.82	3.27	2.86	1.02	3.02
Ca	% m/m	0.40	0.13	0.18	0.68	0.30	0.59
Ti	% m/m	0.43	0.57	0.52	0.56	0.15	0.42
Mn	% m/m	1.76	0.03	0.02	0.09	0.01	0.09
Fe	% m/m	5.96	3.74	5.42	4.95	0.24	5.28
Sr	mg/kg	78	51	61	142	227	134
Zr	mg/kg	232	378	189	200	100	180
Rb	mg/kg	122	124	198	139	58	120
Ba	mg/kg	925	490	868	1088	318	706

indications of a possible continental source for the black bracer come from the archaeological evidence.

The problem over the differences between the red bracer, ON 6588, and the highly curved and sometimes decorated red continental ones was partly resolved by the realisation that the latter were made from differing materials. A rock which can be split into separate layers can be made into a flat bracer, but is not suitable for curved ones, although for these a fine-grained volcanic rock would be ideal. Thus the Langdale tuff was selected for making nearly all the British curved bracers (Woodward and Hunter 2011). There is little information on the stone used for the curved bracers found in continental Europe, but a few are said to be made from tuff, sometimes porphyritic, as for instance a decorated example from Kornwestheim, Lkr. Ludwigsberg, Baden-Württemberg (Sangmeister 1974, 105). Two others made from tuff were reported from the Netherlands (Butler and van der Waals 1966, 122, 124) and Clarke commented on their purple-brown colour (1970, 87). However, examination in the Leiden museum of one of these, from Stroeërzand, Gelderland (Bursche 1933, 85, Taf. vi, 5), indicated manufacture from a sedimentary rock, a fine-grained red sandstone with very small green reduction spots. This material resembles that used for another curved bracer from Unseburg, Kr. Stassfurt, Germany (Sangmeister 1974, 131, no. 20), seen in the Landesmuseum für Vorgeschichte in Halle, though in this case the dark red stone has large reduction spots. For both these examples a Permian/Triassic source for the rock is thought likely. By contrast, igneous rock is thought to have been used for another German example recorded from Leihgestern, Lkr. Giessen, Hessen, with the suggestion that the stone is a tuff (*tuffstein*) from the red beds (*rotliegendes*) of the Lower Permian (Sangmeister 1951, 81). The stone used to make another curved red bracer from Darmstadt Waterworks (Clarke 1970, 306 fig. 198; Hessisches Landes-museum, Darmstadt) also appears to be a Permian igneous rock, porphyritic rhyolite with a likely source at Bad Münster am Stein-Ebernburg (Heim 1960; Falke 1972). Here there are dramatic, 300 m high cliffs of red rock on either side of the river Nahe. This locality is not far from the River Rhine, and must have been well known since it falls on the edge of one of the areas where Bell Beaker finds are concentrated, as shown, for instance, by distributions of pottery as well as bracers (Harrison 1980, figs 1 and 37).

It appears that at least two distinctive materials were used to make the continental curved red bracers and these must now be ripe for further investigations. These red bracers, however, barely relate to ON 6588, with only one possible link, since the concept of colour, especially red, is one that might have influenced the choice of the Caerfai shale to provide a second wristguard. There is, however, a chronological difficulty with this theory, since it is likely that most of the red continental European bracers, with their curved shape and multiple holes, are somewhat later in date than the Amesbury Archers's bracers.

Archaeological Considerations

Turning to the archaeological aspects of the investigation, the apparent selection of a Cambrian mudstone from Pembrokeshire to make a single red bracer is not readily understood. A look at the map, however, provides some possible explanations. Saint David's Head, although a long way from Boscombe Down, is one of the Welsh locations closest to Ireland, so that travellers may have come this way *en route* to Ross Island, where early copper working has been dated to between 2400 and 1900 BC (O'Brien 2004, 155). In the case of the Amesbury Archer, however, this seems less likely, since none of his three knives was made from the Ross Island A-metal. Another reason for journeys to Ireland would have been to acquire metal for gold working and this might have included a desire to use gold for making basket-shaped ornaments, which are also known from two Irish finds (O'Connor 2004, 207–11; pp. 129–37) as well as from the graves of the Amesbury Archer and the 'Companion', although the Amesbury Archer's own ornaments are apparently not made from Irish gold.

It may be, though, that the suggested interest in Caerfai Bay had some connection with the significance of the Preseli bluestones. The first arrival and subsequent re-arrangement of the bluestones at Stonehenge have not as yet been firmly dated (Parker Pearson *et al.* 2007, 618; Pitts 2009, 190). A recent idea is that the bluestones were first positioned in the Aubrey Holes, forming part of Stonehenge I, which can be dated from *c.* 3000 BC (Parker Pearson *et al.* 2009, 32). This phase of Stonehenge is contemporary with the makers of Grooved Ware, and another interpretation is possible, based on a survey of stone axes found in late Neolithic pits with this pottery (Roe, in prep.). It was found that the axes from Grooved Ware pits were most frequently made of greenstones from Cornwall, while second in popularity were axes from Penmaenmawr in north Wales. Noteworthy is the fact that no bluestone axeheads have been recorded from these pits, suggesting that the Preseli stone may not have come into use until sometime later.

The black stone used to make ON 6600 gives rise to a different set of discussion points and some possibly relevant links between Britain and the Continent during the Copper Age have already been suggested above. It is not difficult to find comparable black two-holed bracers from Germany, with a number of recorded examples from the middle Rhine area. In addition to those already mentioned, another such bracer was found with a Bell Beaker at Dirmstein, Lkr. Bad Dürkheim, Rheinland-Pfalz (Gebers 1978, 29, Taf. 30, 9), while a number of stray finds are also known. Beakers with plaited cord ornament have been recorded from the same area, as well as elsewhere (Gersbach 1957, 11). Only one bracer, an elaborate, decorated red example of Sangmeister's curved type A, from Worms, Rheingewann, was directly associated with a Beaker having such ornament (Gebers 1978, 105, Taf. 52). However, others did come from the same sites as these Beakers, including a two-holed grey bracer found in one of three crouched burials at Eppelsheim, Lkr. Alzey-Worms, Rheineland-Pfalz (Gebers 1978, 30, Taf. 48, 10). In spite of such potential parallels with the burials at Boscombe Down, a notable feature of the Bell Beaker burials in this area is the almost complete absence of tanged copper knives and daggers, although one was recorded from Mauchenheim, Lkr. Alzey-Worms, Rheineland-Pfalz (Gebers 1978, 56, Taf. 70, 38). Another relevant omission from the central Rhineland is that of ornaments of gold.

One area where both gold ornaments and tanged copper daggers have been recorded is Bavaria (Heyd 2007a, 336, 344, 348, fig. 6). Numerous bracers are also known from cemeteries along the upper Danube (Heyd 2007a, 349, fig. 12 b), although not many appear to be of the simple, two-holed variety. One such example, from Augsburg, has already been mentioned. A similar one, said to be made from a light brown/grey slate, was found with a Beaker and a tanged dagger in grave 1 at Trieching (Kreiner 1991, 154) which is radiocarbon dated to 2460–2340 cal BC (3915±28 BP; Heyd 2000, 472; lab. no. not given). Heyd places this burial, with its simple 2-holed bracer, at the beginning of his chronological scheme for Beakers (phase A1), with a starting date in the Alpine foreland of *c.* 2500 BC (Heyd 2007a, 332, fig. 4).

Discussion

The earliest bracers might not have been made in France or Germany. As suggested by Case (2004c, 207), their ultimate origin may have been in Iberia, which provides early radiocarbon dates (eg, Müller and van Willigen 2001) and

where numerous finds of two-holed bracers are known (Sangmeister 1964a, 97, Abb. 2). From Iberia, Beakers and bracers could have been taken northwards up the Atlantic towards Ireland, and also north-eastwards to the south of France, another region with a number of finds and some early radiocarbon dates (Müller and van Willigen 2001). The Beaker folk, ever mobile, could then have brought their pottery and bracers to the Rhineland by travelling up the River Rhône, arriving in the middle of the 3rd millennium BC or thereabouts at the upper reaches of both the Danube and the Rhine.

Finely made stone bracers, such as the ones from the grave of the Amesbury Archer, were probably not intended for everyday use, a conclusion reached initially as a result of the pilot survey for the *Ritual in Early Bronze Age Grave Goods* Project by Woodward *et al.* (2006) and independently by Fokkens *et al.* (2008). Fokkens *et al.* were able to show that a high proportion of bracers from burials were positioned on the outer arm – as was the case with the Amesbury Archer's black bracer, ON 6600 – so that they were probably worn for display (*ibid.*, 118, fig. 10) rather than for protection from the bowstring. Fokkens *et al.* also commented that the use of stone from distant sources would have added to the value of the bracers (*ibid.*, 124). Both of the bracers buried with the Amesbury Archer were found in pristine condition, so that they must have been both valued and carefully stored to prevent breakage. A two-holed bracer of similar type was found in a decorated bone box inside a tomb at Anghelu Ruju in Sardinia (Bray 1964, 82, pl. x), and so had been protected from damage. Bracers have been found in burials in central Europe and elsewhere with other prestigious objects, which may include gold items and also equipment for metal working (Turek 2004).

These deposits seem to suggest not just craft skills and, possibly, specialisation, but also high social ranking, and subsequent burial with an element of symbolic deposition (*ibid.*). It is in this kind of context, with symbolic connections not just to archery, but also to smithing, that the two wristguards from the grave of the Amesbury Archer can be viewed.

Conclusions

The two bracers from the grave of the Amesbury Archer were made from varieties of stone that are exceptional in a British context. Both were manufactured in a continental style, although the best geological candidate there is at present for the red bracer ON 6588 is a Welsh rock, and this is consistent with the results of the geochemical analyis (Table 20), while the craftsmanship was presumably carried out by an incomer from continental Europe. If this bracer had indeed been made of Welsh rock, then the use of a rock from Pembrokeshire need not have been an isolated event, since, apart from the transport of the Preseli bluestones to Stonehenge, this area of Wales would have been on a direct route to Ireland, a source of valued gold. It could be that the inspiration of a red bracer was brought back from a trip to Ireland in search of gold, since it is here that high quality, two-holed red bracers of red jasper have been found in some numbers.

The black bracer, ON 6600, seems more likely to be of continental European origin and to be made from a specific material as yet unidentified, though there are some clues that could be pursued further. An examination of the materials used to make Continental bracers could establish what specific varieties of stone were selected and whether the stone of ON 6600 fitted the description of one such material. This bracer was worn on the outer part of the Amesbury Archer's lower arm, as if it were a badge of status or a symbol of achievement, which could have been along the lines of the successful shooting of a number of wild boars or else moving human targets.

That the Amesbury Archer was a person of high status cannot be in doubt, and he was in all likelihood well thought of for his skills, including those in archery and metalworking. We cannot be certain where he began his journey to Salisbury Plain, but the river Rhine could have provided an easy passage for parts of it, so that a logical starting point would have been somewhere along its upper reaches. Clues in the archaeological record also suggest that a possible starting point could lie in southern Germany. The black bracer could have been acquired here or during the journey through the middle Rhine area, although the actual stone might have come from a more distant source, which would no doubt have been one of special significance.

Geological Analysis of the Bracers
by Rob Ixer and Peter Webb

The results presented here are mainly based on work carried out as part of a Leverhulme-funded pilot project on Beaker bracers. Further analysis was carried out during a subsequent, three year Leverhulme project, *Ritual in Early Bronze Age Grave Goods* and are detailed in the ensuing publication (Woodward and Hunter 2011).

Experimental methodology
Each bracer was petrographically described using a x 10 hand lens/low power binocular microscope and without knowledge of their geochemistry. Particular attention was paid to any breaks/fractures in the artefact as they provided 'fresh', unpolished surfaces and the true colour of the rock. All lithological features, including mean grain size, presence of clasts, megacrysts, fossils, veining, bedding, laminae, and foliation planes were noted and measured. The colour of the polished and any broken, natural surface was recorded and standardised using the Geological Society of America's rock color chart. A lithological identification for each bracer was made based upon these macroscopic characteristics.

Both of the bracers were analysed using a Spectrace TN9000 portable X-ray fluorescence (PXRF) spectrometer. The methodology largely followed procedures described by Potts *et al.* (1997a; 1997b) and Williams-Thorpe *et al.* (1999). Measurements were made with the PXRF analyser in lab. stand configuration and samples were excited sequentially using Cd-109, Fe-55, and Am-241 sources for count times of 100, 60, and 20 s respectively. X-ray spectra were quantified using the instrument manufacturer's algorithms, which are based on region-of-interest peak integration and a fundamental parameter matrix correction. As the samples generally had an elongated, often rectangular, wafer shape, two measurements were made, where possible one on each side of the wafer and the average taken as representative of the bulk composition of the sample. Corrections were made for (a) surface topography (that is, deviations from an ideal flat analysis surface) using procedures described by Potts *et al.* (1997a) and b) calibration bias, based on the average deviation from parity between recommended and analysed values of approximately 25 reference materials analysed as compressed powder pellets. In general, this correction amounted to ±10%. As most of the 26 bracers included in the study samples were generally fine-grained, an average of two measurements was sufficient to account for any mineralogical effects (Potts *et al.* 1997b). The comparability of analytical data derived during this project was monitored by analysing in duplicate two control samples (one powder pellet of a microgranite and one of a dolerite), at the start of each operating session. Consistency of the data was considered to be satisfactory.

ON 6600
A medium grey (N5 on the Geological Society of America rock colour chart) fine-grained, micaceous, laminated metashale/slate showing fissility along foliation planes/

laminae. The lithology is similar to that of the Stonehenge bracer (Woodward *et al.* 2006, no. 26); bracer ON 6600 is slightly coarser-grained but both are made from dark metasedimentary rocks. The closest suitable rocks in Britain would be within the Devonian–Carboniferous metasediments of Cornubia (Devon and Cornwall) known as the killas, but other possible origins could include the Palaeozoic rocks of south Wales and the English Lake District. Despite a superficial visual resemblance the bracer does not have the polish of porcellanite and together with the presence of white mica and the low Fe content (see below) this precludes the bracer from being porcellanite.

The bracer has an unusual rock composition as seen in Table 20 (above) with very little Fe (0.24%) or Mn (0.01%). The low Fe suggests it is not comparable with the Northern Ireland sources for porcellanite, the rock-type used in the manufacture of IPC Group IX axes and noted for its abundant iron oxides. This is in agreement with the petrographical assessment. There is little K and even less Ca present, yet there are relatively high levels of Sr. Except for the Fe and relative levels of Sr and Zr, there are some compositional resemblances to a bracer from Mildenhall, Suffolk, and to the two jasper bracers Ireland A and Ireland B (Woodward *et al.* 2006). The geochemistry of the bracer would be compatible with it being a highly siliceous rock and the petrography favours a metasediment.

ON 6588

A dark reddish brown (10R 3/4) indurated, laminated, micaceous mudstone. Thin, slightly coarser grained bands are present and have taken a slightly different polish. The lithology is a mudstone with minor fine siltstone laminae. The widespread occurrence of similar rock types means that the red bracer would be difficult to provenance. Suitable Devonian or Permo-Triassic red mudstones crop out on the coast in Cornubia but red mudstones also occur within coastal exposures of the Cambrian and Devonian of south Wales and beyond. The red bracer is quite different compositionally from the black bracer (Table 20), with much higher K (2.86%), Ba and Rb, as well as Fe (4.95%) contents. However, in terms of Ca, Ti, and Mn it bears some resemblance to the bracers found at Mildenhall, Suffolk and Tytherington/Corton, Wiltshire (Woodward *et al.* 2006), both of which are petrographically identified as metasediments, although the bracers themselves are in fact different in form. Despite its colour both the macroscopical characteristics and geo-chemistry indicate that the bracer is not red jasper and

so it cannot share a geological origin with the Irish red bracers (*ibid.*). Both the petrography and geochemistry suggest that the bracer is an indurated sediment/metasediment.

'Cushion' Stone
by Stuart Needham

A 'cushion' stone (ON 6593; Pl. 39; Fig. 38) had been placed behind the Amesbury Archer's back (Fig. 36). Extant length 90.5 mm, maximum width 65 mm, maximum thickness 30.3 mm, weight 261.4 g.

Condition

One corner appears to be missing from an original trapezoidal block, probably lydite, which is a muddy chert or siliceous mudstone (P. Webb pers. comm.). Although the fracture has been ground smooth, it still undulates. Limited areas on both faces are rough textured depressions either not fully smoothed by grinding or subsequently roughened; some if not all have the appearance of being damage during use complicated by possible secondary modification to maintain functionality. Otherwise, the whole surface – whether faceted, curved, or undulating – is extremely smoothly polished.

Small spalls, or chips, have become detached from the intact acute corner as well as the apex on the opposite side; these might have been caused by deliberate percussion.

Morphology

All the original sides of the surmised trapezoidal block had a flattish central strip with facets of variable angle and width chamfering the body angles to front and back. Two of these chamfers, on the obverse face, are in fact double-facets. Overall the block thickens from the shorter of the long sides towards the longer but, while the obverse face is basically flat with undulations, the reverse is strongly convex except where two large scalloped depressions intervene. The scallops are smooth except where small flakes have subsequently been detached and may be residual flake beds from the original dressing of the block. Nevertheless, their gentle concavity may have lent themselves to particular usage.

Surface features observed under the microscope are detailed by Cowell and Middleton (below).

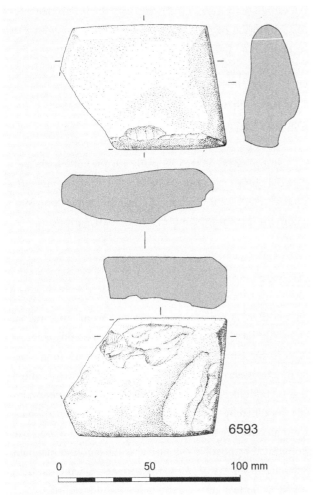

Figure 38 Grave 1289 (Amesbury Archer); 'Cushion' stone ON 6593

Plate 39 'Cushion' stone ON 6593 from the grave of the Amesbury Archer

The 'Cushion' Stone and Metalworking

Drawing meaningful parallels for this object is hampered by the lack of unambiguous evidence for function (Cowell and Middleton p. 117 below) and by the fact that similar stone equipment shows relatively little standardisation in form. In fact, a wide variety of such equipment occurs in British and continental European Beaker/Early Bronze Age graves, as well as other contemporary contexts (for example Brandherm 2009). Detailed study has been sporadic and has tended to concentrate on the more carefully shaped and finished forms. Yet miscellaneous stone equipment is frequent in barrows in Britain, often deriving from the mound rather than grave groups; this can be seen, for example, from the catalogue of William Greenwell's barrow-excavated material (Kinnes and Longworth 1985; Lynch 2001, 403). The stones concerned range from heavily shaped to well-chosen pebbles which required less modification. In terms of functionality and significance, it may be a mistake to discriminate too rigidly between these paths of selection and working, but functions can be diverse – hammer, anvil, polishing, grinding, whetting – and relate to production and maintenance well beyond just metalworking. Moreover, individual blocks may have had multiple simultaneous functions. The discussion of block-like stone equipment that follows is necessarily selective.

The Amesbury Archer's 'cushion' stone has evidently received much care in its finish and yet its shape was evidently not especially regular. Undulations in the faces and varying edge faceting are thought to be original features and may indicate a lack of concern for regularity or, rather, they may actually indicate a positive desire for variability in profiles to give flexibility in its function. This point was made by Butler and van der Waals in their classic study of the Dutch examples of 'cushion' stones (1966, 63–75).

Clarke described stones in five British Beaker graves as 'pebble hammers' (Clarke 1970, no. 652, 820, 1306, 1368, 1451), but there are also two better shaped stones that he regarded as 'polished and faceted hammerstones' (*ibid.*, 219, 221, 445); overall he suggested a four-fold categorisation of Beaker-associated metalworking stones (*ibid.*, 573–4, fn. 56). The hammer from Winterbourne Monkton, Wiltshire (Annable and Simpson 1964, no. 75), has a roughly ovate plan and a sub-triangular section and was also described by Clark as a 'Smith's serpentine hammer' (1970, fig. 898), although Piggott (1973, 344) thought it need be no more than a personal whetstone. The example from Amesbury barrow G54, Wiltshire, is extremely neatly fashioned into a rectanguloid block, symmetrical from end to end and with bowed and highly polished faces (Clark 1970, fig. 890). Piggott had it as a 'stone polisher' (1973, 343–4, fig. 14, d). Both these graves are best dated now to Early Bronze Age Period 2 (Needham and Woodward 2008), a little later than the Amesbury Archer. Amesbury G54 contained a flint dagger, a type that does not occur in association with metalwork, so it would be intriguing if the stone block from that grave was for metalworking.

Rather similar to the last example, although trapezoidal, is a quartzite 'hammer/hone' recovered during excavations at Newgrange, Co. Meath, Ireland. It was found amidst Beaker occupation material beneath cairn-edge slip on the old land surface, a horizon that also yielded other stone objects potentially relating to metalworking and a bronze flat axe (O'Kelly and Shell 1979). The typology of the axe suggests a date around or a little before 2000 BC, but this is only a broad indicator for other material on this land surface.

In Upton Lovell barrow G2a, Wiltshire, two successive burials were recognised by Cunnington (1806), but their respective grave goods were not necessarily fully disentangled. Most of the many stone, bone, and boars' tusk accompaniments seem to have been associated with the lower, presumably primary, burial probably dating to Period 3 (Needham 2005; 206, fig. 3; Needham and Woodward 2008, 6, fig. 3). These included Neolithic flint axes and Early Bronze Age battle-axes, the former presumably as relics, but other stones fell into less obvious types. One is a neatly fashioned thick discoidal block with chamfered perimeter from both faces and another carries a groove on one face, recalling the more regularly shaped 'arrowshaft smoothers' found in occasional graves.

Another stone from the Upton Lovell assemblage has, however, assumed much more interest recently because of the discovery by Colin Shell that it bears gold traces; he argues

that these are ancient traces because some can be observed going underneath an area of calcite accretion and they also have an appropriate composition (Shell 2000). The block is described as a 'slate burnisher', is *c.* 70 mm long and 35 mm wide, and has a rather club-like shape, but its character suggested to Shell that it may not have been primarily a gold-working tool. The narrower end seems to be neatly fashioned into a shallow dome (*ibid.*, fig. 1).

Two stone blocks were among finds made at the centre of a small cairn at Kirkhaugh, Northumberland – a site which produced one of the gold basket ornaments. One is a neatly fashioned rectanguloid block, 62.5 x 38.5 x 16 mm, with one end chamfered symmetrically from both faces (Maryon 1936, 213, 215, fig. 3, g). Maryon describes it as having a 'smooth semi-polished surface'. The site appears to have started as a ring cairn enclosing an area only about 3 m in diameter; no skeletal remains were recovered, but they may have been present originally and subsequently decayed.

Another noteworthy context for stone blocks is a Collared Urn burial from Sandmill, Wigtownshire, Dumfries and Galloway (Clarke *et al.* 1985, 295–6, fig. 7.31). Two of three blocks are described as modified pebbles, one being rectanguloid, the other more trapezoidal. The third is more irregular with concave sides and a thicker rounded projection at one end; one face bears a linear groove, recalling one of the Upton Lovell pieces. The grave group also included a stone battle-axe, a fragmentary bronze knife/razor, and a bone pin, and should again be of Period 3.

Closer in date to the Amesbury Archer's piece would be two stone blocks said to have been found with a copper flat axe at Hindlow, near Buxton, Derbyshire (Needham 1979, 282, 269, fig. 4.3; circumstances unknown, but see Hart 1981, 50, for other sites in the vicinity). Both are likely to have originated as pebbles which were then substantially modified by shaping and use resulting in strong chamfering around much of their perimeters. The different grain size and qualities of the stones suggest they served different stages in an abrasion and percussion process for which metalworking is a highly plausible candidate.

In addition to these examples from datable contexts, there are undoubtedly a good number of potentially contemporary stray finds. Frances Lynch, for example, has brought together a variety of polishers, often very well crafted, that appear to mimic the shape of axes (Lynch 2001). Although the lack of contexts must leave uncertain how many are strictly relevant to this discussion, the shape of an example such as from Penicuik, Midlothian, which matches closely that of broad-butted trapezoid copper axes, is strongly suggestive of an early date (*ibid.*, 402, fig. 2, 2). There are in fact a number of axe-like polishers in grave contexts; in addition to the Food Vessel associated example from Killicarney, Co. Cavan, mentioned by Lynch, there are others with Food Vessels in Scotland and Ireland (Simpson 1968, 206, fig. 49), as well as examples from Beaker graves, as in schist at Clinterty, Aberdeenshire, or in flint at Garton Slack 163, East Yorkshire (Clarke 1970, nos 1305, 1443). The writer is aware of yet others: a small axe/?polisher in dark grey stone from a cremation burial in a cairn at Topped Mountain, Co. Fermanagh (Waddell 1990, 88–9), and a rather crudely shaped axe-like block of pinkish brown sandstone from a cist at Upper Boyndlie, Aberdeenshire (Marischal Museum, Aberdeen). These are not necessarily all of the same character and function but they do suggest a tradition of creating axe-shaped working stones was taken up in these islands following a principle established on mainland Europe.

Amongst the best known group of related stone blocks on the Continent at this date are those from Dutch Beaker graves (p. 216 below). It was the first real study and characterisation of these objects that led Butler and van der Waals to the appellation *cushion stones* (1966, 63). The objects are from two graves and the hoard from Wageningen, Gelderland, all in the central Netherlands, with the addition of two stray finds. They were interpreted as metalworking equipment, but they are varied in form and some are clearly reworked from earlier objects – in one case a stone axe butt end, in another a grooved maul (a type known to be associated with mineral extraction). Amongst the rest of the group, most have a fairly regular rectanguloid form, although varying in size so as to allow dual interpretation as anvils and hammers (*ibid.*, 63). Two objects in the well-furnished Lunteren grave, however, were less regular. Butler and van der Waals also noted that the blocks can have faceted angles, as on the Boscombe Down object; 'their variety of planes from almost flat to slightly convex and with their facets and varying angles, are well suited for the hammering of metal' (*ibid.*, 71). Disappointingly, no metal traces were found on these objects despite being subjected to X-ray fluorescence analysis.

Butler and van der Waals drew attention to a few other similar objects from dispersed locations, among them a crisp rectangular block from a Beaker grave at Stedten, Mansfeld-Südharz, Saxon-Anhalt (Fig. 79). Another important group of Beaker graves with equipment interpreted as for metalworking comes from central Europe (Bertemes and Heyd 2002, 217, fig. 12). They are concentrated in Moravia and Bohemia in the Czech Republic, with a scatter of examples to the west and north-west (p. 217 and Fig. 76, below).

Dirk Brandherm's work in Iberia is also recognising more 'cushion' stones and other stone implements from funerary contexts in a region where the majority are still from settlement sites (Brandherm 2009). Even so, they appear only in restricted regions and over limited time periods – notably the Beaker period in central and northern Portugal and the Argaric Early Bronze Age in south-east Spain (*ibid.*, 179). Whatever the precise significance of these sets of equipment in terms of the status of the interred person, their inclusion in graves was clearly regionally specific and time dependent. In many parts of Europe, including Britain, funerary occurrence is sporadic to non-existent, so there was no universal compunction to identify the smith through grave offerings, if this is what such inclusions signify.

Despite the lack of clinching analytical evidence, the stone block found with the Amesbury Archer is more than a basic grinding or polishing stone. The indications of surface marks and spalls are that this block has been used fairly intensively and it is therefore curious that no ancient traces of metal could be identified, although this has also been the case for other 'cushion' stones. One possible explanation for the lack of gold traces might be the use of a leather pad over the stone when beating out sheet gold. Nevertheless, the very fine grain and generally smooth polished finish would be suitable as a base against which to finish metalwork, whether of copper or gold. Likewise the versatility offered by the varied profiles of edges would be a positive advantage in sheet metalworking, and it is surely no coincidence that working blocks of this particular character appear at the same time as the earliest metalwork in many regions.

The 'cushion stone', assuming that this object has been correctly interpreted as for metalworking, inevitably raises the question of whether the Amesbury Archer himself was the metalworker. The more abundant continental evidence for similar equipment at this date is reviewed below (pp. 212–22). Despite ambiguities in the functional interpretation of many of the artefacts concerned, collectively they make a persuasive case for a genuine connection with metalworking. In an essentially novel metalworking environment, the proclamation of metalworking skills in some graves is perhaps understandable, but this still leaves open to debate whether the Amesbury Archer himself was a metalworker, or whether he was instead regaled with all the appropriate symbols of his culture because of his standing and adventurous life history.

A final comment is merited on the petrography of the stone (see Cowell and Middleton below); if it is correctly identified as lydite, then is worth noting that this is one of the classic rock types (normally black in colour) selected for use as touchstones for determining the approximate composition of gold (Moore and Oddy 1985). This may be coincidental for there is no evidence of such ancient use on the Amesbury Archer's block and it is hard to imagine the need to characterise the purity of the gold at a time when very little was in circulation and it was easily differentiated in other ways from the baser metals.

Examination of the 'Cushion' Stone
by Mike Cowell and Andrew Middleton

In an attempt to identify the material of the 'cushion' stone, it was examined with the aid of a binocular microscope and also qualitatively analysed by X-Ray Fluoresence (XRF) using an air-path instrument equipped with a molybdenum target x-ray tube operated at 45 kV and a beam collimated to irradiate (and hence analyse) an area about 0.5 mm in diameter on the artefact. Further details of the equipment can found in Cowell (1998). It has a fine, even-grained texture; for the most part it is very dark grey-black in colour but there are occasional lighter grey and buff coloured regions (possibly a result of weathering during burial). The XRF analysis suggested that the stone is silica-rich, with significant potash and iron, but little calcium. (It was not possible to analyse for light elements such as sodium, magnesium, or aluminium).

These observations did not permit identification of the stone, although the low level of calcium excludes the possibility that the stone is a fine-grained limestone. Subsequent analysis with Energy Dispersive X-Ray Fluorescence (EDXRF) and Scanning Electron Microscope by E. Pernicka at the Bergakademie, Technische Universität Freiberg, has suggested that the stone is lydite, a form of chert. The stone was also examined microscopically for wear marks and surface deposits of metal for potential evidence that it had been used in metalworking processes. Investigation of metal traces was also carried out by non-destructive qualitative XRF analysis of several areas on the stone.

The stone is slab-shaped with five almost linear edges. The shortest edge seems to be an old break so that originally the stone may have been trapezoidal (Needham p. 113 above). The two main faces are relatively flat although one has a buff coloured hollow area. The faces are mainly characterised by a very smooth texture carrying many small thin scratches. These are generally not more than 10 mm in length, mainly linear and of random orientation. They are uniform over the surface, with no areas having a higher frequency of scratches, and seem likely to have resulted from natural abrasion or general handling. Three of the longer edges of the stone are slightly rounded and the transition from one of the faces (that without the brown hollowed area) is slightly faceted and characterised by deeper parallel scratches orientated almost at right angles to the edge. On the edges themselves the scratches are finer, more consistent with the main faces, with a slight preference for orientation along the long axis of the edge. The consistency of the deeper abrasions indicates that they are not natural and that they resulted from deliberate abrasion on a coarse material. This may have been to form or straighten the edges but it is also possible that these abrasions are the outcome of using the stone to work another material. The finer scratches along the edges are also unlikely to be natural and suggest that the edge has been rubbed against a relatively finely textured material. As above, this may have been to form or finish the edge or, alternatively, the result of working another material.

As noted above, there are some lighter grey areas on the stone and one of these occurs on the shortest edge of the stone. This particular edge is flat and has very smooth sections at the ends with a light grey area between. Examination of this latter area shows it to have an angular or crystalline surface and at first it was though this might be a percussion surface, ie, where damage had occurred due to it being lightly struck or pressed onto another material. However, further examination of other similar coloured areas on the stone, some along the main faces and others near the edges where percussion would be very unlikely due to their orientation, show identical features. It therefore seems more likely that the area on the short edge is due to weathering during burial, as suggested above for the light grey areas in general.

The microscopic and XRF examination, concentrating particularly on scratches and other recesses, failed to find any evidence for metal traces; likewise, none were noted by Needham during his inspection of the whole surface under low magnification at the British Museum. In contrast, the later analysis using Scanning Electron microscope in Freiberg identified metal traces of two distinct compositions – silver and copper-rich gold – and as neither of these compositions is recorded for the north-west European Chalcolithic and as they were not apparent when the stone was examined previously, they are regarded as modern.

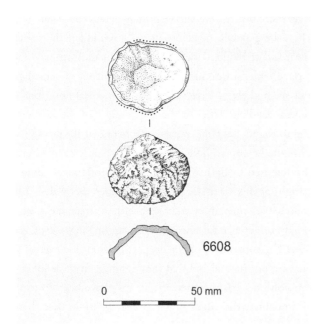

Figure 39 Grave 1289 (Amesbury Archer); iron pyrites nodule ON 6608

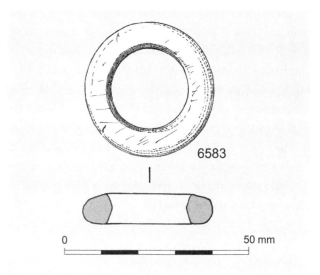

Figure 40 Grave 1289 (Amesbury Archer), shale ring ON 6583

Iron Pyrite

A piece of iron pyrite (ON 6608; Fig. 39), an iron sulphide that occurs naturally in the Chalk, was found by the Amesbury Archer's face (Fig. 36). It is 43 mm long, 35 mm wide, and 3 mm thick. It has extensive signs of use along the longer sides that are consistent with the mineral having been struck with flint to create sparks to light fires. In addition, one small complete and 17 fragments from the outer shell of iron pyrite nodules were recovered. One was found during the excavation, while all the others were from samples 7342 and 7348 and it is likely that many of these fragments occurred naturally in the Chalk. Some, however, may be fragments of nodules that were used in fire-making sets (pp. 34 and 95 above).

Three heavily worn fabricators or strike-a-lights were also found in the grave (ON 6586–7, 7345.1). None of these was associated with pyrites nodule ON 6608 but ON 6586 has iron staining. This was probably caused by proximity to a piece of iron pyrite that had fragmented and which was not identified during excavation.

Shale Belt Ring

by Alison Sheridan and Mary Davis

A shale belt ring (ON 6583; Fig. 40) had been placed in front of the Amesbury Archer's knees (Fig. 36). It is a plain, symmetrical black ring with a flattish D-shaped section. It has an external diameter of 34 mm and an internal diameter of 20 mm. The ring width is 7 mm and the maximum ring thickness 8.55 mm. The material was identified as Kimmeridge shale by one of the authors (MD) and by the late J.M. Jones (see below).

The interior of the ring is very slightly bowed, its shape suggesting that the hole had been cut from both sides of the roughed-out parent disc and the resulting facets had then been ground smooth. The ring's surface is smooth but not highly polished, and the flattish 'upper' and 'lower' sides, and part of the outside of the ring, retain traces of the slight natural irregularities in the stone's texture. The degree of polish varies from area to area, with the flattish surfaces duller than much of the outer edge, and with the outer parts of the hoop's inner surface slightly shinier than its middle. Judging from its disposition, this pattern of variable sheen is more likely to relate to differential polish at the time of manufacture rather than to use-wear. There are no obvious signs of use wear, such as a localised hollow produced by the rubbing of a belt, and so this item need not have been very old when deposited in the grave.

The raw material used for the belt ring was determined using three techniques: microstructural examination using a scanning electron microscope (SEM), qualitative compositional analysis using energy dispersive X-ray analysis (EDS) in the SEM, and examination of a minute detached fragment as a polished specimen, using reflected light microscopy at a magnification of x600. The first two kinds of analysis were undertaken by MD using a CamScan MaXim 2040 analytical SEM with a low vacuum chamber, plus an Oxford

Instruments Link Isis energy dispersive X-ray spectrometer; the low-vacuum setting negated the need to apply a conductive coating to the object. This analysis revealed that the material contained appreciable amounts of iron, plus a higher oxygen to carbon ratio than has been seen in other black materials such as jet, lignite and cannel coal (eg, Davis forthcoming). The fact that it did not contain zirconium accorded with the microstructural (and indeed macroscopic) indications that the material is not jet. Confirmation that the material best matches Kimmeridge shale was provided by the oil-emersion reflected light microscopy undertaken by J.M. Jones, who had access to an extensive reference collection of raw materials.

Discussion

Even though its position in the grave suggests that this item had not been on the deceased's body at the time of burial, it is assumed to have been a belt ring, by analogy with continental European examples (as discussed, for example, by Clarke in his review of this artefact class in 1970, 571–2) and with other, slightly later, British examples whose position with respect to the body is known (eg, cist 6 Borrowstone Farm, Aberdeenshire, and Stanton Harcourt, Oxfordshire, where bone rings were found in the hip area: Shepherd 1986, 13, illus. 13, a; Grimes 1960, figs 66–7). (There is currently no evidence that these rings had been used for an alternative purpose, as securing rings for quiver straps for example, although this possibility cannot be ruled out.) Its possible mode of use, whereby each end of a belt is passed through the ring and knotted, has been shown to be feasible through experimental reconstruction undertaken in connection with this project (cf. Clarke 1970, fig. 144 for the use of perforated or 'handled' examples).

Clarke had observed that some examples had been deliberately roughened on part of their surface as an anti-slip device (ibid., 571); whether the 16 mm wide patch of not-so-polished surface on the outer edge of the hoop served this purpose is uncertain. Although not all examples have been found with archery gear, the wearing of a belt would help to keep the wearer's clothing out of the way during shooting. These objects appear to be predominantly or exclusively associated with males.

Circular belt rings – as distinct from earlier British Neolithic elliptical belt sliders (which Clarke mistook to be derived from Beaker examples: 1970, 100) – represent the adoption of a continental European fashion. Clarke

emphasised the wide distribution of belt rings in earlier Corded Ware/Battle Axe contexts in northern Europe, and argued that this artefact type was adopted by users of Beaker pottery in east-central Europe and the middle Rhine (ibid., 99, 571–2), whence its use spread to Britain. The suggested continental European precursors include 'handled' forms as well as the plain ring form as seen here, and they are most commonly found in bone, with amber examples known from northern Europe. Both plain and 'handled' forms are found in Britain, with examples including the plain bone ring from Wilsford barrow G1 (with a Wessex/Middle Rhine/Step 2 Beaker: ibid., fig. 139; Lanting and van der Waals 1972) and the aforementioned handled bone example from Stanton Harcourt (with a Northern/Middle Rhine/Step 2 Beaker: Clark 1970, fig. 261). It appears that Clarke was basically correct in suggesting a Rhenish and/or east-central European origin for the British examples; belt rings are not a regular feature of Iberian Beaker funerary assemblages (with a rare exception, in bone, noted from El Pago de la Peña, Zamora: Delibes de Castro 1978; Garrido-Pena 1997, 191, pl. 102.16).

The use of belt rings continued in Britain during the currency of Beaker pottery, with variant plain and edge- or transversely-perforated examples emerging, some with decoration (Clarke 1970, fig. 143). Several of these later examples are made of Whitby jet and similar looking materials (Sheridan and Davis 1998; 2002), and more rarely of amber (as at Raunds, Irthlingborough) barrow 1, Northamptonshire (Healy and Harding 2004, 183, fig. 63; Harding and Healy 2007; Davis forthcoming), and Ferry Fryston, West Yorkshire (Howard-Davis 2007). Several bone examples also exist: see, for example, Ritchie (1970) for some Scottish finds.

The choice of Kimmeridge shale – a non-local substance – as the raw material is in keeping both with the calibre of many of the grave goods in this grave, and with the use of this particular material in Beaker graves of the third quarter of the 3rd millennium BC. Kimmeridge is roughly 67 km as the crow flies from Amesbury, but accessible by sea and up the Avon 1–2 days' travel. While one might regard Kimmeridge shale as a southern English substitute for Whitby jet, there is, however, no unequivocal proof of the use of Whitby jet in pre-23rd century Beaker contexts (even though it had previously been used, and moved around the country as a precious and probably amuletic material, during the 4th and early 3rd millennia). The material used for the tiny disc beads in the early composite necklace from Chilbolton, Hampshire, where the primary burial is broadly contemporary with the Amesbury Archer, and Devil's Dyke,

120

Sussex, is shale (probably or definitely from Kimmeridge: Russel 1990; Kinnes 1985, 15–17). It would appear that the 'take-off' period for the use of Whitby jet was the last quarter of the third millennium – Needham's 'fission period', when the use of Beaker pottery and associated artefacts in Britain expanded and diversified (Needham 2005).

If, then, Kimmeridge shale need *not* have been used as a substitute for jet in the Amesbury assemblage, the question arises: was it selected for use just because it was a rare, distinctive, and probably aesthetically pleasing substance – or might it have been ascribed special powers or symbolic significance as well? It does not have the electrostatic property of jet or amber, nor would it have burned in the same distinctive way as these materials (although it does admittedly produce sulphorous fumes and black smoke when burnt); it is these properties that are most likely to have led to a belief in the magical powers of jet and amber (Allason-Jones 1996). However, it is quite possible that colour symbolism did play a part in its choice, given that this does seem to have been a factor in the choice of stone used for the red and black bracers in the Amesbury assemblage. Colour symbolism may also have been involved in the manufacture of the Beakers, with some being a bright red colour. Quite what was the specific significance of red and black is, however, a matter for speculation.

Finally, as regards the deposition of the ring, and indeed other grave goods, away from the body, there is a good (albeit slightly later) parallel for this practice from the aforementioned barrow 1 at Raunds, where an amber belt ring and a set of five V-perforated jet buttons were found (along with other artefacts) beyond the feet; they had probably been deposited in an organic container. This burial (of an adult male) has been dated to 2100–1930 cal BC (UB-3148, 3681±47 BP: Healy and Harding 2004; Harding and Healy 2007).

Copper Dagger and Knives

by Stuart Needham

The copper dagger (ON 6613) was found under the Amesbury Archer's right shoulder and the two copper knives in front of the chest (ON 6620) and the knees (ON 6598)

respectively (Pl. 40; Figs 36; 41). They were studied before and after conservation.

Copper Dagger ON 6613
Condition

A smooth patinated surface is partially intact, mainly light green, but dull green at the top of the blade on both faces. At the blade tip and tang end the patina has flaked patchily o a fractionally lower surface, which is slightly textured but still mainly even, and purple-tinged brown with some orangy spots.

Blade edges are consistently very thin, but only the uppermost stretches show the blade's original outline. The slightly notched and wavy outlines below result from erratic and minor corrosion loss. The centre of the damaged tip is marginally thicker than edges suggesting that the blade was originally longer, though by as little as 2–3 mm. One shoulder is very angular and intact; the other has slight loss along the upper edge. Tang sides and end are all a reduced surface with slight metal loss.

Plate 40 Copper knives from the grave of the Amesbury Archer before conservation: a–c) ON 6620, 6598 and 6613

Morphology and manufacture

Allowing for areas of outline loss, the blade would have had a near triangular shape, one side being gently concave the other perhaps straighter. The lost tip almost certainly would have contracted suddenly in either a linguate or bullet shape. A totally flat mid-blade is delineated by clear but not crisp edge bevels which meet in an acute angle well above the tip (c. 25 mm). The bevels are slightly concave in section and are roughly straight-edged on one face and concave on the other.

The tang expands gradually from its now-rounded butt, the expansion accelerating towards the shoulders. Flattened sides may have been created or accentuated by hammering, to judge from limited stretches of lipping (mini-flanging) up to around 0.4 mm high. An arcuate hilt-line is discernible on both faces, being preserved as a sudden change in patina colour and associated textural differences. Parts of the hilt-lines are also picked out by very slight ridges or grooves. Two tiny lumps on tang face 2 retain a grain structure and are pseudomorphs of an organic hilt (Cowell et al. p. 128 below); the grain is slightly skewed to the long axis.

Dimensions

Extant length 107.0 mm, width of shoulders 32.0 mm, maximum thickness 2.0 mm, thickness at edge bevel c. 1.4 mm, thickness of tang sides 1.1 mm, weight 17.85 g.

Copper knife ON 6598

Condition

Large areas of the tang retain a smooth green patina. A darker green patina on the blade is largely flaked away on face 2, but elsewhere flaking is intermittent and generally confined to edges. The reduced surface is dull, purple-tinged brown with localised orangy brown spots.

The blade edges are thin and sharp, but slightly ragged, probably due to corrosion loss. The more pronounced shoulder is almost intact, the other broken off; despite this difference in condition it is clear that they would not have been exactly symmetrical. There is generally little outline loss around the tang. A fair proportion of patina is intact on one side; the other side is almost totally reduced.

Morphology and manufacture

Allowing for limited outline loss, the blade would have been strongly triangular with just minimal bowing of one side, while the shoulders would appear to have been rounded and prominent but not symmetrical. The tang is long and almost

rectangular with just slight expansion towards the blade. The line of the sides is modified by continuous, somewhat irregular notching, or denticulation. The notches were almost certainly produced by hammering as demonstrated by irregular and slight lipping around many. The indentations at the base of the tang, where it joins the blade, may not, however, be original features.

The mid-blade section is flat inside the bevels, which are set close to their respective edges (the maximum inset being 2.5 mm). The tang section is very slightly swollen. An abrupt change in surface colour and character at the blade/tang junction indicates an arcuate hilt-line that probably continued along the line of the shoulders. A small extraneous pale green patch at the end of the tang on face 1 contains near-longitudinally aligned grain – the pseudomorph of an organic hilt-plate (Cowell et al. p. 128 below).

Dimensions

Length 71.5 mm, extant width of shoulders 23.3 mm, maximum thickness 1.6 mm (around middle of tang), thickness at edge bevels 0.7 mm, maximum thickness of blade 1.4 mm, maximum thickness of tang sides 1.3 mm, width of tang end 11.0 mm, width of tang base 17.1 mm, weight 8.80 g (Fig. 41).

Copper knife ON 6620

Condition

A smooth mid green patina is intact over much of the knife, but is flaked to a fractionally lower surface towards edges and also in centre of blade face 1. This reduced surface is purple-tinged brown mottled with pale dusty green or occasionally orangy brown.

Blade edges are thin, more-or-less sharp, and hold a good even line apart from tiny intermittent irregularities. The tip is similar and there is no reason to suspect preferential outline loss there. The more angular shoulder is intact; the other has tiny loss at the corner. Tang sides are entirely of the reduced surface, but there is no significant loss of outline. Its end is ragged in shape, the deepest notch leading into a hairline crack; there is no evidence to suggest that a rivet hole was present and thinning of the tang suggests it was not much longer when intact.

Morphology and manufacture

The blade is virtually intact, sub-triangular with one side gently concave and the tip probably rounded rather than acute. Shoulders are angular and their slightly sloped upper sides meet the tang in obtuse angles. The tang itself is approaching parallel sided.

There are traces of very slight and diffuse edge bevels, 1.3–1.7 mm wide, between which the blade section is marginally lenticular rather than absolutely flat. Tang faces are, however, flat in section. Its reduced sides retain evidence for more-or-less regular shallow notches, perhaps four on each side. They are likely to have been hammered features, but no surface lipping survives.

An ill-defined arcuate hilt-line at the tang/blade junction is created, in this instance, by an extremely shallow furrow probably made by hammering and/or grinding. One face of the tang just above the hilt-line bears in the patina four or five short transverse incisions or punchmarks. A corrosion-impregnated lump on face 1 of the tang has a longitudinally-aligned grain, being the mineralised remains of an organic hilt (Cowell *et al.* p.128 below).

Dimensions

Extant length 51.7 mm. extant width of shoulders 22.3 mm. width of tang base 13.4 mm, extant width of tang end 9.0 mm, maximum thickness 1.4 (tang/blade junction), thickness at edge bevel *c.* 0.5 mm, maximum thickness of tang sides 1.1 mm, weight 4.30 g (Fig. 41).

Discussion

A brief history of copper dagger/knife study in Britain

In order to appreciate the significance of the copper dagger and knives found with the Amesbury Archer it is necessary to turn to previous studies. Sabine Gerloff reviewed the history of the study of tanged copper daggers and knives up to and including the third quarter of the 20th century (Gerloff 1975, 13–14) and there is no need to do more than reiterate or add a few salient points here. It was once thought that tanged blades were later than flat riveted ones, on the assumption that they were degenerate insular derivations of the first introduced daggers. It was Montelius (1900; 1908) who first recognised their primacy in much of western and northern Europe, seeing them as part of the earliest metallurgy accompanying the spread of Beaker culture.

This became the established opinion thereafter and subsequent metal analyses showed that tanged daggers were of copper, whereas the flat butt-riveted ones were of bronze. At the time when Gerloff was writing in the early 1970s, however,

the two broad types were still set in a relatively compressed chronology, a result of the chronological implications of Sangmeister's reflux horizons. His model suggested that the tanged daggers, along with early metallurgy in general, only reached Britain after the inception of Reinecke A1 on the Continent (ie, *c.* 2200 BC). Since then it has become clear from both reconsideration of relative dating (eg, Burgess 1979; Needham 1979) and a growing number of absolute dates that these arrivals must have preceded A1 and, moreover, that central Europe was not the main source zone. This last point is most graphically illustrated by differences in the composition of metalwork in Chalcolithic north-west Europe and the contemporary material in central Europe (Gerloff 1975, 13, 37; Needham 2002). The Amesbury Archer's copper implements are consistent with these prevailing composition patterns – to be discussed further below.

Gerloff had to work with a rather small number of examples, just 24 (including the 'knife-daggers with projecting butt, no. 237–40), of which three blades without context (no. 8, 17A, 18) are anomalous in form relative to the early insular series and are thus best set aside. Nevertheless, the remaining 21 examples were still varied in size and detailed form and not unrepresentative of western European Beaker tanged daggers generally. Since then a further 16 examples have come to light in Britain, almost doubling the sample and giving much more scope for identifying meaningful trends.

Gerloff had suggested three divisions of tanged daggers and knives, but she left half the known implements ungrouped or only loosely connected to a group (Gerloff 1975, 27–31). Attribution was complicated because classification involved a flexible combination of absolute size and morphological traits; while size was deemed important, it was not used as an overarching defining feature – so, for example, the Winterslow piece was placed with the long Roundway group blades rather than the comparable length Mere group blades. Differentiation between these two types on the basis of 'rounded' or 'drooping' shoulders now looks rather arbitrary; nor does blade shape discriminate between them.

Although Gerloff recognised that the presence of rivet holes or notches in tangs and shoulders could be significant in terms of background or technical development (see also Clarke 1970, 260–1), even here her classification lacks consistency. Although most riveted examples known at the time were small blades ('knife-daggers'), two (no. 12–13) were placed alongside unriveted examples – in her 'group Dorchester' – and four others were left to form a 'not homogeneous' group (Gerloff 1975, 27, nos 14–17).

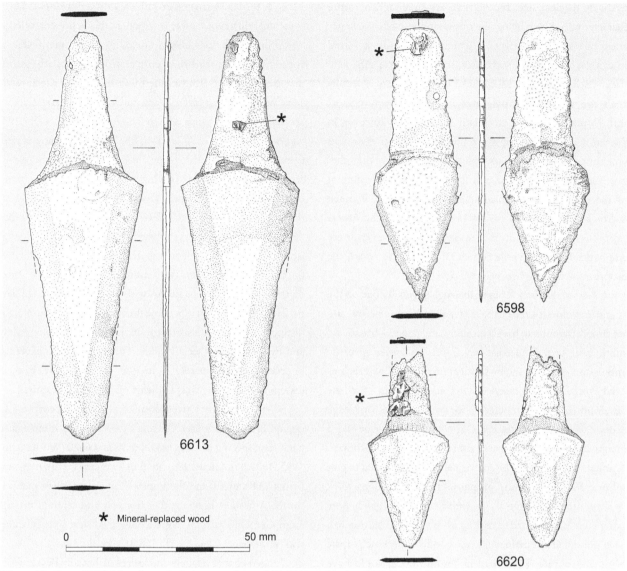

Figure 41 Grave 1289 (Amesbury Archer); copper dagger ON 6613 and knives ON 6620 and 6598. For each object Face 1 is shown on the left and Face 2 on the right

The Amesbury Archer's dagger and knives

Turning now to the Amesbury Archer's three implements, the first point is that all are of copper, as would be expected of the type. This places them essentially in the newly defined Chalcolithic (or Period 1; Allen *et al.* forthcoming). To comprehend developments in style and technology more empirically, two major aspects of form have been classified afresh – tang shape and the presence/absence of rivets – and correlated with one another. These particular attributes form the basis of the new classification because they show the most significant correlations with other types associated in graves; it has been possible to define four main association groups (Ia, Ib, II, III). The overall pattern of correlations and details of relevant finds are given elsewhere (Needham forthcoming). Although not used in defining the main classes,

there are other attributes that can be relevant to function, production tradition and mode of hilt fixing – notably blade length, blade shape and the treatment of tang sides; these are discussed below. The Amesbury Archer's implements lack any rivet emplacements (classification: 'A') and tang shapes are form '3' for the dagger and form '2' for the two knives. These feature combinations (A3, A2) are amongst the earliest for tanged daggers in Britain and were probably mainly current during the earlier half of the Chalcolithic, *c.* 2450–2300 BC.

In the tanged dagger/knife series as a whole blade length ranges widely, from 50 mm to 300 mm, and blade shapes form a spectrum from linguate to triangular. These attributes do not obviously have significant correlations with chronology or associated material. The three tanged copper implements present in the Amesbury Archer's grave are of relatively modest size. Indeed, two are small and of knife character rather than being obvious weapons, while the larger one is of a size (approaching 110 mm) that is usually referred to as a dagger when in such early Beaker contexts. Absolute size in itself may not be strictly relevant to meaning, especially at a stage when metal would presumably have been in short and fluctuating supply (Needham 1999a, 187). However, in the case of the Amesbury Archer's implements there are other important distinctions between ON 6613 and the other two; these are seen in blade proportions and the treatment of the edge bevel. The blade (excluding the tang) is much narrower on ON 6598 (w/l = 0.43) relative to the others (0.65–0.71). Variation in this respect is echoed even more emphatically in the whole British tanged dagger series, the proportions ranging between 0.25 and 0.88.

A second distinction lies in the edge bevels. Those on the larger implement ON 6613, rather than being narrow and seemingly functional, have a more ornate quality – broad and subtly hollowed. The edge bevels on the knives give the impression of being the by-product of repeated whetting as need arose during use. This could account for the development of asymmetry if, for some reason, one edge experienced preferential use, for both have one edge marginally concave, the other marginally convex. Alternatively, this might be an original feature designed to give subtly different functional properties to the two edges.

In contrast, the large blade seems to have been given more symmetry. If wear had necessitated re-sharpening, this had been done skilfully, maintaining the goodly appearance of the blade and bevels. The broad hollowed bevels would have caught the light in a more responsive way than the minimalist bevels on the associated knives.

In terms of shape, the best parallels in Britain for ON 6613 are blades from Mere G6a, Wiltshire (Gerloff 1975, no. 6) and Stuston Common, Suffolk (Pendleton 1999, 193), and for ON 6620, from the Inverurie district, Aberdeenshire (Gerloff 1975, no. 11), and Chilbolton, Hampshire (Russel 1990), although Inverurie lacks any tang-side denticulation, having slight flanges instead. Among the small Irish corpus, those from Kilnagarnagh, Co. Offaly, and an unprovenanced one are good shape matches for ON 6613 (Harbison 1969, no. 3, 7).

Despite the insular focus thus far, the Beaker tanged copper dagger implement series is renowned for its degree of international uniformity and some attention needs to be paid to Continental comparisons. Among Dutch finds, the blades from Ginkelse Heide and Exloo perhaps have most in common with ON 6613 (Butler and van der Waals 1966, 60–

1, no. 6, 9). Squat triangular knives, although present, have somewhat different tang forms (where this is not corroded).

Although French blades are quite numerous, Gallay's corpus (1981) surprisingly contains no particularly good matches for ON 6613. On the other hand there are several squat near-triangular blades with more-or-less sharp shoulders and relatively stout tangs with much resemblance to ON 6598 and 6620 (ibid., no. 52–7, 85–6, 88–90). Tang shape varies from near-parallel sided – type Soyons – to broad trapezoid – amongst type Fontbuisse. Another with a narrow, tapered tang has since been published from Enencourt-Leage, Oise (Blanchet 1984, 93, fig. 39). Two or three examples (coming from both Gallay's types) show evidence of denticulated tang sides, another point of comparison. However, while the trapezoid tanged variant is a feature of the Fontbuisse zone of the Midi, the Soyons blades with their tangs more similar to those found with the Amesbury Archer occur in two distinct areas: three finds distributed down the Rhône valley and two in Centre-Ouest France. These at least are likely to be connected intimately to major axes of early Beaker dissemination to the west and east of the Massif Central.

Squat triangular knives dominate the small corpus of tanged blades from east Germany and Poland, some again paralleling specific features at ON 6598 and 6620 (Wüstemann 1995, 199–206; Gedl 1980, no. 66). The east German group forms a cluster around the upper Elbe. An excellent parallel for the Amesbury knives comes from far into central Europe, from Gemeinlebarn, St Pölten, Lower Austria (Neugebauer and Neugebauer-Maresch 2001, 430, 435, fig. 1.6; 7).

Tanged copper daggers and knives of broadly Beaker type are more frequent finds in Iberia than any other part of the Beaker world, In part the large number is a reflection of the longevity of the type there; Brandherm sees the whole series, a much more diverse series than found in north-west Europe, as spanning the whole of the Iberian Early Bronze Age (Brandherm 2003, 24 fig. 2, end pull-out). This makes the later examples contemporary with at least some of the butt-riveted daggers that span Periods 2–4 in Britain. A good proportion of the implements in Brandherm's corpus retain an omega hilt-line, a feature which in the British sequence seems to replace the standard early arcuate line only as tanged daggers were giving way to butt-riveted ones. There are nevertheless some good matches for the Amesbury blades, as might be expected given the numbers involved. Many Iberian blades, especially among Brandherm's series F, G, H and I, are squat in proportions and comparable to Amesbury ON 6598 and 6620. Intriguingly, some of these series are focussed on the southern half of the peninsula, but G and

H are more often from the northern strip and the Tagus estuary (Lisbon district). Just to pick out one example: a knife from the well-known Chalcolithic fortified site of Vila Nova de São Pedro (Brandherm 2003, no 96) has a broad parallel-sided tang above marked shoulders at the top of a squat triangular blade, an overall shape very similar to ON 6598 and 6620.

This is far from an exhaustive search for continental parallels. Nevertheless, it is clear that good parallels, some of which may be fortuitous because of the limited spectrum of variation within the early Beaker production tradition, are widespread. Of particular interest in the context of Amesbury Archer is that squat triangular variants similar to ON 6598 and 6620 are widespread across the Beaker domains of western Europe, penetrating as far east as the culture in general did. Such a wide distribution has been more generally acknowledged for the more 'classic' Beaker tanged daggers.

Because it is such an unparalleled circumstance, we need to go on to ask why there were three similar implements in the one grave with just one corpse. It is possible that more than one function is implied; one other grave, Dorchester-on-Thames XII, Oxfordshire, has two implements (Gerloff 1975, no. 10, 239) and their blade lengths do in fact bear comparison with the two sizes found with the Amesbury Archer. But this does not help explain why there was yet a third one.

One feature of the Amesbury Archer's instruments – their chemical signature – suggests two very different ultimate histories. Blades ON 6613 and 6620 are very similar in composition to one another (Cowell *et al.* below) and are close in character to *Bell Beaker* metal (BB-metal), which is a regular component of the metal in Chalcolithic graves in Britain; in fact over half of analysed copper daggers/knives have this metal composition. Conformity to the elemental ranges defined for BB-metal in north-west Europe (Needham 2002, 114, fig. 7) is generally good, but the values for antimony (0.4% and 0.5%) are at the very top of that element's range; the same is true of the lead values (0.08% and 0.09%). The method of analysis employed for these fragile objects may not accurately represent their true average composition.

In contrast, ON 6598 has a chemical signature which can be termed *Arsenic-only* metal (As-only metal); arsenic is the only 'impurity' element present above low levels (threshold 0.08%), in this case at 0.6%. This composition seems to correspond well with a good number of copper objects from western France (and further south), but is rarely found in copper metalwork from Britain and Ireland (*ibid.*, 107–9, fig. 5, left).

The metal compositions of the Amesbury Archer's blades thus link them to a much broader composition continuum running from the Lower Rhine, through northern and western France to Iberia (*ibid.*). A few BB-metal compositions have been found in contemporary material further east into central Europe: for example, there are just four in the list of 56 analyses of Bell Beaker metalwork in Austria, Moravia, and Bohemia published by Bertemes and Šebela (1998, 235, table iii). It is significant that none is present amongst the Corded Ware-associated metalwork also listed by those authors. The same pattern applies to As-only compositions in that dataset: whereas five examples come from Bell Beaker contexts, none is from a Corded Ware context. It is clear, therefore, that in central Europe Bell Beaker groups were responsible for the arrival of a limited supply of BB-metal and As-only metal, and this was presumably drawn from their westerly contacts. Again in southern France, where Cabrières metal dominated, BB compositions are exceptional and associated with Bell Beaker contexts, as in the dagger from the La Fare, Alpes-de-Haut-Provence, grave (Ambert 2001, 580, fig. 1). This picture is significant for the Amesbury Archer; it means that even if he brought the dagger and knives with him from the south-east, their contained metal had almost certainly originated in Atlantic Europe.

Despite the clear regional picture, the specific source areas for these two metal compositions are uncertain. A case has been made for northern Spain having been *one* source of BB-metal (Needham 2002); certain mines in Asturias have been shown to have been exploited during the third quarter of the 3rd millennium BC and analysis of ores indicates that appropriate impurity suites were present. There are indications, however, from the distribution of elements through the full spectrum of BB-metal that more than one chemical composition may be involved and this could imply more than one source input. There is also the possibility of some small admixture of other metals during recycling, even at this early date. It is not impossible that similar ores yielding a broadly similar impurity pattern were being exploited elsewhere along the Atlantic façade, conceivably in western France or south-west England. The latter area has been given serious consideration because of the 'radiogenic' character of lead isotope results for the five analysed copper objects with BB-metal signature (Rohl and Needham 1998, 88). The 'radiogenic' character is the result of the close proximity of uranium in the copper ore body, a situation that does also occur elsewhere, although not often.

A better understanding of the internal variations within BB-metal is only likely to come in the future from a

126

programme of lead isotope analyses (assuming sufficient lead present). For the present, it is possible to say with some confidence that the impurity suite defined as BB-metal was introduced to Britain as part of the primary Beaker package and, at this stage, would indicate metal from established exploitation further south in Atlantic Europe. However, it is possible if not likely that in time the Beaker economy stimulated the exploitation of new sources yielding copper with a similar signature in Beaker occupied/acculturated zones, so we cannot assume that all BB-metal was imported from the Continent. In the case of ON 6613 and 6620, the fact that their context is fairly early in the British Beaker sequence might give preference to a continental origin for the metal. The third blade (ON 6598) poses less of a problem since there is no real case for Arsenic-only type compositions having emanated from insular ores exploited in the Chalcolithic or Early Bronze Age. Consequently, it is highly probable that it was made of metal won in either western France or Iberia where Chalcolithic objects of this composition abound. The fact that there are some good form comparisons in these regions allows, moreover, the possibility that it was the knife itself that was imported, not just the metal.

Both copper metal types present in the Amesbury Archer's grave have arsenic as a significant impurity giving them similar working and hardness properties, so the Amesbury Archer or his metalworker would not have been conscious at an empirical level of the difference. Nevertheless if, as suspected, the dagger and knives originated in different metal-producing zones, it is possible that he would have been aware of this either through direct experience of their origins or through the conveyance of oral information with the objects. This could perhaps have given the two apparently similar knives discrete significance in the eyes of the Amesbury Archer. Given the massive changes in the scale and nature of elite social interactions brought to north-west Europe by early Beaker culture, it is entirely feasible that an individual such as the Amesbury Archer could have drawn social capital from the fact that he possessed copper objects from more than one ultimate 'source'.

Hilting

How the tanged copper daggers and knives were hilted is not well understood; no hilts survive for these Beaker implements. The curved hilt-lines that are regularly in evidence suggest that hilt-plates of some relatively hard material which could be cut to shape were placed against either face. This is supported by the vestigial traces of a fine-grained material on

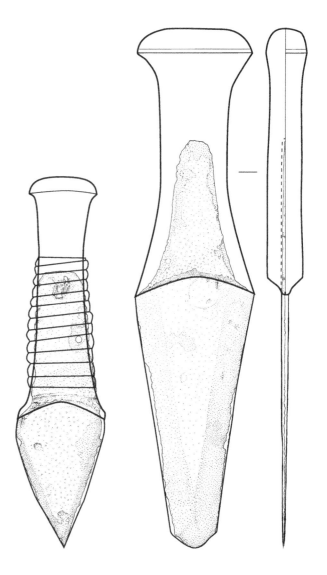

Figure 42 Possible hilt arrangements for knife ON 6620 and dagger ON 6613

all three of the Amesbury Archer's implements – in one case identified to oak (Cowell *et al.* below; Fig. 41). This indicates that the hilt was not simply a leather binding. The key questions for reconstruction are, firstly, would the hilt have been the same width as the tang or broader and, secondly, if broader, was the hilt in one part or two?

The denticulation on the tang sides of the Amesbury knives is a feature that recurs intermittently through the Beaker tanged implement series. Alternatively, other tangs have slight flanging down the sides. Both features would seem to imply that the blades in question had rather narrow hilt-plates leaving the tang's edges just exposed: the sandwich of hilt-plates and tang would then be bound together and where denticulation was present, the first coils of binding would nestle into the notches thus minimising the risk of lateral movement and retaining a tight bind. This may have been important at a time when no rivets pierced through the different components to maintain alignment. One result of this hilt construction would be to leave the binding as the outer, visible layer for much of the handle. In fact rare examples of flint knives/daggers with intact hafts from the west Alpine lake settlements of Charavines and Vinelz, of Final Neolithic date, had external thong-binding for the full length of the handle (Mallet 1992, pl. 33–4; 54). This would be good for hand grip but it does result in a straight hilt-line at variance with the arcuate ones consistently seen on tanged copper blades. It is therefore likely that on the Amesbury Archer's knives the binding did not continue right down to the blade junction (Fig. 42, a). Lower down, the hilt-plates doubtless splayed out, for the arcuate hilt-lines are often seen to extend the full width of the blade at the shoulders. In this mode of hafting, therefore, binding would occupy just a central band of the hilt, providing a contrast with exposed horn or wood above and below.

The hilt arrangement for the dagger could have been rather different (Fig. 42, b). There are no tang denticulations and if the hilt-plates were kept to the width of the tang they would result in a narrow hilt grip becoming even narrower upwards. It seems more likely in this instance that the hilt was wider than the tang. If made in two parts, two issues would need to be solved; firstly, the tang would have to be sunk into a correspondingly shaped recess on the inner face of one or both plates; then, the unit would have to be bound together,

Table 21: Results of X-ray fluorescence (XRF) analysis of the copper dagger and knives from grave 1289 (Amesbury Archer)

%	ON 6613 dagger	ON 6598 knife	OM 6620 knife
Cu	98	99	98
Zn	<0.1	<0.1	<0.1
Sn	<0.05	<0.05	<0.05
Pb	0.08	0.03	0.09
Bi	0.1	<0.03	<0.03
As	1.1	0.6	1
Sb	0.4	<0.1	0.5
Fe	<0.05	<0.05	<0.05
Co	<0.1	<0.1	<0.1
Ni	0.5	<0.03	0.3
Ag	<0.03	<0.03	<0.03

The precision (reproducibility) of the results is c. ±1–2% for copper and c. ±10–30% relative for the other elements. The accuracies cannot be clearly defined for the reasons outlined in the text

again resulting in visible binding (assuming there were no rivets/pegs beyond the tang's limits). Alternatively, a single-piece carved hilt could have been carefully socketed to receive the tang. Since the tang is long and very thin, the cutting of a tightly fitting hole would be nigh impossible; in practice it would probably have to be cut somewhat bigger, the gaps then being neatly wedged to grip the tang. On this reconstruction the mineralised wooden remnants attached to the blade would be from wedges rather than the main hilt. This sort of hilt has been found occasionally on later daggers and knives.

Scientific Examination and Analysis of the Copper Dagger and Knives
by Mike Cowell, Caroline Cartwright, and Susan La Niece

Analysis
The dagger and knives were analysed by X-ray fluorescence under the same operating conditions as for the cushion stone (p. 117 above). The analysis of each was carried out on a small area (about 1 mm²) abraded on the hilt. The abrasion was carried out using a scalpel and, with minimal intrusion, was intended to remove corrosion and expose a metal surface representative of the bulk of the artefact. X-ray fluorescence is essentially a surface analysis technique (with a depth of analysis up to about 100 μm in metalwork) which, for accurate results, requires a homogeneous and uncorroded metal surface. For the dagger (ON 6613), the metal exposed appeared to be almost free of corrosion but for the smaller and thinner knives more red copper oxide (cuprite) seemed to be present in the analysed area. Oxidation and corrosion of the metal will alter its surface composition, to an indefinable extent, because of the differing reactivity and mobility of its elemental components. Therefore, as all the artefacts appear to have some internal corrosion, the accuracy of the quantitative analyses will be less than ideal.

The approximate results obtained are shown in Table 21. All the implements are of impure copper with arsenic being the main impurity. The dagger, ON 6613 and one of the knives, ON 6620, are of very similar composition with comparable amounts of As, Sb, Ni, and Pb but they differ in the presence of bismuth. It is not possible to say if they are likely to be from the same batch of metal but they could have originated from a similar source. The second knife, ON 6598, is significantly different from the other two in having only one principal impurity, arsenic, which is also at a lower concentration than in the other two implements. The arsenic content, assuming it is fully dissolved in, or alloyed with, the copper will modify the metallurgical properties of the implements (see below). Even at these low levels, copper-arsenic alloys, when cold-worked, will work-harden to a modest extent more than pure copper.

The analyses have been compared with the composition groups of Chalcolithic copper-based metalwork from western Europe discussed by Needham (2002). The large and small knives are within the composition range shown by the Bell Beaker metalwork group (BB) which is particularly characterised by high traces of arsenic, medium traces of antimony and nickel, and low (or undetectable) traces of silver. Even if an allowance is made for the possible large systematic errors in the results due to corrosion effects, the composition is still compatible with BB metalwork. The BB group has been sub-divided by lower and higher nickel contents (LNBB and HNBB respectively) and the nickel contents of the knives correspond more closely with the HNBB sub-group. However, due to the uncertain accuracy and the possibility that the nickel contents may be over-estimated, the knives cannot be confidently classified to specific sub-groups. Needham (2002) has noted the similarity in the composition of BB, particularly HNBB, metal with ore sources and artefacts from Spain and the Pyrenees.

The medium sized knife (ON 6598) is made of arsenical copper with only lead otherwise detectable. Its composition corresponds closely with the Chalcolithic metalwork group 'arsenic-only metal' which has a strong geographical association with western France but is also frequent in metalwork from Spain (Needham 2002).

Hafting

On both sides of the tang of the dagger (ON 6613) there are traces of a heavily mineral-replaced wood (Fig. 41) which was examined under an optical microscope. Sufficient diagnostic features were present to allow the identification of the wood to *Quercus* sp. (oak). Oak wood was frequently selected for the hafting of prehistoric metalwork in Britain, second only to the use of ash wood. Wood-like traces on the two knives were too vestigial for identification. On the radiographic image (Pl.

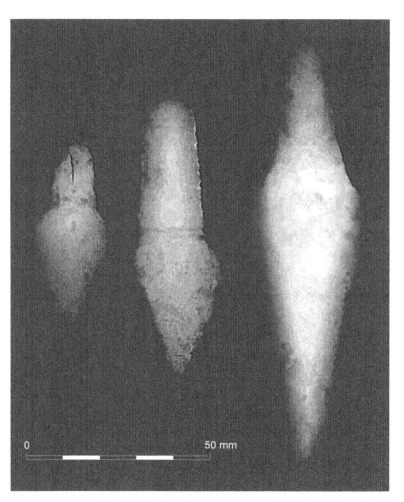

Plate 41 Radiograph of copper knives ON 6620, 6598 and 6613 from the grave of the Amesbury Archer

41) of ON 6598, there are two dark lines across the tang, one near the blade and the other 5–7 mm from the tip of the tang. These would appear to be shallow grooves, whether deliberately incised or caused by wear or corrosion is not known, but it seems reasonable to relate them to the binding of a lost hafting material. There is a faint line across the tang of knife ON 6620, but none is visible on the dagger ON 6613.

Metallography

All of the implements are too thin and fragile to allow safe polishing and etching of a metallographic section; this would be the normal method of revealing metal structure and establishing the processes used to make the knives. Hardness testing was also considered too risky. Radiography is another method of establishing the manufacturing stages for a metal artefact and has the advantage of being totally non-destructive, but it can rarely give as conclusive results as metallography. The radiographs of the two smaller knives are dappled by a network of corrosion pits, which appear darker (ie, less dense). Although some directionality can be observed in these features on the blade of the medium sized knife, there is insufficient evidence to conclude that these indicate working or are residual casting structures. Radiography also revealed hair-line cracks, notably one across the tip of ON 6598, confirming their fragile condition.

The dagger, which is in sounder condition than the knives, is more informative. At high magnification there are no signs of casting porosity and numerous fine linear features can be discerned in the blade. The tentative interpretation of these features is that they are slip lines, particularly evident on the blade. One or two parallel pairs of stronger lines can be seen which closely resemble annealing twins. No grain boundaries are apparent but the grouping of the slip lines suggest equiaxed grains about 3 mm across. If this interpretation is accepted, it indicates that the knife was worked and annealed, followed by cold working of the blade. This would indicate knowledge, on the part of the metal smith, of the properties of the metal and how they could be improved. Tylecote (1986) summarised the effect of different working treatments on copper containing arsenic at the levels seen in these copper knives (0.6–1.0%). It was observed that the influence of arsenic on the strength of copper in the cast or annealed condition is relatively slight, but cold working has a considerable effect, increasing the hardness and much improving the edge as a cutting tool. This would have very clear advantages for an implement such as a knife or dagger.

Gold Basket-shaped Ornaments from Graves 1291 (Amesbury Archer) and 1236

by Stuart Needham

The Amesbury Archer

The two gold basket-shaped ornaments (ON 6446, 6589) were found in front of the knees (Pl. 42; Figs 36; 40). They were studied both before and after conservation.

ON 6589
Condition
The ornament has a dull gold sheen throughout. There is slight buckling of the basket and a sharper bend at the beginning of the tang. The tang end is straight but not quite square to the long axis; under magnification slight irregularities suggest the terminal has been torn off. Otherwise all edges are intact but there are small invasive tears

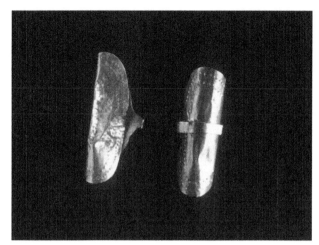

Plate 42 Gold basket ornaments from the grave of the Amesbury Archer ON 6589 (left) and ON 6446 (right)

into the basket either side of where the tang curls around it. In addition, this stretch of the edge had the most buckled surface suggesting that at one time the tang was more tightly drawn round the basket; currently there is a 1 mm gap.

Facets run along the curled basket, perhaps due to the original rolling not achieving a perfectly smooth curve.

Morphology and manufacture
In its pre-curled state the basket would be a slightly asymmetric oval with neat, extremely thin edges, mainly 0.05–0.1 mm. There is a minor asymmetry either side of the basket/tang junction, one side being angular, the other having a short diagonal stretch across the angle; magnification shows the latter to have been modified by a ground bevel on the inside. The tang itself is parallel-sided and thicker than the basket, 0.15–0.3 mm; its sides were finished by grinding, giving varied profiles from rounded to double-faceted, or even triple-faceted. The majority of fine grinding/polishing striations on the tang faces are longitudinal.

Pointillé decoration
There are two rows of dots outlining the basket edge, but broken at the base of the tang. The decoration was impressed from the inside outwards before the object was curled. The outer has 62 dots, of which three are double-struck and one has a tear through it. The inner circuit comprises 51, of which one is double-struck. They are roughly circular, but not very regularly impressed leading to variation in size, mostly 0.2–0.3 mm diameter.

A few dots to either side of the break at the base of the tang are reduced by wear or compression relative to the majority; this is most marked in the two dots closest to the

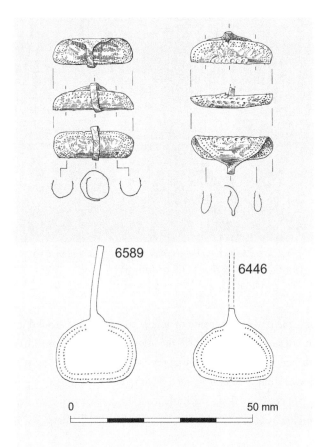

Figure 43 Grave 1289 (Amesbury Archer); gold ornaments ON 6589 and 6446

tang. There is also possible reduction of two or three inner circuit dots just to one side of the current tang position.

Dimensions
Diameter of basket 6–7 mm, maximum width of basket 21.9 mm, width of tang base 1.6 mm, width of tang end (break) 1.5 mm, maximum width of tang 1.8 mm, depth of basket (flattened out) *c.* 15 mm, length of tang *c.* 16 mm, thickness of tang 0.15–0.3 mm, thickness of basket edge 0.05–0.1 mm; weight 0.48 g.

ON 6446
Condition
Unlike its pair, this piece is severely crushed and most of the tang has broken off. The main damage to the basket is a marked fold half way round its curled profile. This fold is rather rounded at either end, whereas in a 10 mm central section it has been sharply crimped – as folded paper. Inset by almost 1 mm from this sharp fold is a row of small contiguous impressions. Individual impressions fall into two shapes: elongate ones aligned perpendicular to the edge and smaller approximately round ones. They are not wholly

regular in disposition and some may be double-struck, but a 7 mm stretch contains a more regular run of 8–10 oval impressions; they give the impression of having been punched with a very finely toothed instrument but, if so, would have had to be struck twice, once from each face. In fact the crimped effect would more readily be produced by a simultaneous pincer-action, but it is hard to envisage such a tool at this period.

The basket edge opposite the tang is buckled, has invasive tears as far as the inner pointillé row and two radial creases – one just beginning to tear. As with its pair, it seems likely that these damage features are ancient and arose from the tight clamping of the tang around the basket.

Morphology and manufacture
Unfurled, the sheet of gold would have had a shape almost identical to its pair (more so than in Fig. 43), even to the point of the asymmetry at the tang/basket junction. It seems possible that they were cut around the same pattern, or one from the other. All basket edges are extremely thin and neat, those of the tang stump a little thicker. A stretch alongside one edge shows evidence for localised folding or lapping of gold folios, pressed back into the surface during the original working.

Pointillé decoration
Two rows of peripheral dots comprise some 76 in the outer row, not entirely evenly spaced, and 62 in the inner row of which four were double-struck. Average dot diameter is 0.2 mm. The rows, which were made from the outside inwards, are not quite complete circuits, there being a break at the base of the tang. They were executed with a fine, near-round ended tool. In the damaged area opposite the tang several dots are more-or-less effaced due to wear or pressure.

Dimensions
Width of basket 22.3 mm, width of tang base 2 mm, depth of basket (flattened out) *c.* 15 mm, length of tang *c.* 4 mm, thickness of basket edge 0.05–0.15 mm, thickness of tang end (break) 0.25 mm, weight 0.41 g.

The 'Companion's' Basket-shaped Ornaments

The two gold ornaments in the 'Companion's' grave (ON 6708) were found, one inside the other, inside the right jaw of the skeleton (Pl. 22; Figs 23; 25) when it was being cleaned after excavation. ON 6708a is the outer ornament, ON 6708b the inner one. Until the final stages of analysis, when it was considered by the author that it was safe to separate them, the objects were left as they were found.

ON 6708a

Condition

A complete ornament with bright gold exterior and matt interior speckled with soil traces. The curvature of the tight curling is not even: there are two rounded angles across the basket, another at the tang/basket junction and two more across the tang (one corresponding to that on the underlapping basket). Edges are generally crisp with little sign of wear. A 4–5 mm stretch of the basket edge is bent inwards; this is currently offset relative to where the tang curls round, but the latter appears to be pulled a little to one side and the bend was undoubtedly caused by the tang being pulled round firmly.

Morphology and manufacture

In uncurled state, the basket would be near elliptical in shape with perhaps a slight asymmetry between the base and the top (leading into the tang). The angles meeting the tang are sharp and approach right-angles. The tang tapers only very gradually. The surface is covered with dense, very fine striations; on the basket they are multi-directional and sometimes overlapping, on the tang, predominantly longitudinal.

Pointillé decoration

Dots, mainly 0.2–0.4 mm in diameter, were impressed from the inside by a fine round-ended tool; there are very occasional minute perforations where the punch has gone through the sheet-metal. Despite the minuteness of the decoration, no dots appear to be double-struck – each is a single clean impression. The outer row has about 95 dots, the inner row about 68 (accurate counts not possible because of stretch concealed by tang). To the naked eye dot spacing looks quite regular, but concentricity is less good and there are occasional kinks in the lines. The rows are not quite complete circuits, there being a break at the base of the tang; dots may be a little less well defined as they approach this break, possibly due to wear.

Dimensions

Diameter of basket 6–7 mm, width of basket 22.2 mm, width of tang base 3.6 mm, width of tang end (curving) c. 2 mm, depth of basket (flattened out) 15.5 mm, length of tang 19.5 mm, thickness of edge ≤0.1 mm, weight 0.39 g.

ON 6708b

Condition

A complete ornament, the exterior bright gold with coppery patches, the interior matt. The curvature of the tight curling is not even throughout: in particular, there is tighter curvature across the middle of the basket, a rounded angle across its base, and an angle across the tang; the latter more or less aligned with an angle on ON6708a. Edges are generally crisp with little sign of wear. The basket base has been indented where the tang curls round it, this time resulting in a more sinuous line, but one clearly related to pressure from the tang.

Morphology and manufacture

In uncurled state, the ornament would be very similar in shape to ON 6708a, although there is a minor difference in the tang end where the sides curve in quickly and are then truncated by a near-flat end. The basket surface is probably covered with dense striations as ON 6708a, but colour makes them harder to observe; on the tang they are both longitudinal and diagonal.

Pointillé decoration

Dots are the same in character as on the pair ornament, but different in number – about 104 in the outer row, about 84 in the inner row. Again the concentricity of the two rows is not especially good relative to one another and the basket edge. Dots are more definitely fainter towards the break, presumably due to preferential wear here.

Dimensions

Diameter of basket 6–7 mm, width of basket 22 mm, width of tang base 3.9 mm, width of tang end (curving) c. 2.7 mm, depth of basket (flattened out) 15.5 mm, length of tang 18.5 mm, thickness of edge c. 0.1 mm, weight 0.38 g.

Basket-shaped Ornaments and Primary Beaker Goldwork

The British gold basket-shaped ornaments have always excited much interest because of their early associations, showing that they are among the earliest goldwork in north-west Europe. The most recent discussions have been by Sherratt (1986), Russel (1990), Barclay and Wallis (1999), and O'Connor (2004). Until fairly recently finds were few – three pairs (Radley, Boltby Scar, Orbliston) and a singleton (Kirkhaugh) – but since 1986 the number has more than doubled (Table 22; also O'Connor 2004, 211). In addition to

Table 22: Atlantic gold basket ornaments

Site	W	D	W/D	Grp	Edge decoration				Internal dec.		Tang dec.	Comments/ references
					1	2	3	4	Bands	no		
Estremoz	46	41	1.0	A	2	–	–	–	–	–	–	V. short tang, ?broken; Armbruster & Parreira 1993, 158–9
Ermegeira A	35	43	0.8	A	2	–	–	–	–	–	–	Taylor 1980, pl. 3j;
Ermegeira B	34	41	0.8	A	2	–	–	–	–	–	–	Armbruster & Parreira 1993, 156–7
Dacomet/Benraw	43	45	0.95	A	3	–	–	–	–	–	–	short tang; Taylor 1980, pl. 3h–i; O'Connor 2004, 208, fig. 18.3
Gilmorton A	34	43	0.8	A	1							Needham 2008a
Gilmorton B	34	c. 43	0.8	A	1							
Cova da Moura	–	–	–	?A	1	–	–	–	–	–	–	Galay & Spindler 1970, 48 fig. 11
Boscombe Down Grave 1A, ON 6589	22	16	1.4	B(i)	2	–	–	–	–	–	–	this volume
Boscombe Down Grave 1B, ON 6446	22	15	1.5	B(i)	2	–	–	–	–	–	–	
Boscombe Down 2A, ON 6708a	22	15.5	1.4	B(i)	2	–	–	–	–	–	–	
Boscombe Down 2B, ON 6708b	22	15.5	1.4	B(i)	2	–	–	–	–	–	–	
Kirkhaugh	35	28	1.25	B(i)	2	–	–	–	2	1	Dots	cross-lines converge to tang base & are bold repoussée; Clarke 1970, 281, fig. 3; Clarke et al. 1985, 86 pl. 4.7, 269
Boltby Scar A	32	19.5	1.7	B(i)	1	–	2	–	–	–	–	Taylor 1980, pl. 3e; Clarke
Boltby Scar B	30.5	19	1.6	B(i)	1	–	2	–	–	–	–	et al. 1985, 187 pl. 5.18, 269
Stogursey	29	18	1.6	B(i)	3	–	2	–	2	2	–	Needham 2001; O'Connor 2004, 207 fig. 18.2
Colledic	?	?	(1.7)	B(i)	1	–	1	–	≥4	4, 3	–	c. half basket extant? Taylor 1994, 46, 59 pl. 20
Chilbolton 2A	26	15	1.7	B(ii)	–	1	2	–	2	7	–	Russel 1990; Kinnes 1994, A17
Chilbolton 2B	25	15	1.7	B(ii)	–	1	2	–	2	5	Line	
Chilbolton 1A	45	(22)	2.0	B(ii)	–	–	2	–	2	3	Line	
Chilbolton 1B	46	22	2.1	B(ii)	–	–	2	–	2	3	Line	
Calbourne	41	21	2.0	B(ii)	–	–	3	–	2	5, 4	–	tang broken off ; secondary perforations; Needham 2008b
Radley A	47	20	2.3	B(ii)	–	–	2	–	2	6	Line	Case 1977b, 24, fig. 4.12–13; Taylor 1980, pl. 3d; Clarke et al. 1985, 92 pl. 4.13, 265; Sherratt 1986, 63 fig. 1; Barclay & Halpin 1999, 154 fig. 5.4
Radley B	47	20	2.3	B(ii)	–	–	2	–	2	6	Line	
Belleville A	86	28	3.1	C	1	–	1	–	10	3	–	no tang, perforations; Case 1977b, 24, fig. 4.1–4
Belleville B	104	30	3.5	C	1	–	1	–	9	3	–	
Belleville C	84	28	3.1	C	1	–	1	–	10	3	–	
Co. Cavan (?Belleville)	106	30	3.5	C	1	–	1	–	10	3	–	
Ireland, no location A	132	36	3.7	C	–	–	–	–	–	–	–	thin hooked tangs; Case 1977b, 24, fig. 4.7–8; Taylor
Ireland, no location B	128	38	3.4	C	–	–	–	–	–	–	–	1980, pl. 3g
Orbliston A	135	30	4.5	D	1	–	2	1	–	–	–	second ornament lost; Taylor 1980, pl. 3f; Clarke et al 1985, 188 pl. 5.19, 269

Notes: most dimensions taken from publications; those of depth of basket unfurled (D), in particular, are estimates

Key: W – width of basket; D – depth of basket; *Edge decoration:* 1 = number of dot row(s); 2 = number of dashed lines; 3 = number of continuous lines; 4 = number of 'ladders' (row of transverse strokes); *Internal decoration:* Bands = number of bands of cross-lines in total; No. = number of lines per band

the two pairs from Boscombe Down, a further two pairs were excavated from two intercutting Beaker graves at Chilbolton, Hampshire, while singletons have been found by metal-detectorists at Stogursey, Somerset and Calbourne, Isle of Wight. A further pair is said to come from Gilmorton, Leicestershire, but these are not of the British type. There is an even more recently found example, but very fragmentary, from Shorwell, Isle of Wight (Treasure case 2009 T741 – Gill Varndell, pers.comm.; not in Table 22). Reappraisal of the function of the ornaments and the development of the type in Britain is thus timely in the context of the important Boscombe Down contexts.

No recent finds have been added to the tiny Irish group of closely related ornaments – an unprovenanced pair and a singleton from Dacomet, Co. Down (or Benraw, Co. Down – Briggs 2004). The first French example, a fragment, has however been recognised from just across the channel at Colledic, Brittany (Taylor 1994, 46, 57, pl. 20), but this barely begins to fill the large distributional gap between the British group and two finds from Portugal often seen to be related – a pair from Gruta da Ermegeira, Estramadura, and a singleton from Estremoz, Évora (Armbruster and Parreira 1993, 156–9).There is also a fragment of gold sheet with peripheral dots (apparently piercing the sheet) from Cova da Moura, a small cave near Torres Vedras, Estramadura, which is probably from a basket ornament of this type (Taylor 1968, 261; Gallay & Spindler 1970, 48 fig. 11; Kunst & Trindade 1990, 45 no 28, pl. 6l; Perea 1991, 25, 28).

There are two principal issues relating to external relationships. The first concerns how these Atlantic style basket ornaments interrelate with similar ornaments further east in Europe; this has been thoroughly discussed recently by O'Connor (2004). The second is about the internal development of the Atlantic style and, in particular, where it originated. The search for an external origin for the specific insular form with its ribbon-like tang of modest length and a broad (sometimes extremely broad) basket is hampered by the dearth of specific parallels abroad and any close dating for them.

Although their frequency in Britain relative to other Atlantic regions may encourage the idea that the style emanated in Britain, for a variety of taphonomic reasons this is a dangerous conclusion based on recovered numbers alone. However, the possibility that their virtual absence in western France is a function of poor recovery is undermined by the fact that Chalcolithic contexts there containing Beaker material (usually late use of megalithic tombs) have yielded a range of small sheet-gold trinkets of other forms (Eluère

1982, 124–9). Similarly, the two or three finds from Portugal would also seem to be a paltry record for Iberia as a whole, given its enormous archive of Beaker contexts, some with associated goldwork. The Portugese examples match very few of the north-west European ones, only really Dacomet/Benraw (Taylor 1968, 261; 1994, 46) and the new pair purporting to be from Gilmorton, Leicestershire (Needham 2008a). Similarly, reconstruction of the Colledic fragment would suggest it was of a different shape from the British basket-shaped ornaments (Taylor 1994, 46, 57, pl. 20); the alignment of the groove bands can be assumed to be parallel to the long axis of the tang which implies a sub-triangular shape for the basket.

At present therefore there is no evidence that this style of ornament gained any great popularity in other parts of Atlantic Europe, nor is there specific evidence for chronological primacy in any of those regions. Moreover, finds of the deep basket form (group A below) are currently split between Iberia and Britain/Ireland, so these are equivocal regarding place of origin even if they were the primary form, which itself is far from certain. A far more economic explanation of the current evidence might be that Atlantic basket-shaped ornaments were first devised in Britain, where they then enjoyed a currency for two or more centuries, and were later imitated with modifications elsewhere in the Atlantic zone. In Britain itself, later basket ornaments dating to the Early Bronze Age are different in form from the gold examples and are now of bronze (Barclay and Wallis 1999).

This leaves the question as to whether the British series was inspired by similar ornaments (with either one or both ends flattened) which appear further east in Europe. Andrew Sherratt, in fact, considered the full spectrum of interrelated ornaments to extend to 'willow-leaf' forms and, even further, to coiled wire ornaments that had no flattened ends and which are much larger in diameter – *Noppenringe* (Sherratt 1986, 62, 64). These appeared first in Corded Ware contexts up to half a millennium earlier than any of the spatulate-ended ('oar-ended'), or basket varieties and any connection with the very differently styled British ones is tenuous indeed.

Brendan O'Connor (2004, 208–10) has most recently surveyed the varied spectrum of helically coiled and tube-curled 'basket' ornaments. The absolute chronologies now established show that while some regional variants probably overlapped in time with the British series, notably the central European helically coiled type from Bell Beaker contexts (eg, Vandkilde 1996, 184, fig. 175; Heyd 2001, 392–3, fig. 4A), others are wholly or substantially later and of no particular relevance here. Few if any of the examples claimed at one time or another to be Irish (or British) exports to mainland Europe would now be accepted as such (O'Connor 2004). The lost example from the Wasosz hoard, western Poland, for example, seems to have a very delicate hooked tang and the transverse grooves across the broad oval 'basket' (which is not obviously curled) occupy a single band in the middle (Gimbutas 1965, 51, fig. 17); this combination of features is not really matched in the British Isles.

All this serves to emphasise the essential independence of the British/Atlantic series, even if the initial idea was seeded from elsewhere. The general basket ornament idea could perhaps have been drawn from the contemporary central European Beaker type, but again it is difficult on present independent chronological evidence to determine which series started earliest, and therefore in which direction the idea is likely first to have travelled. While the Amesbury Archer's isotopic inheritance might be seen as grounds for a north-western passage of transmission, it needs to be remembered that he himself was accompanied at death not by central European style ornaments, but by insular ones. It is, though, an intriguing coincidence that the Amesbury Archer should have hailed from the very region deep into Europe that had its own spatulate-ended ornaments of precious metal (Hásek 1989). This type has the peripheral dot rows present on the Boscombe Down basket-shaped ornaments, but also internal crosses. Is it just conceivable that he carried with him to Britain the idea of this ornament type, and that when later 'recreated' at his instigation something rather different emerged?

Even within the Atlantic series of basket-shaped ornaments there is some variation in decoration and form that may have chronological and geographical significance. Marked variation is found in the proportions of the 'basket' part of the ornament taken in its unrolled state – the object would be flat when the goldworker was defining the shape. Using the simple ratio of width (perpendicular to tang) to depth (w/d), it is possible to divide the series into four convenient groups (Table 22; Fig. 44) which have a number of other significant correlations.

Group A includes six examples whose baskets are less wide than deep; they are not far from circular but, in practice, can be slightly drawn out asymmetrically towards the tang, making them slightly onion-shaped. The known examples have already been mentioned above and are listed in Table 22. The group is united in having simple decoration of one, two or three perimeter dot rows. They also differ from the classic British ones (group B) in their tangs, which tend to be

narrower and stouter; indeed Estremoz and Dacomet/Benraw are rod-like spikes. Although the baskets are curled a little in the Gilmorton pair, and others suggest that original curvature has been flattened out (eg, Ermegeira), they do not give the impression of having been tightly curled with tang wrapped around in the classic British fashion. They may therefore have functioned or hung differently.

Group B are more oval and now distinctly longer on the width axis, although again there is often asymmetry on the tang axis. The w/d ratios range between 1.25 and 2.3, with a focal range of 1.4–1.7. Fifteen examples (12 occurring as pairs) are all from Britain south of the Scottish border, and the fragment from Colledic, Brittany, is a variant in shape at least (above). The group is profitably split further. Nine examples, group B(i), have peripheral dot rows like group A, but only the four from Boscombe Down have that motif alone. Significantly, group B(i) are all modest ovals (w/d ≤1.6), whereas the remaining seven ornaments have wider baskets. The other five of group B(i) anticipate the peripheral lines and/or internal bands of lines which are systematically present on B(ii). On the Kirkhaugh ornament the lines are strong ribs relative to other line decoration in the series and are extremely competently executed (Clarke et al. 1985, 86, pl. 4.7). In group B(ii) the peripheral dot rows have been omitted and only the dashed line on one of the Chilbolton pairs might reflect them. Significant also is that in the dominant transverse line decoration we see a multiplication of lines, numbering from three to seven within each band.

Group C comprises elongate oval baskets, or plaques, w/d 3.0–3.7, and all are from Ireland. The unprovenanced pair is plain and flat despite having thin hooked tangs; they are conceivably unfinished, but may alternatively never have been intended to be curled, being attached or suspended differently. In this context it may be significant that the four Co. Cavan ornaments (of which at least three are from Belleville) are also flat plaques. They lack any tang, having instead a pair of central perforations, thereby linking them to the circular discs more frequent at this date in Ireland (Case 1977b). These four also deviate from the group B in showing multiplication of the *bands* of transverse lines, 9 or 10 bands rather than just two.

Finally, a single example has such an elongate basket (w/d 4.5) that it has been placed alone in group D. This surviving example of the pair from Orbliston, Moray, is indeed an 'outlier' in other respects. As well as two peripheral lines and a dot row, it has a peripheral row of strokes arranged ladder-like; this may betray influence from the more complex designs on gold discs. It also appears to have the largest tube diameter

135

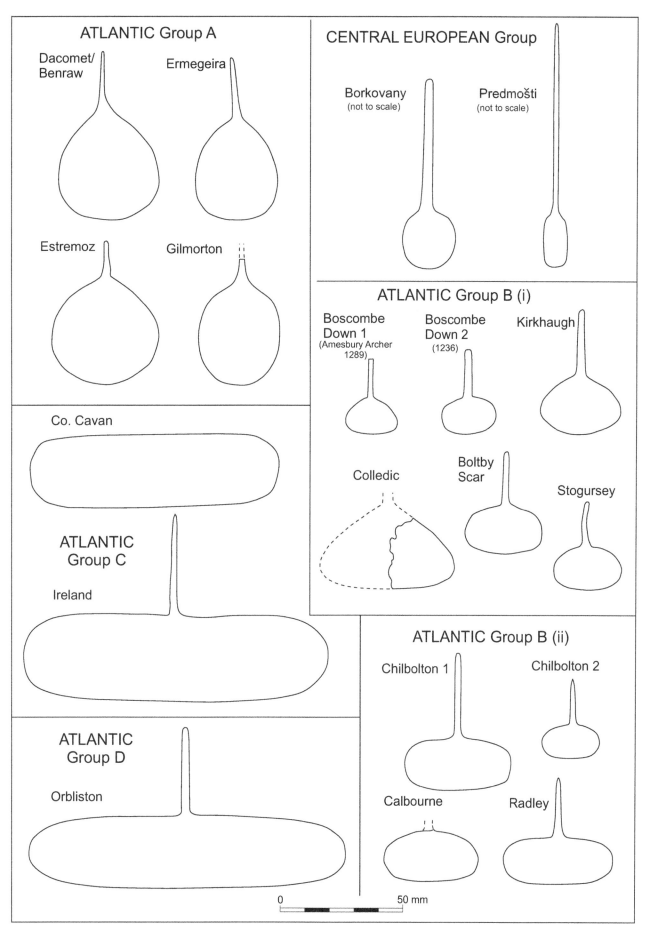

Figure 44 Classes of Atlantic Gold Basket Ornaments

of the British series and it is by far the most northerly findspot for the type. The lunula from the same site, if truly associated, would suggest that this find is also late in the sequence, probably not before the last quarter of the 3rd millennium BC.

Although these groups have been described and seriated in Table 22 as if they present a unilinear progression, it should not be inferred that the whole series of linkages has only temporal significance. In fact it is clear that there are also key geographical shifts and so actual sequences may be region-specific. With relatively few finds in any one region, even southern England, such detail will be difficult to discern as yet. Moreover, there are indications that not all functioned in exactly the same way.

Among group B, of prime importance for Boscombe Down, four finds are in definite or possible association with Low-Carinated Beakers and other diagnostic artefacts (three being radiocarbon dated) and should belong essentially to what has been termed Beaker phase 1, or the earlier Chalcolithic (Needham 2005; forthcoming). Among this small group, it seems possible that the Boscombe Down ornaments are the earliest. This depends on the argument that simplicity of design and execution would tend to be early in an emergent phase of metalworking. The same argument might place group A as early in broad terms; they could thus represent a regionally complementary tradition to group B(i), although this would be blurred by acceptance of the Gilmorton provenance. The only other object type associated with group A is a plain sheet-gold sub-rectangular 'diadem' at Estremoz, which is very simple and plausibly early, but not yet closely datable. If the Chilbolton, Calbourne, and Radley group B(ii) specimens were a development from group B(i), this sequence nevertheless takes place *within* Beaker phase 1 (earlier Chalcolithic) in Britain. Even Irish group C and Orbliston need not be much later.

Something needs to be said about the relationship between the two pairs of ornaments from Boscombe Down given the proximity of the two graves and indications of close contemporaneity. The very similar design of the two pairs, even extending to similar basket dimensions, helps support an argument for closeness in time. The only substantive difference in design between the two pairs lies in the number of dots which rises from 51/62 in the inner rows and 62/76 in the outer rows of those found with the Amesbury Archer to 68/84 and 95/104 respectively with the 'Companion's.' This might conceivably be construed as due to greater finesse owing to developing craft skill.

Another important difference between the two pairs has emerged from the metal analysis (La Niece below). Little is understood of the contemporary exploitation of gold sources at present, but the difference in the copper level between the two pairs of basket ornaments from Boscombe Down, intriguingly echoed in the two pairs from Chilbolton, might signify discrete sources rather than variability within one alluvial gold catchment. La Niece's set of comparative analyses, undertaken using the same technique, emphasises that the lower copper content of the 'Companion's' ornaments is more typical of primary Beaker goldwork from Britain. This is interesting in the light of the radiocarbon dates which place the 'Companion' a little later than the Amesbury Archer. Silver levels fluctuate somewhat in early Beaker goldwork, but this is not unexpected because silver is naturally present in gold in varied proportions. Contemporary Irish objects almost all conform to the main British pattern, with copper well below 1% (Warner 2004). So too do the results for slightly later goldwork – lunulae and Wessex-type objects. Warner has suggested that rather small variations in the levels of copper and especially tin in gold artefacts may be due to regionally varied workshop practices (*ibid.*, 76), but this seems unlikely given the smallness of the variation and in the context of this primary stage of gold-working.

It is therefore possible to suggest very tentatively that the higher copper in the Amesbury Archer's ornaments and the larger pair from Chilbolton could be indicating their manufacture from gold from a different source area. Cultural context alone makes it attractive to see this as continental gold being brought along the primary Beaker exchange networks. The introduction of some continental gold to Britain at this stage would hardly be surprising, for it would appear that goldworking was an integral element of the Beaker technological repertoire as it first spread across western Europe.

The ornaments under consideration here have been hotly debated in terms of their function. The traditional identification as earrings was challenged by Sherratt who saw links with a wider series of rings more probably serving to adorn hair tresses (Sherratt 1986; 1987b). In order not to confuse morphological categorisation with function, the neutral term 'basket ornament' previously adopted by the present writer has been maintained. However, the Boscombe Down examples actually shed important new light on function.

There are problems with Sherratt's assumption of cross-culturally common function, particularly since the range of forms he considered is extremely varied (Russel 1990, 166).

Russel, in studying the four excavated Chilbolton examples, consistently found evidence for wear on most of the tang, but not on the part closest to the basket; this in conjunction with a lack of scratches inside the baskets led him to conclude in favour of the traditional interpretation that they were worn as earrings (*ibid.*, 164–6). The present writer has not re-examined these pieces, but Russel's detailed observations can actually be interpreted very differently. If the basket enclosed a soft material one would not expect scratches; on the contrary, the material might tend to continually polish the inner surface. Moreover, the lack of wear on the basal end of the tang could mean that, rather than having been protected by flesh, it was concealed by string or ribbon used to secure the ornament to whatever it was wrapped around.

Some general points can be made about the British group B basket ornaments which may help with regard to the debate on function. Firstly, it may be questioned whether their very thin, ribbon-like tangs are well suited to penetrating through (already) pierced flesh; a narrower but stouter tang, such as found on Atlantic group A basket ornaments, would be more easily accommodated thus. The diameters of the curled baskets are variable, even within group B: the smallest is around 6–7 mm, as at Boscombe Down, and they range up to about 15–16 mm at Orbliston. Although several of them are distorted or fragmentary, this is post-use damage and the tight curling of the tang on the less distorted examples would not lend itself to repeated threading through a piercing; had this happened on a regular basis one would expect to see considerable evidence for repeated bending leading ultimately to stress cracks. On the contrary, the tangs give the impression of having been curled into place just once, then remaining *in situ*. If fixed permanently on the body it is hard to see these delicate ornaments surviving so well; there would be particular risk of crushing during sleep. These difficulties apply equally to the hair tress and earring interpretations.

The specific evidence from the Boscombe Down ornaments is that all four show deformation or tearing of the rim of the basket at the point where the tang wrapped round it. In fact this pattern of deformation can also be seen on the two larger of the Chilbolton ornaments (Russel 1990, 165, fig. 7, 10A–B). This suggests, obviously, that the tang was originally tightly curled around the basket; but it also implies an opposing force. In other words, gentle pressure was being exerted from within the curled tube, thus pushing outwards the parts of the basket not constrained by the tang. A tightly bunched tress of hair trying to expand as soon as the restriction slackened would be one possibility, but other

compressed soft materials, such as cloth or braids of rope, could result in similar physical effects. More important is the negative implication that these ornaments did not hang loosely from body, clothing, or anything else.

The contexts of the basket ornaments are of limited help. The Amesbury Archer's pair was in front of his knees. The two in the 'Companion's' grave were nested one inside the other and found inside the jaw (Pl. 22) and this may imply they were not in their use positions. The position at the skull is, however, more in line with that at Barrow Hills, Radley, grave 4A: the ornament assumed to be from the lobe of the right ear '…had slipped down to the nape of the neck, the other had worked down into the gravel beneath the left ear' (Williams 1948, 5) (Fig. 74, below). Similarly, the larger pair at Chilbolton was 'adjacent to the head', although not more precisely located (Russel 1990, 156). The smaller pair at that site was recovered from sieved soil from 'round the body' of the same, primary skeleton; however, given the small vertical distance (<100 mm) between the primary skeleton and the floor of the secondary grave cut, it is not impossible that this pair was actually associated with the secondary grave. The soils enveloping the two skeletons were not dissimilar, so the distinction may have been poor; moreover, the excavator considered it possible that the primary burial had been disturbed at the time of recutting (Russel 1990, 156–7).

Collectively, therefore, there is evidence in favour of these ornaments most often being at the head of the deceased individuals – hence the two proposed functions of earrings and tress-rings. But if the arguments advanced above seem to militate against them being a permanent appendage to the human body (or a removable tress ring), then perhaps it is worth considering instead a removable headdress or collar, to which the gold ornaments were permanently attached. Such an explanation allows the ornaments to be protected from undue damage at night and perhaps even in everyday life. The special garment might only be worn for special occasions, including, of course, the funeral. In the case of the Amesbury Archer's grave, one can imagine that a headdress/collar was for some reason placed in front of the knees. In the case of the 'Companion's' grave, one is left to conclude that the goldwork was divorced from its normal context for some reason.

In total contrast to the subtle pressure damage features just discussed is the pronounced crimping of the basket of ON 6446. This is indicative of a deliberate, and indeed carefully executed, action, conceivably intended to decommission the object during the funeral rites.

Conclusions

The Boscombe Down metalwork is consistent with various other evidence for an early date within the British Beaker grave sequence. All three tanged copper implements from the Amesbury Archer's grave have typological characteristics which are best placed in the early Chalcolithic. The presence of three in a single grave is exceptional: only the Dorchester-on-Thames grave in Britain has more than one (see p. 228 below for one with four in central Europe – Předmostí). In part the explanation may lie in functional differentiation, for the two smaller implements received different edge preparation or maintenance from the larger one and this may imply an emphasis on functionality while the larger blade served more emphatically as a denoter of status (although this does not rule out its actual use). Duplication of the copper knives is still, however, curious, although it is possible that they were valued as discrete items because they were known to have come from distinct metal production spheres; this is archaeologically discernible through two different chemical signatures. It is probable that both copper types present were metal originally obtained in the Atlantic zone of continental Europe.

Within the Atlantic gold basket ornament tradition, the Amesbury Archer's examples belong to a genuinely British style (group B). Patently, this insular style must already have emerged, either through external stimulus or internal development, before the Amesbury Archer and 'Companion' were laid to rest. This would seem to imply that although those two individuals were amongst the early 'pioneers', they were not at the absolute bow-wave of Beaker expansion into Britain unless the invention of group B basket-shaped ornaments was instantaneous at the point of first arrival. Although the Atlantic basket ornaments have a spectrum of relationships to more or less similar ornaments across Beaker/Early Bronze Age Europe, it is far from certain whether any continental type is early enough to have potentially served as prototype. The most likely source of external stimulus, if such there was, is the small series of coiled spatulate-ended ornaments from early Beaker contexts in central Europe. Alternatively, it may be necessary to consider an indigenous invention based on an existing simple gold-sheet working tradition within pioneer Beaker communities. The stylistic seriation presented above suggests an internal evolution and this may have occurred over as little as two or three centuries (c. 24th–22nd centuries BC).

A case has been made for the two pairs of basket ornaments being made of gold from different sources, possibly continental Europe for the Amesbury Archer's and Ireland for the 'Companion's'. Whatever the ultimate source of the gold, there can be little doubt that the ability to work it into simple ornaments existed within Britain as attested by the insular group B style, and indeed perhaps locally as implied by the putative metalworking block in the Amesbury Archer's grave (pp. 113–17 above).

The adoption of copper working locally is also feasible, for the techniques required for producing flat knives and daggers are only a little more complex. However, local copper working is not as such demonstrated by the Boscombe Down graves, since both the morphology and composition of the Amesbury Archer's tanged implements are well matched in continental Europe and it remains possible that all three were imports in their current forms. Nevertheless, copper working was certainly underway in Ireland by the 24th century BC to allow the production of distinctive axes of Lough Ravel type (O'Brien 2004, 557–64). Two tanged daggers in Irish A-metal from Britain attributed to association group I could be as early (Sutton Courtenay, Oxfordshire and Hundon, Suffolk; Gerloff 1975, no. 7, 3; Needham forthcoming), but there is nothing yet to say whether they were made in Ireland or Britain. At a more general level, however, it can be surmised that it is unlikely that there would have been any significant time lag between the first Beaker arrivals and the first metalworking simply because that technology was so obviously central to the constitution of the Beaker 'culture'.

Subtle damage on all four gold ornaments proves to be very important to the debate on function; it is argued that it results from the gentle pressure of a body of hair, cloth or similar compressible material enclosed *within* the curled forms. A review of the few known contexts for the type and a consideration of pragmatic issues relating to their use contribute to the suggestion that they were actually not attached to any part of the human body, but instead furnished a removable item of clothing, notably a headdress or collar. In stark contrast is the pronounced crimping of ON 6446 from the Amesbury Archer's grave; this is argued instead to be due to a deliberate and controlled act of decommissioning.

Examination and Analysis of the Gold Ornaments and Comparative Primary Beaker Goldwork
by Susan La Niece

The ornaments from the graves of the Amesbury Archer (ON 6589 and 6446) and the 'Companion' (ON 6708) are very similar in size and appearance. Both are cut from sheet-gold, and decorated with a two row pointillé border punched with

Table 23: Analysis of gold ornaments in grave 1289 (Amesbury Archer using Energy Dispersive X-ray analysis (EDX) in a scanning electron microscope (SEM), and of other Pimary Beaker Gold objects using EDX and Surface X-ray fluorescence (XRF)

Object type	Find place	Identification no.	% Au	%Ag	%Cu	Analytical method
Pair basket ornaments	Boscombe Down (Amesbury Archer)	Grave 1289, ON6589	90.0	8.3	1.7	EDX on abraded metal
		Grave 1289, ON 6446	87.8	10.6	1.6	
Pair basket ornaments		Grave 1236, ON 6708a (outer)	89.0	10.9	0.2	EDX on abraded metal
		Grave 1236, ON 6708b (inner)	89.1	10.6	0.2	
Pair of basket ornaments	Boltby Scar, N. Yorkshire	BM1940.4-4.1	88.9	10.0	<0.2	EDX on abraded metal
		BM1940.4-4.2	89.4	10.6	<0.2	
Basket ornament	Stogursey, Somerset	BM2000.7-1.1	94.6	4.9	0.5	EDX on abraded metal
Basket ornament	Calbourne, Isle of Wight	2005/T113	88	12	0.5	XRF - on surface
Basket ornament	Radley, Oxfordshire		82	6.8	0.8	#
Pair of basket ornaments	Chilbolton, Hampshire	BM A1986.1-16.10a	89	9.4	1.5	XRF – on surface*
		BM A1986.1-16.10b	89	9.5	1.3	
Pair of basket ornaments		BM A1986.1-16.14	89	10.8	0.3	XRF – on surface*
		BM A1986.1-21,15	89	11	0.2	
Bead		BM A1986.1-21,17	90.6	9.3	<0.1	XRF – on surface*
Proto-lunula	Braithwaite	BM PE88	90	10	0.3	XRF – on surface
Diadem?	nr, Winchester	2005/T21	91	8	1	XRF – on surface
Disc	Kilmuckridge, Co. Wexford	BM 1849.3-1.31	90.5	9.5	<0.2	EDX on abraded metal
Disc	nr. Douglas, Co. Cork	BM 1854,2-27.2	93.0	7.0	<0.2	EDX on abraded metal
Disc	Cobham, Kent	2004 T431	88.2	11.7	<0.2	EDX on abraded metal
Disc	Kirk Andreas, Isle of Man	BM Townley coll.	90.6	8.7	0.7	EDX on abraded metal
Disc	Cow Down, Wiltshire		93	7	tr.	XRF – on surface
Disc	Tyn-ddol, Dyfed		93–4	6–7	<0.1	EDX on surface †
Disc - pair	Lake, Wiltshire	BM 1895.7-23.55a	91.0	8.7	0.3	EDX on abraded metal
		BM 1895.7-23.55b	90.0	9.7	0.3	
Disc - pair		BM 1895.7-23.55c	86.6	13.0	0.5	EDX on abraded metal
		BM 1895.7-23.55d	85.3	13.9	0.8	

The precision (reproducibility) of the above results for EDX on abraded metal is *c.* ±1% for gold, *c.* ±10% relative for silver and *c.* ±30% relative for copper. The accuracies are likely to be similar. The precision for the results obtained by XRF surface analysis is similar, but the accuracies cannot be determined because of the unknown corrosion losses from the surface metal.
*analysis by Duncan Hook, British Museum, in Russel (1990); † Treasure report. Mary Davis, National Museum of Wales.
analysis by Peter Northover, Department of Materials, Oxford University (Northover 1995, 518)

a blunt point from the inside face (Pls 42–4; Figs 25; 43). The surfaces of the pair from the grave of the Amesbury Archer show fine parallel striations which suggest that the sheet-gold was smoothed before being cut and decorated (Pl. 43).

The gold was analysed by Energy dispersive X-ray analysis (EDX) in a Scanning Electron Microscope (SEM), see the first four items in Table 23. The analysis of each ornament was carried out on a tiny patch of clean metal exposed by making a small scratch in the surface of the gold of the tangs. This preparation cuts through the weathered surface which is likely to be altered by corrosion. Indeed, preliminary analysis of the uncleaned surface of the ornaments did show higher levels of gold and correspondingly lower copper, typical of corrosion loss over a lengthy burial period. It should be noted that where surface analyses are reported in Table 23 for comparative pieces, the real values for the alloy

are likely to be a little poorer in gold and correspondingly richer in copper because of this corrosion loss at the surface. For a full discussion of this problem and assessment of the extent of the losses in Bronze Age gold, see Hook and Needham (1989).

The pair of ornaments ON 6708 from the grave of the 'Companion' are sufficiently similar to each other in composition to have been cut from the same sheet of gold. The pair from the grave of the Amesbury Archer, on the other hand, differ significantly from them and to a minor extent from each other. Only silver and copper were detected in the gold alloy. Other elements were looked for but not found, in particular tin which has a detection limit of 0.3% by this method. Silver is present in all the pieces at levels which might be expected to be found in naturally occurring alluvial gold (Hartmann 1980). The origin of the copper in

Plate 43 Enlarged detail of the decoration on gold ornament ON 6446 from the grave of the Amesbury Archer (1289) (upper top)

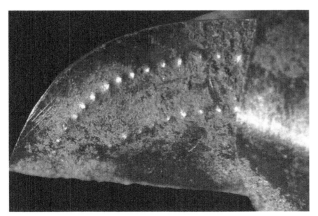

Plate 44 Enlarged detail of the decoration on gold ornament and ON 6708 from the grave of the 'Companion' (1236) before conservation

the alloy is less well established. The copper content seems rather low to be a deliberate alloying ingredient, but 1.7% is more than might be expected from Hartmann's analyses of British and Irish gold sources.

Analysis was carried out of similar Primary Beaker gold ornaments (cf. Eogan 1994, 12–22) in the British Museum using the same method. These results, together with X-ray fluorescence analyses of the unabraded surface of comparable published goldwork are also given in Table 23. As noted above, the surface analyses will differ from those of the abraded metal analyses in under-estimating the percentages of copper and silver in the alloy.

The results in Table 23 show a general trend for the Primary Beaker gold of silver contents (5–14% silver) typical of alluvial gold and copper contents which are consistently low (<1% copper). This trend can also be seen from the analyses of Irish basket ornaments and discs by Hartmann (1970; 84) and collated by Taylor (1980, fig. 23). The pair of basket ornaments from the earlier of the two burials at Boscombe Down (copper *c.* 1.7%) form a notable exception

to the generally low copper compositions of the pieces from Britain and Ireland. However, a parallel is offered by two of the basket-shaped ornaments from Chilbolton, which have a copper content of *c.* 1.5%. The possibility of deliberate addition of copper to the gold cannot be excluded but the most plausible explanation for these 'high copper' exceptions seems to be that they were made of gold from a different geological source to the other, and later, British and Irish ornaments.

Pottery
by Rosamund M.J. Cleal

There were five Beakers arranged around the body of the Amesbury Archer (Fig. 45). Two (ON 6609–10) were in front of the face and one (ON 6590) behind the head. The other two were either side of the feet, ON 6596 placed between the feet and the pelvis and ON 6597 in front of the feet. All the vessels were thin-sectioned (Williams p. 154 below) and sampled for lipid analysis (Mukherjee *et al.* pp. 154–6 below).

Methods

The pottery was examined at x10 magnification, prior to vessel reconstruction, and was counted and weighed in the sherd groups identified during excavation. As all the pottery is soft in absolute terms, 'soft' and 'hard' are used here to indicate the ease with which a fingernail can scrape or be pushed into the fabric along a broken edge, ie, easily or with some difficulty. Fabrics are recorded as 'hackly' or 'smooth' in section; these relate to the quality of the fabric itself rather than degrees of abrasion. Hackly fabrics show jagged breaks, caused mainly by the compactness of the fabric and the size and frequency of inclusions; smooth is self-evident.

Condition was normally recorded as 'fresh', 'fair', or 'worn' for surfaces and edges separately, depending on the degree to which prominences in section are worn and surfaces and decoration show wear, and in comparison with absolute freshness as seen in sherds which have been recently fired in modern experimental work. So, 'fresh' implies more or less fresh from firing; 'worn', a condition in which the prominences even in hard hackly fabrics are at least partially smoothed and surface decoration is beginning to be obscured by wear; and 'fair', neither one extreme nor the other.

Frequency and shape of inclusions were estimated with the use of charts for comparison (Prehistoric Ceramics

Research Group 1995, 46–7), percentages being for area not weight; these should be regarded as very approximate as the grog inclusions in particular were often almost impossible to distinguish from the matrix.

ON 6590: All-Over-Comb Beaker

This almost complete comb-decorated Beaker (Fig. 46) is represented by 34 sherds weighing a total of 509 g. It had been placed behind the head of the inhumation and was found crushed, lying on its side with its mouth to the north (Fig. 45).

Fabric

The fabric is hard and shows a hackly fracture in section; very few inclusions are visible at x10 magnification but include grog (with quartz sand inclusions) ≤5 mm maximum dimension, although most are smaller. The grog is difficult to distinguish from the matrix, but at least one fragment shows what appears to be the surface of the sherd from which it was derived. Other inclusions include some fine well-rounded quartz sand grains (probably less than 5%), rare, fine well-calcined flint (≤2 mm, most ≤1 mm) in squarish, blocky pieces and also rare to sparse fine dark grains ≤1 mm. A single sherd has a small white inclusion which was not identifiable. This description accords well with the petrology identified by thin-section (Williams, p. 154 below), in which the dark grains are identified as iron oxides. The vessel is well made with thin walls (6–7 mm in the lower body, 4–5 mm in the neck region and 4–5 mm at 10 mm below the rim).

Decoration

The vessel is decorated virtually over its whole external surface by square-toothed comb impressions in which the individual tooth impressions measure approximately 1 x 1 mm (Pl. 45, a). The comb appears to have been in the region of 15–20 mm long with 11–12 teeth. (Comb impressions can vary depending on how the decorator was holding the comb for each of its impressions: the ends may not always be pressed into the clay with as much force as the middle, leaving a slightly shorter impression than the comb's real length because of the curvature of the pot's surface).

There do not appear to be any intentionally wider undecorated zones within the overall pattern, although the width of the gaps between the lines does vary. The impressions appear to have been made when the clay was still quite soft (ie, they are very clearly imprinted). Although there is some white material in some of the comb impressions this does not appear to be deliberate white infilling such as is found on some comb-decorated Beakers and it is likely to be post-depositional. The surfaces are very well-smoothed but not burnished.

Colour

The exterior appears to be well-oxidised to fairly clear shades of red and orange (Munsell 2.5YR 5/6 (red)–5YR 5/6-6/6 (yellowish-red–reddish-yellow). The interior is pale brown (7.5 YR 6/6 reddish-yellow) and the core black. The depth of oxidation is up to 2 mm on the exterior edge of the core, but commonly 1 mm.

Condition

The condition is good but not fresh. There seems no reason to assume that the breaks between the sherds are other than post-depositional, with one exception. In this case a single sherd did not show the clear core colour in section, but rather a paler more 'oxidised' colour along one join. This may have been a crack which occurred during firing which therefore became oxidised because air could reach the core; alternatively, however, the colour change could perhaps be due to leaching, as is seen sometimes in worn sherds in which the edges have clearly been exposed for a long time. In either case it raises the possibility that the vessel was already damaged when it entered the grave. Overall the impression given by the vessel is that it did not enter the grave fresh, and that it may have been used for some time before burial, although not long enough to become noticeably worn; this, however, is a subjective impression.

ON 6596: All-Over-Cord Beaker

This possibly incomplete Beaker (Fig. 46) with twisted cord impressions is represented by 81 sherds, weighing a total of 591 g. It had been placed behind the waist of the inhumation and was found crushed, lying on its side with its mouth to the north (Fig. 45).

Fabric

The fabric is hard and compact, with a smooth fracture, containing moderate (at least 10% by area) fine sand and grog (≤1 mm); the surfaces are smooth, not sandy in feel. The grog is sub-angular and generally paler in colour than the matrix. Williams notes (p. 154 below) that the percentage of grog was higher in the thin section from this pot than from the others and this is consistent from examination macroscopically.

142

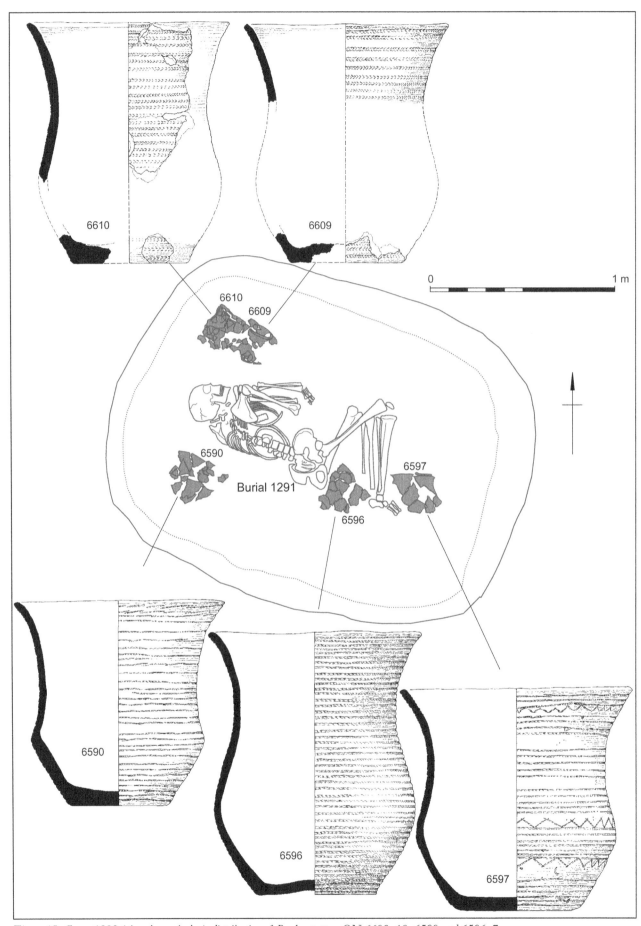

Figure 45 Grave 1289 (Amesbury Archer); distribution of Beaker pottery ON 6609–10, 6590 and 6596–7

Occasional flint and iron oxide inclusions also occur, the latter as round to oval grains with a maximum dimension of 6 mm.

Decoration

The impressions are of lines of Z-twisted cord impressions (ie, from an S-twisted cord). Some striations are visible within the impressions, representing impressions of the individual fibres within the cord. The decoration covers the exterior from rim to base with no undecorated zones.

Colour

The exterior is generally well-oxidised to a clear orange-red (Munsell 2.5YR 5/6 red and 5YR 5/6 yellowish-red) and the interior to a pale orange-brown (Munsell 7.5YR 6/6 reddish-yellow and 5YR 6/6 reddish-yellow). The core is black.

Condition

This vessel gives the general impression that it may have been slightly older when put in the grave than the other four, although this is a largely subjective impression as the vessel is not markedly worn. Surfaces were fair to slightly worn, edges were fair. Overall the traces of wear seemed to be around the middle of the body, while beneath the rim the surfaces showed little or no wear.

ON 6597: Comb-decorated Beaker

This Beaker, decorated with zones of comb impressions (Fig. 46), is represented by 29 sherds, weighing 533 g. It had been placed by the feet of the inhumation and was found crushed, lying on its side with its mouth to the north (Fig. 45).

Fabric

The fabric is hard and compact with a slightly hackly fracture. Grog and sand inclusions are present but the grog in particular was difficult to distinguish from the clay matrix. Occasional flint fragments are present (although not in every sherd), most of which were >2 mm maximum dimension; at least one piece was cortical and 6 mm in length. No dark grains were visible at x10 magnification. The pot appears well-made, with walls 4 mm thick just below the rim. The surfaces are well-smoothed but not burnished.

Colour

The exterior may only be partially oxidised, and shows shades of brown, including Munsell 7.5YR 4/6 strong brown. The

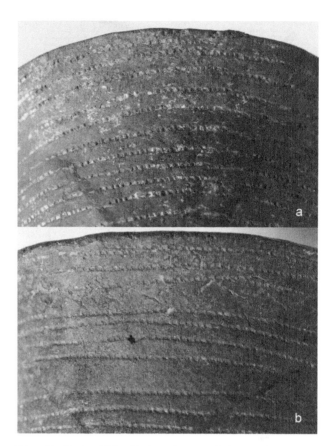

Plate 45   Beaker ON 6597 from the grave of the Amesbury Archer: detail of zoned comb decoration, and b) beaker zoned comb decoration and fringe motif

interior is also relatively dark, at around Munsell 10YR 4/2 (dark greyish-brown).

Decoration

Decoration is of zones of comb impression in which the teeth are rectangular (averaging 1.0 x 1.5 mm) and the comb about 25 mm long (as impressions – ie, perhaps having shrunk by 10% in firing). Six zones of parallel horizontal lines of comb impression alternate with five zones not so filled but in which a zig-zag motif is appended from the edge of one of the bordering zones (Pl. 45, b). Different combs have been used for the linear impressions and the fringe: that for the fringing seems to have had four teeth, that for the long impressions about 12.

Condition

The surfaces and edges are in fair condition; the breaks have some white deposit along them, probably from precipitation of salts from groundwater that had percolated in. About 90% of the rim is present, and it is possible that the vessel was not quite complete when it entered the grave. The rim seems

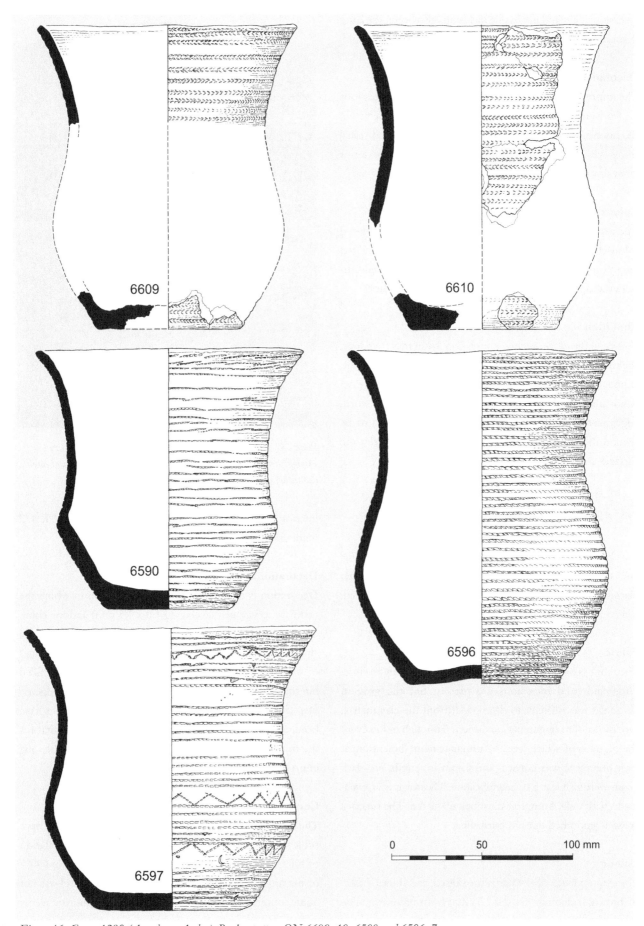

Figure 46 Grave 1289 (Amesbury Archer); Beaker pottery ON 6609–10, 6590 and 6596–7

particularly worn; however, the fact that the vessel is clearly only incompletely oxidised suggests that the firing conditions were different from those for the vessels which show more complete oxidation (ie, they will have had more air in the firing, at least towards the end, and therefore better combustion and probably a higher temperature). The fabric of this vessel may consequently be softer and less resistant to wear than that of the other Beakers.

ON 6609: All-Over-Cord (Plaited Cord) Beaker

This Beaker, decorated all over with impressions of plaited cord (Fig. 46), is represented by 77 mostly small sherds, weighing 339 g, plus about 88 crumbs weighing in total 58.5g (therefore giving a vessel total of 397.5 g). This Beaker was one of two (ON 6609–10) that had been placed in front of the face of the dead man; they were both crushed, lying on their sides with their mouths to the north (Fig. 45).

Fabric
The fabric is soft – a fingernail may be easily pushed into it, even after drying out – and grog and sand are discernible at x10 magnification, although the grog fragments are difficult to distinguish from the matrix. Very rare white angular fragments 1–2 mm in maximum dimension are probably the bone identified in thin-section (Williams, p. 154 below) although they would have been difficult to identify as bone without thin-sectioning as they show none of the structure or colouring which can sometimes be used to distinguish bone from other non-reactive inclusions. It seems unlikely that the bone was a deliberate inclusion, given its rarity in the vessel. The presence of grains of glauconite is attested by thin-sectioning, but because of the dark colouring of much of the vessel it is difficult to distinguish these macroscopically.

Colour
The upper 15–20 mm below the rim appears to be unoxidised (10YR 5/2–5/3 greyish-brown to brown); beneath this, for about 50–60 mm there is a zone, at least around some of the vessel, in which the surface is at least partially oxidised (7.5YR 5/6–6/6 strong brown–reddish-yellow), but over the majority of the body, which cannot be reconstructed, the surfaces appear to be unoxidised or incompletely oxidised (around 7.5YR 5/6 strong brown). The distinctive dark colour around and below the rim may have been caused by firing the vessel inverted: as a layer of ash built up at the base of the fire

Plate 46 a) Beaker ON 6609 from the grave of the Amesbury Archer: plaited cord impression, b) Beaker ON 6610 from the grave of the Amesbury Archer: plaited cord impression, c) pitted surface of Beaker ON 6610.

oxygen may be cut off entirely to the narrow portion of rim buried in the ash. (The writer's own experimental firing has produced this effect, unintentionally, in an otherwise open fire). In one or two places the exterior surface is a clearer reddish colour, indicating that the clay is red-firing and that the pot could have been red if fired in conditions giving free access to air. However the condition of most of the vessel suggests that air was fairly restricted during firing.

Decoration

The decoration is of lines of what appear to be plaited cord impressions, extending from the rim to the base apparently without any undecorated zones (Pl. 46, a). Cord-impressed decoration is usually impressed as spirals of cord, but as the pot only partially survives this is not determinable. In the first four or five lines beneath the rim, however, the impressions face in the opposite direction to those on the rest of the body, showing that the cord had been turned round and impressed the other way. This enables a maximum length for the piece of cord to be calculated (it could be shorter, if there were joins in the impressions in the missing part of the upper body) probably around 2 m. (A range of between approximately 1.8–2.3 m was obtained on a similar size of vessel).The possibility that the cord impressions were made with the bowstring of a Beaker-period bow was considered, as this length would be acceptable as belonging to such a bow and since it is known from modern bows that strings can be plaited, rather than simply plied, but there seem to be no known examples in archaeological contexts (A. Sheridan, pers. comm.; illustrated in Lepers 2005, figs 7.1; 7.3; 7.17).

The cord itself is very fine and at x10 magnification does not appear fibrous. The impressions are very slightly asymmetric, falling clearly neither into Gersbach's (1957) plaited (*Flechtschnur*) or crocheted (*Häkelmaschen*) forms; in attempted replication of the two techniques the writer has found the impressions difficult to distinguish, with crochet appearing sometimes asymmetric rather than even (as is in fact shown in Gersbach 1957 Taf. 3, 3 compared with Taf. 5, although it is asymmetry which is meant to be key in identifying plaiting) because of the way the threads have pulled through the loop. (In crochet, although the threads are pulled through together, in one action, and should therefore be even, they sometimes come through unevenly, therefore mimicking the asymmetry of plaiting). The term 'plaiting' has been preferred here as it is the more usual usage in Britain (eg, in Clarke 1970) but it is possible that it is actually crotcheted cord which is present.

Condition

This vessel is in a very poor condition and very little of it could be reconstructed. The surviving total weight of just under 400 g seems too little for a complete vessel – the others in the grave, apparently of similar size and wall thickness, are 500–600 g in weight – but all the vessel appeared to be represented during excavation and it appears likely, from the condition of the vessel under excavation, when it was found to be very soft, that some of the vessel completely disintegrated during burial and excavation. For this reason an accurate weight cannot be given. The poor condition does not seem to be caused by wear so much as by disintegration and the same is true of the other All-Over-Cord (plaited) vessel ON 6610.

ON 6610: All-Over-Cord (Plaited Cord) Beaker

This Beaker with all-over plaited decoration (Fig. 46) is represented by 142 sherds, plus 45 g of crumbs, weighing a total of 534 g. It is strikingly similar to ON 6609 which it was found next to in front of the face of the inhumation, their mouths tipped away from him and facing to the north (Fig. 45).

Fabric

The fabric is fairly hard (not scratched easily by the fingernail, although some sherds are softer than others) and shows a hackly fracture. Moderate quartz sand and angular grog (<1 mm) are visible, with occasional well calcined flint (>2 mm maximum dimension). One pebble-like oval inclusion, which is probably flint, is visible, 7 x 4 mm, and there are some small inclusions which are likely to be mica.

Colour

None of the sherds appears to be fully oxidised and the surface colours are fairly dull or dark. The exterior varies from Munsell 5YR 5/4 (reddish-brown) to 6/4 (light reddish-brown) to at darkest 10 YR 4/3 (brown). The core is black, with a thin exterior skin (mostly 1 mm thick but 2 mm in places) coloured as for the surface; the interior is generally darker than the exterior, at around 2.5YR 3/2 very dark greyish-brown.

Decoration

The same comments apply here as for ON 6609. Although there are changes in the direction in which the cord was applied, these occur at different points in the profile to ON 6609 (Pl. 46, b).

Condition

This vessel, like ON 6609, is in a very poor condition, and both are particularly so relative to the other three vessels in the grave. In particular many of the sherds show pitting and degradation of the surfaces which this writer has not seen to such a degree in other Beakers in similar chalk contexts and it seems likely that there is some reason inherent in the quality of the pots themselves which has contributed to this (Pl. 46, c). A possible reason for such severe degradation is that the vessels were not completely converted to ceramic in the firing and have partially decayed since. This might have been related to a desire to keep the surfaces unoxidised and so achieve darker shades than the clearer colours of the other Beakers. Achieving darker colours, probably by clamping down the firing with organic material, carries a risk of depressing temperatures and not, therefore, achieving the temperature range needed to cause what is sometimes colloquially termed the 'ceramic change' or, more technically, the decomposition of the various clay minerals in the fabric (Rye 1981, 106–11; Rice 1987, 80–109). The resulting pots might appear to be fired but would begin to break up if in contact with liquids for any length of time and would not survive in damp conditions as well as vessels fired at a higher temperature. A possible scenario which would be consistent with this appearance is that they were created as burial goods, were made and fired not long before the funeral and either did not

hold liquids or only contained them for a short period before burial. The survival of considerable but different weights of sherd material suggests that disintegration had gone further in ON 6609 than in 6610, possibly because the fabric was slightly better fired in the latter (recorded as a slightly harder fabric here). In both cases the fact that very few conjoins were found, relative to the proportion of each pot surviving as suggested by the weight, suggests that disintegration may have taken place preferentially along edges of post-depositional breaks.

Pot Histories – 'Life' Before the Grave

It will be argued below that the vessels represent two pairs and a single vessel, which had different histories before reaching the grave.

The 'pre-existing' pair: All-Over-Comb (ON 6590) and Comb-zoned (ON 6597) Beakers

Any examination of the illustrations of these vessels will demonstrate their high degree of similarity, a feature made more obvious if the profile of one is imposed over the other (Pl. 47; Fig. 47). Handling the reconstructed vessels only emphasises this similarity. Both appear slightly asymmetric, particularly in the upper body, a shared feature which could be the result of a particular potter's motor skills or visual perception. (This is noticeable when a group of people pot together, and I have noticed it in my own potting). The percentage of upper body against total vessel height is also, in both cases, 68%. A comparison of the horizontal lines of comb impression on the two vessels (by overlaying drawings at 1:1) shows a very similar spacing between the lines in their groups; again, it is this sort of detail which can be a reflection of individual potter's motor habits, albeit within the framework of the decorative scheme. In condition they are comparable too; neither is absolutely fresh, but nor do they show any particularly obvious signs of wear. The rim of ON 6597 shows slightly more wear than 6590, but as argued above, it is possible that this is due to a slightly lower temperature firing leaving the vessel more vulnerable to wear; in both cases it seems clear that they were not freshly made for the burial. The fabrics for the vessels are similar but not identical, ON 6597 not showing, at x10 magnification, the dark grains (iron oxides) visible in the other. As the iron oxides will be a natural component of the clay while certainly the grog and

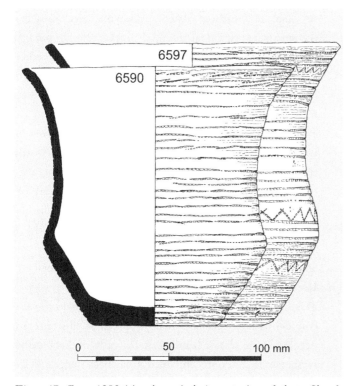

Figure 47 Grave 1289 (Amesbury Archer); comparison of the profiles of Beakers ON 6590 and 6597

Plate 47 Beakers ON 6590 and 6597 from the grave of the Amesbury Archer

possibly the flint and sand are additives, this could be interpreted as a potter applying the same recipe to slightly different clay sources; both could be local, but need not necessarily be so.

The 'made for the grave' pair: Beakers ON 6609 and 6610

The similarity of form and decoration, varying only in slight details (such as the points at which the direction of the impressions change) strongly suggest that these two vessels were made together (Fig. 46). Added to this is that the fabrics are very similar, and both contain glauconite, which is absent from the other vessels, it seems likely that these were made as a pair for the burial. Their very degraded condition may, as argued above, be the result of incomplete firing which would have rendered their useful life short and as glauconite and clay is available locally it is tempting to see these vessels as having been made somewhere in the local area. As Smith (1973) found both clay and greensand in his excavation at West Amesbury on the Stonehenge Avenue, and other deposits have been found since, it is possible that the vessels were made somewhere close to the Avon, in the period between the death and burial of the Amesbury Archer.

The 'singleton': All-Over-Cord Beaker ON 6596

This vessel seems to stand alone in form and decoration, in not sharing either with any of the other four vessels (Fig. 46). In fabric too this vessel is different; Williams reports (p. 154

below) that in thin-section it could be seen to include more grog than any of the other four and it lacked the glauconite of the other cord-impressed vessels.

Discussion

As the radiocarbon dates place the five Beakers accompanying the burial among the earliest Beaker pottery in the British Isles, it is reasonable to suppose that, whether or not they were made in Britain, their makers will have drawn on ceramic traditions from outside these islands which they had encountered in Britain or abroad. While it is to be expected that such vessels would show clear features in common with Beakers in near-mainland Europe, it is worth examining the vessels individually to determine whether that is the case and, if it is, to try to elucidate the network of associations and references which their makers embodied in them.

The All-Over-Cord Vessel (ON 6596) and All-Over-Cord (Plaited) Vessels (ON 6609–10)

The three cord-impressed Beakers find parallels in north-west continental Europe, as their form and all-over-cord decoration are classic features of the early Beakers in the Netherlands, a country in which it has been suggested by some that Beakers originated and where numerous finds are known from burials. Comparable 'Dutch' Beakers were first defined as type IIb by van der Waals and Glasbergen (1955), but it is arguable that the connection with the vessels in the grave of the Amesbury Archer may not be a direct one. Beaker ON 6596 has an exaggeratedly sinuous profile, falling into Needham's 'S' Profile Low-bellied class (Needham 2005, fig. 10), with 68% of the profile of the vessel above the maximum belly diameter, a relatively prominent belly and a concave upper body. This form is clearly related to Beakers found around the Lower Rhine but the resemblance is not straightforward. Case described, in relation to van der Waals and Glasbergen's type 2IIb Beakers, two related variations on the type, one having slender and 'flowing' profiles, the other comprising similar vessels but with flaring rims, higher shoulders and narrow bases (Case 2004b, 21). Case noted that there is a skewed distribution of both forms outwards from the Netherlands: little or no presence northwards, and little westwards, the majority of those outside the Lower Rhine occurring upstream, in the Middle Rhine region (*ibid.*). Although ON 6596 is slender, its profile is more bulbous at the belly than the gently sinuous Dutch Beakers of Case's 'flowing' type such as that from Mallem, Gelderland, which he cites as an exemplar of that variety (Case 2004b, 21, fig. 3, 4; Lanting and van der Waals 1976, fig. 15). The other variety among type IIb Beakers to which Case drew attention was a squatter All-Over-Cord type, more widespread and clearly related to Maritime Beakers in form; he gives as an example one from Poses, Eure, in northern France (Case 2004b, fig. 3) which seems to provide a particularly striking parallel for ON 6596 (Billard and Penna 1995, fig. 12). Both the vessel from Poses and ON 6596 have upper body percentages of around 68%, exaggeratedly sinuous profiles rather than carinated, with markedly concave upper bodies, and no internal rim decoration. Case's close examination and sub-division of 2IIb Beakers, particularly in relation to the 'squatter' type which embraces forms which fall into Needham's Low-Carinated type (such as that from Bathgate, West Lothian, Case 2004b, fig. 3, 6) serves as a reminder of the range of forms to be found under the 2IIb 'umbrella', variation which in part may be due to the dissemination of the type, with potters working at one or more removes from vessels that were made in the Lower Rhine.

In Britain and Ireland there are few close parallels in form for the All-Over-Cord vessel (ON 6596), the only one in Clarke (1970) approaching it closely in form being from a burial at Grassington, North Yorkshire (1970, fig. 30). Among Beakers found since the publication of Clarke's corpus, there is an All-Over-Cord Beaker from grave 206 at Barrow Hills, Radley, with a sinuous profile but its belly is higher than that

of ON 6596 and the Radley pot has a 'bottle-shaped' form not shared by the Amesbury vessel (Barclay and Halpin 138–9, 204, fig. 4.75, P74; Needham 2005, fig .10, 1). Beaker ON 6596's geographically closest parallel is probably vessel ON 2B from the grave of the Boscombe Bowmen (Fig. 14) which has a more rounded belly and is more concave in the upper body than the other uncarinated vessels from that grave (cf. Barclay p. 43 above).

Interpretation of the two Beakers with the plaited cord impression (ON 6609–10) is rendered difficult by their incomplete survival but they appear to be more gently sinuous than ON 6596, possessing neither prominent bellies nor angular carinations. ON 6610 has the deepest reconstructable profile and although the point of maximum body diameter is missing, the lack of carinated sherds and generally smoothly sinuous nature of the profile suggests that it, and probably 6609 too, is a closer match for Beakers like the Mallem example than is ON 6596.

The decoration of ON 6609–10 is much less common than that of ON 6596, both within and outside Britain and Ireland. Complex cord impressions (ie, arrangements other than single evenly spaced rows of twisted cord with twists in the same direction) occur relatively frequently on Beakers in the Lower Rhine, western France and elsewhere in north-western Europe (Gersbach 1957, 10–11), and include plaiting, crochet, and impressions of multiple lines in what appear to be attempts to mimic plaiting or crochet. Laure Salanova states that she has not recognised the plaited or crocheted types of *Flechtschnur* or *Häkelmaschen* defined by Gersbach among French Beakers, recognising instead what she refers to as groups of two or three rows sometimes with opposing twist types (ie, Z and S) (Salanova 2000, 149, fig. 90). The use of different lengths of cord with twists in different directions arranged in opposition as they appear in crochet or plaiting would seem intended to mimic those techniques. In the British Isles all-over plaited cord appears to be absolutely rare. Some examples known from sherd material have to be assumed to derive from completely All-Over-Plaited vessels but that cannot be certain, although Clarke certainly presumed that to be the case (Clarke 1970, 54). There are, however, vessels with related impressions (that is, arrangements such as Salanova describes) at Mount Pleasant, Dorchester, Dorset (p. 49 above) and elsewhere in Wessex, and some of these are clearly in all-over schemes of decoration. Longworth notes the vessels from Mount Pleasant as having paired lines of twisted cord with the twists in the same direction, on a form very reminiscent of both plaited cord vessels ON 6609–10 and the All-Over-Cord

Beaker ON 6596 (eg, Longworth 1979, fig. 47, P132) while others with similar decoration, and with simple twisted cord decoration, are squatter and more like the forms of ON 6590 and 6597 (*ibid.*, P131 and P139). One other Dorset example of what appears to be true plaited cord is included by Clarke from Hilton, north-east of Dorchester (Clarke 1970, 54, fig. 48a). The other English example cited by Clarke is from an occupation site at Downton, Wiltshire. Here two sherds, probably from the same Beaker, carry in one case a row of four lines of cord-impression, with the twists all facing the same way (ie, not crocheted or plaited) and in the other, two lines (ApSimon 1962, fig. 13, 15, 16). Double cord lines are also seen on a Beaker (represented only by a sherd) from Horslip long barrow, near Avebury (Ashbee *et al.* 1979, fig. 8, P13), from the upper fill of the long barrow ditch. Even closer to the burial of the Amesbury Archer, and approximately contemporary, the Boscombe Bowmen vessels show a remarkable concentration of cord-impression of different types (Figs 14–15). Only one (ON 6/23), with a carination and markedly concave upper body, appears to have true plaiting, while one has paired lines with opposed twists which appear to be too widely spaced to be plaiting and may be an attempt to mimic it. This group seems to include (in addition to one Cord-Zoned-Maritime Beaker) profiles of the two sub-types of 2IIb mentioned by Case (ie, flared rim, and sinuous types) (Barclay, p. 39 above; Fig. 14, ON 2A–B), and of the squatter, carinated type, in one place (Fig. 14, ON 5), with in addition a possibly extremely low-carinated Beaker with cylindrical upper body (Fig. 15, ON 19).

The comb-impressed vessels (ON 6590 and 6597)

As argued above, these vessels are so similar in form and in the spacing of the impressed lines that they are arguably by the same hand. Their carinated form and proportions place them within Needham's (2005) Low-Carinated Group. Although in their case their decoration does not include the characteristic features of herringbone or lattice which would place them among clearly Maritime-Derived vessels in that group, their antecedents are nonetheless essentially Maritime Beakers and there is a suspicion that the decoration on ON 6597 is in zones, even if they are not clearly defined.

Needham has discussed the European relations of the Low-Carinated form at length (Needham 2005, 178–88) and observes that the form is 'found in significant numbers between Brittany and the Rhine' (*ibid.*, 179). In his illustrations of continental European Low-Carinated vessels those closest in form to ON 6590 and 6597 appear to be vessels from Brittany, largely because of the rather low carinations of the

vessels buried with the Amesbury Archer compared with British Beakers of this type in general and in comparison with similar Beakers from the Lower and Middle Rhine. (Needham summarises the upper body of British Low-Carinated Beakers as 'typically 55–60% of total body height', *ibid.*, 183). Overall, a comparison of the ON 6590 and 6597 with Needham's illustrations of Low-Carinated Beakers from continental Europe (*ibid.*, fig. 4a–b) and his figure of British Low-Carinated vessels highlights, rather, the slightly idiosyncratic nature of the comb-impressed vessels buried with the Amesbury Archer, particularly in the marked concavity of the upper body, an idiosyncrasy which seems to be shared more often with other British vessels than with those from continental Europe.

Brittany has been regarded as a possible source of some Beakers in the past but on the whole rejected, particularly by Clarke. This is largely because, among other features, Beakers in Brittany have lower carinations; fabrics and colour tend to be different; dished and dimpled bases are common in Brittany but not in Britain; and internal rim decoration is common in Britain but not generally found in Brittany (Clarke 1970, 65). Needham essentially supports this, although he allows the possibility of some influence from that direction, while noting that 'for some reason Brittany did not become a springboard for major Beaker dissemination to south-west Britain' (Needham 2005, 179). It is conceivable, however, that while in general this area contributed little to the range of Beaker production in Britain, perhaps in limited areas and for a short time there was some contact between makers and users of Beakers in Britain and in Brittany and that this contact left its mark in a fairly limited range of surviving vessels in southern England. Among Beakers from Brittany, those from Men-ar-Rompet, Côtes d'Armor (Needham 2005, fig. 4a, 2–3) show a particular similarity in form to ON 6590 and 6597, although some of the Breton vessels are undecorated (Salanova 2000, 261, Br205, 265, Br219, and Br221). In addition, this site (a gallery grave on the northern coast of Brittany; Patton 1993) is noted as having Beakers which, because of their similar profiles and the fact that they were deposited nested, are considered likely to have been produced by a single hand and to have been made for the occasion (Salanova 2002, 156, fig. 4).

Within Britain, the angular form of ON 6590 and 6597, with the upper body comprising more of the total body height than is typical of the Low-Carinated type of Needham's, is widespread but not common and occurs in both comb-decorated Beakers of Clarke's 'European' type, that is to say all over comb decorated, and in All-Over-Cord

Beakers. It is, for example, very strongly shared by a Beaker with unusual, Maritime-Derived decoration from Barrow Hills, Radley, grave 4660 (Barclay and Halpin 1999, 63, 204–6, fig. 4.23, P27) and by the vessel from the primary burial at Chilbolton, (Russel 1990, 161–2, fig. 5, 1; Needham 2005, fig. 5, 14 and 4). A larger example of the form is another with clear Maritime-Derived decoration from the final blocking of the West Kennet Long Barrow, Wiltshire (Piggott 1962, fig. 14, B8).

Vessels showing parallels to ON 6590 and 6597 in both form and decoration within Britain are few and, literally, far between. Probably the closest parallel for the comb-zoned vessel 6597, is a Beaker from Brantham Hall in eastern Suffolk (Clark 1931, 356, fig. 5). This vessel, from the burial of a woman and a child, was one of three Beakers. It has a chevron infill in three zones which, in the photographs (*ibid.*) rather than the Clarke drawing (1970, fig. 106), appear to be pendant in places. This vessel is so similar in size, profile, and decoration to the example buried with the Amesbury Archer that it is difficult not to conclude that both pots may have been made by, if not the same potter, then at least potters who had worked together or seen similar Beakers; this may seem fanciful but the Amesbury Archer had travelled greater distances than that between East Anglia and Wessex.

Thus, the decoration of ON 6597 does not only hint at one specific contact at a distance; it suggests wide-ranging contacts within the British Isles. The fringe triangle motif as seen on ON 6597 is a rare one; it is rare everywhere, occurring sporadically in continental Europe and with no particularly discernible pattern. Within Britain its distribution is markedly northern although many of these finds are later in date. Taking the Beakers illustrated in Clarke (1970) as a 'snapshot' (but including the Brantham Hall vessel, which is illustrated poorly in Clarke), there were at that time a total of 38 occurrences of the triangle fringe motif on reconstructable Beakers. Of these 27 (71%) were from Scotland, three (8%) from East Anglia, four (10.5%) from Yorkshire, and four from southern England. Of these last, one each comes from Cornwall, Hampshire, Surrey, and Bedfordshire (Sewell: Clarke 1970, pl. 3; Kinnes 1985, 11–13). The vessel buried with the Amesbury Archer is not the only find of the motif in the south of England since Clarke's work was published: a single small sherd with a pendant triangle was discovered as a stray find on Bishop's Cannings Down, 5 km south-west of the Avebury complex of monuments (Cleal 1992b, 61, fig. 44, 7). The relatively common occurrence of this motif on later, short-necked Beakers, mostly in the north, could result from the motif

having been rare to begin with, when it may have been as much southern as northern, but subsequently more widely adopted in the north and largely abandoned in the south (although a sherd with this motif from Fengate, Cambridgeshire is probably to be associated with later Beakers; Gibson 1982, 152–3, fig. Fen.15.2. No other instance is known to this writer).

There are few close parallels for the combination of form and decoration of the All-Over-Comb vessel, as those closest in form tend to have more complex decoration, such as that from West Kennet Long Barrow, cited above (Piggott 1962, fig .14, B8), or two from Thickthorn Down long barrow, or from Blackbush, the latter two sites in Dorset (Drew and Piggott 1936, 83, fig. 1–2; Clarke 1970, fig. 66; 69). An All-Over-Corded Beaker also from the West Kennet Long Barrow, which is fragmentary, is clearly strongly carinated and may be of this form, but its upper body is missing (Piggott 1962, fig. 14, P7; Case 1995b, fig. 7, 1). An All-Over-Comb Beaker from Winterbourne Gunner, Wiltshire (Musty 1963, fig. 1, A), is also strongly carinated (although, as illustrated, it appears atypical in form, with a particularly exaggerated carination). Three other sherds from near this vessel (all the sherds being in a disturbed context) belong to at least one 'much larger' cord-impressed Beaker, and the excavator considered that more than one vessel may be represented; the mention of one 'shoulder' suggests that at least one of the cord-impressed vessels may have been carinated (Musty 1963).

Making and choosing pots for the grave

The Amesbury Archer vessels do quite clearly have different histories of use, as shown by their varying condition. All except the two with complex cord impression appear to have been used prior to their deposition, but were in good enough condition to have been deposited complete or near-complete. Both the comb-decorated vessels (ON 6590 and 6597) and the All-Over-Corded vessel (ON 6596) show slight signs of wear, around the rim in the case of the All-Over-Corded vessel, and possibly around the bodies of the two comb-impressed vessels, but in neither case was this substantial and the degree of wear would not support an interpretation of them as ancient vessels or 'heirlooms'. It seems likelier that they were used in daily life by the deceased or by his companions or family and may have been used for some time before his death. The fact that the fabrics are fairly soft, and that a degree of mobility is assumed at this time, would suggest that a use-life of a few years might be all that was reasonable to assume. The two All-Over-Cord (plaited) vessels, however, are much more likely to have been made for the burial. Although the residue analysis results were meagre, ON 6610 at least did produce evidence that it had held dairy products (Mukherjee *et al.* p. 156 below). The condition of these two vessels in the grave was extremely poor, as although they lay together in front of the face in two easily definable Beaker-shaped groups, they were in such poor condition that it was not possible for either vessel to be reconstructed physically. While there were clearly two vessels present (see Fig. 45; Pl. 23), the combined weight of the surviving sherds (931 g) was less than would be expected for two vessels (but considerably more than would be expected for one). In addition, the surviving sherds were very degraded, with severe pitting and disintegration of the fabric. Pitting has been noted in the Beaker pottery from Raunds where it was suggested that this was a result of the contents and it was most marked around the part of the Beakers holding liquid (Healy and Harding 2004, 180; Harding and Healy 2007) It is possible that this has been a contributory factor with these two vessels, as it is true that the best preserved parts of the vessels appear to be the parts of the rims uppermost as they lay in the grave (ie, the parts least likely to be in contact with the contents of the pot once it was on its side, because of the slightly outward profile of the form of the pot towards the rim). It also seems likely, however, that the pots may have been less well fired than the others and that this has contributed to their condition at discovery. Both pots are noticeably darker than the other Beakers in the group and to achieve this clamping down of the firing is likely to have occurred. It seems possible that the clamping down was done too early and the pots poorly fired so that, in the damp conditions of the grave, partial disintegration took place. This would account for the fact that the combined weight of the sherds lies only between the expected weight of two vessels and for the poor condition of the sherds which have survived. If this is a correct interpretation of their condition it would also have made them very vulnerable in use. All these factors – the fact that they are clearly a pair, the likelihood that they were poorly-fired and unlikely to have been robust, the lack of signs of wear, the selection of them to hold a foodstuff for the dead man in the grave, and their clearly local fabric – all combine to suggest that although they belong to a tradition firmly traceable to mainland Europe and particularly to the Netherlands, they were made locally and probably for the occasion of the funeral, using materials from the valley of the Avon, perhaps even from close to Stonehenge and its Avenue, where both redeposited greensand and clay are attested at West Amesbury (Smith 1973).

Finally, the multiple deposition of vessels must be considered. Up to now the burial of the Amesbury Archer represents the greatest number of Beakers deposited in a single event in the British Isles but although the number is unusually high, multiple Beakers are not unknown. In the 1970 listing of Beakers by David Clarke deposition of two Beakers in a grave is shown to be common, but there are only five groups of three Beakers in reliable associations (1970, 438–47), four of which being identified as accompanying female burials (the other being a cremation of unknown sex) and all except the Brantham Hall group coming from northern England or Scotland. Other groups of three have been found since 1970, and there are some cases in which disturbed burials may represent original deposits of at least three vessels. As mentioned above, there is a possible multiple burial of as many as three Beakers at Winterbourne Gunner, Wiltshire and a similarly disturbed group may be represented by the Cord-Zoned Maritime, All-Over-Corded and a very fragmentary Wessex/Middle Rhine Beaker from barrow Wilsford G54, also in Wiltshire (Smith 1991, fig. 12, P6–8). As at Winterbourne Gunner, the original grave at Wilsford appears to have been disturbed and the group scattered, in this case by a later burial, but the hint of multiplicity and the likely earliness of the Beaker types seems a common factor, shared also by the burial from Brantham Hall cited above. At Wilsford the putative group includes a Wessex/Middle Rhine Beaker, and this type has not been discussed here as the grave of the Amesbury Archer does not include any of this type, but two factors are worth noting. Firstly, the Wilsford vessel is represented by relatively few sherds and Smith notes that its proportions as illustrated were modelled on the better-preserved clearly Wessex/Middle Rhine Beaker from Winterslow Hut (Smith 1991, 29); it is possible, therefore, that the vessel was actually of a squatter form than shown, was not a classic Wessex/Middle Rhine vessel at all, and was potentially closer to the Low-Carinated type. Secondly, there is a relatively recent find of what in Needham's scheme is classifiable as something between a Tall Mid-Carinated and a Short-Necked vessel associated with a burial close to Amesbury G1, south west of Stonehenge. A radiocarbon date of 2460–2290 cal BC (Leivers and Moore 2008, 25–30) (Table 30, below), so placing it, whatever its type, with the very early Beakers under discussion here and so rendering it possible that the similar vessel from Wilsford G54 is equally early. An interesting sideline on this is that the three burials suggested as having multiple Beakers – five certainly in the case of the Amesbury Archer, three each at Winterborne Gunner and Wilsford G54 and probably some of the Boscombe

Bowmen– are all situated at a distance of several kilometres from Stonehenge (approximately Wilsford 2 km, Winterbourne Gunner 10 km, and the Amesbury Archer and Boscombe Bowmen *c.* 5 km), as if the burial of multiple vessels was in some way inversely related to proximity to the monument.

A recent find from Scotland – Upper Largie, in the Kilmartin valley, Argyll, Argyll and Bute – recently analysed by Sheridan, seems also to illustrate the pattern of multiple deposition with early Beaker types and the northern preference for this practice. There, three Beakers were present (All-Over-Corded, Cord-Zoned-Maritime (CZM), and broadly Maritime-Derived comb-zoned) and Sheridan has argued for direct connections with the Netherlands in the case of that group (Sheridan 2008a).

Summary

It would be satisfying, particularly as the buried man has a proven life history outside the British Isles, to be able to identify with confidence a source area for the tradition in which the five buried vessels were made, but this is not the case, except in the broadest terms. It is clear that the cord-impressed vessels are related to early Dutch Beaker traditions, but this is not the same thing as saying that the man or his family or associates had learnt their potting around the Lower Rhine. Some direct contact may have been involved, but at least one vessel very similar to the Amesbury Archer All-Over-Corded Beaker was deposited at Poses, Eure, in northern France. As it was in a burial showing more Dutch than northern French features, this may represent direct movement, but it could also indicate an area in which 'Dutch' styles could have been encountered outside the Lower Rhine. Even the complex cord impressed Beakers ON 6609 and 6610, although similar to finds from the Lower Rhine or Netherlands, also show, in their cord impressions, similarities to Beakers arguably of ultimately 'Dutch' derivation from northern and western France, particularly Brittany and the Loire (eg, from the river Loire at Ancenis, where Harrison notes that some were 'very reminiscent indeed of the oldest Dutch types '(Harrison 1980, 112)). All of this can be taken as a caution against assuming that the occurrence of Beakers showing features clearly originating in the Lower Rhine are the result of direct contact with that area, and the pots could, for example, have been made by potters from the Lower Rhine area (Salanova 2000).

With Low-Carinated vessels, that group also shows some hints of contact with areas other than the Lower Rhine. The form (although not, particularly, the decoration) is found more in the Middle than the Lower Rhine, and also occurs in Brittany. The particular similarities of form with some vessels from Men-ar-Rompet on the north Breton coast have been highlighted, and the predilection for multiplicity in pot deposition and for the deposition of very similar vessels made for the grave (albeit undecorated in that case) has some resemblance to the selection (and probably production) of a pair of vessels for the burial of the Amesbury Archer. Finally, if we are to look within Britain and Ireland for potential contacts, the possible links to the east have been explored, as exemplified by Brantham Hall in Suffolk, and to the north and east in the case of the fringe motif, although many of those vessels are later in date. To the south and west of Boscombe Down, the Beakers from Mount Pleasant, Dorset are an intriguing mixture, at least some of which have similarities with both the Amesbury Archer's group, in the use of complex cord impression, and in Low-Carinated forms. The proximity of these Beakers, at a potentially early date and close to a part of the coast with relatively easy access to Brittany (Sherratt 1996, fig. 1) also hints that early southern British Beakers may owe something to Brittany and other areas of the French western seaboard. In this connection, two features are also worth introducing into the argument, although they have only general rather than particular relevance to the Amesbury Archer burial. Firstly, the occurrence in the grave of the Boscombe Bowmen, in a collection of Beakers which belong to more than one episode of burial, of a Cord-Zoned-Maritime Beaker at a clearly early date (p. 49 above) also hints that there could have been links between this area and the western coastal areas of France, where Cord-Zoned-Maritime Beakers are relatively common. These links are reinforced by other occurrences of Cord-Zoned-Maritime Beakers in Wessex including Wilsford G54, Wiltshire (Smith 1991, fig. 12, P6-8) and Christchurch (Clarke 1970, fig. 78, E313), Mount Pleasant (Longworth 1979, fig. 50, P177) and at Wyke Down 2 henge (in Cranborne Chase), all in Dorset (Cleal 2007, fig. A4.12, P17–19). Secondly, a feature of note is the interest in long mounds shown by the users of some of the potentially early Low-Carinated vessels (that is, those most similar in form to ON 6597 and 6590). Clarke noted the Thickthorn Down Beakers, deposited with secondary burials cut into the top of that Dorset long barrow, as 'the most Breton-like of the British series' (1970, 79, fig. 65) and the vessel from West Kennet long barrow has a similarly very low carination (upper body 69%; 70% in the Thickthorn vessel). It is perhaps pressing the limits of the evidence to suggest that the people who deposited these Beakers were reproducing in some half-remembered form actions associated with long mounds on the other side of the English Channel, but it is not entirely impossible. It is, if nothing else, a reminder that the Amesbury Archer's Beakers, rather than presenting a coherent set of references to a single area of continental Europe, belonged to a time in which the makers and users of Beakers have left us hints of a rich and mixed background of contacts and associations which stretch across both the British Isles and through much of nearer Continental Europe. Given the varied histories and references in the other objects placed with the Amesbury Archer, this is perhaps not surprising.

Petrology of the Beakers
by David Williams

Small samples from all five vessels were submitted for a detailed examination in thin section under the petrological microscope. The object of the analysis was to characterise the fabric of all five vessels through the identification and texture of the non-plastic inclusions present in the clay. With this information it should be possible to see whether all five vessels were made with the same range of raw materials and, possibly, to suggest a likely source or sources for their production.

Under the microscope it is clear that all five vessels contain frequent angular pieces of grog, ie, small previously fired and broken pottery that was added to the clay by the potter as a form of temper during the preparation of the clay prior to firing. This would not only give the vessel walls stability but also help to open up the clay for drying before the firing stage. The percentage of grog is higher in ON 6596 (Fig. 46) than for the other four pots. Also present in all the samples are ill-sorted grains of quartz, pieces of flint, the latter mostly small-sized but with a few larger, angular-shaped pieces, some shreds of muscovite mica in the groundmass, and a little opaque iron oxide. The grog contains a similar range of inclusions as is to be found in the clay matrix. ON 6609–10 also contain a moderate disaggregation of well-rounded dark brown pellets of glauconite which are scattered randomly throughout the clay matrix. None of the remaining four samples seems to contain any glauconite.

In addition, ON 6609 also contains a few small pieces of bone within the clay matrix. It is not possible to differentiate as to whether these are human or animal bones. It is interesting to note that two Beakers from a group of three with bone and glauconite in the fabric were recovered from nearby Butterfield Down (Cleal 1996). From the description,

the bone content seems to be more frequent in the two Butterfield Down vessels than is the case with the Beakers in the grave of the Amesbury Archer, but considering the rarity of bone? tempering in this period, indeed in any period, the presence of glauconite and the close proximity of all three finds, a similar source is a strong possibility.

Amesbury and Boscombe Down are situated on the Middle Chalk, with some flint (Geological Survey 1" Map of England Sheet Nos. 298/82). Glauconite is commonly associated with Greensand formations and there are Upper Greensand deposits some four miles to the south west and eight miles to the north west of the site (Reid 1903). All of the non-plastic inclusions described above could in theory have been obtained at no very great distance and, on this basis, there seems little reason to suspect anything other than a fairly local origin for all five vessels.

Organic Residue Analysis
by Anna J. Mukherjee, Richard P. Evershed, and Alex Gibson

Samples from the Beakers placed in the grave of the Amesbury Archer were analysed using the same materials, methods, and instrumentation used for the analyses of the vessels from the grave of the Boscombe Bowmen (grave 25000, pp. 55–6 above), with samples taken from the base, body, and rims of all five vessels.

High temperature gas chromatography analysis
High temperature GC analyses were performed on the solvent extracts of a sub-sample of each potsherd, the results of this screening are summarised in Table 24 on a sample by sample basis, giving the total lipid content per gram of powdered sherd and a brief description of lipid components. Samples containing sufficient quantities of lipid were selected for further analyses by GC-C-IRMS (as indicated by an asterisk).

The total lipid content per gram of powdered sherd was relatively low in most of the sherds analysed, the highest concentration being seen in vessel ON 6610 (Fig. 48). The extracts from vessels ON 6609 and ON 6610 comprised free fatty acids, mono-, di-, and triacylglycerols which are highly indicative of a degraded animal fat. It is known that the triacylglycerols (TAGs), which form the major constituents of fresh animal fats, can be hydrolysed to diacylglycerols (DAGs), monoacylglycerols (MAGs), and free fatty acids during vessel use and burial (Evershed et al. 1992). The extract

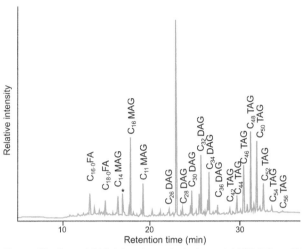

Figure 48 Grave 1289 (Amesbury Archer); partial HTGC profile illustrating the distribution of components characteristic of degraded animal fat in the lipid extracts from the Beakers in the grave

from vessel ON 6590 comprised only monoacylglycerols and free fatty acids whereas vessels ON 6596 and ON 6697 contained only trace amounts of lipid.

In the burial environment the TAGs are more stable to degradation than DAGs and are less susceptible to leaching than fatty acids. Furthermore, it has been shown in previous studies that TAGs can be indicators of broad lipid origin (Dudd and Evershed 1998; Kimpe *et al.* 2001; 2002).

Triacylglycerol distribution

Distributions of TAGs preserved in ancient fats can provide evidence complimentary to compound-specific $\delta^{13}C$ values. HTGC is used to provide TAG 'fingerprints' which can be used to make tentative distinctions between remnant animal fats of different origins. For example, bovine adipose fats contain saturated TAGs of total acyl carbon numbers between C_{44} and C_{54} and porcine fats posses a 'narrow' distribution, ie, TAGs range from C_{46} to C_{54}. In contrast, milk fats are quite distinctive due to their characteristic 'wide' TAG distribution ranging from C_{40} to C_{54}. It should be stressed, however, that distributions of TAGs alone are not sufficient for reliable determination of lipid origin but can be used to support interpretations based on the more robust stable isotopic criterion. Moreover, TAGs frequently do not survive in remnant fats, thus completely obviating their use.

The TAGs were preserved in two of the vessels (ON 6609–10) so it was possible to consider the TAG distribution (Fig. 49). Vessel ON 6610 has a wide TAG distribution indicative of a ruminant dairy fat. However, the TAG distribution for vessel ON 6609 is less diagnostic and could

Table 24: Major lipid components detected in samples from Beakers in grave 1289

Sample	Lipid concentration ($\mu g\,g^{-1}$)	Lipid components
ON 6590	66	FFA, MAG
ON 6596	12	Trace
ON 6597	20	Trace
ON 6609	40	FFA, MAG, DAG, TAG
ON 6610*	274	FFA, MAG, DAG, TAG

be indicative of either a ruminant adipose fat or a degraded ruminant dairy fat.

GC-C-IRMS analysis

Only one vessel (ON 6610) had a lipid concentration suitable for isotope analysis (Fig. 50) and exhibited $\delta^{13}C$ values of a predominantly ruminant dairy fat origin. A scatter plot is used to display results obtained from stable isotope analysis of lipid extracts. Data obtained for modern reference animal fats from species known to have been the major domesticates exploited in British prehistory are grouped within ellipses, onto which the data for archaeological pottery can be overlaid. The $\delta^{13}C$ values for the $C_{18:0}$ fatty acid are more depleted in ruminant milk fats than in ruminant adipose fats thus enabling the distinction between milk fat and adipose fat in ruminants (Dudd and Evershed 1998; Copley *et al.* 2003).

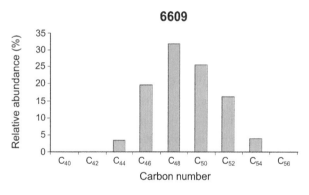

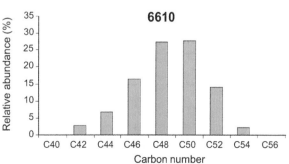

Figure 49 Grave 1289 (Amesbury Archer); distributions of triacylglycerols in the lipid extracts from the Beakers in the grave

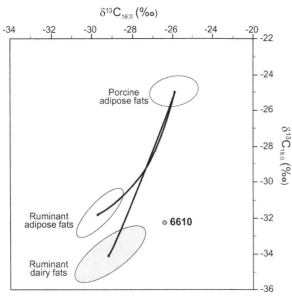

Figure 50 Grave 1289 (Amesbury Archer); plot showing δ¹³C values for reference animal fats represented by p = 0.684 sample confidence ellipses

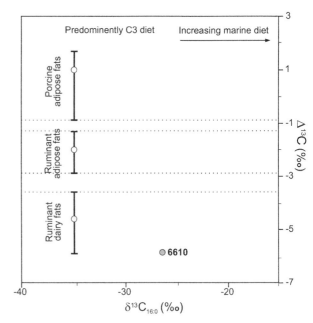

Figure 51 Grave 1289 (Amesbury Archer); distribution of porcine and ruminant fats in the lipid extracts from Beaker ON 6610

The less depleted $\delta^{13}C$ values for the $C_{16:0}$ and $C_{18:0}$ fatty acids in non-ruminant fats compared to those in ruminants are believed to be due to differences in diet, physiology and in the metabolic and biochemical processes involved in the formation of body fats in ruminant and non-ruminant animals. Work is currently being undertaken in order to investigate how their different digestive physiologies and metabolism affect specific diet-to-tissue fractionations (Mukherjee and Evershed, unpublished data).

Another way to consider the data is to calculate the difference between the $\delta^{13}C$ values for the two major fatty acids ($\Delta^{13}C$):

$$\Delta^{13}C = \delta^{13}C_{18:0} - \delta^{13}C_{16:0}$$

Values in the region of 3.3–6.3‰ indicate ruminant dairy fats, values from 1.0–2.8‰ represent ruminant adipose fats while values from –0.7 to –1.9‰ indicate porcine adipose fats. The $\Delta^{13}C$ value for vessel ON6610 is indicative of a ruminant dairy fat (Fig. 51).

Discussion

A summary of the lipid assignments for each of the five vessels from the Amesbury Archer burial is presented in Table 25. Lipid concentrations deemed to be significant were observed in three of the five vessels: while the lipids found in ON 6609 and ON 6610 could be identified as degraded animal fats, the residue extracted from vessel ON 6590 is very poorly preserved and can be only tentatively identified as a highly degraded animal fat. Analysis of the TAG distributions was possible for vessels ON 6609 and ON 6610. In both cases the distributions are characteristic of ruminant fats and vessel ON 6610 is likely to be a ruminant dairy fat. Only vessel ON 6610 was suitable for stable isotope analysis; the $\delta^{13}C$ values of the $C_{16:0}$ and $C_{18:0}$ and the $\Delta^{13}C$ value confirms that the extract has a ruminant dairy fat origin. One possible explanation is that the pots were sealed with milk upon firing and that the low concentrations of lipids may suggest that the pots were not used for cooking (p. 147 above).

Table 25: Lipid assignments from TLE, TAG distribution, δ¹³C and Δ¹³C values from Beakers in grave 1289 (Amesbury Archer)

Sample no.	Assignment from TLE	Assignment from TAG distribtion	Assignment from δ¹³C values	Assignment from Δ¹³C value
ON 6590	Animal fat	–	–	–
ON 6596	–	–	–	–
ON 6597	–	–	–	–
ON 6609	Animal fat	Ruminant adipose/ dairy fat	–	–
ON 6610	Animal fat	Ruminant dairy fat	Ruminant dairy	Ruminant dairy

Antler Objects

Pin

Pin ON 6601, probably of antler, is 138 mm long, with a rounded cross-section 5–3 mm in diameter, tapering rapidly to a point (Pl. 48; Fig. 52). The head was originally 'T'-shaped with flared wings. The end of the surviving wing has a rectangular boss at its end. The missing wing was broken in antiquity: the break is not fresh and it was not caused during excavation. The pin was found on, and parallel to, the black bracer (ON 6600) on the left forearm of the dead man, with the pointed end pointing upwards toward his face (Fig. 36). It is possible that it was tucked under the hide or cord bindings that fastened the bracer to a hide sleeve or backing rather than being worn, but it seems unlikely that it was used to secure the bracer in some way. The intact wing was facing outwards, while the broken one was next to the forearm. The length of the pin suggests that, if it was used to fasten clothing, it was used for a large item of clothing such as a cape or cloak.

The only comparable pin known from Britain comes from Barrow Hills, Radley, grave 4660. Made from animal bone it is of a similar length (144 mm) but is broken at the tip. The wings are much more squat than in ON 6601 and this may partly be a result of the pin being made from bone rather than antler (Barclay and Halpin 1999, 63–4, fig. 4.23, WB 4; Needham 1999b). In considering the Radley example, Needham suggested that it belonged to the diverse family of hammer- and/or crutch-headed pins of bone, antler, and metal (Needham 1999a). The grave, which also contained a copper knife and a Maritime-Derived Beaker, should be relatively close in date to the Amesbury Archer's.

The lack of comparable finds in Britain might indicate that that the pin is of a continental European style. While this seems likely, and a range of later prehistoric bone and antler pins is known from western Europe (Roudil 1977; Beeching and Lambert 1977–78), few of them can be compared with ON 6601. Some pins are hammer-headed and a few are known in copper, such as that from Commequiers, Vendée (Joussaume 1981, 398, fig. 182, 2; 232, 11). However, few are well dated (eg, the example from Donzère, Drôme) and it is likely that they span the Neolithic to Bronze Age.

Curiously, and perhaps coincidentally, the best parallel for the general shape of ON 6601 is a much smaller – only half the size – and earlier pin from Vinelz, Kanton Bern, in western Switzerland (Strahm 1971) (Fig. 53). The pin was 'excavated' along with other hammer-headed examples in 1881–2 from the lakeside settlement at Vinelz (Fénil) 'Alte Station' when it was exposed by canalisation work (Ischler 1923, 29, 42, 203–7, no. xviib, Abb. 11, 2). The site has since been renamed as Vinelz, 'Strandboden-Ländti' (Winiger 1989, 157–62, no. 141.20, No. 14.121) and its overall occupation dated by dendrochronology to 2734–2626 BC (Winiger 1993, 60–78).

Such antler pins were initially taken to be prototypes for metal ones (Ischler 1923, 42, Abb. 11, 2) but this logic was

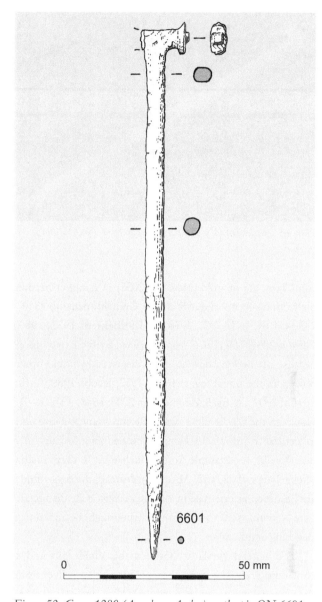

Figure 52 Grave 1289 (Amesbury Archer); antler pin ON 6601

inverted by Strahm who argued that this and related Swiss examples were imitations of metal hammer-headed pins of Únětice date, thus suggesting a longer and later currency for Corded Ware (Strahm 1971, 75–7, 153–5, Abb. 32–3; 1979, 62). However, subsequent and systematic work on the Swiss Late Neolithic lake villages has made it clear that these small antler pins are found principally in western Switzerland (Strahm 1979, 54–7, fig. 8) and can be dated to 2700–2500 BC (Hafner 2002, 523, Abb. 6; Hafner and Suter 2003, 19, Abb. 10, 4; 2005, 445, Abb. 5F, 4; 9, 61–6).

Extensive consideration has been given to the similarities between hammer-headed pins found in Corded Ware contexts, particularly in eastern Europe, with those from the Black Sea and the Caucasus region (eg, Childe 1931) where most are also of antler or horn, but a few, including examples

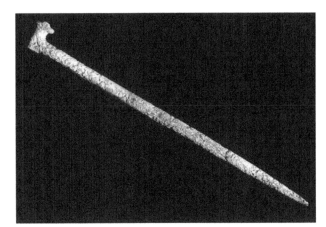

Plate 48 *Antler pin ON 6601 from the grave of the Amesbury Archer*

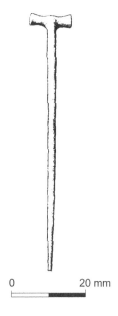

Figure 53 Antler pin from Vinelz, Switzerland

0   20 mm

from Troy, are of gold (Mansfeld 2005). A hammer-headed pin from Bleckendorf, Kr. Stassfort, Germany dated to 2840–2490 cal BC (KIA-162, 4080±20 BP; Behrens 1952; 1989, Furholt 2003, 189, Taf. 73) has attracted particular attention because of the long distance links displayed by it and other objects in the burial (eg, Behrens 1952; Jacobs 1989, 9–10; Strahm 2007, 56, fig. 8; Zimmerman 2007, 56–8, Abb. 36–7). However, the Bleckendorf pin, while important, is a rare find in central Europe and hammer-headed pins occur only occasionally, for example from Franzhausen, Lower Austria (Neugebauer 1992, 152, Abb. 3, 7). Instead, the Swiss finds are best seen as one type in a range of regionally distinctive Late Neolithic pins to which other types might be added (eg, Beeching and Lambert 1977–78, 32–3).

The general similarity between the Vinelz pin and a contemporary, and very much larger, pin made of silver from the Remedello cemetery in north Italy (Cornaggia Castiglioni 1971, tav. x, 5) has long been noted (eg, Forssander 1936, 4, Abb. 6; 10). The burial (BS II) with which the Remedello pin was found has been dated to 2880–2470 cal BC (Beta-35224; ETH-6196, 4070±70 BP; Biagi 1989; de Marinis 1997; Bagolini and Biagi 1990 *passim*). Two composite pins made of silver and an organic material(s) have been identified recently in a slightly later, Rinaldone cemetery at Porte delle Sette Miglia, Rome (Anzidei *et al.* 2007; A. Dolfini, pers. comm.) It is possible that the terminal mouldings on the Amesbury Archer's pin derive from such composite pins.

The Remedello pin remains unique in being made entirely from silver and while the BS II burial does not appear to have been of notably higher status in that cemetery (Cornaggia Castiglioni 1971), early objects of silver in eastern and central Europe are seen to have been of high status (Primas 1995). It has also been noted that the copper daggers found in the

Remedello cemetery were, unlike the axes, made in an arsenical copper alloy that gave them a silver like finish (Hansen 2002, 165). The gold hammer headed pins from Troy (Mansfeld 2005) also suggest that at least some of these pins were used to display status. The similarities in shape between the pin buried with the Amesbury Archer and earlier pins from an area in which isotope analysis suggest he may have lived (p. 188 above), and in size and to a less extent shape with the Remedello pin, may be fortuitous. But there is also a possibility – nothing more – that the pin buried with the Amesbury Archer carried with it echoes of distant lands and status.

Spatula
by Phil Harding

A spatula of red deer antler (ON 6612; Fig. 54) was found by the right shoulder at the edge of the cache of objects by Beaker ON 6609 (Fig. 36). It is 95 mm long and 17 mm wide, and made of a splinter of antler that retained traces of the marrow on the inside. The groove along one side may have been caused by groove and splinter working. One end was rounded while the opposite end was flattened.

Spatulae have been found frequently in Beaker burials in Britain and suggestions as to their function have included tools for potting and netting (Thurnham 1871, 436–7), components of composite bows (Clark 1963, 51), and leather workers' tools. The interpretation of spatulae for leather working was proposed by Smith and Simpson when they undertook the first detailed assessment of these objects following the discovery of a spatula associated with a Beaker and cache of other objects placed behind the skull of the burial in a barrow on Overton Hill, Wiltshire (Smith and Simpson 1966). They listed 11 spatulae made of antler or bone from eight graves with Beakers (*ibid.*, tab. I, app. v). most of which were Wessex/Middle Rhine or Southern Beakers. The Mere G6a grave, Wiltshire, also contained a bracer and two gold discs (Hoare, 1810, 44; Case 1977a; fig. 1, 8–17;

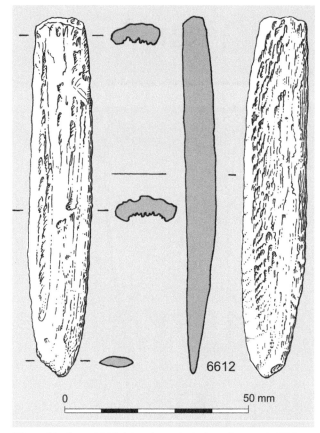

Figure 54 Grave 1289 (Amesbury Archer); antler spatula ON 6612

1995b, fig. 2, 1–5, 13–17; 2001, 363–6, fig. 1, 8–17; 2; 2004b, fig. 1, 8–17).

All of these spatulae were certainly or probably found with male inhumation burials and the associated finds included flint or copper daggers, barbed and tanged arrowheads, awls, scrapers/knives, and other objects of worked flint. The grave at Mere G6a was suggested to contain both a male and female. Drawing on recent historical evidence, Smith and Simpson noted that similar spatulae had been used to burnish leather and as at Overton Hill, the spatula was associated with a bronze awl and knife, these objects represented a leather worker's tool kit. They were equally content to apply this interpretation to all other spatulae (*op. cit.*, 135).

Clarke drew attention to the fact that antler and bone spatulae are frequently found with archery equipment and suggested that they might be parts of composite bows, quivers, or archery tools. Reviewing this suggestion, Ashbee (1988, 42) noted that spatulae occurred either as a 'long' variety, approximately 250 mm (10 in) in length, or a 'short' variety, about 125 mm (5 in) long.

Although Smith and Simpson's interpretation of spatulae as leather working tools was generally accepted (eg, Healy and Harding 2004, 185), uncertainty about it has also been expressed (Foxon 1990). Their possible use as multi-purpose tools (Barclay and Halpin 1999, 94) or in composite bows (Gdaniec 1996, 656) has been suggested and a further interpretation of spatulae as flint working tools has also been proposed. In examining the tips of the four antler spatulae from a burial of either Beaker or Early Bronze Age date at Easton Lane, Hampshire, Olsen compared them with experimental examples and argued strongly that they were pressure flaking tools (Olsen in Harding 1989, 104). This interpretation is compatible with the consistent connections with archery equipment (cf. Woodward *et al.* 2005, 44).

The use of antler for flaking, including pressure flaking, has been well documented ethnographically (Evans 1897) and the use of spatulae as pressure flaking tools has been tested experimentally by the author, who has shown them to be an efficient tool for this task. Long strips of antler (such as Ashbee's 'long' spatulae) flex, store energy, apply leverage, and make flaking more efficient. With use the flaker becomes worn down and the advantages of the additional leverage are lost. Eventually they become too short, turning into Ashbee's 'short' spatulae, and are no longer efficient. It could be argued that this reflects the practice of including worn or broken implements with the graves of Beaker burials, although the differences in their size they may reflect the selection of slightly different tools for different tasks.

Spatulae also occur in a number of burials in continental Europe that have been interpreted as those of flint workers (pp. 222–4 below), and 'Ötzi' carried a short antler-tipped flaker held in a wooden handle (Egg and Spindler 1992, 62–4, Abb. 23, Farbtaf. xi)). Although there is little evidence for the use of antler in flint knapping during the Neolithic and Bronze Age in Britain, bifacial flint daggers (eg, H.S. Green *et al.* 1982) were undoubtedly produced with soft hammers, of which antler is a likely candidate. Antler tines were also used in Continental Europe (Mathiassen 1939) during the Neolithic and Early Bronze Age for indirect percussion and probably for pressure flaking.

Other Objects
by A.P. Fitzpatrick

Two strips of antler (Fig. 55) were found in front of the dead man, some 270 mm apart and on a similar alignment (Fig.

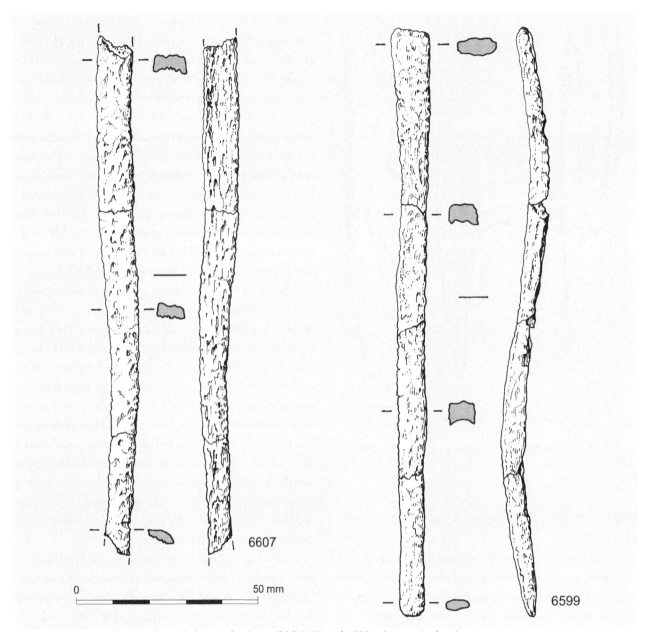

Figure 55 Grave 1289 (Amesbury Archer); antler objects (ON 6607 and 6599) of uncertain function

36). They are similar in size, shape, and manufacturing technique.

ON 6607: rectangular, slightly tapering, antler strip, both ends missing: 135 mm long, *c.* 9 mm wide, *c.* 4 mm thick. Broken into three pieces. Found in front of the arms.

ON 6599: rectangular and apparently complete antler strip with narrow end squared to a tip. The wider end is squarer. Sinuous profile and rectangular in section: 151 mm long, *c.* 7 mm wide, *c.* 5 mm thick. Broken into four pieces. Found in front of the knees.

The possibility that these fragments are from a single object that has been broken and moved slightly due to post-depositional factors seems to be precluded by the fact that one of them (ON 6599) is apparently complete. They are either two separate objects or, possibly, parts of a single composite object. Their function is not known.

The complete example, ON 6599, may be compared with the spatulae discussed above. Although such spatulae are often rounded in section, as in ON 6612 above, they are occasionally rectangular, as at Chilbolton (Foxon 1990, fig. 6, 2) and Barrow Hills, Radley, grave 203 (Barclay and Halpin 1999, fig, 4.79, WB 13). If ON 6599 were to be interpreted as a spatula it would mean that there are both longer and shorter examples in the Amesbury Archer's grave, as was the case at Easton Lane where there were two longer examples, 340 mm and 328 mm long, and two shorter examples, 270 mm and 240 mm long (Harding 1989). The broken object, ON 6607, could also be a spatula and though shorter than ON 6599 its ends are missing. As well as Easton Lane, multiple spatulae are known from the Green Low (three) and Mouse Low (two), both Derbyshire and Ferrybridge, West Yorkshire, burials (Smith and Simpson 1966; Duncan 2005).

It is possibly that the antler strips are from a single composite object made of antler and perhaps wood, but it is not considered likely that they are reinforcements for a composite bow. All the direct evidence for Neolithic, Beaker, and Bronze Age bows, which is set out below, is for self-bows, ie, made from a single piece of wood. In addition, the total length between the furthermost tips of the two antler strips is only 556 mm, too short a distance for them to have been reinforcements for bow ends.

Bell Beaker bows

The evidence for Neolithic and Bronze Age bows in Britain, Ireland, and western Europe is consistently for self-bows. The presence of composite bows, ie, wooden bows with reinforcements of another material, usually of antler or horn and backed with sinew, has been suggested largely from the evidence of representations, but there is no unequivocal evidence (Rausing 1997).

Several Neolithic bows, up to 1.75 m long, are known from Britain and Ireland, and they, as well as the construction and use of replicas, were surveyed comprehensively by Clark (1963). These one-piece or self-bows were usually made from yew and their effectiveness is beyond doubt (Prior 2000). Although only three Bell Beaker or Bronze Age bows were known when Clark wrote, they were all self-bows, the first from near Cambridge, the second from De Zilk, Noordwijkerhout, Zuid Holland, and the third from Stadskanaal, Onstwedde, in north-east Holland (Clarke 1963, 67–8, fig. 12, 5, 13–14). The use of self-bows in the Neolithic and Bronze Age has been affirmed by subsequent finds and surveys in continental Europe (Glover 1979; Di Donati 1991; Lanting *et al.* 1999; Egg and Spindler 1992; Suter *et al.* 2005, 506–10, Abb. 16–25). In addition, a Middle Bronze Age miniature self-bow (455 mm long) made of antler has been found at Isleham, Cambridgeshire (Gdaniec 1996, 656).

Two self-bows are partly or wholly contemporary with the burial of the Amesbury Archer. That from Stadskanaal is radiocarbon dated to 2840–2230 cal BC (GrN 4069, 3970±65

BP; Lanting *et al.* 1999, 8) and a recently discovered bow from Barrysbrook, Co. Offaly, Ireland, is dated to 2400–2040 cal BC (Murray 2004; GrA-23116, 3970±45 BP). In the Bell Beaker burial cist 6 at Borrowstone Farm, Aberdeenshire, a length of sinew was found in front of the arm and it and a quantity of wood and possibly hide clutched in the hand were interpreted as possible evidence for the former presence of a bow (Shepherd 1986, 13, fig. 13a; 2460–2140 cal BC, GrA-29082, 3820±40 BP; 2460–2140 cal BC, GrA-29083, 3835±40 BP).

In his study of prehistoric archery in north-west Europe, Clark argued that composite bows were developed in environments in which wood with the toughness and resilience necessary for a good self-bow was absent, environments such as the tundra of Siberia (Clark 1963, 50–1). It has been suggested, however, that composite bows were made in the Beaker period.

In studying Bell Beaker and Early Bronze Age bow-shaped pendants (suggested on pp. 60–1 above to be quiver decorations), Piggott proposed that representations of bows on carvings from Göhlitsch, Germany and Sion, Le Petit-Chasseur, Switzerland were depictions of short, composite, recurve bows. The Göhlitsch slab is from a Corded Ware context (Clark 1963, pl. ix; Rausing 1997, 38–9, fig. 8) though the representations on the stelae from Petit-Chasseur are of Bell Beaker date. Piggott also remarked on the expanded terminals of the bow-shaped pendants, suggesting that they were much more pronounced than those on self-bows. Piggott concluded, of the Göhlitsch and Petit-Chasseur representations, that 'clearly a short rather than longbow is intended' and they also 'imply the possibility of short and probably composite bows' (Piggott 1971, 89). No other evidence to support the existence of Bell Beaker composite bows was presented or has been found subsequently (Rausing 1997).

It must be doubted whether these depictions can be taken as accurate and naturalistic indications of size. This is particularly true of the Alpine stelae which, while they provide accurate representations in many regards (eg, Heyd and Harrison 2007), use a convention of representing objects against the torso. This and the physical nature of the medium – stone slabs – both restrict the size at which larger objects might be depicted. Similarly, the boar's tusks or animal ribs that bow-shaped pendants are made from are naturally curved. Consequently, the case for composite Bell Beaker bows cannot yet be regarded as proven.

Evidence might yet be forthcoming, however. It has been suggested that three longitudinally split cattle ribs from the

162

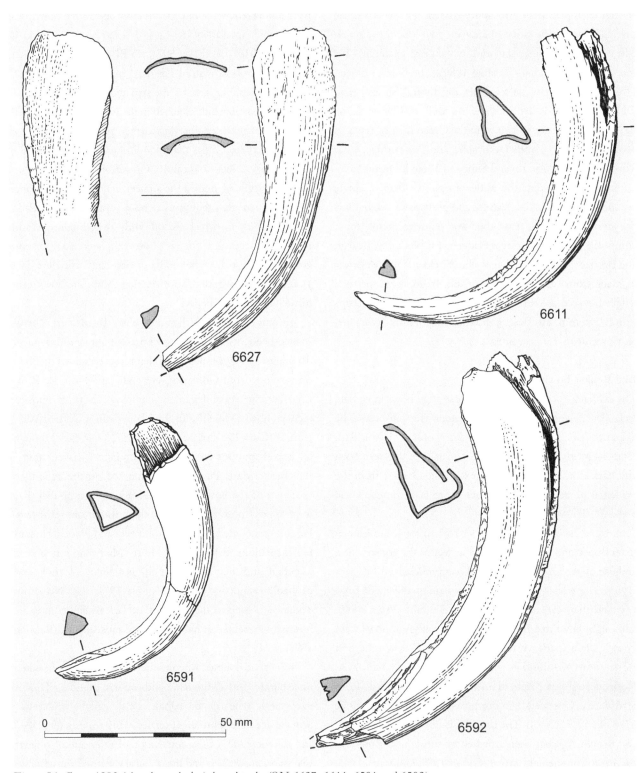

Figure 56 Grave 1289 (Amesbury Archer); boars' tusks (ON 6627, 6611, 6591 and 6592)

primary grave in barrow 1 at Raunds, Northamptonshire, where the burial is dated to 2210–1930 cal BC (UB-3148, 3681±47 BP) may have been the reinforcements for a composite bow (Healy and Harding 2004, 186–7, fig. 63–4; 2008). Elsewhere it can be noted that some burnt wooden remains from a Globular Amphora Culture burial at

Bożejewice, Kuyavian-Pomerania Voivodeship, Poland, dated to 3030–2340 (Gd-888, 4140±120 BP) have been interpreted as representing a composite bow, although again the evidence is not decisive (Kosko and Klochko 1987; Sarauw 2007, 76). The antler strips in the grave of the Amesbury Archer cannot confidently be interpreted as being from a bow and on this evidence it seems likely that if a bow was placed in the grave, it would, as with other Bell Beaker examples, have been a self-bow.

Boars' Tusks
by A.P. Fitzpatrick, Stephanie Knight, and Pippa Smith

Four boars' tusks were found, two in front of the head (ON 6611 and 6627) and two behind it (ON 6591–2) (Fig. 36). All are mandibular tusks from the right side of adult male animals (Fig. 56). All the tusks are in poor condition and the survival of the enamel surface is variable. Not enough dentine survives to allow the tusks to be aged.

ON 6611: tusk, medium sized, male, lower right side. Possibly worked to enhance the point. The inside edge is more worn than the other tusks but the surface is not sufficiently polished to confirm this. 95 mm long.

ON 6627: tusk, medium sized, male, lower right side. Worked into a rounded flat scoop/spoon shape with two sides cut away and the reverse is very smooth. The tusk is widest at the root end. The missing tip is due to damage in excavation. 95 mm long, scoop 22 mm wide.

ON 6591: tusk, small, male, lower right side. No working is clearly visible but the tip may have been flattened and shaved. 70 mm long.

ON 6592: tusk, small, male, lower right side. No working is clearly visible. The missing tip is due to excavation damage. 111 mm long

Although alteration to the tips of the tusks has often been interpreted as deliberate modification it is possible that it arises from natural wear (Hillson 1986, 129, fig. 1.89; Woodward *et al.* 2005, 45). However, the two tusks placed in front of the face had clearly been modified, one as a scoop, the other as a point. No certain evidence for use wear was observed.

Boars' tusks are rarely found in Bell Beaker graves in Britain, so their occurrence in the graves of the Amesbury Archer, the Boscombe Bowmen, and the 'Companion' is noteworthy. In central Europe tusks have been suggested to be metalworkers' tools, perhaps for planishing or burnishing objects (p. 222 below). The two tusks found behind the back of the Amesbury Archer are adjacent to the cushion stone

(Fig. 36), strongly suggesting that they had a similar purpose. Like the cushion stone, the tusks were examined by Ernst Pernicka at the Bergakademie, Technische Universität Freiberg for traces of ancient metals but in view of the pitted surfaces of the tusks, analysis was not considered to be practicable.

Radiocarbon dates were obtained from two tusks to provide independent dating for the grave and also to establish whether any were much earlier than the burial as had been suggested for a tusk placed in the primary burial (grave 30426) at Raunds (Irthlingborough) barrow 1 (Healy and Harding 2004, 186; Harding and Healy 2007). Tusk ON 6611 from in front of the dead man and tusk ON 6592 from behind his back yielded dates consistent with the date from the human bone (p. 169 below; Table 27). This also raises a question about the date from the Raunds grave, one of a series for the contents of the grave obtained from several laboratories over several years.

Oyster Shell
by Sarah F. Wyles

ON 6623 (Fig. 57): oyster shell; right valve; 65 mm long, 56 mm wide.

This single oyster valve was found in front of the Amesbury Archer's chest (Fig. 36). A small notch was probably made during opening the oyster and a central perforation, 8 mm long by 3 mm wide, appears to have been bored from both sides, suggesting that it may have been worn as a pendant. On the left side of each face there are lowered areas, *c.* 3 mm long, which are not fully bored through and might have been caused by wear. The inner surface of the shell was covered in a concretion deposit, as a result of depositional processes.

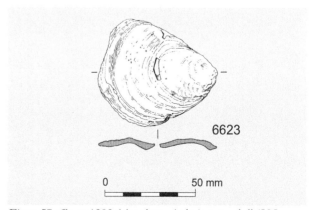

Figure 57 Grave 1289 (Amesbury Archer); oyster shell (ON 6623)

As European oysters all belong to the same family it is not possible to differentiate specimens that lived in the Mediterranean from those living around the coasts of Britain and Ireland. Evidence from infestation of shells might be more geographically diagnostic but in this case there are only slight traces of infestation by a polychaetic worm. Oysters are not common finds in later prehistoric contexts in Wessex. Occasional examples of marine mollucs have been found close to Durrington Walls; scallops were identified in the Late Neolithic pits at Ratfyn, Wiltshire (Stone 1937) and Woodlands (Stone 1948, 300, fig. 32), and mussels at Ratfyn and Woodhenge (Cunnington 1932, 77).

At Woodlands it was suggested that shells were used as a temper in Grooved Ware pottery and a subsequent study has shown that shell in Grooved Ware pots at Ratfyn, Woodlands, and also the nearby Chalk Plaque Pit (Harding 1988) was all from oyster (Cleal *et al.* 1994, 446; Cleal 1995a, 190).

Other than the use of cockle shells to decorate Beakers (Salanova 2000), including in Britain (Clarke 1970) (and note the possible use of a cockle shell to crimp one of the gold ornaments, p.224 below), the use of marine shells, particularly for ornaments, is quite rare in continental Europe during the Bell Beaker period although in Bavaria some spondylus shells were incised with crosses and perforated for use as pendants. This contrasts with the Neolithic when shells were widely used as ornaments (eg, Jeunesse 2003, 27–30, fig. 6). Although Mediterranean whelk shells (*Columbella rustica*) perforated for threading onto necklaces are frequent finds in Bell Beaker contexts at Petit Chasseur, Sion, Switzerland, which lies in the southern ranges of the Alps (Gallay 1989), this is atypical. Such shells occur only occasionally in Bell Beaker burials in southern Germany; in grave 5 at Barbing and grave 5 at Sendling (Heyd 2000, 293–4). Other occasional finds from coastal regions may be noted, for example a cockle shell from the south of France at Dolmen des Adrets IV (Brignole, Dép. Var) (Lemercier 2004, 251, fig. 199, 307, 56) or a large unperforated mussel from the megalithic tomb at Cañada del Carrascal, Mairena del Alcor, Sevilla, in Spain (Leisner and Leisner 1943, 214, Taf. 67, 7). These serve primarily to emphasise how little marine shells were used.

Pendants are no more common than shells, though a bone disc from the early Bell Beaker child's grave 919 at Barrow Hills, Radley made from the scapula of a large mammal, probably cattle, may be noted (radiocarbon dated to 2840–2140 cal BC, OxA-1874, 3930±80 BP; Barclay and Halpin 1999, 57, 236, fig, 4.14, WB 2).

The perforated oyster, perhaps used as a pendant in the grave of the Amesbury Archer is, then, a rare find. It may have been a memento of a journey, but where that might have been to or from, cannot yet be determined.

PART III

Chapter 6

Chronology and the Radiocarbon Dating Programme

by Alistair Barclay and Peter Marshall with T.F.G. Higham

Eleven measurements were obtained from the graves of the Boscombe Bowmen (25000) (Table 26), the Amesbury Archer (1289) and the 'Companion' (1236) (Table 27). The dating programme was undertaken at the Radiocarbon Accelerator Unit, Oxford.

Ten of the 11 samples submitted, eight on human bone and two on boar's tusks, were subject to collagen extraction (Law and Hedges 1989; Hedges *et al.* 1989) followed by gelatinisation and ultrafiltration (Bronk Ramsey *et al.* 2004a). The single cremated bone sample was pre-treated following the procedure described in Lanting *et al.* (2001). They were all measured by Accelerator Mass Spectrometry as described by Bronk Ramsey *et al.* (2004b). The laboratory maintains a continual programme of quality assurance procedures, in addition to participation in international inter-comparisons (Scott 2003) which indicate no laboratory offsets and demonstrate the validity of the precision quoted.

Radiocarbon Results and Calibration

The radiocarbon results from the three graves are quoted in accordance with the international standard known as the Trondheim convention (Stuiver and Kra 1986). They are conventional radiocarbon ages (Stuiver and Polach 1977).

Calibrations of the results (Tables 26–7), relating the radiocarbon measurements directly to calendar dates, are outlined in Figure 58. All have been calculated using the calibration curve of Reimer *et al.* (2004), and the computer program OxCal v4.0.5 (Bronk Ramsey 1995; 1998; 2001; 2009). The calibrated date ranges cited in the text are those for 95% confidence. They are quoted in the form recommended by Mook (1986), with the end points rounded outwards to 10 years. The ranges quoted in italics are posterior density estimates derived from mathematical modelling of given archaeological problems (see below). The ranges in plain type in Tables 26–8 have been calculated according to the maximum intercept method (Stuiver and Reimer 1986). All other ranges are derived from the probability method (Stuiver and Reimer 1993).

General approach

A Bayesian approach has been adopted for the interpretation of the chronology from the graves of the Boscombe Bowmen, Amesbury Archer, and the 'Companion' (Buck *et al.* 1996). Although the simple calibrated dates are accurate

Table 26: Radiocarbon measurements from grave 25000 (Boscombe Bowmen)

Lab. no.	Burial/bone deposit	Sample	$\delta^{13}C$ (‰)	Radiocarbon age (BP)	Calibrated date BC (95% confidence)	Posterior density estimate cal BC (95% probability unless otherwise stated)
OxA-13542	25010 spoil heap, machine removed grave fill; adult male	25010a human r femur	-20.70	3955±33	2580–2340	*2500–2340 (87.4%)*
OxA-13543	25008 bone dep, in grave; disarticulated, adult male	25008b human r femur	-20.65	3822±33	2470–2200	*2470–2310*
OxA-13681	25010 spoil heap, machine removed grave fill; disarticulated, subadult	25010b human r femur	-21.10	3825±30	2340–2140	*2460–2290*
OxA-13598	25007; articulated juvenile (5–6 yr)	25010e Human l femur	-21.40	3889±32	2470–2230	*2410–2270 (90%)*
OxA-13624	25004; articulated adult male (30–40 yr)	25005 ON 11 human r femur	-20.90	3845±27	2460–2200	*2340–2200*
OxA-13972	25006; cremation burial, infant	25006 human long bone	-21.10	3613±28	2110–1950	*2040–1920 (80.9%)*
OxA-13599	25001; articulated juvenile (6–7 yr)	25010f human l femur	-21.40	3681±30	2190–1950	*2140–1970*

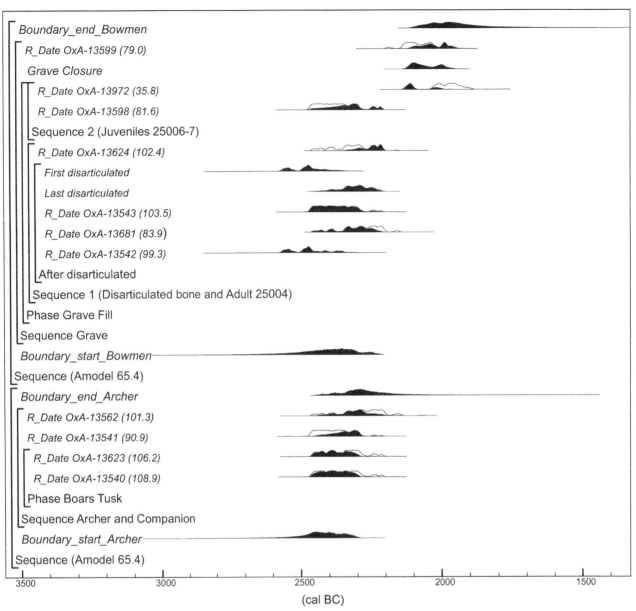

Figure 58 Probability distributions of dates from graves 25000 (Boscombe Bowmen), 1289 (Amesbury Archer), and 1236. Each distribution represents the relative probability that an event occurs at a particular time. For each of the dates, two distributions have been plotted: one in outline, which is the result of simple calibration, and a solid one, based on the chronological model used. Distributions other than those relating to particular sample dates correspond to aspects of the model (eg estimations of closure of the Boscombe Bowmen grave (25000), first and last disarticulated bone). The square brackets and the OxCal keywords define the model's structure

estimates of the dates of the samples, this is usually not what archaeologists really wish to know. It is the dates of the archaeological events represented by those samples which are of interest. Here, it is the chronology of the graves that is under consideration, not the dates of the samples themselves. The dates of this activity can be estimated by not only using the scientific dating information from the radiocarbon measurements on the samples, but also by using archaeological information about the relationships between samples.

Fortunately, methodology is now available which allows the combination of these different types of information to produce realistic estimates of the dates of interest. It should be emphasised that the *posterior density estimates* produced by this modelling are not absolute. They are interpretative *estimates*, which can and will change as further data become available and as other researchers choose to model the existing data from different perspectives. For example we have used two models based on 'different' readings of the archaeological evidence.

Table 27: Radiocarbon measurements from grave 1289 (Amesbury Archer) and 1236

Lab. no.	Sample	$\delta^{13}C$ (‰)	Radiocarbon age (BP)	Calibrated date BC (95% confidence)	Posterior density estimate BC (95% probability unless otherwise stated
Amesbury Archer (grave 1289)					
OxA-13541	human right femur	-20.6	3895±32	2470–2280	*2380–2290*
OxA-13540	ON 6611 boar's tusk	-21.3	3877±33	2470–2210	*2380–2290*
OxA-13623	ON 6592 boar's tusk	-20.1	3866±28	2460–2210	*2380–2290*
'Companion' (grave 1236)					
OxA-13562	human right femur	-20.4	3829±38	2460–2140	*2350–2260 (59.7%)*

The technique used is a form of Markov Chain Monte Carlo sampling, and has been applied using the program OxCal v4.0.5 (http://c14.arch.ox.ac.uk/). Details of the algorithms employed by this program are available from the online manual or in Bronk Ramsey (1995; 1998; 2001; 2009). The algorithm used in the models described below from grave 25000 (the Boscombe Bowmen) can be derived from the structure shown in Figure 59.

Objectives

The objectives of the radiocarbon dating programme were:

- to place the graves of the Boscombe Bowmen (25000), the Amesbury Archer (1289), and the 'Companion' (1236) into a chronological sequence;
- to compare this sequence with the Late Neolithic and Beaker pits, monuments, and graves at Boscombe Down;
- to provide a precise chronological sequence for these elements of the Boscombe Down finds and to compare them with other locally available chronologies (ie, Durrington Walls and Stonehenge), and with selected Beaker burials and early copper mines (eg, Ross Island) elsewhere in Britain and Ireland.

Human bone and animal bone object selection procedure

With the human bone the same bone, such as the adult right femur, was selected for sampling to avoid the possibility of inadvertently dating the same individual more than once. This was particularly important when dealing with the disarticulated remains from the grave of the Boscombe Bowmen, where bones could not always be assigned to one individual but rather to a minimum number of individuals.

In the case of the juvenile burials from the grave of the Boscombe Bowmen the left femur had to be selected because the right ones were not preserved. The human bone samples were selected by Jacqueline McKinley and sampled at the Radiocarbon Accelerator Unit, Oxford under the supervision of Tom Higham. Two separate samples from the Amesbury Archer were submitted yielding a statistically indistinguishable result and two boar's tusks from the grave were also dated.

Results and Models

The graves of the Boscombe Bowmen (25000), the Amesbury Archer (1289), and the 'Companion' (1236)

In addition to the 11 dates from the early Beaker graves reported in this volume, a further 29 samples from selected features of Late Neolithic and Early Bronze Age date from the excavations at Boscombe Down have been incorporated into the radiocarbon models (Fig. 61; Table 28). The locations of these features are shown on Figure 3. Full details and a complete list of these measurements will appear in Volume 2 (Powell and Barclay in prep.).

Eight measurements were made on samples of human bone from the grave of the Boscombe Bowmen (25000). Two (OxA-13624 and OxA-13598) are on articulated skeletons (25007: juvenile and 25004: mature adult) that were on the base of the grave. The right femur of the adult burial (25004) was recovered in an articulated position and, although the femur from 25007 was recovered from recently disturbed grave fill (25010e), its attribution to this burial is considered to be highly likely (see McKinley, p. 20 above). In addition three measurements were obtained on disarticulated right femurs. One (OxA-13543; 25008b adult) was from a bundle of bones (25008) that was stratigraphically beneath the articulated legs of burial 25004 at the base of the grave (Fig. 6, above). The remaining two femurs were recovered from the recently disturbed grave fill (25010), although there is a high probability that these had been displaced from the *in situ* bone deposit 25008 during the service trench work. One femur belongs to a second adult (OxA-13542; 25010a) and the other to a sub-adult (OxA-13681; 25010b). A small (7 g) deposit of cremated human bone from an infant (25006) was

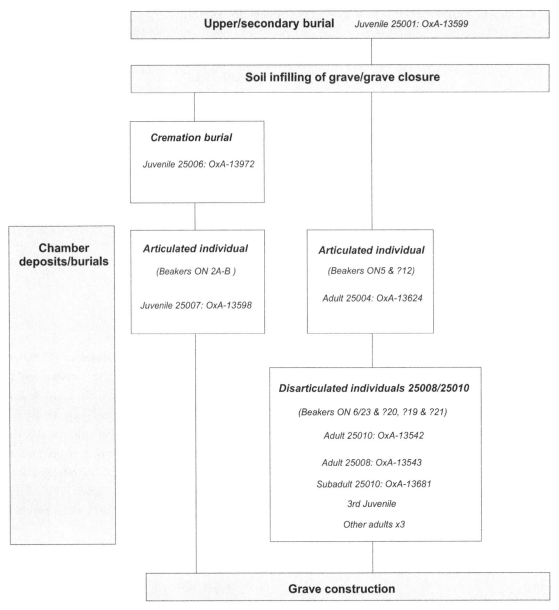

Figure 59 Grave 25000 (Boscombe Bowmen): Radiocarbon Model 1

found above and intermingled with the bones of the juvenile, 25007. Its position relative to the inhumed bone suggested, at the time of excavation, that it should be broadly contemporaneous. A single date on cremated long bone was obtained (OxA-13599; 25006). Lastly, a single date (OxA-13972) was obtained for juvenile burial 25001 that was recovered from the upper fill of the grave of the Boscombe Bowmen (25005) and was therefore stratigraphically later (Fig. 5, above). This measurement (OxA-13599) is on a left femur, recovered from recently disturbed grave fill (25010/20f), and identified as almost certainly deriving from this burial (see McKinley, p. 20 above).

Interpretation of the Boscombe Bowmen burial sequence and the radiocarbon models

Two alternative chronological models for the grave of the Boscombe Bowmen (25000) are presented below. The difference between the two models is based on archaeological interpretation of the grave deposits. The prior information for each model is outlined in Figures 59–60.

The remains of eight, possibly nine, individuals (five radiocarbon dated) along with eight Beaker pots, and other objects of bone and flint were buried in a wooden lined grave that may have been sealed with and accessed by a lid. The probability that the cremated remains of a juvenile (25006)

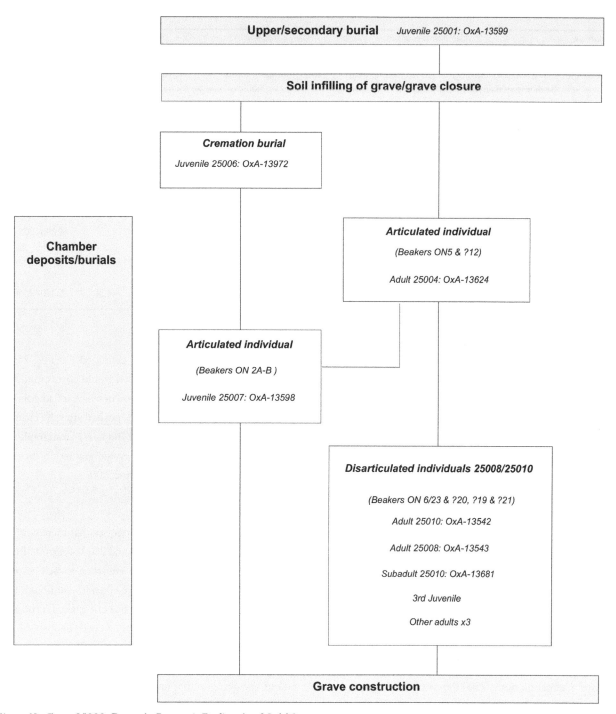

Figure 60 Grave 25000 (Boscombe Bowmen): Radiocarbon Model 2.

were added prior to the infilling of the chamber is discussed on p. 28. The chamber was filled with soil, which could represent a closing event for the use of the chamber, assuming this was a deliberate act. This event is recognised in both models and must have happened after the deposition of the cremated remains and some time before the interment of juvenile 25001. The remains of juvenile 25001 were inserted into the top of the infilled grave.

In total the remains of up to 11 people are recognised and feasibly each could represent a separate burial event. Alternatively the remains of more than one individual could have been placed during a single burial event. The length and probable size of the grave suggests that it was never intended to hold more than a small number of contemporaneous burials although it was clearly larger than would be necessary to hold a single individual. This would strongly support the

Table 28: Selected radiocarbon dates from Boscombe Down

Lab. no.	Burial/bone deposit	Sample	δ¹³C (‰)	Radiocarbon age (BP)	Calibrated date BC (95% confidence)
NZA-32486	Flat grave, crouched burial (10025) assoc. with Beaker material in upper fill of grave	10288 human l. femur	-21.1	3812±25	2340–2150
NZA-32510	Cremation burial assoc. with Late Neolithic pit/post alignment	13412 human long bone shaft	-22.6	3934±30	2560–2310
NZA-32788	Primary Beaker burial, partially disturbed, in round barrow; burial placed in chamber/lined grave	6012 human l. ulna from articulated skeletal remains	-20.8	3835±25	2460–2200
NZA-32506	Deposit of Beaker pottery (comb zoned & finger-nail rusticated) & animal bone in upper fill grave 10025	cattle bone	-21.9	3770±30	2290–2060
NZA-32494	Beaker burial 12134 with long necked Beaker	12125 human l. distal femur	-21.2	3664±30	2140–1950
NZA-32485	Pit 10152 with human skull & femur frags & Beaker pottery (2 comb zoned impressed vessels)	human humerus	-21.0	3779±30	2296–2060
NZA-32490	Single grave 13377, burial of v. tall individual; long necked Beaker	13385 human l. fibula	-21.1	3734±25	2200–2040
NZA-32495	25010 Beaker burial with short necked Beaker	25049 human l. distal femur	-20.6	3774±30	2290–2060

suggestion made here that the grave was intended (or at least used) for a series of sequential burials (see Chapter 2 above).

The burials on the base of the grave comprise the juvenile burial (25007), the mature adult burial (25004), and a mass of disarticulated remains from which a minimum of four individuals (juvenile, subadult and two adults) have been suggested (see McKinley pp. 20–1 above). The interpretation of the burial sequence is hampered both by the processes of burial deposition and post-depositional factors. Due to the ambiguity in the evidence the following models were considered:

Model 1

In this model the following depositional, stratigraphic, and/or spatial factors are considered (Fig. 59): after construction of the burial chamber the earliest deposits include the disarticulated bone (25008/25010) and the juvenile burial 25007, although there is no stratigraphic relationship between the two. Cremation burial 25006 must be later than juvenile 25007 and the individuals represented by the disarticulated bone deposits (25008 including 25010) must be earlier than the articulated burial 25004 with which they are stratigraphically associated. The assumption is made that the temporal relationship between 25004 and 25007 is unknown. It is argued that the cremated remains are so closely associated with the bones of 25007 that the chamber must still have been open at the time of deposition. The possibility that the cremated bone was deposited within a secondary grave cut is dismissed (see p. 28 above). The implication is that the chamber was open and relatively free of grave fill

until after the deposition of the cremated remains, 25006. The filling of the chamber with soil would correspond with the 'closure' of the grave or a period in which it had gone out of use. Juvenile burial 25001 was deposited after the chamber had filled (or been filled) with soil and is at a stratigraphically higher level within grave 25001. It is stratigraphically the latest of the burial deposits within grave 25000.

Model 2

This model is similar to 1 but recognises that there could be a sequence between burials 25004 and 25007 (Fig. 60). In this model the disarticulated remains are taken to belong to an early phase of burial (one or more episodes), although their relationship with burial 25007 remains uncertain. It is possible that the bones represent bodies that had been deposited intact along with their associated grave goods (Beakers ON6/23 and ?ON20), and subsequently moved towards the southern end of the grave so that juvenile burial 25007 (with Beakers ON2A–B) could be placed. The possibility that the adult burial 25004 disturbed that of juvenile burial 25007 is considered by McKinley (see p. 28 above) and this relationship is acknowledged in this model. The disarticulated bone was then further manipulated by the placing of the adult burial 25004, which also respects the position of the juvenile and the associated pots. Beaker ON5 and possibly ON12 were placed near this adult's head, as other available space is occupied by bundles of human bone.

In this model burial is seen as individual and sequential, although the overall time span could be quite short.

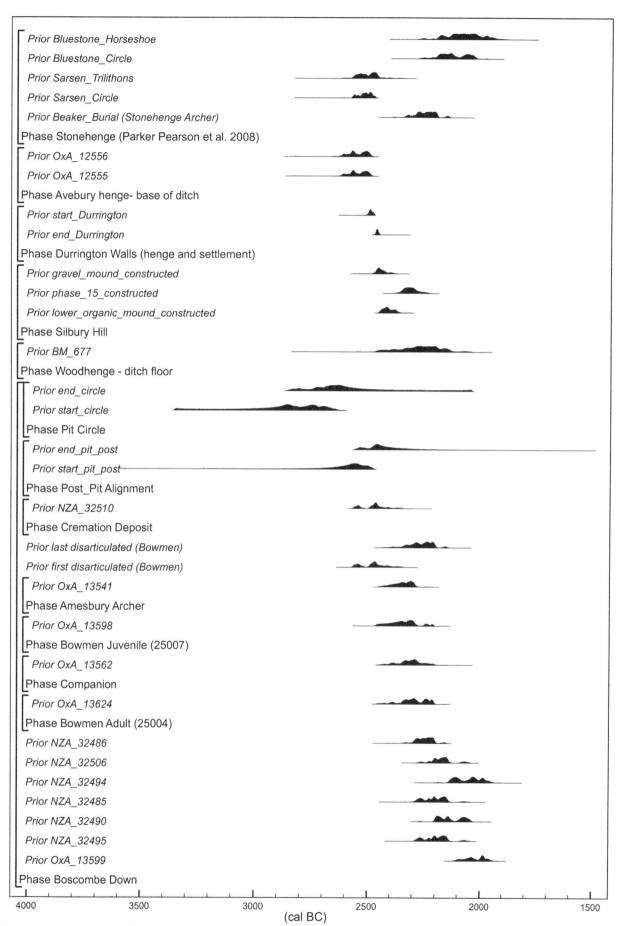

Figure 61 Probability distributions (posterior density estimates) and calibrated distributions for key sites in Wessex and selected Late Neolithic and Beaker features at Boscombe Down

Table 29: Probability (%) order of radiocarbon dates for selected burials from Boscombe Down

	Order	Cremation burial: pit alignment NZA-32510	Amesbury Archer OxA-13541	'Companion' OxA-13562	Adult 25004 OxA-13624	Juvenile 25007 OxA-13598	Bowmen grave Lastdisart	Beaker burial 10025 NZA-32486	Bowmen grave Firstdisart	Beaker burial NZA-32788
Cremation burial: pit alignment	NZA-32510	0.0	95.6	97.6	99.8	95.1	98.1	99.9	47.3	99.4
Amesbury Archer	OxA-13541	4.4	0.0	100.0	94.4	57.2	73.1	96.1	3.6	90.6
'Companion"	OxA-13562	2.4	0.0	0.0	80.3	40.3	52.2	82.2	2.0	75.0
Adult 25004	OxA-13624	0.2	5.6	19.7	0.0	13.8	0.0	49.7	0.0	43.3
Juvenile 25007	OxA-13578	4.9	42.5	59.7	86.2	0.0	61.0	84.9	4.1	79.5
Bowmen grave	Lastdisart	1.9	27.0	47.8	100.0	39.1	0.0	82.2	0.0	74.8
Beaker burial 10025	NZA-32486	0.1	3.9	17.8	50.3	15.1	17.8	0.0	0.1	42.4
Grave 25000 (Boscombe Bowmen)	Firstdisart	52.7	96.4	98.1	100.0	96.0	100.0	99.9	0.0	99.6
Beaker burial	NZA-32788	0.6	9.4	25.0	56.7	20.4	25.2	57.6	0.4	0.0

The table should be read from the left hand column across each row. The stated value (%) is the probability that the radiocarbon date listed in the left column is older than each radiocarbon date in the row (eg, the % probability that cremation burial NZA-32510 is older than the Amesbury Archer OxA-13541 is 95.6% = 0.956 probability)

The Amesbury Archer and the 'Companion'

There is no direct stratigraphic relationship between the Amesbury Archer, the 'Companion', or the grave of the Boscombe Bowmen. However, there is an archaeological argument for interpreting the burial of the 'Companion' as later than that of the Amesbury Archer because of the typology of the gold ornaments found in both graves (pp. 129–31 above). The burials in all three graves are linked by similar material culture.

Burial Order of the three graves and other early graves from Boscombe Down

Table 29 provides an assessment of the relationship between selected burial dates from Boscombe Down including the Late Neolithic cremation burial (NZA-32510), the Amesbury Archer, 'Companion', four individuals from the Bowmen grave, 'flat grave' inhumation burial 10025 (NZA-10025), and primary barrow burial (NZA-32788). The last two graves were located near to the Late Neolithic pit circle (Fig. 3, above).

Details of NZA-32486, 32510, and 32788 can be found in Table 28 and will be published in full in Volume 2 (Powell and Barclay in prep.). The earliest burials are the cremation burial (NZA-32510) and the first disarticulated individual from the grave of the Boscombe Bowmen. The date of the

Amesbury Archer is later than both, of a similar age to Boscombe Bowmen juvenile 25007, and probably earlier than all of the other selected burials. Both the juvenile 25007 and the Amesbury Archer could be slightly earlier than the youngest of the disarticulated individuals. The 'Companion' is younger than both the Amesbury Archer and this juvenile and probably of a similar age to the last disarticulated burial, and he is potentially older than the Boscombe Bowmen adult 25004 and burial 10025, both of which could have died at a similar time. The last disarticulated individual in the grave of the Boscombe Bowmen probably died before both these burials. The person buried at the centre of the barrow (NZA-32788) probably died just before individuals 25004 and 10025. Table 29 provides a probability order using the OxCal function for selected burial dates from Boscombe Down based on the prior information used in model 1. Model 2 with slightly different (additional) prior information produces a near-identical outcome of order probabilities, and for this reason is not shown. Based on model 1 the earliest burials are the cremation burial (NZA-32510) and the first disarticulated individual. The date of the Amesbury Archer is later than both, of a similar age to the juvenile in the grave of the Boscombe Bowmen 25007 and probably earlier than all the other selected burials. Both the juvenile 25007 and the Amesbury Archer burials could be slightly earlier than the youngest of the disarticulated burials. The 'Companion' is younger than both the Amesbury Archer and this juvenile and probably of a similar age to the last disarticulated burial. He is potentially older than the Boscombe Bowman adult 25004 and burial 10025, both of whom could have died at a similar time. The last disarticulated individual probably died before both these burials. The person buried at the centre of the barrow (NZA-32788) probably died just before 25004 and 10025.

The three radiocarbon dated articulated burials (25001 = OxA-13599, 25004 = OxA-13624, and 25007 = OxA-13598) were all sampled for strontium and oxygen isotopes (p. 13 above) and in all three cases the radiocarbon dates can be considered to be direct measurements on the respective skeletons. In the case of the other two adults sampled for the isotope analysis (from part of the disarticulated bone group 25008/25010 = OxA-13542–3) the radiocarbon dates are not directly associated and although the measurements are on right femurs that could be from the same individuals this cannot be demonstrated with complete certainty as more than two adults are represented (see McKinley below). If the assumption is made that the dated femurs belong with the respective mandibles, then there is the possibility that the three male adults were alive at a similar time.

For the three individuals (25004, 25008, and 25010) to have travelled at the same time, the two represented by disarticulated remains OxA-13542–3 (ages at death c. 23–30 and 25–30 yrs, respectively) must have died and been buried in the grave up to 10 years before 25004 (age at death c. 35–45 yr) if their respective age at death is considered (see McKinley above). This is not in total agreement with the modelled results (see below and χ^2 text) as the three measurements are statistically inconsistent (T'=9.7; ν=2; T'(5%)=6.0); only 25008 and 25004 could be of a similar age, while 25010 is probably older (with the caveat that the dated bones may not actually belong with the mandibles, see above).

Chronology of the Burials and Wider Implications

The results of the chronological models and calibration plots are shown in Figures 58 and 61 and in summary the models show that the burials of the Boscombe Bowmen, the Amesbury Archer, and the 'Companion' belong to an early phase of Beaker activity that starts between *2480 and 2340 cal BC (at 68% probability)* (Amesbury Archer) and *2510 and 2300 cal BC (at 68% probability)* (Boscombe Bowmen) (Model 1; the Model 2 results are almost indistinguishable).

The earliest date (OxA-13582) is associated with one of the disarticulated individuals from the grave of the Boscombe Bowmen. However, the date of the earliest individual (here referred to as 'First disarticulated') is calculated by modelling all of the available dates on disarticulated bone from the grave. Model 1 indicates that the difference between this inhumation (First disarticulated) and the Late Neolithic cremation burial from the pit alignment is between *150 and 160 years (at 95% probability)*. In other words either could be earlier, although the gap between the two could be up to at least 150 years. Both burials could be older than all of the others under discussion here. Within the grave of the Boscombe Bowmen the span of time represented by the disarticulated burials could have lasted just one or three human generations or considerably longer, up to 10 or more generations (*100–250 years at 68% probability and 30–310 years at 95% probability*; Model 2 would produce a near identical result). This model indicates that the grave was 'closed' (no longer an accessible chamber) at some point between *2120 and 1970 cal BC (at 95% probability)*. This date would approximate to the end of the Beaker phase at Boscombe Down and the onset of an Early Bronze Age phase (associated with Food Vessels and Collared Urns) (Powell and Barclay in prep.).

The OxCal 'Order' function has been used to sequence the burials in the three graves that do not have direct stratigraphic links (Table 29). The earliest of the disarticulated bones in the grave of the Boscombe Bowmen grave is earlier (*First disarticulated burial 2400–2310 BC at 68% probability*) than the articulated remains of the juvenile 25007 (*2360–2290 BC at 68% probability*) and adult 25004 (*2330–2200 BC at 95% probability*) in the same grave, the Amesbury Archer (*2380–2290 BC at 68% probability*) and the 'Companion' (*2350–2260 BC at 59% probability*). The juvenile 25007 is older than the adult 25004 but probably of a similar age to the Amesbury Archer. The Amesbury Archer is older than the 'Companion', while the latter could be of a similar age to adult 25004 in the grave of the Boscombe Bowmen.

Although the five measurements on the individuals from the Bowmen grave are not statistically consistent (T'=12.1; ν=4; T'(5%)= 9.5), the results do suggest that the individuals died within a relatively short period of time of each other. The juvenile inhumation burial 25004 (OxA-13598) and the disarticulated burial 25010 (OxA-13542) are statistically consistent and could be of the same age (T'=2;ν=1; T'(5%)= 3.8) as could the adult inhumation burial 25004 (OxA-13624) and the disarticulated burials 25008 (OxA-13543) and 25010 (OxA-13681) (T'=2; ν=2; T'(5%)= 6.0). The latter is more inline with Model 2 (see above).

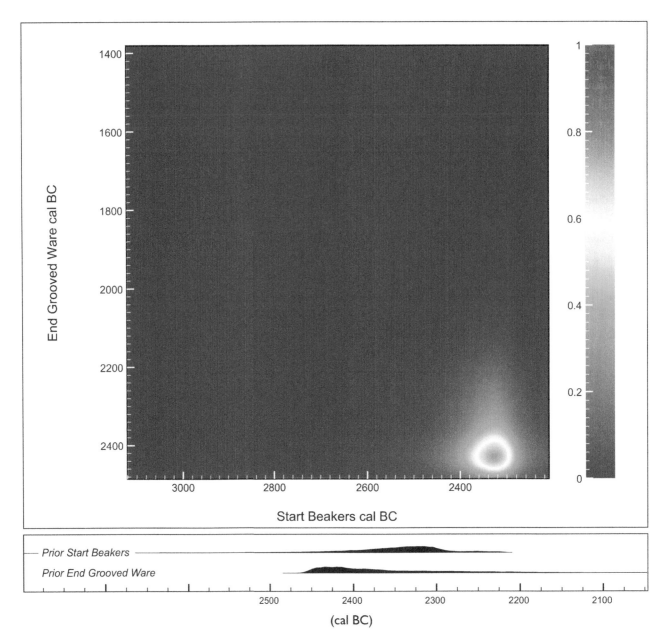

Figure 62 Posterior Density Estimates for the start of Beaker associated activity and the end of Grooved Ware associated activity at Boscombe Down. Lower: individual distributions for the two parameters (start_Beakers, end_Grooved Ware); Upper: a probability contour plot generated from plotting the distributions of the two estimated parameters – start_Beakers, end_Grooved Ware. The colour scale on the right hand side denotes the probability (red is high) that any overlap between the final use of Grooved Ware and the first use of Beaker pottery was relatively short.

However, the date of each individual comes from a single radiocarbon measurement and therefore the validity of the model could be further tested if additional dates were obtained (ie, at least two measurements per individual). However, due to the nature of the calibration curve, further dates are unlikely to improve the level of precision achieved so far.

All the Beaker burials in the three graves (the Amesbury Archer, the Boscombe Bowmen, and the 'Companion') are older than and, therefore, were made before grave 10025

(NZA-32486), while the primary burial (6033) within barrow 6037 is of a similar but slightly younger age to the adult burial 25004 (OxA-13624) from the grave of the Boscombe Bowmen. The model also shows that the cremation burial of an infant (25006) and the inhumation burial of a juvenile (25001) found stratigraphically above the adult burial 25004 in the grave of the Boscombe Bowmen were made up to 200 years later than burial 25004 (*140–270 years at 66% probability*). This suggests that a significant interval could separate the final Beaker burial in 25000 and the closure of the grave from

177

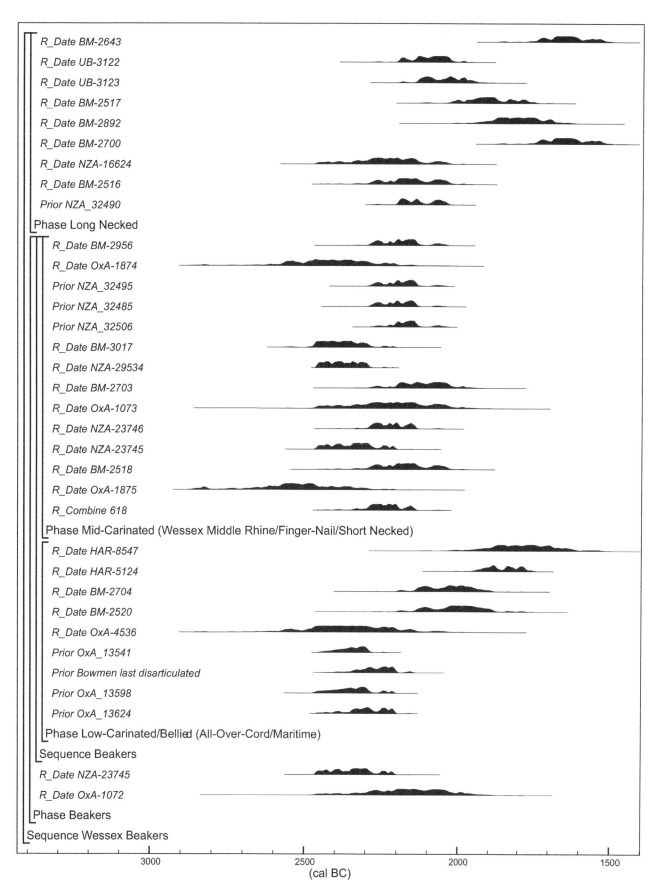

R_Date BM-2643
R_Date UB-3122
R_Date UB-3123
R_Date BM-2517
R_Date BM-2892
R_Date BM-2700
R_Date NZA-16624
R_Date BM-2516
Prior NZA_32490
Phase Long Necked
R_Date BM-2956
R_Date OxA-1874
Prior NZA_32495
Prior NZA_32485
Prior NZA_32506
R_Date BM-3017
R_Date NZA-29534
R_Date BM-2703
R_Date OxA-1073
R_Date NZA-23746
R_Date NZA-23745
R_Date BM-2518
R_Date OxA-1875
R_Combine 618
Phase Mid-Carinated (Wessex Middle Rhine/Finger-Nail/Short Necked)
R_Date HAR-8547
R_Date HAR-5124
R_Date BM-2704
R_Date BM-2520
R_Date OxA-4536
Prior OxA_13541
Prior Bowmen last disarticulated
Prior OxA_13598
Prior OxA_13624
Phase Low-Carinated/Bellied (All-Over-Cord/Maritime)
Sequence Beakers
R_Date NZA-23745
R_Date OxA-1072
Phase Beakers
Sequence Wessex Beakers

3000   2500 (cal BC)   2000   1500

Figure 63 Probability distributions of radiocarbon dated Beaker burials from Boscombe Down and other sites in Wessex

burial 25007, which could be associated with the nearby ring ditch (probably a barrow) presumed to be of Early Bronze Age date. These results are summarised in Figure 61. The cremated human remains (*2500–2400 BC at 65% probability*) from one of the post-pits of the pit/post alignment are probably earlier than the phase of Beaker burials and this deposit is probably earlier than the first individual represented amongst the disarticulated remains in the grave of the Boscombe Bowmen.

Comparison with selected Beakers from Wessex and the Upper Thames Valley and the chronological relationship with Grooved Ware from Boscombe Down

The Beakers associated with the Boscombe Bowmen and Amesbury Archer burials include All-Over plaited Cord, Cord-Zoned-Maritime, All-Over-Cord and Comb and 'European' style vessels. There is the suggestion that, on Boscombe Down, Wessex/Middle Rhine, short-necked or mid-carinated Beakers, as well as rusticated vessels, are later in date (after 2300 cal BC) (NZA-32506, NZA-32485, NZA-32495), while forms with long or short upright necks are later still (NZA-32490, NZA-32494). Based on the measurements currently available for the project, then, this suggests that overall the Beaker phase at Boscombe Down lasted 400–500 years (or between 16 and 20 human generations), starting in the late 25th century and ending either during the 21st or 20th century BC (Fig. 61). This is in broad agreement with Needham's scheme for the funerary use of Beakers (2005, 209–10, fig. 13), although it also suggests that his so-called 'fission horizon' – as Sheridan (2007, 99) has suggested for Scotland – may have occurred at a slightly earlier date (*c.* 2300 cal BC) than he had suggested. It also seems that Needham's third and final phase: 'Beaker as past reference', could on current evidence be largely absent from at least the local sequence.

Despite the small sample size, the Boscombe Down sequence of dates does provide a consistent set of results that approximates to the typo-chronologies advanced previously by Case (1977a) and Lanting and van der Waals (1972), although overall the sequence appears condensed into a 500 year span.

Figure 63 presents a comparative plot of a selection of Beaker burial dates (Table 30; cf. Needham 2005, tables 1–7) from Wessex and the Upper Thames with those from Boscombe Down. The dates have been grouped into broad categories according to Clarke's styles of Beaker (1970) and into what are generally considered to be early, middle and late types following the earlier work of Case (1977a). The first

group includes All-Over-Cord/Comb and Maritime/European vessels (AOC/M), the second Wessex/Middle Rhine, All-Over Finger-Nail (mostly aplastic) and short-necked forms (Northern styles) and the third, long-necked Beakers (Southern styles).

When the Boscombe Down Beaker dates are compared with those from the selected sites they highlight the potential problematic dates from elsewhere, in particular those from Barrow Hills, Radley (BM-2704, BM-2520, OxA-1874 and 1875) and Balksbury, Hampshire (HAR-5124) (Fig. 63: compare with the results from Boscombe Down, in particular OxA-13541 and OxA-13598). The reliability of a number of older measurements has been challenged (eg, Ashmore *et al.* 2000; Sheridan 2007, 93–6; Lanting 2007, 42; p. 196 below) (Table 30). The date for the inhumation burial with low carinated/Maritime Derived vessel from Balksbury, Hampshire is generally accepted as being too late (Cleal 1995b; Needham 2005, 185, table 1). The dates for the Barrow Hills burials could also be seen as problematic. Those associated with the two burial deposits in grave 919 appear too early by perhaps 100–200 years for the types of Beaker vessels. A date no earlier than the one for the Amesbury Archer (OxA-13541) or Barrow Hills, grave 4A (OxA-4536) would be expected on typological grounds for the pottery, despite the presence of what are acknowledged as potentially early copper rings (Needham 1999a, 186). Given that the rings could have been intended for an adult rather than a juvenile, they could be older than the person buried and, therefore, the possibility that they are heirlooms should be considered. Similarly the dates for Barrow Hills 4660 (BM-2704), with an atypical Comb-Zoned Maritime Beaker and tanged copper knife, and 203 (BM-2700), with an All-Over-Cord S-profile Beaker appear too young by at least 200 years. In all these cases this will only be resolved through a further dating programme. Given that a number of the results can be seen as problematic, then the rather late date for Radley burial 206 may also be questioned as being too late.

If an allowance is made for the various problematic results then, for the earlier part of the Beaker sequence, the radiocarbon dates do appear to support the suggestion that All-Over-Cord and Cord-Zoned-Maritime Beakers are amongst the earliest forms. All-Comb-Zoned Maritime Beakers (ie, the Chilbolton vessel) are potentially slightly later. The temporal position of the classic slender Wessex/Middle Rhine vessel is typified by vessels from Wilsford G1 (A303), Wiltshire (NZA-29534), Thomas Hardye School (NZA-23745-6), Dorset and Barrow Hills 950 (BM-2703). The earliest dates are those for Wilsford G1 (NZA-29534, 2465–

Table 30: Selected radiocarbon dated burials in Wessex and the Upper Thames mentioned in the text

Site and burial	Lab. no.	δ¹³C‰	Radiocarbon age (BP)	Calibrated date BC (95% confidence)	Sample	Beaker
A303/Wilsford G1, Wiltshire, grave 1502	NZA-29534	–	3878±20	2465–2285	human bone, some disturbance	Wessex/Middle Rhine
Alington Avenue, Dorset, grave 127	HAR-9662	–	3810±120	2580–1910	human bone	–
Balksbury, Hampshire, grave 2286	HAR-5124	–	3530±30	1950–1750	human bone	Wessex/Middle Rhine
Barnack, Cambridgeshire, grave 28	BM-2956	–	3770±35	2300–2040	human bone	Wessex/Middle Rhine
Barrow Hills, Radley, Oxfordshire, Barrow 4A	OxA-4356	-21.4	3880±90	2580–2040	human bone	Maritime Derived
Barrow Hills, Radley, grave 4660	BM-2704	-21.3	3650±50	2200–1890	human bone	Maritime Derived
Barrow Hills, Radley, Barrow 201, grave 203	BM-2700	-20.9	3360±50	1760–1510	human bone	Southern style/long neck
Barrow Hills, Radley, Barrow 201, grave 206	BM-2520	-21.8	3630±60	2200–1780	human bone, all destroyed in dating	All-Over-Cord
Barrow Hills, Radley, grave 919, double burial	OxA-1874 / OxA-1875	-21 (est) / -21 (est)	3930±80 / 3990±80	2630–2150 / 2860–2280	human bone	Zone incised/barbed wire disarticulated bone in Wessex/ Middle Rhine/European style
Chilbolton, Hampshire, primary burial (16)	OxA-1072	–	3740±80	2460–1920	human bone, burial disturbed	Wessex/Middle Rhine/ European style
Chilbolton, secondary burial (15)	OxA-1073	–	3780±80	2470–1970	human bone	aplastic, finger-nail impressed (FN)
Oxford, Gene Function Centre, Oxfordshire, grave 204	NZA-16624	-21.0	3792±60	2470–2030	human bone	S4 Final southern Beaker Group/Step 7
Thomas Hardye School, Dorset, grave 1605, burial 1738	NZA-23746	-21.0	3789±30	2300–2130	human bone, disturbed	Wessex/Middle Rhine
Thomas Hardye School, grave 1643, burial 1823	NZA-23745	-20.9	3859±30	2470–2200	human bone	Wessex/Middle Rhine
Fordington Farm, Dorset, grave 59	UB-3305	–	3767±47	2340–2030	human bone (?both femurs)	–
Fordington Farm, grave 70	UB-3304	–	3715±54	2290–1950	human bone (?both femurs)	–
Stonehenge, Wiltshire, burial 4028	OxA-4886	-21.2	3960±60		human bone	
Stonehenge, Wiltshire, burial 4028	OxA-4044	-20.7	3785±70		human bone	
Stonehenge, Wiltshire, burial 4028	OxA-5045	-20.6	3825±60	combined 2440–2140	human bone	
Stonehenge, Wiltshire, burial 4028	OxA-5046	-20.6	3775±55		human bone	
Stonehenge, Wiltshire, burial 4028	BM-1582	-21.8	3715±70		human bone	

2285 cal BC) and Thomas Hardye School grave 1643 (NZA-23745 2460–2280 cal BC). Both could be as early as, or slightly later than, the Amesbury Archer (OxA-13541 2440–2280 cal BC model 1) and Boscombe Bowmen juvenile (25007 OxA-13598 2460–2280 cal BC 79% probability model 1) burials and certainly as early, if not earlier than the 'Companion' (OxA-13562 2350–2240 cal BC at 63% probability or 2440–

2200 cal BC at 95% probability model 1) and the Boscombe Bowmen adult 25004 (OxA-13624 2340–2200 cal BC 95% probability model 1). The single date for Shrewton 5K (BM-3017) can also be seen as slightly too early (see Needham 2005, tab. 4; Sheridan 2007, fig. 11.3) and its real age could be expected to be no earlier than 2300 cal BC (cf. Sandhole, Aberdeenshire: OxA-V-2172-23, 3845±32 BP, 2400–2210 cal

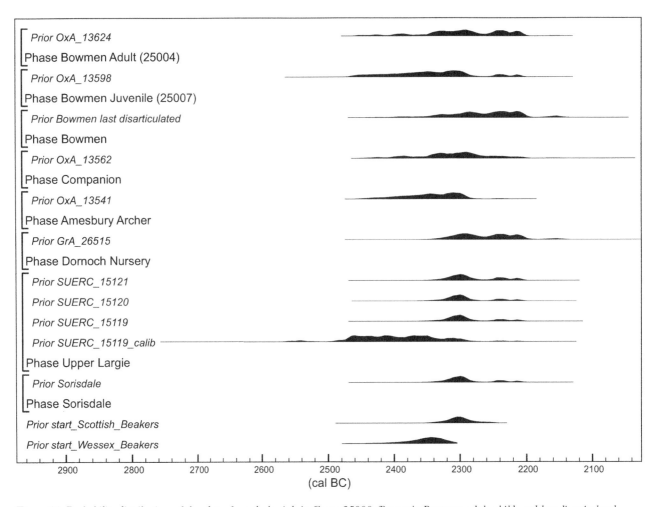

Figure 64 Probability distributions of key dates from the burials in Grave 25000 (Boscombe Bowmen; adult, child, and last disarticulated burial), 1289 (Amesbury Archer), and 1236, and a comparison with selected graves from Scotland and the modelled start dates for Beakers in Wessex and in Scotland

BC at 68% confidence or 2470–2200 cal BC at 95% confidence; and Boatbridge Quarry, South Lanarkshire: OxA-V-2168-42, 3824±32 BP, 2340–2200 cal BC at 68% confidence or 2460–2140 cal BC at 95% confidence), bringing it broadly in line with the Boscombe Bowman adult (25004), burial 1238, and the Stonehenge burial. The re-dating of this grave as part of the Beaker People Project should help resolve this uncertainty.

The Boscombe Down project, along with other recent investigations (eg, the A303 and Thomas Hardye School: Leivers and Moore 2008; Gardiner *et al.* 2006) appear to be producing a typologically coherent sequence from which other older results (ie, those obtained pre-2005) from Wessex can be reviewed.

In contrast to the first appearance of Beaker activity, the final use of Grooved Ware associated activity on Boscombe Down appears to have effectively ceased within the late 25th century or early 24th century cal BC (Models 1–2 have near

identical results: *Start Beaker 2400–2300 cal BC, End Grooved Ware 2460–2320 cal BC*). This relationship between Grooved Ware and Beaker associated activity is shown in Figure 62. This period of overlap between Beaker and Grooved Ware activity and practices may approximate to the beginning of a British Chalcolithic phase, the start of which could be marked by the burials of the Boscombe Bowmen juvenile 25007 (*2460–2280 cal BC at 79% probability*) and the Amesbury Archer (*2440–2290 cal BC at 95% probability*). However, within the Boscombe Bowmen grave is at least one burial that could pre-date that of the juvenile 25007. This person could have died one or more generations before the other two burials and in the early or mid-25th century cal BC (*2500–2350 cal BC at 68% probability*). The possibility that one, if not two, pots (ON6/23 All-Over plaited Cord and 20 Cord-Zoned-Maritime) of what should represent the earliest Beaker types in Britain may belong to this early phase of burial, although the evidence is ambiguous (see p. 49 above). The relationship

Table 31: Selected radiocarbon dated burials in Scotland mentioned in text (no δ¹³C measurements)

Site and burial	Lab. no.	Radiocarbon age (BP)	Calibrated date BC (95% confidence)	Sample	Beaker
Upper Largie, Argyll & Bute	SUERC-15119	3915±40	2550–2280	charcoal (hazel), same level as grave goods	Cord-Zoned-Maritime, Maritime Derived, All-Over-Cord
	SUERC-15120	3900±35	2480–2280	charcoal (oak), post-pipe in ring ditch	
	SUERC-15121	3880±35	2480–2200	charcoal (oak), fill of ring ditch	
Sorisdale, Isle of Coll	OxA-14722	3879±32	2470–2200	human bone	All-Over-Cord
	BM-1413	3884±46	2630–2030	human bone	
Dornoch Nursery, Highland	GrA-26515	3850±40	2470–2150	cremated bone, young adult, *poss.* assoc. with adult burial with whom grave goods considered to be assoc. but which contained insufficient collagen to produce a radiocarbon date	All-Over-Cord

between the end of Beaker-associated activity and the uptake of Collared Urn and Food Vessel pottery and associated practices will be examined in Volume 2 (Powell and Barclay in prep.), although this is likely to have happened in the 21st century cal BC.

Comparisons with Beakers from Scotland and from the Ross Island, Ireland, copper mine

In order to establish whether Beakers in Wessex appeared earlier in the burial record than those from Scotland (see Sheridan 2007), both sets of available dates were modelled with the resulting start dates presented in Figure 64 (Table 31). This revealed that in Wessex the use of Beakers probably started during *2420–2300 cal BC (at 95% probability)* or *2373–2318 cal BC (at 68 probability)*, while in Scotland it was slightly later, beginning at some point during *2340–2250 cal BC (at 95% probability)* or *2320–2280 cal BC (at 68% probability)*. However, this result may be misleading as the earliest Beakers in Scotland (eg, Newmill, Perth and Kinross) are under-represented with radiocarbon dates, since the bodies had decayed away (Sheridan 2008a, 253, fig. 21.9, 1). Typologically, there is little, if anything, in the Scottish record which suggests that Beakers appeared in Scotland later than in the south of England (see Clarke 1970, 281; and also note in particular the occurrence of plaited cord impressed sherds from Archerfield, East Lothian and Glenluce, Wigtown (*ibid.*, 286 48 b–c) that are likely to be from similar Beakers to the ones from the Bowmen and Archer graves). Of the earliest Scottish Beaker burials, direct comparison cannot be made with that from Upper Largie, Kilmartin, Argyll and Bute (Sheridan 2008) as the dates are on charcoal (albeit from a short-lived species) and charred plant remains that have an uncertain association and age offset with the actual burial (which did not survive). There is no doubt, however, that the Upper Largie burial is one of the earliest in Scotland.

Of the other early Scottish Beaker burials (Fig. 72), the AOC Beaker associated individual from Sorisdale on Coll (OxA–14722 *2340–2270 cal BC at 77% probability*) is probably slightly earlier than the AOC Beaker associated individual at Dornoch Nursery, Highland (GrA-26515 2340–2190 cal BC at 93% probability). If these burials are compared with those from Boscombe Down then the one from Sorisdale is likely to be younger than the burial of the 'Companion' (*2350–2240 cal BC at 64% probability*) but older than the last Beaker burial in the grave of the Boscombe Bowmen, adult 25004 (*2330–2200 cal BC at 95% probability*). The models (1 and 2) suggests that the Amesbury Archer (83% probability) was buried before all of the currently dated Beaker burials in Scotland, while the burial of the juvenile in the grave of the Boscombe Bowmen (69% probability) could be of a similar age or earlier than the Beaker burial tradition in Scotland, and the 'Companion' (55% probability) could be of a similar date to the beginnings of Beaker burial in Scotland. At present the evidence seems to suggest that the earliest Beaker contact in Britain was probably in southern Britain.

The radiocarbon dates from Ross Island (Co. Kerry, Ireland) copper mine and work camp (O'Brien 2004) were also reviewed. Thirty-three measurements are available for the Beaker/Early Bronze Age activity from material recovered from spoil and underlying contexts. The calibrated results on a series of bone and charcoal samples are shown in Figures 65–6 (O'Brien 2004, table 22). As part of the Ross Island report, Lanting (2004, 312–14) provides a detailed critique of the results and his conclusion that mining could have started around 2400 cal BC is not disputed here. Figure 66 shows that at least three bone dates (GrA-7526-7, GrA-7534) are of approximately the same age as eight of the 10 measurements on charcoal (T'=9.2; ν=10; T'(5%)= 18.3), indicating the possibility that any charcoal age offset is minimal as Lanting alludes to (2004, 313). The 2400 cal BC start date would not be at odds with the earliest type of

182

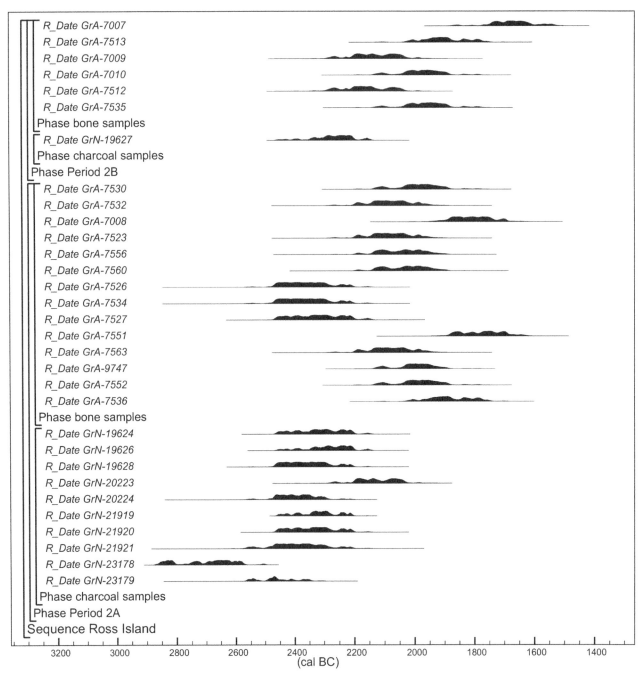

Figure 65 Probability distributions of radiocarbon dates from Ross Ireland work camp (information from Lanting 2004)

Beaker pottery from the site (Brindley 2004, 337). Broadly speaking the earliest phase of mining is therefore of similar date to the earliest Beaker activity at Boscombe Down.

Boscombe Down and Wessex: a local and regional history

The models indicate activity on Boscombe Down for much of the 3rd millennium cal BC. The following sequence (Fig. 61; Table 32) is based on Model 1. Prior to the first Beaker burials a number of pit- and post-defined structures and

monuments were constructed, many pits containing deposits that included Late Neolithic Grooved Ware pottery were dug, and at least one cremation burial was deposited.

Figure 61 shows that the Boscombe Down pit circle (*start 2960–2660 BC at 68% probability, end 2750–2480 BC at 62% probability*) is likely to be broadly contemporary with a post-built structure and perhaps slightly earlier than the pit and post alignment (*start 2640–2490 BC at 68% probability, end 2750–2480 BC at 62% probability*). The cremation burial associated with the pit/post alignment is of slightly later date

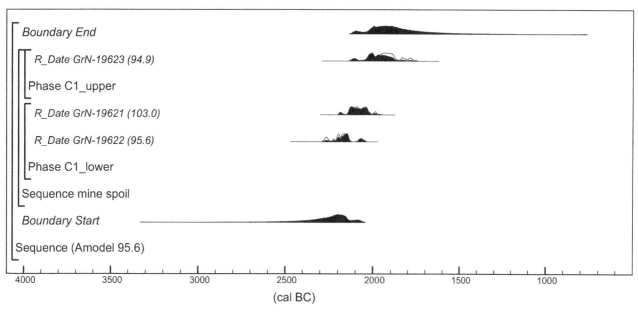

Figure 66 Probability distributions of radiocarbon dates from Ross Ireland mine (information from Lanting 2004, phasing from O'Brien 2004)

(*2560–2440 cal BC at 68% probability*). They all pre-date the Boscombe Down Beaker phase, with the possible exception of the pit/post alignment cremation burial and firmly belong with the Grooved Ware activity on the site.

The Boscombe Down pit/post alignment could be of a similar age to the sarsen settings at Stonehenge if the interpretation based on Parker Pearson *et al.* 2008 is accepted (trilithons *2560–2470 cal BC at 68.8% probability* and circle

2540–2490 cal BC at 62% probability) and the settlement and construction of the Durrington Walls henge (M. Parker Pearson, pers. comm. *Start 2500–2480 cal BC at 68% probability, end 2470–2460 cal BC at 68% probability*), if the argument that these monuments are contemporary is accepted. It is probable that the earliest individual, some of whose disarticulated remains were buried in the grave of the Boscombe Bowmen (prior First disarticulated *2500–2340 cal*

Table 32: Sequence of burial deposits based on Order Table 29 and modelled dates
(Beaker phases after Needham 2005)

Phase	Grave 25000 (Boscombe Bowmen)	Other burials
2300– Beaker Fission Horizon– Bronze Age	*Adult 25004*	
Secondary emergent Beaker set/package		
		Grave 10025
?Stonehenge bluestone settings		
Silbury Hill secondary phases		
		Barrow burial 6033
	Last disarticulated	
2450–2300 BC Chalcolithic		*Burial 1238*
Grooved Ware/Beaker	*Juvenile 25007 – other disarticulated burials*	
Primary Beaker Set/package		
Silbury Hill primary phase		*Amesbury Archer 1291*
–2450 Final Neolithic– Grooved Ware		*Post/pit cremation burial*
	?First disarticulated	
Pit/post alignment, Durrington Walls & ?Stonehenge sarsen settings		

BC, 87%), could have been alive when this activity was taking place, perhaps in the early part of the 25th century cal BC (see p. 175 above). This person probably died sometime before the individual whose cremated remains (see pp. 182–3 above) were recovered from the pit and post alignment at Boscombe Down. This activity could also be broadly contemporary with the burial of a goat and the final infilling of the chambers of the West Kennet long barrow (Bayliss *et al.* 2007a, 97).

It is also possible that the first person to be buried in the grave of the Boscombe Bowmen had lived before the construction of the first mound at Silbury Hill near Avebury (*2450–2410 cal BC at 59% probability*). The other individuals represented amongst the disarticulated bones are likely to have lived and died during the construction of Silbury Hill (*gravel mound 2470–2430 cal BC and phase 15 2350–2292 cal BC at 68% probability*: J. Leary, pers. comm.; Bayliss *et al.* 2007b). With the exception of the possible early individual, the people represented amongst the early Beaker burials at Boscombe Down all lived and died between the currently suggested dates of the construction of the sarsen settings at Stonehenge (*2570–2480 BC at 95% probability and 2580–2430 BC at 93% probability*) and the placing of the Bluestone horseshoe and circle (*2240–2030 BC at 92% probability*).

The burial in the enclosure ditch at Stonehenge (*2350–2190 BC at 91% probability, 2290–2200 BC at 68% probability*) is of a similar date to the articulated adult male 25004 in the grave of the Boscombe Bowmen (*2330–2200 cal BC at 95% probability, 2290–2200 cal BC at 68% probability*). Both could be slightly later than the burial of the 'Companion'. The single date (*2340–2190 BC at 60% probability*) from the primary fill of the Woodhenge ditch that is shown in Figure 61 is difficult to evaluate. At face value it appears later than expected and could perhaps be taken to indicate that the henge ditch post-dates the post settings; however, further dating is required to clarify the date of its construction and use. The single date is, however, comparable with the three burials discussed above.

Figure 61 illustrates that the henge at Avebury was probably earlier (*start 2620–2490 BC at 95% probability*) than the settlement and henge at Durrington Walls (*2480–2450 BC at 95% probability*), both of which pre-dated Silbury Hill and the early Beaker burials at Boscombe Down. It is therefore possible that the Durrington Walls henge could be a copy of the enclosure at Avebury, with the possible implication that the sarsen stone settings at Avebury could pre–date those at Stonehenge (see also Pollard and Cleal 2004 and Bayliss *et al.* 2007b).

It can be suggested from Figure 61 that the henges at Avebury and Durrington Walls and the sarsen settings at Stonehenge were constructed before the appearance of Beaker associated material culture, while the construction of Silbury Hill was broadly contemporaneous with the first appearance of Beaker graves (the local and regional Chalcolithic phase: Needham 2005). The Bluestone settings at Stonehenge, the horseshoe and circle, seem on present evidence to have been erected after 2300 cal BC, and at the start of the Early Bronze Age.

On Boscombe Down the main period of overlap between the first Beaker burials and the final use of Grooved Ware could have been quite short, perhaps no more than 50–75 years (<3 generations) spanning the end of the 25th century and the earlier half of the 24th century cal BC (Fig. 62). This implies that, in this area, the initial contact with the Beaker network and the full adoption of the Beaker set or package was relatively rapid and widespread by 2300 cal BC.

Chapter 7

A Summary of the Strontium and Oxygen Isotope Evidence for the Origins of Bell Beaker individuals found near Stonehenge

by C.A. Chenery and J.A. Evans

Background to Isotopic Analysis of Human Remains

Oxygen and strontium isotopes are fixed in tooth enamel biogenic phosphate at the time of tooth formation. Biogenic phosphate is extremely robust and the isotope signature of enamel does not change during life, nor is it altered in the burial environment. Oxygen isotopes are derived primarily from ingested fluids and reflect the isotopic value of available meteoric/ground/drinking water. Strontium isotopes are derived from food and relate to the geology of the area where the food was produced. As strontium and oxygen isotopes behave independently of one another, they allow two parameters for investigating an individual's place of origin and migration patterns.

This review presents isotope data from the teeth of 12 individuals from the area around Stonehenge but principally from Boscombe Down (12/14) (Table 33). Some of these results (samples 1–4) will be reported on more fully in Volume 2 (Powell and Barclay in prep.) but they are summarised here to provide an assessment of the immediate context for the early Bell Beaker graves. The data include three of the males and two juveniles interred in the grave of the Boscombe Bowmen (Evans *et al.* 2006; p. 32 above) and the Amesbury Archer and the 'Companion' (p. 87 above), both also adult males. One of the juveniles from the grave of the Boscombe Bowmen, burial 25001 (sample 12), dates to the Early Bronze Age. To investigate place of origin and migration patterns, when available, two teeth, representing mid-childhood and early adolescence, were chosen for analysis.

Dentine from three individuals from Boscombe Down, including the adult male 25004 from the grave of the Boscombe Bowmen, was analysed for strontium to assess the local environment signal and facilitate the identification of individuals who spent their childhood locally in the Stonehenge

area (Table 34). The same methods followed used for the analyses of the Amesbury Archer and the Boscombe Bowmen (pp. 32 and 87 above) and they are summarised below.

Sample Preparation

Core enamel and crown dentine were removed from the tooth samples and mechanically cleaned using tungsten carbide dental tools following the procedure given in Montgomery (2002). For strontium, all further preparation and analysis was carried out within the class 100, HEPA-filtered laboratory facilities at the NERC Isotope Geosciences Laboratory (NIGL), Keyworth, UK. The isotope compositions of strontium were obtained using a Thermo Triton thermal ionisation multi-collector mass spectrometer. The reproducibility of the international strontium standard, NBS 987, during a period of analysis gave ± 0.001% (2σ, n=25). All samples were corrected to the accepted value of $^{87}Sr/^{86}Sr = 0.710250$ to ensure that there was no induced bias through mass spectrometer drift. Strontium isotope data are presented as $^{87}Sr/^{86}Sr$ ratios. Laboratory contamination, monitored by procedural blanks, was negligible.

Oxygen Isotope Analysis

Silver Phosphate Method

Biogenic phosphate was converted to silver phosphate after the method of O'Neil *et al.* (1994) and is briefly summarised here. The core enamel samples were crushed to a fine powder and cleaned in hydrogen peroxide for 24 hours to remove organic material. The peroxide was evaporated to dryness and the sample dissolved in 2M HNO_3. The sample solutions were transferred to clean polypropylene test tubes and each

Table 33: Isotope analyses from Bell Beaker date burials, Boscombe Down and surrounding area

Sample no.	Location	Tooth	Sr ppm	$^{87}Sr/^{86}Sr_n$	$\delta^{18}O_{SMOW}$	$\delta^{18}O_{SMOW}$ drinking water	Project code and burial/context
1	Boscombe Down	pM2	62.56	0.70795	17.3	-7.7	Project 56240,
		M3	77.06	0.70796	16.8	-8.7	Grave 5293; burial 5292
2	Boscombe Down	pM2	108.5	0.70927	17.5	-7.2	Project 53535,
		M3	188.8	0.70931	17.9	-6.3	Grave 25051, burial 25049
3	Boscombe Down	pM2	55.13	0.70785	18.0	-6.0	Project 56240,
		M3	44.96	0.70800	17.6	-7.0	Grave 5290, burial 5289
4	Normanton Down	pM2	37.85	0.70784	17.8	-6.6	Project 50538,
		M3	50.45	0.70804	17.5	-7.1	burial 1515
5	Stonehenge	pM2	51.72	0.70823	17.6	-6.9	Stonehenge 1978, burial 4028
		M3	44.16	0.70791	17.5	-7.3	burial 4028
6	Boscombe Down: Bowmen	pM2	48.98	0.71344	17.5	-7.3	Project 53535,
		M3	58.91	0.71143	17.3	-7.6	grave 25000, burial 25004
7	Boscombe Down: Bowmen	pM2	76.65	0.71309	16.9	-8.5	Project 53535,
		M3	85.7	0.71174	17.0	-8.2	grave 25000, ON 11
8	Boscombe Down: Bowmen	pM2	39.78	0.71352	17.5	-7.1	Project 53535,
		M3	45.19	0.71187	17.4	-7.4	grave 25000, context 25010
9	Boscombe Down: Amesbury Archer	pM2		0.71034	16.2	-10.0	Project 50875,
		M3		0.70940	16.2	-10.0	burial 1291*
10	Boscombe Down: 'The Companion'	pM2		0.70855	17.0	-8.3	Project 50875,
		M3		0.70949	16.4	-9.5	burial 1238*
11	Boscombe Down: Bowmen	pM2	54.67	0.70983	17.6	-6.9	Project 53535, grave 25000, burial 25001 (Early Bronze Age)
12	Boscombe Down: Bowmen	pM2	55.14	0.70973	17.7	-6.8	Project 53535, grave 25000, burial 25007

Key:
*Sr isotope data provided by P. Budd
Project code:
50538: A303 Stonehenge Highway Improvements (Moore and Leivers 2008); 50875: Boscombe Down, excavations 2002; 53535: Boscombe Down: Lower Camp Watching Brief, 2003–4; 56240: Boscombe Down excavations, 2004

sample was treated with 2M KOH followed by 2M HF to remove Ca from the solution by precipitation. The following day, the samples were centrifuged and the solution was added to beakers containing silver amine solution and silver phosphate precipitated, filtered, rinsed and dried.

Analytical measurement was by Continuous Flow Isotope Ratio Mass Spectrometry (CF-IRMS) using the method of Vennemann *et al.* (2002). The instrumentation is comprised of a TC/EA (thermo chemical elemental analyser) coupled to a Delta Plus XL isotope ratio mass spectrometer via a ConFlo III interface, all by Thermo Finnigan. All reported isotope ratios are expressed using the delta (δ) notation in parts per thousand (permil: ‰) relative to a standard: δ(‰) = $((R_{sample}/R_{standard}) - 1) \times 1000$. Each sample was analysed in triplicate. AgPO4 ppt from NBS120C gave 21.71±0.16, (1σ, n = 10).

Drinking water values, where cited, are calculated using Levinson *et al.* after a +1.4‰ correction to the (Levinson *et al.* 1987) intercept value (19.4‰) to correct for standard differences between laboratories. Details of this method can be found in (Chenery *et al.* 2010). It should be noted that other drinking water conversion equations, such as that of Daux *et al.* (2008), will produce slightly different drinking water values. An uncertainty of *c.* ±0.35 (1σ) on calculated drinking water values is typical based on the reproducibility of NBS120C as given above.

Results

The data are presented in Table 33 and Figure 67. The results of this study are plotted along with previous studies of tooth enamel samples from near Stonehenge. There is a wide variation in both the strontium and oxygen isotopes from individuals buried near Stonehenge which attests to the diversity of origins of the burial population in the area. The Boscombe Bowmen form a distinctive group of data because of the radiogenic (high) strontium ratios their enamel

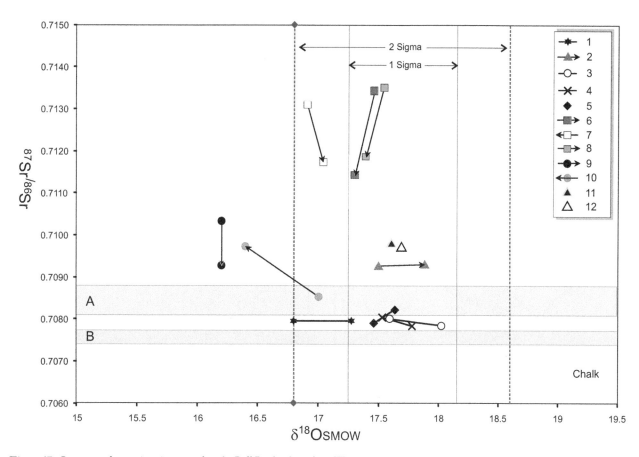

Figure 67 Oxygen and strontium isotope values for Bell Beaker burials in Wessex. Sample numbers as Table 33

displayed and the consistent shift seen in the three individuals between the strontium isotope composition of their early premolar and their later 3rd molar teeth. This shows that all three individuals moved during their childhood in a consistent manner (Evans *et al.* 2006b). The main types of rock that are likely to provide a suitable site for the early childhood premolar teeth of the three adults are granites and early Palaeozoic, or older, rocks. In Britain such rocks can be found in Scotland (Millar 1990 and references therein), the Lake District (Evans 1996a), Wales (Evans 1989; 1996b; Shand *et al.* 2001), and south-west England (Darbyshire and Shepherd 1985). Of these areas, Wales, which has links at this time with Wessex, is the closest.

If an origin for these individuals outside Britain is considered, the following regions are, on geological grounds, a possibility; south-east Ireland (O'Conner *et al.* 1998), Brittany and the Massif Central of France (Negrel *et al.* 2003), the Palaeozoic rocks of Portugal (Tassarini *et al.* 1996) and the Black Forest (Schutowski *et al.* 2000). Much of northern France can be excluded, as it is dominated by chalk and gives river water values below 0.71 (Negrel and Petelet-Giraud 2005) and Norway and Sweden can be ruled out as they are

dominated by old Proterozoic rocks that give high $^{87}Sr/^{86}Sr$ values, generally above 0.72 (Åberg 1995), and are probably too radiogenic to provide a possible homeland. Their oxygen isotope composition (−6 to −8.7) is within the UK range (Chenery *et al.* 2010) and also consistent with much of France (Lecolle 1985) and Germany (Rozanski 1995; Tütken *et al.* 2004).

The two juveniles (25001, who lived in the early Bronze Age, and 25007) found with the Boscombe Bowmen are very close in both oxygen and strontium isotope composition. They are within the 1σ range of UK oxygen values and have an elevated strontium isotope composition that shows they

Table 34: Dentine data from Boscombe Down (all M3)

Sample no.	Location	Sr ppm	$^{87}Sr/^{86}Sr_n$	Project code & burial/context no.
1	Boscombe Down	228	0.7077	Project 56240, burial 5292
2	Boscombe Down	238	0.708358	Project 53535, burial 25049
3	Boscombe Down: Bowmen	184	0.707765	Project 53535, grave 25000, burial 25004

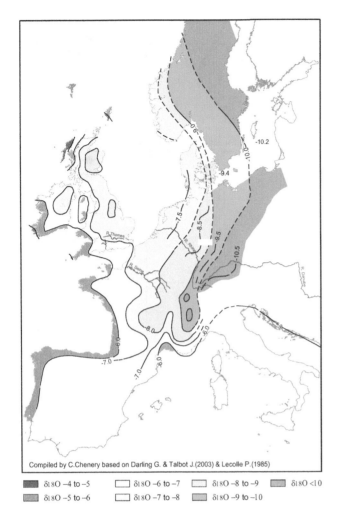

Compiled by C.Chenery based on Darling G. & Talbot J.(2003) & Lecolle P.(1985)

δ18O –4 to –5   δ18O –6 to –7   δ18O –8 to –9   δ18O <10

δ18O –5 to –6   δ18O –7 to –8   δ18O –9 to –10

Figure 68 Distribution of oxygen isotope values in north-west Europe

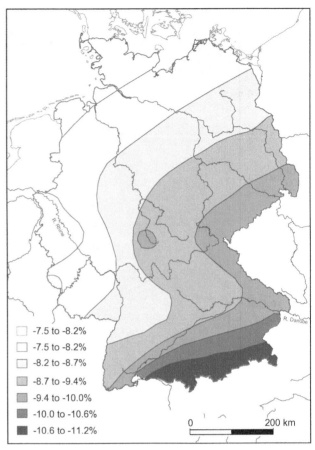

☐ -7.5 to -8.2%
☐ -7.5 to -8.2%
☐ -8.2 to -8.7%
▨ -8.7 to -9.4%
▨ -9.4 to -10.0%
■ -10.0 to -10.6%
■ -10.6 to -11.2%

0   200 km

Figure 69 A drinking water map of Germany (after Rozanski 1995)

are not from an area underlain by Chalk, ie, they are not 'local' to the Stonehenge area.

The oxygen isotope composition of the Amesbury Archer (1291) is distinctive. It is too low (too 'cold') to have been formed in the UK and is consistent with a broadly north–south zone of Europe from south Norway/Sweden down to eastern Germany (Figs 68–9).

Burial 1238 (the 'Companion') shows the largest shift in oxygen isotope composition between two teeth of any of the individuals in this study, indicating a significant move between areas of different climate during his childhood. He records a change from a $\delta^{18}O_{SMOW}$ value of 17, or –8.3 drinking water, which is near the lower end on UK values, to a even 'colder' value of 16.4 (–9.5) which is outside the 2σ range of recorded UK values (Chenery *et al.* 2010). His strontium isotopes show a shift from a value consistent with living on the Chalk Downs to a more elevated value for later childhood within the range of the Archer's strontium isotope range.

Burial 25049 from Boscombe Down is similar to the juveniles from the grave of the Boscombe Bowmen. Both teeth are within the UK 1δ range for $\delta^{18}O_{SMOW}$ value with strontium isotope values above those attributed to the Chalk Downs of the UK. The data from remaining individuals from Boscombe Down (burials 5289, 5292 and 6445), Stonehenge, and Normanton Down/Wilsford G1 are consistent with all of them having spent their childhood on Chalk terrain in southern England.

Figure 70 presents strontium isotope data from human tooth enamel from sites in continental Europe published in the last 10 years. The data from Bell Beaker individuals found close to Stonehenge (presented here and by Evans *et al.* 2006a) are displayed in the lower section. The 'Stonehenge' data are grouped, as shown by the shaded boxes, into 1) locals (ie, those individuals who have $^{87}Sr/^{86}Sr$ compositions within the range of dentine values, which provide a reasonable estimate of chalk biosphere, 2) non-locals, those individuals who do not have a 'chalk dwellers' signature, and 3a and 3b), the early and late childhood composition of the Boscombe Bowmen.

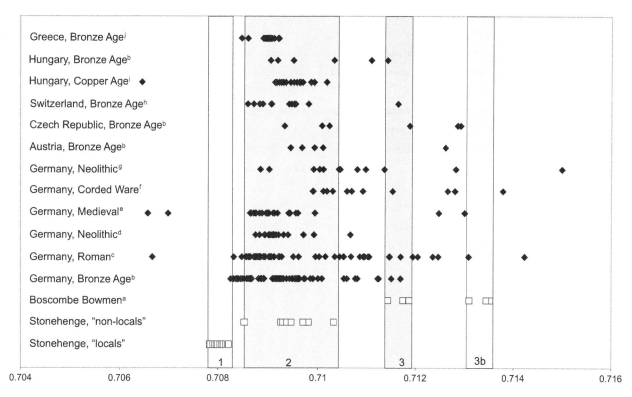

Figure 70 A comparison of human tooth enamel $^{87}Sr/^{86}Sr$ composition from continental Europe compared with data from individuals found close to Stonehenge. a) Evans et al. 2006; b) Grupe et al. 1997; c) Schweissing and Grupe 2003; d) Price et al. 2006; e) Haeblar et al. 2006; f) Haak et al. 2008; g) Nehlich et al. 2007; h) Chiaradia et al. 2003; i) Giblin 2009; j) Nafplioti 2008

The published studies represent the composition of human tooth enamel found at specific sites and most discuss the evidence for local versus non-locals at the specific locations. For the purpose of this comparison the data are used to give a snapshot of the range of compositions found in number of countries predominantly during the Bronze Age, which encompasses the Chalcolithic (which included the Bell Beaker period), but data from Neolithic (Nehlich *et al.* 2007), Roman (Schweissing and Grupe 2003) and medieval (Haeblar *et al.* 2006) sites are also included as they provide further data from continental Europe.

The aim of this comparison is to look at the type of isotope composition that typifies continental Copper Age–Bronze Age populations and compare them with the data from the Stonehenge area to assess the possible continental origins of individuals. The first notable observation is that the low strontium values seen in the population designated as 'local to Stonehenge' are not represented by any of the continental European sites. The values are essentially unique to the UK with the possible exception of one or two individuals found at the Altdorf and Ausberg Bell Beaker cemeteries in southern Germany (Grupe *et al.* 1997). This supports our tentative designation that these values typify

individuals raised on Chalk supported landscape as found across southern England and that these individuals may be designated 'local.' The four samples from Germany and Hungary that have values below 0.707, are likely to be from areas founded on young volcanic rocks.

The second group of individuals found at Stonehenge includes the Amesbury Archer who, based on the evidence of the oxygen isotopes, was raised outside Britain; the 'Companion' whose later tooth could suggest time spend outside UK in a cooler climate, and the two juveniles from the Boscombe Bowmen grave (25001: Early Bronze Age and 25007: Bell Beaker) and BD25049 (Bell Beaker). The oxygen isotopes drinking water values from the two Boscombe Bowmen juveniles and BD25049 are between –6.3 and –7.2. These values are consistent with a UK origin but are also found in Europe predominately through central France and the French/Italian Mediterranean coast and the north-west corner of Germany (Figs 68–9).

The strontium isotope composition of the Amesbury Archer and the 'Companion' are hence consistent with continental Copper Age–Bronze Age populations from much of central Europe. The origins of BD 25049 and the Boscombe Bowmen juveniles are consistent with either a UK or continental European origin but neither the oxygen or strontium isotopes are clearly diagnostic.

In conclusion, the strontium values seen in many of these individuals of below *c.* 0.7088, are rare/absent in most continental European Copper Age–Bronze Age populations and suggest that these are indicative of individuals raised in Britain on Chalk substrate. Oxygen isotopes support this in that the oxygen isotope data for such individuals is within the range of observed UK tooth enamel values.

The strontium isotope composition of the Boscombe Bowmen is also unusual when compared with continental populations in that it is unusually high, particularly for the early teeth. The Boscombe Bowmen data are consistent in both strontium and oxygen with a UK origin, but areas of the continent, that yield a similar combination of isotope signature, cannot be ruled out. The oxygen isotope composition of the Amesbury Archer is diagnostic of an origin outside Britain. His drinking water value of –10 is found in south-east or west Germany and up into Scandinavia and his strontium isotope composition is typical of many of the Bronze Age populations from such areas. The 'Companion' has a combined signature that is consistent with an early childhood in south-east England in a Chalk founded area but later childhood values suggest a domicile closer on conditions to that of the Amesbury Archer.

Chapter 8

The Local and European Settings

Something of the significance of the three early Bell Beaker graves comes from their proximity to Stonehenge and other Late Neolithic monuments that date to the first half of the 3rd millennium BC (eg, Darvill 2006; Lawson 2007; Richards 2007)(Fig. 2). From the site of the grave of the Boscombe Bowmen it is possible to look into the interior of the massive Durrington Walls henge, *c.* 3 km to the north and on the other side of the River Avon. Stonehenge lies *c.* 4 km west from the grave of the Boscombe Bowmen, from which it is separated by both the valley of the River Avon and King Barrow Ridge. The point at which the Stonehenge Avenue meets the Avon at West Amesbury and where a small henge has recently been discovered, is only 2.4 km north-west of the grave of the Amesbury Archer.

Durrington Walls and Stonehenge were amongst the most important sites in Britain in the 3rd millennium BC. The graves of the Boscombe Bowmen, the Amesbury Archer and the 'Companion' date to the 24th century BC, not long after these great temples had either been or were being built. Both Durrington Walls and Stonehenge required great commitment of labour to build them. The henge at Durrington Walls is one of the largest monuments known in Britain, a little bigger than the slightly earlier great henge at Avebury, 30 km to the north. Although Durrington Walls and Stonehenge may be the largest and most famous of these temples, they were not the only ones. In addition to the example recently discovered at West Amesbury, henges are known at Coneybury and Woodhenge. At Boscombe Down a Late Neolithic pit circle whose size might be compared with Stonehenge and the southern circle at Durrington Walls (Darvill 2006, 161, fig. 58; Pl. 3) has been found, as has an alignment of timber posts (Fig. 3, p. 4 above). It seems probable that other related and contemporary monuments await discovery in the areas around Boscombe Down, Durrington Walls, and Stonehenge.

With the notable exception of the Durrington Walls village which pre-dated the henge, Late Neolithic settlement evidence in the immediate vicinity that can be shown to be broadly contemporary with these temples is scarce. Houses are otherwise only known from below the Durrington 68 barrow. While pits of Late Neolithic date which often, but

not always, contain deliberately placed deposits of objects and wild foods are not uncommon finds, they are not necessarily direct indicators of settlements. Several such pits have been found at Boscombe Down (Fig. 3) and several others are known in the vicinity of Durrington Walls, sometimes forming extensive scatters (Darvill 2005, 56–1, ill. 37; 2006, 114–16; Lawson 2007, 95–6). It also seems likely that a chalk plaque found in a Romano-British pit at Butterfield Down had originally been placed in a Late Neolithic pit (Rawlings and Fitzpatrick 1996, 22–3, fig. 14, pl. 4). With the exception of Stonehenge (Parker Pearson *et al.* 2009), Late Neolithic burials are rare (p. 195 below), although a cremation burial has been found in the pit alignment at Boscombe Down (pp. 182–3 above).

Despite the systematic sampling and analyses of the charred plant remains from the Grooved Ware pits at Boscombe Down (Powell and Barclay in prep.), only one pit contained cereal grains; a small quantity of naked barley and emmer. Such sparse evidence for the cultivation of crops is typical at this time and the apparent rarity of contemporary houses may be associated with this. The Late Neolithic landscape may have been less divided and domesticated than is often envisaged and the area around Boscombe Down was apparently dominated by temples.

Although the shape and date of these temples is well understood at a general level, and the layout and orientation of all of them is thought by many to reflect the rising and setting of the sun on the shortest and longest days, much important detail about both the shape and date of the stone settings is uncertain (eg, Cleal *et al.* 1995; Case 1997; Whittle *et al.* 2007; Parker Pearson *et al.* 2009). This is not the place to rehearse the evidence in any detail as the state of knowledge was summarised recently by both Darvill (2006, 93–156) and Lawson (2007, 82–99) and the internal sequences of many of the principal sites are currently under review as part of the Stonehenge Riverside Project (Larsson and Parker Pearson 2007; Parker Pearson *et al.* 2007; Thomas 2007; Pollard and Robinson 2007; Darvill and Wainwright 2009; Parker Pearson *et al.* 2009).

What may be said is that the building of these temples required immense effort which has been interpreted variously as showing that society was organised by chiefs or by an astronomer-priesthood. An alternative view argues that the building of the temples does not reflect the existing situation but what was to follow as the building of the temples helped create new social orders (Barrett 1994, 24–32; Brodie 1998, 50). At Durrington Walls the southern circle was made from timbers from long lived oaks trees that would have had to have been felled and brought to the site and building the henge involved the excavation of an enormous ditch using antler picks and creating a bank from the upcast. At Stonehenge the creation of the stone settings involved bringing the smaller bluestones from the Preseli Hills of north Pembrokeshire, Wales, over 220 km away and the larger sarsens from possibly as far as 40 km away on the Marlborough Downs. The effort required to shape and move the sarsen stones into place was huge. Calculations of how few people or beasts of burden might have been needed to move stone and timbers or to excavate ditches bring a modern rational and often minimalist logic to the task. Instead, part of the enterprise may have been to involve as many people as possible and perhaps from as far away as possible. The consequences of failure might have increased but so too might have the rewards.

It was into this context that the first people bringing the Bell Beaker Set of objects and the ideas that they embodied arrived (Brodie 1998, 50). Neither settlement nor funerary contexts provide much evidence for contact with the indigenous Late Neolithic Grooved Ware using groups and the radiocarbon dated local chronology set out above (Chapter 6) also suggests that there may have been little chronological overlap. It has been suggested that the number of people using the Set was small and their relationship with Late Neolithic communities may have been 'interstitial', representing 'migration by infiltration' (Brodie 1998, 50; cf. Needham 2005, 182; 2007, 41–2). These first contacts may have been seasonal (eg, Case 1995a, 26; 1998, 408–10; 2004b, 22; 2007, 245–6).

Bell Beaker burials have attracted most attention partly because evidence for Bell Beaker settlements is scarce, usually being represented by a few pits or post-holes (cf. Brück 1999). Those features often contain lithics and pottery of types that comprise a distinct 'domestic assemblage' that, while related to the Beakers found in graves, is also quite distinctive (Gibson 1982; Bamford 1982; Case 1993). Evidence for such finds from Wessex is slight (Allen 2005) but includes the settlement at Downton, Wiltshire, which is unusual in that it has some evidence for buildings (Rahtz 1962). More typical finds are the groups of pottery from pits from Dean Bottom,

Wiltshire (Cleal 1992a) and Bestwall Quarry (Ladle and Woodward 2009, 204–13, 356–7, fig. 135–40) and post-holes at Middle Farm, Dorchester, both in Dorset (Cleal 1997, 101, fig. 65, 31–6). Even though the pottery assemblages from these features may not be large, they typically contain fineware pottery related to the Wessex/Middle Rhine Beakers found in graves. When these finds are considered alongside the regular finds of Beaker 'domestic pottery' (eg, Ladle and Woodward 2009, 212) and the large assemblage from site IV at the Mount Pleasant henge (Wainwright 1979; p. 49 above), they suggest that Bell Beaker settlements may prove to have been rather more widespread than often imagined. However, at present the clearest evidence for the early stages of the Bell Beaker network found in Wessex comes from graves.

While these graves include the earliest dated Beaker pottery in Britain, they do not necessarily date the arrival of the Bell Beaker Set, which will have been before the earliest burials. How much earlier is not yet known but as yet, there is no convincing evidence for Beaker pottery being found in other, earlier, contexts that are securely stratified and radiocarbon dated (Parker Pearson et al. 2007, 634–6, table 2).

The Bell Beaker Network

The isotope analyses indicate that the Amesbury Archer (burial 1291), perhaps the adjacent burial 1238, and quite possibly several of the Boscombe Bowmen had travelled between Britain and continental Europe. Their graves, dating to the 24th century BC, are amongst the earliest Bell Beaker ones currently known in Britain. It seems likely that they, and those who travelled with them, were amongst the first people whose arrival brought the Bell Beaker Set of objects and the ideas that they embodied to Britain. The distribution of Bell Beaker objects, often found in graves, is widespread, if discontinuous (Fig. 72, below), and the interpretation of individual Bell Beaker graves, with similar burial rites and comparable objects in widely separated areas, in parts of central, western, and Mediterranean Europe, has vexed archaeologists for generations (cf. Clarke 1976; Harrison 1980), and continues so to do (eg Nicolis 2001b; Czebreszuk 2004a; Turek 2006a; Guilaine 2007; Vander Linden 2007).

The 'Three Age' system and the importance of the introduction of different metals still underpins the way in which understandings of European prehistory are organised. In particular, the importance of the adoption or acceptance of metallurgy as a factor that caused social change, and as a device in increasing social differentiation, is still – rightly or wrongly – emphasised in many works (Roberts 2009a; 2009b; Roberts *et al.* 2009). The use of the term 'Copper Age' or Chalcolithic does little to alter this, although a wider discussion of this point lies beyond the scope of this report (see Allen *et al.* forthcoming). It is clear, though, that over much of temperate Europe metallurgy pre-dates the appearance of the 'Beaker Folk' and that even at a later date, metallurgy was not necessarily introduced by groups using the Bell Beaker Set of objects of the types that were placed in the grave of the Amesbury Archer (eg, Vander Linden 2004, 43; 2006a).

In continental Europe the Bell Beaker period is widely regarded as having been superseded by the full Early Bronze Age by *c.* 2200 BC, and there is evidence in Britain too for the adoption of bronze by this date (eg, Gerloff 2007, 122, 128, table 13.1). In Britain, however, the use of Bell Beaker derived pottery and objects continued after this date (eg, Needham 2005, 209–10) and in consequence much of what is called the 'Beaker period' in Britain covers a time that on technological grounds can be called 'Early Bronze Age' and this has led to considerable confusion.

Earlier interpretations among Anglophone scholars of the 'Beaker Folk' have been divided into three broad camps. In the first, the explanation is sought through ethnicity and immigration; in the second it is sought through status; and in the third it is sought through beliefs (Brodie 1998, 45–8).

In the ethnic hypothesis, Bell Beaker assemblages (sometimes described as 'packages' of material) were taken as symbols of ethnicity and thought to mark the arrival of immigrant 'Beaker People.' Although this interpretation fell out of fashion, it can now be clearly demonstrated that Bell Beaker funerary practices were quite different to what they succeeded and may be regarded as intrusive, leading to a similar conclusion, but arrived at by a very different route (eg, Heyd 2001).

The idea of the travel and migration of individuals and small groups using the Bell Beaker assemblage has also been steadily rehabilitated in more recent works of synthesis across central and western Europe (eg, Brodie 2001; Heyd 2001; Salanova 2001, 96; 2007; Vankilde 2005a, 96, 102; Heyd 2007a; Harrison and Heyd 2007; Sarauw 2009, 28). Craniological studies are still considered to support migration (eg, Budziszewski 2003) and this is being complemented by the development of dental morphology techniques (eg, Piguet *et al.* 2007, 262–6). Now, irrespective of interpretive fashions, isotope analysis studies in continental Europe (eg, Price *et al.* 1998; 2004; Heyd *et al.* 2003) and in Britain (Parker Pearson 2006), including those on the Amesbury Archer and the Boscombe Bowmen, have demonstrated that such mobility did take place. Within Britain further evidence may come from the graves at Upper Largie and Sorisdale on the western coast of Scotland (Sheridan 2008a; 2008b).

In the second hypothesis, Bell Beaker assemblages were seen as being associated in some way with the appearance across Europe of more individualising status hierarchies or ideologies (Shennan 1976; Burgess and Shennan 1976). This idea, popularised by Gordon Childe's conception of the Bronze Age (1930), has been developed in models based either on prestige goods (eg, Thorpe and Richards 1984) or on symbols of status (eg, Barrett 1994). What can be termed a 'ranked society,' where societies are led by local chieftains or tribal leaders, is often implied.

The third interpretation, of beliefs, appears in a number of guises and in many ways further develops the status interpretation. Bell Beaker assemblages have been seen as representing a cult package in which the Beakers symbolise male drinking rituals, participation in which was restricted to certain groups (Sherratt 1987a; Rojo-Guerra *et al.* 2006). Case has suggested that the core of the Bell Beaker package – bow and arrow, knife, and Beaker – was a symbolic hunting set, providing for the hunting of big game, undertaken in either the world of the living or the dead, its ritual killing, and the ritual drinking of its blood (Case 1998; 2004a; 2005).

Lastly, some have sought to explain these similarities through, or as, a 'phenomenon' and to interpret the material remains as a 'set'. For example, 'we interpret the Set as the remains of a new knowledge, an ideology' (Strahm 2004a, 122; cf. Salanova 2000, 15–17). This Bell Beaker network or phenomenon, whose formulation is in many ways similar to an archaeological culture but with echoes of a religious belief, may also have allowed for the use of some form of shared language or even a proto-Celtic Indo-European language (Gallay 2001).

All these hypotheses, which are not mutually exclusive, have some appeal, appearing to explain certain aspects or manifestations in certain times or places, with Bell Beaker using groups often being considered as the first socially differentiated and male dominated European people. However, none is entirely convincing as a pan-European explanation (eg, Brodie 2001), probably because there is no single explanation. Many regions did not adopt the Bell Beaker Set and the regions where it was adopted appear as nodes within a network or as Harrison has expressed it, as 'islands' in a discontinuous distribution although the similarities they share with neighbouring islands allows them to be grouped in broad provinces of 'southern', 'eastern' and

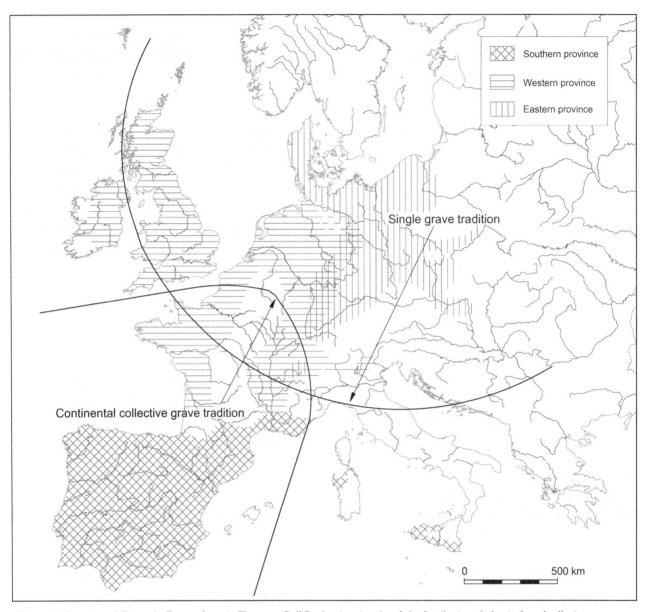

Figure 71 Location of Boscombe Down, the main European Bell Beaker 'provinces' and the distribution of the single and collective grave traditions c. 2400 BC

'western' Europe (Harrison 1980, 11–12; cf. Vankilde 2005a, 98; Sarauw 2009, 31) (Fig. 71). It is also clear that there is greater similarity between the evidence from single burials, which enact idealised representations of social identities, than that from settlements. But an emphasis on this aspect often neglects local variations. Some scholars therefore identify difference and diversity (Vander Linden 2004a; 2006a; 2006b; 2007) or put another way, that which is 'similar but different' (Czebreszuk 2004b).

The evidence from Boscombe Down, which in itself has considerable variation, is just one small part of this complex European network.

Chapter 9

Bell Beaker Mortuary Rites in Wessex

The early Bell Beaker graves at Boscombe Down lie at the start of the Bell Beaker sequence in Britain and for this reason attention is restricted here to finds that are either earlier or broadly contemporary with them. The distribution of these 'early Bell Beaker burials' is widespread but infrequent (Fig. 72).

The Beakers placed in these graves are of All-Over-Cord, Maritime or Wessex/Middle Rhine type. The All-Over-Cord and Maritime types belong to Lanting and van der Waals' Steps 1–2 and to Needham's Phases 1 and 2 of Bell Beaker finds in Britain, which he characterised as 'Beaker as circumscribed, exclusive culture, c. 2550–2250 cal BC' (2005, 209, fig. 13; Needham and Woodward 2008, fig. 3). All-Over-Cord and Maritime Beakers are found across Europe and are what Salanova has described as 'standard' international types (2000, 173–92). Wessex/Middle Rhine Beakers are part of the regionally distinctive styles that partly overlapped with but largely succeeded the international forms. The radiocarbon dated sequence from Boscombe Down (Chapter 6) suggests that in Wessex this regional phase started slightly later and ended rather earlier than suggested by Needham. Burials that have been radiocarbon dated to the currency of these Beakers (pp. 178–80 above) and selected finds from the Upper Thames Valley are also considered (cf. Lawson 2007, 131–76). Just how few dated graves there are can be seen in Table 30.

In Britain, the 'typical' Beaker grave is usually thought of as an individual interment, a concept that has almost become an archetype. In large measure this is due to the widely-held view that in Britain Bell Beaker burials represent the introduction from continental Europe of a rite that emphasised the individual in contrast to the community thought to be represented by burials made in Neolithic tombs.

In southern England earthen long barrows and megalithic tombs have now been shown to have passed out of widespread use over a thousand years before the arrival of the Bell Beaker Set (Whittle et al. 2007). Subsequent Middle and Late Neolithic individual interments of unburnt or cremated human are absolutely rare which hinders any assessment of mortuary rites in these periods (Cleal 2005, 116–17). The Late Neolithic cremation burials from Stonehenge are rare finds, whose closest parallels are to be found in the slightly earlier cemeteries around Dorchester-

on-Thames, Oxfordshire (Cleal et al. 1995, 163–4; Whittle et al. 1992; Parker Pearson et al. 2009). The recent recognition of other cremation burials associated with ring ditches in the Thames Valley at Imperial College Sports Ground, near Heathrow (Barclay et al. 2009) and the slightly later single cremation burial at Boscombe Down are noteworthy (pp. 182–3 above; Vol. 2).

In Wessex it seems that the chambers within earthen long barrows were seldom reused for burials accompanied by Beakers. At West Kennet, close to Avebury, some remains from the secondary fills date to the Late Neolithic and the chambers were apparently blocked around the middle of the 3rd millennium when Beaker pottery began to be used (Piggott 1962, 26–30, 68–71, 73–4; Thomas and Whittle 1986, 139–50; Case 1995b, 8–15, fig. 7–8; Bayliss et al. 2007a, 90–3; Bayliss et al. 2007b, 44; Parker Pearson et al. 2007, 634–5). Burials of this date may also be present at Stonehenge (Parker Pearson et al. 2009, 29) while unaccompanied single inhumations have been dated to the Late Neolithic from pit 942 Barrow Hills, Radley (Barclay and Halpin 1999, 89, fig. 4.41–3) and Horton, Berkshire (Barclay et al. 2009, 6).

Sometimes Bell Beaker burials might be placed in the mounds of long barrows (Field 2006, 153–6) and at Thickthorn Down, Dorset, at least two Bell Beaker graves, one of which (no. 1) contained a double burial, were cut into the mound of the barrow (Drew and Piggott 1936, 80–4, pl. xvi; xviii). Close to Avebury again, Beaker pottery was found in the ditches of the Horslip long barrow and Beaker pottery and barbed and tanged arrowheads were found in the ditches of the South Street long barrow (Case 1995b, 8).

While there is, as yet, insufficient evidence to suggest continuity in mortuary rites from the Late Neolithic (as had been argued by Gibson (2004; 2007; cf. Sheridan 2008b, 63), their potential contribution to Bell Beaker rites should not be discounted.

Early Bell Beaker Burials

While these Late Neolithic burials are rare so, perhaps inevitably, are early Bell Beaker burials and this has often been taken to indicate that they represent a minority group and usually an elite one (eg, Case 2004a, 200). Only a handful of burials from across Britain can be shown by radiocarbon dating to be broadly contemporary with the early graves at Boscombe Down (Fig. 72). This apparent rarity is not entirely due to many early graves not being covered by barrows and so being harder to locate. In some cases graves that might be suspected to be early in date do not have material that can be radiocarbon dated. Nor, despite the primacy often ascribed to prehistoric Wessex, should it be assumed that it is the only region where early Bell Beaker burials are to be expected.

The initial assessment of the early Bell Beaker burials from Wessex summarised below also confirmed that a reconsideration of their radiocarbon dating was necessary and this has been set out above (p. 178). In the specific case of the Boscombe Bowmen it was evident that, ideally and as with the Amesbury Archer, two samples should have been submitted from each of the individuals represented and that the mandibles from which the isotope samples were obtained should also have been dated. However, in relation to dating Beaker pottery, the conclusion of the British Museum 'Beaker dating programme' undertaken in the 1980s, that typo-chronological schemes were not supported by the radiocarbon dates (Kinnes *et al.* 1991) can, for present purposes, be set aside. This is partly because of the reservations expressed in the comments that followed the publication (*ibid.*; cf. Lanting 2007) and the fact that few determinations were obtained from graves likely to be of early date. Improved dating procedures have now yielded more reliable dates, though this also means that many existing radiocarbon dates cannot now be considered as reliable (cf. Cleal 2005, 118; Sheridan 2007). As the radiocarbon modelling set out above shows (p. 178), the dates broadly support the typological sequences set out by Lanting and van der Waals (1972) and Needham (2005). It also allows accompanied burials that are not radiocarbon dated to be placed in a relative sequence and used for comparative purposes here.

Apart from Chilbolton, the early graves in Wessex considered here are, from Wiltshire; Avebury Avenue (Stone 29a) (Smith 1965, 230, fig. 78, P350; Cleal 2005, 118–19, 131), Bulford Camp (de Shortt 1946), and the three times excavated but only once recorded grave at Wilsford cum Lake G54 (Smith 1991, 23–30, figs 10–12). Slightly later Wiltshire graves containing low-carinated Wessex/Middle Rhine Beakers are the double burial at Mere barrow G6a and the burial at Roundway barrow G8 (eg, Piggott 1973, 342, fig. 13, c–d; Case 1977a; fig. 1, 8–17; 1995b fig. 2, 1–5, 13–17; 2001, 363–6, fig. 1, 8–17; 2; 2004b, fig. 1, 8–17; Needham 2005, fig. 5,

2). The Roundway G8 burial is considered likely to be slightly later than Mere G6a as it was accompanied by what appears to be an Early Bronze Age flat-headed pin. The bracer from Roundway G8 also has four holes rather than two, which is generally a later trait (Gerloff 1975 32–3; Clarke 1970, 94, fig. 132) and the knife from the grave is significantly larger than the one from Mere G6a, which is also likely to be of chronological significance (Gerloff 1975, 27–9, 32–3, pl. 41, A). The finds from Winterbourne Gunner, near Boscombe Down discussed above (pp. 51 and 151) also seem likely to be from a grave (Musty 1963). Flat grave 1502 next to the Wilsford G1 barrow is slightly later in date.

Early graves from Dorset include the two cut into the Thickthorn Down long barrow. Grave 2 contained a copper awl, while grave 1, which was apparently a multiple burial, contained a stylistically more developed Wessex/Middle Rhine Beaker (Drew and Piggott 1936, 80, no. 1–2, 83, pl. xvii, fig. 1–2; Case 2004b fig. 1, 2–3). A group of burials from Thomas Hardye School, Dorchester, where a possible flat cemetery was superseded by a barrow cemetery, has been radiocarbon dated (Gardiner *et al.* 2006; Table 30). These graves are slightly later than the early graves at Boscombe Down, as are two graves, 59 and 70, at Fordington Farm (Bellamy 1991) which (like burial 1238 at Boscombe Down, the 'Companion'), fall into the oxymoronic category of 'non-Beaker Beaker Burials' (Bellamy 1991).

In Oxfordshire there are a number of radiocarbon dated burials from amongst the Barrow Hills, Radley barrow cemetery; flat graves 206, 919 and 4660 and barrow 4A (Barclay and Halpin 1999; Williams 1948). However, as discussed above, many of the existing dates may be too late (Lanting 1997, 40) while that for grave 919 appears too early (see Garwood 1999, fig. 9.4). This grave contained three copper rings (Barclay and Halpin 1999, 55–6, fig. 4.14), finds typical of the early stages of metallurgy in many regions in continental Europe, but the Beakers appear to be later in date. The early date from grave 204 at the Gene Function Centre, Oxford is from a burial accompanied by a typologically late Beaker (Boston *et al.* 2003, 190; Needham 2005, 183, table 1).

The number of early Bell Beaker burials from Wessex may seem surprisingly small and while the dating programme currently being undertaken as part of the Beaker People Project (Parker Pearson 2006) will provide a much larger set of determinations, at present there are few other radiocarbon dated regional sequences in southern England (eg, Jones and Quinnell 2006, 54–6). The regional context of occasional early graves elsewhere, for example Margate on the Isle of Thanet, Kent dated to 2460–2200 cal BC (Wk-18733,

197

Figure 72 Selected sites in Britain and Ireland that are mentioned in text

3852±33 BP) is not known (Moody 2008, 82, fig. 35; 38). In Scotland by contrast, a robust national sequence has been established (Sheridan 2007) and some early burials with high quality and early dates are relevant here(p. 181 above). In addition to the dated burials from Upper Largie, Sorisdale, and Dornoch Nursery (Sheridan 2007; 2008a; Lanting 2007, 31), the Bathgate, West Lothian finds, which are probably from burials(s), are also likely to be early in date (Lanting and van der Waals 1972, 40, 42; Sheridan 2007, 104–5; 2008a, 257, fig. 2.10, 3). Sheridan also identified some potentially early graves where the burials have not survived and so cannot be radiocarbon dated.

When Bell Beaker burials of all dates from Britain are considered, a broad distinction may be made between the south and north (Brodie 2001, 489–90). In the south of the country males were generally placed on their left side with their head to the north facing east. There is less information available about the burials of females but they seem to have been placed on their right side with the head to the south. Given the very small number of early Bell Beaker burials known from southern England, it is difficult to confidently distinguish any particular regional orientation but a preference for all burials in Wessex to be oriented north–south has been noted since William Stukeley (Burl 1987, 120–1). Burials aligned east–west are exceptional (Lanting and van der Waals 1972, 37).

However, the early burials in Wessex seem to be oriented slightly differently: north-west to south-east. Despite the differences between a collective and single graves, the Amesbury Archer, burial 1238 (the 'Companion') and the articulated adult male 25004 in the grave of the Boscombe Bowmen all lay on their left sides with their heads to the north-west, and juvenile 25007 in the grave of the Boscombe Bowmen may have done too. Other examples of this orientation include the female burial at Thickthorn Down whose head was at the south-east, the well-furnished male burial in grave 1643 at Thomas Hardye School, all the male graves at Barrow Hills, Radley; graves 203, 206, 950, 4660, and barrow 4A, and possibly the original burial at Wilsford cum Lake G54.

In some cases this north-west to south-east alignment was adhered to faithfully. After the primary burial at Chilbolton was disturbed only its feet remained in their original positions but the body was rearranged so that it was aligned north-west to south-east with the head, which was placed upside down, to the north. The secondary burial was laid in the same position. As so few contemporary burials are known from Wessex, the significance of this difference from the majority

of north–south oriented burials is not known though it appears, in part at least, to be chronological.

Recent discoveries of north–south oriented burials include grave 1502 at Wilsford G1, probably grave 1605 at Thomas Hardye School which is slightly later than grave 1643, and the Balksbury, Hampshire burial 2286 (an adolescent, possibly but not certainly female, buried on their left side: Wainwright and Davies 1995, 9, 82, fig. 10). All these burials were accompanied by Wessex/Middle Rhine or related types of Beaker

Burials such as these have usually been interpreted as symbolising the wider Bell Beaker network and this has resulted in considerations of the social status portrayed by them being rare. Where it has been done it has – as with in the study of other periods – usually been based on the number and quality of the grave goods (eg, Thomas 1991; Barclay and Halpin 1999, 284, tab. 9.3). The most comprehensive consideration of social status as represented by grave goods is by Case who distinguished five Groups (2004a, 197):

1. 'Quite rich burials invariably of men (where reliably identified) with beaker pottery and exceptional objects.
2. More frequent burials of men and women with generally more mundane objects: scrapers, awls etc.; and arrowheads only with men.
3. Rare children's burials with beaker pottery and generally more mundane objects still (e.g. flint flakes).
4. Quite frequent men's, women's and children's burials with beaker pottery only.
5. Finally, men's, women's and children's burials, forming part of the beaker associated burial groups and without contrasting associations, by themselves without beaker-pottery.'

The 'exceptional objects' in Group 1 were not defined but had been set out in an earlier paper where the five 'levels' were defined. The objects associated with level 1 were listed as copper or bronze knives, bracers, spatulae, stone battle axes, flint daggers and ornaments of gold or amber (Case 1977a, 81–2; 1998, 406). Case interpreted rich burials as those of the chief of a tribe or clan, and many of those burials were surmounted by barrows.

Bell Beaker Barrows

Although many Bell Beaker graves, particularly those with wooden chambers of the sort found in the grave of the

Amesbury Archer and probably that of the Boscombe Bowmen were surmounted by mounds (Ashbee 1976; Bellamy 1991, 127; Healy 2004, 61), there is no evidence for ring ditches encircling the early graves at Boscombe Down. Even so the presence of the wooden chambers would have meant that not all the spoil could be returned to the grave and this might have provided the material for small mounds that could have covered the graves. The location of the grave of the Amesbury Archer was apparently marked well enough to allow the burial of the 'Companion' to be made close to it within one or two generations.

The earliest example of a more complicated Bell Beaker monument in Wessex comes from Chilbolton, Hampshire (Russel 1990). Here the ring ditch was *c.* 5 m in diameter. It was also discontinuous, having two opposed causeways, and such discontinuous ditches are associated quite frequently with graves that contain relatively early Beakers (Stone 1938; Bellamy 1991, 127–8, tab. 6; Russel 1990, 169, Ashbee 1976, 26–7). With diameters often less than 10 m, Bell Beaker barrows in southern England are often small in relation to Early Bronze Age and, indeed, Neolithic (Kinnes 1979), examples.

Early accounts provide some of the best descriptions of these modest monuments. Near to Stonehenge the Wilsford South barrows G51–54 were recorded as 'small barrows scarcely elevated above the soil' (Colt Hoare 1810; Burl 1987, 116, H. Case 2003, 186). The Mere G6a barrow, until it was excavated by Colt Hoare, had escaped the attention of antiquarians because of 'its insignificance, and slight elevation' and Leslie Grinsell only relocated it in 1950 because of 'the exuberant growth of buttercups' on it (Grinsell 1957, 182; Burl 1987, 118). Piggott and Piggott noted that the earlier barrows at Crichel Down were 'small and inconspicuous mounds, none rising more than few inches above the down and with small diameters of about 20' (6.09 m), and were indeed only discovered in the course of the work on the larger and more conspicuous barrows in their neighbourhood' (Piggott and Piggott 1944, 52). The excavation of barrow 5 at Long Crichel (on Launceston Down) less than a kilometre from Crichel Down revealed that the primary grave, which contained a Wessex/Middle Rhine Beaker, was surrounded by a ring ditch 8 m in diameter and covered by a mound 0.3 m high (C. Green *et al.* 1982, 41, fig. 2).

This evidence suggests that if ring ditches or gullies surrounding earlier Bell Beaker graves were used as quarries, they could not have produced a sufficient quantity of rubble to create a large burial mound. Additional mound material could have been provided if the topsoil was removed from the berm, as appears to have been done at Barrow Hills,

Radley, barrow 4A (Williams 1948, 3). However, where substantial barrows were eventually created, as at Amesbury G51 (Ashbee 1976) or at Barnack (Donaldson 1977), these barrows either marked the closure of the grave after it had been used for a series of interments or the end of the use of the enclosed area for what was effectively a flat cemetery.

Wooden Chambers in Graves

Most of the burials considered above have been regarded as 'typical' Bell Beaker single burials but closer examination reveals that several of them provide evidence for rites of secondary burial. Something of the complexity of these rituals is due to the not infrequent occurrence, in Wessex at least, of wooden chambers in early Bell Beaker graves. The size of these chambers varies but all of them would have allowed the graves to have been reopened. The best known examples are those with larger wooden chambers that were often surmounted by barrows (Ashbee 1976; Bellamy 1991, 127; Healy 2004, 61) but it seems increasingly likely that the presence of a wooden structure was also a frequent feature in smaller graves. The evidence for these structures and the burials found in them is reviewed in detail below, starting with graves surmounted by barrows.

Barrows

The best preserved example of a wooden chamber yet excavated is from Amesbury G51. This barrow forms part of the Cursus group of barrows that runs immediately to the north-west of Stonehenge. Although the chamber is later in date than the early graves at Boscombe Down, it provides the best evidence for such a wooden chamber and is directly relevant here.

Interpreted by Ashbee as a mortuary house, remains of this wooden chamber had survived (Ashbee 1976, 6–8, 27–34, fig. 2–6, pl. 2). The grave was 3.35 m long, 2.28 m wide and 1.82 m deep from the contemporary ground surface. The wooden chamber placed within it had four rectangular corner posts suggested to have been up to 1.82 m square. The walls were made from planks in the region of 76 mm thick and an impression of one of them survived in the chalk face of the rubble packing. Narrow slots were found on the base of the grave parallel to but just within the line of the boards. These may represent a rebate for the end boards that may have been fixed to the corner posts by mortise and tenon joints.

Striations on the walls of the grave indicate that it had been excavated using antler picks.

The rubble packing was found only in the lower 0.68 m of the grave. The upper surface of the packing was horizontal and had traces of what were considered to be the eaves of a superstructure. The packing was described as rock hard, perhaps being caused by water percolation which had cemented the chalk rubble together. Ashbee suggested that this percolation could have been caused by the run off from a sloping room, going on to suggest that 'this would mean that a house-like rectangular structure was half buried, but exposed and visible in the grave pit for a measurable period before the barrow was built' (Ashbee 1976, 8). Other, later, examples of wooden chambers from Amesbury 71 and Sutton Veny, both in Wiltshire, were also discussed by Ashbee (*ibid.*, 28). The chamber at Amesbury G51 was originally excavated by William Cunnington in 1805, who recorded that three skeletons were found at the three different levels and the lower two burials were accompanied by Beakers. The type of Beaker placed with the primary burial is not now certain but it may have been of Wessex/Middle Rhine type (Ashbee 1976. 2, 13, 27, fig. 14; Clarke 1970, 501, 1038F).

A comparable chamber was present at Chilbolton (Russel 1990). This grave is earlier than Amesbury G51 and broadly contemporary with the early graves at Boscombe Down with which its dimensions are more comparable. The Chilbolton grave was a sub-rectangular pit, up to 2.50 m long, 1.75 m wide and 0.70 m deep. The outer fill, from top to bottom, was a packed chalk rubble that had also preserved its vertical face. In this case there was not a step in the side of the grave. A darker strip of soil at the base of the west side of the rubble may have derived from the timber chamber that the grave was interpreted as containing (Russel 1990, 156–7, fig. 2). As discussed above, the two shallow ditches that surrounded the grave could not have provided the material for a barrow of any size.

The well-furnished primary burial at Chilbolton was described as having been disturbed and was semi-articulated (Fig. 74, below). It was suggested that this happened when a secondary burial was inserted into the wooden chamber, disturbing the corpse or skeleton, though natural processes such as animal disturbance could also have contributed. Almost all of the bones of the primary burial were present but the head was upside down and few of the vertebrae and ribs were in place. Most of the ribs were in a group to the east of the body and the vertebrae were jumbled in the general area of the spine. No arm bones were articulated with the torso and one of them had been placed at the southern

end of the grave beyond the feet along with a tibia and a fibia. The hand belonging to this arm was at a higher level in the grave. One femur had been placed as if *in situ* but it had been reversed and his feet are thought to have been displaced slightly (Russel 1990, 156). Two pairs of gold ornaments were attributed to the primary burial but it is just possible that one pair should be associated with the secondary burial, as the heads of the two burials were very close, albeit at a different levels (p. 137 above).

Other early graves whose size and shape, particularly their depth and the presence of vertical or stepped sides, suggest they contained wooden chambers include the probably primary central grave 1 in barrow 5 at Long Crichel (Launceston Down) (Green *et al.* 1982), grave 1643 at Thomas Hardye School (Gardiner *et al.* 2006, 38, fig. 9, c), Barrow Hills, Radley, barrow 4A (Williams 1948), Wellington Quarry, Herefordshire (Harrison *et al.* 1999, 3–5. fig. 3–4), and the primary burial (28) at Barnack, Cambridgeshire (Donaldson 1977, 208, 227, fig. 8, pl. xxviii–xxix). The 'great deal of charred wood' described by Colt Hoare in the Mere G6a grave (1810, 44) might have been the mineral replaced remains of a wooden chamber.

There were also wooden chambers in the two Phase 1 pre-barrow graves at Fordington Farm, Dorset (Bellamy 1991, 108–9, fig. 1–3, pl. 2–4). Radiocarbon dates indicate that these unaccompanied burials are broadly contemporary with early Bell Beaker burials (Table 30) (the so-called 'non-Beaker Beaker burials': Case 2004a). In grave 59 the disarticulated remains of two individuals were all placed on the base of the grave and 'the bones of each individual had been carefully and separately arranged in the pit' (Bellamy 1991, 108). Grave 70 contained the disarticulated remains from three people and 'the bones of each individual were neatly and separately arranged' (Bellamy 1991, 108). A wide range of bones was absent from the Fordington Farm burials including the pelvis, scapula, humerus and mandible, was absent. In this case it would appear that the bones had been removed.

This evidence suggests that wooden chambers may have been relatively common in early Bell Beaker graves that were later covered by barrows. They also provide important evidence for successive burials and also for secondary burial rites. The graves into which the chambers were placed are typically oval or sub-rectangular in shape. However, the profile of the earlier graves – the Boscombe Bowmen; the Amesbury Archer; Chilbolton; Barrow Hills, Radley, barrow 4A; and perhaps Long Crichel barrow 5 – is vertical. The wooden chambers found in the earlier graves are relatively modest in size, and the graves were not especially deep. The 'step' in the side of the grave, which might have provided a surface to support a roof for the chamber is not present in the Amesbury Archer or Chilbolton graves, though it may be present at Wellington Quarry. Deeper graves such as Amesbury G51 or Barnack are later than the Boscombe Down examples. At all these graves, however, evidence of a hard-rammed packing deposit between the edge of the grave and the outside of a wooden or wicker chamber or structure is found regularly.

Flat Graves

Several flat graves provide similar evidence. The excavation of grave 1502 next to the Wilsford G1 barrow, which forms part of the Normanton Down barrow group close to Stonehenge, found that parts of the lower body were missing from what was otherwise a generally well-preserved burial. Here, it was suggested that this was due to deliberate disturbance (Leivers and Moore 2008, 28–9, fig. 14–16). However, the size of the grave, which is not dissimilar to some of those later covered by barrows, and the quantities of charcoal, suggest that a wooden structure might have been present. Grave 1643 at Thomas Hardye School may also have had a wooden structure (Gardiner *et al.* 2006, 38).

At Barrow Hills, Radley, grave 206, only a small amount of human bone was present, slightly above the floor of the grave (Barclay and Halpin 1999, 173, fig. 4.73–4). It was suggested that the activities responsible for the presence of only small quantity of human bone had occurred before the grave was closed but the size and shape of the grave, and the small hollows in the base of the grave, are all consistent with the presence of a wooden coffin or chamber. Also at Barrow Hills, grave 950 was suggested to have contained a wooden monoxylous 'tree trunk' coffin in which the body of an adult male was placed in either an articulated or deliberately dismembered state before 'the corpse was then exhumed before being dumped back into the grave as two deposits' (Barclay and Halpin 1999, 59). Human bone and objects are also suggested to have been removed at this stage. The possibility that a cut mark on the medial clavicle indicated deliberate dismemberment was considered but it was concluded that it was more likely that the bone was damaged when the grave was re-opened. The re-opening of the grave would have been made easier by the presence of a wooden chamber or coffin. Similar arguments for the robbing of graves or for burials being made when the corpse was in an

advanced state of decomposition have also been made for the later Bell Beaker graves at Barrow Hills, barrow 15, grave 1 and at nearby also Stanton Harcourt XV, I/1 (Hamlin 1963; Riley 1982, 79; Case 1982, 113; Case 2004a, 196; Barclay and Halpin 1999, 160–2; Boyle 1999, 175, tab. 7.2).

The Addition and Removal of Human Remains

The evidence reviewed above is fine grained and limited but it demonstrates that several earlier Bell Beaker flat graves contained structures of wood or other organic materials that would have allowed the grave to be reopened. The human remains found in these graves also suggest that early Bell Beaker mortuary rites in Wessex were more complex than the usual interpretation of single burial might allow.

At Chilbolton the absence of some of smaller bones (toe and wrist bones) from the primary burial might be explained by natural processes. However, the missing left fibula and some ribs may have been removed deliberately when the secondary burial was made and at which time the primary was thoroughly disturbed, but then rearranged to appear like an articulated skeleton (Russel 1990, 157). In the much deeper graves 59 and 70 at Fordington Farm barrow, the absence of bones from the tightly packed arrangements of bones seems likely to be deliberate. There is no suggestion that the bones had been buried or exposed elsewhere previously.

Two graves from Barrow Hills, Radley, illustrate the diversity in what appear to be single burials in flat graves. Only a small quantity of bone was present in grave 206 and it is possible that the remainder of the burial may have been removed. In grave 950 most – but not all – of the skeleton was present despite the extensive disturbance but the right humerus, right scapula, and the first cervical vertebra; all larger bones, were absent.

This absence of bones is seen in other burials. There is also considerable diversity in the way disarticulated bones were placed. Sometimes, as at Barrow Hills, Radley, grave 950, no order is discernable in the ways that the bones were placed in the grave (Barclay and Halpin 1999, 59, figs 4.18–9). At Fordington Farm, the bones were placed in groups in which all the bones came from one individual. At Barrow Hills, Radley, grave 206, the small number of bones, mainly leg bones but also a skull fragment, had been placed together (Barclay and Halpin 1999, 133–5, fig 4.73).

When these graves were reopened is hard to assess. At Chilbolton, the individual elements of the primary burial were completely rearranged before the insertion of the secondary burial (Russel 1990, 157). The primary burial must have decomposed to a state in which it was either fully or partly disarticulated in order for this reordering of the body to have taken place. How long these processes of decay took would have varied according to the local micro-environments. It is suggested that the length of time could vary between a few months and 5 years (Evans 1963; Henderson 1987).

On occasion, apparent disturbance to a burial might be explained by natural agencies such as burrowing animals, as has been suggested for the burial placed in the ditch at Stonehenge (Evans 1984, 15) but it seems likely that the reopening of graves and reordering of bodies was a regular part of early Bell Beaker mortuary rites in southern England. This could also include the removal of bones, possible reasons for which include:

- their removal as part of a secondary burial rite;
- their removal when additional burials were placed in the grave;
- their removal when items were removed from the grave;
- their removal when additional items were placed in the grave.

The removal of objects from the grave, which is not necessarily the same as 'grave robbing' can be difficult to demonstrate archaeologically unless fragments of objects are left in the grave (cf. Neugebauer 1994; Randsborg 1998). Similarly, items that had been added would be hard to identify archaeologically unless they have significant differences from those already present in the grave. On occasions Beakers themselves may have been curated before their eventual deposition (Woodward 2002) and some objects in graves were clearly old and/or broken, for example the fragmentary wristguard from Wellington Quarry (Harrison *et al.* 1999).

However, the rearranged primary burial at Chilbolton still contained rare and valuable objects, which included at least one set of gold ornaments, a gold bead, and a copper knife. The fact that the bones had been replaced in an approximate position also suggests that the reopening of the grave was not in order to remove grave goods.

Too little evidence is currently available for more precise patterns – if they existed – to be identified. The emphasis appears to be on single burial and this is of a different character from the regular occurrence in the Early Bronze Age of multiple and disarticulated burials represented by bones that are often scattered through the fill of the grave without any apparent order (Petersen 1972).

In this context of secondary burial rites in Wessex and beyond, the successive and disarticulated burials of the Boscombe Bowmen might seem more readily intelligible. However, the isotope analyses suggest that the men buried in grave 25000 were not from Wessex.

Chapter 10

The Journeys of the Boscombe Bowmen

Three points about the grave of the Boscombe Bowmen are clear. First, that it contains what are amongst the earliest radiocarbon dated Bell Beaker burial in Britain. Secondly, the accompanied Bell Beaker burial rite has no clear antecedents in the British Late Neolithic. Thirdly, even in the context of the emerging complexity of secondary burial rites, there are no ready contemporary parallels in Wessex or southern England for what appears to be the successive interments within a timber chamber.

The earliest individuals buried in the grave can be shown to have migrated to Wessex and to have followed the same migratory pattern. The strontium isotopes indicate that they were travelling in their childhood and it can be shown that they were in one area at around the age of 5 years and in a second one by the age of 13 years. Neither of these areas was close to Wessex. It is not known if this represents one journey that will have taken at least 8 years or several shorter journeys. Within mainland Britain, Wales, which is over 150 km from Boscombe Down, is the nearest area that can supply the appropriate $^{87}Sr/^{86}Sr$ values for the early childhood strontium values of the men.

It is possible that at least two of the men were born at approximately the same time. The similar shape of their heads and wormian bones suggests – but does not demonstrate with certainty – that they came from a related community. This need not mean that they were related biologically.

Only one of the skulls of the Bowmen was complete enough for cranial measurements to be made, with the consequence that there is insufficient data to assess against the numerous interpretations of the shape of heads amongst Bell Beaker populations and their possible significance (eg, Brodie 1994; Budziszewski *et al.* 2003, 157, fig. 3–4; Desideri and Eades 2004). It was possible to gain an impression of general shape of the back of the heads of five of the Bowmen individuals (Pl. 10) and superficially at least, their shapes appear similar; quite short and broader at the back. This is consistent with the brachycranial form widely considered to be characteristic of Bell Beaker populations.

This might be interpreted as suggesting that the men whose journeys could be studied by isotope analyses, and perhaps all of the men in the grave, were closely related. They

Figure 73 The 'Boscombe Bowmen', possible locations of strontium values

may be from the same community, and possibly from the same family. This would be consistent with the osteological evidence for close relationships between the people buried in some small cemeteries in Bavaria and Lower Austria (Heyd 2007a, 337).

Where the men travelled from is less clear (Fig. 73). Wales is the closest area in mainland Britain that provides suitable $^{87}Sr/^{86}Sr$ values, followed by the Lake District, Cumbria. Beyond Britain the following regions are, on geological grounds, also possible sources; south-east Ireland, Brittany, and the Massif Central of France, the Palaeozoic rocks of Portugal and the Black Forest in south-west Germany. However, the $\delta^{18}O$ drinking water compositions indicates that a western source would be more likely. The archaeological evidence from these regions is sketched below.

Britain and Ireland

The area closest to Boscombe Down with comparable biosphere values is Wales and a connection with it would echo that demonstrated independently by the geological provenance of the bluestones erected at Stonehenge, *c.* 4 km away from Boscombe Down. The source of these stones has been suggested by petrological and chemical analyses to be a small area in the Preseli Hills in south-west Wales (Green 1997, Scourse 1997, Thorpe *et al.* 1991, Williams-Thorpe *et al.* 1997), and even if more eastern sources in Wales are included, in relative geographical terms the area is very small.

However, the evidence currently available does not allow it to be determined with any confidence when the bluestones were brought to Stonehenge. The limited stratigraphic evidence from Stonehenge and the few radiocarbon dates that are regarded as reliable can be interpreted differently. On the one hand it has been argued that the bluestones were brought to Stonehenge and erected in the Aubrey Holes around 2900 BC, centuries before the Boscombe Bowmen lived (eg, Parker Pearson *et al.* 2009, 31–3; Pitts 2009, 189). On the other hand it has been argued that the bluestones were brought to Stonehenge at a later date although whether this was before the arrival of the sarsen stones (eg, Bayliss *et al.* 2007b, 46; Darvill and Wainwright 2009, 13, 16) or after (eg, Case 1997, 165–6) is uncertain. The latter possibilities would be broadly contemporary with the Boscombe Bowmen who lived in the 25th–24th centuries BC. An association with Wales was initially suggested (Fitzpatrick 2004, 14–16) but the subsequent Bayesian modelling of the radiocarbon dates has shown that the grave is one of the earliest Bell Beaker examples in Britain. If the Boscombe Bowmen were either to have come from Wales or to have travelled to Wales from Wessex when they were children, this would, on the evidence currently available, have been contemporary with the arrival of the Bell Beaker Set in Britain. This might have been contemporary with the transportation of some (but not all) of the bluestones.

Very little early Bell Beaker material is currently known from Wales (Fox 1925; Grimes 1951, 50; Griffiths 1957), and although as elsewhere in Britain, burial rites in the 3rd

millennium BC are poorly understood, no grave that may be compared with that of the Boscombe Bowmen has been recorded. Several well-dated examples show that the building of megalithic tombs in Wales had generally passed out of use by the later fourth millennium BC but there is some evidence for their use in the later third millennium. For example, three burials from the Thornwell Farm, Gwent, Severn-Cotswold tomb are radiocarbon dated to the later third millennium BC (OxA-18885, 3802±28 BP; Ox-A18896, 3876±28 BP and Ox-A 18900, 3838±29 BP,) and All-Over-Ornamented pottery was found in the chamber (S. Burrow pers. comm.). A small number of burials of this date have also been identified at other sites by radiocarbon dating, for example in the passage at Parc le Breos Cwm, West Glamorgan (Whittle and Wysocki 1998, 147, 173–5, tab. 2, fig. 16). The only Beakers of early type that are currently known from megalithic tombs are the All-Over-Ornamented sherds from Thornwell Farm, and Tinkinswood, Glamorganshire again in south Wales (S. Burrow, pers. comm.).

Otherwise Beakers from megalithic tombs in Wales are of later types, for example from Capel Garmon, Denbighshire (Grimes 1951, 33–5). The probable single burial from Pengeulan, Cwmystwyth, Ceredigion with a gold disc of Bell Beaker date is a rare find. It seems unlikely to be coincidental that this upland find is not far from the copper mine of Copa Hill (Timberlake 2003, 112–13; Timberlake *et al.* 2004; A. Gwilt, pers. comm.). This mine has yielded some of the earliest radiocarbon dates (on charcoal) of any mine in Wales with prospection and mining is tentatively suggested to have started early in the second half of the 3rd millennium BC (Timberlake 2003, 55, 104).

The other region within Britain indicated by the isotopes as a potential place of childhood residence for the Boscombe Bowmen is the Lake District. However, early Bell Beaker material is absent from this region and although stone axes from Great Langdale were widely distributed during the Early Neolithic (eg, Bradley and Edmonds 1993), and monument types such as stone circles and henges are found in both regions, there are no obvious links between Wessex and the Lake District in the mid-3rd millennium BC (Evans 2008).

Turning west to Ireland, there are strong connections in the Early, and to a lesser extent, the Late Neolithic between western Britain and Ireland (Cummings and Fowler 2004). However, on the evidence currently available, the appearance of the Bell Beaker Set in Britain and Ireland was broadly contemporary in Britain. Some of the earliest evidence comes from the copper mine at Ross Island, Co. Kerry in south-west Ireland (O'Brien 2004; 2007, 20–30) and this is broadly contemporary with the burials of the Boscombe Bowmen (pp. 181–2 above). In Ireland Bell Beaker burials are frequently associated with the small megalithic 'wedge tombs' and while relatively little is yet known about the burial rites practised in them, it did include collective burial (Brindley and Lanting 1992; Walsh 1995; Case 1995a; 2004a; 2005; Schulting *et al.* 2008; Carlin 2011).

While there is currently little or no evidence for the early appearance of the Bell Beaker Set in Wales or the Lake District, or for an earlier appearance in Ireland, this is not necessarily the case for the other possible sources of the elevated $^{87}Sr/^{86}Sr$ values for the early childhood values of the Boscombe Bowmen where the use of the Bell Beaker Set was already well established.

Continental Europe

Although the common perception of Bell Beaker mortuary rites in Britain is of single burial, as we have seen this was often in the context of rites of secondary burial. In the context of continental Europe this is unsurprising. Single burial was the most frequent rite in the areas of the Lower and Middle Rhine that have often been seen as the area of origin of Beaker pottery in Britain, and beyond that throughout the Bell Beaker 'East Group' of central Europe. However, collective burial as seen in the grave of the Boscombe Bowmen was the most frequent rite across much of France, Portugal, Spain, and also southern Switzerland (eg, Harrison 1980; Chambon 2004; Salanova 2003b; 2004a, 66; fig. 4; 2007, 213–17; Vander Linden 2006, fig. 112) (Fig. 71).

While this distinction is true at a broad level, as Salanova has observed, it is difficult to divide Europe absolutely on this basis. In the Paris Basin some single burials are also known and, unlike megalithic tombs with Bell Beaker objects, these graves are found in both the east and west of the region (Billard *et al.* 1998; Salanova 2004a, 66, fig. 4).

Single graves are also found in the central Spanish Mesetas including the well-furnished burial at Funete Olmedo, Valladolid (Harrison 1980, 142) and the same is true in Portugal, where single inhumation burials have been identified in tombs (Salanova 1998a; 2001; 2003b; 391, fig. 3–4; Vander Linden 2006, 162). The difficulties of interpreting secondary burial rites are well known (eg, Chambon and Leclerc 2003; Salanova 1998a, 322–3; 2003b; pp. 201–2 above). Nonetheless, Salanova has demonstrated that in some tombs the distribution of objects of Bell Beaker type is consistent with them having been placed in the tomb

accompanying successive single burials (Salanova 1998a, 322–3; 2005, 165; Vander Linden 2006, 162).

Even within central Europe where there is much greater emphasis on single burial, double burials are also known. Whether all cremation burials are those of single individuals is much less certain. As an example the multiple burials within a single grave at Tvořiház, Znojmo, Moravia (Bálek *et al.* 1999) may be noted. In contemporary Corded Ware contexts multiple burial is more common and in some examples, such as Eulau, it seems clear that these were of family groups (Haak *et al.* 2008).

In Brittany *c.* 20% of the numerous megalithic tombs have yielded finds of Bell Beaker type. Not far to the east in the Paris Basin, *c.* 350 megalithic tombs mainly belonging to the, earlier, Seine-Oise-Marne culture are known but only 13, all in the west of the region, have yielded Bell Beaker finds. In the south of France the presence of Bell Beaker finds in the Pyrenees is described as 'quasi-systématique' but in the Département of Gard where over 200 megalithic tombs are known, only two have yielded finds of Bell Beaker type. A similar variability is evident in Portugal where megalithic tombs are abundant (Salanova 2003b; 2004a, 69–73; 2007, 387–8, fig. 1–2; Chambon and Salanova 1996).

Many of these megalithic tombs were examined at an early stage in the development of excavation techniques with the consequence that the records do not allow detailed examination. In Brittany the granitic geology means that human bone was often poorly preserved but in all of France, out of the hundreds of tombs that have yielded finds of Bell Beaker type, only three have demonstrated an incontestable association between burials and the artefacts.

In the Massif Central, Brittany, and Portugal, most Bell Beaker graves are collective. Seeking comparanda for the grave goods buried with the Boscombe Bowmen is not straightforward. The pottery was made close to Boscombe Down and it was selected from the styles that were current in Wessex at the time of the deaths of the Bowmen as adults or older teenagers, not the styles that were current in the places whence they had travelled as children. Additionally there are strong similarities between Beakers, across western Europe, especially the 'international types' of All-Over-Cord and Maritime (eg, Salanova 2000).

Barbed and tanged arrowheads are also found widely in western Europe. They are common in France, especially in western France and the Atlantic coast generally, although the type continued to be used into the Early Bronze Age (eg, Joussaume 1981, 502–4, fig. 240; 242; Verron 2000, 189–202, fig. 114; L'Helgouac'h 2001). This type is also found in the

Netherlands and it was adopted in Italy (Barfield 2001, 515–16). In central Europe, by contrast, hollow-based arrowheads are the norm (eg, Heyd 2000, 275–8) and winged or barbed and tanged examples occur only occasionally (eg, Borkovany 1/59, (with *Lockenringe*) (Dvorak *et al.* 1996, Taf. 1A, 3). For this reason the regular occurrence of hollow-based arrowheads in Ireland (Green 1980; Case 1995a, 24; Woodman *et al.* 2006, 132, 135), is notable.

Of the two French regions whose geology is compatible with the results of the strontium analyses, bone is generally poorly preserved in the Massif Central with the consequence that very little is known of the mortuary rituals practised there in the 3rd millennium BC (Chambon 2004, 69). However, the region is adjacent to the oxygen isotope zone characteristic of the Amesbury Archer (Fig. 68) and this might be thought to be relevant. Comparisons can also be made with some elements of the pottery found with the Boscombe Bowmen, for example ON 6/23 is similar to a cord decorated 'S'-profiled Beaker from the 'Dolmen d'Ustau de Loup', St-Gervazy, Puy-de-Dôme (Daugas *et al.* 1972, 90, fig. 5; Bill 1984, 164, Abb. 1, Phase 1). At least three antler pendants are also known from eastern France: La Baume-sous-Rouche, Loisia, Jura (Treinen 1970, 274, fig. 48, 11; Bill 1973, Taf. 8, 7.8), Chagny, Vertempierre, Saône et Loire (Treinen 1970, 274, fig. 48, 11; Bill 1973, Taf. 8.2, 3), and Collonges-Les-Bévy, Côte-d'Or (Treinen 1970, fig. 48, 12) but none of these has the small loop seen on the example from the grave of the Boscombe Bowmen (ON 18).

There is more evidence from Brittany, mainly from megalithic tombs (Salanova 1998a, 322–3; 2003b; 2007b). Brittany has been suggested as a 'homeland' for the Boscombe Bowmen (Sheridan 2008b, 27; Parker Pearson *et al.* 2007, 636) though Salanova has repeated the earlier observation of how few links between Beaker pottery in Brittany and Britain are apparent (eg, 2000, 181–4, fig. 114; Lanting and van der Waals 1972, 36; pp. 54 and 149 above).

At the same time very strong similarities between the Beaker pottery of Portugal and Brittany have long been recognised (eg, Salanova 2000, 191–21; 2001, 94–6, fig. 4; Cardoso *et al.* 2005). The oxygen isotope data currently available are not well developed but they do not support a Portuguese origin for the Boscombe Bowmen (p. 187 above). Even so, Portugal should be noted as it provides extensive evidence for Bell Beaker material with numerous collective graves using dry-stone corbel vaulted-tombs rather than passage graves, and also settlements (Harrison 1977, 24–67) and it is widely seen as one of the regions, if not the region, in which the Bell Beaker network emerged (eg, Kunst 2001,

81–6; Case 2007, 238–41). The possible Iberian origins for the insular series of gold basket-shaped ornaments found in Britain and Ireland are well known (Taylor 1980, 22, pl. 3, j; 1993, 46, pl. 13; 1994, 46, 57, pl. 20; O'Connor 2004, 208; pp. 133–4 and 233). Comb-decorated Maritime Beakers are particularly frequent in Portugal and very occasional examples of plaited All-Over-Cord Beakers are known too (Jorge 2002). In contrast, despite the very wide ranging distribution of antler pendants in Europe, with many finds from northern Italy and also Sardinia and Greece, only one is known from Iberia.

The Black Forest region in south-west Germany is also partly coincident with the oxygen isotope zone characteristic of the Amesbury Archer discussed below and it might be tempting to consider a common origin. However, relatively few Bell Beaker finds are known from this region and they are mainly related to the 'East Group' (Sangmeister 1964b, 81, Karte 1–4; 1984, 81; Heyd 2000) though the 'International' types of Beaker occur to the north of the Black Forest (*ibid.*). To the north of the Black Forest, the practice of multiple burial is a very distinctive trait of the late Corded Ware groups of the Tauber valley (Dresely 2004) and an increasing number of Bell Beaker burials are known west of the Rhine (Salanova and Heyd 2007). While no examples of the antler pendant found in the grave of the Boscombe Bowmen have yet been found in south-west Germany, they are found in regions to the north and east as well as to the south and west (Fig. 21).

Parallels for the objects buried with the Boscombe Bowmen are not only to be found in the areas with which the isotopes are consistent. In particular the similarities of the Beaker pottery with Lower Rhine, and area in which All-Over-Cord ornament is frequent, should be noted. The similarity between ON 6/23 from the grave of the Boscombe Bowmen as reconstructed (noting the uncertainty about is profile p. 40 above) and a Type 2IIb Beaker from Swalmen, Bessel, Limburg, is striking (Lanting and van der Waals 1974, fig. 25, fig. 10, BM 127). This echoes the situation in western France, where although All-Over-Cord Beakers are made from local clays, the use of cord appears to be introduced from the Lower Rhine. Some graves in northern France that contain All-Over-Cord Beakers have been interpreted as the graves of migrants from the Lower Rhine region (Salanova 2003a).

These difficulties in attempting to identify any 'homeland' are further exacerbated by the wide distribution of early Bell Beaker material culture across western Europe, with the possibility that this was the result of a deliberate attempt to create uniformity (Harrison and Mederos Martin 2001, 112).

The more heterogeneous material culture from settlements and which is also likely to reflect preceding local traditions (eg, Piguet *et al.* 2007, 262), may well eventually provide a better indication than the more homogeneous funerary evidence.

Conclusion

On the basis of this evidence, archaeological connections can be suggested with most of the regions of continental European whose geology could provide the ^{87}Sr/^{86}Sr values found in the Boscombe Bowmen, and with other regions too.

There is a strong tradition of artefact studies in prehistoric studies and perhaps inevitably analyses tends to be drawn to them. What may be emphasised here, however, is how different, and apparently atypical, is the pattern of mobility seen amongst the Boscombe Bowmen. It is not repeated in the evidence from the isotope analyses of the other burials from Boscombe Down and it is not seen in any of the continental European studies where mobility has been demonstrated (eg, Price *et al.* 1998; 2004; Chapter 7), though the same methods have not been used in all the studies. As well as the multiple locations evidenced in childhood, an important feature is the length of time that elapsed between the two isotope signatures, at least 6 years. This could suggest one longer or a series of shorter journeys between, for example the Massif Central and Brittany, and possibly Portugal. It also raises the possibility that they moved to different areas at different ages *from* the same place, which might not have been the one at which they were eventually buried (*pace* Evans *et al.* 2006). That is to say they have travelled from the same place once before they were 5 or 6, and again by the time they were 13. Subsequent journeys in adulthood cannot currently be demonstrated by the isotopic analyses of teeth. Childhood mobility, albeit more local, is also seen in the juvenile 25007 and also 25001, the latter being of Early Bronze Age date.

The international nature of the finds in the grave, with wide-ranging connections evident in the pottery, arrowheads and antler pendant, make it difficult to rank one region above the other as a possible source. The collective burial rite is characteristic of the much of western Europe but the grave was apparently used only for males, recalling the bi-polar single burial rite typical of much of central Europe. At least some of these men had the status of a warrior but, as shown below, this was common across the Bell Beaker network. The presence of one and possibly a second juvenile need not occasion surprise and the burial of children accompanied by Beakers was regarded by Case as quite frequent amongst Bell Beaker burials in Britain (2004a, 197l; p. 198 above), though how typical this is for early Bell Beaker burials is less certain.

This evidence further emphasises the extensive mobility of the period and the suggestion that the Boscombe Bowmen came from beyond Britain is consistent with their position as one of the earliest Bell Beaker graves in Britain, and with the practice of collective burial. It is not clear how much emphasis should be placed on the presence of males and no females in the grave but the physical similarities between the Boscombe Bowmen, including the certain and possible juvenile, and the fact that some of the adults made very similar journeys at the same ages and possibly at the same time, indicates that they belonged to a close-knit group.

Chapter 11

The Construction of Social Identities

The single burials of the Amesbury Archer and burial 1238 (the 'Companion') provide a sharp contrast with the collective burial of the Boscombe Bowmen. The Amesbury Archer is one of the most lavishly furnished Bell Beaker individual burials yet found in Europe. In Britain the very few broadly contemporary and comparably well furnished graves in Britain are; Chilbolton, Barrow Hills, Radley, grave 4660 and barrow 4A, and Wellington Quarry, Herefordshire, and the slightly later graves from Mere G6a, Roundway G8, and Thomas Hardye School 1643, all of which have been considered above (pp. 197–200, Fig. 74; Table 35).

Russel noted of the Chilbolton grave that none of the objects placed with the primary burial is uncommon as an individual item but as an assemblage they are of exceptional richness and diversity (Russel 1990, 171). That view perhaps understated the rarity of the two pairs of gold basked-shaped ornaments and the possibility that both they, and the copper knife, came from continental Europe. The same might be said of the grave goods buried with the Amesbury Archer (Needham 2005, 207). These offerings include multiple examples of the key elements of the Bell Beaker Set: pottery, copper knife, bracer, and arrowhead.

Case interpreted these rich burials as those of chief of a tribe or clan (p. 198 above) where the significance of the objects lay not in the commemoration of dynastic families but in the creation of myths. Those myths were about conquering the ideological domain and the creation of symbolic ancestors who legitimated the right of their descendents over a territory

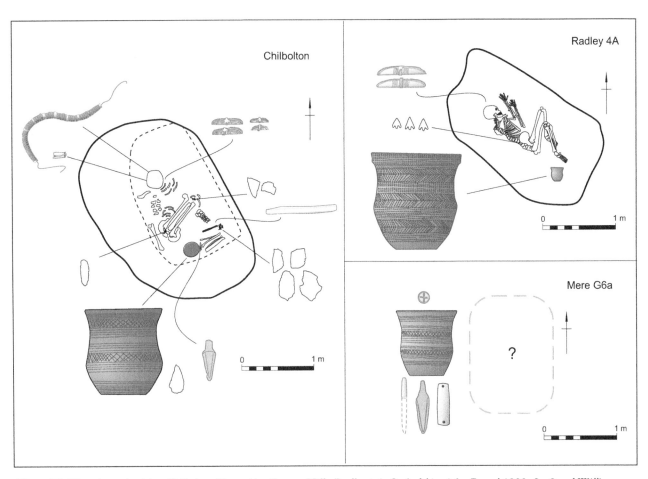

Figure 74 The primary burial at Chilbolton, Hampshire; Barrow Hills, Radley 4A, Oxfordshire (after Russel 1990, fig. 2 and Williams 1948, pl. II, a); and finds from the Mere G6a, Wiltshire, burial (after Case 1977a; fig. 4:3)

Table 35: Grave goods in selected well-furnished early Bell Beaker graves in southern England

Site	Burial	Weaponry	Tools	Ornaments	Pots
Amesbury Archer	M	arrowhead (x18) bracer (x2) copper knife (x3) flint knife (x2)	metalworker's stone pressure flaker (?x3) scraper (x8) knife (naturally backed flake) (x 8) strike-a-light (x3) flakes	gold ornament (x2) shale belt-ring	Beaker (x5)
Chilbolton	M	copper knife	pressure flaker strike-a-light flake (x6)	gold ornament (x4) gold bead shale beads	Beaker
Barrow Hills, Radley, barrow 4A	M	arrowhead (x3)		gold ornament (x2)	Beaker
Barrow Hills, grave 4660	M	arrowhead (x2) copper knife	pressure flaker flint blade	bone wing-headed pin	Beaker
Mere G6a	M	bracer copper knife	pressure flaker	gold ornament (x2)	Beaker
Thomas Hardye School, grave 1643	M	arrowhead (x3) bracer copper knife	flakes (?x3)		Beaker
Roundway G8	?	bracer copper knife		copper ?pin	Beaker
Wellington Quarry	?	arrowhead (x4) arrowhead blank (x3) bracer copper knife	knife (x5) flakes		Beaker

and who might also be called upon from time in case of need (2004a, 200; 2004b, 29; 2007, 249–50).

In proposing this, Case was drawing on the close similarities in well-furnished single burials of men found across Europe. The Amesbury Archer came from continental Europe as his mourners may have done too and the reasons why he was afforded such a well-furnished burial need to be seen in this wider context. Although found in Wessex, the style of his burial is, in large measure, continental European and this context is examined below.

Warrior Status

The warrior status of Bell Beaker males in single graves is almost an archetype (Pl. 49) but it is only rarely possible, as with burial 25004 in the grave of the Boscombe Bowmen, to identify single burials in collective graves and the association of grave goods with particular individuals is difficult. Nonetheless, the panoply of bow and arrow, bracer, and dagger is widely regarded as one of the defining characteristics of the Bell Beaker Set (eg, Salanova 1998a; Case 2004a; 2004b; 2007; Heyd 2004a; 2007a; Fokkens *et al.* 2008). Across central and western Europe, flint and chert

arrowheads are the most common type of offensive weapon used in hunting and warfare. In central Europe small bow-shaped pendants are found regularly in graves with arrowheads and it is possible that they ornamented quivers. There is no doubt that bows and arrows were used as weapons and this shown dramatically by the burial in the ditch at Stonehenge. This 25–30 year old man was buried wearing a bracer and he was killed by the bow. The remains of three barbed and tanged arrowheads were found with him, the broken tip of one embedded in his sternum; others had left marks on his ribs (Evans 1984, 15–17, 190, fig. 11–14, 17–20, 21, b–d; Pitts 2001, 112).

Bracers are much less frequent funerary finds than arrowheads, irrespective of whether their purpose was as much symbolic as functional (Sangmeister 1964a; Smith 2006; Fokkens 2008; though Delgado and Risch (2008) have suggested they were used as whetstones). In Britain, bracers decorated with gold capped rivets are known from Barnack, Cambridgeshire and Culduthel Mains, Highland, emphasising their role in making and displaying status and this is underlined by the famous gold bracer, probably of Early Bronze Age date, from Agua Branca in northern Portugal (Harrison 1980, 139, fig. 96), and by the later Breton *brassard-ornements* of precious materials.

Plate 49 The burial of the Amesbury Archer (1291)

Copper knives have, as with the Amesbury Archer, been found next to the chest and upper left arm of burials so regularly as to suggest they were worn or displayed there (Heyd 2000, 270; Zimmermann 2007; Fokkens 2008, 112–16). These knives are usually considered to be daggers for stabbing and while just how effective they were as weapons is open to question, with Case considering them as blades used to deliver the *coup de grâce* in hunting (eg, Case 2004a; 2007; p. 193 above), they could cause fatal blows in close combat (Zimmermann 2007). Perhaps as important was their role as a symbol of status (Zimmermann 2007; Heyd 2007a, 344–7). Although copper axes could conceivably been used as weapons, they were not placed in graves.

With three copper knives and two flint ones, a quiver's worth of arrows and two bracers, it is clear that the Amesbury Archer was ascribed the status of a warrior, or hunter, or both. His burial might be seen as yet another, albeit well-furnished, formulaic or stereotypical presentation of an idealised type (eg, Needham 2005, 207; Fokkens 2008; Sarauw 2007; 2009, 36) indicating a ranked, segmentary society evolving towards a chiefdom type (Heyd 2007a, 358–61).

The Bell Beaker itself is integral to the Bell Beaker Set and Salanova has argued that its role as a funerary vessel was fundamental to the expansion of the Bell Beaker Network (eg, Salanova 2000). The contents of Beaker pots have been much discussed. The idea of them being used for an alcoholic drink such as mead consumed in male feasts and drinking competitions has been a popular one (Sherratt 1987a) and although there is some evidence for drinks such as mead from Spanish finds (Rojo-Guerra *et al.* 2006), the evidence from Britain, as elsewhere, is not clear cut (Guerra-Doce 2006; pp. 54–8 and 154–6). Beeswax and plant waxes that might have been used to sweeten mead have been found only occasionally (Šoberl *et al.* 2009, 7) and in the graves of the Boscombe Bowmen and the Amesbury Archer, dairy based and plant-oil based products are indicated. Elsewhere in Britain the 'distinctive yellowish soil spilling out from its neck' from the Wessex/Middle Rhine Beaker placed in the Barnack grave was compared by the excavator to 'cold porridge' (Donaldson 1977, 208, 227, fig. 8) and as Shepherd pointed out the horn spoon found inside a Beaker from a multiple burial at Broomend of Crichie, Aberdeenshire, suggests that the contents of that Beaker had been viscous (1986, 10). All of this evidence is consistent with the preliminary results of wider studies that suggest that Beakers contained a wide range of food and drink (Guerra-Doce 2006). The precise contents of the Bell Beaker may not have been as important as the provision of food or drink in the otherworld and the ways in which it was presented and consumed.

Access to objects of gold or copper was also important in displaying status. But as Salanova, following Godelier (1996) pointed out in relation to the Bell Beaker Set, precious goods cannot by definition be used in daily life, as they are abstracted and projected into an imaginary world of symbols and power. They are rare because of the materials from which they are made or the time invested in their manufacture, attractive or considered to be so, and, finally, included in a sphere of exchange with comparable objects (Salanova 1998a). As we have seen, Case developed this idea, suggesting that the package of bow and arrow, knife, and Beaker, the core of the Bell Beaker Set was a symbolic hunting set.

In two comparative studies of Bell Beaker graves from Portugal, Spain, France, The Netherlands and Britain, Salanova noted that the quality of the pots in the graves, while often interpreted as prestige goods, showed few correlations between age, sex or other types of grave good (1998a; 2003a). In Britain Clarke's study had demonstrated that flint arrowheads, bracers, tanged copper knives, and flint daggers or knives, bone belt rings, antler spatulae, pyrite nodule, and strike-a-lights were found to occur exclusively in male graves (Clarke 1970, 448, app. 3.3) and this has been supported by subsequent finds (Brodie 2001, 490, fig. 2). Salanova also confirmed that what is thought of as the characteristic Bell Beaker assemblage was, as asserted previously, associated with males (Salanova 1998a, 316). Heyd's study of south German graves also systematically set out a comparable and equally clear gender division in the placing of objects in graves. Copper knives were found in only 3% of all graves (2000; 2007a, 341–51).

In contrast to the varied orientations of the other categories of grave examined (p.198 below), men buried with weapons were invariably aligned north–south with the head to the north. In the Netherlands the body was usually oriented east–west (1998a, 317) and a similar orientation was evident in the study of the Iberian graves (2003a). Salanova concluded that this rite was used to distinguish a particular group or male caste, noting that this burial rite was followed quite rigidly in contrast to the seemingly much more fluid rites for females. A similar observation was made in relation to Bell Beaker burials in the Upper Thames by Sofaer Derevenski (2002, 201–2). In this context it is noteworthy that the grave of the Amesbury Archer is not aligned north–south.

However, a knife, bracer, and arrowhead(s) are rarely present in any single grave. In Salanova's 1998 study only two graves from France, the Netherlands and Britain contained this symbolic panoply of a warrior (Salanova 1998a). These were Aremberg, Département Nord, France, which two pots that are very similar and may have been made for the grave (Salanova 2000, 331 and pers. comm.) and Lunteren, The Netherlands, which is the grave of a metalworker.

The burials of the East Group in central Europe display a rigid bipolar patterning. Here, females and males were almost invariably buried north–south with the women placed on their right side facing south. The men were placed on their left side facing east (eg, Havel 1978; Müller 2001). A study of only those burials whose sex had been identified reliably established several subtleties in the association of higher status grave goods with gender (Müller 2001). Arrowheads were found to be almost exclusively with male burials ($N = 41/42$) but 18% of copper knives were found with female burials ($N = 6/33$). Eleven per cent of the bracers were also found with female burials ($N = 5/46$). From this evidence, Müller concluded that gender was only one of the ways by which social status was ascribed. Turek has also made a similar point using some, but not all, of the burials considered by Müller (Turek 2002). Unlike Müller's study, in some cases the attribution of sex is on the basis of the position and orientation of the body – a more questionable approach. Six female burials from Bavaria, Bohemia, and Moravia were accompanied by copper knives. Turek suggests that these knives are smaller than usual and are therefore symbolic representations. Two of these female burials were accompanied by bracers; a fragment in Záhlinice grave 48/49 and two in Tišice grave 77/79, one of which was on the forearm in the usual position (Fig. 75). Four graves (Brandýsek 22, Radovesice 117/78, Tišice 77/99 and Záhlinice 48/49) contain copper awls which are usually – but not always – found with females. Three of these six burials also include precious metal ornaments: Radovesice grave 117/78 and Tišice 77/99 contain gold sheets from composite objects, and Záhlinice 48/49 two silver tress rings. The evidence for the wearing of gold and electrum ornaments from burials in central Europe, where they are consistently found by the temples, suggests that they were worn as tress rings.

When considered in a wider European context, it is clear that this number of female burials with copper knives is regionally distinctive (Zimmermann 2007, 81–2), but within the region, which is nonetheless extensive, these finds are widely distributed. This suggests that in some regions some

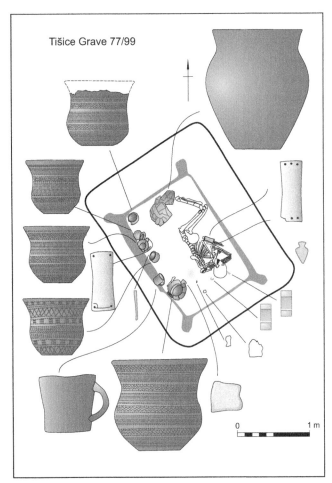

Tišice Grave 77/99

0   1 m

Figure 75 The Tišice, Bohemia, grave 77/99 burial (after Turek 2004, fig. 1)

objects, notably the knife and bracer, were used to construct social status in ways which were nor sex, or perhaps gender, specific. In the case of the Boscombe Down burials the Amesbury Archer had the status of the warrior and the presence of five arrowheads in the grave of the Boscombe Bowmen suggests that one or more of them, but perhaps not all, may also have had this status. The 'Companion' was not buried with any weaponry.

Ascribed Status

That some of these statuses may have been ascribed or inherited at birth or at an early stage of childhood, and were therefore not necessarily age-dependent, is shown by the occasional well furnished child burials. For example, what might be the earliest metal objects in Britain, three copper rings, were buried with a child in Barrow Hills, Radley, grave 919 (p. 196 above).

In central Europe, grave 6 at Lehovice, in Moravia, was that of a 9–10 year old child, buried on the left side – a

characteristically male position – with a copper knife, hair ornaments made of coiled wire (some of gold, others of copper), and five pots. In the multiple cremation burial of the Tvořiház, Distr. Znojmo, Moravia, a dagger, bracer, bone ring, four decorated Beakers, and a jug were found with the remains of a *c.* 10 year old (Bálek *et al.* 1999; Heyd 2007a, 353–4, fig. 16). A similarly well furnished gave is known from Žabovřesky nad Ohři in Bohemia (Medunová and Ondráček 1969, 439–40, tab. II; Müller 2001, 598; Turek and Černý 2001, 609; Dornheim *et al.* 2005, 52). Also in Bohemia, at Radovesice 53/80–I, the cremation burial of a child was accompanied by a bracer, an antler bow pendant, arrowheads, and v-bored buttons (Turek and Cerny 2001, 609).

Further west in Bavaria, a *c.* 5–7 year old child was buried at Landau-Südost, grave 1. The grave was much longer than necessary. In addition to the grave goods, including bow-shaped pendants, which were placed near the body, a further group, including a bracer, two arrowheads, a strike-a-alight and a Beaker, was placed some distance beyond the child's feet. It was suggested that the grave was so large because it contained a full size bow and two arrows indicating that in this instance warrior status was inherited, not achieved, although other interpretations, such as the putative bow being part of a cenotaph, are of course possible. Also in Bavaria, a bracer was also included in an infant grave at Königsbrunn (Kociumaka 1995; Heyd 2004a, Abb. 5–6, 13; 2004b; 2007a, 352, fig. 14–15). This raises questions about the social status of the juvenile(s) buried in the grave of the Boscombe Bowmen.

Bell Beaker Metalworkers

In Britain several attempts have been made to distinguish the 'occupation' of individuals on the basis of the grave goods placed with the deceased by their mourners, for example whether they were a craftsman (Smith and Simpson 1966; Clarke 1970, 260–5; Brodie 1997, 303–4; 1998; 2001). The cushion stone in the Amesbury Archer's grave symbolises a connection with metalworking and may identify him as a metalworker (pp. 114–16 above). It seems likely that this is an important factor in explaining why his burial was so well-furnished. As the evidence for Bell Beaker metalworkers has not been systematically assessed before, it is summarised below.

Copper and Bronze Age metalworkers' tools made from stone were first identified and examined by Butler and van der Waals in the context groups of stone tools found in burials at Lunteren and Soesterberg in The Netherlands

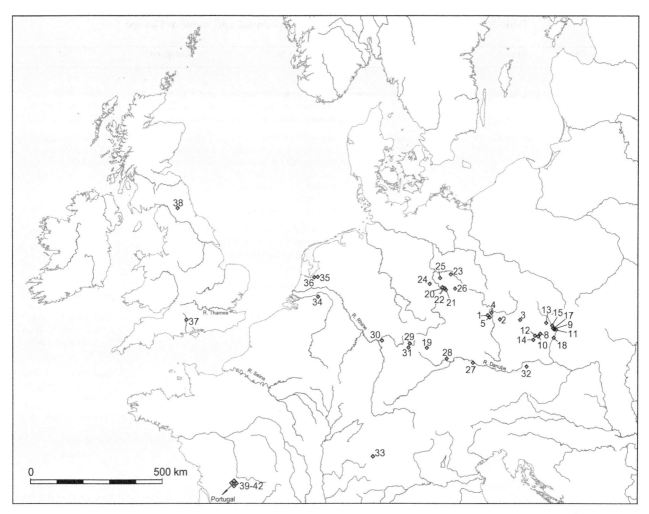

Figure 76 Distribution of Bell Beaker metalworkers' burials in central and western Europe. 1 Brandýsek grave 2; 2 Bylany by Český Brod grave 2; 3 Hrochův Týnec-Stičanyave grave 2/84; 4 Neratovice, grave xvi; 5 Stehelčeves Findspot I; 6 Stehelčeves Findspot III, grave 1; 7 Stehelčeves Findspot III, grave 2; 8 Brno-Řečkovice II, grave 1/34; 9 Holešov, grave X; 10 Ježeřany-Maršovice; 11 Kostelec by Holešov, grave A; 12 Lhánice, grave 3; 13 Luderov, grave 1; 14 Prosiměřice, grave A; 15 Předmostí Pit B/grave 1; 16 Předmostí Pit C /grave 2; 17 Turovice; 18 Veselí nad Moravou; 19 Dietfurt an der Altmühl, grave 2; 20 Bottendorf; 21 Eulau; 22 Grosskayna; 23 Sandersdorf; 24 Nohra Grave 16; 25 Stedten; 26 Zwenkau; 27 Künzing Bruck grave 9; 28 Mitterharthausen; 29 Heidingsfeld; 30 Dienheim; 31 Tückelhausen; 32 Ragelsdorf Platten Graves 1 and ?3; 33 Petit Chasseur; 34 Beers-Cuijk, Gassel II; 35 Lunteren, 'de Valk'; 36 Soesterberg; 37 Amesbury Archer; 38 Kirkhaugh; 39 São Pedro do Estoril; 40 Gruta da Portucheira, cave 2; 41 Bobadela; 42 Orca de Seixas

(Butler and van der Waals 1966; Clarke 1970, 573–4; Needham p. 116 above). Drawing on archaeological and historical examples they suggested that the differently shaped tools could have been used as hammers, whetstones and cushion stones. The term cushion stone was coined because some of these square or rectangular shaped stones resembled the styles of 1960s sofa cushions. Cushion stones were suggested to have been multipurpose metalworking tools that could have been used as both hammers and anvils.

Butler and van der Waals identified other metalworker's stone tools in western Europe and undertook metallurgical analyses using X-ray fluorescence spectrometry. Their work was supplemented by experimental studies of Early Bronze Age stone hammers (Hundt 1975) and more recently metalworkers' stone tools have been dealt with more systematically (Armbruster 2001; 2006) and a number of studies have, independently, examined the graves of Copper Age craft workers in general (Batorá 2002a; 2002b; Turek 2003; 2004; Bertemes 2004a) and Bell Beaker metalworkers in particular (Moucha 1989; Müller 1987; Bertemes *et al.* 2000; Bertemes and Heyd 2002). Experimental studies are currently being undertaken to further clarify the function of the complete range of tools (Freudenberg 2009).

The placing of tools and moulds in burials has its ultimate origins east of the Pontic (Bátora 2002a; 2002b) and it seems likely that it was transferred westwards as part of the

Table 36: Bell Beaker metalworkers' burials in central and western Europe

	Country/Name	Region	Sex/age	Stones	Other	Comment	Ref
Czech Republic							
1	Brandýsek grave 2	Okr. Kladno	M	axe-shaped hammer	3 pots (1= Bell Beaker) 2 other vessels, ?attribution to grave uncertain	said to be 'at the head'; grave not illus.	Kytlicová 1960, Abb. 6.1; Moucha 1989, 215, no. 1
2	Bylany by Český Brod grave 2	Okr. Kolin	?	rectangular cushion stone	multiple burial, inhumation with 1–2 cremation burials; with inhumation 1: bracer, 2 Bell Beakers. 2 a'heads; with cremation 3: 5 pots (2= Bell Beakers), flint knife, arrowhead	unclear if placed with inhumation 1 or cremation 3	Pič 1910; Moucha 1989, 215, no. 2, Abb. 1, 4; Turek 2006, Fototab. 1
3	Hrochův Týnec-Stičanyave grave 2/84	Okr. Chrudim	M	large cushion stone; cushion stone, 'multi-facetted tool' (hammer?)	2 pots (1=Bell Beaker) + other vessels not certainly attributed to disturbed grave		Moucha 1989, 25, no. 3, Abb. 1, 1–3
4	Neratovice, grave xvi	Okr. Mělník	double grave	hammer, not illus.	3 arrowheads, 'retoucher'	by feet	Hájek 1968, 77; Moucha 1989, 215, no. 5
5	Stehelčeves Findspot I	Okr. Kladno		hammer (broken axe, tip still sharp?), hammer	Bell Beaker, copper knife, bracer, arrowshaft smoother		Hájek 1961; Moucha 1989, 215, no. 5, Abb 1, 5; Zimmermann 2007, Abb. 56
6	Stehelčeves Findspot III, grave 1	Okr. Kladno	M	smith's hammer (axe), anvil, whetsone	4 pots (2 Bell Beakers), copper knife & chisel, 2 bracers, boar's tusk		Knor 1966; Hájek 1968, 118; Moucha 1989, 215–16, no. 7
7	Stehelčeves Findspot III, grave 2	Okr. Kladno	M	hammer (axe)	3 Bell Beakers, copper knife, bracer, 22 arrowheads, scraper, flakes, antler object, boar's tusk pick?		Knor 1966; Hájek 1968, 118; Moucha 1989, 215–16, no. 7; Zimmermann 2007, 140, C75
8	Brno-Řečkovice II, grave 1/34	Brno-Město	M	?	4 stones	by legs	Langová & Rakovský 1981, 29; Dvorak 1992, 18, Taf. 6, B
9	Holešov, grave X	Okr. Kroměříž	M	2 cushion stones, hammer, from axe?	2 pots (1 Bell Beaker, 1 polypod), bracer, 9 arrowheads, knife, scraper?, several flakes	1 cushion stone behind waist; 1 behind feet, with axe; grave partly destroyed by grave 420 of Nitra group EBA cemetery	Ondráček & Šebela 1985, 84, Abb. 164–5, Tab. 45–6; Moucha 1989, 216, no. 1
10	Jezeřany-Maršovice	Okr. Znojmo	M,30–40	7 stones, at least 2 cushion stones	2 Bell Beakers, silver tress ring, under lower jaw, bracer, 13 a'heads of imported flint, small blades, bow-shaped pendant, boar's tusk	stones & tusk in group behind waist; barrow, probably in chamber	Langová & Rakovský 1981; Růžičková, 2008, 47–8, tab. 12–13
11	Kostelec by Holešov, grave A	Okr. Kroměříž	Barrow	cushion stone	Bell Beaker, arrowheads		Červinka 1911, 118, Obr. 17; Moucha 1989, 216, no.2, Abb. 1, 7
12	Lhánice, grave 3	Okr Třebíč	M	'few flat stones'	pot, animal bone		Hájek 1951, 28, obr. 18; Langová & Rakovský 1981, 29
13	Luderov, grave 1	Okr. Oloumec		2-part? sandstone mould for knife	9 Bell Beakers, large copper awl		Böhm 1929; Hájek 1966, 214, Abb.5–6
14	Prosiměřice, grave A	Okr. Znojmo	M, 30–50	anvil, smith's hammer, poss. 2 cushion stones	2 pots (1 Bell Beaker), 10 arrowheads, 7 in tight group, oriented towards feet, scraper, flat piece bone	by feet; barrow chamber?	Pernička 1961; Moucha 1989, 216, no. 3

Table 36 (continued)

	Country/Name	Region	Sex/age	Stones	Other	Comment	Ref
15	Předmostí Pit B/grave 1	Okr. Přerov	?	axe, hammer or cushion stone,	Bell Beaker, 2 gold tress rings+frags 1–2 in electrum, 4 copper knives, 2 bracers, 5 arrowheads, 2 boar's tusks		Benešová-Medunová 1962; Hájek 1966 Moucha 1989, 216, no. 4
16	Předmostí Pit C /grave 2	Okr. Přerov	?	axe/hammer, axe	4 pots (3 Bell Beakers), copper knife, 2 bracers		Benešová-Medunová 1962; Hájek 1966, 211–12, Abb.1–2; Moucha 1989, 216, no. 4
17	Turovice	Okr. Přerov	?	hammer, cushion stone	Bell Beaker, 2 gold tress rings, copper knife, 2 bracers, 3+ arrowheads, 2 flint flakes	barrow	Červinka 1911, 119, Obr. 23; Hájek 1966, 212–14, Abb.3; Moucha 1989, 216, no. 5; Bertemes & Heyd 2002, 216–17
18	Veselí nad Moravou	Okr. Hodonín	?M	2 stones; 1 rhomboidal; 1 trapezoidal	2 pots (jug & dish, poss. Epi-Corded Ware Carpathian Culture (ESKK) type rather than Bell Beaker), bracer, boar's tusk	stones & tusk in front of feet	Langová & Rakovský 1981, 29; Staňa 1959

Germany

19	Dietfurt an der Altmühl, grave 2	Lkr. Neumarkt, Oberpfalz, Bavaria	no bone	2 axes, hammer/axe, flatter stone	undecor. Bell Beaker, 2 arrowheads, scraper	stones probably behind back.	Goetze 1987
20	Bottendorf	Lkr. Artern Halle	?	rectangular axe/cushion stone	undecor. Bell Beaker		Müller 1987, 177, Abb. 1, c–d
21	Eulau	Kr. Naumburg Sachsen-Anhalt	?	axe like, but with squared sides?	undecor. Bell Beaker		Müller 1987, 177, Abb. 2, a–b
22	Grosskayna	Lkr. Saalekreis Sachsen-Anhalt	?	small axe	undecor. Bell Beaker		Müller 1987, 177, Abb. 1, a–b
23	Sandersdorf	Kr. Bitterfeld Sachsen-Anhalt	?	long faceted stone/axe-like	decor. Bell Beaker		Müller 1987, 177–8, Abb. 2, c–d
24	Nohra Grave 16	Kr. Nordhausen Thüringen	?F	3 axes	decor Bell Beaker, 3 faceted stone chisels, flint flakes	Poorly recorded, attribution to grave (1 of few Bell Beakers in Únetiče cemetery) uncertain. Grave photographed after objects removed;. 'chisel-like' tools not well known in Bell Beaker graves, may be later date. The date of 2130–1760 cal BC BLN–3752, 3580± 50 BP supports this	Schmidt-Thielbeer 1955, 99–100; Abb. 3, Taf. xiii, 4; xxi, 3; Müller 1987, 177; Müller & van Willingen 2001, 78–9, fig. 12; Görsdorf 1993 (for date)
25	Stedten	Lkr. Mansfeld-Südharz (formerly Eisleben) Sachsen-Anhalt	M	cushion stone? sandstone so poss. anvil or hammer	Bell Beaker, copper knife, 3 arrowheads (1 hafted), boar's tusk, antler spatula & pressure flaker, adult pig bones/meat	below feet; stone cist, floor covered with limestone wash	Matthias 1964; Müller 1987, 178; Freudenbrg 2009 15, 18, Anm. 15.

Table 36 (continued)

	Country/Name	Region	Sex/age	Stones	Other	Comment	Ref
26	Zwenkau	Lkr. Leipzig Sachsen	crem. double?M adult & poss. F adult	2 flat polishing stones, 3 pumice whetstones, silicaceous stone (*Kieselscheifer*), 2 amphbolite axe-shaped hammers, heavily worn	Bell Beaker, 4 x4 mm diam. gold discs, 4 arrowheads, amber bead, 2 arrowshaft straighteners	'Bohemian' style Bell Beaker; axes have traces of metal; polishing stones & whetstones traces of wear; ?another grave nearby, with 2 Bell Beakers	Campen 2001; 2004; Hille 2003, 104–5; Conrad 2007, 6, 9–10 Taf 1, 1; 2, 2, 4, 5, 8; M. Conrad, pers. comm.
27	Künzing Bruck grave 9	Lkr. Deggendorf Bavaria	M adult	cushion stone?, traces of wear on upper surface, triangular stone (*Kalkstein*) with smooth surfaces, triangular sandstone with no traces of wear, arrowshaft smoother, axe frag with traces of gold	2 Bell Beakers, copper awl, bracer, 5 arrowheads, 2 scrapers, 5 boar's tusks	axe and triangular stones by feet.	Schmotz 1991; 1992, 56, Abb. 14; Bertemes *et al.* 2000
28	Mitterhart-hausen	Lkr. Straubing-Bogen Bavaria	M	small axe	traces of copper & 1 small sheet, bracer, arrowhead, flakes, 3 arrowshaft smoothers, 2 boar's tusks (partly stained green)		Hundt 1958, 14, Taf. 6, 10; Heyd 2001, 280–1, Taf. 75, 9
29	Heidingsfeld	Stkr. Würzberg Bavaria	?	axe, cushion stone?	Bell Beaker		Pescheck 1958, 84–5, Abb. 4–5; Taf. 10, 9; Heyd 2000, 282
30	Dienheim	Lkr. Mainz-Bingen Rheinland-Pfalz	?	2 axes + 2 smaller, 1 with frag. horn handle	Bell Beaker (but close to Corded Ware), flint knife, flake		Koster 1965–6, 53, Taf. 19, 7–11; Gebers 1978, 28–9, no. 27a, Taf. 39, 1–7; Heyd 2000, 283
31	Tückelhausen	Lkr. Würzberg Bavaria	?	axe, poss from grave		graves disturbed	Schröter & Wamser 1980, 295, Abb. 6, 1; Heyd 2000, 282
Austria							
32	Ragelsdorf Platten Graves 1 & ?3	Bez. Holla-brunn Lower Austria	?	possible axes			Hetzer 1949, 100–3; Heyd 2000, 282
Switzerland							
33	Petit-Chasseur	Valais	?	1 cushion stone?,	poss. other stone tools	collective burial, Dolmen M XI	Gallay & Chaix 1984, 123, pl. 1, 1413
The Netherlands							
34	Beers-Cuijk, Gassel II	Noord-Brabant	?	poss. sandstone hammerstone	Bell Beaker, gold hair clips, amber pendant, 2 flint flakes	finds found in dredging in localised area. Uncertain if hammerstone & flakes associated	Drenth & Hogestijn 1999; van der Beek 2004, 171–2, fig. 18
35	Lunteren, 'de Valk'	Veluwe	?	large quartzite cushion stone + hammer-stone, small cushion stone, micaceous quartzite whet-stone, greywacke axe	2 Bell Beakers, copper awl, bracer, 6 arrowheads	Stones found in 2nd excavation of barrow by F.C. Bursch?	Butler & van der Waals 1966, 63–72, 125–31, figs 11–13, 37, 44–6
36	Soesterberg	Utrecht	?	quartzite cushion stone, quartzite hammerstone, sandstone hammer	Bell Beaker?, 2 boar's tusks, bracer? lump granite		Butler & van der Waals 1966, 63–72, 132–3, figs 14–15, 44

Table 36 (continued)

	Country/Name	Region	Sex/age	Stones	Other	Comment	Ref
	United Kingdom						
37	Amesbury Archer	Wiltshire	M 35–45	cushion stone	this volume		
38	Kirkhaugh	Northumberland	?	cushion stone, hammerstone?	Frag. coarse pottery (Bell Beaker?), gold hair tress, arrowhead, saw/knife (or strike-a-light?), iron nodule, 6 worked flakes, 2 cores, flakes		Maryon 1936, 213, 215, fig. 3, g; 4
	Portugal						
39	São Pedro do Estoril	Cascais, Lisboa	?	2 cushion stones, ?polished basalt	group includes bracers, copper knives, chalk cylinders, bone points.	hypogeum, collective grave (Find Group 7), cushion stones found in SE of Tomb 1	Leisner *et al.* 1964, 27, 53, Estampa C, 11–12; D, 15–16, Leisner 1965, 107, Taf. 85.2, 5–6; Brandherm 2009, 172, fig. 2
40	Gruta da Portucheira, cave 2	Matacães, Torres Vedras	?	metalworking stones		collective grave	Leisner 1998, Brandherm 2009, 172
41	Bobadela	Oliveira do Hospital, Coimbra	?	poss. cushion stone, no. 79		megalithic collective grave	Leisner 1998, 139, Taf. 104, 79; Brandherm 2009, 172
42	Orca de Seixas	Moimenta da Beira, Viseu	?	1 cushion stone (no. 3), 2 poss. hammerstones (nos 1 & 5)		megalithic collective grave	Leisner 1998, 15, Taf. 3, 1, 3, 5; Brandherm 2009, 172, fig. 3

Yamnaya package before being adopted and adapted in Bell Beaker mortuary rites along with other Yamnaya elements such as copper knives and hair ornaments of precious metal (Harrison and Heyd 2007). Across central and western Europe approximately 40 graves, principally Bell Beaker but with a few Corded Ware examples (to which the Veselí nad Moravou burial (no. 18) might, perhaps, be added), have been suggested to be those of metalworkers (Fig. 76; Table 36). As a result, stone tools thought to have been used by Bell Beaker metalworkers can now be identified with some confidence, particularly in central Europe in Harrison's 'eastern province' (1980, 12) or East Group (eg, Heyd 2007a). Most of these finds are broadly contemporary with the Amesbury Archer and provide important comparanda.

These burials of metalworkers are usually single burials and typically those of adult males; only one grave contains a multiple burial: Bylany by Český Brod grave 2 (Table 36, no. 2). Bertemes and Heyd calculated that in central Europe these graves comprise less than 1% of male Bell Beaker burials and less than 0.1% of Corded Ware examples (2002, 217).

Although often described as the burials of smiths, it is apparent that these graves only rarely contain evidence for the processing or casting of metals. Instead, the stone tools from the great majority of graves are for use in the final stages

of finishing objects, which could be undertaken by cold working the metals. Only one burial, from Luderov, contains a mould, in this case for a knife (Böhm 1929; Hájek 1966).

This contrasts with the situation in Copper Age Eastern Europe, particularly in Ukraine and the Black Sea region in Yamnaya and Catacomb culture contexts, where a significantly higher proportion of graves contain clay crucibles, tuyères, and moulds for casting objects. The types of clay object that were placed in the grave varied regionally with most moulds being unused and while some also contain stone tools, most do not. Many of these graves are slightly earlier than the Bell Beaker and Corded Ware finds from central and western Europe but those of the Catacomb culture, which provides the largest number of finds, are broadly contemporary (Pustovalov 1994; Batorá 2002a; 2002b).

In central and western Europe the quality of the evidence available is, inevitably, variable. Some graves were discovered by chance (eg, Předmostí Pit B/grave 1 and Pit C/grave 2) or examined by early excavations (eg, Bylany by Český Brod grave 2, Kostelec by Holešov grave A, Turovice). Other more recent finds are not yet fully published (eg, Stehelčeves Findspot I and Findspot III, graves 1 and 2). In some cases the stones were not identified as metalworking tools when

218

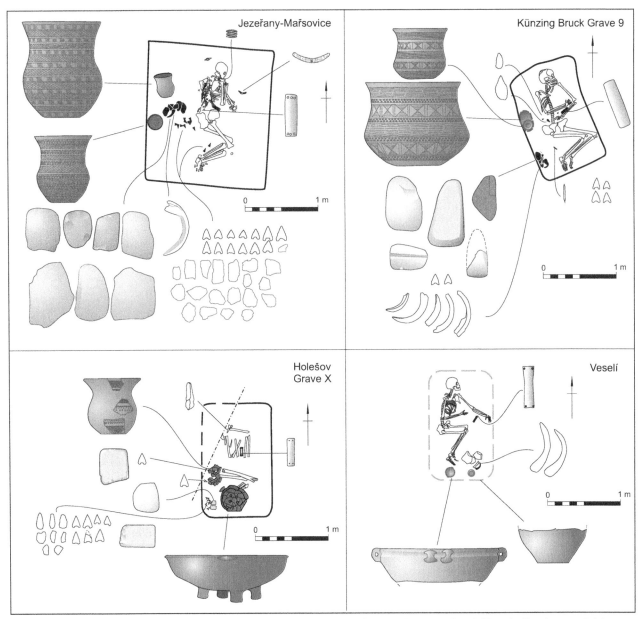

Figure 77 Plans of metalworker's burials: Jezeřany-Maršovice (after Langová and Rakovský 1981, obr. 2); Künzing Bruck, grave 9 (after Schmotz 1992, Abb. 12-14); Holešov, grave X (after Ondráček and Šebela 1985, obr. 164); and Veselí (after Staňa 1959, tab. 4)

the graves were published and the information available in the primary publication is limited (eg, Jezeřany-Maršovice; Veselí).

There are, however, an increasing number of well-recorded and published burials with groups of metalworkers' stone tools (eg, Holešov grave X, Künzing Bruck grave 9, and Zwenkau) (Fig. 77). From these it is clear that the stone tools found in these graves were used for finishing objects. None has evidence for earlier stages in the extraction and processing of ore.

Although mining is relatively well-studied (Timberlake 2001, 2003, 51; O'Brien 2004; Ambert and Vaquer 2005),

evidence for Bell Beaker metalworking is surprisingly scare. Although it is well attested in Iberia within major settlements such as Zambujal (Kunst 1997), there are only occasional traces from France (Mille and Bocquet 2004), Britain (Simpson *et al.* 2006, 139–40, fig. 12.2), and central Europe. Occasionally, however, groups of stone tools are found in non-funerary contexts where they can be interpreted as metalworking tools, as seems to be the case with an example from Newgrange, Co. Meath, Ireland (O'Kelly and Shell 1979, O'Kelly *et al.* 1983).

Stone Tools

As Needham observes above (p. 114), the ways in which the stone metalworking tools were used is not always immediately obvious. In studying those from Lunteren and Sjoesteberg, Butler and van der Waals identified five types:

1 Cushion stones (which could be used as an anvil and/ or as a hammer).
2 Slab-shaped grinding stones or whetstones.
3 Hammers (made from irregularly shaped stones).
4 Broken or blunted stone axeheads.
5 Large stone hammers (with a groove around the middle for attaching them to a wooden handle or a withy).

In practice, most of the stone tools are of two types; either cushion stones or small axe-shaped hammers. Even though these types are quite well-defined they have been described and interpreted in different ways. Similar looking axe-shaped stones have been called both axeheads and hammers, while larger cushion stones have been described as anvils and smaller ones as forging hammers (eg, Moucha 1989). This inconsistency in definition and description reflects a situation in which details of use wear are rarely given (cf. Butler and van der Waals 1966; Schmotz 1992; Conrad 2007; Freudenberg 2009), and few comparative studies have been undertaken since Butler and van der Waals' work.

The large hammer is known only from Soesterberg. With the groove around the middle for attaching it to its handle it is similar to the rilled stones used as hammerstones or mauls in the mining of ores and their processing before smelting (eg, O'Brien 2004, 338–556). A further object might be added to the finds from The Netherlands. A small roughly flaked and partially polished flint axehead from Lunteren was not considered to be a metalworking tool (Butler and van der Waals 1966, 129, no. 7, fig. 13b, 7). However, in view of the number of axeheads that can now be identified with other stone metalworking tools in graves in central Europe, the Soesterberg piece may also have been a metalworking tool that could be incorporated within Butler and van der Waals's fourth category of 'axes (broken off from and modified from earlier stone axes)'. Other types of tool found less frequently include medium-sized flat stones up to *c.* 150 mm long (eg, Künzing Bruck grave 9 and Zwenkau) and these may have been used as anvils. Given the immense variability in the size and hardness of the stones that could have been selected to be made into, or used as, metalworkers' tools, considerable typological diversity should be expected.

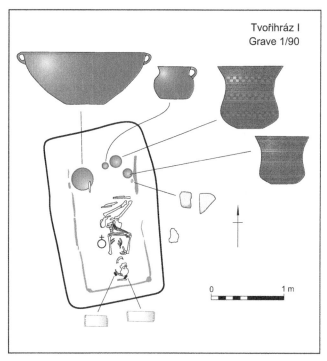

Figure 78 Plan of Tvořiház grave I, Moravia, burial (after Bálek et al. 1999, tab. 3–4

In four instances so-called arrow shaft straighteners/ polishers have been found with metalworking stones in graves: Künzing Bruck grave 9 (1 example), Zwenkau (2 examples), Mitterharthausen (3 examples), and Stehelčeves Findspot I (1 example). Although their use as smoothing the shafts of arrows is often asserted (eg, Heyd 2000, 283, Taf. 75), this interpretation is not supported unequivocally by use-wear analyses and it has been suggested that they are grooved whetstones (Woodward *et al.* 2005, 39, illus. 1, 1–4; 2) and at present their function(s) cannot be determined. In central European graves the objects are often found either singly or in pairs (eg, Šlapanice II 6/35, Moravia; Dvořák and Hájek 1990, 13, Taf. xxiii).

Lastly, two small but clearly worked stone objects, perhaps tools, were found by the feet in a well furnished female burial at Tvořiház, Distr. Znojmo, Moravia (Bálek *et al.* 1999, 12, Tab. 3, 8–9, size no. 8 = 25 x 34 x 23 mm: no. 9 = 25 x 30 x 43 mm) (Fig. 78). Their purpose is not known and they are much smaller than the metalworker's tools considered here but they emphasise that not all stone tools found in graves are necessarily metalworking tools.

Stone type
The type of stone chosen for the tools has rarely been well described. Where it has, the stones are often hard, igneous, rocks but softer sedimentary sandstones were also chosen. The Lunteren and Soesterberg finds are described as of

micaceous quartzite, presumably selected from glacial erratics. The cushion stone buried with the Amesbury Archer is probably of lydite (p. 113 above), a form of chert, which is found widely across Europe. At Zwenkau the two axe-shaped hammers, both of which are heavily worn, are of amphibolite and one of the three whetstones is described as being of a siliceous schist but the other two whetstones are described as being of pumice. The São Pedro do Estoril finds (Table 36, no. 39) are described as being of basalt.

The cushion stone from Stedten is a sandstone, which has led to doubt being expressed as to how effective it would have been as a tool (Butler and van der Waals 1966, 72; Müller 1987, 178; Freudenberg 2009, 15, 18, Anm. 15), even though some sandstones can be 'hard.' The possible hammerstone from Beers-Cuijk, Gassel II is also a sandstone and the same reservations apply but both objects exhibit traces of wear. Sandstones were also chosen for tools in Künzing Bruck grave 9, the two largest of which had traces of wear, although the axehead containing traces of metal is a diabase/dolerite.

Metallurgical analyses

Where metallurgical analyses of stone tools have been undertaken the results have been mixed. The tools from the Amesbury Archer (p. 117 above), Lunteren and Soesterberg graves have been analysed but did not yield any evidence for ancient metalworking. Negative evidence was also reported from experimental studies using replica Early Bronze Age axeheads (Hundt 1975). However, X-ray microscopy using an electron microprobe has revealed traces of metal within the structure of a number of tools.

The axehead from Künzing Bruck grave 9 retained a mixture of copper and gold in a ratio of 1:3 (25:75%) within the microstructure of the stone with metal flakes of up to 30μ being recorded. Because most of the stone tools were too large to fit into the analysis chamber, only the axehead from Künzing Bruck grave 9 could be examined (Bertemes *et al.* 2000, Bertemes and Heyd 2002, 216). However, the high silver content in the metal profile, which has some resemblances to modern jeweller's silver, is noteworthy, giving rise to the suspicion that there may have been contamination from a modern gold ring. Other tools reported to have traces of metal are the axehead from Turovice (Bertemes *et al.* 2000, 59) and the two axeheads from Zwenkau (Conrad 2007, 9).

Although graves of late Corded Ware smiths are less frequent than Bell Beaker examples (Bátora 2002a; see also Zimmermann 2007, 76–9), with only four currently identified, two stone tools from graves in Moravia have yielded traces of metal; Střelice (Bertemes and Heyd 2002, 217) and

Těšetice, both Distr. Olomouc (Šebela 1999, 152–3, pl. 108–9; 206; Bátora 2002a, 199). The cushion stone from Těšetice is described as having traces of copper.

Groups of Stone Tools

The interpretation of a grave as that of a metalworker on the basis of the presence of stone tools needs to be approached with caution. As Moucha (1989, 216) and Bartelheim (2002, 34, considering the Early Bronze Age) have cautioned, stones could simply be whetstones for sharpening the blades of metal objects.

Of the 36 certain or possible single graves scheduled in Table 36, 13 are not considered further here, either because of insufficient evidence or because they contain only single axeheads. Although Copper Age finds of one or two axeheads have been accepted as metalworker's tools by several writers (eg, Moucha 1989; Heyd 2000, 280–3; Bátora 2002a; 2002b), and Turek observes that axeheads are otherwise very rare in Bell Beaker graves in central Europe (Turek 2004, 150–1), in the absence of metallurgical analyses it remains possible

Table 37: Groups of stone metalworking tools from Bell Beaker metalworkers' burials

Burial	*No. stones*	*Cushion stone*	*Boar's tusks*
Brno-Řečkovice II, grave 1/34	4	no data	–
Dienheim	4	no	–
Dietfurt an der Altmühl, grave 2	4	no	–
Heidingsfeld	2	?	–
Holešov, grave X	3	✓	–
Hrochův Týnec-Stičanyave grave 2/84	3	✓	–
Jezeřany-Maršovice	7	?	1
Künzing Bruck grave 9	5	✓	5
Lhánice, grave 3	'a few'	no data	–
Lunteren	4, poss. 5	✓	–
Předmostí pit B/grave 1	2	✓	2
Prosiměřice grave A	2	✓	–
Soesterberg	3	✓	2
Stehelčeves Findspot I	2	no	–
Stehelčeves Findspot III, grave 1	3	?	1
Turovice	2	✓	–
Veselí nad Moravou	2	?	2
Zwenkau	5	✓	–

that the objects are simply axeheads rather than axe-shaped metalworker's hammers (cf. Lynch 2001). Few publications are precise about whether the axehead has a cutting edge, for use as an axe or a flat face, for use as a hammer. One consequence of this decision is to exclude many of the finds from north Germany published by Müller (1987). The multiple find from Dienheim with four axeheads is, however, included because of its similarity to the larger groups of metalworking stones.

While the same reservations about single finds might also apply to cushion stones, as in the case of the Amesbury Archer (Pl. 50) they represent a type of object that was invented for the manufacture of metal objects, and which was a novelty in Britain and Ireland. It seems highly unlikely that it would have been an heirloom, unless within the context of previous use on the Continent. Cushion stones were apparently only made for metalworking and an assessment of those graves in which more than one type of stone tool is found shows that, unlike axeheads, they are often found with other types of stone tool (Table 37). There is considerable ariety in the shape and size of cushion stones. Many, like that in the grave of the Amesbury Archer, have carefully facetted edges. Others, for example the (sandstone) stones from Künzing Bruck, grave 9, do not appear to be worked into shape, even though they bear traces of wear. As a result there is a question over two of the single finds where the identification of stones as cushion stones is not certain (Předmostí Pit B/ grave 1 and Bottendorf).

Of the 26 graves that are considered further here, 18 contain more than one stone with the Zwenkau grave appearing to contain two examples of each type of stone tool (Table 37). Of the 26 graves, two from Moravia contained groups of multiple stones about which little information is available (Lhánice grave 3, and Veselí) and the single grave with a casting mould, Luderov, does not contain any other metalworking tools and so it is not excluded for comparative purposes. While the quality of evidence is variable, the variety in shape of the stones is noteworthy (cf. Fig. 77) and it is considered sufficient to counter Bartelheim's reservations that the association of these stone tools with metalworking is unclear (2002, 34). Eight of the 18 graves definitely contain cushion stones and a further five possibly do. Three definitely do not contain 'cushion' stones and there is insufficient data for the remaining two. This suggest that cushion stones occur in c. 50% of those graves with groups of metalworkers' tools with sufficient data for the stones to be identified to broad type. Unusually, the finds from Nohra grave 16 could be

interpreted as representing three pairs of hammers and 'chisels', but the association of the Beaker is uncertain and the burial seems likely to be of later, Únetiče, date.

Two cushion stones were found at Lunteren, Holešov grave X, and Zwenkau, and perhaps at Prosiměřice grave Λ. Those graves which contain only cushion stones are; Bylany by Český Brod grave 2, Kostelec by Holešov grave A, Předmostí Pit B/grave 1, the Amesbury Archer, and possibly Bottendorf and Stedten.

In central Europe metalworking stones are rarely found in front of the corpse or by the head. Instead they are often found by the feet and legs and behind the back but apparently not by the chest and in this they form part of a consistent pattern of where objects were placed (Havel 1978). Examples of metalworking tools found by the feet are: Holešov grave X, Künzing Bruck grave 9, Prosiměřice grave A, Veselí, and possibly Stedten (Figs 77, 79). The single hammer at Neratovice grave xvi is described as being placed by the feet, while the stones at Brno-Řečkovice II, grave 1/34 are described as being by the legs. Finds placed behind the waist or back include Dietfurt an der Altmühl, grave 2 (probably, as bone did not survive), Holešov, grave X, Jezeřany-Maršovice, and the Amesbury Archer. In one instance, Brandýsek grave 2, the stone was placed by the head next to a Bell Beaker (apparently in front of it). In this case the body was laid on the right hand side, which is typical for female burials though the osteological analysis suggested that the dead was possibly male (Kytlicová 1960). In view of the number of female graves with copper knives in central Europe, some of which are very well-furnished (pp. 211–2 above), the possibility that this burial was of a woman should not be discounted.'

Plate 50 The cushion stone and boars' tusks ON 6591–2 from the grave of the Amesbury Archer (1289)

Boars' Tusks

It has been suggested that boars' tusks were used as metalworkers' tools, perhaps as planishing or burnishing tools. Tusks have been found in five of the 18 graves that contain more than one stone metalworking tool (Table 37) and in a further two examples containing only single tools; the Amesbury Archer (Pl. 50) and Předmostí Pit B, grave 1 and possibly Stedten, and Stehelčeves Findspot III, grave 2. This comprises *c.* 20% of all the probable and possible burials, a significant proportion but they are not as common as the 'nearly always' stated by Bertemes and Heyd would imply (2002, 217). Two tusks were also found in the Mitterharthausen grave along with a small axehead or possible axe-shaped hammer.

Boars' tusks – sometimes perforated for suspension – were also regularly placed in graves that do not contain metalworking tools in central Europe (eg, Heyd 2000, 298–9; Turek 2004, 150) and sometimes in Britain too. Accordingly the presence of tusks in a grave, as with the Boscombe Bowmen and the 'Companion', should not automatically be associated with metalworking. In Britain one tusk has been found in a female burial (Brodie 2001, tab. 2).

However, in the graves of three metalworkers, the tusks were physically associated with the metalworking tools, suggesting a direct association. The Jezeřany-Maršovice burial had a single tusk, Veselí two and at Künzing Bruck grave 9, five tusks were found amongst the stone tools, suggesting they may all have been placed in the grave in a bag or other organic container. At Stedten an antler spatula and a pressure flaker were found alongside the possible metalworking stone

and a boar's tusk, also suggesting that they were placed in the grave in a bag (Fig. 79).

As with two of the tusks placed with the Amesbury Archer (and also with the Boscombe Bowmen and 'Companion') there is some evidence for the modification of the tusks. One of the Veselí tusks is described as having been used as a scoop, while Předmostí Pit B/grave 1 contained two tusks, one of which has been sharpened. In the grave of the Amesbury Archer tusk ON 6627 has been worked into a scoop and was smooth on the reverse, while ON 6611 was probably sharpened (Fig. 56; p. 163 above). How a scoop would or have been used in the relatively simple cold working metalworking techniques in which metalworking stones were used is not clear. Boar's tusks are much less frequent finds in Britain than continental Europe so the presence of them in all three early Bell Beaker graves at Boscombe Down is intriguing, especially as the example in the grave of the Boscombe Bowmen has been worked into a scoop (Fig. 20).

Bell Beaker Flintworkers?

The presence both of one (or perhaps three) antler spatulae, possibly used for pressure flaking to retouch flint objects, and numerous flint blanks, suggests that the Amesbury Archer was also a flint-worker. This skill will have been ubiquitous.

By comparison with the burials of Bell Beaker metalworkers, those of flintworkers have reached much less attention. This is largely due to there being fewer of them in central and western Europe, although beyond the Bell Beaker world, in eastern Europe, graves of flintworkers are more frequent than graves of metalworkers (Bátora 2002a, 207–11). In continental Europe the presence of antler spatulae (pp. 158–9 above) in graves is one of the criteria that has been used to identify the deceased as flintworkers.

In his survey of craftsmen's graves Bátora (2002a, 211) cites only two from central Europe: Stedten and Samborzec (Figs 79–80). At Stedten two antler objects, one of which was a spatula, were placed in the bag by the feet of the dead man (Matthias 1964; Fig. 79). Another German find is from Warmsdorf, Kr. Stassfurt, where the grave goods included a Beaker, a flint knife, an arrowhead, a scraper and a blade fragment (Agthe 1989, 60, 103, nr. 27, Abb. 30; Zimmermann 2007, 10, Abb. 64).

The burial at Samborzec in southern Poland (Fig. 80) was found in a small cemetery and differed from the other nine burials in several regards (Kamieńska and Kulczycka-Leciejewiczowa 1970; Budziszewski *et al.* 2003). Most of the

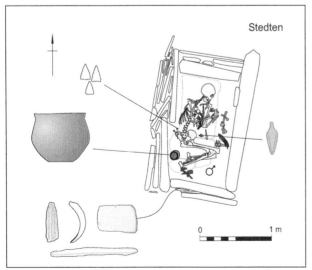

Figure 79 Plan of the Stedten, (Salle: Sachsens/Anhalt), Germany, metalworker/flintworker's? burial (after Matthias 1964, Abb. 1–2)

graves were oriented broadly north-south with men lying on their left side with their head to the north. Women were placed on their right with their head to the south. However, this 50–60 year old man was buried in a large grave (no. III) in a supine position with his head facing east but his legs and arms akimbo; a position typical of high status male burials in the region (Budziszewski *et al.* 2003, 160–3, fig. 7; 2470–2150 cal BC, Ki-7923, 3850±50 BP). The size of the grave, the number of objects which include a copper knife, an arrowhead, and a bracer, and the quality of the three pots, were interpreted by the excavators as reflecting both the high status of the deceased, and the age to which he had lived.

A further example is grave 116/78 at Radovesice (Fig. 80). Placed alongside this male burial, which had been disturbed in modern times, were two pots, a copper knife, a bracer, and an arrowhead. By the man's feet were a group of finds, again perhaps placed in an organic container, that included a boar's tusk, an antler spatula, a copper awl (possibly used in flintworking), and 21 flint flakes. It is possible that this grave also contained stone metalworking tools as four stones were found with the tusk and spatula but were discarded on excavation (Turek 2004).

How frequently antler or bone tools were placed in graves is uncertain, particularly as descriptions of items whose purpose is not well understood are (as with metalworkers' stone tools) not always helpful. An antler object in the metalworker's grave of Stehelčeves Findspot III/ grave 2 has been described variously as a 'hoe' (Hájek 1968, 118), an 'axe' (Moucha 1989, 216) and a 'flint retoucher' (Zimmermann 2007, 140, C75). Another example is 'flat piece of bone' found with one of the stone tools in the metalworker's burial at Prosiměřice (Pernička 1961, 29).

In Britain, finds of antler spatulae subsequent to Smith and Simpson's work (1966, 134–41, fig. 5, table 1; p. 158 above) include the well furnished and broadly contemporary primary burial at Chilbolton (Russel 1990, 166–7, fig. 6, 2) and the important – but later – group of spatulae, bone point, and flint flakes from burial 2752 at Easton Lane, Hampshire (Fasham *et al.* 1989; p. 159 above). Other finds include graves 203 and 4660 at Barrow Hills, Radley (Barclay and Halpin 1999, 63, 141, 235–6, fig. 4.22–3, WB3; 4.76; 4.79, M13) and the later finds of graves 4013/12 at Gravelly Guy, Oxfordshire (Lambrick and Allen 2004, 52–4, fig. 2.10, 2.18, pl. 2.3–4) and SK 19 at Ferrybridge, West Yorkshire (Roberts 2005, 45–6, 163–4, figs 32, 34, pl. 10–12; Duncan 2005).

Each one of the 15 burials with which these spatulae have been found have been adult males, although Mere G6a was a double burial, and many of the burials broadly contemporary

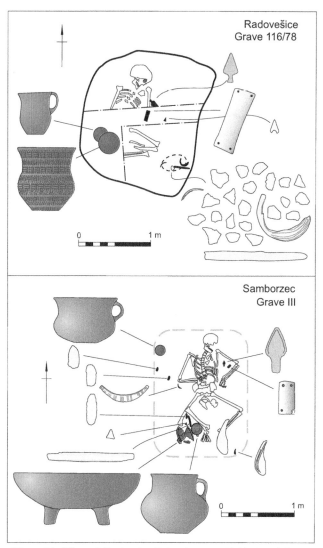

Figure 80 Plans of Radovesice, Bohemia, grave 116/78 and the Samborzec, Sandomierz, Poland flintworker's burials (after Turek 2004, fig. 4; 2006, obr. 78 and Kamieńska and Kulczycka-Leciejewiczowa 1970, fig. 12)

with the Amesbury Archer can be considered to have been of high status. Both the Chilbolton and Easton Lane graves included flint flakes that could be used as blanks for new objects. The number of multiple finds should also be noted: four at Easton Lane, three at Green Low and the Amesbury Archer and two at Ferrybridge and Mouse Low. Clarke (1970, 203), may have slightly overstated the association in graves with archery equipment but barbed and tanged arrowheads were present in nine of the 15 graves: graves 203 and 4660 at Barrow Hills, at Easton Lane, Gravelly Guy, and the later graves at Green Low and Haddon Field (Derbyshire), Mouse Low (Derbyshire).

The spatula with the Amesbury Archer was placed by his right shoulder/face but the spatula in the disturbed primary burial at Chilbolton was lying close to the feet and this was also the case with Barrow Hills, grave 4660. The burial at Easton Lane was also disturbed but here three of the four spatulae seem to have been placed behind the back along with a bone point or awl, and the fourth (found near the knees) may also have been originally. The spatulae were also placed behind the back at Barrow Hills, grave 203 along with a bone point or awl, and in the later grave A at Amesbury G51. In this regard the placing of the tools by the feet or back in these graves is closer to continental European practice than is the case with the Amesbury Archer.

It may at least be said that the few central European graves that have been identified as those of flintworkers all contain knives of either copper or flint and arrowheads, and two contain bracers. This suggests that the men were all of high status and at Stedten and Radovesice 116/78 they may have been metalworkers. It has also been argued in the context of the burial of a contemporary Corded Ware flint-worker at Koniusza, where the flints came from at least four sources, that the ability or obligation to produce arrowheads was one of a warrior not a craftsman (Budziszewski and Tunia 2000, 129; 2550–2290 cal BC, GrN-12516, 3925±30 BP). This suggests that while flintworking skills were sometimes distinguished in burials, other skills or statuses may have been afforded more importance.

Other Crafts

Graves that might be distinguished as those of other craftspeople or 'artisans' such as potters have not been identified, though antler spatulae could have been used to decorate some early forms of Bell Beakers, and their use as potting tools has been suggested (p. 158 above). However, potting is represented in the grave of the Amesbury Archer by the pair of pots that seems to have been made for the grave (ON 6609–10). In Britain the poor quality of Beakers sometimes placed in graves has been remarked on many times (eg, Brodie 2001, 490; Boast 1995, 71–2). This was not the case with the pots made for the grave of the Amesbury Archer. These were finely made and carefully decorated. That two of them the matching ON 6609–10 were not robust may have been a deliberate choice perhaps because, they were only going to be used once, or in another world. They were also decorated in a style that is very rare in Britain.

Potting may also be signified in the grave of the Amesbury Archer by the damage to one of the gold ornaments. This was folded, or crimped, over and it bears rows of impressions from what appears to have been one or

two toothed instruments (p. 130 above) such as pottery stamps (Simpson 2004; Harrison 1977, 47, fig. 26): or a cardium shell as these were widely used to decorate Maritime and derived Beakers. The damage recalls that to the gold plate from Landau Südost grave 9 which was broken in two when it was found, although the grave had been disturbed (Husty 2004, 47, Abb. 16).

The Status of Metalworkers

The number of objects buried with the Amesbury Archer appears consistent with the frequently expressed view that Bronze Age smiths were of high social status (eg, Bertemes 2004b, 214; Kristiansen and Larsson 2005, 52–7). In part this reflects the special properties often ascribed to the making of metal as an exclusive technology and one which is widely regarded as having strong ritual and magical associations (eg, Cowie 1988; Budd and Taylor 1995; Kristiansen and Larsson 2005, 53–7).

This view is encapsulated by Randsborg's comments about the full Bronze Age that when:

> 'on the rare occasions where manufacturing or agricultural tools are found, they are usually well-furnished graves. In other words they appear as an additional element in the definition of the important status and the role of the dead … crafts were carried our by people whose status was primarily defined by their kinship in society (cf. Rowlands 1971). It is by no means unthinkable that for example the manufacture of fine metal goods was the prerogative of leading individuals; in other words, that the 'chief' and the 'smith' were one and the same person or belonged to the same social level' (Randsborg 1984, 188).

How skilled artisans or crafts people were symbolised in central European Bell Beaker burials has been discussed by Turek (2003; 2004). Turek divided the crafts represented in burials into an archery package, and a metalworking package. The interpretation of the tools associated with working flint arrowheads and other flint tools was seen by Turek as unproblematic. In considering metalworking, Turek asks what scale of craft specialisation might be anticipated at, or shortly after, the introduction of Bell Beaker metallurgy? He suggested that early copper metallurgy was established on a limited scale; with no evidence of either mass production or craft specialisation. Given the rarity of early metal objects in

225

the archaeological record, he suggests that it is unlikely that the men buried with metalworking tools were full time specialists in metal production.

Instead, Turek suggested that the metalworking tools need not indicate that the man they were buried with was necessarily a smith. Instead they symbolised the control of the new technology and the dead men are seen as having had a privileged access to what is regarded as an esoteric knowledge or exclusive technology. Turek suggests that this comes from a particular social category and personal status which, he suggests, allowed the control of what is called 'strategic *technologies* and raw-materials' (2004a, 151).

The burials of these metalworkers, almost invariably of men, are almost universally considered as being among, if not the, most well-furnished graves in their local context (eg, Moucha 1989, 216; Bátora 2002b, 43, 46; Bartelheim 2002, 35; Bertemes 2004b, 152–3; Delgado and Risch 2006; Zimmermann 2007, 88; Brandherm 2009). This is largely on the basis of the objects placed in the grave and is summarised below.

The status of a warrior is frequently represented in these graves. Archery, is represented by arrowheads and bracers with flint arrowheads being found in over half (20) of the graves of certain or possible metalworkers. In three cases the arrows were recorded as being found close together suggesting that they were in a quiver (Jezeřany-Maršovice, Künzing Bruck grave 9 and Prosiměřice, grave A). The same may also have been the case with the groups from Holešov grave X and Lunteren but the distribution of the arrowheads in the grave of the Amesbury Archer shows that they were not placed in the grave in a quiver, even if they represent a quiver full of arrows.

Bracers have been found in 14, possibly 15 metalworker's graves. Most of these graves also contain arrowheads and those that do not were often poorly recorded raising the possibility that small objects were overlooked (eg, Stehelčeves Findspot I; Findspot III, grave 1 and Předmostí, Pit C/grave 2). However, the well-recorded Veselí grave did not contain arrowheads (though the burial might be assigned to an Epi-Corded Ware Carpathian Culture ((ESKK)) context) and they were recorded from Předmostí, Pit B/grave 1, indicating that there is not an absolute correlation between arrowheads and bracers. Many more graves across Europe contain only arrowheads.

In addition to the Amesbury Archer, seven other certain or possible metalworker's graves contained copper knives: Stehelčeves Findspot I; Findspot III, graves 1 and 2; Předmostí, Pit B/grave 1 and Pit C/grave 2; Stedten, and Turovice (Table 36). As well as copper knives, the Amesbury

Plate 51 Copper knife ON 6613 and flint knife/dagger ON 6570 from the grave of the Amesbury Archer.

Archer also had two flint knife/daggers placed with him (Pl. 51). While not as skilled in their execution as the some of the later bifacially flaked flint daggers found in Britain (eg, Clark 1932; H.S. Green *et al.* 1982; Lomborg 1972), the two flint knife/daggers in the Amesbury Archer's grave were the best made of the numerous flint objects and their profile also seems to imitate those of copper knives.

Outwith the northern Netherlands, northern Germany and Scandinavia, flint knives (or daggers) are not particularly frequent in Bell Beaker contexts in continental Europe. Little more than a dozen are currently known from central Europe, though on some occasions finds have been interpreted initially as projectile points or just 'points' rather than as knives, suggesting that the true number may be higher (Zimmermann 2007, 99–113). This also seems to be suggested by some recent finds from Bavaria at Eitensheim grave 19 (Meixner and Weinig 2003, 29–30, Abb. 18) and Atting 'Aufeld' graves 4777 and 4799 (Engelhardt 2006, 33, Abb. 33–4; 35, 1–2).

226

Two early burials from southern Germany (Heyd's Phase A2a) from Landau an der Isar, Kr Dingolfing-Landau, and Oberstimm, Kr Pfaffenhofen, each contained copper and flint knives, demonstrating their contemporaneity. As Heyd suggested, this shows that objects made from different materials could perform the same function (2007a, 275). On this basis the Amesbury Archer might be considered as having been furnished with five high status knives or daggers, three of metal and two of flint (Pl. 51).

Precious metal ornaments are found at Jezeřany-Maršovice, Předmostí, Pit B/grave 1, and Turovice, although the tiny fragments of gold from Zwenkau are excluded as they may derive from the manufacture of ornaments. Gold ornaments also occur in graves in north-west Europe at Beers-Cuijk, Gassel II, Kirkhaugh, and with the Amesbury Archer.

A systematic comparative analysis of metalworkers' graves is more difficult. Bell Beaker cemeteries across Europe are typically small, with rarely more than 20 graves and there are subtle chronological and geographical variations in the number and type of objects placed in graves (Heyd 2001; 2007a, 347–51). Only two metalworker's graves occur in medium-sized cemeteries. At Holešov, where the cemetery contained 10 graves, and Künzing Bruck where there were nine graves. These samples are too small to provide a reliable statistical basis but it can at least be said that in relation to the other graves in the cemeteries (which were in use for several generations), both of the metalworker's graves did contain a higher number of artefact types.

Funerary architecture can be taken as another indicator of social status (Turek 2006b, 173–6) and ring ditches indicating the presence of barrows over graves have been found at six sites: Jezeřany-Maršovice, Kostelec by Holešov grave A, Lunteren, Prosiměřice grave A, Soesterberg, and Turovice. At both Jezeřany-Maršovice and Prosiměřice, grave A there was certain or probable evidence for the existence of wooden chambers. The Lunteren grave is described as notably wide and deep (Butler and van der Waals 1966, 127). However, in some cemeteries where the grave of a metalworker was not apparently covered by a mound other graves do have ring ditches. This was the case at Künzing Bruck (grave 8) and Dietfurt an der Altmühl (grave 1).

The image that emerges of Bell Beaker metalworkers, particularly in central Europe, is that they often had the status of a warrior, equipped with a bow and arrow and accompanied with a bracer. Copper knives that may have been used as daggers were also often carried. The hair and faces of at least some of the metalworkers were adorned with ornaments of precious metal. In this regard the metalworkers carried the objects they were involved in making. Some of the graves had wooden chambers, a feature being identified with increasing regularity across central (and western) Europe, and some were covered by barrows. On the few occasions in which the graves of metalworker's have been found in small or medium-sized cemeteries they are the most well furnished both with regard to the number of objects and the number of artefact types placed in them.

This image is a composite one, drawn from evidence of variable quality and slightly different dates scattered across central and western Europe but it is consistent with the view that these craftsmen were part of an elite (Heyd 2007a, 360). Few graves conform to an ideal type. The Amesbury Archer (Pl. 50) is one.

While it might, on this basis, be tempting to see the Amesbury Archer in relation to a classic formulation of a centralised prestige goods economy, particularly in relation to the supply of metals, the situation is more subtle. Some of the skills represented such as potting and flintworking were widespread and graves containing Beakers and/or arrowheads are common. Nor was there any single social persona; the Amesbury Archer was also an incomer, someone who had lived with disability and, as the genetic link with the 'Companion' shows, part of a family group. Even so, one of the outstanding characteristics of his burial is the sheer number of objects placed with it.

Überaustattung *in Bell Beaker Graves*

The mourners of the Amesbury Archer placed an exceptionally large number of offerings in his grave. While this has been interpreted as signifying great status, the number of grave goods is so large that it has led some to suggest that the grave was reopened after the burial was completed and further objects placed in it (J.C. Barrett, pers. comm.; A. Gibson, pers. comm.). As the burial was placed within a timber chamber this could have been done without leaving any archaeological trace other than the addition of these objects. Other possible explanations for the number of grave goods include the inclusion of heirlooms, perhaps from an earlier burial. The damage (if accidental) to the tang of one of the gold ornaments, the wear on one of the copper knives, and the presence of an All-Over-Cord Beaker that might be earlier than the other Beakers, are objects that could be interpreted as heirlooms (cf. Woodward 2002). Other possible explanations are a cenotaph or the former presence of a child whose slight remains did not survive although this seems unlikely as the calcareous chalk geology generally preserves bone well, as is the case with the skeleton of the Amesbury Archer.

The removal of objects should also be considered briefly. The absence from the burial of one rib might be because of its removal as part of the type of secondary burial rites evident in early Bell Beaker graves in southern England. In the Bronze Age across continental Europe Randsborg demonstrated that the 'plundering' of well-furnished male burials is quite widespread (Randsborg 1998). The evidence suggests that some highly significant items, and occasionally body parts, were removed shortly after the burial and as well-furnished females burials were not treated in this way, Randsborg suggests that the plundering may represent the deliberate 'killing' of elite status.

However, one of the characteristics that distinguishes the grave of the Amesbury Archer in relation to many other graves, is not just the overall number of objects but the number of them of which there are *multiples*. The flint arrowheads have been suggested to have been made mostly by the same person and two pairs of Beakers have been identified amongst the five Beakers, with one pair suggested to have been made for the grave. This does not suggest that these objects were added to the grave at a later date. Of the other objects that occur in multiples, excluding the gold ornaments, the discovery of pairs of bracers is by no means unknown. As has been shown above, bracers and copper knives occur in the graves of some females in central Europe, suggesting that in some areas at least they symbolised a status way that was not exclusive to gender.

The regular though infrequent occurrence of over-provisioning in graves and hoards in prehistoric Europe was examined by Hansen (2002) who showed that the extravagant and seemingly unnecessary use of valuable objects was a widespread phenomenon practised by Copper Age and – most notably – Early Bronze Age elites in regions as diverse as Wessex, Armorica, central Germany, Mycenae, and Ur. He called this *Überaustattung* (cf. Vankilde 2005b, 273–4).

The number of objects, their quality and the often rare and precious materials which they were made of, were all used to define very high, if not supreme status. In some cases immense mounds were raised over graves. Examples from funerary contexts include the gold dagger and silver shaft hole axehead from Mala Gruda tumulus in Montenegro, the placing of multiple daggers – sometimes more than 10 – in Armorican 'dagger graves', and the size of the tumulus over the Leubingen grave, which also had a prodigious quantity of

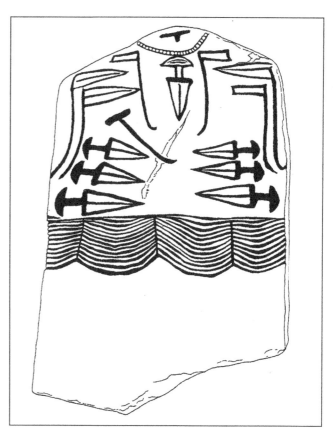

Figure 81 The Arco stele

objects, including metalworking tools, placed in it. The re-current representation of multiple objects on the Remedello Copper Age stele at Arco in northern Italy (Fig. 81), if interpreted as self-representations, is another example of over-provision (Hansen 2002).

Such over-provision by placing multiple examples of objects is a regular, though not frequent, occurrence in Bell Beaker graves in continental Europe.

Bows and arrows

The largest group of multiple finds in the grave of the Amesbury Archer is the arrowheads – some 17 barbed and tanged arrowheads and one probable triangular example – and it is possible that most of them were made by the same person (p. 91 above).

In central Europe, large groups of arrowheads are known from metalworkers burials; 22 at Stehelčeves Findspot III, grave 2; 13 at Jezeřany-Maršovice (Fig. 77) and 10 each from Prosiměřice, grave A and Holešov, grave X. However, large groups of barbed and tanged arrowheads are also known from early Bell Beaker graves in Britain; 18 from Thames Valley Business Park from a probable grave with a comb decorated Beaker, and 11 from grave 137 at Mucking, Essex, which included an All-Over-Combed Beaker (p. 99 above).

Bracers

In Britain two bracers have been found in two, possibly three, other graves: Tring, Hertfordshire (where they were both placed by the feet of the deceased), Newlands, Oyne, Aberdeenshire, and possibly Liveras chambered tomb, Broadford Bay, Isle of Skye (Smith 2006, 54). In continental Europe there are at least eight finds of multiple wristguards from single graves and four of these are from the graves of metalworker's: Předmostí, Pit B/grave 1, Pit C/grave 2, Stehelčeves Findspot III, grave 1, and Turovice (Table 36). The other finds are from Brno-Holásky-II grave 13/38 (Dvořák 1992, 10, Taf. 14), Hulín I grave 95/204 (Růžičková 2008, 47, Tab. 11), Lysolaje grave 6, Prague-West (Hájek 1968, 64–5), and Tišice 77/79 (Turek 2002; 2004, 150, fig. 1).

Copper knives

Finds of two copper knives (or daggers) in a grave are very rare across Europe. Other than the grave of the Amesbury Archer only two instances are known and in neither is the grave well recorded. At Brno-Holásky-II-60/38, which has two knives (Dvořák 1992, 15, Taf. 26), the records made at the time of discovery during quarrying and the objects attributed to the grave are contradictory, leading Dvořák to express some doubt as to whether the grave goods are from one grave group (Dvořák 1992, 15, Taf. 26). The finds from the two well furnished graves at Předmostí were only reported to archaeologists a fortnight after their discovery (Benešová-Medunová 1962) and although the attributions to two graves has been widely accepted (eg, Hájek 1966, 211–14), there must be some reservations about them. Nonetheless, Pit B/grave 1 is thought to have contained four copper daggers, one of which is significantly larger than the others. The grave also contained five arrowheads, two gold tress rings and another one, possibly two, of electrum, two bracers, two boar's tusks, a Beaker, and two stone metalworking tools.

Beakers

The number of pots placed with the Amesbury Archer is unusual for two reasons: first, their number – five – and secondly, the probable occurrence of two pairs of pots, one pair (ON 6609 and 6610) suggested to have been made for the grave, and the other pair (ON 6590 and 6597) to have been made by the same potter (pp. 147–8 above). The number of Beakers from the grave of the Boscombe Bowmen, eight, is also high but it is a collective burial. The case has been made above that the pots may have been placed in the grave in pairs (pp. 39–40) though it may or may not be coincidental that the remains of seven or eight individuals of Bell Beaker date were identified.

In his corpus of British finds Clarke recorded 28 or more occurrences of two Beakers being found in single graves, and four instances of three Beakers, all later graves from northern England and Scotland (1970, app. 3.1: graves with three Beakers; Dilston Park, Hexham (no. 675) and North Sunderland (no. 695) both Northumberland (no. 675); Nether Criggie, Dunnottar, Aberdeenshire (formerly Kincardine-shire) (no. 1683; 2280–2030 cal BC, OxA-V-2166-46, 3741±32 BP), and Keir, Belhelvie, Aberdeenshire (no. 1460; 2200–2030 cal BC, OxA-V-2172, 3715±32 BP). Some of these Beakers form 'nested sets' of different sizes. However, the Boscombe Down graves and perhaps Wilsford G54 and Winterbourne Gunner, and Upper Largie, contained three Beakers, demonstrating that the placing of multiple Beakers was also practised early in the British sequence (pp. 152–3 above).

While the number of Beakers placed with the Amesbury Archer is atypical for Britain, the number can again be both matched and exceeded by the number placed in some central European single graves. This observation must be qualified in that, generally, more pots were placed in graves in central Europe than in western Europe. However, unlike in Britain, these pots were often mainly *Begleitkeramik* or accompanying pottery, with only one or two Beakers present. In many graves the only pottery is *Begleitkeramik*. However, some graves are distinctive in the number of decorated Beakers they contain. The well furnished female burial at Tišice 77/79 (Fig. 75) contains seven pots, five of which are decorated Beakers, the other two being a handled jug and a large urn. Exceptionally, the metalworkers grave at Luderov, which is the only one to have contained a mould (for a knife), rather than metalworking tools, contained nine decorated Beakers and a copper awl. Although the placing of multiple vessels is not typical of single graves in France (Salanova 1998b, 2, 4; 2000), the placing of multiple Beakers is known from collective graves in Brittany though it is not possible to associate these vessels with individual burials.

Other objects

The gold basket-shaped ornaments found in the graves of the Amesbury Archer and 'Companion' graves, normally occur as pairs, but two pairs occur in the Chilbolton primary grave (but see p. 136) and probably also in Předmostí, Pit B/grave 1.

Most of the other objects are singletons, such as the antler pin and the shale ring, or they are of types that occur as multiples elsewhere. There are three, possibly more, antler spatulae in the grave of the Amesbury Archer, and four are known from the Easton Lane grave; there are also multiple finds from the Green Low (three), Ferrybridge (two), and Mouse Low (two) graves. The multiple flint objects are less easy to parallel and while they may echo some of the groups of flint deposited in Late Neolithic Grooved Ware pits, including at Boscombe Down (Powell and Barclay in prep.), many of the arrowheads, at least, may have made by the same person (p. 91 above). Flint objects also occur in many of the graves of metalworkers in central Europe (Table 36) with the possible metalworker's grave at Radovesice 116/78 containing 21 flakes apparently paced in an organic container (Fig. 80).

Conclusion

The frequency with which these multiple finds occur in the graves in central Europe containing metalworkers' tools is evident. All four of the Bohemian and Moravian graves with large groups of arrowheads are of possible metalworkers, as are four of the eight graves in central Europe with multiple finds of bracers (Předmostí, Pit B/grave 1, Pit C/grave 2, Stehelčeves Findspot III, grave 1, and Turovice), and one of the two graves with multiple copper knives (Předmostí, Pit B/grave 1). If the flint examples are included, the Amesbury Archer was buried with five knives. The grave with the largest number of Beakers, Luderov, is again of a possible metalworker.

Only Předmostí, Pit B/grave 1 is comparable in the number of types of object placed as multiples, and as its finds were recovered by workmen it seems likely that smaller flint objects and sherds of pottery are under-represented. One of the copper knives is significantly larger than the other three, which is also the case in the grave of the Amesbury Archer.

While graves of possible metalworkers are often suggested to be 'rich' and part of a social elite (Heyd 2007a, 360), the number of instances of over-provision as set out by Hansen (2002), suggests that at least some of them, such as at Předmostí, Pit B/grave 1 and the Amesbury Archer, may have been of the highest social status.

Chapter 12

The Journeys of the Amesbury Archer and the 'Companion'

The oxygen isotope analyses for the Amesbury Archer indicate that he spent part of his later childhood somewhere in a zone stretching from the Alps to Scandinavia (Fig. 68). The results of the strontium analysis are consistent with the southern part of this zone, in particular with the complex geologies comprised of material derived from the Alps but buried under later sediments. They do not support an origin in the northern, Scandinavian, part of the zone defined by the oxygen isotopes.

Although the Bell Beaker Set is found in Denmark, Poland, and central and northern Germany, the styles of material culture in these regions are different from that found with the Amesbury Archer. While the central German material forms part of the East Group (Hille 2003; Conrad 2007; cf. Heyd 2007a) or 'eastern province' (Harrison 1980, 12; Fig. 71), the finds on the North German plain and in Scandinavia appear quite distinct (Czebreszuk and Szmyt 2003; Vankilde 2005a; Sarauw 2007). They might instead now be classified as the regional group of the north European lowlands (Heyd 2007a, 328, fig. 1; 2007b).

In contrast, the objects buried with the Amesbury Archer are principally western in style, notably the pottery and arrowheads and arguably also the gold ornaments, with some widespread 'international' types such as the bracers and copper knives. At present the Bell Beaker finds in Denmark, Poland, and central and northern Germany cannot be shown to be any early than the burial of the Amesbury Archer with the more northerly finds appearing to be later in date. The archaeological evidence is therefore broadly consistent with the results of the strontium analyses in suggesting that, when a child, the Amesbury Archer lived in the southern part of the zone identified by the oxygen isotopes. The areas where there are most similarities are in the Alps and Alpine forelands of Switzerland and some parts of south-west Germany, although most of the German material belongs to the East Group.

The isotope analysis of the teeth of the 'Companion' also revealed significantly different oxygen isotope compositions. The results from the first permanent tooth are consistent with him having been born in Wessex but those from the later tooth are much more similar to that of the Amesbury Archer.

This suggests that the 'Companion' spent his earlier childhood in Wessex, but that in later childhood, about 12–16 years, he was resident elsewhere, perhaps in continental Europe. The few objects placed with the 'Companion' offer no indications about this journey. The boar's tusk may have been associated with metalworking and such tusks are also found in graves of the Boscombe Bowmen and the Amesbury Archer. As with the Amesbury Archer the gold basket-shaped ornaments were not worn in the usual way at burial (considered here to have been as tress rings). In this case the ornaments may have been suspended from a cord around the 'Companion's' neck. In view of the genetic link between the Amesbury Archer and the 'Companion', and the possibility raised by the radiocarbon dating that the two men were not one, but two, generations apart, this might suggest that links were maintained to a traditional, ancestral, homelands. The 'Companion', therefore, may have made a journey to continental Europe although the different isotope values do not immediately suggest that this was to the same circum-Alpine region from which the Archer had travelled previously.

Even so, it is not possible to precisely identify the Archer's 'homeland' through either isotope or archaeological analyses. There are several reasons for this which have been set out in Chapter 10 in relation to the Boscombe Bowmen, but perhaps the most important is that the 'journey' identified by isotope analysis might well have comprised several shorter journeys rather than one longer one. It is also important that unrealistic expectations should not be placed on techniques such as isotope analysis whose potential is clear but whose application to archaeological data is relatively new and where fine calibration for variables such as climatic change is yet to emerge. Even if it were possible to identify a distinctive archaeological culture for a 'homeland' or those places visited during the journeys, the cumulative result is likely to have been one where any distinctive local traits would have been dissipated and the resulting impression would be cumulative and international. These difficulties are further exacerbated by the 'international' nature of much of the early Bell Beaker material culture across western Europe.

Nonetheless, as with Boscombe Bowmen (pp. 205–7 above), the existing data should be considered briefly. South-west Germany and the Massif Central have been briefly considered above. Relatively few Bell Beaker finds are known from Switzerland and most have been made in the north and west of the country (Besse 2006). With the exception of the megalithic cemetery at Petit Chasseur in Valais in the south of the Alps (cf. Harrison and Heyd 2007), few burials are known (Bill 1976; Degen 1976). As a result there is the unusual situation of almost as many settlements being known as burials (Othenin-Girard 1997; von Berg 2002; Combe and Rieder 2004).

One object buried with the Amesbury Archer has been compared with finds from Switzerland. The antler pin is a similar shape, but much larger in size, to an antler pin most probably of Corded Ware association, from the settlement at Vinelz on the shore of Lake Biel. However, there is no overlap in date between the likely Auvernier date for this pin or the large silver pin from Remedello in northern Italy. It is possible that the size of the pin buried with the Amesbury Archer indicates that it was a copy of a large pin of precious metal but its size may simply have been dictated by the type of costume that it pinned.

Other similarities in the finds buried with the Archer are, again, more general. For example, the hanging triangles on the lower zone of a Bell Beaker from Cortalloid/Potat-Dessous (Kt. Neuchâtel; von Burg 2002, Abb. 55) might be compared with those on pot ON 6597 (Pl. 52), but such motifs can also be found elsewhere, and cord decoration is common (Salanova 2000, 113–14). Decorated Beakers in Switzerland have often been linked with examples to the north-east, from Bavaria and Bohemia (eg, Degen 1976), but there are also links to Alsace to the north-west, to Baden-Württemberg to the north-east (eg, Heyd 2000, 353–5; 2004b, 185–6, Abb.1), and to the north where some All-Over-Ornamented Beakers in the Upper Rhine have carinated rather than sinuous profiles (Sangmeister 1964b, 94). It is interesting to note that at the settlement at Alle Noir Bois, Kt. Neuchatel, a significant proportion of the small quantity of decorated pottery was imported to the site from the north over distances of at least 50 km (Othenin-Giraud 1997, 84, fig. 58). Whether this represents the movement of people and materials or the finished vessels is not clear.

Two-holed bracers of Sangmeister's Type G, the type buried with the Amesbury Archer, have also been found in Switzerland (eg, Saint-Blaise, Kt. Neuchâtel) but as shown above (p. 107–11) this type, which appeared at an early date but continued in use until the Early Bronze Age, is very

Plate 52 Beaker ON 6597 from the grave of the Amesbury Archer

widely distributed (Sangmeister 1964a, 96–101; 1974, 122; Heyd 2000, 348, 472). Although Sangmeister noted the relative rarity of this type in central Europe in comparison with Iberia (1964a, 95, Abb.2), it is uncertain if this remains the case. In central Europe most Type G bracers are grey and only very rarely red and Roe argues above (p. 112) that the black bracer buried with the Amesbury Archer may be continental European in origin as no satisfactory match for the rock has been found among British sources. Plancher-les-Mines (Haute Saône) in the southern part of the Vosges is suggested as a possible source for the rock, and this is just to the north-west of Switzerland. The suggestion that the red bracer (ON 6588) was made from shale at Caerfai Bay, near St David's, Pembrokeshire, not far from the sources of the bluestones at Stonehenge (p. 109 above), does not alter its distinctively early and typically continental form and it is distinctive amongst British and Irish finds. Even here, a continental European source for the red bracer cannot be excluded entirely.

The other objects placed in the grave of the Amesbury Archer are no more diagnostic geographically. Although many have clear continental European parallels, they are often widespread. The arrowheads can only be said to be a type that occurs principally but not exclusively in western Europe and the Beakers are north-west European types. In the case of the belt ring (pp. 118–20 above), several finds made from bone are known from southern (Treinen 1970, 94, fig. 48, 14–16) and western France (Joussaume 1981, 502, fig. 230, 35–6). The find from Pago de la Peña in Spain has been considered to demonstrate links with central Europe (Harrison 1977, 65) but the only example of Bell Beaker date there seems to be the bone ring bone from the multiple cremation burial in grave 2/91 at Tvořiház, Distr. Znojmo, Moravia (Bálek *et al.* 1999, 35, tab. 8, 16).

In the current state of knowledge it is difficult to regard the Beakers, bracers or copper knives buried with the Amesbury Archer as other than early and 'international' types. The chronology of the Swiss material may, however, be more interesting than any similarities with individual objects in the grave of the Amesbury Archer. In Switzerland, the Bell Beaker Set is thought to have been in use between 2400 and 2200 BC after which it was superseded by Early Bronze Age types.

This is consistent with the appearance of the Bell Beaker set in central and northern Europe, but it also follows shortly after the last occupation of lakeside settlements in Switzerland, or at least the use of Auvernier material, which is well dated by dendrochronology to 2450–2400 BC (Pétrequin *et al.* 1985) and perhaps as closely as 2430–20 BC (Gross-Klee 1999). Largely on the basis of the appearance of Bell Beaker material at Sion, Petit-Chasseur, and the disappearance of Auvernier material, Furholt would place the appearance of the Bell Beaker Set in Switzerland as after 2460 cal BC (Furholt 2003, 68; Harrison and Heyd 2007).

In the neighbouring parts of continental Europe that practised single burial there is considerable regional variety in the orientation of the body (p. 211 above) and this might offer some insight into the journeys of the Amesbury Archer and the 'Companion'. Only a very small amount of evidence for either single burial or the final burials in collective graves is available from France (p. 205, Fig. 71 above). Nonetheless it shows that burials were often oriented east–west or west–east even though the body was not regularly placed in one position (Salanova 1998a, 318; 2003a, 164). In the southern Netherlands and neighbouring parts of north-west Germany bone is often poorly preserved but bodies were often appear to have been placed with their head to the east or north-east and facing south or south-east (van der Beek 2004, 168, 176). While this further emphasises the regional variability in this aspect of Bell Beaker mortuary rites in northern and western Europe (eg, Lanting and van der Waals (1976, 2, 72; Salanova 1998a, 321; Sofaer Derevenski 2002), particularly when compared to the bi-polar single burial rites of the 'East Group' in central Europe, it offers little assistance in establishing the journeys of the Amesbury Archer. Perhaps more notable is the shared orientation of the burials in the early graves at Boscombe Down despite the different rites of collective and single burial and the different domiciles of the

dead men when they were young teenagers. This may suggest the orientation is a British one, and it may relate to that of the nearby temples.

The River Rhine or Rhône?

It might be assumed that if the Amesbury Archer was brought up near the Alps or amongst the Alpine forelands or close to the Massif Central (one of the regions in which the Boscombe Bowmen might have lived as children) then the journey that ended in Britain started by following the valley of the River Rhine.

In Britain, particular emphasis has been given to the view that Beakers first appeared in the Lower Rhine and the area of north of the River Main. The Rhineland was unhesitatingly identified by Abercomby as the area from which the 'Beaker peoples' came to Britain (1902; 1912, 66–7). This was largely on the basis of the finds from, and the number of, single burials around the area of the confluence of the Rivers Main and Rhine. This view was epitomised by Clarke's definition of a 'Wessex/Middle Rhine' type of Beaker (1970, 84, 92–4, fig. 93), though the coherency of the Middle Rhine grouping was challenged by Lanting and van der Waals (1972, 30–1). Needham has also suggested that the closest stylistic links of British All-Over-Cord Beakers were with finds from the Middle Rhine (2005, 179) though those Beakers, which form a rather heterogeneous collection, are not of the earliest 'international' types.

In this context, finds of Niedermendig lava from at least four Late Neolithic sites in Wessex should be noted. This rock was widely for quern stones in the Roman and historic periods. At the Sanctuary close to Avebury, fragments of what were identified as Niedermendig lava (by H.H. Thomas of the Geological Survey), presumably from a quern, have been recorded from an apparently well-stratified Late Neolithic context, post-hole 27 (Cunnington 1931, 332). Although finds have been made at other important prehistoric sites in Wessex; from Avebury, the Avebury Avenue, and Stonehenge (Clarke 1970, 100; Megaw and Simpson 1979, 204; Cleal *et al.* 2005), the find from the Sanctuary is the only example where the date of the context appears to be reliable (R. Cleal and J. Pollard, pers. comm.). If this is correct, the quern provides very rare evidence for contact with continental Europe during the Late Neolithic.

The Lower Rhine region, including the Netherlands has been identified by Dutch scholars as the origin of Beaker pottery across Europe as Beakers here can be shown to develop from Corded Ware (Single Grave Culture) pottery (eg, Lanting and van der Waals 1972; 1976; Lanting 2007). The Maritime Beaker, which is regarded as the first 'true' Bell Beaker, emerges from this tradition. This regional model of typological development is widely known as the 'Dutch Model' (Harrison 1980, 16–23). It has proved to be a robust regional model (van der Beek and Fokkens 2001) and there are clear connections, if not necessarily direct ones, between Beakers from the Lower Rhine and the earliest ones in Britain, but the wider applicability of the Dutch model has been doubted.

In considering the material from France, Salanova argued that there is no clear evidence for a progression from All-Over-Ornamented to Maritime types (1998b, 1–2; 2000, 157–71; 2004b) and the identification of a phase when only Maritime Bell Beakers were in use in the Netherlands has also been challenged (eg, Drenth and Hogestijn 2001, 312–13; 2007). Instead, radiocarbon dates now indicate that Maritime Beakers first appeared around the Tagus Estuary in Portugal where they have clear typological antecedents (Kunst 2001; 1993, 248; Case 2004b, 11–22; 2007, 238–43; Needham 2005, 176). Lanting's recent wholesale dismissal of both these radiocarbon dates and a critique of the typological development (Lanting 2007, 13, 37–8) is difficult to sustain.

Reflecting this view, Needham has suggested that the origins of British Beakers should be sought in a rather wider area than the Lower Rhine. This area includes not only the Lower Rhine but much of northern France. In this zone, influences from both Atlantic Europe (ultimately from Iberia) and the Lower Rhine are suggested to have interacted resulting in a 'fusion corridor' (Needham 2005, 176–82, fig. 3). However, Salanova argues that the Bell Beaker Set was not adopted in the Paris Basin suggesting instead that styles of Beaker pottery passed through it but with 'apparently no effect on local cultural development' (2004a, 69).

In identifying the earliest forms of Beaker found in Britain, Needham emphasised the presence of a low-carination but noted that Beakers with low-bellies were also present from the beginning (2005, 179). Some of these low-bellied vessels are 'S'-profiled and several of these are early in date, including examples from the Boscombe Down and other early burials (*ibid.*, 200). This variety in form is reflected in the varied locations of the comparanda for the Boscombe Down Beakers which include northern France, Brittany, and the Lower Rhine. As a result it has not been possible to identify a single region that provided the direct inspiration for the Boscombe Down Beakers (pp. 153–4 above). Thus, while the idea of a journey by the Amesbury Archer down the Rhine might be attractive to British scholarly tradition, the

evidence from the early Bell Beakers from Boscombe Down for links with the Rhineland cannot be regarded as clear cut.

Similar uncertainty surrounds the origins of the British series of basket-shaped gold ornaments of which the Boscombe Down finds are the earliest dated examples (p. 136 above). While some central European inspiration for the insular series is possible, the central European tress rings differ notably in having spiral twists as opposed to the flat tangs seen on the insular and Iberian ornaments (Fig. 44). The closest parallels for the British and Irish finds remain the Portuguese finds from the Estremoz (Évora) area and Ermegeira (Lisboa), close to the Tagus estuary (O'Connor 2004, 208). The dating evidence for these finds is limited but the Ermegeira tomb contained Maritime Beakers and Palmela bowls which does not suggest that it is was in use any later than the earliest insular finds (Leisner 1965, Taf. 12; Harrison 1977, 152). While reservations have been expressed about the reliability of the provenance of the pair of basket-shaped ornaments from Gilmorton, Leicestershire (Needham 2008a; Table 23), some Early Bronze Age finds and a ring ditch are now known from the findspot (W. Scott, pers. comm.), and the form of the Gilmorton ornaments can be compared with the Portuguese finds. In Ireland the Dacomet/Benraw, Co. Down find is the also of a similar shape and, notably, appears not to be of Irish gold (Cahill 2006, 267–8 and pers. comm.; cf. O'Connor 2004, 208). Connections between the pottery of Portugal and Brittany have long been suggested (eg, Cardoso *et al.* 2005) and an Iberian origin for the insular series of basket-shaped ornaments cannot be discounted. This would be consistent with the Atlantic origins of the copper used for the knives buried with the Amesbury Archer and perhaps the knives themselves.

The Amesbury Archer may have been brought up in or near the Alps or the Alpine forelands and the pivotal location of modern Switzerland in central and western Europe is important. It lies astride the Alps and connected to three of the great rivers of Europe – not just the Rhine but also the Rhône and the Danube. The role of the Rivers Rhône and Saône are of central importance and views as whether dominant external influences in modern Switzerland in the Bell Beaker period travelled north or south have alternated though time (Besse 2001), emphasising the difficulties in determining regional influences (eg, Heyd and Salanova 2007, 483). At present, the current orthodoxy is that at this time Switzerland, especially its western and northern regions, looked to the south and west, and not to the north (eg, Bill 1973; Ottaway 1992, 283; Wolf 1992; Besse 2001; Strahm 2007). In studying the Bell Beaker finds from southern France

Lemercier would see the Bell Beaker Set being diffused from southern France northwards up the Rhône valley, with interaction with communities to the east who used Rinaldone style pottery and Remedello metalwork (2004, 467–83). The arrival of the Bell Beaker Set in central Europe, whether as a 'proto-package' with Iberian origins (Harrison and Heyd 2007) or fully formed but then subject to eastern influences, may also have involved the Rhône/Saône axis (Heyd 2001; Salanova 2004b). Typological considerations – but not yet radiocarbon dating – suggest that its arrival in central Europe and Britain and Ireland was broadly contemporary.

Certainty is not possible, but rather than pointing to a journey along the Rhine, these finds might instead suggest journeys along the Atlantic and Channel seaboards. Journeys to the north and west that started in the western Alps seem as likely, if not more so, to have been initially to the south towards the Mediterranean or the west than to the north. A journey towards the Mediterranean coast must have turned to the west at some point, possibly across central France, or further south to follow the River Gironde. A journey west would have led across the Paris Basin

Chapter 13

Conclusions

Radiocarbon and typological dating confirm that the graves of the Boscombe Bowmen, the Amesbury Archer, and the 'Companion' with their different styles of collective and single burial are amongst the earliest Bell Beaker burials currently known in Britain. Isotope analyses demonstrate that many of the men buried in these graves had travelled long distances and at least some came from continental Europe. The burials lie not far from some of the most important temples of the age; Durrington Walls and Stonehenge.

These Late Neolithic temples were built before the arrival of the Boscombe Bowmen, though Stonehenge may still have been being remodelled when the Boscombe Bowmen and the Amesbury Archer were alive. There is little evidence that allows an assessment of the relations between these incomers and the Late Neolithic communities who built the temples. Late Neolithic burials are rare, as are settlements. Late Neolithic and Bell Beaker finds, whether from settlement or funerary contexts, are rarely associated (eg, Case 2001) and the local radiocarbon sequence suggests that there may have been little chronological overlap between the two (p. 180 above). It is possible that the groups to whom the Boscombe Bowmen and the Amesbury Archer belonged chose to maintain a distinctive identity (cf. Needham 2007, 41, p. 192, above).

The earliest of these Bell Beaker graves is that of the Boscombe Bowmen. They were buried in a small collective grave and it seems likely that there was a timber chamber, the reopening of which enabled successive interments to be made. The radiocarbon dating suggests that the burials may have been made over a relatively short period, possibly within one generation. The earliest dated individual died 2500–2340 cal BC, the latest Bell Beaker burials, which were articulated, died 2360–2290 cal BC (juvenile 25007) and 2330–2200 cal BC (adult 25004). On the basis of the last two of the Bell Beaker interments, the burials were flexed inhumations accompanied by grave goods, mainly Beakers but arrowheads and other flint objects, a boar's tusk, and a pendant of antler were also placed with the dead. The remains of earlier burials were moved aside when the next burial was made. Where it was possible to determine the sex of the adults and teenagers buried in the grave, they were all male. Arrowheads are

typically found with male burials and they indicate that some of the deceased had the status of a warrior. No female burials were identified. It seems likely that the individuals came from a closely related community but it is not possible to say that they were related biologically.

This burial rite, individual burial accompanied by grave goods in a collective grave, does not have contemporary parallels in Britain. In the light of the isotope analyses that indicate that some of the adults were not local to Wessex and the fact that many of the grave goods are clearly of continental European inspiration, it seems likely that the rite is intrusive to the region. Where the rite may have been introduced from is uncertain and the international nature of the Bell Beaker Set found in graves emphasises the similarities between regions rather than the differences that are more apparent in the, as yet, rare settlements. While the isotope analyses are comparable with biosphere values from Wales, and there are known archaeological links with the area, there is little if any contemporary early Bell Beaker material from the country. A number of other western European regions provide comparable biosphere values and these include Brittany, the Massif Central, the Black Forest, and perhaps Portugal but there is no necessary correlation between these modern biosphere values and ancient archaeological cultures. The present state of archaeological evidence does not permit any one region to be preferred but on balance a continental European origin seems most likely.

In contrast, the graves of the Amesbury Archer and the 'Companion' are single burials, the type of burial thought to be typical of the Bell Beaker period in Britain. While this remains broadly correct, study of other early Bell Beaker burials in Wessex shows that secondary burial rites were practised and the absence of a rib raise the possibility that this may also have been the case with the Amesbury Archer.

The Amesbury Archer died 2380–2290 cal BC and the 'Companion' 2350–2260 cal BC. Despite the absence of DNA analyses, an unusual non-metric trait in their feet demonstrates that these two men were genetically related. The Amesbury Archer spent some of his childhood in central Europe, probably in the Alpine region, before travelling to Wessex. The Alps stand close to two of the possible places of residence of the Boscombe Bowmen, the Massif Central and the Black Forest in south west Germany. In contrast, the 'Companion' was probably born in Wessex but may have made a journey to continental Europe, possibly to the same region where the Amesbury Archer had lived although the isotope values are not identical. Greater geographical precision is not currently possible and it is perhaps just a coincidence that the left legs of the Amesbury Archer and one of the Boscombe Bowmen (25004) were disabled, especially if the absence of the Archer's kneecap was as a result of a congenital condition rather than an injury.

The grave of the Amesbury Archer contained a wooden chamber but it does not appear to have been surmounted by a barrow. His burial is the best-furnished Bell Beaker example yet found in Britain and, arguably, all of Europe. The grave goods included 18 flint arrowheads, five Beakers, two bracers or wristguards, three copper knives, and a pair of gold ornaments. These objects clearly signify warrior status and high social status. The copper itself and, perhaps, the knives came from continental Europe. The gold used to make the ornaments appears to be continental European but the style of the ornaments is insular. The stone used to make the black bracer appears to be continental European and it is possible that this is also the case for the stone used for the red one. Other grave goods include a wing headed pin that is likely to be of continental European type and a stone metalworking tool, or cushion stone. This tool is of particular signifying in attempting to explain why the burial was so well-furnished.

However, some of the costume fittings and ornaments were not worn but placed by the dead man's knees; the gold ornaments, the red bracer, the shale ring, and the largest of the copper daggers. Whatever these items of costume signified, the Amesbury Archer did not wear them at death. The gold ornaments may have been deliberately damaged at this time.

Much of the material culture placed next to the Archer was still novel to Britain and it may also have included items of clothing. The antler pin might have originally have fastened a cape or cloak and the plaited cord decoration on a pair of the Beakers evokes textiles of the types shown on the stelae from le Petit Chasseur (Harrison and Heyd 2007). The many objects would also have been distinguished by a range of colours and textures and by being beautifully finished, created a collage of blacks, red, and whites, gold and copper set against the timbers of the wooden chamber. All this will have conveyed to the mourners that the offerings were made from materials common and exotic, from sources both near and far. They will have evoked stories, some of which were directly linked to continental Europe, to travel and different tongues. Some of the materials might have been considered to have magical properties (Sheridan 2008b). Many objects were of international types, found across Europe.

In much of continental Europe metallurgy was already long established. This was certainly the case in the Alpine region from which the Amesbury Archer may have travelled (Strahm 1994; 2005; 2007), and the same is also true of some of the regions from which the Boscombe Bowmen might have come (the Massif Central and, possibly, Portugal). This poses the question why the Archer's journey as a metalworker was made at the time that it was – around the time that Bell Beaker 'Set' was adopted in that region – and not centuries before when metallurgy was first adopted there? (Strahm 2005; 2007). The answer may lie in the ways in which the ideas that were shared by what were apparently widely separated groups using the Bell Beaker 'Set' were linked, and the ways in which the adoption of metallurgy was linked to the movement of people (cf. Vander Linden 2007, 349). This is different to the idea of itinerant metalworkers.

While the Amesbury Archer may have had the status of metalworker, and this provides one explanation for his journeys, he was buried far from sources of metal. However, it is consistently the ability to make objects that is represented in the burials of Bell Beaker and Bronze Age metalworkers and not the mining of ores and the production of metal that appears to have been accorded a special status. No metal objects were found at Ross Island, just three scraps of metallurgical waste (O'Brien 2004, 525–32, fig. 241, pl. 98–9). The objects made from the ores, perhaps copper axeheads, were manufactured elsewhere, though the evidence for the manufacture of objects at settlements in temperate Europe is slight (eg, Mille and Bouquet 2004; Simpson *et al.* 2006, 139–40). Accordingly metalworkers need not have been resident close to the sources of metal and in the case of the Amesbury Archer the very *distance* from them may have been important.

The movement of women as one way of distributing the knowledge of making Beakers has been emphasised by Brodie (1998; 2001, 492–5). This interpretation rests on a number of premises. The origin of one of the classic styles of Beaker pottery, All-Over-Cord Beakers, was in the Lower Rhine. Taking potting to have been a skill practised by women, and drawing on the evidence of the isotope studies in Bavaria (Price *et al.* 1988), Brodie suggested than an example of such movement might be represented by the group of Beaker pottery from Oštrikovac in the Morava valley in Bosnia and Herzegovina. The nearest Beaker pottery then known was near Budapest, some 400 km away to the north-west (Brodie 1997, 307–11, fig. 1; 2001, 492–5, fig. 1; Heyd 2007b, 92).

This interpretation places considerable emphasis on the Beaker pot itself (Boast 1995) and the ways in which the All-Over-Cord style was reproduced. Salanova has argued that the role of the Beaker as a funerary vessel was fundamental to the early dispersal of the international or 'standard' types (eg, Salanova 2001). Movement in the opposite direction is symbolised by the introduction of metallurgy which, Brodie suggested, indicates the movement of skilled metalworkers. These were not the Childean prospectors or itinerant smiths often envisaged in the introduction of metallurgy (Childe 1930, 9), but metalworkers who were invited into a community (Brodie 1997, 306; 2001, 494). As Brodie put it; 'there was more information embodied in the head and hands of metalworker than embedded in the substance of a thousand inanimate objects' (2001, 494).

Brodie was followed by Needham (2005, 207–8) but he emphasised instead the movement of men and the transfer of metalworking skills. He suggested that this might help account for the similarities in the burials of adult males with weapons across large areas (Needham 2007, 42). In north-west Europe copper metallurgy could have been an important driver (Salanova 2001) and while the association between the appearance of Beakers there and metallurgy has arguably been overstated (Vander Linden 2007) the association was nonetheless important (Needham 2007, 42; Sheridan 2008a, 257–9; 2008b, 63–9). In some areas where metallurgy was already long established, the status ascribed to metal seems to change after the Bell Beaker 'Set' was adopted (eg, Kunst 1997; Ambert 2001; Roussot-Larroque 2005; Roberts *et al.* 2009, 1018), with a 'new emphasis on metal exploitation and prestige good production' (Heyd 2007a, 360).

In relation to this, the role of alliances and links within and between families in sustaining links across long distance may be emphasised. These have different roles and functions from that envisaged for marriage as a means of acculturation as set out by Brodie. Fosterage is an important mechanism and this might have some relevance to the journeys made by the Boscombe Bowmen, the Amesbury Archer, and possibly also the 'Companion' when they were children. Apprenticeship is an important way of learning skills including how to get access to materials (Vankilde 2005a, 82, 96, 102; Karl 2005; Roberts 2009a; 2009b) and in many societies this has often involved moving away from the home of the immediate family. While these mechanisms can be interpreted as means of integrating societies, they can also be

used to maintain distinctive identities by maintaining family ties and a shared language although other languages may also have been spoken.

In a similar vein, several writers have emphasised the importance of the access to materials such as metal and knowledge about distant places and things (Brodie 2001; Turek 2004, 151–5; Needham 2005, 207, Kristiansen and Larsson 2005; Vankilde 2005a, 102). In the case of Bell Beaker metalworkers the objects made were almost invariably small items of jewellery and weaponry; objects of adornment used to symbolise status (Turek 2004; Bartelheim 2007).

Whether this status was shared by all those involved in the production of metal rather than just those producing objects is less clear. Bartelheim has questioned this, placing the emphasis on the production of objects (2002, 35; 2007, 207). Writing of the full Bronze Age in Cyprus Belgirono has suggested that extraction and processing tasks may have been thought to be 'inferior', while the master metalworkers belonged to a privileged class (2002, 79). A related point is made by both Bertemes, who emphasises the importance of metal not in its own right but in relation to the control of goods as an economic factor (2004a, 148), and by Kristiansen and Larsson, who suggest that later in the Bronze Age, special tools were added to the grave goods of the elite (2005, 57–8).

In many respects the Amesbury Archer could be seen to embody this interpretation. He has a metalworking tool, more if the boar's tusks are also accepted as metalworking tools, but the metal of the copper knives and maybe also the knives themselves come from northern Spain and western France. The presence of two well-made flint knives in the grave of the Amesbury Archer might be seen as a sign that copper was not readily available.

This knowledge of metalworking may have led to the Amesbury Archer being afforded a particular status in Wessex but a comparative study has demonstrated that in those areas of northern Europe where Bell Beaker single burial was practised, metalworkers were also often afforded well-furnished burials. Several of the burials contain multiple objects and this over-provision or *Überaustattung* can be interpreted an indication of the highest social status.

The cushion stone is, then, particularly important to understanding why the Amesbury Archer was afforded such a well-furnished burial by his mourners. It symbolises a connection with metalworking and metallurgy, a technology that was introduced to Britain from continental Europe. The copper knives and gold ornaments buried with him are, at present, the earliest dated metal objects in Britain. The gold ornaments are made from a metal that is probably continental

European in origin, but they are made in a style that is insular. The amount of gold required was small and the skills may have been modest, but the *knowledge* of metalworking, access to the metal, and control of the distribution of the finished objects within the *chaîne opératoire*, the operational sequence, was new and perhaps priceless. This network may well have been continental in scope.

Pending the completion of the ongoing and nationwide Beaker People Project (Parker Pearson 2006), these early burials at Boscombe Down provide the best evidence in Britain for long journeys by specific individuals at this time, but there is also evidence for other broadly contemporary journeys to Britain and Ireland.

To Ireland

The earliest known copper mine in Britain and Ireland is on Ross Island among the Killarney Lakes of Co. Kerry in the south-west of Ireland, where a mine and associated work camp have been excavated (O'Brien 2004; 2007, 29–30). The mining of the readily accessible and high grade copper is suggested to have started between 2500 and 2200 BC. The Ross Island copper has a high arsenic content and the knowledge and skills necessary to produce this metal are likely to have drawn on expertise from continental Europe. In this regard, it can surely be no coincidence that the pottery from the Ross Island work camp is of Beaker type. O'Brien is clear: 'copper metallurgy first appeared in Ireland at a relatively advanced level, probably through contacts with metal-using groups on the continent' (2001, 561; cf. O'Brien 2004, 563–5). The precise nature of this contact is not clear but it must have involved journeys across the Channel and the Irish Sea and the evidence from Ross Island can be interpreted as representing a mining enclave.

The small megalithic 'wedge tombs' of Bell Beaker date that are widely found across Ireland (Brindley and Lanting 1991/92; Walsh 1995; Case 1995a, 25; Schulting *et al.* 2008) have often been suggested to have been introduced from north-western France. The gold basket-shaped ornaments (pp. 133–4 and 233 above) found in Ireland may also have Atlantic, and specifically Iberian, connections. While these connections seem to be with the Atlantic coast, other Irish objects display the same sort of wide-ranging contacts reflected in the early graves at Boscombe Down. In most of western Europe barbed and tanged arrowheads are the most common type but hollow-based forms, which are found more frequently in central Europe, are common in Ireland (Green 1980; Case 1995a, 24

Plate 53 The graves of the 'Companion' (1236) (foreground) and the Amesbury Archer under excavation. The excavation of the burial of the 'Companion' is finishing, that of the Amesbury Archer is set to continue

2001, 375; Woodman *et al.* 2006, 126–55). The number of polypod bowls found in Ireland is also notable (Case 1995a, 20; Carlin 2011) as they are best known in central Europe though they also occur in western European assemblages in small quantities (Piguet *et al.* 2007, 252–2, fig. 4).

To Scotland

Several early Bell Beaker graves have been found in Scotland and there is no reason to think that they are significantly later than those in England (Sheridan 2007, 96–8; p. 181 above). Although these single graves are not numerous the same can be said of England (p. 196 above), and the distribution of the Scottish examples is distinctive. Burials in the Highlands and Islands are as early, if not earlier, than those in the Lowlands which suggests that the Bell Beaker Set was distributed around Scotland both rapidly and widely.

One of the earliest burials is at Sorisdale on the Isle of Coll in the Inner Hebrides (Ritchie and Crawford 1978). Coll lies off the west coast of Scotland and the burial seems likely to reflect contact along the Irish seaboards. Recent isotope analysis suggests that the person may have spent their early childhood elsewhere (Sheridan 2007; 2008a, 253–4, fig. 21.9, 3).

The grave at Upper Largie, Arygll and Bute, has clear Continental connections. The grave, which had probably had a wooden chamber, was within a ring ditch that had a series of posts set in it. The grave goods included two Beakers with Maritime derived decoration; a third was All-Over-Corded. All three have either low-carinations or are 'S'-profiles with low bellies and this typologically early date is confirmed by a radiocarbon date on charcoal from the base of the grave (p. 181 above; Table 31). As Sheridan has emphasised, the setting of posts within the ring ditch and also the Beakers have strong continental links. She argues that these are specifically Dutch and represent the first sign of the links across the North Sea seen in slightly later finds from eastern Scotland (2008a; 2008b, 63–5).

Upper Largie lies in the Kilmartin Valley with ready links to Ireland and at the south-western end of the Great Glen which runs across Scotland. There are sources of copper in the Kilmartin Valley and at the north-eastern end of the Great Glen, the Migdale-Marnoch metalworking tradition was one of the earliest to develop in Britain and displays links with Ireland and continental Europe (Needham 2004). The pivotal location of the Kilmartin Valley at this time is reflected in a range of contemporary monuments and Sheridan suggests that the possible Dutch connection may reflect exploration for metals and their subsequent exploitation (2008a, 258; 2008b, 63). A metallurgical or prospecting context might be also suggested for the burial at Dornoch at the edge of the highlands in north-east Scotland (Ashmore 1989, a possibly secondary cremation burial in the stone cist is now dated to 2460–2200 cal BC (GrA-26515, 3850±40 BP; Sheridan 2007, 99, app. 1; table 4.6)).

This widely distributed evidence from Britain and Ireland is consistent with the suggestions of Case and earlier commentators that the Bell Beaker Set was introduced to Britain and Ireland from different parts of continental Europe (Case 1995a; 2001, 363–5; 2007, 245). The scale of and nature of these contacts remains a matter for debate.

The continental European nature of the burials of the Amesbury Archer, the Boscombe Bowmen and at Upper Largie, indicates that people familiar with Continental rites made the burials. The Boscombe Bowmen seem likely to have been from a small community and to have made their journeys at, or at about, the same time. The close anthropological links of the 'sedentary' individuals buried in small cemeteries in Bavaria and Lower Austria has been pointed out by Heyd who also suggests that the Bell Beaker Set was introduced into central Europe by small migratory groups (Heyd et al. 2003; Heyd 2007a, 337). The impression gained from the isotope analyses of other, slightly later, Bell Beaker burials from Boscombe Down, Normanton Down, and Stonehenge (Chapter 7) is of communities where travel and settlement over long distances is unusual. This is consistent with the evidence from isotope studies from broadly contemporary Bell Beaker cemeteries in central Europe, particularly Bavaria (Price 1999; 2004; Heyd et al. 2003). There, most people did not travel far. Some travelled and settled at distances of up to 100 km, creating an image that is consistent with the regular and perhaps routine movement and intermarriage between closely linked communities.

However, the journeys made by the Amesbury Archer and the Boscombe Bowmen, and perhaps the 'Companion', differ because of their early date in the British Bell Beaker sequence, the distances travelled, even if they and their fellow travellers made several shorter individual journeys, and also in the journeys having started from different locations. The journey or journeys of the Boscombe Bowmen were made over several years while they were children and this is also unusual. These journeys transcend the routine and they were made within a generation of each other. This might suggest that these journeys were associated with something new, in this case the introduction of the Bell Beaker Set to Britain. The reasons for the journeys are not known, if indeed the final destinations were pre-meditated. In the case of the Amesbury Archer the new attitudes to metallurgy that formed part of the Bell Beaker Network or the giving up of Alpine lakeside settlements might provide continental explanations. But such possible reasons for the journeys of the Boscombe Bowmen, which were made before that of the Archer, have not been identified. Events such as the building and rebuilding of Stonehenge, or the opportunity to visit the famous temples of Wessex are possible. The journeys might also be related to those to Scotland and Ireland, forming part of a much wider network. Metallurgy has been argued to be a key factor in those early journeys and they will almost certainly have had international connections. Seen from this perspective and as Stuart Piggott argued long ago (Piggott 1938; cf. Sherratt 1996) where Wessex is, between continental Europe and the metal bearing areas of Britain and Ireland and metallurgy, rather than what it was may have been more important.

What does seem clear is that irrespective of its origins and the precise regional sequences, the appearance of the Bell Beaker Set in central and northern Europe, Britain and Ireland was broadly contemporary and apparently very rapid during the 25th and mainly 24th–23rd centuries BC. Whatever united the Bell Beaker Network (Besse and Strahm 2001; Strahm 2005), it was able to sustain the rapid dispersal of a Bell Beaker ideology or culture over large distances and across a discontinuous distribution.

At Boscombe Down the evidence for long journeys, and apparently from different regions, is found primarily in the early Bell Beaker graves which suggests that this period of long-distance travel was short-lived. The 'Beaker Folk' were long seen as invading warriors and metal prospectors. This reflected on the one hand the importance of individual burial in some regions and the emphasis on warrior status or ideology, and on the other the association of early metal objects in many regions with the Bell Beaker Set. While these points have been over-emphasised in the past and they overlooked the potential importance of local and singular causes for migration, they are not without merit in attempting to understand the movements of small groups over long distances and the way in which those groups maintained cultural identities through family networks (Pl. 53) that spanned great distances and which linked together what were foreign lands. The radiocarbon and typological dates from Britain and Ireland show that these long journeys took place within a few, overlapping generations. The homogeneity of material culture over such wide areas of Europe may reflect similar journeys over what may have been a short, dramatic, time.

Something of those networks and that time is preserved in the remarkable, and very different, burials of the Boscombe Bowmen and the Amesbury Archer.

Bibliography

Abercromby, J., 1902, 'The oldest Bronze Age ceramic type in Britain, its close analogies on the Rhine, its probable origin in central Europe', *Journal of the Royal Anthropological Institute* 32, 373–97.

Abercromby, J., 1912, *A Study of the Bronze Age Pottery of Great Britain and Ireland and its Associated Grave Goods*, Oxford, University Press.

Åberg, G., 1995, 'The use of natural strontium isotopes in environmental studies', *Water, Air and Soil Pollution* 79, 309–22.

Adams, J.C., 1987, *Outline of Fractures*, London, Churchill Livingstone.

Agthe, M., 1989, 'Bemerkungen zu Feuersteindolchen im nordwestlichen Verbreitungsgebiet der Aunjetitzer Kultur', *Arbeit- und Forschungsberichte zur Sächsischen Bodendenkmalpflege* 33, 15–113.

Allason-Jones, L., 1996, *Roman Jet in the Yorkshire Museum*, York, Yorkshire Museum.

Allen, M.J., 2005, 'Beaker settlement and environment on the chalk downs of southern England', *Proceedings of the Prehistoric Society* 71, 219–46.

Allen, M.J., Gardiner, J. and Sheridan, A., (eds), forthcoming, *Is there a British Chalcolithic?: people, place and polity in the later third millennium.* Oxford, Prehistoric Society Research Paper 4.

Ambert, P., 2001, 'La place de la métallurgie campaniforme dans la première métallurgie française', in Nicolis (ed.) 2001b, 577–88.

Ambert, P. and Vaquer, J., (eds), 2005, *La première métallurgie en France et dans les pays limitrophes: Actes du colloque internationale, Carcassone, 28–30 septembre 2002*, Paris, Memoire de la Société préhistorique française 37.

Annable, F.K. and Simpson, D.D.A., 1964, *Guide Catalogue of the Neolithic and Bronze Age Collections in Devizes Museum*, Devizes, Wiltshire Archaeology and Natural History Society.

Anonymous, 1953, 'Fundchronik', *Germania* 31, 109–23.

Anzidei, A.P., Aurisicchio, C. and Carboni, G., 2007, 'Manufatti in argento dalle tombe a grotticella della facies di Ronaldone del territorio di Roma', in *Atti della XL Riunione dell'Istituto Italiano di Preistoria e Protostoria. Strategie di insediamento fra Lazio meridionale e alla Campania centro-settentriale in età preistorica e protostorica*, Florence, Istituto Italiano di Preistoria e Protostoria, 553–9.

ApSimon, A., 1962, 'The prehistoric pottery', in Rahtz 1962, 128–38.

Armbruster, B.R., 2001, 'Zu bronzezeitlichen Werkzeugen der plastischen Verformung im nördlichen und westlichen Europa', in W.H. Metz, B.L. van Beek and H. Steegstra (eds), *Patina: Essays presented to Jay Jordan Butler on the occasion of his 80th Birthday*, Groningen, privately published, 7–26.

Armbruster, B.R., 2006, 'L'outillage en pierre du métallurgiste ancien', in L. Astruc, F. Bon, V. Lea, P.-Y. Milcent and S. Philiberts (eds), *Normes techniques et pratiques sociales. De la simplicité des outillages pré- et protohistoriques. Actes de la Rencontre d'Antibes 2005*, Antibes, XXVIe rencontres internationales d'archéologie et d'histoire d'Antibes, 321–32.

Armbruster, B. and Parreira, R., (eds), 1993, *Inventário do Museu Nacional de Arqueologia. Colecção de Ouriversaria. 1° volume do Calcolitico à Idade do Bronze*, Lisbon, Instituto Português de Museus.

Ashbee, P., 1978, 'Amesbury Barrow 51: excavations 1960', *Wiltshire Archaeology and Natural History Magazine* 70/71 (1975/6), 1–60.

Ashbee, P., 1985, 'The excavation of Amesbury barrows 58, 61a, 61 and 72', *Wiltshire Archaeology and Natural History Magazine* 79, 39–91.

Ashbee, P., 1992, 'Amesbury barrows 61 and 72: a radiocarbon postscript', *Wiltshire Archaeology and Natural History Magazine* 85, 140–1.

Ashbee, P., Smith, I.F. and Evans, J.G., 1979, 'Excavation of three long barrows near Avebury, Wiltshire', *Proceedings of the Prehistoric Society* 45, 207–300.

Ashmore P.J., 1989, 'Excavation of a Beaker cist at Dornoch Nursery, Sutherland', *Proceedings of the Society of Antiquaries of Scotland*, 119, 63–71.

Ashmore P.J., Cook, G.T. and Harkness, D.D., 2000, 'A radiocarbon database for Scottish archaeological samples', *Radiocarbon* 42, 41–8.

Aufderheide, A.C. and Rodríguez-Martín, C., 1998, *The Cambridge Encyclopaedia of Human Palaeopathology*, Cambridge, University Press.

Bagolini, B. and Biagi, P., 1990, 'The radiocarbon chronology of the Neolithic and Copper Age of Northern Italy', *Oxford Journal of Archaeology* 9, 1–23.

Bálek, M., Dvořák, P., Kovárník, J. and Matějíčková, A., 1999, *Pohřebiště Kultury Zvncovitých Pohárů v Tvořiházi (Okr. Znojmo)*, Brno, Pravěk Supplementum 4.

Bamford, H.M., 1982, *Beaker Domestic Sites in the Fen Edge and East Anglia*, Dereham, East Anglian Archaeology 16.

Barber, M., Field, D. and Topping, P., 1999, *The Neolithic Flint Mines of England*, Swindon, English Heritage and Royal Commission on the Historical Monuments of England.

Barclay, A., 1999, 'Summary and reassessment of monuments excavated before 1983–5', in Barclay and Halpin 1999, 149–66.

Barclay, A. and Halpin, C., 1999, *Excavations at Barrow Hills, Radley Oxfordshire. Volume I: the Neolithic and Bronze Age Monument Complex*, Oxford, Thames Valley Landscapes 11.

Barclay, A. and Wallis J., 1999, 'Gold from barrows 4A and 2', in Barclay and Halpin 1999, 183–6.

Barclay, A., Gray, M. and Lambrick, G., 1995, *Excavations at the Devil's Quoits, Stanton Harcourt, Oxfordshire, 1972–3 and 1988*, Oxford, Thames Valley Landscapes: the Windrush Valley 3.

Barclay, A., Lambrick, G., Moore, J. and Robinson, M., 2003, *Lines in the Landscape. Cursus monuments in the Upper Thames Valley: excavations at the Drayton and Lechlade Cursuses*, Oxford, Thames Valley Landscapes Monograph 15.

Barclay, A., Bevan, N., Bradley, P., Chaffey, G., Challinor, D., McKinley, J.I., Powell, A. and Marshall, P., 2009, 'New evidence for Mid–late Neolithic burial from the Colne Valley. West London', *PAST* 63, 4–6.

Barclay, A.J. and Edwards, E. forthcoming. 'The prehistoric pottery', in G. Hey, C. Dennis and C. Bell, *Yarnton: Neolithic and Bronze Age settlement and landscape*, Oxford, Thames Valley Landscapes.

Barfield, L., 2001, 'Beaker lithics in northern Italy', in Nicolis (ed.) 2001b, 507–18.

Barnes, I., Butterworth, C.A., Hawkes, J.W. and Smith, L., 1997, *Excavations at Thames Valley Park, Reading, Berkshire 1986–99: prehistoric and Romano-British occupation of the floodplain and a terrace of the River Thames*, Salisbury, Wessex Archaeology Report 14.

Barrett, J.C., 1994, *Fragments from Antiquity. An Archaeology of Social Life in Britain, 2900–1200 BC*, Oxford, Blackwell.

Bartelheim, M., 2002, 'Metallurgie und Gesellschaft in der Frühbronzezeit Mitteleuropas', in J. Müller, (ed.), *Vom Endneolithikum zur Frühbronzezeit: Muster sozialen Wandels?* Bonn, Universitätsforschungen zur prähistorischen Archäologie 90, 29–44.

Bartelheim, M., 2007, *Die Rolle der Metallurgie in vorgeschichtlichen Gesellschaften. Sozioökonomische und kulturhistorische Aspekte der Resourcennutzung; ein Vergleich zwischen Andalusien, Zypern und dem Nordalpenraum*, Rahden/Westphalia, Forschungen zur Archäometrie und Altertumswissenschaft 2.

Bartelheim, M., Pernicka, E. and Krause, R., (eds) 2002, *The Beginnings of Metallurgy in the Old World*, Rahden/Westphalia, Forschungen zur Archäometrie und Altertumswissenschaft 1.

Barton, C. and Hitchcock, F., (eds), 2008, *Treasure Annual Report 2005/6*, London, Department of Culture Media and Sport.

Bass, W.M., 1987, *Human Osteology*, Columbia, Missouri Archaeological Society.

Bátora, J., 2002a, 'Contribution to the problem of "craftsmen" graves at the end of Aeneolithic and in the Early Bronze Age in central, western and eastern Europe', *Slovenska Archeológia* 50(2), 179–228.

Bátora, J., 2002b, 'K hrobom metalurgov z obdobia eneolitu v strednej, západnej a východnej Európe', in I. Cheben, and I. Kuzma, (eds), *Otázky neolitu a eneolitu našich krajín – 2001. Zborník referátov z 20. pracovného stretnutia bádateľov pre výskum neolitu a eneoliti Čiech, Moravy a Slovenska, Liptovská Sielnica*, Nitra, Archaeologica Slovaca Monographiae Communications 4, 35–46.

Bayliss, A., Whittle, A. and Wysocki, M., 2007a, 'Talking about my generation: the date of the West Kennet long barrow', *Cambridge Archaeological Journal* 17(1) (supplement), 85–101.

Bayliss, A., McAvoy, F. and Whittle, A., 2007b, 'The world recreated: redating Silbury Hill in its monumental landscape', *Antiquity* 81, 26–53.

Beeching, A. and Lambert M., 1977–78, 'L'épingle en os de Donzère (Drôme) et le type dit "en béquille"', *Etudes Préhistoriques* 14 (1981), 31–3.

Beek, G.C., van, 1983, *Dental Morphology: an illustrated guide*, Bristol, Wright.

Beek, Z., van der, 2004, 'An ancestral way of burial. Late Neolithic graves in the Netherlands', in Besse and Desideri (eds) 2004, 157–94.

Beek, Z., van der and Fokkens, H., 2001, '24 years after Oberried: the "Dutch Model" reconsidered', in Nicolis (ed.) 2001b, 301–8.

Behrens, G., 1952, 'Ein neolithisches Bechergrab aus Mitteldeutschland mit beinerner Hammerkopfnadel und Kupfergeräten', *Jahresschrift für Mitteldeutsche Vorgeschichte* 36, 53–69.

Behrens, H., 1973, *Die Jungsteinzeit im Mittelelbe-Saale-Gebiet*, Berlin, Veröffentlichungen des Landesmuseums für Vorgeschichte in Halle 27.

Behrens, H., 1989, 'Zur Problemsituation der Mittelelbe-Saale-Schnurkeramik', *Archäologisches Korrespondenzblatt* 19, 37–46.

Belgirono, M.R., 2002, 'Does tomb no. 21 at Pyrgos (Cyprus) belong to a blacksmith?', in H. Procopiu and R. Treuil, (eds), *Moudre et broyer. L'interprétation fonctionnelle de l'outillage de mouture dans la Préhistoire et l'Antiquité, vol. 2. Archéologie et histoire du Paléolithique au Moyen Age*, Paris, Mémoires de la section d'Histoire des Sciences et Techniques 11, 73–80.

Bellamy, P., 1991, 'The excavation of Fordington Farm round barrow', *Proceedings of the Dorset Natural History and Archaeological Society* 113, 107–132.

Benešová-Medunová, A., 1962, 'Nálezy zvoncovitých pohárů z Předmosti u Přerova', *Sborník Československé společnosti archeologické*, Brno 2, 235–45.

Benz, M. and Willingen, S., van, (eds), *Some New Approaches to the Bell Beaker 'Phenomenon.' Lost Paradise..? Proceedings of the 2nd Meeting of the Association Archéologie et Gobelets, Ffeldberg (Germany), 18th-20th April 1997*, Oxford, British Archaeological Report S690.

Berg, A., von, 2002, 'Die Glockenbecherkultur auf dem Plateau von Bevaix', *Archäologie der Schweiz* 25, 48–57.

Bernhang, A.M. and Levine, S.A., 1973, 'Familial absence of the patella', *Journal of Bone and Joint Surgery* 55A, 1088–90.

Berry, A.C. and Berry, R.J., 1967, 'Epigenetic variation in the human cranium', *Journal of Anatomy* 101, 261–379.

Bertemes, F., 2004a, 'Frühe Metallurgen in der Spätkupfer- und Frühbronzezeit', in Meller (ed.) 2004, 144–9.

Bertemes, F., 2004b, 'Zur Enstehung von Macht, Herrschaft und Prestige in Mitteleuropa', in Meller (ed.) 2004, 150–3.

Bertemes, F. and Heyd, V., 2002, 'Der Übergang Kupferzeit/ Frühbronzezeit am Nordwestrand des Karpaten-beckens – kulturgeschichtliche und paläometallurgische Betrachtungen', in M. Bartelheim, E. Pernicka and R. Krause, (eds), *Die Anfänge der Metallurgie in der Alten Welt Band 1. Forschungen zur Archäometrie und Altertumswissenschaft*, Rahden/Westphalia, Marie Leidorf, 185–228.

Bertemes, F. and Šebela, L., 1998, 'Quelques aspects de la métallurgie du chalcolithique récent et le début de l'Âge du Bronze en Autriche, Bohème et Moravie', in C. Mordant, M. Pernot and V. Rychner (eds), *L'atelier du bronzier en Europe du XXe au VIIIe Siècle avant notre ére, tome II*, Paris, Comité des Travaux Historiques et Scientifiques, 227–39.

Bertemes, F., Schmotz, K. and Thiele, W.-R., 2000, 'Das Metallurgengrab 9 des Gräberfeldes der Glockenbecherkultur von Künzing, Lkr. Deggendorf', in M. Chytrááek, J. Michálek and K. Schmotz (eds), *Archäologische Arbeitsgemeinschaft Ostbayern/West und Südböhmen, 9. Treffen, 23–bis 26 Juni 1999 in Neukirchen b. Hl. Blut, Deggendorf*, Rahden/Westfalen, Marie Leidorf, 53–60.

Besse, M., 2001, 'Bell Beaker common ware: a discussion of its problems illustrated by the Saône-Rhône corridor', in Nicolis (ed.) 2001b, 277–87.

Besse, M., 2006, 'Les archers néolithiques en Pays de Neuchâtel (Suisse)', in B. Arnold, N. Bauermeister and D. Ramseyer (eds), *Archéologie plurielle. Mélanges offerts à Michel Egloff à l'occasion de son 65e anniversaire*, Lausanne, Archéologie Neuchâteloise 34, 37–45.

Besse, M. and Desideri, J., (eds), 2004, *Graves and Funerary Rituals during the Late Neolithic and the Early Bronze Age in Europe (2700–2000 BC)*, Oxford, British Archaeological Report, S1284.

Besse, M., and Strahm. C., 2001, 'The components of the Bell Beaker complex', in Nicolis (ed.) 2001b, 103–10.

Biagi, P., 1989, 'An AMS radiocarbon date from grave BSII of the Copper age cemetery of Remedello Sotto (Brescia, Northern Italy)', *Natura Bresciana* 26 (1991), 299–300.

Bill, J., 1973, *Die Glockenbeckerkultur und die frühe Bronzezeit im französischen Rhonebecken und ihre Beziehungen zur Südwestschweiz*, Basle, Antiqua 1.

Bill J., 1976, 'Die Glockenbeckerkultur in der Schweiz und den angrenzenden Regionen', *Helvetica Archaeologica* 7, 85–93.

Bill, J., 1984, 'Die Glockenbecherkultur in Süddeutschland, der Schweiz und Ostfrankreich (ohne Provence)', in Guilaine (ed.) 1984, 159–73.

Billard, C. and Penna, B., 1995, 'Les sites de Poses "Les Quatres Chemins" et "La Pleine de Poses" (Eure): transition néolithique moyen–récent et campaniforme', in C. Billard (ed.), *Evreux 1993: Actes du 20ème colloque interrégional sur le Néolithique*, Rennes, Revue Archéologique de l'Ouest supplément 7, 273–91.

Billard, C., Querré, G. and Salanova, L., 1998, 'Le phénomène campaniforme dans la basse vallée de la Seine: chronologie et relation habitats-sépultures', *Bulletin de la Société préhistorique française* 95, 351–63.

Blanchet, J.-C., 1984, *Les Premiers Metallurgistes en Picardie et dans le Nord de la France*, Paris, Mémoires de la Société préhistorique française 17.

Boast, R., 1995, 'Fine pots, pure pots, Beaker pots', in Kinnes and Varndell (eds) 1995, 69–80.

Boast, R., 1998, 'Patterns by design: changing perspectives of Beaker variation', in M. Edmond and C. Richards (eds), *Understanding the Neolithic of North-West Europe*, Glasgow, Cruithne Press, 384–406.

Böhm, J., 1929, 'Příspěvky k moravské prehistorii', *Časopis Vlasteneckého Musejního Spolku Olomouc* 41–2, 1929 (1932), 139–52.

Booth, A., St J., and Stone, J.F.S., 1952, 'A trial flint mine at Durrington, Wiltshire', *Wiltshire Archaeological and Natural History Magazine* 54, 381–8.

Boston, C., Bowater, C., Boyle, A. and Holmes, A., 2003, 'Excavation of a Bronze Age barrow at the proposed Centre for Gene Function, South Parks Road, Oxford, 2002, *Oxoniensia* 68, 179–200.

Boyle, A., 1999, 'Human remains', in Barclay and Halpin 1999, 171–83.

Bradley, R., 1970, 'The excavation of a beaker settlement at Belle Tout, East Sussex, England', *Proceedings of the Prehistoric Society* 36, 312–79.

Bradley, R. and Edmonds, M., 1993, *Interpreting the Axe Trade*, Cambridge, University Press.

Brandherm, D., 2003, *Die Dolche und Stabdolche der Steinkupfer- und der älteren Bronzezeit auf der Iberischen Halbinsel, Stuttgart,* Prähistorische Bronzefunde 6, 12

Brandherm, D., 2009, 'The social context of Early Bronze Age metalworking in Iberia: evidence from the burial record', in Kienlin and Roberts (eds) 2009, 172–80.

Bray, W., 1964, 'Sardinian Beakers', *Proceedings of the Prehistoric Society* 30, 75–98.

Brickley, M. and McKinley, J.I., (eds), 2004, *Guidelines to the Standards for Recording Human Remains*, Southampton and Reading, British Association for Biological Anthropology and Osteoarchaeology and Institute for Field Archaeology

Briggs, C.S., 2004, 'A note on the history of the gold ornament from "Dehomet"', in Shepherd and Barclay, (eds) 2004, 214–16.

Brindley, A.L., 2004, 'Prehistoric pottery', in O'Brien 2004, 316–38.

Brindley, A.L. and Lanting, J.N., 1991–92, 'Radiocarbon dates from wedge tombs', *Journal of Irish Archaeology* 6, 19–26.

Brodie, N., 1994, *The Neolithic-Bronze Age Transition in Britain*, Oxford, British Archaeological Report 238.

Brodie, N., 1997, 'New perspectives on the Bell-Beaker culture' *Oxford Journal of Archaeology* 16, 297–314.

Brodie, N., 1998, 'British Bell Beakers; twenty five years of theory and practice', in Benz and van Willingen (eds) 1998, 43–56.

Brodie, N., 2001, 'Technological frontiers and the emergence of the Beaker culture' in Nicolis (ed.) 2001b, 487–96.

Bronk Ramsey, C., 1995, 'Radiocarbon calibration and analysis of stratigraphy: the OxCal program', *Radiocarbon* 37, 425–30.

Bronk Ramsey, C., 1998, 'Probability and dating', *Radiocarbon* 40, 461–74.

Bronk Ramsey, C., 2001, 'Development of the radiocarbon calibration program OxCal', *Radiocarbon*, 43, 355–63.

Bronk Ramsey, C., 2009, 'Bayesian analysis of radiocarbon dates', *Radiocarbon* 51, 337–60.

Bronk Ramsey, C., Higham, T.F.G., Bowles, A. and Hedges, R.E.M., 2004a, 'Improvements to the pretreatment of bone at Oxford', *Radiocarbon* 46, 155–63.

Bronk Ramsey, C., Ditchfield, P. and Humm, M., 2004b, 'Using a gas ion source for radiocarbon AMS and GC-AMS', *Radiocarbon* 46, 25–32.

Brothwell, D.R., 1972, *Digging Up Bones. The Excavation, Treatment and Study of Human Skeletal Remains*, 2nd edn, London, British Museum (Natural History).

Brothwell, D.R., 1973, 'The human biology of the Neolithic population of Britain', *Fundamenta*, Reihe B 8, 280–99.

Brothwell, D. and Zakrzewski, S., 2004, 'Metric and non-metric studies of archaeological human remains', in Brickley and McKinley (eds) 2004, 24–30.

Brothwell, D. Powers, R. and Denston, B., 1976, 'The human skeletal remains from Amesbury barrow 51', in Ashbee 1976, 43–55.

Brück, J., 1999, 'What's in a settlement? Domestic practice and residential mobility in Early Bronze Age southern England', in J. Brück and M. Goodman (eds), *Making Places in the World: themes in settlement archaeology*, London, University College London Press, 52–75.

Buchvaldek, M. and Pleslová-Štiková, E., (eds), 1989, *Das Äneolithikum und die früheste Bronzezeit (C14 3000-2000 b.c.) in Mitteleuropa: kulturelle und chronologische Beziehungen. Actes des XIV Internationalen Symposiums Prag-Liblice*, Prague, Præhistorica 15

Buchvaldek, M. and Strahm, C. (eds), 1992, *Die Kontinentaleuropäischen Gruppen der Kultur mit Schnurkeramik. Schnurkeramik-Symposium 1990*, Prague, Præhistorica 19

Buck, C.E., Cavanagh, W.G., and Litton, C.D., 1996, *Bayesian Approach to Interpreting Archaeological Data*, Chichester, Wiley.

Budd, P. and Taylor, T., 1995, 'The faerie smith meets the bronze industry: magic versus science in the interpretation of prehistoric metal-making', *World Archaeology* 27, 133–43.

Budziszewski, J. and Tunia, K., 2000, 'A grave of the Corded Ware culture arrowhead producer in Koniusza, southern Poland. Revisited', in S. Kadrow (ed.), *A Turning of the Ages. In Wandel der Zeit. Jubilee Book dedicated to Professor Jan Machnik on his 70th Anniversary*, Krakow, Institute of Archaeology and Ethnology, Polish Academy of Sciences, 101–35.

Budziszewski, J., Haduch, E. and Włodarczak, P., 2003, 'Bell Beaker culture in south-eastern Poland', in Czebreszuk and Szmyt (eds), 2003, 155–81.

Buikstra, J.E. and Ubelaker, D.H., 1994, *Standards for Data Collection from Human Skeletal Remains*, Fayetteville, Arkansas, Archaeological Survey Research Series 44.

Burgess, C., 1979, 'The background of early metalworking in Ireland and Britain', in Ryan (ed.) 1979, 207–14.

Burgess, C. and Shennan, S., 1976, 'The Beaker phenomenon: some suggestions', in C. Burgess and R. Miket (eds), *Settlement and Economy in the Third and Second Millennia BC*, Oxford, British Archaeological Report 33, 309–31.

Burgess, C., Topping, P. and Lynch F., (eds), 2007, *Beyond Stonehenge. Essays on the Bronze Age in Honour of Colin Burgess*, Oxford, Oxbow.

Bursch, F.C., 1933, 'Die Becherkultur in den Niederlanden', *Oudheidkundige Mededeelingen uit het Rijksmuseum van Oudheiden te Leiden* 14, 39–123.

Burl, A., 1987, *The Stonehenge People*, London, Guild.

Burnett, S.E. and Case, D.T., 2005, 'Naviculo-cunieform I coalition: evidence of significant differences in tarsal coalition frequency', *The Foot* 15, 80–5.

Butler, J.J. and Waals, J.D., van der, 1966, 'Bell Beakers and early metal-working in the Netherlands', *Palaeohistoria* 12, 41–139.

Cahill, M., 2006, 'John Windele's golden legacy – prehistoric and later gold ornaments from Co. Cork and Co. Waterford', *Proceedings of the Royal Irish Academy* 106C, 219–337.

Campen, I., 2001, 'Grab eines steinzeitlichen Metallhandwerkers?', *Archäologie in Deutschland* 2001(2), 50.

Campen, I., 2004, 'Unscheinbar, aber bedeutsam. Das älteste Gold Sachsens stammt aus einem Steinzeitgrab bei Zwenkau', *Archaeo* 1, 27–9.

Cardoso, J.L., 2001, 'Le phénomène campaniforme dans les basses vallées du Tage et du Sado (Portugal)', in Nicolis (ed.) 2001b, 139–54.

Cardoso, J.L., Querré, G. and Salanova, L., 2005, 'Bell Beaker relationships along the Atlantic coast', in M.I. Prudêncio, M.I. Dias and J.C. Waerenborgh (eds), *Understanding People through their Pottery*, Lisbon, Trabalhos de Arqueologia 42, 27–31.

Carlin, N., 2011, 'Into the west: placing Beakers within their Irish context', in A.M. Jones and G. Kirkham (eds), *Beyond the Core: reflections on regionality in prehistory*, Oxford, Oxbow, 87–100.

Case, D.T., 2003, *Who's related to whom? Skeletal kinship analysis in medieval Danish cemeteries*, Arizona, Arizona State University, unpublished Ph.D. thesis.

Case, D.T. and Burnett, S.E., 2005, 'Tarsal coalition: identification and popular variation', *American Journal of Physical Anthropology* Supplement 40, 85.

Case, H., 1963, 'Notes on the finds [from Stanton Harcourt] and on ring-ditches in the Oxford region', *Oxoniensia* 23, 19–52.

Case, H., 1977a, 'The Beaker Culture in Britain and Ireland', in R. Mercer (ed.), *Beakers in Britain and Europe*, Oxford, British Archaeological Report S26, 71–101.

Case, H., 1977b, 'An early accession to the Ashmolean Museum', in V. Markotic (ed.), *Ancient Europe and the Mediterranean. Studies presented in Honour of Hugh Hencken*, Warminster, Aris and Phillips, 19–34.

Case, H.J., 1982, 'The Vicarage Field, Stanton Harcourt', in Case and Whittle (eds) 1982, 103–17.

Case, H., 1993, 'Beakers: deconstruction and after', *Proceedings of the Prehistoric Society* 59, 241–68.

Case, H.J., 1995a, 'Irish Beakers in their European context', in Waddell and Shee Twohig (eds) 1995, 14–29.

Case, H., 1995b, 'Some Wiltshire Beakers and their contexts', *Wiltshire Archaeology and Natural History Magazine* 88, 1–17.

Case, H., 1997, 'Stonehenge revisited. A review article', *Wiltshire Archaeological and Natural History Magazine* 90, 161–8.

Case, H., 1998, 'Où sont les campaniformes de l'autre côte de la Manche?', *Bulletin de la Société préhistorique française* 95, 403–11.

Case, H., 2001. 'The Beaker culture in Britain and Ireland: groups, European contacts and chronology', in Nicolis (ed.) 2001b, 361–77.

Case, H., 2003, 'Beaker presence at Wilsford 7', *Wiltshire Archaeology and Natural History Magazine* 96, 161–94.

Case, H., 2004a, 'Beaker burial in Britain and Ireland. A role for the dead', in Besse and Desideri (eds) 2004, 195–201.

Case, H., 2004b, 'Beakers and the Beaker Culture', in Czebreszuk (ed.) 2004b, 11–34.

Case, H., 2004c, 'Bell Beaker and Corded Ware Culture burial associations: a bottom-up rather than top-down approach', in Gibson and Sheridan (eds) 2004, 201–14.

Case, H.J., 2007, 'Beaker and the Beaker culture', in Burgess *et al.* (eds) 2007, 238–54.

Case, H.J. and Whittle, A.W.R., (eds), 1982, *Settlement Patterns in the Oxford Region: excavations at the Abingdon causewayed enclosure and other sites*, London, Council for British Archaeology Research Report 44.

Červinka, I.L., 1911, 'O. "zvoncovitých pohárech"', *Časopsis Vlasteneckého spolku musejního v Olomouci* 28, 66–87, 109–25.

Chambon, P., 2004, 'Collective graves in France during the Bell Beaker phenomenon', in Besse and Desideri (eds) 2004, 69–78.

Chambon, P. and Salanova, L., 1996, 'Chronologie des sépultures du IIIe millénaire dans le Bassin de la Seine', *Bulletin de la Société préhistorique française* 93, 103–18.

Chambon, P. and Leclerc, J., (eds), 2003, *Les practiques funéraires néolithiques avant 3500 av. J.-C. en France et dans les régions limitrophes*, Paris, Mémoires de la Société préhistorique française 33.

Charters, S., Evershed, R.P., Goad, L.J., Blinkhorn, P.W. and Denham, V., 1993, 'Quantification and distribution of lipid in archaeological ceramics: implications for sampling potsherds for organic residue analysis', *Archaeometry* 35, 211–23.

Charters, S., Evershed, R.P., Quye, A., Blinkhorn, P. and Reeves, V., 1997, 'Simulation experiments for determining the use of ancient pottery vessels: the behaviour of epicuticular leaf wax during boiling of a leafy vegetable', *Journal of Archaeological Science* 24, 1–7.

Chenery, C., Muldner, G., Evans, J., Eckardt, H. and Lewis, M., 2010, 'Strontium and stable isotope evidence for diet and mobility in Roman Gloucester, UK', *Journal of Archaeological Science* 37, 150–63.

Chiaradia, M., Gallay, A. and Todt, W., 2003, 'Different contamination styles of prehistoric human teeth at a Swiss necropolis (Sion, Valais) inferred from lead and strontium isotopes', *Applied Geochemistry* 18, 353–70.

Childe, V.G., 1930, *The Bronze Age*, Cambridge, University Press.

Childe, V.G., 1931, 'The chronological position of the south Russian Steppe graves in European prehistory', *Man* 31, 128–9.

Choczaj-Kukula, A. and Janniger, C.K., 2009, 'Nail-patella syndrome': http://www.emedicine.medscape.com/article/1106294-overview

Christie, P.M., 1964, 'A Bronze Age round barrow on Earl's Farm Down, Amesbury', *Wiltshire Archaeology and Natural History Magazine* 59, 30–45.

Christie, P.M., 1967, 'A barrow cemetery of the second millennium BC in Wiltshire', *Proceedings of the Prehistric Society* 33, 336–66.

Clark, J.G.D., 1931, 'Notes on the Beaker pottery in Ipswich Museum', *Proceedings of the Prehistoric Society of East Anglia* 6, 356–61.

Clark, J.G.D., 1932, 'Note on some flint daggers of Scandinavian type from the British Isles', *Man* 32, 186–90.

Clark, J.G.D., 1963, 'Prehistoric bows from Somerset, England and the prehistory of archery in north-western Europe', *Proceedings of the Prehistoric Society* 29, 50–98.

Clark, K.A., 2006, *Tracing the Evolution of Organic Balm use in Egyptian Mummification via Molecular and Isotopic Signatures*, Bristol, University of Bristol, unpublished PhD thesis.

Clarke, B., 2000, 'Peace dividend brings archaeological rewards', *Antiquity* 74, 277–8.

Clarke, B. and Kirby, C., 2003, 'A newly discovered round barrow and proposed dispersed linear cemetery at Boscombe Down West', *Wiltshire Archaeology and Natural History Magazine* 96, 215–8.

Clarke, D.L., 1970, *Beaker Pottery of Britain and Ireland*, Cambridge, University Press.

Clarke, D.L., 1976, 'The Beaker network – social and economic models', in Lanting and van der Waals (eds) 1976b, 459–77.

Clarke, D.V., Cowie, T. and Foxon, A., 1985, *Symbols of Power at the Time of Stonehenge*, Edinburgh, Her Majesty's Stationary Office.

Cleal, R.M.J., 1992a, 'The Dean Bottom Beaker pit assemblage', in Gingell 1992, 111–14.

Cleal, R.M.J., 1992b, 'The Neolithic and Beaker pottery', in Gingell 1992, 61–70.

Cleal, R.M.J., 1995a, 'Pottery fabrics in Wessex in the fourth to second millennia BC', in Kinnes and Varndell (eds) 1995, 185–94.

Cleal, R.M.J., 1995b, 'Beaker pottery', in Wainwright and Davies 1995, 55–7.

Cleal, R.M.J., 1996, 'The pottery from pit 2', in Rawlings and Fitzpatrick 1996, 24–7.

Cleal, R.M.J., 1997, 'Earlier prehistoric pottery', in R.J.C. Smith, F. Healy, M.J., Allen, E.L. Morris, I. Barnes and P.J. Woodward, *Excavations Along the Route of the Dorchester By-Pass, Dorset, 1986–8*, Salisbury, Wessex Archaeology Report 11, 86–102.

Cleal, R.M.J., 1999, 'Prehistoric pottery' in Barclay and Halpin 1999, 195–210.

Cleal, R., 2005, '"The small compass of a grave": Early Bronze Age burial in and around Avebury and the Marlborough Downs', in G. Brown, D. Field and D. McOmish (eds), *The Avebury Landscape. Aspects of the Field Archaeology of the Marlborough Downs*, Oxford, Oxbow, 115–32.

Cleal, R.M.J., 2007, 'The pottery of Wyke Down 2 henge', in C. French, H. Lewis, M.J. Allen, M. Green, R. Scaife and J. Gardiner, *Prehistoric Landscape Development and Human Impact in the upper Allen Valley, Cranborne Chase, Dorset*, Cambridge, McDonald Institute Monographs, 313–19.

Cleal, R. and Pollard, J., (eds), 2004, *Monuments and Material Culture. Papers in honour of an Avebury archaeologist: Isobel Smith*, East Knoyle, Hobnob.

Cleal, R.M.J., Cooper, J. and Williams, D., 1994, 'Shells and sherds: identification of inclusions in Grooved Ware, with associated radiocarbon dates from Amesbury, Wiltshire', *Proceedings of the Prehistoric Society* 60, 445–8.

Cleal, R.M.J., Walker, K.E. and Montague, R., 1995, *Stonehenge in its Landscape. Twentieth Century Excavations*, London, English Heritage Archaeology Report 10.

Clough, T.H.McK., and Green B., 1972, 'The petrological identification of stone implements from East Anglia', *Proceedings of the Prehistoric Society* 38, 108–55.

Colt Hoare, R., 1810, *The Ancient History of Wiltshire, Volume I*, London, William Miller, republished 1975, Wakefield, EP Publishing with Wiltshire County Library.

Combe, A. and Rieder, J., 2004, *Plateau de Bevaix 1. Pour une première approche archéologique: cadastres anciens et géoresources*, Neuchâtel, Archéologie Neuchâteloise 30.

Conrad, M., 2007, *Glockenbecherzeitliche Gräber in Nordwestsachsen – Vom Becher(-n) zur Tasse*, Leipzig, Leipziger online Beiträge zur Ur- und Frühgeschichtlichen Archäologie 25: http://www.uni-leipzig.de/~ufg/reihe/files/l25.pdf

Copley, M.S., Rose, P.J., Clapham, A., Edwards, D.N., Horton, M.C. and Evershed, R.P., 2001, 'Processing palm fruits in the Nile

Valley – biomolecular evidence from Qsar Ibrim', *Antiquity* 75, 538–42.

Copley, M.S., Berstan, R., Dudd, S.N., Docherty, G., Mukherjee, A.J., Straker, V., Payne, S. and Evershed, R.P., 2003, 'Direct Chemical evidence for widespread dairying in prehistoric Britain', *Proceedings of the National Academy of Sciences of the United States of America* 100, 1524–9.

Copley, M.S., Bland, H.A., Rose, P., Horton, M. and Evershed, R.P., 2005a, 'Gas chromatographic, mass spectrometric and stable carbon isotopic investigations of organic residues of plant oils and animal fats employed as illuminants in archaeological lamps from Egypt', *Analyst* 130, 860–71.

Copley, M.S., Berstan, R., Dudd, S.N., Aillaud, S., Mukherjee, A.J., Straker, V., Payne, S. and Evershed, R.P., 2005b, 'Processing of milk products in pottery vessels through British prehistory', *Antiquity* 79, 895–908.

Copley, M.S., Berstan, R., Mukherjee, A.J., Dudd, S.N., Straker, V., Payne, S. and Evershed, R.P., 2005c, 'Dairying in antiquity. III. Evidence from absorbed lipid residues dating to the British Neolithic', *Journal of Archaeological Science* 32, 523–46.

Cornaggia Castiglioni, O., 1971, *La Cultura di Remedello. Problematica ed ergologia di una facies dell'Eneolitico padano*, Milan, Memorie della Società Italiana di Scienze Naturali e del Museo Civico di Storia Naturale di Milano, 20(1).

Cotton, J., Elsden, N., Pipe, A. and Rayner, L., 2006, 'Taming the wild: a final Neolithic/Earlier Bronze Age aurochs deposit from West London', in D. Serjeantson and D. Field (eds), *Animals in the Neolithic of Britain and Europe*, Oxford, Neolithic Studies Group Seminar Papers 7, 149–67.

Cowell, M., 1998, 'Coin analysis by energy dispersive x-ray fluorescence spectrometry', in A. Oddy and M. Cowell (eds), *Metallurgy in Numismatics 4*, London, Royal Numismatic Society, 448–60.

Cowie, T.G., 1988, *Magic Metal. Early Metalworkers in the North-east*, Aberdeen, Anthropological Museum, University of Aberdeen.

Cox, M. and Mays, S. (eds), 2000, *Human Osteology in Archaeology and Forensic Science*, London, Greenwich Medical Media.

Cummings, V. and Fowler, C., (eds), 2004, *The Neolithic of the Irish Sea: materiality and traditions of practice*, Oxford, Cardiff Studies in Archaeology.

Cunliffe, B. and Renfrew, C., (eds), 1997, *Science and Stonehenge*, London, Proceedings of the British Academy 92.

Cunnington, M.E., 1929, *Woodhenge. A description of the site as revealed by excavations carried out there by Mr and Mrs B.H. Cunnington 1926–8. Also of four circles and an earthwork enclosure south of Woodhenge*, Devizes, Simpson.

Cunnington, M.E., 1931, 'The "Sanctuary" on Overton Hill, near Avebury', *Wiltshire Archaeological and Natural History Magazine* 45, 300–35.

Cunnington, W., 1806, 'Account of tumuli opened in Wiltshire, in three letters from Mr. William Cunnington to Aylmer Bourke Lambert, Esq. F.R.S. and F.A.S. Communicated by Mr. Lambert', *Archaeologia*, 15, 122–9.

Czebreszuk, J., 2004a, 'Bell Beakers: an outline of present stage of research', in Czebreszuk (ed.) 2004b, 223–4.

Czebreszuk, J., (ed.), 2004b, *Similar but Different. Bell Beakers in Europe*, Poznań, Adam Mickiewicz University.

Czebreszuk, J. and Szmyt, M., (eds), 2003, *The Northeast Frontier of Bell Beakers*, Oxford, British Archaeological Report S1155.

Darbyshire, D.P.F. and Shepherd, T.J., 1985, 'Chronology of granite magmatism and associated mineralization, SW England', *Journal of the Geological Society* 142, 1159–77.

Darvill, T.C., 2005, *Stonehenge World Heritage Site: an archaeological research framework*, London and Bournemouth, English Heritage and Bournemouth University.

Darvill, T.C., 2006, *Stonehenge. The Biography of a Landscape*, Stroud, Tempus.

Darvill, T. and Wainwright, G., 2009, 'Stonehenge excavations 2008', *Antiquaries Journal* 89, 10–19.

Daux, V., Lecuyer, C., Heran, M.A., Amiot, R., Simon, L., Fourel, F., Martineau, F., Lynnerup, N., Reychler, H. and Escarguel, G., 2008, 'Oxygen isotope fractionation between human phosphate and water revisited', *Journal of Human Evolution* 55, 1138–47.

Davis, M., forthcoming, 'Analysis of buttons from barrows 1 and 6' in J. Harding and F. Healy forthcoming, *The Raunds Area Project. A Neolithic and Bronze Age Landscape in Northamptonshire. Volume 2, Supplementary Studies*, Swindon, English Heritage, 396–400.

Degen, R., 1976, 'Gräber der Glockenbecherkultur aus Allschwil', *Helvetica Archaeologica* 7, 75–84.

Delgado, S. and Risch, R., 2006, 'La tumba No 3 de Los Cipreses y la metallurgia Argárcia', *AlbercA* 4, 21–50.

Delgado, S. and Risch, R., 2008, 'Lithic perspectives on metallurgy: an example from Copper and Bronze Age south-east Iberia', in L. Longo and N. Skakun (eds), *'Prehistoric Technology' 40 years later: Functional studies and the Russian legacy*, Oxford, British Archaeological Report S1783, 235–53.

Delibes de Castro, G., 1978, 'Sobre la arandela de hueso de la tumba campaniforme de Villabuena del Puente (Zamora)', *Revista de Guimares* 88, 357–63.

Dellestable, F., Péré, P., Blum, A., Régent, D. and Gaucher, A., 1996, 'The "small-patella" syndrome; hereditary osteodysplasia of

248

the knee, pelvis and foot', *Journal of Bone Joint Surgery* 78B, 63–5.

Desideri, J. and Eades, S., 2004, 'Le peuplement campaniforme en Suisse. Nouveaux apports de la morphologie crânienne et dentaire', in Besse and Desideri (eds) 2004, 99–109.

Donaldson, P., 1977, 'The excavation of a multiple round barrow at Barnack, Cambridgeshire, 1974–1976', *Antiquaries Journal* 57, 197–231.

Donato, F., di, 1991, 'Italian prehistoric bows', *Journal of the Society of Archer-Antiquaries* 34, 51–5.

Dornheim, S., Lissner, B., Metzler, S., Müller, A., Ortolf, S., Sprenger, S., Stadelbacher, A., Strahm, C., Wolters, K. and Wiermann, R.R., 2005, 'Sex und gender, Alter und Kompetenz, Status und Prestige: Soziale Differenzierung im 3. vorchristlichen Jahrtausend', in J. Müller (ed.), *Alter und Geschlecht in ur-und frühgeschichtlichen Gesellschaften*, Bonn, Universitätsforschungen zur prähistorischen Archäologie 126, 27–71.

Drenth, E. and Hogestijn, W.J.H., 1999, 'De klokbekercultuur in Nederland: de stand van onderzoek anno 1999', *Archeologie* 9, 99–149.

Drenth, E. and Hogestijn, W.J.H., 2001, 'The Bell Beaker culture in the Netherlands: the state of research in 1998', in Nicolis (ed.) 2001b, 309–32.

Drenth, E. and Hogestijn, W.J.H., 2007, 'Bekers voor Baker. Nieuwe ideën over de oorpsrung en ontwikkeling van klokbekers in Nederland', in J.H.F. Bloemers (ed.), *Tussen D26 en P14: Jan Albert Baaker 65 jaar*, Amsterdam, Amsterdams Archeologisch Centrum, 33–146.

Dresely, V., 2004, *Schnurkeramik und Schnurkeramiker im Taubertal*, Stuttgart, Forschungen und Berichte zur Vor-und Frühgeschichte in Baden-Württemberg 81.

Drew, C.D. and Piggott, S., 1936, 'Excavation of Long Barrow 163a on Thickthorn Down, Dorset,' *Proceedings of the Prehistoric Society* 2, 77–96.

Dudd, S.N. and Evershed, R.P., 1998, 'Direct demonstration of milk as an element of archaeological economies', *Science* 282, 1478–81.

Dudd, S.N., Evershed R.P. and Gibson, A.M., 1999, 'Evidence for varying patterns of exploitation of animal products in different prehistoric pottery traditions based on lipids preserved in surface and absorbed residues', *Journal of Archaeological Science* 26, 1473–82.

Duncan, H.B., 2005, 'Bone artefacts' in Roberts (ed.) 2005, 163–5.

Dvořák, P., 1992, *Gräberfelder der Glockenbecherkultur in Mähren I (Bez. Blansko, Brno-město, Brno-venkov), Katalog der Funde*, Brno, Mährische Archäologische Quellen.

Dvořák, P. and Hájek, L., 1990, *Die Gräberfelder der Glockenbecherkultur bei Šlapanice (Bez. Brno-venkov) Katalog der Funde*, Brno, Mährische Archäologische Quellen.

Dvořák, P., Matějíčková, A., Peška, J. and Rakovský, I., 1996, *Gräberfelder der Glockenbecherkultur in Mähren II (Bezirk Břeclav), Katalog der Funde*, Brno-Olomouc, Mährische Archäologische Quellen.

Egg, M. and Spindler, K., 1992, 'Die Gletschermumie vom Ende der Steinzeit aus den Ötztaler Alpen. Vorbericht', *Jahrbuch des Römisch-Germanischen Zentralmusuems Mainz* 39, 1–113.

Eluère, C., 1982, *Les Ors Préhistoriques*, Paris, L'Age du Bronze en France 2.

Engelhardt, B., 2006, 'Bemerkungen zu den neu entdeckten Glockenbechergräbern von Atting "Aufeld"', *Das Archäologische Jahr in Bayern 2005*, 31–21.

Eogan, G., 1994, *The Accomplished Art. Gold and Gold-working in Britain and Ireland During the Bronze Age (c. 2350–650 BC)*, Oxford, Oxbow Monograph 42.

Evans, H., 2008, *Neolithic and Bronze Age Landscapes of Cumbria*, Oxford, British Archaeological Report 463.

Evans, J. 1897, *The Ancient Stone Implements of Great Britain*, London, Longmans

Evans, J.A., 1989, 'Short paper: a note on Rb-Sr whole-rock ages from cleaved mudrocks in the Welsh basin', *Journal of the Geological Society* 146, 901–4.

Evans, J.A., 1996a, *Final Report on Rb-Sr whole-rock dating of mudrock suites from the Lake District and Southern Uplands*, Nottingham, British Geological Survey, NERC (National Environment Research Council) Isotopes Geosciences Laboratory Report 187.

Evans, J.A., 1996b, 'Dating the transition of smectite to illite in the Palaeozoic mudrocks using the Rb-Sr whole rock technique', *Journal of the Geological Society* 153, 101–8.

Evans, J.A., Chenery, C.A. and Fitzpatrick, A.P., 2006, 'Bronze Age childhood migration of individuals near Stonehenge, revealed by strontium and oxygen isotope tooth enamel analysis', *Archaeometry* 48, 309–22.

Evans, J.G., 1984, 'Stonehenge – The environment in the Late Neolithic and Early Bronze Age and a Beaker-Age burial', *Wiltshire Archaeology and Natural History Magazine* 78, 7–30

Evans, W.E.D., 1963, *The Chemistry of Death*, Springfield, Illinois, Charles Thomas.

Evershed R.P., 1993, 'Biomolecular archaeology and lipids', *World Archaeology* 25, 74–93.

Evershed, R.P., 2008, 'Experimental approaches to the interpretation of absorbed organic residues in archaeological ceramics', *World Archaeology* 40, 26–47.

Evershed, R.P., Heron, C. and Goad, L.J., 1990, 'Analysis of organic residues of archaeological origin by high temperature gas chromatography and gas chromatography-mass spectrometry', *Analyst* 115, 1339–42.

Evershed, R.P., Heron, C. and Goad, L.J., 1991, 'Epicuticular leaf wax components preserved in potsherds as chemical indicators of leafy vegetables in ancient diets', *Antiquity* 65, 540–4.

Evershed, R.P., Heron, C., Charters, S. and Goad, L.J., 1992, 'The survival of food residues: new methods of analysis, interpretation and application', in A.M. Pollard (ed.), *New Developments in Archaeological Science*, London, Proceedings of the British Academy 77, 187–208.

Evershed, R.P., Vaughan, S.J., Dudd, S.N. and Soles, J.S., 1997, 'Fuel for thought? Beeswax in lamps and conical cups from the late Minoan Crete', *Antiquity* 71, 979–85

Evershed, R.P., Arnot, K.I., Collister, J., Eglington, G. and Charters, S., 1994, 'Application of isotope ratio monitoring gas chromatography-mass spectrometry to the analysis of organic residues of archaeological origin', *Analyst* 119, 909–14.

Evershed, R. P., Stott, A. W., Raven, A., Dudd, S. N., Charters, S. and Leyden, A., 1995, 'Formation of long-chain ketones in ancient pottery vessels by pyrolysis of acyl lipids', *Tetrahedron Letters* 36, 8875–8.

Evershed, R.P., Dudd, S.N., Charters, S., Mottram, H., Stott, A.W., Raven, A., Bergen, P.F., van and Bland, H. A., 1999, 'Lipids as carriers of anthropogenic signals from prehistory', *Philosophical Transactions of The Royal Society of London* B354, 19–31.

Evershed, R.P., Dudd, S.N., Copley, M.S., Berstan, R., Stott, A. W., Mottram, H., Buckley, S. and Crossman, Z.M., 2002, 'Chemistry of archaeological animal fats', *Accounts of Chemical Research* 35, 660–8.

Evershed, R.P., Dudd, S.N., Anderson-Stojanovic, V.R. and Gebhard, E.R., 2003, 'New chemical evidence for the use of Combed Ware pottery vessels as beehives in ancient Greece', *Journal of Archaeological Science* 30, 1–12.

Falke, H., 1972, 'The continental Permian in north-and south Germany', in H. Falke (ed.), *Rotliegend: Essays on European Lower Permian*, Leiden, International Sedimentary Petrographical Series 15, 43–113.

Fasham, P.J., Farwell, D.E. and Whinney, R.J.B., 1989, *The Archaeological Site at Easton Lane, Winchester*, Winchester, Hampshire Field Club Monograph 6.

Field, D., 2006, *Earthen Long Barrows. The Earliest Monuments in the British Isles*, Stroud, Tempus.

Finnegan, M., 1978, 'Non-metric variations of the infracranial skeleton', *Journal of Anatomy* 125, 23–37.

Fitzpatrick, A.P., 2004, 'The Boscombe Bowmen', *Current Archaeology* 193, 10–16.

Fokkens, H., Achterkamp Y. and Kuijpers, M., 2008, 'Bracers or bracelets? About the functionality and meaning of Bell Beaker wrist-guards', *Proceedings of the Prehistoric Society* 74, 109–40.

Forrest, A.J., 1983, *Masters of Flint*, Lavenham, Terence Dalton.

Forssander, J.E., 1936, *Der Ostskandinavische Norden während der ältesten Metallzeit Europas*, Lund, Skrifter Utgivna av Kungliga Humanistiska Vetenskapssamfundet i Lund, 22.

Fox, C., 1925, 'On two Beakers of the Early Bronze Age recently discovered in south Wales', *Archaeologia Cambrensis* 7 series 5, 1–31.

Foxon, A., 1990, 'Antler spatula', 166–7, in Russel 1990, 153–72.

Freudenberg, M., 2009, 'Steingeräte zur Metallbearbeitung – einige neue Aspekte zum spätneolithischen und frühbronzezeitlichen Metallhandwerk vor dem Hintergrund des schleswig-holsteinischen Fundmaterials', *Archäologisches Korrespondenzblatt* 39, 1–19.

Furholt, M., 2003, *Die absolutchronologische Datierung der Schnurkeramik in Mitteleuropa und Südskandinavien*, Bonn, Universitäts-forschungen zur prähistorischen Archäologie 101.

Gall, W. and Feustel, R., 1962, 'Glockenbecherfunde im Stadtgebiet von Weimar', *Ausgrabungen und Funde* 7, 220–6.

Gallay, A., 1989, *Le site préhistorique du Petit Chasseur (Sion, Valais) 7. Secteur oriental*, Lausanne, Cahiers d'Archéologie romande 47–8.

Gallay, A., 2001, 'L'énigme campaniforme', in Nicolis (ed.) 2001b, 41–57.

Gallay, A. and Chaix, L., 1984, *Le site préhistorique du Petit Chasseur (Sion, Valais). Le Dolmen M XI*, Lausanne, Cahiers d'Archéologie romande 31.

Gallay, G., 1981, *Die kupfer- und altbronzezeitlichen Dolche und Stabdolche in Frankreich*, Munich, Prähistorische Bronzefunde 6.5.

Gardiner. J., Allen, M.J., Powell A., Harding, P., Lawson, A.J., Loader, E., McKinley, J.I., Sheridan, A. and Stevens , C., 2006, 'A matter of life and death: Late Neolithic, Beaker and Early Bronze age settlements and cemeteries at Thomas Hardye School, Dorchester', *Proceedings of the Dorset Natural History and Archaeological Society* 128, 17–52.

Garrido-Pena, R., 1997, *El Campaniforme en la Meseta Central de la Península Ibérica (c. 2500–2000 AC)*, Oxford, British Archaeological Report S892.

Garwood, P., 1999, 'Radiocarbon dating and the chronology of the monument complex', in Barclay and Halpin 1999, 293–309.

Gebers, W., 1978, *Endneolithikum und Frühbronzezeit im Mittelrheingebiet. Katalog*, Bonn, Saarbrucker Beiträge zur Altertumskunde 28.

Gedl, M., 1980, *Die Dolche und Stabdolche in Polen*, Munich, Prähistorische Bronzefunde 6.4.

250

Gerloff, S., 1975, *The Early Bronze Age Daggers in Great Britain, and a reconsideration of the Wessex Culture*, Munich, Prähistorische Bronzefunde 6.2.

Gerloff, S., 2007, 'Reinecke's ABC and the chronology of the British Bronze Age, in Burgess *et al.* (eds) 2007, 117–61.

Gersbach, E., 1957, 'Schnur-und Häkelmaschenverzierung auf westeuropäischen Glockenbechern', *Jahrbuch der Schweizerischen Gesellschaft für Ur- und Frühgeschichte* 46, 1–12.

Gdaniec, K., 2006, 'A miniature antler bow from a Middle Bronze site at Isleham, (Cambridgeshire), England', *Antiquity* 70, 652–7.

Giblin, J.I., 2009, 'Strontium isotope analysis of Neolithic and Copper Age populations on the Great Hungarian Plain', *Journal of Archaeological Science* 36, 491–7.

Gibson, A., 1982, *Beaker Domestic Pottery*, Oxford, British Archaeological Report 103.

Gibson, A., 1993, 'The excavation of two cairns and associated features at Carneddau, Carno, Powys, 1989–90', *Archaeological Journal* 150, 1–45.

Gibson, A., 2004, 'Burials and beakers: seeing beneath the veneer in Late Neolithic Britain', in Czebreszuk (ed.) 2004b, 173–92.

Gibson, A., 2007, 'A Beaker veneer? Some evidence from the burial record', in Larsson and Parker Pearson (eds) 2007, 47–64.

Gibson, A. and Sheridan, A., (eds) 2004, *From Sickles to Circles. Britain and Ireland at the time of Stonehenge*, Stroud, Tempus.

Gimbutas, M., 1965, *The Bronze Age Cultures of Central Europe*, The Hague, Mouton.

Gingell, C.J., 1992, *The Marlborough Downs: a Later Bronze Age landscape and its origins*, Devizes, Wiltshire Archaeological and Natural History Society Monograph 1.

Gingell, C.J. and Harding, P.A., 1981, 'A method of analysing the technology of flaking in Neolithic and Bronze Age flint assemblages', in F.G.H. Engelen (ed.), *Third International Symposium on Flint, 24–27th May 1979 Maastricht*, Sittard (Nederlandse Geologische Vereniging), Staringa 6, 73–6.

Glover, W., 1979, 'A prehistoric bow fragment from Drumwhinny Bog, Kesk, Co. Fermanagh', *Proceedings of the Prehistoric Society* 45, 323–7.

Godelier, M., 1996, *L'énigme du don*, Paris, Fayard.

Goetze, B.-R., 1987, 'Glockenbecher-Gräber von Dietfurt an der Altmühl', *Archäologisches Korrespondenzblatt* 17, 169–75.

Görsdorf, J., 1993, '14C-Datierungem des Berliner Labors zur Problematik der chronologischen Einordnung der Bronzezeit in Mitteleuropa', in K. Rassmann (ed.), *Spätneolithikum und frühe Bronzezeit im Flachland zwischen Elbe und Oder*, Lübstorf, Beiträge zur Ur- und Frühgeschichte Mecklenberg-Vorpommern 28, 97–117.

Gray, H. St George, 1908, 'Report on the Wick Barrow excavations', *Proceedings of the Somerset Archaeological and Natural History Society* 54, 1–78.

Green, C., Lynch, F. and White, H., 1982, 'The excavation of two round barrows on Launceston Down, Dorset (Long Crichel 5 and 7)', *Proceedings of the Dorset Natural History and Archaeological Society* 104, 39–58.

Green, C.P., 1997, 'The provenance of the rocks used in the construction of Stonehenge', in Cunliffe and Renfrew (eds) 1997, 257–70.

Green, H.S., 1980, *The Flint Arrowheads of the British Isles*, Oxford, British Archaeological Report 75.

Green, H.S., Houlder, C.H. and Keeley, L.H., 1982, 'A flint dagger from Ffair Rhos, Ceredigion, Dyfed, Wales', *Proceedings of the Prehistoric Society* 48, 492–501.

Griffiths, W.E., 1957, 'The typology and origins of Beakers in Wales', *Proceedings of the Prehistoric Society* 23, 1957, 57–90.

Grimes, W.F., 1951, *The Prehistory of Wales*, Cardiff, National Museum of Wales.

Grimes, W.F., 1960, *Excavations on Defence Sites, 1939–1945. I: Mainly Neolithic–Bronze Age*, London, Ministry of Works Archaeological Reports 3.

Grimes, W.F., 1964, 'Excavations in the Lake Group of Barrows, Wilsford, Wiltshire, in 1959', *Bulletin of the Institute of Archaeology University of London* 4, 89–121.

Grinsell, L.V., 1957, 'Archaeological gazetteer', in R.B. Pugh and E. Critall (eds), *Victoria History of the Counties of England. History of Wiltshire I, Part 1*, London, University of London Institute of Historical Research, 21–279.

Gross-Klee, E., 1999, 'Exkurs. Glockenbecher: ihre Chronologie und ihr zeitliches Verhältnis zur Schnurkeramik aufgrund der C14-Daten, 55–61, in B. Eberschweiler, 'Die jüngsten endneolithischen Ufersiedlungen am Zürichsee', *Jahrbuch der Schweizerischen Gesellschaft für Ur-und Frühgeschichte* 82, 39–64.

Grupe, G., Price, T.D., Schroter, P., Sollner, F., Johnson, C.M. and Beard, B.L., 1997, 'Mobility of Bell Beaker people revealed by strontium isotope ratios of tooth and bone: a study of southern Bavarian skeletal remains', *Applied Geochemistry* 12, 517–25.

Guerra-Doce, E., 2006, 'Exploring the significance of Beaker pottery through residues', *Oxford Journal of Archaeology* 25, 247–59.

Guilaine, J., (ed.), 1984, *L'Âge du cuivre européen. Civilisations à vases campaniformes*, Paris, Centre national de la recherche scientifique.

Guilaine, J., (ed.), 2007, *Le chalcolithique et la construction des inégalités. Tome I. Le continent européen*, Paris, Errance.

Guilaine, J., Claustre, F., Lemercier, O. and Sabatier, P., 2001, 'Campaniformes et environnement culturel en France méditerranéenne', in Nicolis (ed.) 2001b, 229–76.

Haak, W., Brandt, G., Jong, H.N., de, Meyer, C., Ganslmeier, R., Heyd, V., Hawkesworth C., Pike, A.W.G., Meller, H. and Alt, K.W., 2008, 'Ancient DNA, strontium isotopes and osetological analyses shed light on social and kinship organization of the later Stone Age', *Proceedings of the National Academy of Sciences of the United States of America* 105, 18226–31.

Haeblar, K., Zintl, S. and Grupe, G., 2006, 'Lebensbedingungen und Mobitität im frühmittelalterlichen Perlach', *Bulletin de la Société Suisse d'Anthropologie* 12, 47–62.

Hafner, A., 2002, 'Vom Spät- zum Endneolithikum. Wandel und Kontinuität um 2700 v. Chr. in der Schweiz', *Archäologisches Korrespondenzblatt* 32, 517–31.

Hafner, A., and Suter, P., 2003, 'Das Neolithikum in der Schweiz': http://www.jungsteinsite.uni-kiel.de./pdf/2003_hafnersuter_text.pdf

Hafner, A. and Suter, P.J., 2005, 'Neolithikum: Raum/Zeit–Ordnung und neue Denkmodelle', *Archäologie im Kanton Bern* 6, 431–98.

Hájek, L., 1939, 'Půlměsícovitá spinadla kultury zvoncovitých pohárů', *Památky Archeologické* 32, 1939 (1946) 20–9.

Hájek, L., 1951, 'Nové nálezy kultury zvoncovitých pohárů', *Archeologické rozhledy* 3, 27–30.

Hájek, L., 1961, 'Kostrový hrob kultury zvoncovitých pohárů ze Stehelčevsi', *Památky Archeologické* 52, 138–48.

Hájek, L., 1966, 'Die älteste Phase der Glochenbecherkultur in Böhmen und Mähren', *Památky Archeologické* 67, 210–41.

Hájek, L., 1968, *Kultura zvoncovitých pohárů v Čechách*, Prague, Archeologické Studijní Materiály 5.

Halpin, C., 1987, 'Irthlingborough', *Current Archaeology* 9, 331–3.

Hamlin, A., 1963, 'Excavation of ring-ditches and other sites at Stanton Harcourt', *Oxoniensia* 28, 1–19.

Hansen, S., 2002, '"Überausstattungen" in Gräbern und Horten der Frühbronzezeit', in J. Müller, (ed.), *Vom Endneolithikum zur Frühbronzezeit: Muster sozialen Wandels?*, Bonn, Universitäts-forschungen zur prähistorischen Archäologie 90, 151–73.

Harbison, P., 1969, *The Daggers and Halberds of the Early Bronze Age of Ireland*, Munich, Prähistorische Bronzefunde 6,1.

Harbison, P., 1976, *Bracers and V-Perforated Buttons in the Beaker and Food Vessel Cultures of Ireland*, Bad Bramstedt, Archaeologia Atlantica Research Report 1.

Harding, J. and Healy, F., 2007, *The Raunds Area Project. A Neolithic and Bronze Age Landscape in Northamptonshire*, Swindon, English Heritage: htpp//www.english-heritage.org.uk/server/show/ConWebDoc/13537.

Harding, P., 1988, 'The chalk plaque pit, Amesbury', *Proceedings of the Prehistoric Society* 54, 30–7.

Harding, P., 1989, 'Flint and the burial group in 1017' in Fasham *et al.* 1989, 99–107.

Harding, P., 1991, 'The worked stone: stratified groups from Rowden and Cowleaze', in P.J. Woodward, *The South Dorset Ridgeway. Survey and excavations 1977–84*, Dorchester, Dorset Natural History and Archaeological Society Monograph 8, 73–87.

Harding, P., 1992, 'The flint', in Gingell 1992, 123–33.

Harding, P., 1997, 'Associated flints', in I. Barnes, C.A. Butterworth, J.W. Hawkes and L. Smith, *Excavations at Thames Valley Park, Reading, Berkshire, 1986–88*, Salisbury, Wessex Archaeology Report 14, 24–6.

Harrison, R.J., 1977, *The Bell Beaker Cultures of Spain and Portugal*, Harvard, American School of Prehistoric Research Bulletin 35.

Harrison, R.J., 1980, *The Beaker Folk. Copper Age Archaeology in Western Europe*, London, Thames and Hudson.

Harrison, R. and Heyd, V., 2007, 'The transformation of Europe in the third millennium BC: the example of "Le Petit Chasseur I + III" (Sion, Valais, Switzerland)', *Prähistorische Zeitschrift* 82, 129–214.

Harrison, R.J. and Mederos Martin, A., 2001, 'Bell beakers and social complexity in central Spain', in Nicolis (ed.) 2001b, 111–24.

Harrison, R.J., Jackson, R. and Napthan, M., 1999, 'A rich Bell Beaker burial from Wellington Quarry, Marden, Herefordshire', *Oxford Journal of Archaeology* 18, 1–16.

Hart, C.R., 1981, *The North Derbyshire Archaeological Survey to AD 1500*, Chesterfield, North Derbyshire Archaeological Trust.

Hartmann, A., 1970, *Prähistorische Goldfunde aus Europa*, Berlin, Studien zu den Anfängen der Metallurgie 3.

Hartmann, A., 1980, 'Analyses of British prehistoric gold and some British ores', in Taylor 1980, 138–41.

Hásek, I., 1989, 'Die ältesten Gold-und Silberfunde Mitteleuropas', in Buchvaldek and Pleslová-Štiková (eds), 1989, 49–54.

Havel, J., 1978, 'Pohřební ritus kultury zvoncovitých pohárů v Čechách a na Morave', *Præhistorica* 7/*Varia Archaeologica* 1, 91–117.

Healy, F., 1984, 'Discussion', in Lambrick and Allen 1984, 61.

Healy, F. and Harding, J., 2004, 'Reading a burial: the legacy of Overton Hill', in A. Gibson and A. Sheridan (eds), *From Sickles to Circles: Britain and Ireland at the time of Stonehenge*, Stroud, Tempus, 176–93.

Hedges, R.E.M., Bronk Ramsey, C. and Housley, R.A., 1989, 'The Oxford Accelerator Mass Spectrometry facility: technical developments in routine dating', *Archaeometry* 31, 99–113.

Heim, D., 1960, 'Über die Petrographie und Genese der Tonsteine aus dem Rotliegenden des Saar-Nahe Gebietes', *Beiträge zur Mineralogie und Petrographie* 7, 281–317.

Hitchcock, C. and Nichols, B.W., 1971, *Plant Lipid Biochemistry*, London and New York, Academic Press.

Helms, M., 1988, *Ulysses' Sail*, Princeton, University Press.

Henderson, J., 1987, 'Factors determining the state of preservation of human remains', in A. Boddington, A.N. Garland and R.C. Janaway (eds), *Death, Decay and Reconstruction*, Manchester, University Press, 43–54.

Hetzer, K., 1949, 'Beiträge zur Kenntnis der Glockenbecherkultur in Österreich', *Archaeologia Austriaca* 4, 87–115.

Heyd, V., 2000, *Die Spätkupferzeit in Süddeutschland*, Bonn, Saarbrücker Beiträge zur Altertumskunde 73.

Heyd, V., 2001, 'On the earliest Beakers along the Danube', in Nicolis (ed.) 2001b, 387–409.

Heyd, V., 2004a, 'Nuova individualizzazione e internazionalizzazione: I gruppi della cultura della ceramica cordata e del bicchiere campaniforme lungo il corso superiore del Danubio', in F. Marzatico and P. Gleirscher (eds), *Guerrieri, Principi ed Eroi, fra il Danubio e il Po dalla Preistoria all'Alto Medioevo, Catalogo della mostra, 19 guigno–7 novembre 2004*, Trento, Castello del Buonconsiglio, 125–33.

Heyd, V., 2004b, 'Überregionale Verbindungen der süddeutschen Glockenbecherkultur anhand der Siedlungen', in V. Heyd, L. Husty and L. Kreiner 2004, *Siedlungen der Glockenbecherkultur in Süddeutschland und Mitteleuropas*, Büchenbach, Arbeiten zur Archäologie Süddeutschlands 17, 181–202.

Heyd, V., 2007a, 'Families, prestige goods, warriors and complex societies: Beaker groups of the 3rd millennium cal BC along the Upper and Middle Danube', *Proceedings of the Prehistoric Society* 73, 327–79.

Heyd, V., 2007b, 'When the West meets the East. The eastern periphery of the Bell Beaker phenomenon and its relation with the Aegean Early Bronze Age', in I. Galanki. H. Thomas, Y. Galanakis and R. Laffineur (eds), *Between the Aegean and Baltic Seas. Prehistory across Borders*, Aegaeum 27, 91–104.

Heyd, V. and Harrison, R., 2007, 'Sion, Aosta e le transformazioni nell'Europa del terzo millennio a.C.', in S. Casini and A.E. Fossati (eds), *Le Pietre Degli Dei. Statue-stele dell'età del rame in Europa. Lo stato della ricerca*, Bergamo, Notizie Archeologiche Bergomensi 12, 143–73.

Heyd, V., Winterholler, B., Böhm, K. and Pernicka, E., 2003, 'Mobilität, Strontiumisotopie und Subsistenz in der süddeutschen Glockenbecherkultur', *Berichte der Bayerischen Bodendenkmalpflege* 43/44, 109–35.

Hille, A., 2003, 'Die Glockenbecherkultur in Mitteldeutschland. Ein Zwischenbericht', in Czebreszuk and Szmyt (eds) 2003, 101–6.

Hillson, S.W., 1979, 'Diet and dental disease', *World Archaeology* 2, 47–62.

Hillson, S.W., 1986, *Teeth*, Cambridge, University Press.

Hillson, S., 1996, *Dental Anthropology*, Cambridge, University Press.

Hobson, D.M.,1978, *The Plymouth Area*, London, Geologists Association Guide 38.

Holden, J.L., Phakley, P.P. and Clement, J.G., 1995a, 'Scanning electron microscope observations of incinerated human femoral bone: a case study', *Forensic Science International* 74, 17–28.

Holden, J.L., Phakley, P.P. and Clement, J.G., 1995b, 'Scanning electron microscope observations of heat-treated human bone', *Forensic Science International* 74, 29–45.

Hook, D.R. and Needham, S.P., 1989, 'A comparison of recent analyses of British Late Bronze Age gold work with Irish parallels', *Jewellery Studies* 3, 15–24.

Howard-Davis, C., 2007, 'The amber belt ring', in F. Brown, C. Howard-Davis, M. Brennand, A. Boyle, T. Evans, S. O'Connor, A. Spence, R. Heawood and A. Lupton, *The Archaeology of the A1(M) Darrington to Dishforth DBFO Road Scheme*, Lancaster, Lancaster Imprints 12, 307–8.

Humble, J., 1990, 'Grave goods: the building blocks in the interpretation of Beaker burials', in. C. Halpin (compiler), *The Work of the Central Excavation Unit 1988–9*, London, English Heritage, 7–8.

Hundt, H.-J., 1958, *Katalog Straubing I. Die Funde der Glockenbecherkultur und der Straubinger Kultur*, Kallmünz, Materialhefte zur Bayerischen Vorgeschichte 11.

Hundt, H.-J., 1975, 'Steinerne und kupferne Hämmer der frühen Bronzezeit', *Archäologisches Korrespondenzblatt* 5, 115–20.

Husty, L., 2004, 'Glockenbecherzeitliche Funde aus Landau a.d. Isar', in V. Heyd, L. Husty and L. Kreiner 2004, *Siedlungen der Glockenbecherkultur in Süddeutschland und Mitteleuropas*, Büchenbach, Arbeiten zur Archäologie Süddeutschlands 17, 15–102.

Ischler, T., 1923, *Die Pfahlbauten des Bielersees,* Biel, Heimatkundliche Monographien 4.

Ixer, I. and Webb, P.C., 2011, in Woodward and Hunter 2011, Chapters 2 and 3.

Jacobs, J., 1989, 'Jungsteinzeitliche Metallfunde auf dem Gebiet der DDR', *Zeitschrift für Archäologie* 32, 1–17.

Jay, M. and Richards, M., 2007, 'The Beaker People Project: progress and prospects for the carbon, nitrogen and sulphur isotopic analysis of collagen', in Larsson and Parker Pearson (eds) 2007, 77–82.

Jenkins, V., 1991, 'Inhumations' 119–21, in P. Bellamy, 'The excavation of Fordington Farm round barrow', *Proceedings of the Dorset Natural History and Archaeological Society* 113, 107–132.

Jerome, J.T.J., Varghese, M. and Sankaran, B., 2009, 'Congenital patellar syndrome', *Romanian Journal of Morphology and Embryology* 50, 291–3.

Jessup, R.F., 1933, 'Early Bronze Age beakers', *Archaeologia Cantiana* 45, 174–8.

Jeunesse, C., 2003, 'Les pratiques funéraires du Néolithique ancien danubien et l'identité rubanée: découvertes récentes, nouvelles tendances de la recherche', in Chambon and Leclerc (eds), 2003, 19–32.

Jones, A.M. and Quinnell, H., 2006, 'Cornish beakers: new discoveries and perspectives', *Cornish Archaeology* 45 (2008), 31–69.

Jones, M.U. and Jones, W.T., 1975, 'The crop mark sites at Mucking, Essex, England', in R. Bruce-Mitford (ed.), *Recent Archaeological Excavations in Europe*. London, Routledge and Kegan Paul, 133–87.

Joussaume, R., 1981, *Le néolithique de Aunis et de Poitou occidental dans son cadre atlantique*, Rennes, Travaux du Laboratoire d'Anthropologie, préhistoire, protohistoire et quaternaire Armoricains.

Jorge, S.A., 2002, 'Um vaso campaniforme cordado no Norte de Portugal: Castelo Velho de Freixo de Numão (Va N.a de Foz Côa). Breve notícia', *Revista da Faculdade de Letras. Ciências e técnicas do património* 1 ser 1, 27–50.

Kamieńska, J. and Kulczycka-Leciejewiczowa, A., 1970, 'The Neolithic and Early Bronze Age settlement at Samborzec in the Sandomierz district', *Archaeologia Polona* 12, 223–46.

Karl, R., 2005, 'Master and apprentice, knight and squire: education in the "Celtic" Iron Age', *Oxford Journal of Archaeology* 24, 255–71.

Kienlin, T.L. and Roberts, B. W., (eds), 2009, *Metals and Societies. Studies in Honour of Barbara S. Ottaway*, Bonn, Universitätsforschungen zur prähistorischen Archäologie 169.

Kimpe, K., Jacobs, P. A. and Waelkens, M., 2002, 'Mass spectrometric methods prove the use of beeswax and ruminant fat in late Roman cooking pots', *Journal of Chromatography* A968, 151–60.

Kinnes, I., 1977, 'The finds', in Donaldson 1977, 209–16.

Kinnes, I., 1979, *Round Barrows and Ring-ditches in the British Neolithic*, London, British Museum Occasional Paper 7.

Kinnes, I.A. 1985, *Beaker and Early Bronze Age Grave Groups, British Bronze Age Metalwork, Associated Finds Series* A7–16. London, British Museum.

Kinnes, I.A., 1994, *Beaker and Early Bronze Age Grave Groups, British Bronze Age Metalwork, Associated Finds Series, A17–31*, London, British Museum.

Kinnes, I.A. and Longworth, I.H., 1985, *Catalogue of the Excavated Prehistoric and Romano-British Material in the Greenwell Collection*, London, British Museum.

Kinnes, I. and Varndell, G., (eds), 1995, *Unbaked urns of Rudely Shape. Essays on British and Irish pottery for Ian Longworth*, Oxford, Oxbow Monograph 55.

Kinnes, I., Cameron F., Trow, S. and Thomson, D., 1998, *Excavations at Cliffe, Kent*, London, British Museum Occasional Paper 69.

Kinnes, I., Gibson, Ambers, J., Bowman, S. and Boast, R., 1991, 'Radiocarbon dating and British Beakers. The British Museum programme', *Scottish Archaeological Review* 8, 35–78.

Kimpe, K., Jacobs, P. A. and Waelkens, M., 2001, 'Analysis of oil used in late Roman oil lamps with different mass spectrometric techniques revealed the presence of predominantly olive oil together with traces of animal fat', *Journal of Chromatography* A937, 87–95.

Knor, A., 1966, 'Nécropole à Stehelčeves près de Kladno (Bohême)', in J. Filip (ed.), *Investigations Archéologiques en Tchécoslovaquie. Etat actuel des recherches et leur organisation*, Prague, Academia, 107–8.

Knowles, F.H.S., 1944, *The Manufacture of a Flint Arrow-head by Quartzite Hammer-stone*, Oxford, Pitt Rivers Museum Occasional Paper on Technology 1.

Knüsel, C., 2000, 'Activity related changes', in V. Fiorato, A. Boylston and C. Knüsel (eds), *Blood Red Roses: the archaeology of the mass grave from the battle of Towton AD 1461*, Oxford, Oxbow, 103–18.

Koch, H., 2006, 'Neue Grabfunde der Glockenbecherkultur aus Irlbach', *Das Archäologische Jahr in Bayern 2005*, 25–8.

Kociumaka, C., 1995, 'Gräber der Glockenbecherkultur aus Königsbrunn', *Das Archäologische Jahr in Bayern 1994*, 60–2.

Kociumaka, C. and Dietrich, H., 1991, 'Ein Gräberfeld der Glockenbecherkultur vom Sportgelände der Universität Augsburg', *Das Archäologische Jahr in Bayern 1991*, 67–8.

Kosko, A. and Klochko, V.I., 1987, 'A late Neolithic composite bow', *Journal of the Society of Archer-Antiquaries* 30, 15–23.

Köster, C., 1966, 'Beiträge zum Endneolithikum und zur Frühen Bronzezeit am nördlichen Oberrhein', *Prähistorische Zeitschrift* 43–4, 2–95.

Kreiner, L., 1991, 'Neue Gräber der Glockenbecherkultur aus Niederbayern', *Bayerische Vorgeschichtsblätter* 56, 151–61.

Kristiansen, K. and Larsson, T.B., 2005, *The Rise of Bronze Age Society. Travels, Transmissions and Transformations*, Cambridge, University Press.

Kuna, M. and Matoušek, V., 1978, 'Měděná industrie hrob kultury zvoncovitých pohárů ve středni Evropě', *Præohistorica* 6, 65–89.

Kunst, M., 1997, 'Waren die "Schmiede" in der portugiesischen Kupferzeit gleichzeitig auch die Elite?', in B. Fritsch, M. Maute, L. Matuschik, J. Müller and C. Wolf, (eds), *Tradition und Innovation. Prähistorische Archäologie als historische Wissenschaft. Festschrift für Christian Strahm*, Stuttgart, Internationale Archäologie, Studia honoraria 3, 541–50.

Kunst, M., 2001, 'Invasion? Fashion? Social Rank? Consideration concerning the Bell Beaker phenomenon in Copper Age fortifications of the Iberian peninsula', in Nicolis (ed.) 2001b, 81–90.

Kytlicová, O., 1960, 'Eneolitické pohřebiště v Brandýsku', *Památky Archeologické* 51, 422–74.

Ladle, L. and Woodward, A., 2009, *Excavations at Bestwall Quarry, Wareham 1992–2005. Volume 1. The Prehistoric Landscape*, Dorchester, Dorset Archaeological and Natural History Society Monograph 19.

Lambrick, G. and Allen, T., 2004, *Gravelly Guy, Stanton Harcourt, Oxfordshire. The Development of a Prehistoric and Romano-British Community*, Oxford, Thames Valley Landscapes 21.

Langová, J. and Rakovský, I., 1981, 'Objekty kultury zvoncovitých pohárů z Jezeřan-Maršovic, *Archeologické rozhledy* 33, 19–36.

Lanting, J.N., 2004, 'Ross Island: radiocarbon dates and absolute chronology', in O'Brien 2004, 305–16.

Lanting, J.N., 2007–08, 'De NO-Nederlandse/NW-Duitse klokbekergroep. Culturele achtergrond, typologie van het aardewerk, datering, verspreidung en graafritueel', *Palaeohistoria* 49/50, 11–326.

Lanting, J.N. and Waals, J.D., van der, 1972, 'British Beakers as seen from the Continent', *Helinium* 12, 20–46.

Lanting, J.N. and Waals, J.D., van der, 1974, 'Oudheidkundig onderzoek bij Swalmen. I Praehistorie. Opgravingen in de jaren 1936–1938 en 1968–1973', *Oudheikundinge Mededelingen uit het Rijksmusum van Oudheden te Leiden*, Nieuwe Reeks 55, 1–111.

Lanting, J.N. and Waals, J.D., van der, 1976a, 'Beaker culture relations in the Lower Rhine Basin', in Lanting and van der Waals, (eds), 1976, 1–80.

Lanting, J.N. and Waals, J.D., van der (eds), 1976b, *Glockenbecher-symposion Oberried*, Bussum/Haarlem, Fibula-van Dishoeck.

Lanting, J.N., Kooi, B.W., Casparie, W.A. and Hinte, R., van, 1999, 'Bows from the Netherlands', *Journal of the Society of Archer-Antiquaries* 42, 7–10.

Lanting, J.N., Aerts-Bijma, A.T., and Plicht, J., van der, 2001, 'Dating of cremated bones', *Radiocarbon* 43, 249–54.

Larsson, M. and Parker Pearson, M., (eds), 2007, *From Stonehenge to the Baltic. Living with Cultural Diversity in the Third Millennium BC*, Oxford, British Archaeological Report S1692.

Last, J., (ed.), 2007, *Beyond the Grave. New Perspectives on Barrows*, Oxford, Oxbow.

Law, I.A. and Hedges, R.E.M., 1989, 'A semi-automated bone pretreatment system and the pretreatment of older and contaminated samples', *Radiocarbon*, 31, 247–53.

Lawson, A.J., 2007, *Chalkland: an archaeology of Stonehenge and its region*, East Knoyle, Hobnob.

Lécolle, P., 1985, 'The oxygen isotope composition of landsnail shells as a climatic indicator – applications to hydrogeology and paleoclimatology', *Chemical Geology* 58, 157–81.

L'Helgouach, J., 1984, 'Le groupe campaniforme dans le Nord, le Centre et l'Ouest de la France', in Guilaine (ed.) 1984, 59–80.

L'Helgouach, J., 2001, 'Le cadre culturel du campaniforme armoricain', in Nicolis (ed.) 2001b, 289–99.

Leisner, V., 1965, *Die Megalithgräber der Iberischen Halbinsel. Der Westen. Teil 1*, Berlin, Madrider Forschungen 1.3.

Leisner, V., 1998, *Die Megalithgräber der Iberischen Halbinsel. Der Westen. 4. Lieferung*, Berlin, Madrider Forschungen 1.

Leisner, G. and Leisner, V., 1943, *Die Megalithgräber der Iberischen Halbinsel. Erster Teil: der Süden*, Berlin, Römisch-Germanische Forschungen 17.

Leisner, V., Paco, A, do. and Ribeiro, L., 1964, *Grutas Artificiais de São Pedro do Estoril*, Lisbon, Fundação Calouste Gulbenkian.

Leivers, M. and Moore, C., 2008, *Archaeology on the A303 Stonehenge Improvement*, Salisbury, Wessex Archaeology for the Highways Agency.

Lemercier, O., 2004, *Les campaniformes dans le sud-est de la France*, Lattes, Monographies d'Archéologie Méditerranéenne 18.

Leonard, M.A., 1974, 'The inheritance of tarsal coalition and its relationship to spastic flat foot', *Journal of Bone and Joint Surgery* 56B, 520–26.

Lepers, C., 2005, *Arcs et flèches. Historie et savoir-faire*, Liège, Bulletin de la Société Royale Belge d'Études Géologiques et Archéologiques (Les Chercheurs de la Wallonie) numéro hors-série.

Levinson, A.A., Luz, B. and Kolodny, Y., 1987, 'Variations in oxygen isotope compositions of human teeth and urinary stones', *Applied Geochemistry* 2, 367–71.

Lippmann, E. and Müller, D.W., 1981, 'Zwei Gräber der Glockenbecherkultur bei Erfurt-Gispersleben', *Ausgrabungen und Funde* 26, 236–42.

Lomborg, E., 1972, *Die Flintdolche Dänemarks. Studien über Chronologie und Kulturbeziehungen des südskandinavischen Spätneolithikums*, Copenhagen, Nordiske Fortidsminders B1.

Longworth, I.H., 1961, 'The origins and development of the primary series in the Collared Urn tradition in England and Wales', *Proceedings of the Prehistoric Society* 27, 263–306.

Longworth, I.H., 1971, 'The Neolithic pottery', in Wainwright and Longworth 1971, 48–155.

Longworth, I.H., 1979, 'The Neolithic and Bronze Age pottery', in Wainwright 1979, 75–124.

Longworth, I.H., 1981, *Collared Urns of the Bronze Age in Britain and Ireland*, Cambridge, University Press.

Lynch, F., 1970, *Prehistoric Anglesey*, Llangefni, Anglesey Antiquarian Society.

Lynch, F., 2001, 'Axes or skeuomorphic cushion stones; the purpose of certain "blunt" axes', in W.H. Metz, B. L. van Beek and H. Steegstra, (eds), *Patina: Essays presented to Jay Jordan Butler on the occasion of his 80th Birthday*, Groningen, privately published, 399–404.

Makristathis, A., Schwarzmeier, J., Mader, R.M., Varmuza, K., Simonitsch, I., Chavez J.C., Platzer, W., Unterdorfer, H., Scheithauer, R., Derevianko, A. and Seidle, H., 2002, 'Fatty acid composition and preservation of the Tyrolean Iceman and other mummies', *Journal of Lipid Research* 43, 2056–2061.

Mallet, N., 1992, *Le Grand Pressigny: ses relations avec la Civilisation Sâone-Rhône*, Le Grand Pressigny, Centre d'Études et Documentation Pressigniennes/Supplément au Bulletin de la Société des Amis du Musée du Grand Pressigny.

Manby, T.G., 1980, 'Bronze Age settlement in eastern Yorkshire', in J. Barrett and R. Bradley (eds), *Settlement and Society in the Later British Bronze Age*, Oxford, British Archaeological Report 83, 307–70.

Manchester, K., 1983, *The Archaeology of Disease*, Bradford, University Press.

Mansfeld, G., 2005, 'Das frühbronzeitliche Grab von Korinto/Achalgori und seine weitreichenden Beziehungen (Überlegungen zum Phänomen der Hammerkopfnadeln)', *Metalla* 12(1/2), 23–68.

Maran, J., 1998, *Kulturwandel auf dem griechischen Festland und den Kykladen im späten 3. Jahrtausend v. Chr. Studien zu den kulturellen Verhältnissen in Südosteuropa und dem zentralen sowie östlichen Mittelmeerraum in der späten Kupfer- und frühen Bronzezeit*, Bonn, Universitätsforschungen zur prähistorischen Archäologie 53.

Marinis, R.C., de, 1997, 'The eneolithic cemetery of Remedello Sotto (S) and the relative and absolute chronology of the Copper Age in northern Italy', *Notizie Archeologiche Bergomensi* 5, 33–51.

Maryon, H., 1936, 'Excavation of two Bronze Age barrows at Kirkhaugh, Northumberland', *Archaeologia Aeliana* 4th series 13, 207–17.

Mathianssen, T., 1939, 'Bundsø. En Yngre Stenålders Boplats paa Als', *Aarboger for Nordsk Oldkyndighed og Historie* 1, 1–198.

Matthias, W., 1964, 'Ein reich ausgestattetes Grab der Glockenbecherkultur bei Stedten, Kr. Eisleben', *Ausgrabungen und Funde* 9, 19–22.

McKinley, J.I., 1994, *The Anglo-Saxon Cemetery at Spong Hill, North Elmham. Part VIII: the cremations*, Dereham, East Anglian Archaeology 69.

McKinley, J.I., 1997, 'Bronze Age 'barrows' and the funerary rites and rituals of cremation', *Proceedings of the Prehistoric Society* 63, 129–45.

McKinley, J.I., 2004a, 'Compiling a skeletal inventory: cremated human bone', in Brickley and McKinley (eds) 2004, 14–17.

McKinley, J.I., 2004b, 'Compiling a skeletal inventory: disarticulated and co-mingled remains', in Brickley and McKinley (eds) 2004, 13–16.

McKinley, J.I., 2008a, 'The human remains', in R. Mercer and F. Healy, *Hambledon Hill, Dorset, England. Excavation and survey of a Neolithic monument complex and its surrounding landscape*, Swindon, English Heritage Archaeological Report, 477–521.

McKinley, J.I., 2008b, 'Human remains', in C. Ellis and A.B. Powell, *An Iron Age Settlement Outside Battlesbury Hillfort, Warminster, and Sites along the Southern Range Road*, Salisbury, Wessex Archaeology Report 22, 71–83.

Medunová-Benešová, A., 1962, 'Nálezy zvoncovitých pohárů z Předmosti u Přerova', *Sborník Československé společnosti archeologické* 2, 235–45.

Medunová, A. and Ondráček, J., 1969, 'Birituální pohřebiště lidu s kulturou se zvoncovitých pohárů u Lechovic, Okr. Znojmo', *Archeologické rozhledy* 21, 437–45.

Megaw, J.V.S. and Simpson, D.D.A., 1979, *Introduction to British Prehistory*, Leicester, University Press.

Meixner, D. and Weinig, J., 2003, 'Ein Friedhof der Glockenbecherkultur bei Eitensheim', *Das Archäologische Jahr in Bayern 2002*, 28–30.

Meller, H., (ed.), *Der geschmiedete Himmel. Die weite Welt im Herzen Europas vor 3600 Jahren*, Halle/Salle, Landesamt für Denkmalpflege und Archäologie Sachsen-Anhalt – Landesmuseum für Vorgeschichte Halle/Saale.

Messing, S.D., 1957, 'Further comments on resin-coated pottery: Ethiopia', *American Anthropologist* 59, 134–5.

Millar I.L., 1990, *Caledonian and pre-Caledonian events in Moine rocks of the Cluanie area, Inverness-shire*, London, University of London, unpublished thesis.

Mille, B. and Bouquet, L., 2004, 'Le métal au 3e millénaire avant notre ère dans le Centre-Nord de la France', in M. Vander Linden and L. Salanova (eds), *Le troisième millénaire dans le nord de la France et en Belgique*, Lille, Anthropologica et Præhistorica 115/Mémoire de la Société préhistorique française 35, 197–215.

Molleson, T.I., 1993, 'The human remains', in D.E. Farwell and T.I. Molleson, *Excavations at Poundbury 1966–80. Volume 2: the cemeteries*, Dorchester, Dorset Natural History and Archaeological Society Monograph 11, 142–214.

Montelius, O., 1900, *Die Chronologie der ältesten Bronzezeit in Nord-Deutschland und Skandinavien*, Brunswick, Archiv für Anthropologie, Völkerforschung und kolonialen Kulturwandel 25–26.

Montelius, O., 1908, 'The chronology of the British Bronze Age', *Archaeologia* 61, 97–162.

Montgomery, J., 2002, *Lead and Strontium Isotope Compositions of Human Dental Tissues as an Indicator of Ancient Exposure and Population Dynamics*, Bradford, University of Bradford, unpublished thesis.

Moody, G., 2008, *The Isle of Thanet from Prehistory to the Norman Conquest*, Stroud, Tempus.

Mook, W.G., 1986, 'Business Meeting: recommendations/resolutions adopted by the twelfth international radiocarbon conference', *Radiocarbon* 28, 799.

Moore, D.T. and Oddy, W.A., 1985, 'Touchstones: some aspects of their nomenclature, petrography and provenance', *Journal of Archaeological Science* 12, 59–80.

Moore, C.N. and Rowlands, M., 1972, *Bronze Age Metalwork in Salisbury Museum*, Salisbury, Salisbury and South Wiltshire Museum Occasional Publication.

Morteani, G. and Northover, J.P., (eds), 1995, *Prehistoric Gold in Europe. Mines, Metallurgy and Manufacture*, Dordrecht, Kluwer.

Mottram, H.R., Dudd, S N., Lawrence, G.J. Stott, A.W. and Evershed R.P., 1999, 'New chromatographic, mass spectrometric and stable isotope approaches to the classification of degraded animal fats preserved in archaeological pottery', *Journal of Chromatography* A 833, 209–21.

Moucha, V., 1989, 'Böhmen am Ausklang des Äneolithikums und am Anfang der Bronzezeit', in Buchvaldek and Pleslová-Štiková (eds), 1989, 213–18.

Mount, C., 1995, 'New research on Irish Early Bronze Age cemeteries', in Waddell and Shee Twohig (eds) 1995, 97–112.

Müller, A., 2001, 'Gender differentiation in burial rites and grave-goods in the eastern or Bohemian-Moravian group of the Bell Beaker culture', in Nicolis (ed.) 2001b, 589–99.

Müller, D., 1987, 'Gräber von Metallwerkern aus der Glockenbecherkultur des Mittelelbe-Saale-Gebietes', *Ausgrabungen und Funde* 32, 175–9.

Müller, J. and Willingen, S., van, 2001, 'New radiocarbon evidence for European Bell Beakers and the consequences for the diffusion of the Bell Beaker phenomenon', in Nicolis (ed.) 2001b, 59–80.

Murray, C., 2004, 'The Barrysbrook bowstave' PAST 46, 3–4.

Muška, J., 1981, 'The settlement and cemetery sites of the Bell Beaker culture at Radovesice by Bílana', in J. Herla (ed.), *Archeological News in the Czech Socialist Republic*, Prague and Brno, Institute of Archaeology, Czechoslovak Academy of Sciences, 51.

Musty, J., 1963, 'Beaker finds from south Wiltshire', *Wiltshire Archaeology and Natural History Magazine* 58, 414–16.

Nafplioti, A., 2008, '"Mycenaean" political domination of Knossos following the Late Minoan IB destructions on Crete: negative evidence from strontium isotope ratio analysis (Sr-87/Sr-86)', *Journal of Archaeological Science* 35, 2307–17.

Needham, S., 1979, 'The extent of foreign influence on Early Bronze Age axe development in southern Britain', in Ryan (ed.) 1979, 265–93.

Needham, S.P., 1999a, 'Radley and the development of early metalwork in Britain', in Barclay and Halpin 1999, 49, 56, 63, 102, 138, 143, 149, 153, 155, 160, 165, 186–192.

Needham, S.P., 1999b, 'Wing-headed pin', in Barclay and Halpin 1999, 236.

Needham, S.P., 2001, 'Stogursey (1), Somerset: Bronze Age gold "basket ornament"', *Treasure Annual Report 1998–9*, London, Department of Culture, Media and Sport, 10.

Needham, S., 2002, 'Analytical implications for Beaker metallurgy in north-west Europe', in Bartelheim *et al.* (eds) 2002, 99–133.

Needham, S.P., 2004, 'Migdale-Marnoch: sunburst of Scottish metallurgy', in Shepherd and Barclay (eds) 2004, 217–45.

Needham, S., 2005, 'Transforming Beaker culture in north-west Europe: processes of fusion and fission', *Proceedings of the Prehistoric Society* 71, 171–217.

Needham, S., 2007, 'Isotopic aliens: Beaker movement and cultural transmissions' in Larsson and Parker Pearson (eds) 2007, 41–6.

Needham, S., 2008a, Gilmorton. Leicestershire: two Copper Age gold basket ornaments (2006 T154)', in Barton and Hitchcock (eds), 2008, 17–18.

Needham, S., 2008b, Calbourne, Isle of Wight: Early Bronze Age gold basket ornament (2005 T113)', in Barton and Hitchcock (eds), 2008, 17.

Needham, S., forthcoming, 'Magnetic monuments meet mysterious metals: the British Chalcolithic, clash of cultures or meeting of minds, in Allen *et al.* (eds), forthcoming.

Needham, S. and Woodward, A., 2008, 'The Clandon Barrow finery: a synopsis of success in an Early Bronze Age World', *Proceedings of the Prehistoric Society* 74, 1–52.

Needham, S.P., Lawson, A.J. and Green, H.S., 1985, *Early Bronze Age Hoards, British Bronze Age Metalwork, Associated Finds Series, A1–6*, London, British Museum.

Negrel, P. and Petelet, E., 2005, 'Strontium isotopes as tracers of groundwater-induced floods: the Somme case study (France)', *Journal of Hydrology* 305, 99–119.

Negrel, P., Petelet-Giraude, E., Barbier, J. and Gautier, E., 2003, 'Surface water – groundwater interactions in an alluvial plain: chemical and isotopic systematics', *Journal of Hydrology* 277, 248–67.

Nehlich, O., Montgomery, J., Evans, J., Richards, M., Dresely, V. and Alt, K., 2007, 'Biochemische Analyses Stabiler Isotope an prähistorischen Skelettfunden aus Westerhausen, Ldkr. Harz', *Jahresschrift für Mitteldeutsche Vorgeschichte* 91, 1–21.

Neugebauer, J.-W., 1992, 'Quellen zur Chronologie der späten Schnurkermik im Unteren Traisental, Niederösterreich', in Buchvaldek and Strahm (eds) 1992, 143–55.

Neugebauer, J,-W., 1994, 'Zum Grabraub in der Frühbronzezeit Niederösterreichs', in K. Schmotz (ed.), *Vorträge des 12. Niederbayerischen Archäologentages*, Buch am Erlbach, Marie L. Leidorf, 109–48.

Neugebauer, J.-W. and Neugebauer-Maresch, C., 2001, 'Bell Beaker culture in Austria', in Nicolis (ed.) 2001b, 429–37.

Newcomer, M.H. and Karlin, C., 1987, 'Flint chips from Pincevent', in G. de G. Sieveking and M.H. Newcomer (eds), *The Human Uses of Flint and Chert*, Cambridge, University Press, 33–6.

Nicolis F., 2001a, 'Some observations on the cultural setting of the Bell Beakers of northern Italy', in Nicolis (ed.) 2001b, 207–27.

Nicolis F., (ed.), 2001b, *Bell Beakers Today. Pottery, people, culture, symbols in prehistoric Europe*, Trento, Provincia Autonoma di Trento, Servizio Beni Culturali, Ufficio beni Archeologici.

Nicolis F., 2002, 'Gli ornamenti del popolo del "bicchiere campaniforme"', in L. Galioto, J. Heiligmann and G. Wesselkamp (eds), *AttraVerso le Alpi – uomini, vie escambi nell'antichità*, Stuttgart, Archäologisches Landesmuseum Baden-Württemberg, 111–17.

Northover, J.P., 1995, 'Bronze Age gold in Britain', in Morteani and Northover (eds) 1995, 515–32.

Nugent, I.M., Ivory, J.P. and Cross, A.C., 1995, *Key Topics in Orthopaedic Surgery*, London, Taylor and Francis.

O'Brien, W., 1995, 'Ross Island and the Origins of Irish-British Metallurgy', in Waddell and Shee Twohig (eds) 1995, 38–48.

O'Brien, W., 2001, 'New light on Beaker metallurgy in Ireland', in Nicolis (ed.) 2001b, 561–76.

O'Brien, W., 2004, *Ross Island: Mining, Metal and Society in Early Ireland*, Galway, Bronze Age Studies 6.

O'Brien, W., 2007, 'Miners and farmers: local settlement contexts for Bronze Age mining', in Burgess *et al.* (eds) 2007, 20–30.

O'Conner, P.J., Kennan, P.J. and Aftalion, M., 1988, 'New Rb-Sr and U-Pb ages for the Carnsore Granite and their bearing on the antiquity of the Rosslare Complex, southeastern Ireland, *Geological Magazine* 125, 25–9.

O'Connor, B., 2004, 'The earliest Scottish metalwork since Coles', in Shepherd and Barclay (eds) 2004, 205–16.

O'Connor, T., 1984, 'The Beaker-Age burial', 13–17, in Evans 1984, 13–17.

O'Kelly, M.J. and Shell, C., 1979, 'Stone objects and a Bronze axe from Newgrange, Co. Meath', in Ryan (ed.) 1979, 127–44.

O'Kelly, M.J., Cleary, R.M. and Lehane, D., 1983, *Newgrange, Co. Meath, Ireland: the late Neolithic–Beaker period settlement*, Oxford, British Archaeological Report S190.

O'Neil, J.R., Roe, L.J., Reinhard, E. and Blake, R.E., 1994, 'A rapid and precise method of oxygen isotope analysis of biogenic phosphate', *Israel Journal of Life Science* 43, 203–12.

Ogden, A.R., 2005, *Identifying and Scoring Periodontal Disease in Skeletal Material*, Bradford, University of Bradford Biological Anthropology Research Centre, unpublished manuscript.

Ohnuma, K. and Bergman, C.A., 1982, 'Experimental studies in the determination of flaking mode' *Bulletin of the Institute of Archaeology University of London* 19, 161–70.

Ondráček, J. and Šebela, L., 1985, *Pohřebiště nitranské skupiny v Holešově*, Kroměříž, Studie muzea Kroměřížska '85.

Orton, C., Tyers, P. and Vince, A., 1993, *Pottery in Archaeology*, Cambridge, University Press.

Othenin-Girard, B., 1997, *Le Campaniforme d'Alle, Noir Bois (Jura Suisse)*, Porrentruy, Cahiers Archéologie Jurasienne 7.

Ottaway, B., 1992, 'Copper artifacts of the Corded Ware complex', in Buchvaldek and Strahm (eds) 1992, 283–9.

Parker Pearson, M., 2006, 'The Beaker People project: mobility and diet in the British Early Bronze Age', *The Archaeologist* 61, 14–15.

Parker Pearson, M., 2007, 'The Stonehenge Riverside Project: excavations at the east entrance of Durrington Walls', in Larsson and Parker Pearson (eds) 2007, 125–44.

Parker Pearson, M., Cleal, R., Marshall, P., Needham, S., Pollard, J., Richards, C., Ruggles, C., Sheridan, A., Thomas, J., Tilley, C., Welham, K., Chamberlain, A., Chenery, C., Evans, J., Knüsel, C., Linford, N., Martin, L., Montgomery, J., Payne, A. and Richards, M., 2007, 'The Age of Stonehenge', *Antiquity* 81, 617–309.

Parker Pearson, M., Chamberlain, A., Jay, M., Marshall, P., Pollard, J., Richards, C., Thomas, J., Tilley, C. and Welham, K., 2009, 'Who was buried at Stonehenge?', *Antiquity* 83, 23–39.

Patrick, P. and Waldron, T., 2003, 'Congenital absence of the patellae in an Anglo-Saxon skeleton' *International Journal of Osteoarchaeology* 13, 147–9.

Patton, M., 1993, *Statements in Stone. Monuments and Society in Neolithic Brittany*, London, Routledge.

Pelle, E. and Mammone, T., 2005, *Topical Regulation of Triglyceride Metabolism, United States Patent Application Publication No. US*

2005/0244359 A1, Arlington, United States Patent and Trademark Office.

Pendleton, C.F., 1999, *Bronze Age Metalwork in Northern East Anglia. A Study of its Distribution and Interpretation*, Oxford, British Archaeological Report 279.

Perea, A., 1991, *Orfebrería Prerromana. Arqueología del oro*, Madrid, Consejeria de Cultura.

Pernicka, R.M., 1961, 'Eine unikate Grabanlage der Glockenbecherkultur bei Prosiměřice, Südwest-Mähren', *Sborník Prací Filozofické Fakulty Brněnské Univerzity* 10, E–6, 9–54.

Pescheck, C., 1958, *Katalog Würzberg I. Die Funde von der Steinzeit bis zur Urnenfelderzeit im Mainfränkischen Museum*, Kallmünz, Materialhefte zur Bayerischen Vorgeschichte 12.

Petersen, F., 1972, 'Traditions of multiple burial in Later Neolithic and Early Bronze Age England', *Archaeological Journal* 129, 22–55.

Pétrequin P. and Jeunesse, C., (eds), 1995, *La Hache de Pierre: Carrières vosgiennes et échanges de lames polies pendant le Néolithique (5400–2100 av .J.-C.)*, Paris, Errance.

Pétrequin, P., Chastel, J., Giligny, F., Pétrequin, A.-M. and Saintot, S., 1988, 'Réinterprétation de la Civilization Saône-Rhône. Une approche des tendances culturelles du Néolithique final', *Gallia Prehistoire* 30, 1–89.

Píč, J.L., 1910, 'Nové hroby se zvoncovitými nádobami', *Památky Archeologické* 24, 1–8.

Piggott, S., 1938, 'The Early Bronze Age in Wessex', *Proceedings of the Prehistoric Society* 4, 52–106.

Piggott, S., 1962, *The West Kennet Long Barrow. Excavations 1955–56*, London, Ministry of Works Archaeological Report 4.

Piggott, S., 1963, 'Abercromby and after: the Beaker cultures of Britain re-examined', in I. Ll. Foster and L. Alcock (eds), *Culture and Environment. Essays in Honour of Sir Cyril Fox*, London, Routledge and Kegan Paul, 53–91.

Piggott, S., 1971, 'Beaker bows: a suggestion', *Proceedings of the Prehistoric Society* 37(2), 80–94.

Piggott, S., 1973, 'The later Neolithic: single-graves and the first metallurgy *c.* 2000–*c.* 1500 B.C.', in E. Crittall (ed.), *Victoria History of the Counties of England. History of Wiltshire I, Part 2*, London, University of London Institute of Historical Research, 333–51.

Piggott, S. and Piggott, C.M., 1944, 'Excavations of barrows on Crichel and Launceston Downs, Dorset', *Archaeologia* 90, 47–80.

Piguet, M. and Besse, M., 2009, 'Chronology and Bell Beaker common ware', *Radiocarbon* 51, 817–30.

Piguet, M., Desideri, J., Furestier, R., Cattin, F. and Besse, M., 2007, 'Population et histoire des peuplements campaniformes: chronologie céramique et anthropologie biologique', in M.

Besse (ed.), *Sociétés néolithiques. Des faits archéologiques aux fonctionnements socio-économiques*, Lausanne, Cahiers d'archéologie romande 108, 249–78.

Pitts, M.W., 1978, 'On the shape of waste flakes as an index of technological change in lithic industries', *Journal of Archaeological Science* 5, 17–37.

Pitts, M., 2001, *Hengeworld* (rev. edn), London, Arrow.

Pitts, M., 2009, 'A year at Stonehenge', *Antiquity* 83, 184–94.

Pollard, J. and Cleal, R.M.J., 2004, 'Dating Avebury', in Cleal and Pollard (eds), 2004, 120–9.

Pollard, J. and Robinson, D., 2007, 'A return to Woodhenge: the results and implications of the 2006 excavations', in Larsson and Parker Pearson (eds) 2007, 159–68.

Potts, P.J., Webb, P.C., and Williams-Thorpe, O., 1997a, 'Investigation of a correction procedure for surface irregularity effects based on scatter peak intensities in the field analysis of geological and archaeological rock samples by portable X-ray fluorescence spectrometry', *Journal of Analytical Atomic Spectrometry* 12, 769–76.

Potts, P.J., Williams-Thorpe, O. and Webb, P.C., 1997b, 'The bulk analysis of silicate rocks by portable X-ray fluorescence: the effects of sample mineralogy in relation to the size of the excited volume', *Geostandards Newsletter: Journal of Geostandards and Geoanalysis*, 21, 29–41.

Prehistoric Ceramics Research Group 1995, *The Study of Later Prehistoric Pottery: general policies and guidelines for analysis and publication*, Salisbury, Prehistoric Ceramics Research Group Occasional Papers 1 & 2.

Price, T.D., Grupe, G. and Schröter, P., 1998, 'Migration in the Bell Beaker period of central Europe', *Antiquity* 72, 405–11.

Price, T.D., Wahl, J. and Bentley, R.A., 2006, 'Isotopic evidence for mobility and group organisation among Neolithic farmers at Talheim, Germany, 5000 BC', *European Journal of Archaeology* 9, 259–84.

Price, T.D., Knipper, G., Grupe, G. and Smrcka, V., 2004, 'Strontium isotopes and prehistoric migration: the Bell Beaker period in central Europe', *European Journal of Archaeology* 7, 9–40.

Price, T.D., Johnson, C.M., Ezzo, J.A., Ericson, J. and Burton, J.H., 1994, 'Residential mobility in the prehistoric Southwest United States – a preliminary study using strontium isotope analysis', *Journal of Archaeological Science* 21, 315–30.

Primas, M., 1995, 'Gold and silver during the 3rd mill. cal. BC', in Morteani and Northover (eds), 1995, 77–93.

Prior, S., 2000, 'Recreating the Neolithic Meare Heath Bow – reassessing the past through experimental archaeology', *Journal of the Society of Archer-Antiquaries* 43, 44–7.

Pustovalov, S.Z., 1994, 'Economy and social organisation of northern Pontic steppe-Forest-steppe pastoral populations:

2750–2000 BC (catacomb culture), in *Nomadism and Pastoralism in the Circle of Baltic-Pontic Early Agrarian Cultures 5000–1650 BC, Baltic-Pontic Studies,* 286–134.

Rahtz, P.A., 1962, 'Neolithic and Beaker Sites at Downton, near Salisbury, Wiltshire', *Wiltshire Archaeological and Natural History Magazine* 58, 116–42.

Rahtz, P.A. and Greenfield, E., 1977, *Excavations at Chew Valley Lake, Somerset,* London, Department of the Environment Archeological Report 8.

Randsborg, K., 1984, 'A Bronze Age grave on Funen containing a metal workers tools', *Acta Archaeologia* 55 (1986), 185–9.

Randsborg, K., 1998, 'Plundred Bronze Age graves. Archaeological and social implications', *Acta Archaeologia* 69, 113–38.

Rausing, G., 1997, *The Bow. Some Notes on its Origins and Development,* Manchester, Simon Archery Foundation.

Raven, A.M., Bergen, P.F. van, Stott, A.W., Dudd, S.N. and Evershed R.P., 1997, 'Formation of long-chain ketones in archaeological pottery vessels by pyrolysis of acyl acids', *Journal of Analytical and Applied Pyrolysis* 40/41, 267–85.

Raymond, R., 1990, 'Prehistoric pottery', in Richards 1990, 188–91.

Rawlings, M.N. and Fitzpatrick, A.P., 1996, 'Prehistoric features and a Romano-British settlement at Butterfield Down, Amesbury, Wiltshire', *Wiltshire Archaeological and Natural History Magazine* 89, 1–43.

Regan, M.H., Case, D.T. and Brundige, J.C., 1999, 'Articular surface defects in the third metatarsal and third cuneiform: nonosseous tarsal coalition', *American Journal of Physical Anthropology* 109, 53–65.

Reid, C., 1903, *The Geology of the Country Around Salisbury,* London, Memoirs of the Geological Survey of England and Wales.

Reimer, P.J., Baillie, M.G.L., Bard, E., Bayliss, A., Beck, J.W., Bertrand, C., Blackwell, P.G., Buck, C.E., Burr, G., Cutler, K.B., Damon, P.E., Edwards, R.L., Fairbanks, R.G., Friedrich, M., Guilderson, T.P., Hughen, K.A., Kromer, B., McCormac, F.G., Manning, S., Bronk Ramsey, C., Reimer, R.W., Remmele, S., Southon, J.R., Stuiver, M., Talamo, S., Taylor, F.W., van der Plicht, J. and Weyhenmeyer, C.E., 2004, 'IntCal04 terrestrial radiocarbon age calibration, 0–26 Cal Kyr BP', *Radiocarbon* 46,1029–58.

Rice, P.M., 1987, *Pottery Analysis. A Sourcebook,* Chicago, University Press.

Richards, J.C., 1990, *The Stonehenge Environs Project,* London, English Heritage Archaeology Report 16.

Richards, J., 2007, *Stonehenge. The Story so Far,* Swindon, English Heritage.

Rieder, K.H., 1987, 'Ein weiterer Bestattungsplatz der Glockenbecherkultur aus Oberstimm', *Das Archäologische Jahr in Bayern 1986,* 46–50.

Riley, D.N., 1957, 'Neolithic and Bronze Age Pottery from Risby Warren and other occupation sites in North Lincolnshire', *Proceedings of the Prehistoric Society* 23, 40–56.

Riley, D.N., 1982, 'Radley 15, a late Beaker ring-ditch', in Case and Whittle (eds) 1982, 76–80.

Ritchie, J.N., 1970, 'Beaker pottery in south-west Scotland', *Transactions of the Dumfriesshire and Galloway Natural History and Antiquarian Society* 47, 123–36.

Ritchie, J.N.G. and Crawford, J., 1978, 'Recent work on Coll and Skye: (i) Excavations at Sorisdale and Killunaig, Coll', *Proceedings of the Society of Antiquaries of Scotland* 109, 75–84.

Roberts, B.W., 2009a, 'Production networks and consumer choice in the earliest metal of western Europe', *Journal of World Prehistory* 22, 461–81.

Roberts, B.W., 2009b, 'Origins, transmissions and traditions: analysing early metal in western Europe', in Kienlin and Roberts (eds) 2009, 129–41.

Roberts, B.W., Thornton, C.P. and Pigott, V.C., 2009, 'Development of metallurgy in Eurasia', *Antiquity* 83, 1012–22.

Roberts, C. and Cox, M., 2003, *Health and Disease in Britain from Prehistory to the Present Day,* Stroud, Sutton.

Roberts, C. and Manchester K., 1997, *The Archaeology of Disease,* Stroud, Sutton.

Roberts, I., (ed.), 2005, *Ferrybridge Henge. The ritual landscape,* Leeds, Yorkshire Archaeology 10.

Rodríguez Casal, A.A., 2001, 'The Galician Maritime Beaker complex in the cultural framework of the Copper Age of western Europe', in Nicolis (ed.) 2001b, 125–37.

Rose, F., 2011, in Woodward and Hunter 2011, Chapters 9, 10 and catalogue.

Roe, F. and Woodward, A., 2009, 'Bits and Pieces: Early Bronze Age stone bracers from Ireland', in M. Edmonds and V. Davis (eds), *Stone Tools in Analytical and Cultural Perspective, Current Research:* Internet Archaeology 26, http://intarch.ac.uk/journal/issue26/index.html.

Rogers, J. and Waldron, T., 1995, *A Field Guide to Joint Disease in Archaeology,* Chichester, Wiley.

Rohl, B. and Needham, S.P., 1998, *The Circulation of Metal in the British Bronze Age: the application of lead isotope analysis,* London, British Museum Occasional Paper 102.

Rojo-Guerra, M.Á., Garrido-Pena, R., Garciá-Martínez-de-Lagrán, Í., Juan-Tresseras, J. and Matamala, J.C., 2006, 'Beer and Bell Beakers: drinking rituals in Copper Age inner Iberia', *Proceedings of the Prehistoric Society* 72, 243–65.

Roudil, J.-L., 1977, 'Les épingles en os du sud-est de la France', *Bulletin de la Société préhistorique française* 74, 237–42.

Roussot-Larroque, J., 2005, 'Première métallurgie du sud-ouest atlantique de la France', in Ambert and Vaquer (eds) 2005, 159–74.

Rowlands, M.J., 1971, 'The archaeological interpretation of prehistoric metalworking', *World Archaeology* 3, 210–24.

Royal Commission on Historical Monuments, 1970, *An Inventory of Historical Monuments in the County of Dorset. Volume II. South-East*, London, Royal Commission on Historical Monuments.

Rozanski, K., 1995, 'Climatic control of stable isotopes in precipitation as a basis for palaeoclimatic reconstruction', in B. Frenzl, B. Stauffer and M.M. Weiss (eds), *Problems of Stable Isotopes in Tree Rings, Lake Sediments and Peat Bogs as Climatic Evidence for the Holocene*, Stuttgart, Palaoklima-forschung–Palaeoclimate Research 15, 171–86.

Russel, A.D., 1990, 'Two Beaker burials from Chilbolton, Hampshire', *Proceedings of the Prehistoric Society* 56, 153–72.

Růžičková, R., 2008, *Lukovité závěsky kultury zvoncovitých pohárů ve střední Evropě*, Brno, University of Brno, unpublished dissertation: http://is.muni.cz/th/110092/ff_b/BC-Luko-vite_zavesky.pdf

Ryan, M., (ed.), 1979, *The Origins of Metallurgy in Atlantic Europe*, Dublin, Stationary Office.

Rye, O.S., 1981, *Pottery Technology. Principles and Reconstruction*, Washington, Taraxacum.

Rye, O.S., 1988, *Pottery Technology. Principles and Reconstruction*, reprint, Washington, Taraxacum.

Sakamoto, K., Munechika, H., Ishikawa, S. and Fujimaki, E., 1999, 'A case report of congenital absence of the patella analyzed with magnetic resonance imaging', *Journal of Musculoskeletal Research* 3, 239–44.

Salanova, L., 1998a, 'Le statut des assemblages, campaniformes en contexte funéraire: la notion de "bien de prestige"', *Bulletin de la Société préhistorique française* 95, 315–26.

Salanova, L., 1998b, 'A long way to go… The Bell Beaker chronology in France', in Benz and van Willingen (eds) 1998, 1–13.

Salanova, L., 2000, *La question du Campaniforme en France et dans les Iles anglo-normandes: productions, chronologie et rôles d'un standard céramique*, Paris, Société préhistorique française et Comité des travaux historiques et scientifiques.

Salanova, L., 2001, 'Technological, ideological or economic European union? The variability of Bell Beaker decoration', in Nicolis (ed.) 2001b, 91–102.

Salanova, L., 2002, 'Fabrication et circulation des céramiques campaniformes', in J. Guilaine (ed.), *Matériaux, productions, circulations du Néolithique à l'Age du Bronze*, Paris, Errance, 151–68.

Salanova, L., 2003a, 'Heads north: analyses of Bell Beaker graves in western Europe', *Journal of Iberian Archaeology* 5, 163–9.

Salanova, L., 2003b, 'Les sépultures mégalithiques et le phénoméne campaniforme' in V.S. Gonçalves (ed.), *Muita Gente, Poucas Antas? Origiens, espaços e contextos do megalitismo*, Lisbon, Instituto Portguês de Arqueologia, 385–93.

Salanova, L., 2004a, 'The frontiers inside the western Bell Beaker block', in Czebreszuk (ed.) 2004b, 63–76.

Salanova, L., 2004b, 'Le rôle de la façade antlantique dans la genèse du Campaniforme en Europe', *Bulletin de la Société préhistorique française* 101, 223–6.

Salanova, L., 2007, 'Les sépulture campaniformes: lecture sociale', in Guilaine (ed.) 2007, 213–28.

Salanova, L. and Heyd, V., 2007, 'Du collectif à l'individu, de la région à l'Europe: le IIIe millénaire avant J.-C., entre le Bassin parisien et la vallée rhénane', in F. Le Brun-Ricalens, F. Valotteau and A. Hauzeur (eds), *Relations interrégionales au Néolithique entre Bassin parisien et Bassin rhénan*, Luxembourg, Archaeologia Mosellana 469–93.

Sangmeister, E., 1951, *Die Jungsteinzeit im nordmainischen Hessen 3. Die Glockenbecherkultur und die Becherkulturen*, Melsungen, Schriften zur Urgeschichte 3.1.

Sangmeister, E., 1964a, 'Die schmalen "Armschutzplatten"', in R. von Uslar and K.J. Narr (eds), *Studien aus Alteuropa 1, Festschrift für Kurt Tackenburg. Kurt Tackenburg zum 65. Geburtstag am 30 Juni 1964*, Cologne, Bonner Jahrbucher Beiheft 10, 93–122.

Sangmeister, E., 1964b, 'Die Glockenbecher in Oberrheintal', *Jahrbuch des Römisch-Germanischen Zentralmusuems Mainz* 11, 81–114.

Sangmeister, E., 1974, 'Zwei Neufunde der Glockenbecherkultur in Baden-Württemberg. Ein Beitrag zur Klassifierung der Armschutzplatten in Mitteleuropa', *Fundberichte aus Baden-Württemberg* 1, 103–56.

Sangmeister, E., 1984, 'Die "Glockenbecherkultur" in S-W Deutschland', in Guilaine (ed.) 1984, 81–97.

Sarauw, T., 2007, 'Male symbols or warrior identities? The "archery burials" of the Danish Bell Beaker Culture', *Journal of Anthropological Archaeology* 26, 65–87.

Sarauw, T., 2009, 'Danish Bell Beaker pottery and flint daggers – the display of social identities?', *European Journal of Archaeology* 11, 23–47.

Savory, H.N., 1972, 'Copper Age cists and cist-cairns in Wales: with specific reference to Newton, Swansea, and other "multiple-cist" cairns', in F. Lynch and C. Burgess (eds), *Prehistoric Man in Wales and the West. Essays in honour of Lily F. Chitty*, Bath, Adams and Dart, 117–39.

Savory, H.N., 1977, 'The prehistoric finds', in P. Charlton, J. Roberts and V. Vale, *Llantrithyd: a ringwork in South Glamorgan*, Cardiff, Cardiff Archaeological Society, 57–60.

Scheuer, L. and Black, S., 2000, *Developmental Juvenile Osteology*, London, Academic Press.

Schmidt-Thielbeer, E., 1955, 'Ein Friedhof der frühen Bronzezeit bei Nohra, Kr. Nordhausen', *Jahresschrift für Mitteldeutsche Vorgeschichte Halle* 39, 93–114.

Schmotz, K., 1991, 'Eine Handwerkerbestattung des Endneolithikums aus Künzing, Lkr. Deggendorf, Ndb,' in J. Prammer (ed.), *Ausgrabungen und Funde in Altbayern 1989–1991*, Straubing, Katalog des Gäubodenmusuems Straubing 18, 35–9.

Schmotz, K., 1992, 'Ein Gräbergruppe der Glockenbecherkultur von Künzing, Lkr. Deggendorf,' in K. Schmotz and F. Schopper (eds), *Vorträge des 10 Niederbayerischen Archäologentages, Buch am Erlbach*, Buch am Erlbach, Ebner, 41–68.

Schmotz, K., 1994, *Eine Gräbergruppe der Glockenbecherkultur von Osterhofen-Altenmarkt*, Deggendorf, Archäologische Denkmäler im Landkreis Deggendorf 9.

Schröter, P. and Wamser P., 1980, 'Eine Etagen-Doppelbestattung der Glockenbecherkultur von Tückelhausen, Stadt Ochsenfurt/ Unterfranken', *Fundberichte aus Hessen* 19/20, 287–325.

Schulting, R.J., Sheridan, A., Clarke, S.R. and Bronk Ramsey, C., 2008, 'Largantea and the dating of Irish wedge tombs', *Journal of Irish Archaeology* 17, 1–17.

Schutowski, H., Wormouth, M. and Hansen, B., 2000, 'Residential mobility of mediaeval Black Forest miners – a strontium isotope study', *Abstract, 12th Congress of the European Anthropological Association*, Cambridge, European Anthropological Association.

Schweissing, M.M. and Grupe, G., 2003, 'Stable strontium isotopes in human teeth and bone: a key to migration events of the late Roman period in Bavaria', *Journal of Archaeological Science* 30, 1373–83.

Scott, E.M., 2003, 'The third international radiocarbon intercomparison (TIRI) and the fourth international radiocarbon intercomparison (FIRI) 1990–2002: results, analyses, and conclusions', *Radiocarbon* 45, 135–408.

Scourse, J.D., 1997, 'Transport of the Stonehenge bluestones: testing the glacial hypothesis', in Cunliffe and Renfrew (eds) 1997, 271–314.

Šebela, L., 1999, *The Corded Ware Culture in Moravia and in the Adjacent part of Silesia*, Brno, Fontes Archaeologiae Moravicae 23.

Shand, P., Darbyshire, D.P.F., Gooddy, D.C., Darling, W.G., Neal, C., Haria, A.H. and Dixon, A.J., 2001, 'The application of Sr isotopes to catchment studies: the Plynlimon upland catchment of central Wales', in R. Cidu (ed.), *Water-Rock Interaction*, Lisse, Swets ans Zeitlinger, 1577–80.

Shell, C.A., 2000, 'Metalworker or shaman: Early Bronze Age Upton Lovell G2a burial', *Antiquity* 74, 271–2.

Shennan, S.J., 1976, 'Bell Beakers and their context in central Europe', in Lanting and van der Waals (eds) 1976b, 231–40.

Shepherd, I.A.G., 1986, *Powerful Pots: Beakers in north-east prehistory*, Aberdeen, Anthropological Museum, University of Aberdeen.

Shepherd, I.A.G. and Barclay, G.J., (eds), 2004, *Scotland in Ancient Europe: the Neolithic and Early Bronze Age of Scotland in their European context*, Edinburgh, Society of Antiquaries of Scotland.

Sheridan, A., 2007, 'Scottish Beaker dates: the good, the bad, and the ugly', in Larsson and Parker Pearson (eds), 2007, 91–123.

Sheridan, A., 2008a, 'Upper Largie and Dutch-Scottish connections during the Beaker period', in H. Fokkens, B.J. Coles, A.L. van Gijn, J. P. Kleijne, H.H. Ponjee and C.G. Slappendel, (eds), *Between Foraging and Farming. An extended broad spectrum of papers presented to Leendert Louwe Kooijmans*, Leiden, Analecta Praehistorica Leidensia 40, 247–60.

Sheridan, A., 2008b, 'Towards a fuller, more nuanced narrative of Chalcolithic and Early Bronze Age Britain 2500–1500 BC', Bronze Age Review 1, 57–78: http://www.british museum.org/pdf/BAR1_2008_6_Sheridan_c.pdf

Sheridan, J.A. and Davis, M., 1998, 'The Welsh "jet set" in prehistory: a case of keeping up with the Joneses?', in A. Gibson and D. Simpson (eds), *Prehistoric Ritual and Religion*, Stroud, Sutton, 148–62.

Sheridan, J.A. and Davis, M., 2002, 'Investigating jet and jet-like artefacts from prehistoric Scotland: the National Museums of Scotland project', *Antiquity* 76, 812–25.

Sherratt, A., 1986, 'The Radley "earrings" revised', *Oxford Journal of Archaeology* 5, 61–6.

Sherratt, A.G., 1987a, 'Cups that cheered', in W. Waldren and R. Kennard, (eds), *Bell Beakers of the Western Mediterranean*, Oxford, British Archaeological Report S331, 81–114.

Sherratt, A., 1987b, '"Earrings" again', *Oxford Journal of Archaeology* 6, 119.

Sherratt, A., 1996, 'Why Wessex? The Avon route and river transport in later British prehistory', *Oxford Journal of Archaeology* 15, 211–34.

Shortt, H. de, S., 1946, 'Bronze Age beakers from Larkhill and Bulford', *Wiltshire Archaeological and Natural History Magazine* 51, 381–3.

Simpson, D.D.A., 1968, Food Vessels: associations and chronology', in J.M. Coles and D.D.A. Simpson (eds), *Studies in Ancient Europe. Essays presented to Stuart Piggott*, Leicester, University Press, 197–211.

Simpson, D.D.A., 2004, 'Making an impression: beaker combs', in Cleal and Pollard (eds) 2004, 207–14.

Simpson, D.D.A., Murphy, E.M. and Gregory, R.A., 2006, *Excavations at Northton, Isle of Harris*, Oxford, British Archaeological Report 408.

Smith, C.N.S., 1957, 'A catalogue of the prehistoric finds from Worcestershire', *Transactions of the Worcestershire Archaeological Society* new series 34, 1–27.

Smith, G., 1973, 'Excavation of the Stonehenge Avenue at West Amesbury, Wiltshire', *Wiltshire Archaeological and Natural History Magazine*, 68, 42–63.

Smith, I., 1959, 'Excavations at Windmill Hill, Avebury, Wilts 1957–8', *Wiltshire Archaeological and Natural History Magazine* 57, 149–62.

Smith, I.F., 1965, *Windmill Hill and Avebury. Excavations by Alexander Keiller 1925–1939*, Oxford, University Press.

Smith, I.F., 1991, 'Round barrows Wilsford-cum-Lake G51–G54. Excavations by Ernest Greenfield in 1958' *Wiltshire Archaeological and Natural History Magazine* 84, 11–39.

Smith, I.F. and Simpson, D.D.A., 1966, 'Excavation of a round barow on Overton Hill, North Wiltshire, England', *Proceedings of the Prehistoric Society* 32, 122–55.

Smith, J., 2006, '"Stone wrist-guards" in Early Bronze Age Britain: archer's bracers or social symbol?', *Journal of the Society of Archer-Antiquaries* 49, 50–7.

Soar, H.D., 1990, 'Some notes on antique archery arm-guards' *Journal of the Society of Archer-Antiquaries* 33, 45–6.

Sofaer Derevenski, J., 2002, 'Engendering context. Context as gendered practice in the Early Bronze Age of the upper Thames valley, UK', *European Journal of Archaeology* 5, 191–211.

Šoberl, L., Pollard, J. and Evershed, R., 2009, 'Pots for the afterlife: organic residue analysis of British Bronze Age pottery from funerary contexts', *PAST* 63, 6–8.

Spindler, K., 1994, *The Man in the Ice*, London, Phoenix.

Staňa, C., 1959, 'Hrob kultury zvoncovitých pohárů ve Veselí n.Mor', *Přehledy výzkumů*, 32–5.

Stirland, A., 1987, 'A possible correlation between Os acromialie and occupation in the burials from the Mary Rose', in V. Capecchi and E.R. Massa (eds), *Proceedings of the Fifth European meeting of the Palaeopathology Association, 1984*, Siena, Tipografia Senese, 327–34.

Stirland, A., 1990, 'Human remains', in Russel 1990, 167–8.

Stirland, A., 2000, *Raising the Dead*, Chichester, Wiley.

Stirland, A., 2005, 'The crew of the Mary Rose', in J. Gardiner with M.J. Allen (eds), *Before the Mast: life and death aboard the Mary Rose*, Portsmouth, Archaeology of the *Mary Rose* 4, 516–57.

Stone, J.F.S., 1935, 'Some discoveries at Ratfyn, Amesbury and their bearing on the date of Woodhenge', *Wiltshire Archaeological and Natural History Magazine* 47, 55–67.

Stone, J.F.S., 1938, 'An Early Bronze Age grave in Fargo Plantation, near Stonehenge', *Wiltshire Archaeological and Natural History Magazine* 48, 357–70.

Stone, J.F.S., 1949, 'Some Grooved Ware pottery from the Woodhenge area', *Proceedings of the Prehistoric Society* 15, 122–7.

Stone, J.F.S. and Young, W.E.V., 1948, 'Two pits of Grooved Ware date near Woodhenge', *Wiltshire Archaeological and Natural History Magazine* 52, 287–306.

Strahm, C., 1971, *Die Gliederung der Schnurkeramischen Kultur in der Schweiz*, Bern, Acta Bernensia 6.

Strahm, C., 1979, 'Les épingles de parure en os du Néolithique final', in H. Camps-Fabrer (ed.), *L'industrie en os et bois de cervidé durant le Néolithique et l'Âge des métaux*, Paris, Centre national de la recherche scientique, 47–85.

Strahm, C., 1994, 'Die Änfange der Metallurgie in Mitteleuropa', *Helvetica Archaeologica* 25, 2–39.

Strahm, C., 2004, 'Das Glockenbecher-Phänomen aus der Sicht der Komplementär-Keramik', in Czebreszuk (ed.) 2004b, 101–26.

Strahm, C., 2005, 'L'introduction et la diffusion de la métallurgie en France', in Ambert and Vaquer (eds), 2005, 27–36.

Strahm, C., 2007, 'L'introduction de la métallurgie en Europe', in Guilaine (ed.), 2007, 47–71.

Stuiver, M. and Kra, R.S., 1986, 'Editorial comment', in M. Stuiver and R.S. Kra (eds), *Proceedings of the 12th International 14C Conference, Radiocarbon* 28(2B)(Calibration issue), ii.

Stuiver, M. and Polach, H.A., 1977, 'Reporting of 14C data', *Radiocarbon* 19, 355–63.

Stuiver, M. and Reimer, P.J., 1986, 'A computer program for radiocarbon age calculation', *Radiocarbon* 28, 1022–30.

Stuiver, M. and Reimer, P.J., 1993, 'Extended 14C data base and revised CALIB 3.0 14C age calibration program', *Radiocarbon* 35, 215–30.

Suter, P.J., Hafner, A. and Glauser, K., 2005, 'Lenk-Schnidejoch. Funde aus dem Eis – ein vor- und frühgeschichtlicher Passübergang', *Archäologie im Kantons Bern* 6, 499–522.

Tassarini, C.C.G., Medini, J. and Pinto, M.S., 1996, 'Rb-Sr and Sm-Nd geochronology and isotope geochemistry of central Iberian metasedimentary rocks (Portugal)', *Geologie en Mijnbouw* 75, 69–79.

Taylor, J.J., 1968, 'Early Bronze Age gold neck-rings in western Europe', *Proceedings of the Prehistoric Society* 34, 259–65.

Taylor, J.J., 1980, *Bronze Age Goldwork of the British Isles*, Cambridge, University Press.

Taylor, J.J., 1994, 'The first golden age of Europe was in Ireland and Britain (circa 2400–1400 B.C.)', *Ulster Journal of Archaeology* 57, 37–60.

Terence O'Rourke 2002, *Land South of Boscombe Road, Amesbury. Environmental Statement,* Bournemouth, Terence O'Rourke, unpublished report.

Thevenot, J.-P., 1961, 'Le tumulus no. 1 de "Vertempierre" à Chagny', *Revue Archéologique de l'Est et du Centre Est* 12, 164–9.

Thomas, J., 1991, 'Reading the body: Beaker funerary practice in Britain', in P. Garwood, D. Jennings, R. Skeates and J. Toms (eds), *Sacred and Profane,* Oxford, Oxford University Committee for Archaeology Monograph 32, 33–42.

Thomas, J., 2007, 'The internal features at Durrington Walls: investigations in the southern circle and western enclosures', in Larsson and Parker Pearson (eds) 2007, 145–57.

Thomas, J. and Whittle, A., 1986, 'Anatomy of a tomb – West Kennet revisited', *Oxford Journal of Archaeology* 5, 129–56.

Thomas, N., 1956, 'Excavations and field-work in Wiltshire, 1956', *Wiltshire Archaeological and Natural History Magazine* 56, (1958), 231–52.

Thorpe, I.J. and Richards, C.C., 1984, 'The decline of ritual authority and the introduction of Beakers into Britain', in R. Bradley and J. Gardiner (eds), *Neolithic Studies. A Review of Some Recent Research,* Oxford, British Archaeological Report 133, 67–84.

Thorpe, R.S., Williams-Thorpe, O., Jenkins, D.G. and Watson, J.S., 1991, 'The geological sources and transport of the bluestones of Stonehenge, Wiltshire, UK', *Proceedings of the Prehistoric Society* 57(2), 103–157.

Thurnham J., 1871, 'On ancient British barrows, especially those of Wiltshire and the adjoining counties (Part II, round barrows)', *Archaeologia* 43, 285–552.

Tilmann, N., 1938, 'The Rhenish Schiefergebirge', *Proceedings of the Geologists Association* 49, 225–60.

Timberlake, S., 2001, 'Mining and prospection for metals in early Bronze Age Britain – making claims within the archaeological landscape', in J. Brück (ed.), *Bronze Age Landscapes. Tradition and Transformation,* Oxford, Oxbow, 179–92.

Timberlake, S., 2003, *Excavations on Copa Hill, Cwmystwyth (1986–1999). An Early Bronze Age Copper Mine within the Uplands of Central Wales,* Oxford, British Archaeological Report 348.

Timberlake, S., Gwilt, A. and Davies M., 2004, 'Copper Age/ Early Bronze Age gold disc from Banc Tynddol (Penguelan, Cwmystwyth Mines, Ceredigion)', *Antiquity* 78, project gallery: http://www.antiquity.ac.uk/projgall/timberlake/index.html

Treinen, F., 1970, 'Les poteries campaniformes en France', *Gallia Prehistoire* 13(1), 55–107; 13(2), 263–332.

Trotter, M. and Gleser, G.C., 1952, 'Estimation of stature from long bones of American whites and Negroes', *American Journal of Physical Anthropology* 10, 463–514.

Trotter, M. and Gleser, G.C., 1958, 'A re-evaluation of estimation of stature based on measurements of stature taken during life and of long bones after death', *American Journal of Physical Anthropology* 16, 79–123.

Turek, J., 2002, '"Cherchez la femme!" Archeologie ženského světa a chybějící doklady ženských pohřbů z období zvoncovitých pohárů v Čechách', in E. Neustupný (ed.), *Archeologie nenalézaného,* Čeněk, Pilzen and Prague, 217–40.

Turek, J., 2003, 'Řemesiná symbolika v pohřebním ritu období zvoncovitých pohárů. Suroviny, výroba a struktura společnosti v závěru Eneolitu', in L. Šmejda and P. Vařeka (eds), *Sedmdesát neustupných let. Sborník k životnímu jubilee prof.Evezena Neustupného,* Plzeň, Čeněk, 199–217.

Turek, J., 2004, 'Craft symbolism in the Bell Beaker burial customs. Resources, production and social structure at the end of the Eneolithic period', in Besse and Desideri (eds) 2004, 147–56.

Turek, J., 2006a, 'Období zvoncovitých pohárů v Europě', *Archeologie ve Středních Čechách* 10, 275–368.

Turek, J., 2006b, 'Beaker barrows and houses of the dead', in L. Smejda, *Archaeology of Burial Mounds,* Pilzen, University of West Bohemia, ArchaEOlogica series, 170–9.

Turek, J. and Černý, V., 2001, 'Society, gender and sexual diamorphism of the Corded ware and Bell Beaker populations', in Nicolis (ed.) 2001b, 601–12.

Tütken, T., Vennemann, T.W. and Pfretschner, H.-U., 2004, 'Analyse stabiler und radiogener Isotope in archäologischem Skelettmaterial: Herkunftsbestimmung des karolingischen Maultiers von Frankental und Vergleich mit spät-pleistozänen Großsäugerknochen aus den Rheinablager-ungen', *Prähistorische Zeitschrift* 79, 89–110.

Tylecote, R.F., 1986, *The Prehistory of Metallurgy in the British Isles,* London, Institute of Metals.

Tyrrell, A., 2000, 'Skeletal non-metric traits and the assessment of inter- and intra-population diversity: past problems and future potential', in Cox and Mays (eds) 2000, 289–306.

Vander Linden, M., 2004, 'Polythetic networks, coherent people: a new historical hypothesis for the Bell Beaker phenomenon', in Czebreszuk (ed.) 2004b, 35–62.

Vander Linden, M., 2006a, *Le phénomène campaniforme dans l'Europe du 3e millénaire avant notre ère. Synthèse et nouvelles perspectives,* Oxford, British Archaeological Report S1470.

Vander Linden, M., 2006b, 'For whom the Bell Tolls: social hierarchy vs social integration in the Bell Beaker Culture of southern France (third millennium BC)', *Cambridge Archaeological Journal* 16, 317–32.

264

Vander Linden, M., 2007, 'What linked the Bell Beakers in third millennium BC Europe?', *Antiquity* 81, 343–52.

Vandkilde, H., 1996, *From Stone to Bronze: the metalwork of the Late Neolithic and earliest Bronze Age in Denmark*, Moesgård, Jutland Archaeological Society Publications 32.

Vankilde, H., 2005a, 'A review of the Early Late Neolithic period in Denmark: practice, identity and connectivity', *Offa* 61/62, 75–109: http://www.jungsteinsite.uni-kiel.de/pdf/2005_vandkilde_low.pdf.

Vankilde, H., 2005b, 'A biographical perspective on Ösenringe from the Early Bronze Age', in T. Kienlin (ed.), *Die Dinge als Zeichen: Kulturelles Wissens und materieller Kulture*, Bonn, Universitätsforschungen zur prähistorischen Archäologie, 127, 263–81.

Vennemann, T.W., Fricke, H.C., Bake, R.E., O'Neil, J.R., and Colman, A., 2002, 'Oxygen isotope analysis of phosphates: a comparison of techniques for analysis of Ag3PO4', *Chemical Geology* 185, 321–36.

Verron, G., 2000, *Préhistoire de la Normandie*, Rennes, Ouest-France Université.

Webb, A., 1994, 'Just ornament, or funerary replica, or release aid?' *Journal of the Society of Archer-Antiquaries* 37, 40–1.

Vu, L.P. and Mehlman, C.T., 2010, 'Tarsal Coalition': http://emedicine.medscape.com.article/1233780-overview

Waals, J.D., van der, 1984, 'Bell Beakers in continental northwestern Europe', in Guilaine (ed.) 1984, 3–35.

Waals, J.D. van der and Glasbergen, W., 1955, 'Beaker types and their distribution in the Netherlands', *Palaeohistoria* 4, 5–63.

Waddell, J., 1990, *The Bronze Age Burials of Ireland*, Galway, University Press.

Waddell, J. and Shee Twohig, E., (eds), 1995, *Ireland in the Bronze Age*, Dublin, The Stationary Office.

Wainwright, G.J., 1979, *Mount Pleasant, Dorset: excavations 1970–71*, London, Report of the Research Committee of the Society of Antiquaries of London 37.

Wainwright, G.J. and Davies, S.M., 1995, *Balksbury Camp, Hampshire. Excavations 1973 and 1981*, London English Heritage Archaeological Report 4.

Wainwright, G.J. and Longworth, I.H., 1971, *Durrington Walls. Excavation 1966–1968*, London, Report of the Research Committee of the Society of Antiquaries of London 29.

Wait, G.A., 1985, *Ritual and Religion in Iron Age Britain*, Oxford, British Archaeological Report 149.

Walsh, P., 1995, 'Structure and deposition in Irish wedge tombs: an open and shut case?', in Waddell and Shee Twohig (eds) 1995, 113–27.

Warner, R., 2004, 'Irish gold artifacts: observations from Hartmann's analytical data', in H. Roche, E. Grogan, J. Bradley, J. Coles and B. Raftery (eds), *From Megaliths to Metals: essays in honour of George Eogan*, Oxford, Oxbow, 72–82.

Webb, A., 1994, 'Just ornament, or funerary replica or release aid?', *Journal of the Society of Archer-Antiquaries* 37, 40–1.

Wells, C., 1977, 'The human bones', in Donaldson 1977, 216–27.

Whimster, R.P., 1981, *Burial Practices in Iron Age Britain: a discussion and gazetteer of the evidence c. 700 BC–AD 43*, Oxford, British Archaeological Report 90.

Whittle, A. and Wysocki, A., 1998, 'Parc le Breos Cwm transepted long cairn, Gower, West Glamorgan: date, contents, and context', *Proceedings of the Prehistoric Society* 64, 139–82.

Whittle, A., Atkinson, R.J.C., Chambers, R. and Thomas, N., 1992, 'Excavations in the Neolithic and Bronze Age complex at Dorchester-on-Thames, Oxfordshire, 1947–1952 and 1981', *Proceedings of the Prehistoric Society* 58, 143–201.

Whittle, A., Barclay, A., Bayliss, A., McFayden, L., Schulting, R. and Wysocki, M., 2007, 'Building for the dead: events, process and changing world views from the thirty-eight to the thirty-fourth centuries cal. BC in southern Britain', *Cambridge Archaeological Journal* 17(1) (supplement), 123–47.

Wiermann, R. R., 2004, *Die Becherkulturen in Hessen. Glockenbecher-Schnurkermik-Riesenbecher*, Rahden/Westphalia, Freiburger Archäologische Studien 4.

Williams, A., 1948, 'Excavations in Barrow Hills, Radley, Berkshire, 1944' *Oxoniensia* 13, 1–17.

Williams, B.P.J. and Stead, J.T.G., 1982, 'Cambrian of Newgate–St. David's area', in M.G. Bassett (ed.), *Geological Excursions in Dyfed, South-West Wales*, Cardiff, National Museum of Wales, 27–50.

Williams-Thorpe, Green, C.P. and Scourse, J.D., 1997, 'The Stonehenge bluestones: discussion', in Cunliffe and Renfrew (eds) 1997, 315–18.

Williams-Thorpe, O., Potts, P.J. and Webb, P.C., 1999, 'Field-portable non-destructive analysis of lithic archaeological samples by X-ray fluorescence instrumentation using a mercury iodide detector: comparison with wavelength-dispersive XRF and a case study in British stone axe provenancing', *Journal of Archaeological Science* 26, 215–37.

Wilson, C.E., 1981, 'Burials within settlements in southern Britain during the Pre-Roman Iron Age', *Bulletin of the Institute of Archaeology University London* 18, 127–69.

Winiger, J., 1989, *Bestandesaufnahme der Bielerseestationen als Grundlage demographischer Theoriebilding*, Bern, Ufersiedlung am Bieler See 1.

Winiger, J., 1993, 'Dendrodatierte Schnurkeramik der Schweiz', *Præhistorica* 20, 9–118.

Wolf, C., 1992, 'Schnurkeramik und Civilisation Saône-Rhône in der Westschweiz: ein Beispiel für die Auseinandersetzung zwischen einer lokalen und einer überregionalen Kulturerscheinung', in Buchvaldek and Strahm (eds) 1992, 187–98.

Woodman, P., Finlay, N. and Anderson, E., 2006, *The Archaeology of a Collection. The Keiller-Knowles collection of the National Museum of Ireland*, Dublin, National Museum of Ireland Monograph Series 2.

Woodward, A., 2002, 'Beads and Beakers: heirlooms and relics in the British Early Bronze Age', *Antiquity* 76, 1040–7.

Woodward, A., Hunter, J., Ixer, R., Maltby, M., Potts, P., Webb, P., Watson, J. and Jones, M., 2005, 'Ritual in some early Bronze Age grave goods', *Archaeological Journal* 162, 3–64.

Woodward, A., Hunter, J., Ixer, R., Roe, F., Potts, P.J., Webb, P.C., Watson, J.S. and Jones, M.C., 2006, 'Beaker Age bracers in England: sources, function and use', *Antiquity* 80, 530–43: http://www.antiquity.ac.uk/projgall/woodward/

Woodward, A, and Hunter, J., 2011, *An Examination of Prehistoric Stone Bracers from Britain*, Oxford, Oxbow.

Wüstemann, H., 1995, *Die Dolche und Stabdolche in Ostdeutschland*, Stuttgart, Prähistorische Bronzefunde 6.8.

Zimmermann, T., 2007, *Die ältesten küpferzeitlichen Bestattungen mit Dolchbeigabe*, Mainz, Monographien des Römisch–Germanischen Zentralmuseums 71.

Index

by Susan M. Vaughan

Page numbers in *italics* denote illustrations. Places are in Wiltshire unless indicated otherwise.

Lightning Source UK Ltd.
Milton Keynes UK
UKOW06f1611271113

221939UK00006B/16/P